Independence

The State of Israel and the Arab–Israeli Conflict

Jacob L. Mosak

Copyright © 2024 by Allan Mosak

All rights reserved. No part of this book, whole or in part, may be stored, reproduced, transmitted, or translated in any form or by any means whatsoever, manually or electronically, without prior written permission from the copyright holder, except by a reviewer who wishes to quote brief passages in connection with a review written for inclusion in newspapers or magazines. The rights of the copyright holder will be strictly enforced.

ISBN:
Hardcover: 979-8-3302-0602-5
Paperback: 979-8-3302-0606-3
E-book: 979-8-3302-0603-2

Publishing services were provided by JewishSelfPublishing. The copyright holder acts as the publisher and is solely responsible for the content of this book, which does not necessarily reflect the opinions of JewishSelfPublishing.

www.jewishselfpublishing.com
info@jewishselfpublishing.com
(800) 613-9430

Contents

List of Abbreviations .... *v*

Preface .... *vii*

Introduction .... *ix*

1 The Balfour Declaration 1
2 Negotiating the Mandate 19
3 Military Intrigues 38
4 Herbert Samuel's Mixed Legacy 61
5 Churchill Partitions the Mandate 92
6 The 1929 Massacres and the Passfield White Paper 112
7 The 1939 White Paper for Palestine as an Arab State 141
8 Churchill Keeps the 1939 White Paper in Force 188
9 The US Supports Britain's 1939 White Paper Policy 218
10 The Truman–Attlee Rift Over Immigration Policy 245
11 The Bankruptcy of Britain's Palestine Policy 281
12 The United Nations Special Committee on Palestine 309
13 The UN General Assembly Votes for Partition 335
14 The Battles against the Creation of the Jewish State 371
15 The Drama of the Rebirth of the Jewish State: Israel 414
16 The War to Liquidate the Newly Reborn Israel 459
17 The Mediator's Revised Peace Plan 504

18	Armistice and Admission of Israel to UN	534
19	The Suez War of 1956	561
20	The Six-Day War	581
21	The United Nations' Principles for Peace	615
22	Conclusion	640

Appendix 1: Excerpts from United Nations General Assembly Resolution 181(II) Concerning the Future Government of Palestine, November 29, 1947 ... 657

Appendix 2: United Nations Security Council Resolution 61, November 4, 1948 ... 659

Appendix 3: A Selection of Calls from the Palestine Liberation Organization for the Annihilation of Israel ... 661

Appendix 4: United Nations Security Council Resolution 242, November 22, 1967 ... 665

Bibliography ... 667

Index ... 689

List of Abbreviations

OETA	Occupied Enemy Territories Administration
PA	Palestinian Authority
PLO	Palestine Liberation Organization
UN	United Nations
UNGA	United Nations General Assembly
UNISPAL	United Nations Information System on Palestine
UNRWA	United Nations Relief and Works Agency
UNSC	United Nations Security Council
UNSCOP	United Nations Special Committee on Palestine

Preface

OUR FATHER, DR. JACOB L. MOSAK, died just before his hundredth birthday. He was a brilliant scholar—a world-class economist at the United Nations who hobnobbed with world leaders. He spent decades researching Israel's history and staying current in relation to its daily events, and he was even present at the United Nations sessions when the vote to create Israel took place.

The primary reason why our father wrote this book was to tell the story of the creation of the State of Israel, setting the record straight and countering anti-Zionist propaganda. Recent polls taken in the United States demonstrate a generational divide in support for Israel. While most older Americans continue to support Israel, a growing number of people aged under thirty-five support the Palestinians. Many of these young people even approve of Hamas' attacks against Israeli civilians and consider Israel to be a "colonialist enterprise" wherein "European settler Jews" forcefully dispossessed the supposedly indigenous Palestinians from their land.

The growing manifestations of anti-Zionism and anti-Semitism on college campuses across the United States—and even in the United States Congress—demonstrate why this book, with its accurate and thoroughly researched history of the creation of the State of Israel, is so vital. In a detailed yet extremely readable way, it provides a history of the creation of the State of Israel from the Balfour Declaration through the 1967 Six-Day War. It shows how the Palestinians have consistently denied Israel's right to exist, while Israel has demonstrated again and again its willingness to compromise and live in peace with its neighbors.

This book was written for an additional reason: to describe the many formidable challenges that threatened the creation of the State of Israel, including the quest for world recognition, the struggle for economic survival, and the need to defend itself against multiple Arab nations who swore to destroy it even before it had achieved statehood. A deeply religious Jew, our father felt that it was only through God's love of the Jewish people that Israel was, against all odds, able to build a modern, prosperous country.

Our father completed the manuscript of this book shortly before he died, trusting his family to find the right venue for its publication. We are very grateful to Eliyahu Miller and his staff at JewishSelfPublishing for enabling us to fulfil his wishes. It has been a pleasure working with Eliyahu on this project. He provided expert guidance through the entire process and made sure that all the work was carried out with the highest level of professionalism. Special thanks are extended to Elisheva Ruffer for her careful and thorough editing of the manuscript; to Amy Hall for the excellent, detailed index; and to Shanie Cooper for the beautiful cover design.

Our thanks also go to all the family members who encouraged our father during the many years that he worked on the book, read and commented on its multiple drafts, and contributed from their areas of expertise to various aspects of its publication. We are especially indebted to our daughter and niece, Adina Moshavi, without whose help and guidance in editing and assembling the manuscript this book might never have been published.

We have made very minor style changes to our father's manuscript but have not updated any references to "present-day" events. In the small number of cases where the citations did not provide complete bibliographic details, reasonable efforts were made to locate the original source and supply the missing information.

Richard and Allan Mosak
July 2024

Introduction

THE ARAB–ISRAELI CONFLICT HAS ENDURED for so long for one reason only: the persistent refusal of the Arabs to accept the epic rebirth of the Jewish State of Israel within its ancient national and religious homeland. In a recent op-ed article in *The New York Times*,[1] Mahmoud Abbas, president of the Palestinian National Authority and of the Palestine Liberation Organization (PLO), noted the United Nations General Assembly (UNGA) vote on November 29, 1947 in favor of partitioning Palestine into two states and lamented, "Minutes after the State of Israel was established on May 14, 1948, the United States granted it recognition. Our Palestinian state, however, remains a promise unfulfilled."

This lament brings to mind the classic story of the young man who, after killing his parents, appeals for sympathy from the court, because he is an orphan. The fact—as can be readily confirmed from the comprehensive online records of the United Nations Information System on Palestine (UNISPAL)—is that the Arab states declared the 1947 UNGA Resolution null and void, insisting that it "murdered the United Nations (UN) Charter." Matching their words with deeds, the Arabs launched a guerrilla war to prevent the rebirth of the Jewish State in accordance with the Resolution, with the guerrilla leader, Abd al-Qadir al-Husseini, who invaded Israel from Egypt, blockading Jewish Jerusalem's lifeline to food and water and threatening its hundred-thousand Jewish population with extinction. Furthermore, with

---

1. Mahmoud Abbas, "The Long Overdue Palestinian State," *The New York Times,* May 17, 2011.

the end of the British Mandate for Palestine on May 15, 1948, when the Arabs, like the Jews, were free to set up their state in Palestine under the UNGA Resolution, they gave no thought to establishing an independent Arab state in Palestine. Instead, on the very day of Israel's rebirth, the Arab states jointly invaded Israel with their regular armies in a determined attempt to annihilate it. As UN Secretary-General Trygve Lie bitterly complained at the time:

> The Arab states launched their invasion of Palestine with the end of the Mandate. This was armed defiance of the United Nations, and they openly proclaimed their aggression by telegraphing news of it to United Nations Headquarters.[2]

Having declared the Resolution for partition null and void as well as having launched their aggression to demolish Israel in "armed defiance of the United Nations," the Arabs now complain that the Resolution's promise of a Palestinian state remains unfulfilled.

Ironically, Abbas continues, to this day, to reject the Resolution's promise of a Jewish state, at the same time as he laments the non-fulfillment of the Resolution's promise of a Palestinian state for which the Arabs alone are responsible. In his op-ed article, he notes only that the Resolution partitioned Palestine into two states, carefully omitting the fact that it partitioned Palestine into two specifically defined states: an Arab state and a Jewish state.

Abbas's emphatic and repeated insistence that he will never recognize Israel as a Jewish state[3] can only mean that even the "moderate" Palestinian leadership continues to refuse to accept the right of the Jewish people to their state in Palestine. This refusal is not a mere

---

2. Trygve Lie, *In the Cause of Peace: Seven Years with the United Nations* (New York: Macmillan, 1954), 173.
3. See "PA Chairman Mahmoud Abbas: I Will Never Recognize a Jewish State," MEMRI, Special Dispatch, No. 4235, November 1, 2011, accessed on August 10, 2023, online at https://www.memri.org/reports/pa-chairman-mahmoud-abbas-i-will-never-recognize-jewish-state-capturing-israeli-soldier.

semantic issue to be shrugged aside as trivial in comparison to the final-status issues, such as borders and security. On the contrary, the refusal raises the question of the meaning of any Arab-Israeli peace pact. Is such a pact intended to put a total end to all Arab claims on Israel and to usher in lasting Arab-Israeli peace, or is it really intended only as one further stage in the policy of "phased liberation" of all Palestine, including all Israel—the policy that Yasser Arafat and the PLO announced in 1974[4] and never formally rejected? No territorial concessions can end a war that the Arabs regard as only a phase in the liberation of all Palestine, including Israel, as Hamas does to this day and as seems implicit in Abbas's emphatic rejection of Israel as a Jewish state.

Abbas's repeated refusal to accept Israel as a Jewish state is all the more troubling because it constitutes a total repudiation of the policy adopted by Yasser Arafat and the Palestinian National Council in 1988, when it issued its Declaration of Independence of a State of Palestine.[5] This declaration based the right of the Palestinian people to independence explicitly on "the adoption of General Assembly Resolution 181(II) of 1947,"[6] which, as the declaration specifically noted, "partitioned Palestine into an Arab and a Jewish state." Invited to address the UNGA on December 13, 1988, Arafat called the UNGA resolution for the partition of Palestine Israel's "birth certificate" and likewise emphasized that it "provides for the establishment of two states, one Arab–Palestinian and the other Jewish."[7] Two days later,

---

4. Palestinian National Council, Cairo, June 9, 1974.
5. United Nations General Assembly, Declaration of State of Palestine—Palestine National Council, Annex III, Document A/43/827, S/20278 (November 15, 1988), accessed on August 7, 2023, online at https://www.un.org/unispal/document/auto-insert-178680.
6. For pertinent excerpts from UNGA Resolution 181(II), see Appendix 1.
7. United Nations General Assembly, Provisional Verbatim Record of the 78th Meeting, held at the Palais des Nations, Geneva, on Tuesday, December 13, 1988: General Assembly, 43rd session, Document A/43/PV.78 (January 3, 1989), accessed on August 7, 2023, online at https://digitallibrary.un.org/record/55459?ln=en.

UNGA passed Resolution 43/177, thereby acknowledging the PLO declaration and upgrading its "observer" status to the label "Palestine," but UNGA also reaffirmed Israel's right as a Jewish state in a preambular paragraph, "Recalling its Resolution 181(II) of November 29, 1947, in which, inter alia, it called for the establishment of an Arab state and a Jewish state in Palestine." This 1988 resolution was adopted according to a vote of 104 to 2, with the Arab states voting unanimously in its favor.

In his bid to the UN Security Council on September 23, 2011 to admit Palestine as a UN member state, Abbas referred to the 1947 UNGA Resolution and to his own role in the 1988 Declaration of Independence, but he again omitted all reference to the fact that the 1947 UNGA Resolution calls for both an Arab state and a Jewish state in Palestine. Abbas's current emphatic repudiation of the PLO's past (equally emphatic) announcement of its acceptance of Israel as a Jewish state raises a basic question of Palestinian credibility regarding the peace effort.

Arab dogma has maintained from the very beginning that the Jews are not entitled to a state and has insisted that the State of Israel is only a Zionist, racist, colonialist implantation of an alien European people into the Arab Middle East, originating around the end of the nineteenth century. In support of this dogma, the Arabs have created their own fictional history of the Jewish people based on a political rewriting of millennia of Jewish history. The PLO charters, both the founding Palestinian National Charter of 1964 established by the Arab League under Gamal Abdel Nasser's leadership, and the revised charter established under Yasser Arafat's guidance (July 17, 1968), declare UNGA Resolution 181(II) of 1947 for the partition of Palestine into an Arab state and a Jewish state illegal and pronounce both the Balfour Declaration and the League of Nations Mandate for establishing a Jewish national homeland in Palestine null and void. By way of explanation, both charter versions add that claims of historical or religious ties of Jews with Palestine are incompatible with the facts of history. Arafat and the Palestinian Authority (PA) have even gone so far as to repeatedly insist that no Jewish Holy Temple ever stood in Jerusalem.

These charges hold in contempt the Hebrew Bible, together with the Oral Torah embodied in the encyclopedic Mishnah and Talmud with their accounts of the central role in Jewish life over approximately a thousand years that the Jewish Holy Temples stood on Jerusalem's sacred Temple Mount. And it holds in equal contempt the New Testament, with its ample records of the role of Jerusalem's Holy Temple in the birth of Christianity. The Gospels record, for example, the trip by the parents of Jesus to Jerusalem's Holy Temple shortly after his birth, even noting that the visit was in accordance with the Jewish rites described in Leviticus 12. The Gospels also report many trips to Jerusalem's Holy Temple, both by Jesus' parents and by Jesus himself, for the Passover holiday, again in accordance with Jewish rites.[8]

Remarkably, the PLO's contempt for the Hebrew Bible's records of the building of Jerusalem's Holy Temple by King Solomon even appears to fly in the face of the Moslem holy book, the Koran, which treats the Hebrew Bible with reverence as "the Book" that "Allah gave to Moses in guidance to the children of Israel" (Sura 17:2) and embraces the biblical heroes Moses, David, and Solomon along with the patriarchs Abraham, Isaac, and Jacob as predecessor prophets to Mohammed. Yet, Arafat and his followers would have us believe that the biblical accounts of King Solomon's building of Jerusalem's Holy Temple and all the biblical prophetic pronouncements regarding that Holy Temple are mere fiction.

---

8. Deuteronomy 16:16; see for example, Luke (2:22–24): "When the time came for their purification according to the law of Moses…and to offer a sacrifice according to what is said in the law of the Lord (see Leviticus 12)," the parents of Jesus brought the newborn child to the Holy Temple. See also in Luke: "Now, his [Jesus'] parents went to Jerusalem every year at the feast of the Passover" (2:41), "And when he was twelve years old, they went up according to custom" (2:43), and "When the feast was ended, as they were returning, the boy Jesus stayed behind in Jerusalem."

Perhaps most surprisingly, Yasser Arafat and today's PA leadership have evidently forgotten that even the PLO's own Declaration of Independence issued in 1988 acknowledges the historical and religious ties of the Jewish people to Palestine, including the existence of the Jewish Holy Temple. In a paean to Palestine, the Declaration's preamble characterizes Palestine as "the land of the three monotheistic faiths," and it affirms the existence of the Jewish Holy Temple, declaring, "The call went out from Temple, Church, and Mosque that to praise the Creator, to celebrate compassion and peace, was indeed the message of Palestine."[9]

In their denial of the Jews' national and religious ties to the Land of Israel, Arabs maintain that the UN decision in favor of the establishment of Israel was the result of the world's guilt over the Holocaust and that Arabs should not have to pay for the West's moral failures.[10] Radical Moslems, such as Iran's former president Mahmoud Ahmadinejad, persist in their denial of the unspeakable Holocaust, evidently under the illusion that denial of the Holocaust does away

---

9. The Preamble is included in the text of the Declaration of Independence: Palestinian National Council, "Palestinian Declaration of Independence," *MidEast Web*, accessed August 7, 2023, online at http://www.mideastweb.org/plc1988.htm.

10. The Arabs, incidentally, were not as innocent as their propaganda maintains. Grand Mufti Haj Amin al-Husseini, who organized Arab massacres of Jews in Palestine in the 1920s and 1930s, collaborated with Hitler in Berchtesgaden, assisted in the annihilation of Jewish communities in the Balkans, and planned for the introduction into the Middle East of Hitler's "Final Solution" to exterminate its Jews after the anticipated Nazi victory.

   Additionally, Hamas, in its founding Hamas Charter of 1988 even awaits an Islamic "Final Solution," when all the Jews will be wiped off the map: "The Day of Judgment will not come about until Moslems fight the Jews, killing the Jews, when the Jew will hide behind stones and trees. The stones and trees will say, 'O Moslems, O Abdullah, there is a Jew behind me, come and kill him'" (Hamas, "Hamas Covenant 1988," *The Avalon Project, Yale Law School*, accessed August 7, 2023, online at https://avalon.law.yale.edu/20th_century/hamas.asp).

with the moral right of the Jews to statehood. But this right to statehood in Palestine is based not on the Holocaust but on the Jewish people's enduring historical, national, and religious ties to the Land of Israel, ties that the Jews never severed, regardless of repeated expulsions by foreign conquerors. The League of Nations recognized the significance of these ties a generation before the Holocaust when, in 1922, its Council decided unanimously in favor of the establishment of a Jewish homeland in Palestine. As the text of the Mandate for Palestine places on record, "Recognition has thereby been given to the historical connection of the Jewish people with Palestine and to the grounds for reconstituting their national home in that country."

Hebrew is Israel's national language today, not because of the Holocaust but because (centuries before the birth of Islam) it is the language of the Jewish Bible, the language spoken by Israel's biblical kings and prophets, the language of the prayer books composed by Israel's rabbis that continue to be used to this day—three times daily, wherever Jews pray. Not many of the world's nations who today denigrate the Jewish claim to Palestine can claim such long-lasting ties to their lands as the Jewish people have maintained to their Land.

Neither do the historical, national, and religious ties to Palestine, particularly to Jerusalem, relate only to ancient history long since gone, and neither are they irrelevant today, as so many anti-Zionists so passionately maintain. Contrary to widespread belief, Jewish life in the Holy Land did not come to an end two thousand years ago, with the Roman destruction of Jerusalem's Holy Temple in the year 70 CE, and it did not come to an end because of the rise of Christianity. It has continued and endured to this day without interruption, despite Roman, Arab, and Moslem conquests of the Land—and in the face of religious persecution and extreme economic hardship. Only little more than sixty years after the Roman Empire destroyed the Holy Temple in the first Jewish War of Liberation (66–70 CE), Israel's Jews recovered sufficiently to challenge the Romans a second time, in a renewed war of liberation under the leadership of Shimon Bar Kochba (132–135 CE). Bar Kochba defeated the Roman armies stationed in Palestine and liberated part of the Land, such that Hadrian (117–138 CE) had to call in his imperial armies from as far as Britain and Germany for his costly victory over the Jews. Enraged over the enormous casualties the Jews had inflicted upon his armies, Hadrian sought to wipe out even the memory of the name of the Land of Israel, renaming the country Palestine in commemoration of Israel's biblical enemies, the Philistines. The Roman-given name did not gain much currency among the Arabs, and the Arabs who came to live there in the seventh century CE, following their seizure of the Holy Land under Omar I, did not call themselves Palestinians. The name "Palestine" does not even appear in the Koran.

The first four centuries following the birth of Christianity were, in fact, a period of remarkable Jewish religious creativity in Palestine despite the traumatic Jewish defeat in its second War of Liberation and the new conflicts that arose from the emergence of Christianity. Around the end of the second century CE, Rabbi Yehudah Hanasi, president of the Sanhedrin (the Jewish supreme judicial and legislative body), compiled the Mishnah, the fundamental Jewish code of law, which constitutes the Oral Torah taught by Israel's rabbis over the centuries. The Mishnah provides, inter alia, an extensive picture of Jewish life in Israel—political, economic, social, and religious—including the focal role of Jerusalem's Holy Temple and Temple Mount.[11]

---

11. The Mishnah in *Middot* provides a detailed blueprint of the Beit Hamikdash, Israel's Holy Temple in Jerusalem, setting out the area on the Temple Mount where the Holy Temple stood, the dimensions of each of the Temple Courts, and the location of each of the Temple sections. Tractate *Keilim* (1:6–9) describes the ten levels of sanctity pertaining to the Holy Land, Jerusalem, and the Temple Mount. Israel is holier than all other lands in the world: agricultural products such as the *bikkurim*, the "first fruits," offered at the *Beit Hamikdash* on the Temple Mount, are acceptable only from crops grown in Israel. Jerusalem is holier than the rest of *Eretz Israel*: Meat from the Temple sacrifices and the second tithes of Israel's crops may be consumed only in Jerusalem. *Har Habayit*, "the Temple Mount," is more sacred than the rest of Jerusalem: Persons with a sexual disease that renders them ritually impure may not enter it. The

The massive Jerusalem Talmud, which, inter alia, greatly expands upon the Mishnah and updates the history of Jewish national and religious life in the Land of Israel/Palestine, was completed around the middle of the fifth century CE.

The Holy Land continued as a major center for Jewish religious creativity even under Arab and Moslem rule. Hebrew poets of the seventh and eighth centuries CE in the Galilee created a large body of liturgical poetry that forms part of the Jewish holiday prayers still recited in synagogues today. In the tenth century CE, Torah scholars in Tiberias completed the *Masorah*, providing the authoritative standard for pronunciation, punctuation, and proper understanding of the biblical texts.[12] In the sixteenth century CE, Jewish life was centered around the town of Safed (Tzfat), where Rabbi Yosef Karo (1488–1575) completed the *Shulchan Aruch*, the comprehensive and updated code of Jewish law that has ever since governed Orthodox Jewish life everywhere, and where Rabbi Yitzchak Luria (1534–1572) and his followers developed Kabbalah, the philosophical doctrines of Jewish mysticism. To this day, Friday-night synagogue services begin with a song of Sabbath greeting, "Lechah Dodi," composed by Rabbi Shlomo Halevi Alkabetz (c. 1500–1576), a leading kabbalist of Safed.

A significant upsurge in Jewish migration to the Holy Land occurred in the nineteenth century, long before the rise of political

---

Cheil, "Temple area enclosure," is holier than the rest of the Temple Mount: Persons who became ritually impure from contact with the dead may not enter the Temple enclosure. Continuing with the higher gradations of sanctity of the various parts of the Holy Temple, where entry becomes more and more restricted, the Mishnah concludes with the tenth and highest level of sanctity, reserved for the Temple's Holy of Holies, where only the *kohen gadol*, the high priest, may enter. Even he is permitted entry only on the holiest day of the year, Yom Kippur, and only for the performance of the special rites required of him there on that day.

12. The *Masorah* involves the creation and application of a set of vowel signs for vowels that are absent in the Hebrew alphabet, together with a distinct musical notation system for the chanting of the Hebrew Bible in synagogues.

Zionism. At the beginning of the century, a group of about five hundred followers of the leading European rabbinic authority, the Vilna Gaon, ushered in a new wave of migration to Safed, Tiberias, and, especially, Jerusalem. As the British historian, James Parkes, wrote, "What 'The Land' meant to the Jewish people can be seen from the statistics of the population of Jerusalem. In 1872, the Jewish population just outnumbered the combined Christian and Moslem inhabitants: Jews—10,600, Christians—5,300, and Moslems—5,000. In 1899, the comparable figures were: Jews—30,000, Christians—10,900, and Moslems—7,700."[13]

It is this Old Jerusalem in which the Jewish population already exceeded the combined Christian and Moslem populations in the nineteenth century—before the rise of political Zionism, which the world now knows as Arab East Jerusalem. The world has ignored the fact that the area became Arab only as a result of the Mufti-led pogroms in the 1920s and 1930s, culminating in the expulsion of Old Jerusalem's entire Jewish population by Transjordan's Arab Legion in 1948, when it seized the city during the Arab War on Israel. Regrettably, the nations of the world and the human rights lobbies remained silent during the nearly two-decade long Jordanian rule (1948–1967) over the area, when it ethnically cleansed Old Jerusalem of its Jewish population, razed its synagogues, and desecrated its Mount of Olives cemetery. In addition, the Jordanians prohibited Jewish worship at the Kotel Hama'aravi, the Western Wall of the Temple Mount, in violation of its armistice agreement with Israel. These nations have all discovered their voices only since June 1967, repeatedly condemning as illegal any change instituted by Israel in East Jerusalem, including resettlement of Jews in the Jerusalem area where so much of ancient Jewish history was written and where Jews once again became, already in the nineteenth century, a majority of the total population.

---

13. James Parkes, *Whose Land? A History of the Peoples of Palestine* (New York: Taplinger, 1971), 230.

The PLO has accompanied its fictional rewriting of Jewish history in Palestine with a redefinition of the Jewish people themselves. The PLO Charter's pronouncement (Article 20) that "Claims of historical or religious ties of Jews with Palestine are incompatible with the facts of history" is followed by the charge, "Judaism, being a religion, is not a nationality. Neither do Jews constitute a single nation with an identity of its own." This definition of the Jewish people, unknown and unimaginable throughout Jewish history until it was created by opponents of Zionism, brings to mind Humpty Dumpty's comment to Alice in *Through the Looking Glass*, "When I use a word, it means just what I choose it to mean, neither more nor less."

Here, Palestinian Arabs, without a distinct Palestinian language, literature, or religion—who never in all Arab and Moslem history had a state of their own, who (as discussed in the chapters that follow) sought to be part of Syria after World War I, who overwhelmingly approved a referendum to annex Palestine's West Bank to Jordan in 1950, and whom even the Arab states in voting on the principles for Arab-Israeli peace in 1967[14] did not recognize as a people entitled to a state of their own, begin their request for recognition of their newly discovered claim as a distinct people by a denial of the peoplehood of the Jewish people, whose roots as a people date back more than three thousand years and whose contribution to world civilization over the ages has been universally recognized.

True, Judaism is a religion, but it is the religion of the Jewish people, and it is deeply rooted in the Land of Israel, with its capital in Jerusalem and with Jerusalem's Temple Mount its most sacred site. The significance of Jerusalem in the Jewish faith is sufficiently evident from the mere fact that the Hebrew Bible names Jerusalem no less than 667 times, and the name "Zion," a synonym for Jerusalem, from which stems the term "Zionism"— so widely maligned in many UN

---

14. United Nations Security Council, Resolution 242, The Situation in the Middle East, Document S/RES/242 (November 9, 1967), accessed on August 7, 2023, online at https://documents-dds-ny.un.org/doc/RESO-LUTION/GEN/NR0/240/94/PDF/NR024094.pdf?OpenElement.

circles—appears an additional 154 times.[15] The Hebrew Bible requires the Jew to make a pilgrimage to the Holy Land's Holy Temple three times a year—on the holidays of Passover, Shavuot, and Sukkot. Each of these holidays is intimately tied to Israel's agricultural festivals, celebrating crops grown in the Land of Israel. And the most sacred holiday, Yom Kippur, is totally centered on the high priest's services conducted only in Jerusalem's Holy Temple. Indeed, so intimately intertwined with the Holy Land is the Jewish religion that the rabbis declared, more than a thousand years before the birth of Islam, "A Jew living outside the Land of Israel lives as if he has no God."[16]

This is not merely ancient Jewish history that is of no relevance today. For two thousand years, Jews everywhere have continued to pray three times daily for the return of the Jewish people to independence and national sovereignty in the Land of Israel. On every memorable occasion in the life cycle, Jews continue to bear Jerusalem in mind. The blessings recited everywhere under the canopy at Jewish weddings include a prayer that the sounds of joy and happiness of bride and groom may once again be heard in the cities of Judea and the streets of Jerusalem. And no such Jewish wedding is complete before the groom has broken a glass to commemorate the destruction of Jerusalem's Holy Temple. Every year since 70 CE, pious Jews all over the world continue to fast on Tishah B'Av, from one sunset to the next, chanting the biblical Book of Lamentations in mourning of the destruction of the Jewish Holy Temple in Jerusalem. And every year, Jews begin the Passover Seder (the ritual feast held at the beginning of the Jewish festival of Passover) with, "Today, we are here; next year, may we be in the Land of Israel" and end it with "Next year, in Jerusalem."

In the face of such enduring historical, national, and religious ties dating from the beginning of Jewish history, the PLO and PA would

---

15. Abraham Even-Shoshan, *A New Concordance of the Torah, Prophets, and Writings* (Jerusalem: Kiryat Sefer/Baker Book House, 1989).
16. *Talmud Bavli, Ketubot* 110b.

– 1 –

The Balfour Declaration

THE REBIRTH OF ISRAEL IN the ancient Jewish national homeland—a situation with which the Palestinian Arabs have yet to reconcile themselves—is the outcome of a concatenation of apparently chance events that in combination seem no less than providential. That diaspora Jewry, having suffered unspeakable persecution (massacres, mass expulsions, forced conversions, inquisitions, and destructions of entire communities), was able to maintain for two thousand years its dream of the promised Redemption and the restoration of Jewish sovereignty in the Holy Land is itself a remarkable manifestation of religious faith that is unparalleled in all history. Beginning in the final quarter of the nineteenth century, Jewish circles in Czarist Russia—aroused by the evolving nationalist movements in Europe and in a state of despair because of the persecution and pogroms they faced—decided the time had come for Jews to translate this dream into reality. A small group calling itself Chovevei Zion ("Lovers of Zion") began in the 1880s a mass movement of settling in Israel, denoting the move an *Aliyah*, a cultural and spiritual elevation, *livnot u'l'hibanot bah*—"to build the Land and be rebuilt in it." In the 1890s, a second *Aliyah*, expanded in size and more significantly in scope, began developing the manifold cultural, political, and governmental institutions that a reborn Jewish national homeland would require. Among those who came to Israel during this second *Aliyah* was David Ben-Gurion (1886–1973), the leader of Mapai (an acronym for the democratic socialist party—*Mifleget Poalei Eretz Yisrael*, "Workers' Party of the Land of Israel") and the first prime minster of the State of Israel—officially reborn only forty-two years after Ben-Gurion's arrival in Israel in 1906.

The founding of political Zionism in Western Europe shortly after the rise of the practical Zionism of the Chovevei Zion movement in Czarist Russia was even more extraordinary in that its founder, Theodor Herzl (1860–1904), was a theretofore totally assimilated Jewish journalist and playwright from Austria. Shocked by the anti-Semitic Dreyfus affair in "enlightened" France, Herzl suddenly appeared on the Jewish scene in February 1896 and electrified the Jewish community with the publication of his book, *Der Judenstaat* ("The Jewish State"), in which he maintained that the only solution to the Jewish problem was the establishment of the Jewish state in the ancient Jewish national homeland. In ringing language, Herzl wrote:

> Palestine is our unforgettable historic homeland… The Jews who will it shall achieve their State. We shall live at last as free men on our own soil, and in our own homes peacefully die. The world will be liberated by our freedom, enriched by our wealth, magnified by our greatness, and whatever we attempt there for our own benefit will redound mightily and beneficially to the good of all mankind.[1]

Herzl won instant acclaim within the Zionist circles, and by the end of 1896, all Zionist Jewry recognized him as their leader. In 1897, he organized the First Zionist Congress in Basel, Switzerland, which about two hundred delegates from seventeen countries attended. The Congress established the Basel Program for the establishment of "a home for the Jewish people in Israel secured under public law." The steps outlined in the program for achieving this goal included the promotion of settlement in Israel, the establishment of public institutions for uniting all Jewry behind the Zionist goal, and gaining

---

1. "Texts Concerning Zionism: Excerpts from Herzl's 'The Jewish State,'" *Jewish Virtual Library*, accessed April 16, 2023, https://www.jewishvirtuallibrary.org/excerpts-from-quot-the-jewish-state-quot.

support from governments for the Zionist goal.[2] The Basel Congress established the World Zionist Organization and elected Herzl as its president. Among the delegates who attended the subsequent annual sessions of the Zionist Congress was Chaim Weizmann (1874–1952), the first president of the State of Israel.

Embarking almost immediately upon a series of high-level diplomatic engagements, Herzl met with the world leaders who held power in the Ottoman Empire, including the German kaiser, the pope, the vizier of the Empire, and the sultan himself, as well as with the cabinet ministers of Czarist Russia and of Great Britain. His goal was to enlist their support for a Jewish national home in Palestine. All turned him down, but in 1903, the British colonial minister, under the then Prime Minister Arthur Balfour (1902–1905), offered the Jews a home in British East Africa, now part of Kenya and Uganda.

Worried about the urgent need to save Jews who were suffering from pogroms and persecution in Czarist Russia, Herzl brought to the Sixth Basel Congress a proposal to consider British East Africa as a temporary place of refuge until a national home could be re-established in Israel. The proposal created a storm in the Congress, where the Russian delegates under Weizmann's leadership, fearful that the proposal would sidetrack the Zionist goal for a Jewish national homeland in Israel walked out of the Congress. The delegates who remained voted in favor of investigating the offer, but the offer was rejected at the Seventh Zionist Congress held in 1905, a year after Herzl had succumbed to stress and disease. Like the biblical Joseph in Egypt, Herzl requested that his body be reburied in Israel when the State of Israel would be reborn. In 1949, the fledgling State of Israel honored his request and his body was reinterred on Mount Herzl.

✡ ✡ ✡

---

2. "Zionist Congress: First Zionist Congress & Basel Program," *Jewish Virtual Library*, accessed April 16, 2023, https://www.jewishvirtuallibrary.org/first-zionist-congress-and-basel-program-1897.

The failed Uganda program set off a chain of highly improbable events which in combination led to the Balfour Declaration, the League of Nations Mandate for Palestine, and ultimately the rebirth of the State of Israel. The first link in that chain was the unexpected meeting in 1906 between Chaim Weizmann and Arthur Balfour, the author of the Balfour Declaration of 1917. Profoundly frustrated by the crisis in the Zionist movement generated by his rejection of the British offer of Uganda as a place of refuge, Weizmann decided in 1904 to suspend his Zionist activity and to leave for England to devote himself completely to a career in chemistry, in which he had undertaken research as a student in Germany. It so happened that Arthur James Balfour, Britain's former prime minister who had made the offer of Uganda to the Zionists, was living in Manchester at the beginning of 1906. His government had fallen in December 1905, and he had come to Manchester to run for a seat in Parliament in the following month's election.

Balfour had a lifelong interest in the Jews and their history. As his niece and biographer, Blanche Dugdale, wrote, he believed that the "Christian religion and civilization owes to Judaism an immeasurable debt, shamefully ill repaid."[3] He had as yet almost no appreciation, however, of Zionist aspirations. Puzzled by the refusal of the Zionist Jews to accept his government's offer of settlement in Uganda, he welcomed the opportunity, at a meeting arranged by a Manchester Zionist, to hear an explanation from Chaim Weizmann, leader of the opposition, to the offer. It is interesting to read Weizmann's explanation as to why he and other Russian Jews (secular Jews for the most part) had been so adamantly opposed to the offer:

> I dwelt on the spiritual side of Zionism. I pointed out that nothing but a deep religious conviction expressed in modern political terms could keep the movement alive and that this conviction had to be based on Palestine and Palestine alone.

---

3. Blanche E. C. Dugdale, *Arthur James Balfour, vol. 1, 1848–1906* (London: Hutchinson, 1936), 324.

Any deflection from Palestine was—well, a form of idolatry. I added that if Moses had come into the Sixth Zionist Congress when it was adopting the resolution in favor of the Commission for Uganda, he would surely have broken the tablets once again. We knew that the Uganda offer was well meant, and on the surface, it might appear the more practical road. But I was sure that quite apart from the availability and the suitability of the territory—the Jewish people would never produce either the money or the energy required in order to build up a wasteland and make it habitable, unless that land were Palestine... Our history has been what it is because of our tenacious hold on Palestine. We have never accepted defeat and have never forsaken the memory of Palestine. Such a tradition could be converted into real motive power, and we were trying to do just that, struggling against great difficulties, but sure that the day would come when we would succeed.

Uncertain whether Balfour really appreciated the significance of Palestine for the Jewish people, Weizmann suddenly had inspiration and asked, "Mr. Balfour, supposing I were to offer you Paris instead of London, would you take it?" Balfour replied, "But Dr. Weizmann, we have London." Weizmann responded, "That is true, but we had Jerusalem when London was a marsh." Impressed by Weizmann's explanation, Balfour asked, "Are there many Jews who think like you?" Weizmann answered, "I believe I speak the mind of millions of Jews...with whom I could pave the streets of the country I come from," to which an impressed Balfour replied, "If that is so, you will one day be a force."[4]

Even more unexpected and seemingly providential was the contribution that Weizmann's research in biochemistry during his student days in Germany was to make to the Allied victory in World War I, a victory that was to provide for the establishment of both the

---

4. Chaim Weizmann, *Trial and Error: The Autobiography of Chaim Weizmann* (New York: Schocken, 1949), 110–111.

Arab states of the Middle East and the rebirth of the Jewish State of Israel. By May 1915, hard-fought battles on the western front and in Gallipoli had created such a grave shortage of ammunition that the resulting "Shell Crisis" forced Britain's Prime Minister Herbert Henry Asquith to reconstitute his cabinet. Thirty thousand tons of acetone, the essential ingredient in the manufacture of explosives, were urgently needed to overcome this crisis. It so happened that during his research in biochemistry in his student days in Germany, Weizmann had focused on processes of fermentation and discovered a process of fermentation of sugar that yielded a mixture of butyl alcohol and acetone.

Upon the outbreak of World War I in 1914, Weizmann, responding to a British War Office circular that invited scientists to report any discoveries of possible military value, offered his discovery in fermentation, free of charge, to the British government. Weizmann's report on his research then came to the attention of Winston Churchill, who offered him a government position with carte blanche authority to obtain the people and facilities required for the manufacture of the huge quantities of the critically needed acetone.[5] Weizmann's vital wartime contribution to overcoming Britain's desperate shortage of ammunition, enabling Britain to escape threatened defeat and go on to victory, opened government doors to him. The government repaid Weizmann by giving him a sympathetic hearing and support for the Zionist program for the return of the Jewish people to their ancient homeland in Palestine.

As important as Weizmann's role was, however, considerations of national self-interest were undoubtedly critical in Britain's decision to enact the Balfour Declaration. A vital consideration, as indicated by the minutes of the War Cabinet meetings, was the conviction within the British cabinet that strong support from Zionist organizations for the war effort in the United States and elsewhere "would be of most substantial assistance to the Allies," particularly since, as

---

5. Weizmann, *Trial and Error*, 133–134, 171–175.

noted below, Germany was competing to secure this goodwill.[6] A concern of commanding importance for many others was the need to deal with competing French interests in the Middle East. As discussed in the next chapter, Zionism would provide Britain with the means to override French claims to a share in governing Palestine, to which Britain had formally consented only a year earlier in the Sykes–Picot Agreement.[7] For some pro-Zionist officials, another significant consideration was the value of a Jewish national home in Palestine for safeguarding British control of the Suez Canal and promoting British interests in the Middle East. According to Richard Crossman, however, "Without the personality of Weizmann, there would have been no Balfour Declaration and no Mandate. There would have been only the slow, painful kind of build-up of Jewish life in Zion which had preceded World War I. And this might well

---

6. J. C. Hurewitz, "The Balfour Declaration of Sympathy with Zionist Aspirations: Minutes of War Cabinet Meetings," in *The Middle East and North Africa in World Politics: A Documentary Record*, ed. J. C. Hurewitz (New Haven: Yale University Press, 1979), Doc. 25, 101–106. On September 3, 1917, the acting foreign minister commented on "the very strong and enthusiastic organization, more particularly in the United States, who were zealous in this matter [of a Jewish State]" and added his "belief that it would be of most substantial assistance to the Allies to have the earnestness and enthusiasm of these people enlisted on our side." On October 4, Balfour reported, "The German government were making great efforts to capture the sympathy of the Zionist movement." At the meeting on October 31, at which the war cabinet authorized him to issue the Declaration, Balfour noted, "He gathered that everyone was now agreed that from a purely diplomatic and political point of view, it was desirable that some declaration favorable to the aspirations of the Jewish nationalists should now be made. The vast majority of Jews in Russia and America, as indeed all over the world, now appeared to be favourable to Zionism. If we could make a declaration favourable to such an ideal, we should be able to carry on extremely useful propaganda both in Russia and America."
7. See Martin Jones, *Failure in Palestine* (London: Mansell, 1986), 2–3.

have been extinguished in the 1930s by the convulsions of Arab nationalism."[8]

✡ ✡ ✡

Even Weizmann's role in Britain's decision to enact the Balfour Declaration would have been of no avail, however, in the presence of a government whose leadership was predisposed to oppose the Zionist aspirations for a Jewish national homeland in Palestine. Herbert Henry Asquith, the very powerful prime minister (1908–1916) who led Great Britain into World War I, was not at all sympathetic to the Zionist cause. Had he remained in power until the very end of World War I, no British declaration expressing support for the establishment of a Jewish national homeland in Palestine would ever have received his approval. It was only the completely unexpected replacement of Prime Minister Asquith by his war minister, David Lloyd George, in December 1916 that paved the way for the Balfour Declaration in 1917.

Winston Churchill considered Prime Minister Asquith one of the greatest peacetime prime ministers Great Britain ever had.[9] According to his biographer, Roy Jenkins, Asquith seemed politically indestructible. He held continuous power for eight-and-a half years, and his cabinet, which included Winston Churchill and David Lloyd George, was considered the most brilliant in English history.[10] Asquith had no interest in Palestine and no sympathy for Zionism or for the Jews. Nearly three years before the Balfour Declaration in January 1915, Sir Herbert Samuel, the first traditional Jew in a British cabinet, had sent a memorandum to Asquith urging Britain to annex Palestine following the hoped-for defeat of the Turkish Empire, to facilitate

---

8. Richard Crossman, *A Nation Reborn* (New York: Atheneum Publishers, 1960), 47.
9. Winston Churchill, "Herbert Henry Asquith," in *Great Contemporaries*, Winston Churchill (London and Glasgow: Collins, 1937), 125.
10. Roy Jenkins, *Asquith: Portrait of a Man and an Era* (New York: Chillmark Press, 1964), blurb.

the immigration there of European Jews, and in due course to give them home rule. Asquith rejected this proposal and commented in his diary entry of January 28, 1915:

> I have just received from Herbert Samuel a memorandum headed, "The Future of Palestine." He goes on to argue, at considerable length and with some vehemence, in favor of the British annexation of Palestine, a country the size of Wales, much of it barren mountain and part of it waterless. He thinks we might plant in this not-very-promising territory about three or four million European Jews and that this would have a good effect upon those who are left behind… I confess I am not attracted by this proposed addition to our responsibilities, but it is a curious illustration of Dizzy's favourite maxim that "race is everything" to find this almost lyrical outburst proceeding from the well-ordered and methodical brain of H.S.[11]

Two months later, Samuel submitted a revised version of his memorandum to the cabinet, omitting the rhetorical peroration that had so astonished Asquith.[12] In his diary entry of March 13, 1915, Asquith again recorded his opposition:

---

11. Herbert Henry Asquith, *Memories and Reflections* (Boston: Little, Brown, and Company, 1928), 70–71. The name "Dizzy" refers to Benjamin Disraeli, an earlier distinguished British prime minister (1868, 1874–80), born a Jew, whose father converted him in childhood to Christianity. He nevertheless remained fiercely proud of his Jewish origins.
12. Herbert Louis Samuel, *Memoirs* (London: Cresset Press, 1945), 142. The peroration in Samuel's memorandum, which had produced such a surprised reaction in Asquith, reads, "The Jewish brain is a physiological product not to be despised. For fifteen centuries, the race produced in Palestine a constant succession of great men—statesmen and prophets, judges and soldiers. If a body be again given in which its soul can lodge, it may enrich the world. Till full scope is granted, as Macaulay said in the House of Commons, 'Let us not presume to say that there is no genius among the countrymen of Isaiah, no heroism among the descendants of the Maccabees'" (John Bowle, *Viscount Samuel* [London: Victor Gollancz,

I think I have already referred to Herbert Samuel's dithyrambic memorandum urging that in the carving up of the Turks' Asiatic dominion, we should take Palestine, into which the scattered Jews would in time swarm back from all quarters of the globe and in due course obtain home rule. Curiously enough, the only other partisan of this proposal is Lloyd George, who, I need not say, does not care a damn for the Jews or their past or their future but thinks it will be an outrage to let the Holy Places pass into the possession or under the protectorate of "agnostic, atheistic France."[13]

1957], 171, cited in Elie Kedourie, *The Chatham House Version* [Hanover, NH: Published for Brandeis University Press by University Press of New England, 1984], 52).

13. Asquith, *Memories and Reflections*, 78. Asquith may have been mistaken. In an article in 1923 on "Palestine and the Jews," Lloyd George showed a very great deal of sympathy for the Jews, writing, inter alia, "Of all the bigotries that savage the human temper, there is none so stupid as the anti-Semitic. It has no basis in reason; it is not rooted in faith; it aspires to no ideal; it is just one of those dank and unwholesome weeds that grow in the morass of racial hatred. How utterly devoid of reason it is may be gathered from the fact that it is almost entirely confined to nations who worship Jewish prophets and apostles, revere the national literature of the Hebrews as the only inspired message delivered by the Deity to mankind, and whose only hope of salvation rests on the precepts and promises of the great teachers of Judah. Yet, in the sight of these fanatics, the Jews of today can do nothing right. If they are rich, they are birds of prey. If they are poor, they are vermin. If they are in favour of war, it is because they want to exploit the bloody feuds of the gentiles to their own profit. If they are anxious for peace, they are either instinctive cowards or traitors. If they give generously—and there are no more liberal givers than the Jews—they are doing it for some selfish purpose of their own. If they do not give—then what could one expect of a Jew but avarice? If labour is oppressed by great capital, the greed of the Jew is held responsible. If labour revolts against capital—as it did in Russia—the Jew is blamed for that also. If he lives in a strange land, he must be persecuted and pogromed out of it. If he wants to go back to his own, he must be prevented. Through the centuries in every land, whatever he does, or intends, or fails to do, he has been pursued by

Asquith himself did not care much for Jews. In one of his letters, he wrote that he dreamed he had been supplanted by Herbert Samuel, "a Jew, an 'Ebrew Jew." Wondering whether that was going to be his fate, he commented, "I take refuge in the beatitude, 'The meek shall inherit the Earth'—and no Jew was ever meek!"[14] Nearly a decade later, after losing his seat in Parliament, Asquith visited the Holy Land, which by then contained about a hundred thousand Jews. His diary entry of November 26, 1924 reads:

> If it were not for these historic associations, no one who could go anywhere else would visit Palestine. It is just what I expected to find—an arid, rocky, hummocky, treeless expanse, with ranges of hills here and there rising to no great height... The Jews are increasing (mainly from the less civilized parts of the east of Europe) as the result of the Zionist propaganda and no doubt are much better looked after and happier here than they were in the wretched places from which they were exported. But the talk of making Palestine into a Jewish "national home" seems to me as fantastic as it always has done.[15]

As might be expected of a statesman of his eminence, Asquith was a man of firm convictions, and as Winston Churchill wrote, he always acted according to those convictions, "showing scorn for arguments, for personalities, and even for events which did not conform to his views."[16] Roy Jenkins noted that when World War I started, Asquith

---

the echo of the brutal cry of the rabble of Jerusalem against the greatest of all Jews—'crucify him!'" (Reprinted in Martin Gilbert, ed., *Lloyd George: Great Lives Observed* [Englewood Cliffs, NJ: Prentice Hall, 1968], 69–72).

14. Stephen Koss, *Asquith* (New York: Colombia University Press, 1976), 176. Another example of Asquith's negative stereotyping of Jews is his comment after having read George Buckle's biography of Disraeli: "He was the only Jew of our time who had real courage—both passive and active—a rare quality in that race."
15. Asquith, *Memories and Reflections*, 260–261.
16. Churchill, "Herbert Henry Asquith," 113–114.

had come to be considered the "natural" head of the government, and that "it required an effort of imagination on the part of his colleagues, his opponents, the electorate, and even himself, to visualize anyone else in his place."[17]

And yet, despite Asquith's seeming indestructibility, his power as prime minister suddenly crumbled, and his government collapsed. What is it that led to Asquith's sudden downfall? Why did one of the greatest prime ministers, who had become such a "natural" head of government that it required an effort of imagination even to visualize anyone else in his place, suddenly become so vulnerable? Remarkably enough, it was a failed romance of the prime minister with a young lady less than half his age that played a key role in this unexpected turn of events. Asquith was then already past sixty, and he had four sons and a daughter by a first marriage and a son and a daughter by a second marriage. Yet, it was a romantic obsession with a young woman, Venetia Stanley, aged twenty-five, a contemporary and close friend of his own daughter, which was largely responsible for his downfall as wartime prime minister.

Roy Jenkins, drawing on Asquith's unpublished private letters, paints a vivid picture of Asquith's relations with Miss Stanley:

> In 1910, he began the first faint trickle of what was later to become a flood of letters to Venetia Stanley. In February 1912, Miss Stanley accompanied Asquith, his daughter, and Edwin Montagu on a Sicilian holiday. Thereafter, the letters became much more frequent. By the outbreak of the War, he was already writing an average of almost a letter a day to her. And they were very substantial letters. Few were under five hundred

---

17. Jenkins, *Asquith*, 332–333. In March 1915, when Asquith threatened to resign, in order to settle a dispute between two cabinet members, he recorded in his diary, "Their mutual anger dissolved like a frost under a sudden thaw, and they both, with a united voice, exclaimed, 'The day you leave that chair, the rest of us disappear, never to return.' And I am sure they meant it."

words in length; many ran to a thousand. During the first three months of 1915, Asquith wrote to her on 141 separate occasions. On one day, Tuesday, March 30, he wrote her four letters of a combined length of just over three thousand words.[18]

In the spring of 1915, Asquith was faced with a grave political crisis over costly military failures on both the western front against Germany and at the Dardanelles against Turkey. In May of that year, the "Shell Crisis" forced him, as already noted, to reconstitute his government in a coalition with the Conservatives. Nevertheless, what preoccupied him throughout this crisis were his own personal problems, because, as Roy Jenkins describes in detail, toward the end of April he sensed that Miss Stanley was breaking off their relationship. On April 22, he wrote to her, begging her to tell him the truth, no matter how hard it might be for him. On Monday, May 10, his hopes rose again after a ten-minute visit with Miss Stanley, and upon returning to Downing Street with Edwin Montagu, his former parliamentary private secretary, who had also been present, he wrote to her:

> I walked back with the Assyrian [Edwin Montagu] from Mansfield Street and we had (as always) good conversation. I don't honestly believe that at this moment, there are two persons in the world (of opposite sexes) from whom I cd. more confidently count, whatever troubles or trials I had to encounter, for whole-hearted love and devotion than you and he: of course in quite different ways and senses.

Immediately thereafter, however, came the shattering blow. The next day, when Asquith went to visit her, he was not permitted to see her. Then, on Wednesday, May 12, Miss Stanley sent him the crushing letter that she had decided to marry Edwin Montagu. Jenkins describes Asquith's anguished reaction:

---

18. Jenkins, *Asquith*, 257–258, 346.

The blow to Asquith was severe. He never reproached Miss Stanley—not even for the suddenness of her action. He never reproached Montagu... But he made no attempt to conceal from either of them or from himself what a heavy blow he had received and how great a change it must make... It was a pity that she chose the moment that she did. Her sustenance of Asquith collapsed at a time when he was in peculiar need of it.[19]

With the heavy blow from Miss Stanley's letter came the collapse of Asquith's political career. As a later prime minister, Sir Harold Wilson, commented:

Modern readers of his various biographies are amazed to see how much he diverted his attention from the conduct of the War to pursue his obsession with Venetia Stanley. On the darkest days of the War on the western front, he would sit at his place in cabinet writing soppy letters to her...and he would frequently desert his duties to be with her... He was shattered by her sudden decision to marry Edwin Montagu... Asquith was no longer capable of acting as a wartime prime minister.[20]

David Lloyd George, Asquith's war secretary, joined the Conservative members of the coalition in challenging Asquith's conduct of the war, and in December 1916, replaced him in a new coalition government. Prime Minister Lloyd George (1916–1922) appointed the former Conservative prime minister, Arthur Balfour, as his minister of foreign affairs (1916–1919), and less than one year later, on November 2, 1917, the Balfour Declaration came, stating that the British government viewed with favor the establishment of a national home for the Jewish people in Palestine.

There is a double irony in the fact that the marriage that so shattered Prime Minister Asquith and led to the new government that

---

19. Jenkins, *Asquith*, 363–366.
20. Harold Wilson, *The Chariot of Israel: Britain, America, and the State of Israel* (London: Weidenfeld and Nicolson/Michael Joseph, 1981), 39–40.

issued the Balfour Declaration was to Edwin Montagu. The first irony is the personal one, noted by his biographer, Roy Jenkins. Edwin Montagu was his most loyal supporter and devoted friend. As Asquith had written to Miss Stanley only two days before the crushing announcement of her decision to marry Montagu, there was no one on whose wholehearted love and devotion he could confidently count as much as on Montagu and Miss Stanley.

The second (and more remarkable) irony lies in its significance for the history of the rebirth of the Jewish State of Israel. Edwin Montagu, like his cousin, Herbert Samuel, was the son of a Jew of traditional background, but in contrast to Samuel, he was a completely assimilated Jew and a passionate anti-Zionist. Although when he joined Lloyd George's government as secretary of state for India, he became a powerful champion for India's independence, he remained throughout his life a fierce opponent of a Jewish state.[21] Like members of the American Council for Judaism thirty years later, who fiercely opposed the UN proposal to establish a Jewish state in Palestine, Montagu and his friends insisted on a thesis theretofore unknown and unimaginable in all Jewish history: that Judaism was only a religion, and Jews were not a people. Worried about possible charges of dual loyalty in their countries of residence, they maintained Jews were only

---

21. Weizmann, *Trial and Error*, 154. Weizmann reports the following comment about Montagu made by Balfour's niece, Blanche E. C. Dugdale, who, like her uncle, was an ardent Zionist: "Mr. [Edwin] Montagu could not extend to his own people the sympathy he evinced later for nationalism in India. He saw the specter of anti-Semitism in every country if its Jews permitted themselves to dream of a territorial center or a national political existence outside their present citizenships. Such aspirations in English Jews he looked upon as traitorous disloyalty to their native land. In the case of Jews living under less happy conditions, he believed that their relations with the countries of their birth would only be worsened. This was not a point of view which never appealed with great force to the non-Jewish populations of the British Empire, many of whom as, for example, the Scotch, are perfectly accustomed to combine strong separate racial consciousness with a wider loyalty."

Englishmen, Americans, or other nationals of the Jewish faith, not a people entitled to a state of their own. Having ceased to observe traditional Jewish practices, they were either ignorant of the basic character of Judaism or simply shrugged aside the fact that Judaism is not simply a religion of faith, but, as discussed in the Introduction, a religion intimately rooted and closely tied to a particular people and a particular place—to the Jewish people and to Israel.

Christian Zionists have always rejected the Montagu thesis. The Christian historian, James Parkes, wrote:

> It is correct to say, 'the Jewish people' and not 'the Jews'; for even when they were scattered in a thousand ghettoes in innumerable different Christian and Moslem countries, the Jews recognized themselves as, and were universally recognized by others to be, a single people. The concepts of Englishmen, Poles or, Americans of the Jewish persuasion is a wholly modern one, a product of emancipation, and has never been applicable to more than a minority of Jewry. During this period, from the second century to the eighteenth, nobody would have challenged the truth of the idea that it was just as accurate to compare Jews with Turks or Frenchmen as to compare them with Christians or Moslems. They were recognized as both a religion and a nation, and it occurred to no one that there was anything inconsistent in the dual attribution. This recognition by themselves and others that they were still a single people reinforces the naturalness of their continued association with the landscape of their independent history and of their lawgivers and prophets. Moreover, their restoration to the Land of Israel was an article of Christian as well as of Jewish belief.[22]

Although Montagu failed to kill the Balfour Declaration, his adamant objections did succeed in delaying its adoption and in watering down the text originally approved by Balfour and Lloyd George. As

---

22. Parkes, *Whose Land?* 137–138.

Weizmann, the Zionist leader who was intimately involved in Britain's issuance of the Balfour Declaration, later wrote:

> A comparison of the two texts—the one approved by the Foreign Office and the prime minister and the one adopted on October 4, after Montagu's attack—shows a painful recession from what the government itself was prepared to offer. The first declares that "Palestine should be reconstituted as the national home of the Jewish people." The second speaks of "the establishment in Palestine of a national home for the Jewish race."[23] The first adds only that the "government will use its best endeavors to secure the achievement of this object and will discuss the necessary methods with the Zionist Organization", the second introduced the subject of the "civic and religious rights of the existing non-Jewish communities" in such a fashion as to impute possible oppressive intentions of the Jews and can be interpreted to mean such limitations on our work as completely to cripple it.[24]

Even so, Montagu's opposition created a deadlock on the question of issuing the Declaration, the government understandably finding it difficult to appear to be more supportive of a Jewish national home than were the Jews. The government felt it desirable, therefore, to seek the support of the United States, which had joined the war against Germany in April 1917.

President Woodrow Wilson, like many Christians who had grown up with the Bible, was a supporter of Zionism. As the historian Peter Grose records, Wilson had informed Rabbi Stephen Wise in June 1917 that he would be ready to respond whenever he and Justice Brandeis, the two leading American Zionists, wished for him to act. Nevertheless, at the beginning of September 1917, when the British government first inquired of the US government's position, Wilson

---

23. The final text refers to "the Jewish people," not "the Jewish race."
24. Weizmann, *Trial and Error*, 207. Britain did in fact subsequently interpret it thus in the 1939 white paper.

hesitated. In October 1917, Balfour sent a second inquiry, this time noting reports that the Germans were "making great efforts to capture the Zionist movement," and Wilson quickly overcame his hesitation, instructing his assistant, Colonel House, that he "concurred in the formula suggested from the other side and would be obliged if [Colonel House] would let them know."[25] As Weizmann subsequently noted, the United States cable in support of the substance of the Balfour Declaration "was one of the most important individual factors in breaking the deadlock created by British Jewish anti-Zionists and in deciding the British government to issue its declaration."[26] The text of the Balfour Declaration, as issued on November 2, 1917, reads:

> His Majesty's Government view with favour the establishment in Palestine of a national home for the Jewish people and will use their best endeavors to facilitate the achievement of this object, it being clearly understood that nothing shall be done which may prejudice the civil and religious rights of existing non-Jewish communities in Palestine or the rights and political status enjoyed by the Jews in any other country.

---

25. Peter Grose, *Israel in the Mind of America* (New York: Schocken Books, 1984), 66–71. In light of the state department's determined opposition to President Truman's pro-Zionist policy in 1947–1948, it is interesting to note that the department's opposition to Zionism was already firmly established at this very early stage during World War I. Secretary of State Robert Lansing was so opposed to any support for Zionism that as Grose points out, Wilson acted on this occasion without consulting him. Subsequently, he found it necessary to overrule his secretary's anti-Zionist position on several occasions.
26. Weizmann, *Trial and Error*, 206–208.

– 2 –

Negotiating the Mandate

THE PATH OF THE BALFOUR Declaration from a unilateral moral obligation of Great Britain to an international legal obligation, which led only a quarter of a century later to the rebirth of the State of Israel in its ancient national homeland, was not a simple one to traverse. The wartime Allies were bound by President Woodrow Wilson's Fourteen Points for achieving "a just and stable peace" (announced early in 1918), according to which the conquered Middle Eastern territories were to be governed by a mandate of the League of Nations, established after World War I. Each territory was to be administered by an approved "Mandatory Power" that would be responsible for nurturing the Mandate territory until it was ready for independence. For Britain to implement the Balfour Declaration, it would need to receive the League of Nation's Mandate for Palestine and the League's approval to incorporate it in the Declaration.

The first step towards the League of Nations agreements was taken during the negotiations at the Paris Peace Conference (January 18, 1919–January 21, 1920). Before the British government representative even went to the Conference, there was some debate within the British government itself concerning whether to take on the Mandate for Palestine. Edwin Montagu, who had joined Lloyd George's government six months after Asquith's fall, was so adamant an opponent of the Balfour Declaration that he favored giving the Palestine Mandate to the United States. In this, he was supported by another anti-Zionist, Lord Curzon, a senior member of Lloyd George's war cabinet who served as acting foreign secretary while Balfour was attending the Paris Peace Conference and who succeeded him in that post after the Conference. Lloyd George, together with Balfour and the majority of his colleagues who supported the Balfour Declaration, carried the day, however, and the government accordingly decided to assume responsibility for Palestine.[1]

Negotiations with France

To receive the Mandate for Palestine, Britain had first to resolve the conflict of its interests in the Middle East with those of its ally, France. Their rivalry in the Middle East dated back to the system of "capitulations," which the European powers including Germany and Russia, as well as France and Britain, had imposed upon the feeble Ottoman Empire during the nineteenth century. As early as 1915, Britain (then still governed under Prime Minister Asquith) drafted a secret agreement with France concerning the post-war division of the Ottoman Empire, covering the entire area of what is now Syria, Lebanon, Iraq, Jordan, and Palestine. The agreement, known as the Sykes–Picot Agreement, was formally adopted in May 1916 in the form of an exchange of letters between the foreign ministers of the two governments.[2]

Under the Agreement, France was to be the power "protecting and advising" Syria (including Lebanon, which had been ruled as the western district of "Greater Syria"), and Great Britain the power "protecting and advising" Transjordan and Iraq. For Palestine, however, account had to be taken of the diverse interests of France, Czarist Russia, and Great Britain. France regarded Palestine as an integral part of Greater Syria; Russia was the "protector" of the Christian Orthodox population there, and Britain considered control of Palestine essential to the security of the Suez Canal—its lifeline in the Middle East. Under the Sykes–Picot Agreement, therefore, Palestine was to

---

1. Wilson, *The Chariot of Israel*, 52.
2. Hurewitz, "Tripartite (Sykes–Picot) Agreement on the Partition of the Ottoman Empire, 26 April–23 October 1916," in *The Middle East and North Africa in World Politics*, Doc. 16, 60–64.

be ruled by an international condominium, with the exact form of administration to be determined after consultation with Russia. A copy of the secret agreement was accordingly sent to Russia.

In 1918, shortly before the end of World War I, Lloyd George's government decided that it was necessary to renegotiate the Sykes–Picot Agreement. Since the United States had entered the war in 1917, and Russia, during the Bolshevik Revolution, had withdrawn from the war, Britain and France would now need to take into account the views of the United States rather than those of Russia. In particular, the Sykes–Picot Agreement needed to be amended to conform with President Wilson's Fourteen Points, calling for the conquered Ottoman territories to be governed according to Mandates of the League of Nations.[3]

The Balfour Declaration then provided Great Britain with the key for locking France out of any share in governing Palestine that it had secured under the original Sykes–Picot Agreement. Five months prior to the issuance of the Balfour Declaration, the Zionist leadership had obtained French recognition that "it would be a deed of justice and of reparation to assist, by the protection of the Allied Powers, in the renaissance of the Jewish nationality in that Land from which the people of Israel were exiled so many centuries ago."[4] The Zionists strongly favored a single power, namely Great Britain, rather than an international condominium, to hold the Mandate in Palestine,[5] and in light of the Balfour Declaration, Britain maintained that it must be that Mandatory Power.

---

3. "Provisional *Modus Vivendi* on the Areas of Special French Interest Under the Sykes–Picot Agreement: Britain and France, 30 September–18 November 1918" in *The Middle East and North Africa in World Politics*, Doc. 31, 118–128.
4. "The British (Balfour) Declaration of Sympathy with Zionist Aspirations: Cambon Letter to Sokolow, 4 June 1917" in *The Middle East and North Africa in World Politics*, Doc. 25, 101–103.
5. "The Zionist Organization's Memorandum to the Supreme Council at the Peace Conference, 3 February 1919" in *The Middle East and North Africa in World Politics*, Doc. 35, 137–142.

France, taking into account its weak bargaining position on Palestine—since it was Britain that had toppled the Ottoman Empire—and hoping to ensure British agreement to a French Mandate over Syria/Lebanon, considered that it had no choice but to yield. It agreed, therefore, under a revised Sykes–Picot arrangement, that in light of the Balfour Declaration, Great Britain should become the sole Mandatory Power in Palestine. In December 1918, French Premier Georges Benjamin Clemenceau accordingly yielded to Lloyd George's request for Palestine to be placed under an exclusive British Mandate.[6] In a *communiqué* issued on February 23, 1919, the French government affirmed that it would neither stand in the way of a British Mandate in Palestine nor prevent the formation of a Jewish state.[7]

Since President Wilson approved the Balfour Declaration prior to its issuance (see Chapter 1), he naturally supported Britain as the Mandatory Power for Palestine.[8] Anti-Israel commentators have argued that the Balfour Declaration was in conflict with Wilson's Fourteen Points. Wilson obviously did not believe so, since he gave his approval to it only months before announcing his Fourteen Points. Indeed, during the Paris Peace Conference, President Wilson expressed his deep belief in the eventuality of the creation of a Jewish state, declaring on March 3, 1919, "I am persuaded that the Allied nations, with the fullest concurrence of our own government and people, are agreed that in Palestine shall be laid the foundation of a Jewish commonwealth."[9]

---

6. "Summary Record of a Secret Meeting to Consider the Sykes–Picot Agreement: The Supreme Council at Paris, 20 March 1919," in *The Middle East and North Africa in World Politics*, Doc. 39, 158–166.
7. Jacques Soustelle, *The Long March of Israel* (New York: American Heritage Press, 1969), 64.
8. "Tentative Recommendations for President Wilson by the Intelligence Section of the American Delegation to the Peace Conference, 3 February 1919," in *The Middle East and North Africa in World Politics*, Doc. 34, 132, 136.
9. "Roots of the US–Israel Relationship," *Jewish Virtual Library*, accessed April 16, 2023, https://www.jewishvirtuallibrary.org/roots-of-the-u-s-israel-relationship.

In view of later history, it is interesting to note that at this stage, when Britain was relying upon the Balfour Declaration for its role as the sole Mandatory Power in Palestine, it argued for an expansion of Palestine's boundaries. It maintained that the southern part of Lebanon, including part of the Litani River, needed to be part of Mandatory Palestine so as to provide adequate water resources for its economic development. It also insisted upon the inclusion of Transjordan (later renamed Jordan) in the Palestine Mandate in order to provide a good military frontier east of the Jordan River and a sufficient area for the development of a vigorous national home for the Jewish people. Remarkably, the borders for Transjordan included in the Palestine Mandate extended eastward well beyond the Hejaz railway, which the Zionist Organization had requested at the Paris Peace Conference and which Balfour had considered essential for the Jewish national home.[10] Britain failed, during the lengthy negotiations, to obtain French agreement to its request for the Litani River, and

---

10. According to Balfour, "In deciding the boundaries of Palestine, economic grounds must count much more than military or strategic considerations, and that if the water necessary for successful development lay as far north as the Litani and Hermon, then the Jews must include both these places in Palestine. The eastern boundary of Palestine must be up to but excluding the Hedjaz Railway" (Colonel Richard Meinertzhagen, *Middle East Diary 1917–1956* [New York: Yoseloff, 1960], 25). The Hedjaz Railway, lying just west of Amman and Damascus, was also the boundary requested by the Zionist Organization at the Paris Peace Conference.

An editorial in *The Times* on September 19, 1919 reflecting the same government policy, stated, "The Jordan River will not do as the eastern frontier of Palestine, and in Galilee, Palestine should also include a good part of the Litani River in the narrows between Lebanon and the Hermon range. To realize the biblical ideal of a united people from Dan to Beer Sheba, not only must Palestine have a good military frontier east of Jordan, but access to the waters of the Litani is needed for the economic development of Northern Galilee… Our duty as the Mandatory Power will be to make Jewish Palestine not a struggling State but one that is capable of vigorous and independent national life" (Martin Gilbert, *Exile and Return: The Struggle for a Jewish Homeland* [Philadelphia, PA: Lippincott, 1978], 124).

Lloyd George yielded.[11] France did, however, agree on Transjordan, and an Anglo–French convention signed on December 23, 1920 accordingly determined Transjordan to be part of Palestine.[12]

Negotiations with the Arabs

Given today's militant Palestinian nationalism, it seems natural to assume that Britain's most difficult problem at the Paris Peace Conference must have related to the strong Arab objections to the Balfour Declaration on Palestine. In fact, however, the Arab leadership at the Paris Peace Conference proved even more readily agreeable to the Balfour Declaration than France had initially been toward relinquishing its claim to a share in governing Palestine. As incredible as it may seem in light of later history, the Arab leadership at the Paris Peace Conference warmly supported the Balfour Declaration and the Zionist aspirations of the Jewish people.

The acknowledged Arab leaders at the time were the Sharif of Mecca, Hussein, a direct descendant of Mohammed and Guardian of the Moslem Holy Places of Mecca and Medina,[13] and his son, Feisal, leader of the Arab Revolt against the Ottoman Empire. In October 1915, Hussein had negotiated an agreement with the British High Commissioner for Egypt, Sir Henry McMahon, under which Britain offered to accept the independence of the Arab territories of the Ottoman Empire in return for Hussein's promise of an Arab revolt against the Empire. Arab nationalists and British anti-Zionists have since argued that the Balfour Declaration contravened the McMahon–Hussein agreement and was therefore invalid. McMahon and

---

11. Howard M. Sachar, *A History of Israel: From the Rise of Zionism to Our Time* (New York: Random House, 2013), 116–117.
12. Paul Hanna, *British Policy in Palestine* (Washington DC: American Council of Public Affairs, 1942), 63-64.
13. After the war, Hussein continued to rule in the Hejaz, where Mecca and Medina are located, but in 1924, he was ousted by Ibn Saud, ruler of the Bedouin kingdom of the Nejd, who subsequently united it with the Hejaz into what is now the Kingdom of Saudi Arabia.

senior members of his staff who were actively involved in the negotiations with Hussein (who generally harbored strong anti-Zionist predilections) have all testified, however, that the promise of Arab independence excluded Palestine.

The controversy over whether the McMahon promise of Arab independence included or excluded Palestine stems from the fact that Palestine is not mentioned by name in McMahon's letter to Hussein. Evidently, the name Palestine was not in current use among the Arabs, and the area was therefore defined only in terms that were in use under the Ottoman Empire. McMahon's letter specified two reservations for territories where the promise of independence would not apply. The first exclusion, among other territories, refers to the portions of Syria "lying to the west of the District of Damascus." As Churchill affirmed in the British white paper of 1922, "This reservation has always been regarded by His Majesty's Government as covering the vilayet of Beirut and the independent Sanjak of Jerusalem. The whole of Palestine west of the Jordan was thus excluded from Sir Henry McMahon's pledge."[14]

The second exclusion included those areas that "were not purely Arab" and "where Britain was not free to act without detriment to the interests of her allies." This reservation must surely have been intended to cover, inter alia, Palestine, since Palestine surely could not be said to be purely Arab, and France was well known to have longstanding interests there, which it relinquished only in the revised Sykes–Picot Agreement of 1919.

Remarkably, Hussein and his son Feisal, far from regarding the Balfour Declaration as a violation of the McMahon–Hussein agreement, in fact approved and indeed welcomed the Balfour Declaration, even expressing strong support for the Zionist aspirations as complementing their own national goals. Hussein attested on March 23,

---

14. Winston Churchill, *Palestine: Correspondence with the Palestine Arab Delegation and the Zionist Organisation*, White Paper, CMD 1700 (London: His Majesty's Stationery Office, 1922) ("the 1922 Churchill White Paper").

1918 in *Al Qibla*, the daily newspaper of Mecca, that Palestine was "a sacred and beloved homeland of its original sons, the Jews" and "the return of these exiles to their homeland will prove materially and spiritually an experimental school for their [Arab] brethren." He called on the Arab population in Palestine to welcome the Jews as brethren and cooperate with them for the common welfare.[15] In January 1918, Commander Hogarth, head of Britain's Arab Bureau in Cairo, had informed Hussein of the contents of the Balfour Declaration and reported back that Hussein "seemed quite prepared for the formula and agreed enthusiastically, saying he welcomed Jews to all Arab lands." Hussein remained friendly toward Zionism even after the 1929 Arab massacres of Jews in Palestine.[16]

Even more striking is the attitude of Feisal, the son of Hussein, who was the commander of the Arab army under the tutelage of the famed Lawrence of Arabia in the war against the Ottomans, and the representative of the Arab people at the Paris Peace Conference. Had Feisal believed that the McMahon–Hussein agreement promised Palestine to the Arabs, he surely would have registered that claim at the Paris Peace Conference. Feisal registered no such claim. On the contrary, in what must have seemed at the time as the miraculous fulfillment of Isaiah's prophecy that "Swords will be beaten into plowshares, and nation will no longer lift up sword unto nation,"[17] Feisal expressed his firm belief that Arab and Jewish national aspirations were complementary goals and were even dependent upon one another for their success. Feisal even expressed his support for

---

15. Isaiah Friedman, *Palestine—A Twice-Promised Land? The British, the Arabs, and Zionism, vol. 1, 1915–1920* (New Brunswick, NJ: Transaction Publishers, 2000), 171.
16. James Parkes, *A History of Palestine from 135 AD to Modern Times* (New York: Oxford University Press, 1949), 288–289. Parkes noted, "Hussein's attitude remained friendly towards Zionism, as is shown in his conversations with Colonel Kisch, Chairman of the Palestine Executive, when they met in Amman in 1924 and 1931."
17. Isaiah 2:4.

all necessary measures to encourage the large-scale immigration of Jews to Palestine and their close settlement upon the land, provisions subsequently incorporated in the text of the British Mandate for Palestine.

Even prior to the Paris Peace Conference, Feisal had met with Chaim Weizmann in Palestine in June 1918, where they agreed on a set of remarkable principles that were incorporated in a written agreement drawn up by Feisal's mentor, the famous spokesmen of the Arab world, Lawrence of Arabia. The agreement, signed on January 3, 1919, two weeks prior to the opening of the Paris Peace Conference, states, inter alia, that His Royal Highness, the Emir Feisal, representing the Arab Kingdom of Hedjaz, and Dr. Chaim Weizmann, representing the Zionist Organization, "realizing that the surest means of working out the consummation of their national aspirations is through the closest possible collaboration in the development of the Arab State and Palestine," have agreed upon a set of articles, including, inter alia, the following:

> Article 1. The Arab State and Palestine in all their relations and undertakings shall be controlled by the most cordial goodwill and understanding...
>
> Article 3. In the establishment of the Constitution and Administration of Palestine, all such measures shall be adopted as will afford the fullest guarantees for carrying into effect the British Government's Declaration [the Balfour Declaration] of the 2nd of November, 1917...
>
> Article 4. All necessary measures shall be taken to encourage and stimulate the immigration of Jews into Palestine on a large scale and as quickly as possible to settle Jewish immigrants upon the land through closer settlement and intensive cultivation of the soil...
>
> Article 8. The parties hereto agree to act in complete accord

and harmony on all matters embraced herein before the Peace Congress.[18]

It was not the Balfour Declaration but the Sykes–Picot Agreement, leading to the French Mandate for Syria, to which Feisal strongly objected as having contravened both the McMahon–Hussein Agreement for Arab independence[19] and the promise of Syria for his Kingdom that had been offered to him by members of General Allenby's military administration, with Lawrence of Arabia in the lead. So passionate was Feisal about his claim to Syria that in a footnote, he added a reservation to the effect that he would not be bound by the agreement with Weizmann unless his claim to Syria was recognized.[20]

On February 6, 1919, Feisal presented his case before the Paris Peace Conference, arguing that Syria should be given its independence as had been promised to his father, Hussein, and as earned by the Arabs for their contribution in the war against the Ottoman Empire and that nothing should be done to imperil the future unity of the Arab people.[21] The French Premier Georges Benjamin Clemenceau

---

18. "Feisal–Weizmann Agreement," in *The Israel–Arab Reader*, ed. Walter Laqueur (New York: Penguin Books, 2016), Doc. 8, 18–20.
19. In a letter to the editor of *The Times* on September 11, 1919 (Andrew Clubb, "T. E. Lawrence and the Arab Cause at the Paris Peace Conference," [2005], *Clio History*, accessed May 22, 2023, https://www.cliohistory.org/thomas-lawrence/paris), Lawrence claimed that the Sykes–Picot Agreement offered the French control only in Lebanon and not in Syria, and it was therefore not inconsistent with the McMahon–Hussein Agreement offering Syria its independence.
20. Since the French expelled Feisal from Syria, he was no longer legally bound by the terms of the agreement with Weizmann, even though Britain gave him Iraq in exchange for the loss of Syria. This does not alter the fact that he had repeatedly expressed such warm sympathy for Zionism and that he believed the Balfour Declaration was not inconsistent with the McMahon-Hussein agreement.
21. Clubb, "T. E. Lawrence and the Arab Cause at the Paris Peace Conference."

opposed Feisal's claim for total Syrian independence and insisted upon France's receiving the Mandate for Syria.

Although it was clear from the Paris Peace Conference's poor reception of his presentation that his claim to Syria would be rejected, Feisal did not abandon his agreement with Weizmann. Instead, he again underscored his sympathy for Jewish aspirations in Palestine in a letter he wrote at the Paris Peace Conference on March 3, 1919 to Felix Frankfurter, then representing the American Zionists:

> We Arabs, especially the educated among us, look with the deepest sympathy on the Zionist movement. Our deputation here in Paris is fully acquainted with the proposals submitted yesterday by the Zionist Organization to the Peace Conference, and we regard them as moderate and proper. We will do our best, in so far as we are concerned, to help them through. We will wish the Jews a most hearty welcome home.

In this letter, Feisal also acknowledged the help that the Zionists had given to the Arab cause at the Peace Conference, declaring,

> [Weizmann] has been a great helper of our cause, and I hope the Arabs may soon be in a position to make the Jews some return for their kindness. We are working together for a reformed and revived Near East, and our two movements complete one another... Indeed, I think that neither can be a real success without the other... I look forward, and my people with me look forward, to a future in which we will help you and you will help us, so that the countries in which we are mutually interested may once again take their places in the community of civilized peoples of the world.[22]

In November 1919, Feisal reconfirmed his sympathy for Zionist aspirations once again in a letter to Herbert Samuel, in which he stated:

---

22. "Feisal-Frankfurter Correspondence" in *The Israel–Arab Reader*, ed. Laqueur, 21–22.

> I am firmly convinced that the mutual confidence established between us and the perfect accord in our view, which has permitted perfect understanding between Dr. Weizmann and myself, will maintain that harmony which is so necessary for the success of our common cause.[23]

The Weizmann–Feisal Agreement and Feisal's letters to Frankfurter and to Samuel are remarkable in terms of the contrast they present to the Arab attitudes and claims as they later evolved with support—indeed, under the guidance—of British military administration officials serving in Palestine and these attitudes and claims have intensified since the rebirth of the State of Israel. They also stand in stark contrast to the claim made in anti-Zionist circles that the Balfour Declaration and the League of Nations Mandate for Palestine were issued without regard to the interests of the Arabs and in violation of the McMahon–Hussein agreement.

According to Pierre van Paassen, the understanding and acceptance that Palestine had been excluded from the promise of Arab independence was not limited to Hussein and Feisal among the Arabs:

> None of the great Arab chiefs, from Hussein to Feisal and Ibn Saud, and none of the Arab revolutionary committees, such as those of Syria and Mesopotamia, which plotted the overthrow of the Ottoman power, as much as introduced the subject of Palestine in the negotiations, both secret and open, that were held with British diplomatic agents. Nobody gave Palestine a moment's thought. What is more: Not a single Palestinian Arab, either lord or commoner, appeared at Feisal's headquarters or at the British agency in Cairo, in Baghdad or in Jidda, where negotiations between Britons and Arabs, at one time or another, were in progress during the better part of three years.

---

23. Letter quoted by Herbert Samuel in a lecture on Great Britain and Palestine given before the Jewish Historical Society, November 25, 1935. The quoted excerpt is from Norman and Helen Bentwich, *Mandate Memories 1918–1948* (New York: Schocken Books, 1965), 19–20.

Even after the issuance in November 1917 of the Balfour Declaration, which was by no means a secret document and which was universally interpreted at the time as containing Britain's pledge to shape political conditions in such a way that a Jewish commonwealth might come into existence in Palestine after the war, and of which the Arabs were fully aware, not a word of protest was voiced against the project by any Arabs, either in Palestine or outside.[24]

✡ ✡ ✡

With the preliminary negotiations between themselves and with the Arabs out of the way, the principal Allies met at the San Remo Peace Conference (April 19–26, 1920), to register their formal decisions on the disposition of the territories of the defeated Ottoman Empire. In accordance with the Paris Peace Conference negotiations, the San Remo Conference decided (on April 24, 1920) to place the Ottoman territories under French and British Mandates: France received the Mandate for Syria/Lebanon, and Great Britain received the Mandates for Iraq and for Palestine, including Transjordan. In the Mandate for Palestine/Transjordan, the agreement incorporated the Balfour Declaration, thereby transforming a unilateral British commitment to facilitate the establishment in Palestine of a national home for the Jewish people into an international legal obligation.

The San Remo Agreement was naturally celebrated by Jews all over the world. Weizmann wrote how deeply moved he was when "arriving a few days later at Victoria Station in London, I was met by representatives of the community bearing the Torah—the Scroll of the Law."[25] Even more remarkable, however, was the reaction of the Arab delegation, which also welcomed the Conference's decision to implement the Balfour Declaration under the League of Nations Mandate for Palestine. In light of the persistent enmity of the Arab

---

24. Pierre van Paassen, *The Forgotten Ally* (Washington, DC: Top Executive Media, 2005), 106–107.
25. Weizmann, *Trial and Error*, 261.

states to which the restoration of the Jewish national home has since been subject, one can only react in wonder to the social event at the conclusion of the Conference, as described by Weizmann, "Anybody entering the dining room of the Royal that evening would have found the Jewish and Arab delegations seated together at a really festive board, congratulating each other under the benevolent paternal gaze of the British delegation at a neighboring table."[26]

Enhanced Commitment in the Mandate

The Mandate for Palestine did more than incorporate the Balfour Declaration. It significantly strengthened the substance of the Balfour Declaration: first, in adding a clause giving recognition "to the historical connection of the Jewish people to Palestine and the grounds for reconstituting the Jewish national home in Palestine" and second, in spelling out the specific obligations of the Mandatory Power concerning the facilitation of the establishment of a Jewish national home in Palestine.

As amazing as it may seem, in one more link in the chain of highly improbable events leading to Israel's rebirth in Palestine, the official responsible for this strengthened text was none other than Lord George Curzon, who had long entertained views that were as unsympathetic to Zionism and to Jews as were those of the former Prime Minister Henry Asquith. In 1919, shortly after the end of the Paris Peace Conference, Curzon had replaced Balfour as foreign secretary. Unlike Balfour, Curzon cared little for Jews and did not favor Britain's facilitation of the rebuilding of the Jewish national home in Palestine. As already noted, Curzon had supported Montagu in the effort to have the United States, rather than Great Britain, assume the Mandate for Palestine. And yet, despite his strong personal objections to the Balfour Declaration, it was Curzon who presided over the strengthening of the Declaration in the text of the Mandate for Palestine.

---

26. Weizmann, *Trial and Error*, 260–261.

Curzon's attitude toward the Jews and the return of the Jews to Palestine is evident from his comments made as early as 1883 on a visit to Palestine at age twenty-four. He had then written to a friend: "Palestine is a country to see once, not to revisit... No Jew with his eyes open (and you never saw one with them shut) would think of going back, and if the millennium is only to arrive when they have returned, our descendants will still be expecting it in 3000 AD."

Curzon's attitude did not change significantly at any stage. Thirty-five years later, in March 1919, while serving as acting foreign secretary (in place of Balfour, who was attending the Paris Peace Conference with Lloyd George), he wrote to Balfour about the reports he had seen of a new Zionist program adopted that year:

> I confess that I shudder at the prospect of our country having to adjust ambitions of this description with the interests of the native population or the legitimate duties of a Mandatory Power; and I look back with a sort of gloomy satisfaction upon the warning that I ventured to utter a year and a half ago in the cabinet as to the consequences of inviting the Hebrews to return to Palestine.

In August 1919, he again wrote to Balfour to express his attitude about Weizmann and Zionists in general:

> This is merely a line to say how much startled I am at a letter from Dr. Weizmann to you, dated July 23, in which that astute but aspiring person claims to advise us as to the principal politico-military appointments to be made in Palestine; to criticize sharply the conduct of any such officers who do not fall on the neck of the Zionists (a most unattractive resting place); and to acquaint us with the "type of man" whom we ought or ought not to send. It seems to me that Dr. Weizmann will be a scourge on the back of the unlucky Mandatory, and I often wish you would drop a few globules of cold water on his heated

and extravagant pretensions.[27]

Curzon's personal hostility to the Balfour Declaration, writes his biographer, was implacable. After replacing Balfour as foreign secretary toward the end of 1919, he could barely restrain himself when he saw the draft text of the Mandate. In March 1920, he commented that the entire conception of the draft was wrong, adding:

> It is quite clear that this mandate has been drawn up by someone reeling under the fumes of Zionism. If we are all to submit to that intoxicant, this draft is all right... But I confess I should like to see something worded differently... I am quite willing to water the Palestine mandate, which I cordially mistrust.[28]

And yet, the final text that Curzon approved considerably reinforced the Balfour Declaration. The preamble he approved added a paragraph that noted:

> Whereas recognition has thereby been given to the historical connection of the Jewish people with Palestine and to the grounds for reconstituting their national home in that country.

In addition, the Curzon-approved operating paragraphs of the Mandate for Palestine spell out in explicit terms the Mandatory

---

27. All three of Curzon's letters are presented in Kenneth Rose, *Superior Person: Portrait of Curzon and His Circle in Late Victorian England* (London: Weidenfeld & Nicolson, 1969), 8990. After citing these letters, Rose commented that Curzon's "judgements [were] not infrequently crystallized early in life. Having determined in 1883 that Palestine was an unsuitable national home for the Jews of the Diaspora, he seems to have resented every stage in their subsequent reunion as a personal affront."
28. Quoted in Conor Cruise O'Brien, *The Siege: The Saga of Israel and Zionism* (New York: Simon and Schuster, 1986), 151, citing "Drafting the Mandate" in *Palestine Papers 1917–1922: Seeds of Conflict*, ed. Doreen Ingrams (London: Eland, 2009), 96–97.

Power's obligations concerning the facilitation of the building of a Jewish national home in Palestine, including:

> Article 2. The Mandatory shall be responsible for placing the country under such political, administrative, and economic conditions as will secure the establishment of the Jewish national home, as laid down in the preamble and the development of selfgoverning institutions…
>
> Article 6. The Administration of Palestine, while ensuring that the rights and position of other sections of the population are not prejudiced, shall facilitate Jewish immigration under suitable conditions and shall encourage, in cooperation with the Jewish agency referred to in Article 4 [the Zionist Organization], close settlement by Jews on the land, including State lands and waste lands not required for public purposes.
>
> Article 11. The Administration… shall introduce a land system appropriate to the needs of the country, having regard, among other things, to the desirability of promoting close settlement and intensive cultivation of the land.
>
> The Administration may arrange with the Jewish agency mentioned in Article 4 to construct or operate, upon fair and equitable terms, any public works, services, and utilities, and to develop any of the natural resources of the country, in so far as these matters are not undertaken by the Administration.[29]

Reviewing Curzon's astonishing role in strengthening the Balfour Declaration as incorporated in the Palestine Mandate, the historian Conor Cruise O'Brien wrote:

> If the document originally submitted to Curzon "[reeked] of Judaism" and was the product of a brain "reeling under the fumes of Zionism," the document Curzon eventually sanctioned reeled

---

29. "San Remo Agreement" in *The Israel–Arab Reader*, ed. Laqueur, 34–42.

and reeked only slightly less. Curzon hated what he had to do, but he did it under protest… Reading Curzon's protestations and looking at Israel's legal foundation stone as it left Curzon's hands, I found a line of Racine's coming into my mind: *Le cruel Dieu des Juifs l'emporte aussi sur toi* (The cruel God of the Jews has you beaten too).[30]

A reader of the Bible may find an even closer parallel to Curzon's action in the story of the non-Jewish prophet, Balaam (Numbers 22:2–24:25), who, though eager to pronounce his curse on the Jews, is repeatedly obliged to give them his blessings.

After searching for a rational answer to the extraordinary phenomenon of a British foreign secretary who, despite all his protestations, nevertheless ends up laying the international legal foundations of the State of Israel, Cruise O'Brien further commented:

> If a Zionist of the pious sort were to tell me that the true explanation of this phenomenon was that God had decided that it was time for His people to come home, I should no doubt express polite skepticism. But if the same pious Zionist were then to ask me whether I can discern any explanation, in terms of Britain's material interests, for the British government's reinforcement of the Balfour Declaration, in the circumstances of the early twenties, I should have to say that I can't find any such explanation.

After exhausting his search for a rational explanation, Cruise O'Brien concluded:

> Deep down, I suspect that there was at work a feeling that it would not be lucky to break a promise to the Jews to help

---

30. Cruise O'Brien, *The Siege*, 151–152. The line is from Racine's play, *Athalie*, Act II, Scene V, based on the history in the Bible in Kings II. In Racine's play, Athalya has a vision at night of her dead mother, Jezebel, coming to foretell her daughter that the Jewish God would destroy her, too.

them return to the Promised Land. Efforts were made at the time to show that the Balfour Declaration was, or was not, in conformity with the Covenant of the League of Nations. What mattered far more was that it was felt to be in conformity with a far older Covenant, between God and the Jews, over *Eretz Yisrael*.[31]

Cruise O'Brien's explanation, it would seem, may not be so very far removed from that of the pious Zionist.

---

31. Cruise O'Brien, *The Siege*, 152–155.

– 3 –

Military Intrigues

IMPLEMENTING BRITAIN'S MIDDLE EAST POLICY proved far more taxing than the negotiations with the French and the Arabs at the Paris and San Remo peace conferences. The British military establishment in Cairo, which General Allenby had appointed to administer the Middle East as the Occupied Enemy Territories Administration (OETA), had evolved an imperial agenda of its own that was diametrically opposed to the government policy announced in London. Acting as if it were an independent branch of government instead of an administration charged with implementing official government policy, the military establishment conspired to undo Britain's Middle East policy—both in Syria *vis-à-vis* the French and in Palestine *vis-à-vis* the Balfour Declaration for a Jewish national homeland. Although their conspiracies failed, they nevertheless laid the groundwork for Britain's ultimate failure as Mandatory Power.

Intrigues in Syria

The military intrigues against Britain's agreement to French rule in Syria began early in the war against the Ottoman Empire. The man primarily responsible for putting the anti-French strategy into effect was T. E. Lawrence, an intelligence officer with a most fascinating and complex personality who was serving in Britain's Arab Bureau in Cairo and was attached to Britain's military establishment. Lawrence was assigned in 1916 as "adviser" to Feisal, son of Sharif Hussein of Mecca, to put into effect the Arab Revolt against the Ottoman Empire, which Hussein had promised in his agreement with McMahon, Britain's high commissioner for Egypt. In two short years, he catapulted himself onto the world stage with a fantastic reputation as the hero of the Arab Revolt who was responsible for the defeat of the Ottoman Empire, the consequent collapse of Germany, and the Allied World War I victory. That reputation, as later historians revealed, was based on sheer fiction, a myth that the political and military establishment nurtured as a powerful weapon in their campaign to undo Britain's Middle East policy.

Compounding the irony of Lawrence's role in that strategy was the fact that although he was the outstanding champion of the Arabs and in his capacity as "adviser" to Feisal, he served as their charismatic spokesman at the Paris Peace Conference, he himself did not share the anti-Zionist bias of his Cairo colleagues. On the contrary, he shared the pro-Zionist sympathies of Balfour and Lloyd George, was a great admirer of Chaim Weizmann,[1] and played a major role in facilitating the Feisal–Weizmann Agreement prior to the Paris Peace Conference. Yet, it was Lawrence's anti-French campaign in Syria that was to provide the Arabs and the British anti-Zionist circles with much of the ammunition for their subsequent unyielding battle against a Jewish national home in Palestine.

As early as the spring of 1915, only months after arriving in Cairo, Lawrence began plotting to deprive the French of any hope of implementing Britain's agreement to French rule in Syria. Already then, he suggested in a letter to his mentor on the Middle East, D. G. Hogarth,

---

1. Lawrence's admiration of Weizmann is evident from the first draft of a letter he wrote—but did not send—in response to an angry letter written by the Anglican Bishop in Jerusalem, wherein he demanded the denial of a statement that had been attributed to Lawrence in a book on Zionism and world politics, where he was quoted as having said, "Episcopal dioceses with missionary interests organized anti-Jewish propaganda." Declaring that he had never denied any statement attributed to him, Lawrence added that he would not do so now, "especially as I suspect that you want my denials only to assure yourself a triumph over Dr. Weizmann, a great man whose boots neither you nor I, my dear Bishop, are fit to black" (David Garnett, *The Letters of T. E. Lawrence* [London: Spring Books, 1964], 342–343).

a plan for Britain to gain control of Syria by using Idrissi, the ruler of Asir, on the coast of what is now Saudi Arabia, writing, "If Idrissi is anything like as good as we hope, we can rush right up to Damascus and biff the French out of all hope of Syria."[2] Idrissi remained in Asir, but when Lawrence was assigned as Feisal's "adviser" toward the end of 1916, he and the Cairo establishment saw their opportunity to achieve their goal. If Feisal's Arab forces, rather than the British army, could be made to appear responsible for the victory in Syria, the Arabs would be able to establish their claim to the territory that they had supposedly liberated, and France would be "biffed" out of the Middle East. Whether solely from genuine affection for the Arab people or, at least in part, in order to promote his status as champion of the Arab cause, he transformed himself into "Lawrence of Arabia," living as a Bedouin and adopting Arab dress, speech, and habits.[3] He was successful beyond the wildest dreams of anyone who was associated with the anti-French campaign.

Until nearly the very end of the war against the Ottomans, prospects for success still remained highly doubtful. As late as mid-July 1918, only three months before the collapse of the Ottoman Empire in October, Lawrence himself noted that the Arab Revolt had not yet got under way. As he wrote then to a friend, he still saw his job as being "to foment an Arab rebellion against Turkey... Until now, we have only been preparing the groundwork and basis of our revolt and do not yet stand on the brink of action."[4] And even when he and Feisal finally took action, their operation was in fact irrelevant for the victory over Turkey, as Richard Aldington showed in detail in his devastating biography of Lawrence:

> Much of the effort of the twenty thousand to twenty-five thousand tribesman plus the little regular army of six hundred...was

---

2. Garnett, *The Letters of T. E. Lawrence*, 195–196.
3. See Phillip Knightley and Colin Simpson, *The Secret Lives of Lawrence of Arabia* (London: Panther Books, 1971), 69.
4. Garnett, *The Letters of T. E. Lawrence*, 243–246.

diverted to hanging around on the outskirts of Medina and to attacks on that part of the Damascus–Medina railway which was of least importance strategically... The revolt was limited to the distant Hejaz (which was too far off and too worthless, except for sentimental reasons, to be worth the Turkish effort of recovery) and to desert areas close to the British army, from which small raids could be made with comparative immunity. Beyond those areas, where there was real danger to be found and real damage to be done, the Arabs did nothing but talk and conspire.[5]

Colonel Richard Meinertzhagen, Lawrence's colleague in the intelligence establishment, who probably knew Lawrence best, entered the same judgment in his diary: "Lawrence's desert campaign had not the slightest effect on the main theatre west of Jordan."[6] Years later, upon the publication of Aldington's book, Meinertzhagen added that Lawrence's "desert exploits had not the slightest bearing on Allenby's campaign. In his own words, his was a 'side show of a side show.'"[7] James Parkes, a British historian and Middle East scholar, likewise dismissed the Arab military contribution in the war, writing:

> Though they were fighting for their own freedom, they had to be led, fed, armed, and supplied by the British at British cost and even then only fought when it suited their own plans, and when they had been paid in advance in gold on a scale which would have made mercenaries blush... No nation has ever won its freedom on such terms.[8]

And Pierre van Paassen characterized the Arab Revolt as pure legend, promoted for political ends, writing:

---

5. Richard Aldington, *Lawrence of Arabia: A Biographical Enquiry* (London: Collins, 1969), 209–221.
6. Meinertzhagen, *Middle East Diary*, 28.
7. Meinertzhagen, *Middle East Diary*, 40–41.
8. Parkes, *A History of Palestine*, 286–287.

In spite of Feisal's unquestioned sincerity and political vision, in spite of the tons of gold that Britain poured into Hussein's seemingly bottomless exchequer... in spite, too, of the account of T. E. Lawrence's exploits and experiences given in the *Seven Pillars of Wisdom*, and in spite of everything else that has been said and written on the subject and that is still being said (for the myth of the Revolt in the Desert is part of the basis on which certain Arab politicians hope to build a new political structure in the Near and Middle East), the Arab rising never took place. In the annals of history, the Revolt in the Desert must be placed in the same category as the Trojan War. Lawrence is the Homer of that latter-day Semitic Iliad. It is a legend—pure and simple.[9]

Yet it was this privately admitted "side show of a side show" that Lawrence was able to sell to the world's leading statesmen as the supreme instrument in the defeat of the Ottoman Empire and the Allied victory in World War I.[10] And it was this legend that the Cairo

---

9. Van Paassen, *The Forgotten Ally*, 74–79. Van Paassen added: "Not only did the Palestinian Arabs not rise in revolt, but they assisted the Turks to the extent of waylaying and murdering British patrols and individual soldiers who strayed off the main line of march. Their leaders, all members of the large landowning families, the mufti of Jerusalem Haj Amin Husseini included, served as officers in the Turkish army."
10. Even Winston Churchill was completely carried away by the myth of the Arab Revolt. Characterizing Lawrence's *Seven Pillars of Wisdom* as among the greatest books ever published in the English language, Churchill summarized Lawrence's exploits in language overflowing with hero worship: "In principle, the structure of the story is simple. The Turkish armies operating against Egypt depended upon the desert railway. This slender steel track ran through hundreds of miles of blistering desert. If it were permanently cut, the Turkish armies must perish; the ruin of Turkey must follow, and with it the downfall of the mighty Teutonic power which hurled its hate from ten thousand cannons on the plains of Flanders. Here was the Achilles' heel, and it was upon this that this man in his twenties directed his audacious, desperate, romantic assaults... Here we see Lawrence the

military and intelligence establishment exploited as the instrument for their campaign, not only to ease France out of the Middle East but also to undo the Balfour Declaration.

✡ ✡ ✡

The scheme to establish a plausible Arab military claim to Syria was based on a declaration by Britain's high commissioner for Egypt in June 1918 in response to an inquiry by a delegation of seven Arab leaders then resident in Cairo, according to which "areas emancipated from Turkish control by the action of the Arabs themselves during the present war" would be treated in the same way as "areas in Arabia which were free and independent before the outbreak of war." In regard to both these areas, "His Majesty's Government recognize the complete and sovereign independence of the Arab inhabiting these areas and support them in the struggle for freedom."[11] Even though, as Lawrence himself wrote, the Arab Revolt had not yet got under way by mid-July, 1918, when victory over the Ottoman Empire was already a near certainty, fiction was quickly made to take the place of facts. Lawrence collaborated with Feisal in creating completely fictional accounts of Arab conquests in Syria, ordering a halt before a captured town until the Arabs could enter so that the capture could be credited to them. Several Syrian cities, including Aleppo, were credited in this fashion to Arab conquests. Damascus, the capital of Syria, was similarly to have been surrendered to the Arabs so as to install Feisal there as the king of Syria before the French could arrive. The

---

    soldier. Not only the soldier but the statesman: rousing the fierce peoples of the desert, penetrating the mysteries of their thought, leading them to the selected points of action and often as not firing the mine himself... Through all, one mind, one soul, one willpower. An epic, a prodigy, a tale of torment, and in the heart of it—a Man" (Winston Churchill, "Lawrence of Arabia," in *Great Contemporaries*, p. 134).

11. J. C. Hurewitz, "The Declaration to the Seven" in *The Middle East and North Africa in World Politics*, Doc. 28, 110–112; Elie Kedourie, *England and the Middle East* (London: Mansell Publishing, 1987), 113–117.

plan miscarried, however, when the Australian commander found it impossible to cut off the Turkish retreat without entering the city, and Damascus was surrendered to him. Feisal entered shortly thereafter, however, and the story was circulated that it was he and his Arab army who had captured Damascus. Lawrence then arranged for Feisal to take charge in Damascus.[12]

The military intrigues accelerated under General Louis Bols, whom General Allenby had appointed in December 1919 as OETA administrator, and his chief of staff, Colonel Waters-Taylor. They proposed to Feisal a plan to make him king of Greater Syria, including Lebanon, Palestine, and Iraq, with Bols to serve as the governor general of Palestine and Waters-Taylor as chief secretary. With one coup, the military would have done away with both the Sykes–Picot Agreement for a French Mandate in Syria/Lebanon and the Balfour Declaration for a Jewish national home in Palestine. Meinertzhagen, the intelligence official whom Foreign Minister Balfour had seconded in 1919 to serve as political officer under Allenby, was shocked by the military intrigues against government policy he had discovered and reported them to the Foreign Office.[13]

On March 11, 1920, the Syrian National Congress, sponsored by the British military administration, proclaimed Feisal as the king of Greater Syria, including Lebanon and Palestine. The agreement Feisal had reached with Weizmann in 1919 as well as his letters to Frankfurter and to Samuel—the latter not even four months old—in which he had expressed such warm support for the Zionist national aspirations now seemed to have been forgotten.[14] Meinertzhagen

---

12. Kedourie, *England and the Middle East*, 117–122; Kedourie, *The Chatham House Version*, 33–51.
13. Meinertzhagen, "Memorandum to the Foreign Office," January 26, 1920, cited in Bernard Wasserstein, *The British in Palestine: The Mandatory Government and Arab-Jewish Conflict* (Oxford: Blackwell Publishing, 1991), 61.
14. As discussed in the preceding chapter, Feisal had an excuse in the caveat he had added to the Feisal–Weizmann Agreement: that it would not be

recorded in his diary that "Feisal had been given to understand that the Arabs of Palestine would welcome federation with Syria under one crown—Feisal's crown. Feisal encouraged this move and secretly formed what was known as the 'Palestine Legion,' whose object was to free Palestine from Jewish and British domination."[15]

Feisal's coup, engineered by the military administration, did not succeed for long. The French were willing to compromise but not to surrender all their claims to Syria. Prime Minister Clemenceau is reported to have told Feisal at the Paris Peace Conference: "I would agree with everything you want. But the French nation cannot agree that there shall be no sign of her in Syria to indicate her presence there. If France is not represented in Syria by [her] flag and by [her] soldiers, the French nation will consider it as a national humiliation, as the desertion of a soldier from the battlefield... However, we do not want to send a large force but only a few men... and there will be no objection to have your flag side by side with ours." Lawrence, however, advised Feisal against agreeing to any compromise on a French mandate in Syria.[16] Feisal and Lawrence, accordingly, left the Paris Peace Conference empty-handed, and the British–French agreement giving the Syrian Mandate to France was formally adopted in April 1920 at the San Remo Conference. To protect its Mandate, the French then invaded Damascus, and on July 25, 1920, they put to an end Feisal's brief reign in Syria.

✡ ✡ ✡

---

binding if his ambitions for receiving Syria did not materialize. He jumped the gun, however, by having himself proclaimed king a month before the San Remo Conference in April, at which Britain agreed to assigning the Syrian Mandate to France. About a decade later, Feisal's chief political secretary issued a denial that Feisal had ever made any agreement with the Zionists (Wasserstein, *The British in Palestine*, 36, citing a cable submitted to the Palestine Commission on the Disturbances of August 1929).

15. Meinertzhagen, *Middle East Diary*, 55, 81.
16. John E. Mack, *A Prince of Our Disorder: The Life of T. E. Lawrence* (Cambridge, MA: Harvard University Press, 1998), 269–270.

Although the Lawrence legend failed to dislodge the French from Syria, Lawrence and Allenby's military headquarters had provided the Arab world with a powerful myth that they had won the war against the Ottoman Empire, only to be cheated out of their rights by the politicians at the Paris Peace Conference. Even after the military administration reconciled itself to French rule in Syria, it continued to cultivate the myth among the Arabs as a powerful instrument in the campaign to undermine the Balfour Declaration and the Mandate for Palestine.

In keeping with its promotion of the myth of the Arab Revolt, the military administration totally ignored the role of its Jewish Legion in the liberation of Palestine and Syria. The Jewish Legion, numbering about five thousand volunteers assembled from Palestine, the United Kingdom, the United States, and Canada under the Zionist leaders Joseph Trumpeldor and Vladimir Jabotinsky, began in August 1917 as the thirty-eighth battalion of the Royal Fusiliers under the command of Lieutenant-Colonel John Henry Patterson. It grew in 1918 to five battalions serving under the command of General E. W. C. Chaytor in the ANZAC Mounted Division. The Jewish Legion engaged the Turks in battles in several areas, including the crucial battle of Megiddo and in the crossing of the Jordan River, which helped them gain culminating victories over the Ottoman Empire. Jabotinsky was decorated for leading the effort across the Jordan, and General Chaytor issued an official commendation of the contribution of the Jewish troops: "By forcing the Jordan fords, you helped in no small measure to win the great victory gained at Damascus."[17]

Given the intense promotion of the Lawrence myth by British and Arab leaders in their campaign to repudiate the Balfour Declaration and the Mandate for Palestine, one can only react in wonder at the irony that Lawrence himself, unlike nearly all his colleagues in the

---

17. Citation quoted by John Henry Patterson in his Foreword to Vladimir Jabotinsky, *The Story of the Jewish Legion* (New York: B. Ackerman, 1945), 21.

Cairo Arab Bureau—with the exception, in particular, of Meinertzhagen—approved of and helped further the Zionist cause. Lawrence was passionately opposed to giving the Syrian Mandate to the French, but he endorsed and vigorously supported the Balfour Declaration and the Mandate for Palestine for a Jewish national home in Palestine. In contrast to his colleagues, Lawrence supported Jewish–Arab cooperation, and it was he who arranged the agreement between Feisal, the Arab leader, and Weizmann, the Zionist leader, for the mutual support of the national aspirations of both the Arab and Jewish people. After Lawrence's death in a motorcycle accident in 1935, Chaim Weizmann wrote in commemoration:

> [Lawrence's] faith in the Jewish national home grew correspondingly with the growth and development of Palestine as a result of Jewish efforts. [Lawrence regarded Jewish–Arab cooperation] as of the utmost importance, from the Jewish point of view, but equally in the interests of the Arabs. He thought that the Jews acted as a ferment and were likely to be instrumental in bringing out the latent energies of the Arab people... I cherish his memory on personal grounds and remember with gratitude his help in furthering the cause of the Jewish people.[18]

Intrigues in Palestine

The OETA's opposition to the Balfour Declaration stemmed in large part from its conviction that a Jewish national homeland was bound to endanger British imperial interests. The British military evidently feared that a democratic Jewish state, with a highly motivated people, would quickly demand independence and deprive the British administration of any meaningful power in Palestine. Opposition to a Jewish national home, however, soon took on a broader coloration. With the development of pan-Arab nationalism—nurtured by the

---

18. "Chaim Weizmann" in A. W. Lawrence, ed., *T. E. Lawrence by His Friends* (New York: Doubleday, Doran and Co., Inc., 1937), 193.

British military administration and growing in reaction to the development of the Jewish national homeland—the British military increasingly came to regard Zionism as a threat to Britain's imperial interests in the entire Arab Middle East and indeed in the entire Moslem world, extending as far as the Empire's crown jewel, India, with its large Moslem population.

Other more subjective factors, however, contributed to shaping the administration's political attitudes. Pro-Arab sentiment in Palestine was enhanced by the considerable investment, both ideological and financial, that Britain's military had made during the war in arousing pan-Arab nationalism as a weapon against the Ottoman Empire.[19] More significant, however, was the administration's considerable antipathy to the Jews.[20] In large part, this attitude reflected the anti-Jewish stereotypes that were deeply embedded in Western

---

19. General Clayton, for example, wrote to Mark Sykes at the Foreign Office in April 1918 that since "up to date, our policy has been directed towards securing Arab sympathy [for the war against the Ottoman Empire]," it was not easy "to switch over all at once to Zionism." Three days later, he wrote to Sir Reginald Wingate, who had replaced Sir Henry McMahon as high commissioner for Egypt, that he could not "conscientiously carry out any line of policy which will go against our pledges to the Arabs" and that if pressed too hard, he could "always return to Egypt" (Wasserstein, *The British in Palestine*, 23–24). Clayton's letter indicates the depth of his anti-Zionist sentiment. As shown in the preceding chapter, both the Cairo British Office and the Arab leaders involved understood the pledge of Arab independence contained in the McMahon–Hussein agreement excluded Palestine. Clayton himself confirmed this fact to Herbert Samuel, the first High Commissioner for Palestine, under whom he later served.

20. Richard Crossman, who served in the Anglo–American Commission for Palestine in 1946, wrote, "One of the things which made the officials who administered the Mandate anti-Jewish was the fact that the Jews are logical people who studied the facts and were not afraid to prove that a British official was talking nonsense... He found it difficult to be impartial between an Arab, to whom he could feel paternally superior, and a Jew, who made him feel uncomfortable all through the interview" (Crossman, *A Nation Reborn*, 55).

culture and religion until the end of World War II and have since been regenerated by the Arab world.[21] Anti-Semitism was exacerbated early on by the intensive missionary work among Arabs by various Christian organizations from all over Europe and the United States.[22] With the onslaught of the Bolshevik Revolution in Russia in 1917, it was further bolstered by widespread blame of the Jews for the rise of Bolshevism. The fact that the Jews were among those who suffered most from Bolshevism—with their culture, religion, and institutions destroyed by the Bolsheviks—and that the Russian Jewish leadership in Palestine was firmly opposed to Bolshevism had no bearing on the anti-Semitic attitudes that prevailed within the military administration. The classic "bible" of anti-Semitism, the Czarist-fabricated *Protocols of the Elders of Zion*, which has since infected much of the Arab and Moslem world, was carried into Palestine by British soldiers who had served in Russia on the staff of Grand Duke Nicholas.[23] Vladimir Jabotinsky, the Zionist leader whose Jewish Legion had contributed to the liberation of Palestine and Syria, wrote, "Neither in Russia nor in Poland had there been such an intense and widespread atmosphere of hatred as prevailed in the British Army in Palestine in 1919 and 1920."[24]

---

21. The depth of anti-Semitism prevailing during the first half of the twentieth century, even in Great Britain itself, is clearly evident from Lloyd George's vigorous protest against it in the article cited in Chapter 1. Since the end of World War II, when the shock over the horrors of the Holocaust caused anti-Semitism to recede in the Western world, it is the Arab and Moslem world that has become the epicenter of a highly toxic and contagious anti-Semitism, which has unfortunately spread to Western progressive and intellectual circles, where it is explained away as anti-Israel or anti-Zionism, not anti-Semitism.
22. Colonel Meinertzhagen, for example, reported that General Allenby told him he could not support Zionism, because it was not a Christian movement (Meyer Weisgal, *The Letters and Papers of Chaim Weizmann, Series A*, vol. 7 [London: Oxford University Press, 1975], letter 22, 29–30).
23. Weizmann, *Trial and Error*, 217–218.
24. Jabotinsky, *The Story of the Jewish Legion*, 1945, 171.

✡ ✡ ✡

The military administration began its resistance to the government's policy for building the Jewish national home in Palestine by refusing to allow the circulation of the Balfour Declaration in Palestine until long after the end of World War I. It justified its decision as a wartime necessity, intended to avoid adverse effects on the military campaign against Turkey, but the Balfour Declaration was still not allowed to be published as late as October 1919, nearly a year after the war's end.[25] Not content merely to withhold circulation of the Balfour Declaration, the administration actively employed a number of channels to awaken a sense of Arab nationalism in the Palestinian Arabs, whose leaders had as yet so little sense of Arab nationalism, let alone of a distinct Palestinian nationality, that instead of joining the fight for promised Arab independence, they had loyally served in the war as officers in the Ottoman Empire army. In July 1918, Charles R. Ashbee, civic advisor to Sir Ronald Storrs, Britain's military governor of Jerusalem, wrote in praise of the activities of his office among the Arabs:

> We are preaching nationality in Palestine… We are for the Arabs… We make great capital out of the Arabic tradition that Jerusalem will come back to the Arabs when a new prophet [al-Nebi, i.e., Allenby] shall enter it as conqueror.[26]

The military authorities took their first major step toward creating an Arab demand for the repudiation of the Balfour Declaration immediately after the armistice with Turkey and only four days before the armistice that ended World War I. On November 7, 1918, they circulated to the Jerusalem Arabs an Anglo–French Joint Declaration promising Arab independence in Syria and Mesopotamia, which they

---

25. Palestine Government File Pol/2108, quoted in Kedourie, *The Chatham House Version*, 402, fn. 13.
26. Hanna, *British Policy in Palestine*, 173, fn. 135.

knew well had nothing to do with Palestine. This declaration, intended to reassure Hussein and Feisal on British and French intentions in Syria and Iraq, stated:

> The object aimed at by France and Great Britain in prosecuting in the East the war let loose by the ambition of Germany is the complete and definite emancipation of the peoples so long oppressed by the Turks and the establishment of national governments and administrations deriving their authority from the initiative and free choice of indigenous populations... Far from wishing to impose on the populations of these regions any particular institutions, they are only concerned to ensure by their support and by adequate assistance the regular working of governments and administrations freely chosen by the populations themselves.[27]

The Joint Declaration referred only to Syria and Mesopotamia and made no mention of Palestine. It was issued as a cloak—employing Wilsonian language about nurturing democracy—to hide the true intentions as indicated in the original Sykes–Picot Agreement for division of the Ottoman Empire between Britain and France. Russia's publication of that agreement, following the 1917 Bolshevik Revolution, had embarrassed Britain and France, and they issued the declaration immediately after the armistice with Turkey in an attempt to reassure the Arab leaders by rephrasing the agreement in line with President Wilson's Fourteen Points and with the new plans for League of Nations Mandates in the Arab territories.

---

27. "Anglo–French Declaration," in Hurewitz, *The Middle East and North Africa in World Politics*, Doc. 28, 112. The kind of independence and democratic institutions actually envisaged for the Arab states may be seen in a telling comment by Balfour on the role of advisers mentioned in the Sykes–Picot Agreement, "By an adviser, these documents undoubtedly mean—though they do not say so—an adviser whose advice must be followed" (*Documents on British Foreign Policy [1919–1939], First Series*, vol. 4 [London: His Majesty's Stationery Office, 1951], 344, cited in Cruise O'Brien, *The Siege*, 137).

All the responsible officials in the OETA, including Sir Ronald Storrs, the governor of Jerusalem, who personally circulated the Joint Declaration, knew (as he and other key officials in the Cairo Arab Bureau subsequently each confirmed in writing) that Britain's promise of Arab independence to Hussein excluded Palestine. They were also well aware of the Balfour Declaration to facilitate the building of a Jewish national homeland in Palestine, whose first anniversary the Zionists had just celebrated in Jerusalem. Nevertheless, they did not hesitate to circulate copies of the declaration's promise of independence for Syria and Iraq to the Arabs in Jerusalem, thereby planting the belief that it did apply to Palestine. The same general headquarters that had prohibited the printing or circulation of the Balfour Declaration ordered the distribution of eighteen copies of the Joint Declaration on Syria and Iraq to the Jerusalem Arab elders, later passing it off as a "bureaucratic error" and pretending that the consequent Arab response was not what the authorities had anticipated.

The Jerusalem Arab elders, happily surprised at receiving the Anglo–French Declaration of future independence for Syria and Iraq, immediately declared their interest in the implied offer. Far from claiming that Palestinians have a distinct nationality of their own, they readily opted for being governed as part of Syria. Sir Ronald Storrs, who circulated the declaration, described its impact:

> Hardly had the excitement caused by the Zionist celebrations died down when, in accordance with orders received from GHQ, I distributed… the eighteen copies of the Anglo–French Declaration respecting the inhabitants of Syria and Mesopotamia. The result was instantaneous, but I fear hardly that anticipated by the authorities. On returning to the office the next day, I found a large deputation of Muslims and Christians combined, who announced that they had come to speak to me… They then asked me, formally, (a) whether Palestine formed or did not form part of Syria, (b) whether, if so, Palestinians came under the category of those inhabitants of the liberated countries who were invited to choose their own future, and (c) if not,

why the notices had ever been sent to them at all. I replied to them in general terms, and they left apparently satisfied... but I have since learnt that there have been further meetings... attended by Muslims, Latins, and Orthodox Christians. It is their intention to visit reciprocally each other's churches and mosques as proof of solidarity, and this demonstration once made before the world to put forward officially their acceptance of the Anglo–French Declaration and their desire for a Sherifian [Feisal] government.[28]

The circulation of the Anglo–French Declaration in Jerusalem, compounded by Sir Ronald Storrs's evasive response to the Arab deputation, had its intended effect. The Arabs correctly understood that the British administration was opposed to the establishment of a Jewish national home in Palestine and was promoting instead the concept of a Greater Syria, including Palestine, under Feisal's Sherifian rule. There is little wonder, then, that they accepted the administration's apparent offer of potential Arab independence and came accordingly to maintain that the McMahon–Hussein Agreement concerning future independence for Arab territories was meant to include Palestine. Not even the fact that both Hussein and his son, Feisal, had endorsed the Zionist national aspirations embodied in the Balfour Declaration sufficed to dissuade the Arabs from insisting that the Balfour Declaration was in violation of the McMahon promise to Hussein. Neither the fact that the Allies endorsed the Balfour Declaration and the Mandate for Palestine at the San Remo Peace Conference, nor that the League of Nations formally approved the Mandate for Palestine, which incorporated the Balfour Declaration, served to discourage the Arabs and their anti-Zionist supporters from exploiting a false claim of a British promise of independence to Palestine, to which they had so skillfully been guided by the military administration.

---

28. Wasserstein, *The British in Palestine*, 33.

In addition to its so-called "bureaucratic error" in distributing the Anglo–French Declaration, the military skillfully guided an Arab movement, which it had originally organized and financed as a propaganda weapon against the Ottoman Empire[29] but now found useful as a tool against the government's pro-Zionist policy. It encouraged the first Arab political organization that had been formed (the Christian–Moslem Association) to increase its anti-Jewish agitation in Palestine. The extent to which the Arab agitation was inspired by the British authorities was revealed by Colonel Meinertzhagen, who wrote, "Arab national feeling is based on our gold and nothing else."[30]

The Passover Pogrom and Its Unexpected Consequences

Around the beginning of April 1920, as the crucial date of the San Remo Peace Conference (April 19–26, 1920) was approaching, several officers of General Allenby's military administration conspired with some Palestinian Arabs to carry out a pogrom in Old Jerusalem in an attempt to convince the London government that the Balfour Declaration must be repudiated. The Sunday of Passover (April 4, 1920) coincided that year both with Easter and with the Moslem holiday, Nebi Musa. This Moslem holiday celebrates Moses, the greatest of Hebrew prophets and liberator of the people of Israel from Egyptian

---

29. The role of the British military in Cairo in creating the Arab movement was described by Lawrence in a confidential report in 1918 as follows: "The phrase 'Arab movement' was invented in Cairo as a common denominator for all the vague discontents against Turkey, which before 1916 existed in the Arab provinces. In a non-constitutional country, these naturally took on a revolutionary character, and it was convenient to pretend to find a common ground in all of them. They were most of them very local, very jealous, but had to be considered in the hope that one or the other of them might bear fruit" (T. E. Lawrence, *Secret Dispatches from Arabia* [London, 1939], 158, cited in Samuel Katz, *Battleground: Fact and Fantasy in Palestine* [New York: Taylor Productions, 2002], 65).
30. Meinertzhagen, *Middle East Diary*, 87.

slavery, as a Moslem prophet preceding Mohammed. Weizmann, who had come to Palestine at the time to spend the Passover holiday with his mother in Haifa, met with Allenby, Bols, and Herbert Samuel to discuss the tense atmosphere and impending trouble. Bols assured him, "There can be no trouble, the town is stiff with troops!" He could feel assured that "everything would go off quietly in Jerusalem."[31]

But while Bols assured Weizmann that there could be no trouble, Waters-Taylor, his chief of staff, had prepared the ground for Haj Amin al-Husseini, the half-brother of the Jerusalem mufti, to carry out a pogrom on the holiday. As Meinertzhagen, whom Balfour had seconded to Allenby as chief political officer, discovered and subsequently recorded in his diary, "Waters-Taylor saw [Haj Amin] on the Wednesday before Easter and told him that he had a great opportunity at Easter to show the world that the Arabs of Palestine would not tolerate Jewish domination in Palestine; that Zionism was unpopular not only with the Palestine administration but in Whitehall; and if disturbances of sufficient violence occurred in Jerusalem at Easter, both General Bols and General Allenby would advocate the abandonment of the Jewish home. Waters-Taylor explained that freedom could only be attained through violence."[32] Bols and Waters-Taylor were motivated not only by ideological concerns but undoubtedly even more by their own personal stake in the outcome. As discussed earlier, they had just engineered a coup in Syria, where they had promoted the installment of Feisal as the king of Greater Syria, including Palestine, under whom Bols was to become governor general of Palestine, and Waters-Taylor the chief secretary.

Although General Bols had assured Weizmann that the town was stiff with troops, all British troops and Jewish police had been removed from the Old City for the holiday. Most of Jabotinsky's Jewish battalions, which had fought under Allenby to liberate Palestine, had been disbanded, and the rest had been confined in camp. Not too

---

31. Weizmann, *Trial and Error*, 254–255.
32. Meinertzhagen, *Middle East Diary*, 81–82.

surprisingly, therefore, Arab posters were displayed in Jerusalem on the day of the rioting, declaring, "The government is with us, Allenby is with us, kill the Jews—there is no punishment for killing Jews."[33]

Waters-Taylor was evidently well satisfied with his arrangements, for as a correspondent for *The Times*, then in Palestine, later reported, he "appears to have left Jerusalem for a trip to Jericho at a moment when crowds were already gathering in ominous fashion near the Jaffa Gate."[34] And so, as the historian Conor Cruise O'Brien described the pogrom that ensued:

> While the Christians were celebrating Easter resurrection as a sign of atonement for their sins and the Jews were celebrating their Passover liberation from enslavement in Egypt under Moses' leadership, the Arab mob, led by Haj Amin al-Husseini, the future grand mufti, celebrated their Nebi Musa holiday, honoring Moses by proceeding to beat and kill Moses' people and to rape their women in the Jewish Quarter of Jerusalem's Old City. The Arab police sided with the rioters and had to be withdrawn and disarmed. Not only did the army fail to enter until it was all over, but the police even prevented the Jews from organizing their own defense. When Jabotinsky, with a small group of Jewish soldiers who had served with the British in the war against the Turks, tried to come to their defense, they were arrested. All told, more than two hundred Jews, mostly old men, women, and children, were wounded, and several were killed.[35]

Waters-Taylor was apparently not altogether satisfied with the results of the pogrom. Meinertzhagen learned that two days after the riot, Waters-Taylor called the mayor of Jerusalem to say, "I gave you a fine opportunity—for five hours, Jerusalem was without military protection. I had hoped you would avail yourself of the opportunity,

---

33. Meinertzhagen, *Middle East Diary*, 82.
34. Weizmann, *Trial and Error*, 256.
35. Cruise O'Brien, *The Siege*, 146.

but you have failed."[36] After the pogrom, Haj Amin al-Husseini made his escape, but he was sentenced *in absentia* to ten years in prison.[37] Jabotinsky, who defended the helpless Jews, was stripped of his commission in the British army and had to sit in jail. The administration charged him with having violated article 58 of the Ottoman Code by having "armed the inhabitants of the Ottoman Empire one against the other with the perverse intention of provoking rape, pillage, devastation, and assassinations," and he was sentenced to fifteen years of hard labor in prison.[38]

Commenting on the impact of the pogrom on the Jews, whose memories of the Czarist pogroms were still fresh in their minds, Chaim Weizmann wrote:

> It is almost impossible to convey to the outside world the sense of horror and bewilderment which it aroused in our people, both in Palestine and outside. Pogroms in Russia had excited horror and pity, but little surprise, they were "seasonal disturbances," more or less to be expected round about Easter and Passover festivals. That such a thing could happen in Palestine two years after the Balfour Declaration, under British rule ("The town is stiff with troops!") was incomprehensible to the Jews and dreadful beyond belief.[39]

Sir Ronald Storrs, the military governor of Jerusalem, came a few days later to express his official condolences to Menachem Ussishkin (acting chairman of the Zionist Commission in Weizmann's absence), insisting that the riots were not a pogrom. Ussishkin answered him:

> You, Colonel, are an expert in administrative matters, and I am an expert in the laws of pogroms. I can promise you that there is no difference between the Jerusalem pogrom and the

---

36. Meinertzhagen, *Middle East Diary*, 82–83.
37. Meinertzhagen, *Middle East Diary*, 97.
38. Weizmann, *Trial and Error*, 255; Soustelle, *The Long March of Israel*, 65.
39. Weizmann, *Trial and Error*, 256.

Kishinev pogrom. The organizers of the local pogrom did not show any originality; they followed, step by step, in the ways of the perpetrators of the Russian pogroms... Czar Nicholas also did not interfere with the pogroms—he also oppressed us. Yet does your honour see what befell him? In his place sits Trotsky. All our enemies in the world and in the land of Israel will also meet such an end.[40]

✡ ✡ ✡

Much to the astonishment and consternation of the military administration, the intrigues unexpectedly backfired on the perpetrators. The anti-Zionist military administration itself was removed from power, and it was replaced by a civilian administration under a pro-Zionist Jewish high commissioner. In confident expectation of harvesting the political fruits of the Arab riots promoted by his chief of staff, General Bols wrote to the government in London urging that the Zionist Commission, which had been set up to facilitate the building of the Jewish national home, be abolished.[41] The administration had not reckoned, however, with the chief political officer under General Allenby, Colonel Meinertzhagen, an exceptionally zealous Christian champion of Zionism who was determined to safeguard the government's policy for Palestine from being sabotaged by the Palestine administration. Five months after Balfour seconded him to General Allenby, he wrote in his diary of his painful struggle against the opposition of his colleagues to the Balfour Declaration:

> I find myself alone out here, among gentiles, in upholding Zionism, which does not make matters at all easy... It is heart-breaking work against such opposition, and I sometimes feel inclined to scrap the whole thing and swim with the tide. I freely express my views to all and sundry and produce what I consider to be

---

40. Zionist Archives, quoted in Cruise O'Brien, *The Siege*, 146.
41. Christopher Sykes, *Crossroads to Israel* (Bloomington, IN: Indiana University Press, 1973), 38.

unanswerable arguments, but it takes more than that to break down a combination of obstinate prejudice and a deep-rooted but suppressed anti-Semitic feeling. I am not surprised that people think I must be a Jew, when I stand alone among Christians here as a friend to Zionism.[42]

Immediately after taking up his position in Palestine, Meinertzhagen had organized a small intelligence unit to assist him in his duties as General Allenby's chief political officer. He quickly learned, "Both Ronald Storrs and Waters-Taylor were in close touch with various Arab notables in Jerusalem, the most dangerous of whom was Haj Amin al-Husseini, later mufti of Jerusalem." Meinertzhagen had thus discovered that at about the same time that Waters-Taylor was organizing a coup with Feisal in Syria, he and Sir Ronald Storrs were also conspiring with Haj Amin al-Husseini, the twenty-seven-year-old future Jerusalem mufti, to encourage Arab hostility to the government's pro-Zionist policy. Shocked that administration officials should be actively plotting against their own government, he reported the intrigues to General Allenby in Cairo, but he found Allenby unwilling to act against his officials.[43]

Deciding to risk his own career, Meinertzhagen went over the general's head and wrote directly to the foreign minister. In a letter to Lord Curzon, the new foreign minister, written on April 14, 1920, ten days after the Easter riots, Meinertzhagen submitted a detailed report

---

42. Meinertzhagen, *Middle East Diary*, 65–67. In a remarkable comment on his own feelings, Meinertzhagen went on to add, "And that is the irony of the whole situation, for I am also imbued with anti-Semitic feelings and would wish that Zionism could be divorced from Jewish nationality. But it cannot, and I prefer to accept it as it is than oppose it on grounds of immaterial prejudice. The idea of fighting for Jews against Christians and my own people is most distasteful to me, but it is what I have had to do out here for the last few months. And I feel that the best in Zionism is an ideal well worth fighting for, an ideal which must eventually materialize and win."
43. Meinertzhagen, *Middle East Diary*, 55–56.

on the conspiratorial acts of the Palestine administration against the government's Zionist policy. His letter detailing the military conspiracy happened to reach Curzon at the same time as the letter from General Bols requesting that the Zionist Commission be abolished. Curzon was then attending the San Remo Conference together with Prime Minister Lloyd George and Lord Balfour, and they acted on Meinertzhagen's advice within twenty-four hours. It was not the Zionist Commission but the military administration (OETA) itself that the London government abolished, and both General Bols and Colonel Waters-Taylor were removed from their posts. The British government decided that the military administration in Palestine should be replaced by a civilian administration, headed by a high commissioner. As the first high commissioner, Prime Minister Lloyd George appointed Herbert Samuel, the Jewish official in Asquith's cabinet who, in January 1915, had first presented the proposal for a Jewish national home in Palestine to the former prime minister. Ussishkin's prophecy had materialized far more quickly than he could have anticipated.

– 4 –

Herbert Samuel's Mixed Legacy

THE REPLACEMENT OF THE ANTI-ZIONIST and anti-Semitic OETA by a civilian administration headed by Herbert Samuel, a traditional Jew with known pro-Zionist sympathies, aroused very high expectations within the Jewish community. But Samuel left the Jewish community a mixed legacy: sadly disappointing, despite many administrative accomplishments. In another one of the ironies surrounding the history of Israel's rebirth, whereas the anti-Zionist Lord Curzon had significantly enhanced the Mandate for Palestine (see Chapter 2), the pro-Zionist Herbert Samuel weakened it grievously. Bending over backward so as to be seen as "fair" by the Arabs, he reappointed the most ardent anti-Zionist officials of the former OETA and elevated the most extreme anti-Zionist elements of the Arab leadership. In addition, Samuel significantly watered down the Mandate for Palestine for rebuilding the Jewish national home, introducing a new interpretation of the Balfour Declaration as charging him with two equal Mandates—one for the Jewish people and one for the Arabs. This thesis was later employed by some British governments to favor the assumed Arab Mandate over the actual Mandate for the Jewish people, even to the extent of putting a freeze on the building of the Jewish national home in Palestine.

✡ ✡ ✡

Samuel's appointment as high commissioner and commander in chief in Palestine—the first Jewish ruler in Israel in nearly two thousand years—was received with profound joy in Palestine's Jewish community. Although Samuel had previously shown little interest in

Jewish affairs, once World War I began, he foresaw the opportunity to restore the Jewish national home in Palestine. Only days after Britain declared war on the Ottoman Empire in November 1914, Samuel discussed the possibility with Lloyd George and with Foreign Secretary Sir Edward Grey, noting:

> If a Jewish State were established in Palestine, it might become the centre of a new culture. The Jewish brain is rather a remarkable thing, and under national auspices, the State might become a fountain of enlightenment and a source of great literature and art and development of science.

Lloyd George replied, "He was very keen to see a Jewish state established there," and Sir Grey indicated he "was quite favorable to the proposal and would be prepared to work for it if the opportunity arose."[1]

By the beginning of 1915, however, Samuel had concluded, as Weizmann himself also believed, that given the limited number of Jews in Palestine at the time, the immediate or early establishment of a Jewish state was not practicable and that a more gradual approach would have to be adopted.[2] In his memoranda to Prime Minister

---

1. Samuel, *Memoirs*, 140–142.
2. Remarkably, Colonel Richard Meinertzhagen disagreed with Weizmann and Samuel's philosophy of gradualism. Anticipating the future collapse of Britain's support for Zionism, he urged Weizmann at the Paris Peace Conference to opt for the immediate establishment of a Jewish state. In his diary entry of February 12, 1919, he recorded, "I had a long talk with Weizmann today and advised him to go all out for Jewish sovereignty in Palestine. He might get it now, whereas in a year's time, it will be impossible. I told him that I will help him all I know. I have good reason to believe that Lloyd George and Wilson will support him... But Weizmann thinks the time inopportune and might wreck the whole idea of Mandatory Zionism. I am sure the Arabs will accept anything from the Peace Conference but would never accept a Jewish sovereign state imposed by Great Britain in, say, five years' time. There are vast anti-Semitic forces at work even now in London and elsewhere, but they are as yet incoherent and powerless

Asquith and to his cabinet (see Chapter 1), Samuel therefore proposed only the more modest program, which he described as follows:

> Under British rule, facilities would be given to Jewish organisations to purchase land, to found colonies, to establish educational and religious institutions, and to cooperate in the economic development of the country, and that Jewish immigration, carefully regulated, would be given preference, so that in course of time, the Jewish inhabitants, grown into a majority and settled in the land, may be conceded such degree of self-government as the conditions of that day might justify.[3]

Samuel's proposal was now embodied in the Balfour Declaration and the Mandate for Palestine, which, as Lloyd George and Balfour had stated, looked toward the eventual establishment of a Jewish state in Palestine. The military administration, with its campaign to repudiate the Balfour Declaration, had shocked the Jewish community, but now, with its replacement by a civilian administration, led from July 1, 1920 by a high commissioner who had played such a significant role in promoting the pro-Zionist policy, Jewish hopes were again raised high.[4]

Contemporary diaries reflect the profound emotions generated in Israel by Samuel's appointment. Samuel himself recorded in his memoirs his deeply emotional experience on the special Sabbath, *Shabbat Nachamu*, the Sabbath of Consolation, which follows Tishah B'Av, the fast day commemorating the destruction of Jerusalem's ancient holy Jewish Temples. Of his visit to the central synagogue in Jerusalem's Old City on that Sabbath, Samuel wrote:

---

to intervene in Paris. In five years' time, they will be in a position to deny the Jews their rights" (Meinertzhagen, *Middle East Diary*, 14–15).

3. Leonard Stein, *The Balfour Declaration* (Jerusalem and London: Magnes Press and Hebrew University, 1983), 110.
4. General Allenby's military headquarters in Cairo remained responsible for the maintenance of law and order in Palestine, even after his military administration was replaced by Samuel's civilian administration.

The most moving ceremony that I have ever attended was on my first visit, after my arrival in Jerusalem, to the old and spacious synagogue in the Jewish quarter of the ancient city.[5] As it was the Sabbath, I had walked over from Government House so as not to offend the Orthodox by driving and found the surrounding streets densely thronged and the great building itself packed to the doors and to the roof; mostly by older settlers, some of those who had come to live, and to die, in the Holy City for piety's sake. Now, on that day, for the first time since the destruction of the Temple, they could see one of their own people governor in the Land of Israel. To them it seemed that the fulfillment of ancient prophecy might at last be at hand. When, in accordance with the usual ritual, I was "called to the Reading of the Law" and from the central platform recited in Hebrew the prayer and the blessing, "Have mercy upon Zion, for it is the home of our life, and save her that is grieved in spirit, speedily, even in our days. Blessed art Thou, O Lord, who makest Zion joyful through her children." And when there followed the opening words of a chapter of Isaiah appointed for that day, "Comfort ye, comfort ye my people, saith your God. Speak ye comfortably to Jerusalem and cry unto her, that her warfare is accomplished, that her iniquity is pardoned"—the emotion that I could not but feel seemed to spread throughout the vast congregation. Many wept. One could almost hear the sigh of generations.[6]

---

5. That "old and spacious synagogue in the Jewish Quarter of the ancient city" of Jerusalem, called the Hurva, was reduced to rubble along with all the Jewish Quarter's other synagogues by the Arab Legion of Transjordan in the Arab War against the rebirth of the State of Israel in 1948. It was rebuilt and rededicated on March 15, 2010. The PA protested the rededication and called it a "provocation."
6. Samuel, *Memoirs*, 176. *Shabbat Nachamu*, the Sabbath of Consolation, is the first of seven consecutive Sabbaths of Consolation following the fast of Tishah B'Av, during which the Prophetic readings in synagogues throughout the world are from Isaiah, prophesying the return of the Jews

Samuel had to his credit a wide range of administrative achievements as high commissioner of Palestine. On August 26, 1920, he announced an immigration ordinance that legalized Jewish immigration into Palestine in accordance with the Mandate, and on September 23, he received approval to promulgate a land transfer ordinance that legalized sales of land to the Jews.[7] Sir Ronald Storrs, the military governor under General Allenby whom Samuel reappointed to the same post in his civil administration with the new title of district commissioner of Jerusalem, summarized Samuel's many administrative achievements:

> He set forth the lines on which towns should be planned. He protected antiquities and checked dealings in them... [He] attached as much importance as anybody to the preservation of historic beauty and always supported pro-Jerusalem... He modernized Ottoman copyright and mortgage law and provided for government control of land transactions. He safeguarded the public against the irregular sales of drugs and reorganized the Palestine police... He inaugurated cooperative societies, commissions for weights and measures, and land credit banks, and as a good liberal, he abolished the censorship of the Arab and Hebrew press.[8]

The Encyclopaedia Judaica provides an equally favorable assessment of Samuel's administrative achievements:

> As a capable administrator, Samuel laid the foundations of the country's civil administration. During his term of office, the Jewish population doubled (from 55,000 in 1919 to 108,000 in 1925), extensive Jewish settlement was carried out, and the

---

to the Land of Israel and Jerusalem. The portion read on *Shabbat Nachamu* is Isaiah 40:1–26.

7. Wasserstein, *The British in Palestine*, 90–91.
8. Ronald Storrs, *The Memoirs of Sir Ronald Storrs* (New York: AMS Press, 1973), 415–416.

number of settlements rose from forty-four to a hundred. Official recognition was given to Jewish representative bodies, local councils were organized, and the chief rabbinate was established. Great improvements were carried through in the legal and judicial system, and education, sanitation, and communications were much improved. The Hebrew language was recognized as one of the three official languages of the country.[9]

These accomplishments must be balanced, however, against Samuel's political appointments and his policy decisions, which led to much subsequent grief and virtually guaranteed the ultimate failure of Britain's administration of the Mandate. As a Jewish high commissioner, Samuel evidently felt obliged to bend over backward in favor of the Arab people, even at substantial cost to the prospects for developing the Jewish national home in Palestine. Aware of the special problems a Jew would face as high commissioner, he had hesitated at first to accept the offer of appointment, but after consulting with Zionist leaders, including Weizmann, who favored his appointment, he decided to accept the post. He then wrote to Lloyd George:

> I am quite clear that if the government decided to invite me to fill that post, it is my duty to accept it. The objection which I mentioned to you, that measures which the majority of the population would accept from a non-Jew would be resented if they came from a Jew, could, I believe, be overcome. In the long run, their attitude would depend upon the reasonableness of

---

9. *Encyclopaedia Judaica*, vol. 14 (Jerusalem: Keter Publishing House, 1971), 799. David Ben-Gurion, the first prime minister of Israel, also gave Samuel high praise for his administrative abilities, saying, "As a technical administrator, of course, he was first class. He had long experience of public service; he had a brilliant mind; and he had a civilized sense of history" (Moshe Pearlman, *Ben Gurion Looks Back* [New York: Schocken Books, 1970], 67). Samuel set out in greater detail his administrative accomplishments as high commissioner of Palestine during 1920–1925 in his own *Memoirs*, ch. 15–16.

the measures themselves and upon the manner in which they were presented.

Samuel realized that if his measures were so diluted as to be acceptable to the Arabs, they might then prove unpalatable to the Jewish people, but he believed this could also be overcome. As he added in his letter to Lloyd George:

> The fulfillment of the Zionist program must, from the nature of the case, be gradual and very considerate for the interests of the Arabs and Christians. Jewry in Palestine and throughout the world would be more likely to practice patience, without losing enthusiasm, if the pace were set by an administrator who was known to be in full sympathy with the ultimate aim than if it were set by anyone else.

Thus, Samuel, who had initially believed that Weizmann's goals were too modest and that big things would have to be done quickly in Palestine, had now become the proponent of a pace so gradual and so very considerate of Arab interests as to be acceptable to the Arabs, while the Jews would be expected to be patient without losing enthusiasm.

Samuel evidently failed to appreciate that success would depend not only upon the reasonableness of the Zionist program but even more so upon the reasonableness of the Arab political leadership. With his optimistic faith in human perfectibility, he failed to see that the Arab leadership he was promoting—even more extensively than the OETA before him—was far from reasonable. Of the two leading Arab Palestinian families—the Nashashibis and the Husseinis—it was the extremist Husseini family that the military administration had nurtured and had even encouraged to resort to violence against the Jews, regardless of the material benefit of the Zionist program to the Arab people. Far from removing these harmful British and Arab influences, Samuel filled his own administration with British anti-Zionist officials and enhanced the power of the Husseini clan within the Arab community, in the expectation, presumably, of winning their goodwill and support.

Appointments of Anti-Zionists to Key Administration Posts

The first sign of Samuel's optimistic nature was his decision to reappoint Sir Ronald Storrs as governor of Jerusalem, with only a change of title from governor under the ousted military administration to district commissioner in his own civilian administration. Samuel made this decision immediately upon receiving his own appointment, even though only a year earlier he himself had complained to the government about the anti-Zionist activities of the military authorities in Palestine, specifically including Storrs in this context.[10] Storrs, a clever and highly sophisticated official who much impressed people with his apparent scholarship and his appreciation of the arts, was also a highly devious person with a talent for manipulating people. He was even capable of describing himself as a committed Zionist, but as the historian, Conor Cruise O'Brien, noted, "Whatever he might say, he was existentially anti-Zionist, as a cat is anti-dog."[11]

Storrs had been a prime mover within the anti-Zionist military administration, seeking in his subtle fashion to awaken Arab nationalism against the government's pro-Zionist policy. It was he who, already in 1918 as military governor of Jerusalem, had promoted

---

10. Wasserstein, *The British in Palestine*, 50. It is indicative of Samuel's belief in the perfectibility of all people that for the post of chief secretary of his administration—the highest post, second only to his own as high commissioner—he had initially contemplated appointing Colonel Waters-Taylor, whom he had then described "as an able man and favorable to Zionism" (Wasserstein, *The British in Palestine*, 84–85). But after Meinertzhagen revealed Waters-Taylor's role in conspiring with Haj Amin al-Husseini in the Easter 1920 pogrom that had led immediately thereafter to the downfall of the military administration, Samuel appointed instead General Wyndham Deedes, one of the very few pro-Zionists in his administration.
11. Cruise O'Brien, *The Siege*, 141–142.

Arab resistance to the Balfour Declaration by distributing copies of the Anglo–French Joint Declaration for Arab independence to Jerusalem's elders (see Chapter 3). And it was he, along with Colonel Waters-Taylor, who had established and maintained the contacts with Haj Amin al-Husseini, the leader of the 1920 pogrom against the Jews in Jerusalem.[12] Colonel Meinertzhagen, whose report on the role of Waters-Taylor and Storrs in instigating the Arab riots in April 1920 had led to the replacement of the military administration by Samuel's civilian administration, wrote of Storrs,

> His long residence in the East had orientalized his mind, introducing an exceptionally strong element of intrigue and intellectual dishonesty. Mental somersaults were no effort. He could be an enthusiast for Zionism and the next day suffering from violent Hebraphobia. He was a dangerous man, not knowing the meaning of the words "loyalty" or "sincerity."[13]

---

12. Storrs was incensed by the Zionist attacks against him and their demands for his ouster over his role in the Arab riots. Assuming the robe of innocence, he complained, "The British officer, work as he might, felt himself surrounded, almost opposed, by an atmosphere always critical, frequently hostile, sometimes bitterly vindictive and even menacing. After the Easter riots of 1920 and the November riots of 1921, I had to endure such a tempest of vituperation in the Palestine and World Hebrew Press that I am still unable to understand how I did not emerge from it an anti-Semite for life" (Storrs, *The Memoirs of Sir Ronald Storrs*, 415–416).
13. Meinertzhagen, *Middle East Diary*, 86. Pierre van Paassen (*The Forgotten Ally*, 122–123) was even more scathingly critical of Storrs's role in Palestine: "Sir Ronald Storrs, the first governor of Jerusalem was a fanatical *arabisant*. He idealized everything Arabic... That man had a great deal to do with the shaping of British policy in the early days of the British occupation of Palestine, when the building of the Jewish national home got off to an uncertain start. He, more than anyone else, was responsible for laying the foundation of that anti-Zionist policy of the successive British administrations in Palestine."

Samuel, however, maintained the highest regard for Storrs, painting an admiring picture of him that contrasts sharply with those drawn by Meinertzhagen, van Paassen, and even by Samuel's own son, Edwin.[14] In his *Memoirs*, Samuel paid this remarkable compliment to Storrs:

> His understanding of the oriental temperament; his tactful handling of difficult problems—sectional, ecclesiastical, and personal—[and] his constant watchfulness and energetic efforts to prevent the awkward situations which were continually arising in the complex and often discordant little world of Jerusalem from developing into open conflicts were of the greatest value.[15]

---

14. Edwin Samuel, who knew Storrs well, was as critical as Meinertzhagen in his assessment of Storrs. In his memoirs, published in 1970, Edwin wrote, "Storrs was thoroughly unscrupulous and often behaved like an Italian renaissance prince: Nothing he said could be wholly trusted... He did not care a damn about anything. In fact, he was thoroughly bored with administration. What he really enjoyed was political intrigue" (Edwin Samuel, *A Lifetime in Jerusalem: The Memoirs of the Second Viscount Samuel* [London: Vallentine Mitchell, 1970], 52–53).

15. Samuel, *Memoirs*,155. Sir Ronald Storrs, in turn, had high praise for Samuel's role, writing, "I firmly believe, if a gentile may express an opinion on Jewish affairs (Jews express themselves freely enough on ours) that the names of the Big Four who will go down to history in the rebuilding of Zion will be Theodor Herzl, who saw the vision; Chaim Weizmann, who grasped the occasion; Arthur Balfour, who caused the world to renew the ancient Promise in a modern covenant; and Herbert Samuel, who turned principle into practice, word into fact" (Storrs, *Memoirs*, 462).

    David Ben-Gurion, the first prime minister of Israel, arrived at a less flattering assessment, telling his interviewer in 1964, "I and my friends felt that his administration was very lukewarm to the whole concept of the Balfour Declaration... He had in fact been a warm supporter of the Balfour Declaration when many other Anglo-Jewish leaders had been opposed to it. But arriving as first high commissioner in the country with two rival communities, he was most concerned to show no favouritism between Arab and Jew, the more so because he was himself a Jew. I understood his difficulties. Granted his background, he must have felt a psychological need to show the Arabs that he was not biased. Maybe

One example of Storrs's behavior in religious matters suggests that Samuel's appreciation of his "tactful handling of difficult [ecclesiastical] problems" was overly generous. Samuel, though a leading member of Britain's Liberal Party and though charged with facilitating the development of the Jewish national homeland under the Balfour Declaration and the Mandate, kept intact the Ottoman laws against Jewish rights of freedom of worship in Palestine. Under him and his successors, even the essential ritual of blowing the shofar on the holiest days of the Jewish year, during Rosh Hashanah prayers and at the end of the Yom Kippur services, remained banned at the Temple Mount's Western Wall as a criminal act in violation of the administration's "sacred" status quo. Enforcing the Ottoman law against the Jews at prayers near the Wall, even though in practice, the law was not enforced under the Ottomans, was Storrs's passion. In his *Memoirs*, Storrs relates the troubles he encountered at the Wall when Jews sought to bring chairs with them for use during prayers. Arabs protested that this was forbidden under Ottoman law. Although the law was only on paper, and in practice, Jews had brought chairs with them to the Wall, Storrs issued an order prohibiting Jews from bringing chairs to the Wall. In 1925, on Yom Kippur, the holiest day of the Jewish calendar, when Jews fast from sundown to sundown and are engaged in continuous prayers at their holy sites, Arabs again protested that Jews had brought chairs to the Wall, and Storrs immediately sent an officer to enforce his order. Storrs defended the interruption of services, arguing,

---

his very friendliness to the Zionist cause may have prompted him to lean over even more backward to demonstrate that he was being 'fair.' And I am afraid that this led him to pursue policies and to recommend policies to the British government which were not in keeping with the specific injunctions of the Balfour Declaration and the League of Nations Mandate, by virtue of which the British ruled, which were to promote the establishment of the Jewish national home" (Pearlman, *Ben Gurion Looks Back*, 66–69).

In the Holy Sepulchre and other holy places, infraction of the status quo, even in the most sacred services upon the most holy days, had from time immemorial been dealt with immediately and on the spot owing to the strong probability of its being subsequently regarded as a precedent.[16]

As will be seen in a later chapter, the ban Storrs put into effect at the Western Wall on Yom Kippur in 1925 was similarly enforced in 1928, opening the door to mob incitement that led to widespread Arab massacres of Jews in 1929.

As his deputy, Storrs selected Sir Harry Luke, a senior official since before World War I, of whom Norman Bentwich, the attorney general, wrote that he had "a gentle apprehension of Zionism, because it conflicted with his idea of a colonial officer's essential function: to promote the well-being of the native population."[17] This deputy com-

---

16. Storrs, *Memoirs*, 420–422. Israel's Nobel laureate in literature, S. Y. Agnon, wrote regarding the edict against bringing chairs to the Wall, "On the eve of the New Moon, I went to the Western Wall, as do the people of Jerusalem, who every month on the eve of the New Moon go to the Wall to pray... In the space in front of the Wall, the Mandatory policemen were sitting in their booth... As I was standing there, one of these policemen punched me aside with the whip he held. What had annoyed him, that he was angry? An old, sickly woman brought a stool with her to sit on. The policeman jumped up, kicked the stool so that the old woman fell down, and then took away the stool because she had broken the law passed by the Mandatory lawgivers forbidding anyone to bring a seat to the Wall. The other people praying saw what had happened but said nothing, for who can argue with someone stronger than himself? The old woman, whom I knew, went over and looked at him. The policeman lowered his gaze and gave her back the stool. I went up to her and said, 'The power in your eyes is greater than all England's promises; for England now sends its officials to annul the Balfour Declaration which it once gave us, whereas you annulled that wicked man's evil designs by just looking at him'" (S. Y. Agnon, *Till Now*, reproduced in David Hacohen, *Time to Tell: An Israeli Life 1898–1984* [New York: Cornwall Books, 1985], 167–168).
17. Bentwich and Bentwich, *Mandate Memories 1918–1948*, 76.

missioner of Jerusalem wrote in his memoirs that he considered the Balfour Declaration to be "a contradiction in terms."[18] Evidently, he saw no "contradiction in terms" in his serving under these circumstances as a high-level government official sworn to implement the Mandate in which that declaration was incorporated. In the summer of 1929, when the Arabs carried out their widespread massacres of Jews, Harry Luke, acting High Commissioner of Palestine at the time, treated the massacres as only a quarrel between Arabs and Jews, in which he ghoulishly insisted that the government must remain "neutral and impartial."[19]

Samuel continued his policy of Arab appeasement with his appointment of an architect named Ernest Richmond to the key administration post of assistant secretary (political), a post Storrs arranged for Richmond, "his most charming and hospitable friend and companion," as he called him in his memoirs. In this capacity, Richmond, a bitter and most fanatical anti-Zionist ideologue, served as chief advisor on Arab affairs to the high commissioner.[20]

General Gilbert Clayton, the anti-Zionist former chief political officer to General Allenby, whom Samuel appointed chief secretary of his administration in 1923, described Richmond's functions,

> With regard to Palestine itself, rightly or wrongly, the political section, and more especially the present head thereof, has become the principal medium of personal approach to the government available to the Arab elements and is regarded in

---

18. Wasserstein, *The British in Palestine*, 155.
19. In fact, Luke's claim of neutrality was false. The British police prevented the Jews from defending themselves. Jews caught carrying arms during the Arab massacres were disarmed, imprisoned, and even kept shackled (see Chapter 6).
20. Kedourie, *The Chatham House Version*, 64. According to Richmond's niece, Valentine Vester, the ninety-three-year-old resident owner of the American Colony Hotel in Jerusalem, he was also "violently anti-Semitic" (Steven Erlanger, "The Saturday Profile: A Grande Dame of a Bygone Jerusalem," *The New York Times*, October 29, 2005).

that respect as to some extent the counterpart of the Zionist Organization.

Although Samuel was charged with implementing the Mandate's pro-Zionist policy, the Zionist Organization was outside his administration, whereas its anti-Zionist Arab counterpart was a high-level, salaried administration official.

Despite Richmond's fanatical opposition to the government's Zionist policy, Samuel considered him indispensable. In 1922, when Richmond threatened to resign over a London government proposal to downgrade his office, Samuel intervened, writing,

> [Richmond's resignation] would have considerable political consequences. In the absence of any Arab in the higher ranks of the administration, Richmond who is in close and sympathetic touch with the Arabs, acts as a most useful intermediary. If he were to go, there is no one to take his place.

Interestingly enough, the Colonial Office—to which Lloyd George had transferred responsibility for the Middle East in 1921 (see Chapter 5)—was not as favorably impressed with Richmond's performance as was Samuel. The official dealing with Palestine commented on Samuel's letter:

> I should not personally have one minute's regret if Mr. Richmond resigned. He is by trade an architect, not a secretariat officer at all... He is a declared enemy of the Zionist policy and almost as frankly declared an enemy of the Jewish policy of [His Majesty's Government]... Indeed, I think that the government, so far from losing, would gain greatly by excluding from its secretariat so very partisan a figure as Mr. Richmond and starting again on a strictly non-partisan basis.[21]

---

21. Kedourie, *The Chatham House Version*, 64–65. Richmond did resign in March 1924. The rabid anti-Zionism of the official whom Herbert Samuel considered irreplaceable appears in stark relief in a letter Richmond sent

Humphrey Bowman was yet another opponent of the Mandate for Palestine whom Samuel appointed to head a department in his administration: the Department of Education. Bowman's anti-Zionist attitude, evidently very widely shared by the British officials in Samuel's administration, was clearly expressed in his memoirs: "In his capacity as watchdog, the British official in Palestine, seeing Jewish immigration increase, began to share the Arabs' fear of Jewish domination."[22] This perception, as watchdog *against* Jewish immigration, was shared by the officials of an administration charged with a Mandate that called for the promotion of Jewish immigration and settlement to facilitate the establishment of a Jewish national home in Palestine.

The intensity of the opposition to Jewish immigration displayed by senior officials of Samuel's administration is vividly reflected in a comment by Douglas Duff, a British police officer in Palestine who, after his retirement, authored several books on Palestine. In sharp contrast to the opinion of his superiors, Duff wrote of the Jewish immigrants:

> Their faith and hope, under the most awful and trying conditions, appeared superhuman… They shone with simple joy and the urging of a great faith as they surveyed the shores of *Eretz*

---

to Samuel after submitting his resignation. Turning down Samuel's invitation to a farewell dinner, he wrote, "I have been led gradually and most reluctantly but definitely to a conviction that the Zionist Commission, the Middle East Department of the Colonial Office, and this administration are dominated and inspired by a spirit which I can only regard as evil… I find myself unhappily in complete opposition—complete because the difference is not merely political but of a moral and even religious order… While forming part of this machine, I have tried to alter it. I have failed… Since things are so, I must go. Meanwhile, any act which emphasizes my connection or rather implies my fellowship with it is repugnant to me, for such an act would be an act of dishonesty, because there is no fellowship of spirit. On the contrary, there is enmity—not, I hope, personal, but still enmity" (Wasserstein, *The British in Palestine*, 145–146; Kedourie, 65).

22. Van Paassen, *The Forgotten Ally*, 127.

Yisrael, the home of the Israel that had once stood glorious amongst the peoples of the Earth and which they intended to raise to first rank amongst the landed nations. The determination to remove the insult of homelessness from their race shone in their uplifted faces. It was impossible to watch them and not to be thrilled. But, we had to be seemingly harsh and unfriendly towards them—it did not pay for one's seniors to think that one had any undue sympathy for the returning Jews.[23]

And the anti-Zionist attitude of the administration officials was tainted by anti-Semitism, which was no less prevalent in Samuel's civilian administration than it had been in the previous military administration. Douglas Duff reported that upon Samuel's retirement in 1925:

[His ship was hardly clear of Jaffa Harbour before official English "society" began to snub the Jewish families who had been part and parcel of the grand old game of drinking each other's "pink teas" during the Samuel regime, when, perforce, Mrs. Government Official had had to be civil and courteous to the leaders of the Zionists. Within a few weeks, the cleavage was complete; henceforth, there were two "societies," each in its own water-tight compartment. Anti-Semitism was no longer dangerous, and official British "society" was able to do justice to its long-suppressed feelings.[24]

---

23. Douglas Duff, *Sword for Hire: The Saga of a Modern Free-Companion* (London: J. Murray, 1934), 117–118. Duff came to Palestine in 1921 with the British gendarmerie after Churchill relieved the military establishment of responsibility for law and order and transferred its functions to a civilian police force. As discussed in a later chapter, Duff's fear of arousing the ire of his anti-Zionist superiors placed him in the very unfortunate role at the Western Wall on Yom Kippur in 1928 that led to the Arab massacres of Jews in 1929.
24. Duff, *Sword for Hire*, 155–157. Duff's explanation of the anti-Semitism prevalent in Samuel's administration was similar to that reached by Richard Crossman (see Chapter 3) a decade later. Duff wrote, "I consider,

Appointment of Haj Amin al-Husseini as Grand Mufti

Samuel's appointment of so many anti-Zionist officials to key positions in his administration, particularly the two key appointments of Storrs and Richmond, quickly bore poisoned fruit for both the Jewish community and Great Britain. These two officials set about to restore the leader of the 1920 pogrom to the political arena and to make him undisputed leader of the Arab people and the Moslem religious community. On July 7, 1920, in his first week as high commissioner, Samuel declared an amnesty for those convicted in the military courts for the 1920 Arab pogrom. This amnesty did not include Haj Amin al-Husseini, who had been sentenced *in absentia* to a prison term of ten years for his leading role in the pogrom. After the pogrom, he had fled to Damascus, but when France expelled Feisal from Syria in July 1920, Haj Amin escaped to Transjordan. Samuel came to Amman

---

after years of thought and experience, that the official glories in the subservience of the Arab and resents the independent attitude of the Jew. Most of the Palestine government officials are men whose only claim to distinction was the holding of a temporary commission in Allenby's armies... This type of official liked the manner in which the Arab approached him. He cringed and fawned, praised the official to the skies, flattered and cajoled him, pandered to his vanity, paid him the utmost deference, and made him feel 'no end of a fine chap,' a second Lawrence of Arabia, Clive, and Kitchener all rolled into one. The Jew, on the other hand, was a businessman and expected to be met and dealt with on a business footing. He was too busy erecting his national home, too conscious that the sole ostensible purpose of the Mandate was to facilitate him doing this in security, to bother himself about the forms of Oriental courtesy. He approached the government official as seldom as he could, and when he had to do so, did his business and went away as rapidly as possible. If the promises received from the official did not materialize, he went to higher authority, and the junior man was rapped over the knuckles. This caused resentment and annoyance in the minds of the greater part of our bureaucracy and led to the anti-Semitism which has apparently been so prevalent."

towards the end of August and was persuaded to issue a special pardon for Haj Amin, permitting him to return to Jerusalem.[25]

Arab militant resistance to Zionism could now proceed anew, led by Haj Amin, who returned to Jerusalem in October 1920 in the secure knowledge that in the retention of the strongly supportive governor of Jerusalem from the previous military administration and the appointment of other confirmed anti-Zionists to key positions, the Arabs had powerful official support in Samuel's administration against the building of a Jewish national home. Less than six months after Haj Amin's return to Jerusalem, a remarkable opportunity arose, and Storrs and Richmond took advantage of it to organize an extraordinary political coup on his behalf. This coup constituted a complete victory for the extreme Husseini clan as against the more moderate Nashashibis. Storrs himself noted in his memoirs:

> In the case of Zionism, Husseinis might be said to represent [the] church and extreme Arab nationalism, Nashashibis [the] state and making the best of a bad job. The Husseini family was by far the more indebted to British authorities, who had confirmed the Ottoman appointment of Kamel Husseini, the late mufti... and were directly responsible for the appointment of his successor, Haj Amin.[26]

---

25. Wasserstein, *The British in Palestine*, 92. Vladimir Jabotinsky, serving a fifteen-year prison sentence for having attempted to defend the Jews, refused Samuel's amnesty on the grounds that it equated the leaders of the pogrom with their victims. He appealed his sentence to the courts in London and won his acquittal several months later. But whereas Samuel permitted Haj Amin to return to Palestine, Jabotinsky was exiled (Soustelle, *The Long March of Israel*, 66–67).
26. Storrs, *Memoirs*, 423. It is noteworthy that Storrs refers only to unnamed British authorities as being responsible for Haj Amin's appointment as the mufti, mentioning neither his own role in the affair nor that of his "most charming and hospitable friend," Ernest Richmond.

On March 21, 1921, the mufti of Jerusalem died, and the high commissioner had to select a successor. Although Haj Amin, half-brother of the dead mufti, was then under thirty years old and had very little religious training—indeed, he had served as an officer in the Turkish army during World War I—Storrs and Richmond embarked on a vigorous campaign to have him appointed the new mufti. In accordance with Turkish law still in effect in Palestine, the Moslem leaders were to submit a panel of names from which Samuel, as high commissioner, was to select as mufti one of the three persons receiving the highest number of votes. The election of such a panel was scheduled for April 12, 1921. On April 1, eleven days before the election, supporters of Haj Amin posted a notice in Jerusalem calling upon the Moslems to awake and prevent danger before it occurs. The poster read in part:

> The accursed traitors whom you all know have combined with the Jews to have one of their party appointed mufti... God wants to punish you for having opposed the Moslem government of the caliphate which protected the religion. Will you accept the shame to have a Jewish Zionist mufti and that your religious affairs should become a plaything in their hands?[27]

After such incendiary campaigning, Storrs and Richmond evidently expected Haj Amin's name to feature amongst the top three names on the panel. Indeed, the day before the elections, Samuel, together with Storrs, met with Haj Amin to discuss the question of his appointment as Jerusalem's mufti. Much to their surprise, however, Haj Amin came in fourth on the election list of April 12 and was therefore not eligible to be appointed mufti.

---

27. Kedourie, *The Chatham House Version*, 58–69. The warning on behalf of Haj Amin that his defeat in the election for mufti would represent God's punishment of Arabs for having opposed the Ottoman Empire in the World War is a vivid demonstration of the absence of any sense of Arab nationalism, let alone of a distinct Palestinian nationalism, amongst the extremist Arab anti-Zionists at the time. Haj Amin's appeal was to solidarity with the Moslem religion, not to Palestinian or even Arab nationalism.

Haj Amin and his Husseini clan now mounted a sharp attack against the results of the April 12 election, charging that it was the work of Arab traitors and the Jews. Richmond, supporting the accusations, called for declaring the elections null and void and for appointing Haj Amin as the mufti in accordance with what he claimed were the true wishes of the Palestinian Moslems. When the attorney general, Norman Bentwich, reported that the mufti of Nablus had declared the elections to be valid, Richmond questioned the legal status of that mufti in the matter and commented:

> The chief point to bear in mind is that no opinion emanating from the legal secretary or his entourage or from any one dependent in any degree on the favour of his Department will at the present time be regarded as other than suspect by a very large majority of the people in this country.[28]

Wyndham Deedes, chief secretary for Palestine during the first two years of Samuel's administration, a rare pro-Zionist in the administration leadership, opposed Richmond's proposal, however, and Samuel hesitated to act.

The opportunity for acting upon Richmond's advice arose as a result of an Arab massacre in Jaffe on May 1, 1921 in which 27 Jews and 3 Arabs were killed, and 104 Jews and 34 Arabs wounded. Samuel called upon General Allenby for military help, and this time, the civil administration, unlike the military administration in the Jerusalem pogrom a year earlier, permitted armed Jewish self-defense. When the violence ended seven days later, 47 Jews and 48 Arabs had been killed, and 146 Jews and 73 Arabs had been wounded.[29]

Among the extraordinary steps Samuel now took to placate the Arabs, the most significant, with lasting effect, was the critical decision Samuel made on May 8, 1921, the day after the week-long violence ended, to yield to Richmond's pressure to declare Haj Amin

---

28. Kedourie, *The Chatham House Version*, 67.
29. Cruise O'Brien, *The Siege*, 160.

the grand mufti of Jerusalem. By a devious political maneuver, the candidate who had received the most votes of the Moslem panel was persuaded to withdraw, and Samuel privately informed Haj Amin al-Husseini that he had been appointed grand mufti of Jerusalem.[30] Samuel, a man with a reputation of unquestioned integrity and high democratic ideals, was apparently uncomfortable with his decision, because he never formalized the appointment in writing. Instead, he tacitly allowed Haj Amin to assume the position of grand mufti without any official letter specifying the terms and conditions of the appointment. It was an appointment that Haj Amin thereupon decided was his for life, to shape as he saw fit, and free of any conditions.[31] This appointment was to plague Great Britain and the Jewish people for the rest of Haj Amin's life.

Meinertzhagen, foreseeing the incalculable harm that was bound to result from Samuel's appointment of Haj Amin as grand mufti of Jerusalem, expressed his utter dismay:

> I had trouble with the man when I was in Jerusalem, for with the connivance of Ronald Storrs and Waters-Taylor, he was conducting violent anti-Zionist propaganda, and during the Easter riots of 1920, he delivered incendiary speeches not only against the Jews but against the British, fled to Transjordan and was sentenced during his absence to ten years imprisonment, but later returned on receiving an amnesty. I had much documentary evidence against Storrs and Waters-Taylor proving up to the hilt that he was receiving encouragement from these

---

30. It was under the British, probably with the advice of Storrs as governor of Jerusalem, that the mufti of Jerusalem was first allowed to call himself grand mufti. Under the Ottoman Empire, the Jerusalem mufti was equal in importance to the muftis of the other regions, and the Turkish Sultan was the supreme religious as well as secular authority. But with the sultan removed from power, the British made the mufti of Jerusalem the supreme religious leader of the Moslem Arabs (Kedourie, *The Chatham House Version*, 58–59).
31. Kedourie, *The Chatham House Version*, 66–67.

two highly placed officials, but Allenby declined to use it. And now he is in a position where he can do untold harm to Zionism and to the British—he hates both Jews and British. His appointment is sheer madness. I am particularly annoyed about this, as before I left Palestine in 1920, I left a memorandum with Samuel warning him of appointing the man when it was obvious his predecessor was in failing health and also warning him that Storrs would press for his appointment purely on the grounds of hostility to Zionism. Haj Amin is a strong character and if given a chance could do great harm. He is very ambitious, quite unscrupulous, and grossly dishonest. Sooner or later, his appointment will be bitterly regretted by us.[32]

Despite Meinertzhagen's warning in 1920, it was the advice of Storrs and Richmond that Samuel followed in May 1921. And the appointment to the post of grand mufti was only the first step in Haj Amin's elevation to leadership. Seven months later, in December 1921, Samuel established the Supreme Moslem Council to serve as counterpart to the Rabbinical Council he had established for the Jews. The Moslem Council was to direct the religious affairs of the Palestinian Moslem community, but it also exercised virtually unlimited rights of patronage and control over the Islamic religious hierarchy of Palestine over the Moslem schools, the religious courts, and the Waqf (religious) trust funds.[33] A month later, in January 1922, Haj Amin was elected president of this Council, with the support of Samuel's administration. He thus became both the religious head and the national leader of the Palestinian Arabs, with the financing of his agenda ensured by his role as custodian in control of the Moslem trust funds.[34]

---

32. Meinertzhagen, *Middle East Diary*, 97–98.
33. Sachar, *A History of Israel*, 170–171.
34. Pierre van Paassen has a telling comment on the wealth amassed by Haj Amin as a result of his appointment to this position of president of the Moslem Council: "I recall one day finding the mufti of Jerusalem and his cousin Jemal Husseini in high glee: The Moslems of Java—forty-seven million of them—had just sent him a donation for the repair of the mosque

As the historian, Elie Kedourie, emphasized:

> To have tacitly allowed Haj Amin, in response to agitation engineered by the Husseini clan to become mufti, and that without a letter of appointment defining the length and conditions of his tenure, was to invite the Palestinians to conclude that in Palestine, rent-a-crowd was king, and to allow the Husseinis, already powerful enough in Palestine, to become the self-appointed exclusive and irresponsible spokesman of the Palestinians, whose power their fellow countrymen could, as the sequel showed, challenge only at their peril. It was the Husseinis who directed the political strategy of the Palestinians until 1947, and they led them to utter ruin.[35]

Watering Down the Mandate for Palestine

In addition to appointing Haj Amin as mufti, Samuel also agreed to the Arab demand to put a halt to Jewish immigration. Churchill disapproved, telegraphing Samuel from London a week later, "The present agitation is doubtless engineered in the hope of frightening us out of our Zionist policy… We must firmly maintain law and order and make concessions on their merits and not under duress."[36] The decision to

---

> of Omar, which had been damaged slightly in an earthquake. '*Figurez-vous,*' said the mufti, 'twenty-seven thousand pounds sterling have come in from the Dutch Indies, from Java alone, on my appeal. Last week, a hundred thousand pounds from Afghanistan. And this is only the beginning: British India, Burma, Malaya, Singapore, with its two hundred Moslem millionaires, Morocco, Algiers, and Persia are still to be heard from. Wonderful, isn't it? Now we, too, are going to build a university and schools and model farms like the Jews.'" And Pierre van Paassen, writing in 1943, in the midst of World War II, when the grand mufti was sitting in Berlin as adviser to Hitler on the Final Solution, for killing all the Jews, added, "But the Arab university still exists only on paper…and the mosque was never repaired…and the mufti is in Berlin, not badly off at all!" (Van Paassen, *The Forgotten Ally*, 126–127).

35. Kedourie, *The Chatham House Version*, 69.
36. Gilbert, *Exile and Return*, 133.

halt immigration so shocked the *Yishuv* (the Jewish community living in Palestine before 1948) that the Zionist leadership—including the Zionist Commission, the Jewish National Council (Vaad Haleumi), and the Chief Rabbinate—threatened collective resignation. Samuel countered this threat, however, with his own threat to resign, and the Zionists felt compelled to yield.[37]

Samuel lifted the suspension two months later, but he then introduced a new system of immigration controls, including requirement of a guarantee of available employment. Of far greater long-term significance, however, was his formulation of a new immigration policy, which Churchill incorporated the following year in an official government white paper. Henceforth, Jewish immigration was to be limited in accordance with the "economic absorptive capacity" of the country. Unfortunately, a country's economic absorptive capacity cannot be measured objectively like the weight placed on a scale—its measurement is often in the mind of the measurer. No matter how innocent Samuel's intentions may have been, this ambiguous concept lent itself to purely subjective estimation. It provided later administrations with a useful tool in campaigns to curb Jewish immigration and to halt the building of the Jewish national home. One government report was later to issue the absurd finding that Palestine did not have the economic absorptive capacity for a single additional Jewish immigrant.[38]

---

37. Mosheh Mossek, *Palestine Immigration Policy* (Totowa, NJ: London, 1978), 24. Weizmann was opposed to the threatened resignation, but in private, he protested vigorously against this surprising turn of events. He cabled Balfour from New York, calling attention to the serious effect on Jewish morale and appealing to him to intervene with the prime minister to secure the immediate restoration of immigration (Meyer Weisgal, *The Letters and Papers of Chaim Weizmann, Series A, vol. 10*, [London: Oxford University Press, 1977], letter 176, 191).

38. In addition to restricting immigration, Samuel violated article 6 of the Mandate, which required that the Palestine administration "shall encourage...close settlement by the Jews on the land, including State lands and waste lands not required for public purposes." Yielding to Arab pressure,

Rationalizing his overriding need to be seen as scrupulously "fair" to the Arabs, Samuel noted in his memoirs:

> I had been appointed with full knowledge on the part of His Majesty's Government of my Zionist sympathies and no doubt largely because of them. But I was there to administer the country, not for the benefit of one section of the population only, but for all—not commissioned by the Zionists, but in the name of the King.

Samuel buttressed this policy formulation with an interpretation of the Balfour Declaration that it imposed a dual obligation on the Mandatory Power, writing:

> The Balfour Declaration, it will be remembered, gave two injunctions—first, to foster the establishment of a Jewish national home, second, to do it without prejudice to the civil and religious rights of the rest of the population.[39]

In his first official report as high commissioner, Samuel explained his understanding of his Mandate:

> It is the clear duty of the Mandatory Power to promote the well-being of the Arab population in the same way as a British administration would regard it as its duty to promote the welfare of the local population in any part of the Empire. The measures to foster the well-being of the Arabs should be precisely those

---

Samuel refused to permit Jewish settlement in the Ottoman State land of the Beisan Valley and instead allotted about 120,000 acres of it to a group of Bedouins that was especially formed for this purpose and which, "After acquiring this acreage for a nominal sum, the Bedouins did not even farm it but sold some of it off at exorbitant prices to Jewish immigrants" (Soustelle, *The Long March of Israel*, 69).

39. Samuel, *Memoirs*, 168.

which we would adopt in Palestine if there were no Zionist question and if there had been no Balfour Declaration.[40]

Samuel's concept of "dual obligation" became "preferential obligation to the Arabs" in the 1939 White Paper, according to which the Chamberlain government shut Palestine's doors to Europe's Jews, who were desperately seeking to escape the Holocaust.

✡ ✡ ✡

The issue that aroused the greatest Zionist anxiety was Samuel's plan to establish a representative government in Palestine. Ever confident that the Arabs would accept a moderate Zionist program that was sensitive to their concerns, Samuel sought to establish a system of self-government in which Moslems, Christians, and Jews were to be chosen in proportion to their numbers in the population and to cooperate in governing the country in their joint interest.

Already in his inaugural address at the beginning of July 1920, Samuel had announced that he would form a small advisory council, including leading members of the Moslem, Christian, and Jewish communities, to which all measures of importance would be submitted.[41] This advisory council, established in October 1920, with Samuel as its chairman, consisted of ten British officials and ten Palestinians appointed by Samuel, including four Moslem Arabs, three Christian Arabs, and three Jews.

On May 8, 1921, one day after the Arab riots ended and three days after he had suspended Jewish immigration—the same day that he yielded to Richmond's pressure to appoint Haj Amin as grand mufti—Samuel proposed to Churchill still another concession to the Arabs. As a further stage on the road to self-government, an elected council should replace the council appointed by the high commissioner.[42] Although in its initial stage, the elected council was to remain in

---

40. Wasserstein, *The British in Palestine*, 88.
41. Samuel, *Memoirs*, 157.
42. Wasserstein, *The British in Palestine*, 108–109.

an advisory capacity, Samuel also had in mind—as indeed the Churchill White Paper of 1922, prepared with his advice (see Chapter 5), officially proposed—for the advisory council to later give way to a legislative council. Such a council, with an overwhelmingly hostile Arab majority whose representatives were elected under the leadership of Haj Amin and his Husseini clan, would inevitably have spelled the end of the Mandate for building a Jewish national home in Palestine. The first objective of such a legislative council would have been to put an end to Jewish immigration and the Jewish purchase of land.

Completely oblivious to any such risk and determined to proceed with placating the Arabs after their riots of the preceding month, Samuel made public on June 3, 1921—at a ceremony to mark the King of England's birthday—both his new interpretation of the Balfour Declaration and his proposal for a representative government. In his speech that day to allay Arab fears stemming from what he called the "unhappy misunderstanding" of the Balfour Declaration, he declared that Britain had "never consented and never will consent...to their country, their holy places, and their lands being taken from them and given to strangers" and "will never agree to a Jewish government being set up to rule over the Moslem and Christian majority." Samuel now explained the meaning of the Balfour Declaration to be,

> The Jews, a people that are scattered throughout the world but whose hearts are always turned to Palestine, would be enabled to found here their home, and...some among them within the limits that are fixed by the numbers and interests of the present population should come to Palestine in order to help, by their resources and efforts, to develop the country to the advantage of all the inhabitants.

He declared further:

> [The British Government,] the trustee under the Mandate for the happiness of the people of Palestine, would never impose upon them a policy which that people had reason to think was

contrary to their religious, their political, and their economic interests.

Finally, he added that the government was examining the possibility of establishing representative institutions in Palestine.[43]

In this speech, given while Jewish immigration still remained suspended, Samuel in effect repudiated the Balfour Declaration by offering the Arabs under the leadership of the grand mufti, Haj Amin, a veto of any measure they considered "contrary to their religious, their political, and their economic interests." He repudiated as well his own "unshakable" Zionist policy expressed in London only one and a half years earlier on the occasion of the second anniversary of the Balfour Declaration, when he had declared,

> The policy propounded before the Peace Conference, to which the Zionist leaders unshakably adhere, is the promotion to the fullest degree that the conditions of the country allow, of Jewish immigration and of Jewish settlement…in order that with a minimum of delay, the country may become a purely self-governing commonwealth under the auspices of an established Jewish majority.[44]

No Jewish majority could ever develop under Samuel's policy of representative government.

On July 19, 1921, Weizmann wrote to Samuel of his worries concerning an elective council:

> We all view with the greatest concern the establishment of an elective assembly in Palestine. I understand from Mr. Churchill that all matters concerning the Jewish national home are to be excluded from the purview of this assembly. But this argument, however well meant, is not convincing. The self-appointed

---

43. Mossek, *Palestine Immigration Policy*, 36–37.
44. Samuel's speech is reproduced in Weisgal, *The Letters and Papers of Chaim Weizmann, Series A, vol. 10*, Appendix, 345–346.

Haifa Congress succeeded in impressing the administration of Palestine and has brought about the enforcement of measures derogatory to Zionist aims. How much more power will have a duly elected and recognised assembly?[45]

Out of a sense of deep frustration, Weizmann added:

There is a tendency for the Balfour Declaration and the San Remo decision to be either ignored or interpreted in a manner which may possibly give a certain amount of temporary satisfaction to the Arabs but which destroys the political foundation on which we have been building... Zionism is being gradually, systematically, and relentlessly "reduced"; Jewish public opinion is not reckoned with; we have ceased to exist as a political factor... After a year of great hope, we stand now *dalim v'reikim* [Hebrew for "wretched and empty-handed"].[46]

At a conference three days later with Lloyd George, Balfour, and Churchill—newly appointed colonial minister, with newly transferred responsibility for the Middle East—Weizmann attempted to secure a reversal of Samuel's new policy. Weizmann protested that Samuel's policy negated the Balfour Declaration, because it would never permit a Jewish majority to eventuate, and "it means giving up Palestine." He went on to complain about Samuel's stoppage of immigration, his failure to grant the necessary concessions for development, and the lack of security for the Jewish population.

Lloyd George agreed, telling Churchill that he "mustn't give representative government to Palestine." Churchill demurred, however,

---

45. Weizmann had good reason to be concerned—the Churchill white paper of 1922 that incorporated Samuel's proposal for a legislative council in fact provided for the establishment of a special committee consisting of members of the legislative council "to confer with the administration about matters relating to the regulation of immigration."
46. Weisgal, *The Letters and Papers of Chaim Weizmann, Series A, vol. 10*, letter 213, 218–222.

noting the difficulties Samuel faced because the Balfour Declaration "was opposed by the Arabs, nine-tenths of the British officials on the spot, and some of the Jews in Palestine."[47] Supporting Samuel's proposal, he warned that he "might have to bring the matter to the cabinet."[48]

The following week, Weizmann unburdened himself to the Christian pro-Zionist Wyndham Deedes, Chief Secretary of Palestine, under the high commissioner:

> British public opinion, which three years ago was distinctly in our favour, is being systematically poisoned against us, and I fear chiefly by those "nine-tenths" [of British Administration officials]. Of the Balfour Declaration nothing is left but mere lip service."

In language that might have been expressed by a pious Jew, Weizmann added:

> The God of Israel in His wisdom is trying His people. Ukraine, Poland, Bolshevism—all that is not enough. We must be pogromed in Palestine, submitted there to restrictions and difficulties. Such are the ways of Providence, and I believe faithfully that it is all for the good in the end."[49]

Despite his repeated attempts to placate the Arabs, however, Samuel failed to win over the Arab leadership. The Arabs saw Samuel's policy of compromise as a sign of weakness. It served only to invite

---

47. Some ultra-pious Jews oppose Zionism because they believe Jews are commanded to await instead the coming of the Messiah for their national independence and sovereignty in the Holy Land.
48. Meinertzhagen, *Middle East Diary*, 104–105. Meinertzhagen's reaction was that Churchill was "not too sympathetic" to the Zionist cause, adding, "I suspect he regards it as a nuisance."
49. Weisgal, *The Letters and Papers of Chaim Weizmann, Series A, vol. 10*, letter 228, 234–239.

their further resistance in the expectation of gaining full control in Palestine. They boycotted the elections called by Samuel for a legislative council, they refused his offer to renew the advisory council, and they turned down a British Cabinet Committee offer to establish an Arab Agency with the same responsibility as the Jewish Agency under the terms of the Mandate.[50] Only the Arab refusal of any compromise and their insistence on the total repudiation of the Balfour Declaration saved the Jewish national home from an early death.[51]

---

50. Mossek, *Palestine Immigration Policy*, 73–76.
51. Samuel took pride in the fact that his policy won him the support of several anti-Zionist British officials who had been firmly opposed to the Balfour Declaration. Thus, Edwin Montagu wrote him that although he had been strongly opposed to the Balfour Declaration, he rejoiced in Samuel's success and in his story of progress. In addition, Sir Gilbert Clayton, who had resigned as General Allenby's first chief political officer in Palestine because of his opposition to Zionism, had accepted Samuel's offer to succeed Wydham Deedes as chief secretary because "The 1922 White Paper relieved his anxieties" (Samuel, *Memoirs*, 170–172). But the white paper did not convert Montagu and Clayton to Zionism; they simply understood its potential for harm to the development of the Jewish National Home in Palestine. Clayton's position as Samuel's chief secretary did not deter him from writing to the Colonial Office on July 6, 1923 to advocate "a whittling down of the Zionist activities in Palestine, on the grounds that Arab opposition to Zionism is steadily increasing" (Meinertzhagen, *Middle East Diary*, 133). Samuel himself was obliged to respond on July 18, "refuting the Arab complaint 'that the administrative policy of Palestine is heavily weighted by Zionist influence.'"

– 5 –

Churchill Partitions the Mandate

THE IRONIES ASSOCIATED WITH THE rebirth of the State of Israel were further compounded by Winston Churchill, an ardent Christian Zionist from almost the beginning of his political career, who immediately after being given cabinet responsibility for Palestine in 1921, proceeded to weaken the Jewish national home even further than had Herbert Samuel. In order to solve a problem totally unrelated to issues in Palestine, Churchill partitioned the Palestine Mandate, reducing the land area available for the Jewish national home to less than one-fourth of the original area approved at the San Remo Conference in April 1920. To the Mandate text that had been originally approved, Churchill added a new article that set all of Transjordan aside from the rest of the Palestine Mandate as an exclusive Arab area for Feisal's brother, Abdullah, where the Balfour Declaration for a Jewish national homeland was not to apply. In addition, Churchill incorporated, in an official British white paper, Samuel's reinterpretation of the Mandate, weakening it in the rest of Palestine where the Balfour Declaration was to apply. Only after the Zionist Executive yielded to his demand that its members sign their acceptance of his position, did he put up the amended text of the Palestine Mandate for a vote of ratification by the League of Nations.

The Decision to Partition the Palestine Mandate

Winston Churchill was among the first in British officialdom to identify with the Zionist cause. Already in 1908, he wrote to the English Zionist Federation in Manchester, "I am in full sympathy with the historical aspirations of the Jews. The restoration to them of a center of racial and political integrity would be a tremendous event in the history of the world."[1] In 1920, shortly before the San Remo Peace Conference, at which Great Britain officially received the Palestine Mandate, he wrote a remarkable essay on Jews and Zionism in which he appealed for building up a Jewish national home in Palestine "with the utmost rapidity." Such a center, he declared, would become "not only a refuge to the oppressed from the unhappy lands of Central Europe" but also "a symbol of Jewish unity and the temple of Jewish glory." Churchill added such laudatory comments about Jews as "Some people like Jews and some do not, but no thoughtful man can doubt the fact that they are beyond all doubt the most formidable and the most remarkable race which has ever appeared in the world." Of the system of ethics that the Jews have given to the world, he declared that it is "incomparably the most precious possession of mankind, worth in fact the fruit of all other wisdom and learning together." Churchill went on to envisage the establishment of a Jewish state in Palestine, writing:

> If, as may well happen, there should be created in our own lifetime by the banks of the Jordan a Jewish state under the protection of the British Crown which might comprise three or four millions of Jews, an event will have occurred in the history of the world which would from every point of view be beneficial and would be especially in harmony with the truest interests of the British Empire.[2]

Yet, in another one of the many ironies in the history of Israel's rebirth, whereas Curzon, the anti-Zionist successor to Balfour, significantly strengthened Britain's commitment to the Jewish national

---

1. Oskar K. Rabinowicz, *Winston Churchill on Jewish Problems: A Half-Century Survey* (London: Lincolns-Prager, 1956), 194–195, quoting *The Jewish Chronicle*, February 7, 1908.
2. Article in *The Illustrated Sunday Herald* on February 8, 1920, quoted in Gilbert, *Exile and Return*, 127–129.

home in the Mandate text placed before the San Remo Conference (see Chapter 2), Churchill, the ardent Zionist, significantly weakened the Mandate before putting it up for ratification by the League of Nations.

Churchill's major concern in 1921, when he was put in charge of the Colonial Office with cabinet responsibility for the Middle East, was to settle what he called the alarming problems of the Middle East.

> In the spring of 1921, I was sent to the Colonial Office to take over our business in the Middle East and bring matters into some kind of order. At that time, we had recently suppressed a most dangerous and bloody rebellion in Iraq, and upwards of forty thousand troops at a cost of thirty million pounds a year were required to preserve order. This could not go on. In Palestine the strife between the Arabs and the Jews threatened at any moment to take the form of actual violence. The Arab chieftains, driven out of Syria with many of their followers—all of them our late allies—lurked furious in the deserts beyond the Jordan. Egypt was in ferment. Thus, the whole of the Middle East presented a most melancholy and alarming picture.[3]

Deploring the need to pour in more British manpower and money to suppress the revolt, Churchill pressed the government to establish a Middle East department to coordinate policy in the region. Responsibility was then shared between the India Office, which administered Iraq, and the Foreign Office, which administered the rest of the Middle East, with inputs from the War and Colonial Ministries. Churchill had the powerful support of the famous Lawrence of Arabia, who had launched a campaign along similar lines beginning July 22, 1920, just as the French army was moving into Damascus to topple Feisal from his newly assumed Syrian throne. Capitalizing on his extraordinary post-war reputation as leader of the Arab Revolt, which had allegedly toppled the Ottoman Empire,

---

3. Churchill, "Lawrence of Arabia," in *Great Contemporaries*, 132.

Lawrence began a letter campaign against the India Office's administration of Iraq. After severely criticizing British rule in Iraq—in a letter to *The Times* on July 22, 1920 and in an article in *The Observer* on August 8, 1920—he wrote to *The Sunday Times* on August 22, 1920, with an urgent call for the replacement of the existing British regime in Iraq. Asking, "How long will we permit millions of pounds, thousands of Imperial troops, and tens of thousands of Arabs to be sacrificed on behalf of a form of colonial administration which can benefit nobody but its administrators?" Lawrence urged the transfer of responsibility for the Middle East to another government department.[4] Prime Minister Lloyd George, embarrassed by the Iraqi revolt and the human and financial costs of suppressing it, responded by transferring responsibility for the Middle East to the Colonial Office, with Winston Churchill newly appointed at the beginning of 1921 to head the Colonial Ministry.

Churchill established the Middle East Department in the Colonial Office, staffing it with experts on Arab affairs who had served in Cairo, Palestine, and Iraq. He offered Lawrence the post of Arab adviser and appointed Colonel Meinertzhagen—whom General Allenby had dismissed in 1920 for insubordination (see Chapter 3)—as military adviser and as inspector general of troops in Palestine.[5]

Shortly after organizing this department in March 1921, Churchill, accompanied by Lawrence, convened a conference in Cairo of the key British military and civilian officials of the region, including the high commissioners for Egypt, Palestine, and Mesopotamia. Meinertzhagen's appointment was postponed for personal reasons until May 9,

---

4. Garnett, *The Letters of T. E. Lawrence*, "Letter 127: To the Editor of *The Times*," July 22, 1920, 306–308; "Letter 130: France, Britain, and the Arabs," to *The Observer*, August 8, 1920, 311–315; and "Letter 131: Mesopotamia," to *The Sunday Times*, August 22, 1920, 317.
5. As noted in Chapter 4, although Meinertzhagen had succeeded in having the military administration under General Bols replaced by the civilian administration under Herbert Samuel, the military had been retained in Palestine with responsibility for the maintenance of law and order.

about six weeks after the conference, giving Lawrence a free hand in shaping Churchill's decision, a decision to which Meinertzhagen was very much opposed.

Lawrence, in defiance of the Sykes–Picot Agreement for France to receive Syria, had planned to divide the conquered Arab territories—except for Palestine—among the sons of Sherif Hussein of Mecca. At the end of World War I, he had proposed to Britain's War Cabinet Committee to place Feisal on the throne in Syria and to divide what is now Iraq between two of Feisal's brothers: Abdullah was to get Baghdad and lower Iraq and Zeid the Mosul region in upper Iraq. Hussein was to remain the ruler of the Hejaz in Arabia, with his oldest son, Ali, to succeed him.[6] The French, however, had expelled Feisal from Syria in July 1920, only months after the British had arranged to have him declared king there. Now, at the Cairo Conference, therefore, Lawrence proposed to Churchill that as compensation for the "loss" of Syria, Feisal should be made king of Iraq.

Churchill agreed, particularly since Saiyid Talib, the leading Iraqi candidate for the throne, seemed reluctant to accept British overlordship—and he arranged for Feisal to be "elected" king of Iraq. Lloyd George, worried about the adverse French reaction to the role of the British military administration in setting Feisal on the Syrian throne, had told Churchill it was "essential that real initiative in any demand for Feisal should come from Mesopotamia."[7] Britain's High Commissioner of Mesopotamia, Sir Percy Cox, also reminded Churchill that the Baghdad Arabs had been promised the election of their king would be as free as elections in England, whereupon, according to Lawrence, Churchill replied that so they would be.[8] Talib was then invited as a dinner guest of Sir Percy, where he was kidnapped and sent off for internment in Ceylon. Ignoring all other candidates for the throne, Cox placed before the voters only the question whether

---

6. Garnett, *The Letters of T. E. Lawrence*, 265–270.
7. Knightley and Simpson, *The Secret Lives of Lawrence of Arabia*, 159–160.
8. Aldington, *Lawrence of Arabia*, 305.

they wanted Feisal as their king, and Feisal received more than ninety-six percent of the vote.[9]

The decision to give Iraq to Feisal left Feisal's older brother, Abdullah, to be appeased. Already at the end of 1920, Abdullah had entered Transjordan with the declared intention of invading Syria and restoring Feisal as its king. And now, in March 1921, there came the alarming news that Abdullah had arrived in Amman on the way to attack the French in Syria. Churchill, worried that the French might react by occupying Amman, accepted Lawrence's advice to set aside Transjordan as an autonomous region of the Mandate for Palestine as a throne for Abdullah, where the Balfour Declaration for a Jewish national home would not apply. Herbert Samuel would remain as high commissioner for Transjordan as part of the Mandate for Palestine. At the conclusion of the Cairo Conference, Churchill went on to Palestine, where, on March 28, 1921, he named Abdullah the emir of Transjordan under the general responsibility of the high commissioner for Palestine.

With a stroke of his pen, Churchill, the ardent Zionist, had thus reduced by about three-quarters—from about 45,000 square miles to somewhat over 10,000 square miles—the original area of Palestine that the United Kingdom had insisted at the Paris Peace Conference must be allotted for the Jewish national home. In accordance with Churchill's decision, the Mandate Britain submitted to the League of Nations for formal adoption included a new article 25 that set Transjordan aside as an area of Palestine that would be off limits to the Jewish national home. Until May 22, 1946, when Britain decided to establish Transjordan as an independent state under a shortened name, Jordan, the area remained part of the Mandate for Palestine, with Abdullah, its ruler, serving under the high commissioner for Palestine.[10]

---

9. According to H. St. John Philby, British "adviser" to Ibn Saud, as reported in Aldington, *Lawrence of Arabia*, 305–306.
10. Eugene V. Rostow, "Israel in the Evolution of American Foreign Policy," in Clark M. Clifford, Eugene V. Rostow, and Barbara W. Tuchman, *The*

Article 25 included a proviso that "no action shall be taken which is inconsistent with article 15," which requires that "no discrimination of any kind shall be made between the inhabitants of Palestine on the ground of race, religion, or language." Nevertheless, Britain prohibited all Jewish immigration and Jewish land purchases in Transjordan. In addition, although article 25 also subjects the Mandatory's authority for postponing or withholding the application of the Mandate's provisions in Transjordan to the consent of the Council of the League of Nations, Britain introduced these prohibitions on Jewish immigration and land purchase without the League of Nation's consent and even in the face of disapproval by the League of Nation's Commission for Palestine.[11]

Palestine Question in American History (New York: Arno Press, 1978), 50.
11. Britain prohibited Jewish land purchases even when Transjordan agreed to them. King Abdullah made a private deal with a member of the Zionist Executive for the Jewish development of a large tract of his land. The deal became public knowledge, however, and the government, feeling obliged to yield to Grand Mufti Haj Amin al-Husseini's objections, insisted upon the abrogation of the deal (Emanuel Neumann, *In the Arena: An Autobiographical Memoir* [New York: Herzl Press, 1976], 121–130). In 1932, Weizmann sought to obtain a reversal of the prohibition of Jewish land purchases in Transjordan. Calling attention to the arbitrary separation of Transjordan for reasons having nothing to do with Palestine, he complained to the colonial minister, Sir Philip Cunliffe-Lister, about the "grave injustice involved in all this talk about land congestion in Palestine. Palestine had first been truncated, and then it had been repeatedly thrown up at us, and at the general public, that we were forcing the government to the execution of a policy under impossible economic and physical conditions." The minister replied he was aware that "the Jews had been offered rather large tracts of land for acquisition in Transjordan." He explained, however, that "though it was possible that the Jews could reach agreement with the sheikhs and begin both to acquire land and even to settle in Transjordan, [His Majesty's] Government had to bear in mind that this might eventually involve them in serious complications. Any such settlements would have to be defended, and that would mean the extension of the defence force to cover Transjordan as a whole. This would naturally mean additional

Churchill Yields to Anti-Zionist Pressure

In Palestine, where Churchill had gone immediately after the Cairo Conference, the Arab leadership, emboldened by Samuel's appeasement policies together with Churchill's award of Transjordan to Abdullah, presented him with a petition from the Haifa Congress of Palestinian Arabs protesting the Balfour Declaration and demanding an end to Jewish immigration. In reply, Churchill spelled out his firm support for the Jewish national home in Palestine, declaring:

> It is manifestly right that the Jews, who are scattered all over the world, should have a national centre and a national home where some of them may be reunited. And where else could that be but in the land of Palestine, with which for more than three thousand years, they have been intimately and profoundly associated? We think it would be good for the world, good for the Jews, and good for the British Empire.[12]

On the same visit, Churchill declared before a Jewish gathering on Mount Scopus, where he was warmly greeted despite his decision on Transjordan, "Personally, my heart has throbbed with Zionism since twelve years ago, when I made the acquaintance of Manchester Jewry."[13]

But despite these firm Zionist sentiments, Churchill yielded under the combined Arab and British anti-Zionist pressure—civilian and military—in Palestine and London. He approved Samuel's proposals for weakening the obligations of the Mandate, and neither Weizmann's firm protestations nor the objections of both Lloyd George and Balfour

---

    expense, which Transjordan could not be expected to cover, and of which Parliament would certainly fight shy" (Meyer Weisgal, *The Letters and Papers of Chaim Weizmann, Series B, vol. 2* [New Brunswick, NJ: Transaction Books, 1983], paper 2, 13).

12. Gilbert, *Exile and Return*, 132–133.
13. Rabinowicz, *Winston Churchill on Jewish Problems*, 195, quoting *The Jewish Chronicle*, May 27, 1921.

at the meeting on July 22, 1921 in Balfour's home (see Chapter 4) dissuaded Churchill from supporting Samuel in his plan to establish a representative government in Palestine.

Hubert Young, the assistant secretary of Churchill's Middle East Department, sought strenuously, like Meinertzhagen, to keep Churchill from accepting Samuel's appeasement policies. On August 1, a little over a week after the meeting in Balfour's home, Young wrote to Churchill calling for a Zionist policy that would facilitate "the gradual immigration of Jews into Palestine until that country becomes a predominantly Jewish state." He went on to argue that the phrase "national home" as used in the Balfour Declaration implied no less than full statehood for the Jews of Palestine. There could be no halfway house between a Jewish state and "total abandonment of the Zionist programme." It was, he continued, "insufficient for us merely to tell the Arab delegation that we do not intend to waver in our policy—the fact of the matter is that we *have* wavered, and we must be prepared to take a stronger line."[14]

Even stronger than the Arab pressure was the anti-Zionist pressure emanating from the Cairo military establishment in Palestine, whose garrison had remained in charge of maintaining law and order even after the military administration had been replaced by Samuel's civilian administration. On October 29, 1921, General Congreve, second in command to General Allenby, issued an extraordinary circular to the troops in Palestine under his command, stating:

> Whilst the Army officially is supposed to have no politics, it is recognized that there are certain problems, such as those of Ireland and Palestine, in which the sympathies of the Army are on one side or the other. In the case of Palestine, these sympathies are rather obviously with the Arabs, who have hitherto appeared

---

14. Gilbert, *Exile and Return*, 136. The Arab delegation, to which Young referred, was then on its way to London to protest against the Balfour Declaration.

to the disinterested observer to have been the victims of the unjust policy forced upon them by the British government.[15]

There is little wonder, then, that with such an attitude displayed by the military in charge of law and order, some Arabs felt sufficiently emboldened to stage a pogrom once again in Jerusalem's Jewish Quarter on November 2, 1921, the fourth anniversary of the Balfour Declaration. Five Jews and three of their Arab attackers were killed. The Palestine administration reacted quite feebly, and again, it was the Colonial Office that felt that the administration should have acted more firmly. Gerard Clauson, an official of the Office, wrote the next day that it was a pity "that when the first mob gathered, the police only dispersed it, instead of rounding it up. It was quite certain that this demonstration was deliberately organized."[16]

Two weeks later, on November 15, 1921, the Arab delegation in London hosted a luncheon that was attended by the leading former high-level anti-Zionist officers of the Palestine military establishment, including Waters-Taylor, promoter of the Passover pogrom in 1920. In his diary entry for November 16, Meinertzhagen commented bitterly:

> It is abominable that government officials should be permitted to lend their names in opposition to the policy of the government they serve. I am compelled to believe that obstruction to Zionism is no longer impelled by the Arab ideas and Arab pressure. Obstruction to Zionism is now captained by British officials, who have constituted themselves as advisers to the Arab delegation here in London and who are working against Zionism in Palestine. It is political sabotage of the worst kind. At the present time, it is impossible for the Arab delegation to voice the views of the people of Palestine. They are instead voicing the view of the handful of ex-Palestine officials in London. This makes negotiations between the Arab delegation and

---

15. Weisgal, *The Letters and Papers of Chaim Weizmann, Series A, vol. 10,* letter 316, 333.
16. Gilbert, *Exile and Return,* 140.

the Zionists manifestly impossible... I am still convinced that a declaration to both parties, based on the Draft Mandate, is the only solution for the present impasse. We have pressed this with all the force at our command, and Winston will not act. I am getting tired of knocking my head against brick walls, which I have been doing for the last three years.[17]

Weizmann was equally bitter about the Arab delegation luncheon, chaired by Lord Sydenham, a backer of the notorious Czarist forgery, *Protocols of the Elders of Zion*. He wrote to Shuckburgh, the head of Churchill's Middle East Department:

> The Sydenham lunch is an open scandal from the government point of view. There were six or seven high government officials who have held responsible positions in the Palestine administration and who are openly countenancing an antisemitic and anti-Zionist and anti-government policy. It is a flagrant case of political sabotage. And this sabotage has been going on for years and is going on now. If this policy of drift and indifference is going to last, we shall have a disaster in Palestine, and possibly the Balfour Declaration will be drowned in Jewish blood...
>
> Jews and Arabs have always lived in amity in Palestine. We are there for the past forty years. Every Arab *knew* what our aim is. The problem only became acute since the advent of elements into Palestine which have poisoned the relations and brought them to the present state. Even here in London, with this delegation, we could have come to a peaceful compromise if not for the Gabriels and Taylors and Somersets and *tutti quanti*. They defy the government, they utilise the fact that the government has other business to do and can give very little attention to a comparatively small problem like Palestine, they thrive on prejudice, on misrepresentation, they calumniate—and it is so easy to insult a Jew and a Jewish movement. I see serious dangers ahead... Anything is better

---

17. Meinertzhagen, *Middle East Diary*, 110–112.

than the present mirage of a Mandate which is, to all intents and purposes, not operative.[18]

Although Weizmann and Meinertzhagen failed to persuade Churchill to issue a declaration reaffirming the government's support for the Balfour Declaration, they did succeed in having the Cairo military command removed from its base of operations in Palestine. On November 19, 1921, Meinertzhagen drafted a cabinet paper calling for the transfer of responsibility for the maintenance of law and order from the Cairo military to a civilian gendarmerie under the jurisdiction of the air ministry, as had been established in Iraq. His diary entry for that date read:

> The effect will be beneficial as it will remove the anti-Zionist influence of GHQ at Cairo from Palestinian politics. The whole of the staff in Egypt, from Lord Allenby and General Congreve downwards, have consistently worked against Zionism, and I shall be heartily glad to see that influence removed.[19]

Meinertzhagen's effort might not have succeeded but for Weizmann's forceful intervention with Balfour three weeks later. On December 13, one day after receiving a copy of Congreve's circular order to his troops, Weizmann cabled Balfour in Washington, informing him of the text of the Congreve circular. He added: "Am reluctantly driven to view real difficulty less with Arabs than with certain British elements bent on poisoning Arab-Jewish relations... Urgently invoke your timely intervention to prevent irreparable disaster."[20] This intervention bore fruit. Prime Minister Lloyd George was informed on December 16 of the Congreve circular to his troops, and he agreed to the removal of the British command in Cairo from the garrison in

---

18. Weisgal, *The Letters and Papers of Chaim Weizmann, Series A, vol. 10*, letter 283, 286–289.
19. Meinertzhagen, *Middle East Diary*, 112–113.
20. Weisgal, *The Letters and Papers of Chaim Weizmann, Series A, vol. 10*, telegram to Balfour dated December 13, 1921, 333–334.

Palestine.²¹ Three days later, on December 19, 1921, Churchill called a conference of cabinet officers in charge of ministries concerned with the Middle East. This conference reached agreement that the War Office should retire from Palestine and hand over defense to the air ministry acting on behalf of the Colonial Office. The new gendarmerie would be set up as a civil force directly under the high commissioner.²² Once again, the Cairo War Office had overplayed its hand, and now, it was completely relieved of all responsibility in Palestine.

The Churchill White Paper

With Palestine now policed and governed by Samuel's civilian administration, Great Britain finally submitted the Draft Mandate to the League of Nations at the beginning of 1922 for a vote on its confirmation. Before it was placed on the League's agenda for a vote, however, Churchill issued a white paper on June 30, 1922, setting forth the British government's reinterpretation of the Balfour Declaration.²³ He then demanded the signed acceptance of the white paper by every member of the Zionist Executive before calling for a vote on ratification.

The 1922 White Paper was a bitter pill for the Zionists to swallow. It was largely the work of Herbert Samuel, who had continued to insist upon the need for a new policy statement by the government to "explain" the meaning of the Balfour Declaration. Following a memorandum that Samuel had submitted a month earlier,²⁴ the 1922

---

21. Weisgal, *The Letters and Papers of Chaim Weizmann*, Series A, vol. 10, letter 323, fn. 3, 337.
22. Meinertzhagen, *Middle East Diary*, 113–115.
23. *The 1922 Churchill White Paper*. Prior to the issuance of the 1922 Churchill White Paper, the Arabs had protested that Palestine had been included in the McMahon letter to Sherif Hussein of Mecca, promising British support for independence of Arab lands. The 1922 Churchill White Paper refuted this argument, noting that Palestine had been excluded from the scope of that letter (see Chapter 3).
24. Gilbert, *Exile and Return*, 142.

Churchill White Paper sought to clear away apprehensions of both Arabs and Jews regarding British policy under the Mandate. Referring to the apprehensions expressed by the Arab delegation from Palestine, the 1922 Churchill White Paper noted:

> Unauthorized statements have been made to the effect that the purpose in view is to create a wholly Jewish Palestine. Phrases have been used such as that Palestine is to become "as Jewish as England is English." His Majesty's Government regard any such expectation as impracticable and have no such aim in view. Nor have they at any time contemplated, as appears to be feared by the Arab delegation, the disappearance or the subordination of the Arabic population, language, or culture in Palestine. They would draw attention to the fact that the terms of the [Balfour] Declaration referred to do not contemplate that Palestine as a whole should be converted into a Jewish national home but that such a home should be founded *in* Palestine.

The 1922 Churchill White Paper then went on to reassure the Jews of Palestine that their apprehensions "that His Majesty's Government may depart from the policy embodied in the Declaration of 1917" are also unfounded, "and that the Declaration… is not susceptible of change." After adding that the purpose of the Jewish national home is the free development of "a centre in which the Jewish people as a whole may take, on grounds of religion and race, an interest and a pride," it made the significant declaration that in order to accomplish this, "It is essential that it should know that it is in Palestine as of right and not on sufferance." It continued by stating that for the fulfillment of the government policy, "It is necessary that the Jewish community in Palestine should be able to increase its numbers by immigration." At the same time, however, it introduced Samuel's ambiguous criterion for limiting immigration, namely, "This immigration cannot be so great in volume as to exceed whatever may be the economic capacity of the country at the time to absorb the new arrivals."

During Samuel's term of office, the number of Jews seeking to enter Palestine was not so high as to bring into play the limitation based on absorptive capacity. Nevertheless, the 1922 Churchill White Paper had made the right of Jewish immigration hostage to future government interpretations of "absorptive capacity." Such interpretations would be governed by the prevailing British prejudices and by extraneous policy considerations. This phrase was subsequently to have drastic consequences not only for the development of the Jewish national home in Palestine but even more so for shutting Palestine's doors before both Europe's Jews desperately seeking to escape the Holocaust and Holocaust survivors kept festering after the war in displaced persons camps.

The 1922 Churchill White Paper feature with the greatest potential for injury to the Jewish national home seen at the time, however, was the proposed Constitution for Palestine. The 1922 Churchill White Paper declared,

> It is the intention of His Majesty's Government to foster the establishment of a full measure of self-government in Palestine... The first step was taken when on the institution of a civil administration, the nominated advisory council, which now exists, was established... It is now proposed to take a second step by the establishment of a legislative council containing a large proportion of members elected on a wide franchise... The legislative council would... consist of the high commissioner as president and twelve elected and ten official members.

Although Churchill had assured Weizmann at their meeting with Lloyd George and Balfour in July 1921 that questions affecting the Jewish national home would not be within the purview of the representative government, the 1922 Churchill White Paper did in fact keep immigration within its purview, as Weizmann had fully anticipated. It declared: "It is intended that a special committee should be established in Palestine, consisting entirely of members of the new legislative council elected by the people, to confer with the administration upon matters relating to the regulation of immigration." The protection offered to the Jews regarding their Mandatory rights on immigration was: "Should any difference of opinion arise between the committee and the administration, the matter will be referred to His Majesty's Government, who will give it special consideration."

The 1922 Churchill White Paper also granted the right of appeal to the League of Nations—through the high commissioner and the Colonial Office—to any religious community that felt that the terms of the Mandate were not being fulfilled by the government of Palestine. In the light of subsequent history, it is clear that this protection would have proved worthless. Indeed, a later government exploited the criterion of "absorptive capacity" for the purpose of restricting and even freezing Jewish immigration. There can hardly be any doubt that Samuel's policies, as incorporated in the 1922 Churchill White Paper, represented a major departure from the intent of the Balfour Declaration and the Mandate that called upon Britain to facilitate Jewish immigration. Fortunately for Zionism, the Arabs refused to accept the 1922 Churchill White Paper proposals, insisting upon explicit repudiation of the Balfour Declaration. Had they accepted, they might have been able to stop the development of the Jewish national home in its tracks.

Weizmann, with his philosophy of moderation, his admiration of Great Britain, and his pragmatic approach, reconciled himself without much difficulty to the 1922 Churchill White Paper, writing:

> So long as, through immigration and the investment of capital, the Jews were able to develop the country, its "absorptive capacity" would continue to grow, and immigration would show a steady rise... We know now, though we were not so sure in 1922 that the principle of "absorptive capacity" could, if generously applied, have been the key to the rapid and stable expansion of the *Yishuv*; we also know that it was in fact applied in such a spirit as to prove a stumbling block to Jewish enterprise.[25]

---

25. Weizmann, 291. Other Zionist leaders were not so readily satisfied as Weizmann by a white paper that promised to promote a Jewish center

One very costly effect of the 1922 Churchill White Paper on Jewish life, both before the establishment of the Jewish State and since, was the serious split it generated within the Zionist movement. Vladimir Jabotinsky, founder of the Jewish Legion in World War I and organizer of the Haganah for self-defense during the 1920 riots in Palestine, was then a leading member of the Zionist Executive. Although he had signed the letter of acceptance of the 1922 Churchill White Paper along with all his colleagues, he found, upon reflection, that he could not reconcile himself to it, and he withdrew from the Zionist Executive. Jabotinsky formed his own nationalist party, the Union of Revisionist Zionists, which called for the establishment of a Jewish state, the restoration of the Jewish Legion, and rapid immigration to bring about a Jewish majority in Palestine, including Transjordan. The Revisionists withdrew from the Zionist Organization and formed their own New Zionist Organization to rival it. The split between the mainstream Zionist Organization and the more nationalist Revisionists never healed, even though the specific issues that divided them changed significantly over time. Since then, it has taken shape in the political division between the left wing and secular parties headed

---

rather than Jewish national independence. In a letter to *The Times* in May 1922, the English author, Israel Zangwill, wrote, "The utmost that now seems predictable is a rise of a Semitic Switzerland in which the Jews would have an equal national status with Arabs... As a Jewish political asset, or as the solution of the Jewish problem, it will be comparatively worthless... What the Jews need as a people is not a centre but a circumscribing circumference, such as every other people enjoys—not an 'airy nothing' but 'a local habitation'; not a spiritual sophistication, but a solid surveyable territory. It was this that was supposed to have come to my sorely tried race as the outcome of the Great War; partly as the expression of the nationalist ideals of the war programme. Read a recent book on my shelves, of four hundred pages, devoted to the 'extra-special' slaughter of Jews in all the shambles of Europe, and you will admit that in these days of universally renascent anti-Semitism, a spiritual Zion is no more a solution of the Jewish problem than Mr. Belloc's fantastic scheme of re-established ghettoes" (Gilbert, *Exile and Return*, 143).

by David Ben-Gurion and his heirs and the more nationalist right-wing and religious parties headed by Menachem Begin and his heirs.

The Ratification of the Partitioned Mandate

Although Britain submitted the revised draft Palestine Mandate to the League of Nations for ratification in January 1922, League action had to await the United States' views on the Mandate. Even though the United States was not a member of the League of Nations, it claimed that that as a World War I Ally, it was entitled to be consulted, and it had reserved its position until it could resolve outstanding differences with Great Britain on an open-door trade policy in Palestine. Only on May 22, 1922 was the British delegation to the League of Nations able to announce the United States' agreement on the issue.[26] And a month later, on June 30, 1922, the United States Congress unanimously endorsed the Mandate for Palestine in Joint Congressional Resolution 360:

> Resolved by the Senate and House of Representatives of the United States of America in Congress assembled, that the United States of America favors the establishment in Palestine of a national home for the Jewish people, it being clearly understood that nothing shall be done which should prejudice the civil and religious rights of Christian and all other non-Jewish communities in Palestine and that the holy places and religious buildings and sites in Palestine shall be adequately protected.[27]

---

26. Weisgal, *The Letters and Papers of Chaim Weizmann, Series A, vol. 10*, letter 323, fns. 4 and 5, 337. The convention between the United Kingdom and the United States, safeguarding the American interests in Palestine, signed on December 3, 1924, incorporated the complete text of the Mandate for Palestine (Eli E. Hertz, "Mandate for Palestine: The Legal Aspects of Jewish Rights," *Israel Forever Foundation,* accessed August 8, 2023, online at https://israelforever.org/interact/blog/mandate_palestine_legal_aspects_of_jewish_rights).
27. On September 21, 1922, President Warren G. Harding (1921–1923) signed the joint resolution of approval to establish a Jewish national home in Palestine.

In the meantime, a new obstruction had arisen in Great Britain's House of Lords, where the Arab delegation in London had gained significant support. Balfour, who had recently been made a Lord, delivered his maiden speech on that occasion, defending immigration and Jewish investment as beneficial to the Arabs as well as to the Jews. But the opposition, much of it of an anti-Semitic nature, was in the majority, and on June 22, 1922, the House of Lords voted down the Palestine Mandate by a majority of sixty to twenty-nine.

On July 4th, 1922, the issue came before the House of Commons, where Churchill made an impassioned speech, defending both the Mandate and the Rutenberg concession for electrical energy, which the Lords had strongly criticized, and appealed to the House of Commons to reverse the vote taken by the Lords. Churchill was successful, and the motion in opposition to the Mandate was rejected by an overwhelming majority of 292 to 35 votes.[28]

With this notable reversal by the House of Commons of the vote in the House of Lords, the way was finally clear for a vote in the League of Nations. Under the League's Constitution, a vote in its General Assembly, consisting of all its member nations, had to be preceded by a vote in the League's Council, whose members were chosen by the General Assembly. In the Council, all decisions had to be unanimous, and up to the very last day before the vote, the outcome was far from certain. Obtaining favorable votes from Spain and Brazil posed a serious problem, since no Jews had lived in Spain from the time of their expulsion in 1492, and the number of Jews in Brazil was too insignificant to influence that country's vote.

Once again, a surprising—indeed, completely unexpected—turn of events came to the help of the Zionist cause. In 1918, when the foundations of the Hebrew University in Jerusalem were laid, a professor of The University of Madrid, a Marrano Jew, had sent a congratulatory telegram. The Zionists now turned to him for help, and he responded with enthusiasm. Suddenly, as Weizmann noted, "A great

---

28. Meinertzhagen, *Middle East Diary*, 118–119.

deal of unexpected and—at the moment—inexplicable help came from Spain. Members of the learned societies, the higher clergy, prominent members of the Spanish nobility received the local delegation in the most friendly fashion." Meanwhile, the Zionists in London called on the Spanish representative in the Council, who, it turned out, was to be the president of the session at which the Mandate was to be debated. According to Weizmann, they said to him: "Here is Spain's opportunity to repay in part that long-outstanding debt which it owes to the Jews. The evil which your forefathers were guilty of against us you can wipe out in part."[29] The Spanish representative responded favorably and helped both with Brazil's and his own country's vote.

Lord Balfour introduced the subject of ratification of the Mandate for Palestine before the Council of the League of Nations on July 22, 1922, and it was ratified the same day. Meinertzhagen recorded his reaction on the approval of the Mandate in his diary: "Today is a great day for the Zionists." Three days later, on July 25, he wrote to Balfour:

> I hope you will permit me to congratulate you on the passage of the Palestine Mandate through the League of Nations... To all of us who from the outside have regarded the Zionist policy with enthusiasm, the step is one for which we are all sincerely grateful, and it is to you that much of our gratitude should be expressed. I cannot help feeling more confident that the unsatisfactory state of the Jews of the world is nearing a solution.

In a note added later in his diary, Meinertzhagen summed up his support for Zionism with this notable comment:

> Giving the Jews the opportunity to build their national home in Palestine was the wisest and most constructive act of statesmanship resulting from the First World War; it was also a first-class example of the principle of self-determination and democratic government.[30]

---

29. Weizmann, *Trial and Error*, 292.
30. Meinertzhagen, *Middle East Diary*, 119–121.

– 6 –

The 1929 Massacres and the Passfield White Paper

THE TOXIC EFFECTS OF SAMUEL'S anti-Zionist appointments and of his weakening of the Mandatory obligations to facilitate the rebuilding of the Jewish national home were not yet visible under Herbert Samuel's immediate successor, General Herbert Plumer (1925–1928). Although many Jews, given their unhappy experience with the Cairo military administration, had received Plumer's appointment with some misgivings, he proved to be the most successful of all Palestine's high commissioners. Unlike the Cairo military establishment, which had a determined anti-Zionist and even anti-Semitic agenda of its own, Plumer was a man of law and order who carried out as faithfully as possible the terms of the Mandate for Palestine.

David Ben-Gurion, Israel's first prime minister, considered Plumer "first class…a firm and wise governor," adding that "there was nothing of the umpire about him. He governed, and he governed with no nonsense."[1] Chaim Weizmann reported in some detail on one particular episode that earned Plumer the admiration of the Jewish community. Plumer granted the Jews permission to transfer the regimental colors of the Jewish battalion of World War I from London to Jerusalem and to carry them in formal procession to the Great Synagogue of Jerusalem. A crowd of Arabs came to protest, and Plumer asked his aide to inform them that he had twelve chairs so they might choose twelve representatives to see him. The twelve who entered warned that if the procession took place, they could not be responsible for

---
1. Pearlman, *Ben Gurion Looks Back*, 69.

order in the city, whereupon Plumer replied, "You are not asked to be responsible, gentlemen. I shall be responsible—and I shall be there."[2]

Plumer's successor, John Chancellor (December 1928–1931), was, however, a much weaker man. Under Chancellor, the effects of Samuel's appointments of Haj Amin as grand mufti and of British anti-Zionists to top-level administration posts became manifest in the summer of 1929, when Palestine's Jews were subjected to brutal Arab massacres. And the Colonial Office, now headed by an anti-Zionist minister and drawing upon Samuel's and Churchill's criteria for interpretation of the Mandate (see Chapters 4 and 5), reacted to these massacres in the 1930 White Paper, with the intention of freezing the building of the Jewish national home in Palestine rather than facilitating its growth.

Yom Kippur 1928: British Preoccupation with the Status Quo

The troubles that led to the Arab massacres of Jews in August 1929 began earlier, during the hiatus between Plumer's departure in July 1928 and Chancellor's arrival in December. The district commissioner for Jerusalem, successor to Sir Ronald Storrs, was Edward Keith-Roach, who, like Storrs, was a zealous guardian of the status quo regarding Jewish religious practice—though not Arab practice—at the Western Wall of the Temple Mount. The issue on Yom Kippur eve in 1928 concerned a portable screen the Jews had brought to the Wall to separate men and women during the prayers, a ritual dating back to the practice in Jerusalem's Holy Temple.[3] Such a portable screen at the 1928 Yom Kippur eve services was so troubling to Mr.

---

2. Weizmann, *Trial and Error*, 328–329.
3. A gallery separating the men from the women was provided in the Holy Temple area during the celebration of the holidays (*Mishnah, Sukkah* 5:2 and *Talmud Bavli, Sukkah* 51b). Since that time, Orthodox Jewish synagogues all over the world (and until the nineteenth century, this meant all synagogues) have continued to provide separate sections for men and women in accordance with the practice in the Holy Temple.

Keith-Roach that he ordered the police to remove it, even at the cost of disrupting Jewish services on their holiest day of the year at the most sacred Jewish site.

Douglas Duff, the twenty-seven-year-old police officer with Keith-Roach at the Wall that evening and charged by him with the unhappy task of removing the screen on Yom Kippur morning, has left a detailed account of the event, which casts a light on the less-than-innocent role of Jerusalem's district commissioner in fomenting the trouble at the Wall. According to Duff, he and Keith-Roach were on the Temple Mount in the area of the Mosque of Omar overlooking the Wall on Yom Kippur eve, when the Jews had assembled for the holy day's services. Keith-Roach, looking down, saw the screen standing on the pavement at the Wall and excitedly asked Duff if he had ever seen a screen there in the past. The screen had been there ten days earlier on Rosh Hashanah, the Jewish New Year, and Duff had seen it, but—apparently worried, as he reported in another context (see Chapter 4), that "it did not pay for one's seniors to think that one had any undue sympathy for the returning Jews"—he answered that he did not remember. Keith-Roach's immediate reaction was that the screen was a violation of the status quo, and he turned to several religious sheikhs belonging to the mosque who had just arrived to ask if they had seen the screen. Duff concluded his report with this comment: "The crafty old gentlemen had not, but, always willing to make capital at the expense of the Jews, immediately assumed miens of righteous indignation." Keith-Roach then gave Duff written orders to remove the screen at the continuation of the Yom Kippur services the next morning, which Duff felt obliged to carry out, even in the face of resistance by the congregants.[4]

---

4. Douglas Duff's detailed account appears in his *Sword for Hire*, 247–252. Duff, unhappy with having been ordered to remove the screen at the Wall, wrote: "I suffered very badly in the next few months. Everybody seemed certain that the whole affair was my fault, and I was lucky to be able to produce the written orders I had received or I should have been made an official scapegoat. Amongst the Arabs, however, from one end of

From Yom Kippur 1928 to the 1929 Massacres

Grand Mufti Haj Amin al-Husseini and his followers, emboldened by Jerusalem's district commissioner's profanation of the Yom Kippur services, embarked upon a two-fold program of sustained multiple interferences with the Jewish prayers at the Wall along with a poisonous propaganda campaign against the Jews. Above the Wall, close to the place of Jewish worship, they introduced a *zikr* ritual (a form of Moslem prayer with repeated chanting) with drum and cymbals. As if this violation against Jewish religious rights did not suffice, they also opened a gate to the Arab homes adjoining the pavement to the Wall, transforming the area into a public thoroughfare for trespass by Arabs and their animals during the Jewish prayers.

Somehow, the British guardians of the status quo, which they held so sacred regarding any possible Jewish violations, were able to regard with equanimity these flagrant Arab violations of the status quo concerning centuries-old Jewish religious rights. A contemporary observer in Palestine, Maurice Samuel, noted that when the Jewish authorities protested to the British administration against this indefensible conversion of the Wall area into a public thoroughfare:

> The administration replied that it would have the door closed during hours of worship, which is equivalent to saying that push-cart pedlars will not be permitted to sell their wares in St. Peter's during services... The simile, strong as it may seem, is inadequate. For the Wailing Wall is *always* being visited by Jews from every part of the world, and prayers are being said at every hour of the day.[5]

Palestine to the other, my word was law, they looked on me as a champion of Islam, a thing that irritated me as much as the universal detestation of the Jews."

5. Maurice Samuel, *What Happened in Palestine: The Events of August 1929, Their Background and Their Significance* (Boston, MA: Stratford Company, 1929), 46.

Harry Luke, Samuel's former deputy district commissioner for Jerusalem, who considered the Balfour Declaration "a contradiction in terms" (see Chapter 4), had since risen to the position of chief secretary for Palestine and was serving as acting high commissioner during the hiatus between Plumer and Chancellor. Luke obtained a temporary concession from the mufti to discontinue the *zikr* ritual, but he permitted it to resume shortly afterward. The new high commissioner, John Chancellor, as indifferent as Luke regarding Arab violation of the status quo at the Wall, permitted the *zikr* to continue until March 29, 1930, more than six months after the 1929 massacres.[6] Chancellor's priority was to revive the earlier plans for the establishment of a legislative council for Palestine, and he had Luke spend the first half of 1929 negotiating the formation of such a council with the two main leaders of the Arab Executive Council. They agreed to a proposal to serve on a fifteen-member council consisting of ten Moslem Arabs, two Christian Arabs, and three Jews. In June 1929, before going off on leave to London, Chancellor promised to discuss the proposals there with the colonial minister.[7]

Grand Mufti al-Husseini, seeing that the highest officials of the civilian administration were as sympathetic to his cause as their predecessors in the military administration had been, now felt encouraged to unleash a campaign of unrestrained incitement against the Jews. Exploiting the placement of the portable screen at the Wall for Yom Kippur services, he called upon the Arabs to "strike a blow for the Faith" and to protect Islam's sanctuaries in Jerusalem from being profaned by the Jews. Maurice Samuel, who was in Palestine at the time, gave vivid testimony regarding the prevailing atmosphere in an account published the same year:

---

6. Royal Institute of International Affairs, *Survey of International Affairs, 1930* (London: Oxford University Press, 1931), 272–273.
7. In the end, the plan for a representative government had to be put aside once again, because Haj Amin al-Husseini was opposed to anything less than the repudiation of the Balfour Declaration.

> The extraordinary currency of the belief that the Jews were actually contemplating an attack on the Mosque, or had designs on it, shows the careful work of agitators… Everywhere, the cry is "Defend El Burak" (the Place of the Wailing Wall)… The Knights of El Burak declare that Moslem silence in the face of Jewish impudence would be regarded as cowardice and meanness. The Moslems must depend on themselves in defending their rights.[8]

With this religious appeal, the grand mufti had directed the propaganda campaign toward an attack against Jews rather than against Zionism. All Jews—Zionist, non-Zionist, and even anti-Zionist—were now the enemy in the eyes of the Arabs, aroused by the grand mufti. And as Duff characterized the campaign, "The atmosphere was electric—everyone knew that trouble—Big Trouble—was upon us."[9]

Chancellor did nothing to halt the grand mufti's incitement against the Jews. Instead, his administration yielded to Arab demands to disarm the Jewish settlements, a decision that left the Jews defenseless, while making no serious attempt to disarm the Arabs. As Douglas Duff characterized the poisonous atmosphere:

> The trouble-makers and agitators found fruitful soil to sow their seed. It was easy to convince the peasants and the Bedouin that the British had practically evacuated the country. From thence, it was only a step to say that this had been done purposely in

---

8. Samuel, *What Happened in Palestine*, 91.
9. Douglas Duff, *Galilee Galloper* (London: J. Murray, 1935), 208–210. The Arabs circulated faked photographs showing the Zionist flag flying over the Mosque of the Dome of the Rock, "the mighty mosque hallowed by the miraculous visitation of the prophet, which covers the site of the ancient Holy of Holies on Mount Moriah. That the pictures were crude fakes, with the Zionist flag most transparently added afterwards, did not mean a thing to the fellahin and Bedouins amongst whom they were circulated. The camera could not lie as far as they were concerned, newly introduced to the machine as they were."

order to demonstrate the government's sympathy with Arab nationalist aims and its hatred of all things Jewish. Was not the administration at Jerusalem trying its best to give them a quiet hint to go ahead with the massacre of these Jewish dogs who were slowly filching their land from them? They had only to look around them to be sure of this, for had not all the sealed armouries of the colonies been taken away and the Jews left entirely defenseless? Had there been any serious attempt to stop gun-running or to disarm the Arabs? Were there not plenty of arms and ammunition in every village?[10]

The agitation came to a head in an outbreak of Arab massacres of Jews in August 1929, during High Commissioner Chancellor's absence on vacation in London, when Luke was again acting high commissioner. Despite the many warning signs of impending trouble, Luke failed to take the most elementary precautionary measures that were readily available in Cairo. In reporting on the events leading up to the 1929 massacres, Duff wrote:

> The dullest intelligence in the all-powerful secretariat should have seen the necessity of asking for at least one battalion of Imperial troops to be stationed in Jerusalem. However, things drifted from bad to worse. Consignment after consignment of arms were smuggled on the sea beaches and across the fords of the Jordan and duly stored away against the inevitable and fast-approaching day.[11]

Edwin Samuel, son of Herbert Samuel, and Luke's private secretary at the time, attributed his inaction to his concern that if he called for military reinforcements and trouble failed to break out, he

---

10. Duff, *Galilee Galloper*, 204.
11. Duff, *Sword for Hire*, 253. In *Galilee Galloper* (210), Duff added, "It could have been easily done under the pretense of manoeuvres—there need have been no fear that the Moslems would be enraged by an overt display of force—but no one seemed willing to take the responsibility."

might get a reputation of being "windy."[12] But it appears from Luke's interview with Pierre van Paassen, in the midst of the massacres, that although he failed to act to prevent the likely massacres, he was in fact sufficiently concerned as to alert the Rothschild Hospital in Jerusalem three weeks in advance of the massacres to prepare two hundred beds for an emergency. After the riots broke out, Luke laid the blame on the previous high commissioner, General Plumer, for reducing the security forces stationed in Palestine. Given, however, the incredible explanation Luke gave during this interview for his failure to act to halt the massacres (see the excerpts of the interview below), it may be doubted whether he would have called upon the forces even if they had been available.

On Friday, August 16, 1929, a week before the massacres, the administration permitted an unprecedented riot of more than two thousand Arabs at the Wall of the Temple Mount. After a sheikh of the Al-Aqsa Mosque made an inflammatory speech, the rioters rushed to the Wall to burn Jewish prayer books and to remove and burn prayer petitions that visitors have traditionally inserted into the crevices of the Wall for centuries. This desecration took place the day after Tishah B'Av, the Jewish day of mourning over the Holy Temple's destruction in the year 70 CE, still commemorated, to date, in fasting from sunset to sunset and in special prayers and lamentations. The administration justified its granting permission for this Arab riotous march, because on the previous day:

> In addition to the large number of Jews who proceeded in the ordinary way to the Wall to worship, some hundreds of young Jews exercised their right of access for purposes not confined to the usual practice of prayers but were associated with the making of a speech and the raising of a flag.

Continuing in the spirit of what the administration considered was its required neutrality and impartiality, Britain's Shaw Commission

---

12. Samuel, *A Lifetime in Jerusalem*, 109.

Report on the 1929 massacres referred to the violent Arab demonstration as a "Moslem visit" to the Wall and added, "[The] government are now investigating offences that may have been committed in the events of both days," equating Jews making a speech and raising a flag at the Wall with an Arab riot.[13]

The Arab massacres that followed throughout the Holy Land were precipitated by another incident the day after the Arab riot. On Saturday, August 17, an Arab stabbed a Jewish boy who had attempted to retrieve a football that had accidentally been kicked into an Arab garden. Three days later, the boy died, and the following day, Wednesday, August 21, Jews carried the body through Jaffa Gate, past Moslem quarters, for burial. According to the official Shaw Commission Report:

> [The funeral] became in effect a political demonstration by the Jews against the government and the Arabs... The crowd...broke through the cordon of police, necessitating a baton charge by British police, in the course of which one Jew was seriously and numbers were slightly injured.

The funeral procession was met by a riotous Arab crowd at Jaffa Gate. A senior British officer in command of the armed police came between the Jews and the Arabs, but he did nothing to break up the demonstration. The mob, convinced that the British were on their side against the Zionists, then began their attack on the Jews. As Duff reported:

> Within an hour of the clash at Jaffa Gate, firing was general throughout the Holy City: bombs were being thrown, and motor cars filled with young town Arabs armed with automatic pistols

---

13. The quotes relating to the 1929 massacres not otherwise attributed are from Walter Shaw, *The Report of the Commission on the Palestine Disturbances of August 1929*, CMD 3530 (London: His Majesty's Stationery Office, 1930) ("the Shaw Commission Report"), 57–61, as summarized in Royal Institute of International Affairs, *Survey of International Affairs, 1930*, 275–277.

were careening through the streets of the Jewish suburbs firing indiscriminately at all passersby.[14]

The next day, Thursday August 22, and continuing into Friday morning, August 23, Arabs came rushing into Jerusalem, armed with clubs, knives, swords, and firearms. And although the British police had earlier disarmed Palestine's Jews and left them defenseless, the chief of police, Mr. Saunders, now inexplicably decided to cancel a subordinate's order to disarm the Arab mob descending upon Jerusalem.[15] Instead, Saunders asked the grand mufti why the Arabs were carrying weapons, and he readily accepted the grand mufti's assurance that there was no need to worry. The Arabs, he said, were carrying weapons only from fear of attacks by the Jews.

Later that morning, the grand mufti and one of his colleagues addressed a mass meeting on al-Haram al-Sharif, the Temple Mount, after which the mob rushed out into the city and attacked every Jew they could see and murdered several. The Jerusalem pogrom continued during the night into the next day, and there was still sporadic shooting in parts of the city even a week later.

Yitzhak Ben Zvi, a Zionist leader who succeeded Chaim Weizmann as president of the State of Israel in 1952, called upon Saunders that Friday afternoon to request that he mobilize the Jewish ex-soldiers in Jerusalem and form a special police force for the various districts. Saunders would not agree to the mobilization of the ex-soldiers, but he did agree to deputize some young Jews, and he armed them with rifles, thereby offering at least a partial counter-measure to his decision to cancel his subordinate's order to disarm the rioting Arabs. Acting High Commissioner Luke, however, inexplicably ordered even the deputized Jews to be disarmed and even to be arrested if they were

---

14. Douglas Duff, *May the Winds Blow: An Autobiography* (London: Hollis and Carter, 1948), 186.
15. *The Shaw Commission Report*. A summary by the Royal Institute of International Affairs is available in "The British Mandate for Palestine 1926–1930," *Survey of International Affairs, 1930*.

found carrying arms. This set the stage for Arab massacres of helpless Jews, prevented from defending themselves by direct order of the acting high commissioner.

The Arabs followed up the attacks on Jerusalem's Jews with the massacre of Jews throughout Palestine. Mobs were aroused by rumors spread from mosques that Jews had occupied and attacked or bombed the Mosque of Omar. In old Jewish communities, where the population consisted almost entirely of defenseless, pious Jewish families—generally non-Zionist and, many, even anti-Zionist—the Arab mobs were able to carry out their pogroms with impunity. However, in cities such as Tel Aviv and Haifa as well as in new Zionist settlements where underground Haganah (self-defense) units had been formed, the Jews fought back against the Arab attacks with such arms as they had managed to keep. As Duff noted,

> Jewish colonies were sacked and burnt and many of the colonists thrown on the funeral pyre of their burning buildings. Other colonies were saved by the heroic resistance of the young men and women, fighting with inadequate weapons against their well-armed attackers, for shortly before the rebellion, all the colonies had been disarmed, their sealed armouries removed by a government bowing before Arab agitation.[16]

---

16. Duff, *May the Winds Blow*, 187–188. In *Galilee Galloper* (219–220), Duff had written, "Defence would have been far easier if the rising had occurred some time before, as then, most colonies still possessed the sealed armouries of rifles and ball cartridge with which they had been armed. These, however, in response to Arab agitation, had been removed by a government ever anxious to pour oil on the troubled waters of the moment… The time was indeed ripe for a grand attack that would drive the Jews into the sea. The Arabs themselves were in possession of plenty of arms; every village had dozens of rifles…retrieved from the battlefields of the late war. Hundreds of automatic pistols of the latest type had been smuggled into Palestine… and there was plenty of ammunition on hand."

As was to be expected, the police were generally of little help during the massacres.[17] The Arab police would not oppose the Arab mobs and melted away, and the British police had orders to disarm and imprison any Jew caught with weapons. Three Jewish communities, in addition to Jerusalem, were particularly hard hit. On Saturday, August 24, Motza, an ancient Jewish town close to Jerusalem,[18] was attacked by about thirty Arabs. A Jewish family of four and two of their guests were butchered in their home, and the house was ransacked and burned down.[19] That same day, the most vicious massacre of all was carried out in Hebron, a city sacred in Jewish history as the residence and burial place of the biblical patriarchs and matriarchs, Abraham and Sarah, Isaac and Rebecca, and Jacob and Leah. Jews had lived in Hebron from time immemorial. In 1929, its Jewish population consisted of religious Jewish families and of teenage students attending its yeshivah (a traditional Jewish institution where students study the Talmud and other rabbinic texts)—they were not involved in the political Zionist movement. Around sixty-five defenseless and helpless Jews—men, women, and children—of whom about a third were students at the yeshivah, were slaughtered, and around another sixty were wounded in the massacre.[20] Nearly a week later, on Thursday, August 29, there was a massacre in the town of Safed, a city sacred as the center of development of Kabbalah (Jewish mysticism), which, like Hebron, was populated by a community of pious Jewish

---

17. Several Jewish settlements in the Galilee were helped by the British police. In his *Sword for Hire*, and in his *May the Winds Blow*, Duff described how, with the assistance of the Arab police under his command, he helped save the Jewish settlement, Mishmar Ha'Emek, from the Arab massacres. And in his *Galilee Galloper*, he described how a British officer, nicknamed Abu George, with whom he had served in Nazareth, saved Afula's Jews.
18. In Joshua 18:26, Motza is listed among the Benjamite cities, and in the Mishnah (*Sukkah* 4:5), it is mentioned as a town to which Jews would come to cut young willow branches for use in the celebration of the Sukkot festival.
19. Samuel, *What Happened in Palestine*, 113–114.
20. Samuel, *What Happened in Palestine*, 115–122.

families with no involvement in political Zionism. Eighteen people were killed, including children in an orphanage—their bodies mutilated and burned—and about forty were wounded, and around two hundred houses were looted and burned.[21] Although the government had sufficient advance warning, and British naval forces were available in Haifa, the district commissioner did not call for their help.

The Hebron massacre, in particular, marked a turning point in the history of Jewish–Arab relations as well as in relations between the Jews and the mandatory authority. The massacre was documented in vivid detail in a book by Maurice Samuel, published less than two months after the event. On Friday, August 23, 1929, an Arab informed the Jews that the Arabs were arming. The community rabbis appealed to the Arab governor of Hebron, who reassured them that they had nothing to fear. Nevertheless, an Arab mob broke into the Hebron yeshivah that afternoon and killed the student who had remained there. As Maurice Samuel relates:

> On Saturday morning, before the slaughter began, the rabbis again appealed to the governor for help. Again, they received the same astounding assurances. Bewildered, they turned to Mr. Cafferata, the British officer in charge of the police. From him, too, they received assurances of safety. I find such difficulty in believing this story that I have looked at every record of eyewitnesses without finding a contradiction. For two hours, on the morning of Saturday, August 24, there raged in Hebron a scene which is not easy to parallel even in the medieval annals of the Jewish people. For two hours, neither the governor of Hebron nor the British officer interfered.[22]

Although the Shaw Commission strongly condemned the savage Arab attack in Hebron, it offered no criticism of Mr. Cafferata for

---

21. The gory details of the Safed massacre were recorded by a contemporary observer, David Hacohen, in "The Massacre in Safed: Notes from My Diary," in Hacohen, *Time to Tell*, 37–41.
22. Samuel, *What Happened in Palestine*, 117–119.

failing to intervene for two hours. Instead, it gave him high praise for his courage in preventing a general massacre, and the government subsequently decorated him for his heroism. The Shaw Commission Report reads:

> About nine o'clock on the morning of the 24th August, Arabs in Hebron made a most ferocious attack on the Jewish ghetto and on isolated Jewish houses lying outside the crowded quarters of the town. More than sixty Jews—including many women and children—were murdered, and more than fifty were wounded.[23] This savage attack, of which no condemnation could be too severe, was accompanied by wanton destruction and looting. Jewish synagogues were desecrated, a Jewish hospital—which had provided treatment for Arabs—was attacked and ransacked, and only the exceptional personal courage displayed by Mr. Cafferata—the one British police officer in the town—prevented the outbreak from developing into a general massacre of the Jews in Hebron.[24]

The official version of Mr. Cafferata's role in the Hebron massacre is belied, however, by contemporary documents. Thus, Maurice Samuel continues with his report on the massacre:

> From English papers, I cull a story of the heroism of Mr. Cafferata in attempting to stop the massacre. I look in vain for a single confirmation in the records of Jewish witnesses. They have preserved with gratitude every instance of mercy and kindliness

---

23. Douglas Duff described the Hebron massacre in the following terms: "In one house alone, the little hotel, there were twenty-three corpses, hacked to pieces by sword, dagger, and axe. I have heard the scene in this building described by the officer who led the relief party. The stairs actually ran with blood, which had flowed down and formed a large pool on the ground floor, whilst the ceiling of the dining room dripped blood on to the table below, as most of the victims had been slain in an upstairs room" (Duff, *Sword for Hire*, 258).
24. *The Shaw Commission Report*, 278–279.

which came to their notice. They mention the humaneness of Commander Partridge of Gaza in his treatment of the sick. They recall, both in the memorial and in the individual statements, the gallantry of Arab friends and landlords: "The family Moshe Masha, the family Borowsky, the family of Rabbi Slonim, the family Schnauirson, were thus rescued.' They recall even the unsuccessful efforts of one Arab, Nassar Eldine, to protect the Jews in his house. And they record, with damning unanimity, that Mr. Cafferata did nothing for two hours.[25]

The man singled out for his heroism in the Shaw Commission Report appears in an even darker light in Pierre van Paassen's interview, in the midst of the massacres, with Acting High Commissioner Luke. Van Paassen asked Luke why he did not arm a few thousand Jews to enable the Jews to defend themselves. Luke's ghoulish reply was, "The government is neutral [and] must be impartial in this quarrel between the Jews and Arabs." At this, van Paassen exploded:

> You call that impartiality, when a man like Captain Cafferata of Hebron comes in and calmly relates how he watched the mob invade a rabbi's home and slaughter twenty-seven persons there…watch human beings being killed, he an officer in the British army, with a police guard at his beck and call and a service revolver in his pocket? One or two shots in the air

---

25. The memorial of the Jews of Hebron, as submitted to Palestine's high commissioner, states, "From our knowledge, we say with certainty that it would have sufficed to issue a warning or to fire some shots into the air, and the crowd would have scattered. It was only after there had been sufficient butchery, plunder, and rape and the pogromists were about to attack an English officer that some shots were fired, and the mob dispersed at once." It concludes by accusing, amongst others, "The governor, Abdullah Kardos, and the Commander Cafferata, *who deprived us of the means of appealing for help and defense* [emphasis in Samuel's text], betrayed us with empty promises, and gave the murderers and robbers their opportunity" (Samuel, *What Happened in Palestine*, 119–122).

by Cafferata, and that mob would never have entered Rabbi Slonim's house.

Hardly able to contain himself any longer, van Paassen continued:

> Neutral and impartial, when it is a question of barbarism versus civilization, when it is a case of gangsters attacking peaceful, innocent citizens as those whose bodies I just saw piled up in a house in Hebron?... I can never hope to explain to an American newspaper reader that in the presence of an unprovoked attack by gangs of hoodlums on a peaceful community, the government looked on as an impartial spectator. Americans won't understand that. They expect something else from a government.

In view of Luke's order to disarm even the deputized Jews and to arrest them if caught carrying weapons, a charge of "aiding and abetting" the massacres would seem to be closer to the truth than Luke's self-incriminating excuse of neutrality and impartiality for the administration's dereliction of duty.[26]

High Commissioner Chancellor rushed back from his vacation in England the week after the Hebron massacres and issued a "proclamation" condemning the brutal murders of defenseless Jews. The proclamation included a paragraph announcing the suspension of his negotiations with the colonial minister for constitutional changes in Palestine's government, which he had initiated in London in

---

26. Luke pretended to van Paassen that Jews sworn in as constables who were disarmed and imprisoned when they sought to defend themselves were only being placed in protective custody for their own safety. Van Paassen then questioned why the imprisoned Jews were being kept shackled, to which Luke replied that the government had been taken completely by surprise, and such mistakes were unavoidable. Van Paassen then countered, "If this outbreak took the government completely by surprise, how is it then, that three weeks ago, the government warned the authorities of the Rothschild Hospital here in Jerusalem to have two hundred beds in readiness for an emergency?" (van Paassen, *The Forgotten Ally*, 163–168).

accordance with his promise before leaving for London. The Arabs protested that the high commissioner was prejudging their guilt without a hearing. Chancellor immediately backtracked and issued a second proclamation declaring that the government would, as quickly as possible, investigate the behavior of both sides. The administration's response was well described by Douglas Duff, who wrote:

> They would make a great show of determination and force, acting as if they really meant what they said, and then weakly collapse and, in response to popular clamour, surrender anything that was wanted by the Arabs... Even the proclamation of the high commissioner, who had hurried back from leave and returned just as the rising was crushed, in which he expressed his horror of the savage atrocities of the Arabs, was humbly withdrawn and almost an apology offered to them for the terms that had been used.[27]

Reading the sorry history of this period, it is difficult to avoid characterizing the behavior of the Palestine administration as anything other than a combination of passiveness towards Arab provocation and incitement before the conflagration; of gross negligence and dereliction of duty in the course of the massacres; and of cover up and whitewash afterwards. This time, there was no longer a Colonel Meinertzhagen in office who, in the 1920 pogrom, was willing to sacrifice his career in order to remove the Palestine military administration, for its conspiring with Haj Amin al-Husseini against the Balfour Declaration to facilitate the development of the Jewish national home. Meinertzhagen had retired from government service; the high commissioner, Herbert Plumer, who believed in his responsibility to maintain law and order, had been succeeded by the much weaker John Chancellor; and the pro-Zionist government of Lloyd George and Lord Balfour had been replaced by a government with little sympathy for Zionism. As colonial minister, the pro-Zionist

---

27. Duff, *Sword for Hire*, 278–280.

Leopold Amery (November 1924–June 1929), had been succeeded by Lord Passfield (June 1929–August 1931), who—in contrast to his nephew, Richard Meinertzhagen, had no sympathy for the Zionist cause. Even Chaim Weizmann, who until then had ready access to all British cabinet ministers, found it difficult to receive an appointment with Lord Passfield. And, when Weizmann met with Lady Passfield, she callously commented, "I can't understand why the Jews make such a fuss over a few dozen of their people killed in Palestine. As many are killed every week in London in traffic accidents, and no one pays any attention."[28]

Although Meinertzhagen was no longer in government, he had not lost his intense interest in Zionism. Convinced that "of all the post-war reparations, Zionism is the greatest in its attempt to repair the great wrong done to the Jews during the last two thousand years," he wrote to his uncle on the day of the massacre in Safed, August 29, urging that for peace to prevail in Palestine, the Arabs must be convinced that "Downing Street and every member of the Palestine administration were determined to carry out government in the spirit of the Mandate."[29] On October 4, he had a long meeting with his uncle, hoping to persuade him that the government plan to send a commission of inquiry into the Arab violence would only be a sop to public opinion. What was needed instead, he urged, was an administration that would loyally carry out its obligations to Palestine's Jewish community as spelled out in the Mandate under which it governed. Meinertzhagen came away from the meeting empty-handed. Lord Passfield's mind was made up on an investigation by a government commission.[30]

---

28. Weizmann, *Trial and Error*, 331. Lord and Lady Passfield, better known under their original names, Sydney and Beatrice Webb, were active in the Fabian Society, which had given birth to the British Labour Party. They were also uncritical supporters of Stalin and the Soviet Union.
29. Meinertzhagen, *Middle East Diary*, 138–142.
30. Meinertzhagen, *Middle East Diary*, 143–144.

The Shaw Commission

The commission of inquiry that Lord Passfield set up under the chairmanship of Sir Walter Shaw, a retired chief justice for the colonies, had as its terms of reference, "to inquire into the immediate causes which led to the recent outbreak in Palestine and to make recommendations as to the steps necessary to avoid recurrence." Perhaps as a partial concession to Meinertzhagen's plea, the statement added, "No inquiry was contemplated which might alter the position of Great Britain in regard to the Mandate or the policy, laid down in the Balfour Declaration of 1917 and embodied in the Mandate, of establishing in Palestine a national home for the Jews." Nevertheless, the commission did go on to consider not only the immediate causes of the Arab outbreak but also to assess the underlying causes, on the basis of which it paved the way for a basic shift in government policy. The Shaw Commission Report, published in March 1930, led the government to issue a white paper to "crystallize" the Jewish national home, in repudiation of the Balfour Declaration and the Mandate.

In its report on the immediate causes of the Arab violence, the Shaw Commission did condemn the Arab attacks on the Jews, but, like the Palestine administration, it exonerated the Arab leadership, asserting that the widespread outbreak was spontaneous—not premeditated or organized. The only criticism it directed at the Arab leaders, including Grand Mufti Haj Amin al-Husseini, was that they had not exercised sufficient influence to keep the Arab rioters under control. The Shaw Commission Report considered the peaceful Jewish demonstration at the Wall on August 15, 1929 to be the most significant immediate cause of the Arab violence the following week, as if such a demonstration were the political equivalent of the massacres that followed.[31] The commission had no criticism for the administration's

---

31. The Shaw Commission also accepted the argument of the Arab leadership and the Palestine administration that a decision of the Zionist Organization to enlarge the Jewish Agency to include non-Zionists as well as Zionists was a contributing cause of the Arab violence. It failed to explain how

permission for the violent Arab counterdemonstration the next day, and it absolved the administration from blame for the massacres, ignoring Luke's order to disarm and imprison even deputized Jews during the Arab riots. Instead, it adopted Luke's self-incriminating position that the administration had discharged, to the best of its ability, the difficult task of maintaining neutrality and impartiality between two peoples whose leaders showed little capacity for compromise.

Going on to its consideration of the underlying causes, the commission attributed the Arab outbreak to Jewish immigration and Jewish purchase of Arab land, which, it claimed, aroused Arab fears that they will in time be deprived of their livelihood and come under Jewish domination. Asserting that Jewish immigration in 1925 and 1926 had been larger than could be justified by the country's economic absorptive capacity, a criterion laid down by Churchill in the 1922 Churchill White Paper (see Chapter 5), it proposed that the government should review immigration policy in consultation with non-Jewish representatives in order to prevent a repetition of such excessive immigration.[32] And blaming Jewish land purchases for leading to the creation of a landless and discontented Arab class, it asserted that Palestine could

---

such a decision, of which the mostly illiterate Arab rioters must have been totally ignorant, could have contributed to a spontaneous and unorganized outbreak of violence throughout all of Palestine less than a month after the decision had been made in Zurich. The enlargement of the Jewish Agency at the beginning of August 1929 was in conformity with article 4 of the Mandate, which provided that the Zionist Organization "shall take steps in consultation with His Britannic Majesty's Government to secure the cooperation of all Jews who are willing to assist in the establishment of the Jewish national home."

32. The Shaw Commission also held the relatively high immigration levels of 1925 and 1926 responsible for Palestine's economic depression in 1927 and 1928, ignoring the effects of factors having nothing to do with immigration, including, as noted by Mandates Commission members, an earthquake in 1927 and the depression in agriculture resulting from a combination of drought, the cattle plague of 1926, and the invasion of locusts in 1928.

not support any increase in its agricultural population unless there was a radical change in farming methods.[33] It therefore recommended, as an interim measure, that immigration should be suspended, pending a special scientific inquiry by the government into the possibilities for improving methods of cultivation in Palestine.[34] The government's land policy should then be formulated in accordance with the study's findings, account being taken of the need for providing for the natural increase in the rural Arab population.

The Mandates Commission of the League of Nations, to whom Great Britain was required to report annually on its stewardship of the Palestine Mandate, was highly critical of the Shaw Commission's findings. Members of the League of Nations dissented from the conclusions that the outbreak of Arab violence was spontaneous and unorganized. They cited numerous findings of fact in the Shaw Commission's own report, regarding incitement by the grand mufti and by members of the Moslem hierarchy and the Arab Executive, which demonstrated that, in the words of M. van Rees, "responsibility for what had happened must lie with the religious and political leaders of the Arabs."[35]

---

33. Mr. Snell dissented from the commission's negative assessments of the impact of Jewish immigration and Jewish land purchases on the Arabs, just as he disagreed with the commission's exoneration of the grand mufti and of the Palestine administration for the Arab violence. He also dissented from another charge of the Shaw Commission that the General Federation of Jewish Labor, when issuing immigration permits, allowed itself to be influenced by the political creed of the applicants and not by their professional qualifications. Even Hope Simpson conceded, albeit somewhat reluctantly, that this charge was false.
34. The British government temporarily suspended Jewish immigration in accordance with the Shaw Commission's recommendation. Its decision was seriously questioned at the hearings of the League of Nations Mandates Commission in June 1930.
35. League of Nations Permanent Mandates Commission, *Minutes of the Seventeenth (Extraordinary) Session, Fifth Meeting, June 5, 1930*, Geneva, Switzerland.

The Palestine administration also came in for severe criticism for enforcing a status quo policy at the Wall of the Temple Mount that was never legally defined and was administered in a discriminatory manner. The administration had treated the use of chairs or of a screen to separate men and women at Jewish prayer services as an intolerable violation of the status quo, even though, as Henry Luke had himself testified before the Mandates Commission, there was photographic evidence of their use under the Ottoman Empire.[36] At the same time, it had allowed the Arabs to introduce a series of innovations that, as both the administration and the Shaw Commission acknowledged, had been introduced for the purpose of annoying the Jews and interfering with their rights to conduct prayer services at the Wall. The administration attempted to justify its tolerance of the Arab violations of the status quo with the claim that it could not interfere with Arab action on its own property. League Commission members reminded them, however, that even property rights were limited by public law and could not be exercised in such a manner as to infringe upon the rights of other parties, particularly at holy places. They also questioned why the administration had permitted the Arabs to hold a counterdemonstration at the Wall on the day after the peaceful Jewish demonstration. Why had they not anticipated that such a demonstration was likely to result in disturbances, and why, having permitted the counterdemonstration to take place, had they taken no precautionary measures to prevent such violence?

The conclusions concerning the underlying causes of the riots also met with significant dissent from members of the Mandates Commission. M. van Rees firmly rejected the Shaw Commission's argument that the riots were spontaneous uprisings of the Arab masses, whose underlying cause was the fear that their standard of living was threatened by Jewish immigration and land purchases. On the

---

36. The administration's excuse for its policy of banning Jewish use of chairs or screens as a violation of the status quo at the Wall despite photographic evidence of such usage under the Ottoman Empire was that the Jews had not presented any legal document authorizing such usage.

contrary, he emphasized, the riots were instigated by the Arab leaders, who had reason to fear that their leadership position over the poor Arab masses was being "threatened by the gradual rise in the standard of living in the country as an inevitable consequence of the activities of the Jews."

Several members of the Mandates Commission were also highly critical of the Palestine administration concerning its basic failure to implement the Balfour Declaration for securing the establishment of the Jewish national home in Palestine. Referring to the requirements laid down in article 6 of the Palestine Mandate, M. van Rees pointedly declared that it would be "useless, however, to search for the administration measures taken to *facilitate* Jewish immigration, and the result would be as negative if an enquiry were made as to the State lands and the waste lands on which the settlement of the Jews had been *encouraged* [emphases in the original]."[37]

The Hope Simpson Report

In response to the Shaw Commission's recommendations, the government approved an inquiry by Sir John Hope Simpson, a retired Anglo-Indian official, into the issues of immigration, land purchase, and development in Palestine. The findings of this inquiry, carried out over three months (May–August 1930), were issued in a government report (CMD 3686) in October 1930.[38] Despite the dearth of data and the limitations on the analytical findings (which Hope Simpson himself noted), his report came to the following extraordinary conclusion: "There is at the present time and with the present methods of Arab cultivation, no margin of land available for agricultural settlement

---

37. M. van Rees also criticized the administration's failure to implement article 11 of the Mandate—the promotion of close settlement and intensive cultivation of the land.
38. Sir John Hope Simpson, *Palestine: Report on Immigration, Land Settlement and Development* (London: His Majesty's Stationery Office, 1930) ("the Hope Simpson Report")—reproduced online on UNISPAL.

by new immigrants, with the exception of such undeveloped land as the various Jewish Agencies hold in reserve." To drive his point home, he concluded with the startling pronouncement that "without development, there is not room for a single additional settler, if the standard of life of the fellahin is to remain at its present level."

Perhaps to soften the impact of his conclusion, Hope Simpson added his personal belief that agricultural development could make room "not only for all the present agricultural population on a higher standard of life than it at present enjoys, but for not less than twenty thousand families of settlers from outside." But implementation of a development program, he emphasized, would require a considerable joint effort on the part of Jews, Arabs, and the Palestine administration, and in the meantime, he was opposed to the admission of any more Jewish immigrants for settlement on the land. In effect, Simpson had interpreted the criterion of absorptive capacity formulated by Herbert Samuel and adopted by Winston Churchill in his 1922 White Paper to mean that Palestine's absorptive capacity for Jewish settlement was nil. He took no notice of the fact that the British administration itself had indeed come to the opposite conclusion in its annual report for the year 1925, when it had recognized the contribution the Jews were making to Arab standards of living even in rural areas, declaring, "The Arab rural community benefits largely from increased immigration and industrial activity, which create a large demand for all classes of produce."[39]

Simpson was also negative regarding Jewish immigration for employment in industry, arguing that it was wrong to permit Jewish immigration to fill existing vacancies while there were Arab workmen who could not find employment. Although he had no statistics on the extent of Arab unemployment, he was convinced that it was

---

39. Royal Institute of International Affairs, *Survey of International Affairs, 1930*, 241–242. The Royal Institute of International Affairs correctly noted that even if a direct adverse effect of a concrete kind had been demonstrated to have been produced in certain cases, that would be no warrant in itself for holding the Jews either legally or morally to blame.

considerable and widespread and that Jewish immigration was contributing to it. He himself drew attention to the derived demand for Arab goods and services as well as for Arab employment resulting from Jewish immigration and industrial development. He even called attention to the uncontrolled and unregistered influx of Arab labor from other countries, particularly from Egypt, Syria, and Transjordan, drawn into Palestine by the economic opportunities that the Jewish industrial development of the country created. Nevertheless, the main conclusion that emerged from his report was that until adequate agricultural development materialized through the joint efforts of Arabs, Jews, and the Palestine administration, Jewish immigration and land settlement in Palestine must be curbed. The report attached little significance to the fact that it was only Jewish immigration and Jewish cultivation of the land that was serving as the engine of economic development in Palestine, benefiting both Jews and Arabs. Simpson did not seem to have been perturbed by the fact that in the absence of Jewish immigration and Jewish capital investment for industry and agriculture, the country had been derelict for centuries and that his recommendations to suspend Jewish immigration and land settlement would condemn the Arab masses to continued economic stagnation.

The 1930 Passfield White Paper

The 1930 Passfield White Paper,[40] issued in October 1930, along with the Hope Simpson Report, established a new anti-Zionist government policy for Palestine, which had little relationship to the Palestine Mandate. Evidently, Lord Passfield and his Colonial Office had already decided on a policy of Arab appeasement in the face of the Arab atrocities of the previous year, and the Hope Simpson Report only provided the necessary fig leaf. As Chaim Weizmann noted:

---

40. Lord Passfield (Sidney Webb), *Palestine: Statement of Policy by His Majesty's Government in the United Kingdom*, CMD 3692 (London: His Majesty's Stationery Office, 1930) ("the 1930 Passfield White Paper")—reproduced online on UNISPAL.

Before the report was issued, together with what is now called the Passfield White Paper, the government declared publicly that it intended to suspend immigration, introduce restrictive land legislation, curtail the authority of the Jewish Agency, and, in general, introduce in Palestine a regime which made the appointment of the Simpson Commission either a superfluity or a propaganda instrument for the government's predetermined policy."[41]

The anti-Zionist attitude driving this white paper was evident in both its tone and its substance. It set forth the government's new policy under three headings: 1. security, 2. constitutional development, and 3. economic and social development. Under "security," it declared that "incitements to disorder or disaffection, in whatever quarter they may originate, will be severely punished." The Jewish reaction to this policy formulation toward the Arab violence was well expressed by Chaim Weizmann in his comment, "I think His Majesty's Government must be well aware that there is only one quarter from which disorder, violence, and massacre have originated. We do not massacre—we were the victims of a murderous onslaught."[42]

Under "constitutional development," the white paper followed the lead given in the Shaw Commission Report on the need for a positive statement on the rights of the non-Jewish population. It declared that the government had "always regarded as totally erroneous" the conception that the rights of the Jewish national home constituted the principal feature of the Mandate and that the passages safeguarding the rights of the non-Jewish community were merely secondary considerations, intended only to qualify the Mandate's primary objective. Instead, the government maintained that equal weight must be given to the rights of the Jewish national home and the safeguarding of the rights of the non-Jewish community.

---

41. Weizmann, *Trial and Error*, 332.
42. Weizmann, *Trial and Error*, 334.

To provide for Palestine's constitutional development, the white paper declared that in the interest of the community as a whole, it was necessary to act without further delay to establish self-government in Palestine. Recalling that Herbert Samuel, the proposal's first sponsor in 1922, had met with Arab refusal to cooperate and that Sir John Chancellor, who had revived the proposal in 1929, had also abandoned it, in the face of what the white paper called, in its "neutral" terminology, the "disturbances" of 1929, the white paper declared that the government would now implement its plan, even if the Arabs or Jews refused to cooperate. It would, if necessary, appoint the requisite number of unofficial members to establish the council.

Passing from constitutional issues to economic and social development, the government, following the lead in the Hope Simpson Report, proposed to limit Jewish purchase of land. It adopted the conclusion that a more methodical agricultural development of Palestine was necessary in order to ensure a better use of the land from which both Jews and Arabs were to benefit and announced that the government was studying the financial means of carrying out this development. During the period of development, however, the Palestine administration, which was to be the authority in charge, must control all disposition of land, and transfers of land would be permitted only with the approval of that authority.

The government also adopted Simpson's thesis regarding the negative effects of Jewish immigration upon the economic position of the Arab population. It declared, accordingly, that in determining the rate at which Jewish immigration may be permitted under the principle of economic absorptive capacity enunciated in the 1922 Churchill White Paper, account must be taken of Arab as well as of Jewish unemployment. Moreover, it adopted Simpson's reinterpretation of article 6 of the Mandate, which required that the Palestine administration, "while ensuring that the rights and position of other sections of the population are not prejudiced, shall facilitate Jewish immigration." The 1930 Passfield White Paper defined the article to mean that if Arab people could not obtain work because of Jewish immigration, or if the general labor position was unfavorably affected by Jewish unemployment, the Mandatory Power was required to reduce or, if necessary, suspend such immigration until the unemployed labor of the non-Jewish community could obtain work. Despite the limitations of the Hope Simpson Report, the government had thus decided to follow his lead by giving the Palestine administration the authority to put an indefinite halt to both Jewish immigration and Jewish land purchase.

✡ ✡ ✡

The publication of the 1930 Passfield White Paper created a storm among some British political leaders in all three parties in parliament, who saw the white paper as a repudiation of the Palestine Mandate. Zionist circles rejected the white paper in its entirety. The Vaad Haleumi passed a resolution the next day declaring that the Jewish community would have nothing to do with the legislative council proposed in the white paper.[43] More significantly, Weizmann resigned from his position as president of the Jewish Agency operating under the Mandate, and several leading colleagues resigned with him in protest against the white paper, As Weizmann wrote:

> The Colonial Office, which, having been unable to guarantee the security of the Jewish community in Palestine, having ignored our repeated warnings concerning the activities of the mufti and of his friends of the Arab Executive, having made no attempt to correct the indifference or hostility of British officials in Palestine, now proposed to make us pay the price of its failure. We realized that we were facing a hostile combination of forces in the Colonial Office and in the Palestine administration, and unless it was overcome, it was futile to think of building on the foundations which we had laid down so solidly in the previous years.[44]

---

43. Royal Institute of International Affairs, *Survey of International Affairs, 1930*, 299.
44. Weizmann, *Trial and Error*, 333. Weizmann's eagerness to resume cooperation with Britain in 1931, when Great Britain temporarily reversed

The Royal Institute of International Affairs accurately summarized the Jewish reaction to the white paper as follows:

> ...without precedent or parallel, up to date, in the relations between Jewry and the Mandatory Power. To Jewish minds, the British government's statement of June 1922 had likewise been disappointing, and the reports submitted by the Shaw Commission and by Sir John Hope Simpson were likewise unpalatable. But...the statement of policy of October 1930 was taken by Dr Weizmann and his colleagues on the enlarged Jewish Agency as a gesture of hostility towards the Zionist cause which made it impossible for them personally to cooperate any longer with the government of the Mandatory Power.[45]

---

its anti-Zionist policy, cost him the presidency of the World Zionist Organization for the next four years. The 1930 Passfield white paper also generated a rift within the organization of the Haganah, the Jewish self-defense force, which never healed. The official Haganah policy, under the direction of Mapai, was one of restraint, limited to defending the Jews from attack, and prohibited from initiating any counterattacks of its own. In the spring of 1931, a number of Haganah leaders broke with the policy of restraint and organized an underground movement—the Irgun Tzvai Leumi (National Military Organization, called in brief, the Irgun, or by its Hebrew acronym, Etzel)—aimed to defy Britain's anti-Zionist policy and promote the establishment of the Jewish state in all of Palestine. The Irgun later came under the control of Jabotinsky and his Revisionist Party. At the end of 1943, Menahem Begin, a follower of Jabotinsky, was to take over the direction of the Irgun, in which role he was to play a major part in inducing Britain in 1947 to surrender the Mandate to the United Nations.

45. Royal Institute of International Affairs, *Survey of International Affairs, 1930*, 295.

– 7 –

The 1939 White Paper for Palestine as an Arab State

The 1930 Passfield White Paper's anti-Zionist policy did not remain in effect for very long. In response to pressure from Chaim Weizmann and from the future first Prime Minister of Israel, David Ben-Gurion, British Prime Minister Ramsay MacDonald (1929–1935) sent a letter to Dr Weizmann in February 1931 providing "the authoritative interpretation of the Passfield White Paper."[1] MacDonald's "interpretation" totally reversed the 1939 Passfield White Paper's anti-Zionist policy.[2] The letter to Weizmann, sent as an official document

---

1. *Hansard*, House of Commons, Debates, vol. 248, cc751–7W, February 13, 1931.
2. Ben-Gurion attributed the reversal of the Passfield policy to a surprising source, one more of the unexpected events surrounding the rebirth of Israel in its ancient homeland. He wrote, "Perhaps the strangest aspect of the whole affair was that Ernest Bevin [Britain's rabidly anti-Zionist post-war foreign minister] caused the [Passfield] white paper to be withdrawn. Bevin was not himself a member of parliament, but the union had fifteen representatives in the House of Commons. The Labour Party did not have a majority and was not even the largest party. The Tories enjoyed that distinction. Labour ruled thanks only to the support of the Liberals. A fine young leader of Mapai, David Hos, who got along very well with Englishmen and had established particularly friendly ties with Bevin, was sent to London to discuss the white paper with him. Hos was extremely successful. He and Bevin called each other 'brother,' and when Brother Bevin heard the details of the white paper, which in fact closed the country to Jewish immigration, he told him that he would order 'his boys' to vote against the government if the white paper were not dropped. Bevin in fact

to the League of Nations and as an instruction to the high commissioner in Palestine, affirmed that "the obligation to facilitate Jewish immigration and to encourage close settlement by Jews on the land remains a positive obligation of the Mandate, and it can be fulfilled without prejudice to the rights and position of other sections of the population of Palestine." Unlike the 1930 Passfield White Paper, it recognized that "the constructive work done by the Jewish people in Palestine has had beneficial effects on the development and well-being of the country as a whole." It added that the government "did not prescribe and do not contemplate any stoppage or prohibition of Jewish immigration in any of its categories." And it assured:

> Immigrants with prospects of employment other than employment of a purely ephemeral character will not be excluded on the sole ground that the employment cannot be guaranteed to be of unlimited duration.[3]

The MacDonald letter naturally raised a storm in Arab quarters. The Royal Institute for International Affairs correctly assessed the policy reversal in noting:

> [Both Arabs and Jews] assumed that Mr. MacDonald's letter was a symptom of the Mandatory Power's perturbation at the vigor of the Jewish protest against the [Passfield] white paper, and this

---

went to MacDonald and warned him of what would happen if there were no change in the white paper policy. MacDonald immediately appointed a new cabinet committee headed by Arthur Henderson, a loyal friend of the Zionist movement and a more sincere man than MacDonald. Henderson 'interpreted' Passfield's white paper in a way that turned it upside down. The government approved this interpretation in what it called 'the MacDonald Letter'" (David Ben-Gurion, *Israel: A Personal History* [New York: Funk & Wagnalls, Inc/Sabra Books, 1971], 44; Pearlman, *Ben Gurion Looks Back*, 71).
3. Royal Institute of International Affairs, *Survey of International Affairs, 1930*, 301.

appeared to confirm a suspicion that the white paper, in its day, had been a symptom of the Mandatory Power's perturbation at the vigor of the Arab hostility to the Balfour Declaration and to the Mandate—a hostility which had been evinced, in an alarming manner, in the outbreak of August 1929. These identical Jewish and Arab interpretations of the letter and the white paper displayed the previous policy of Mandatory Power in an unpleasant light and threatened to give a dangerous turn to Arab and Jewish policy in the future.[4]

MacDonald's decision to overturn the 1930 Passfield White Paper policy may have contributed to saving well over a hundred thousand Jews from perishing in the Nazi Holocaust during World War II. Sir Arthur Wauchope, whom MacDonald appointed as Palestine's new high commissioner (1931–1938), facilitated the growth and development of the Jewish national home until 1936, when the grand mufti launched the Arab revolt against Britain. He authorized a major increase in Jewish immigration and settlement in Palestine, providing a safe haven for tens of thousands of Jews fleeing economic oppression in Poland and brutal persecution in Hitler's Nazi Germany. From an average level of under 4,000 per annum in the previous five years, Jewish immigration more than doubled to over 9,500 in 1932 and then more than tripled again to over 30,000 in 1933—the year Hitler rose to power in Germany. As Nazi Germany intensified persecution of the Jews (canceling the German citizenship of all its Jews, driving them out from all professional positions, and confiscating their businesses), authorized Jewish immigration to Palestine surged to over 42,000 in 1934, reaching a peak level of nearly 62,000 in 1935.[5] Given the closed immigration channels in the rest of the world during the

---

4. Royal Institute of International Affairs, *Survey of International Affairs, 1930*, 303–304.
5. Lord Robert Peel, *Palestine Royal Commission Report*, CMD 5479 (London: His Majesty's Stationery Office, 1937) ("the Peel Commission Report"), 279—reproduced online on UNISPAL.

Great Depression of the 1930s, these Jews would undoubtedly have perished along with the rest of European Jewry in the Nazi Holocaust that followed during World War II but for Wauchope's remarkable support of the Jewish national home at this critical juncture.

The Arab Revolt (1936–1939)

But despite Wauchope's role in saving so many thousands of Jewish lives, his administration ended in failure. Wauchope's undoing was his inability to deal with the ever-increasing Arab violence, led by Grand Mufti Haj Amin al-Husseini, culminating in open revolt against Great Britain in 1936. Arab violence against the Jews had continued after the 1929 massacres, at first only on a sporadic basis, but it gathered momentum in 1933—undoubtedly inspired by Hitler's coming to power in Germany on January 30 of that year—when it came to be directed at the British administration as much as at the Jews. In September, the president of the Arab Executive, after a fierce speech against the influx of Jews into Palestine, demanded in a telegram to the high commissioner that the government order an immediate halt to Jewish immigration. The following month, after the Arab Executive declared a "general strike" starting in October, the Arabs attacked public buildings and police in several cities, beginning in Jerusalem and continuing in Jaffa, Nablus, and Haifa.[6]

The difficulties in dealing with the growing Arab violence were exacerbated by much of the entrenched bureaucracy in Wauchope's own administration, whose continued hostility to the Jews and to the Jewish national home only served to aid and abet Arab terrorism. Douglas Duff's experience as head of a police division in the Galilee region in 1931—just before Wauchope's assumption of his post as high commissioner—is especially revealing of the pro-Arab, anti-Jewish attitude prevalent within the administration's police organization. According to Duff, the Arab violence he encountered was not even politically motivated but was simple extortion:

---

6. *The Peel Commission Report*, 80–85.

The Tulkarm *effendi*s had to find money to pay for their little extravagances, and so they applied the screw to the Zionist money bags. A little violence...would bring in the required blackmail, and, accordingly, a reign of terror was maintained close to the colony.

Of the reaction of Palestine's senior British officials, Duff wrote: "I [dared] not do much against the Arabs, even when I knew they were guilty, as Jerusalem frowned on anything that would annoy the 'nationalists,' as these self-seeking, cynical *effendi*s called themselves." After six attacks on the Jewish settlement in the first six weeks of 1931, Duff risked his professional future by introducing an effective system of surveillance. He soon had to abandon the effort, however, because the *effendi*s "moved Heaven and Earth in Jerusalem, with the result that I was quietly told to curtail my patrols and concentrate on the many other crimes that were being committed. I took the hint, and the whole thing recommenced."[7]

The year 1936 saw the Arabs expand their violence to the level of a full-scale revolt. The objective of this First Arab Intifada, led by the grand mufti, was to drive both the Jews and the British out of Palestine. Events occurring outside of Palestine were probably even more significant in the grand mufti's calculations than Wauchope's weakness. In October 1935, Benito Mussolini, Italy's fascist dictator, emboldened by the absence of any meaningful resistance against Hitler's aggressive rearmament program and his expansionist ambitions, invaded Ethiopia. Emperor Haile Selassie made a dramatic personal appeal for assistance to the League of Nations, but the League proved impotent. Great Britain denounced the invasion, and it declared its support for collective resistance, but neither it nor France was willing to act, and in May 1936, Mussolini added, "Emperor of Ethiopia" to the title of "King of Italy." The resulting loss of British prestige and authority was compounded in the Arab world by the exiled Haile Selassie's abject appearance in Jerusalem after his unheard appeal for

---

7. Duff, *Sword for Hire*, 286–290.

help. Hitler followed Mussolini's invasion of Ethiopia by marching his troops into the heretofore demilitarized Rhineland in March 1936, and the British and French, anxious to avoid any risk of war, again remained passive.

The demonstrated weakness of Great Britain and France against Mussolini and Hitler proved very costly for them in the Middle East. The Arab leaders in Egypt, Syria, and Lebanon began pressing for their own national independence, and both Britain and France, worried over the beginnings of German and Italian political inroads into the Arab and Moslem world, yielded to the Arab pressure. In Egypt, the so-called United Front of political parties, formed in the fall of 1935, pressed for a treaty with Britain to achieve Egyptian independence. The negotiations, beginning in March 1936, led in August 1936 to an Anglo–Egyptian Treaty of Alliance, under which Britain recognized Egypt as a sovereign independent state and undertook to support its application for membership in the League of Nations. In Syria, fifty days after a "nationalist bloc" declared a "strike" against France, negotiations, also begun in March 1936, led in September to a Franco–Syrian Treaty of Alliance, under which France agreed to surrender its Syrian Mandate within three years and to support Syria's application for membership in the League of Nations as an independent sovereign state. In November of the same year, the French separated Lebanon, with its significant Christian population, from Moslem Syria and signed a similar treaty with Lebanon.[8]

The grand mufti similarly believed that the time was ripe for him to turn Palestine into another independent Arab state, and the Arabs were fired up in revolt—politically and financially assisted by Hitler and Mussolini—to be rid of both the Mandatory power and the Jewish national home. Wauchope sought to win over the grand mufti by renewing the repeated calls of past administrations to enhance Arab political power through the establishment of a Palestinian

---

8. The Free French granted Syria and Lebanon their national independence in 1941.

legislative council. To meet Jewish concerns, the Arabs would be given no more than fifty percent of the total seats, the remainder to be held by a combination of British officials, British-appointed representatives, and Jews; and authorization of Jewish immigration would be reserved by the high commissioner. Weizmann sought to dissuade him, warning that a legislative council would only enhance the feudal power of the grand mufti and the Husseini clan and promote tyranny—not democracy. He also objected, as he had already to Churchill in 1922, that the administration would not be able to resist Arab pressure to give the council the power to deal with immigration as well.[9] Wauchope remained adamant, however, and his proposal was submitted to parliament, where it was debated in February and March of 1936. The parliament, moved at least in part by the plight of Jewish refugees from Hitler's Germany and by the vigorous Jewish opposition to a legislative council, failed to support it, and the proposal was abandoned.[10]

The grand mufti launched his Arab revolt against the British government the next month, in April 1936, immediately after Britain and France had yielded to the pressures in Egypt and Syria and had announced their readiness to negotiate. The two main rival Arab families, the Nashashibis and the Husseinis, now formed an uneasy

---

9. Despite his strong objections to Wauchope's proposal, however, Weizmann still retained enough confidence in British officialdom to be willing to consider a council with equal numbers of Jews and Arabs and with British officials holding the balance of power. He believed the dangers inherent in such an approach would be offset by the gains in public opinion and that such a council would have the advantage of building bridges between Jews and Arabs (Weizmann, *Trial and Error*, 380–381).
10. *The Peel Commission Report*, 89–92. The Palestine administration was bitter over the defeat of its proposal for a legislative council. As Weizmann informed the 20th Zionist Congress in August 1937, "Voices were raised in Palestinian official circles alleging that the Jews wielded enormous influence in England, that they had staged the debate and thereby gravely added to the difficulties of the Palestine administration" (Weisgal, *The Letters and Papers of Chaim Weizmann*, Series B, vol. 2, paper 30, 279).

coalition under the banner of the Arab Higher Committee, led by the grand mufti. The committee declared a new national strike and called for the establishment of an independent national government for Palestine.[11] The national strike provided the political backdrop for the emergence of an armed Arab revolt, which spread throughout the country under the direction of the grand mufti and his Arab Higher Committee. Arab guerrilla fighters crossed into Palestine from the surrounding countries to join in the attacks.

The grand mufti financed his revolt in part from diversion of the substantial religious funds under his control as head of the Supreme Moslem Council and in part from extortion through intimidation and violence. And the revolt was not a purely Arab and Moslem affair, for the grant mufti had allied himself with Mussolini's fascist Italy and Hitler's Nazi Germany. According to Labour member Philip Noel-Baker, speaking in parliament on the Arab revolt:

> Money, arms, officers, organizers—everything came from Italy and Germany. Already in 1935—I am quoting the editor of *The Quarterly Review*—fifty German agents were sent to Africa and the Near East... In 1936—I am quoting *The Daily Telegraph*—the Jerusalem police intercepted documents proving that the Arab raiders received £50,000 from Germany and £20,000 from Italy for the purpose of strengthening their resistance. We know that British officers in Palestine talk freely of the German and Italian arms and money that the terrorists have received. We know that the landmines by which British soldiers have been murdered could not be made and could not be operated by the Arabs... We know that Dr. Goebbels has established a propaganda school for Arabs in Berlin.[12]

---

11. *The Peel Commission Report*, 96ff.
12. *Hansard*, House of Commons, Debates, vol. 347, cc2045, May 22, 1939. Herbert Morrison added his warning concerning the Nazi and fascist inroads the next day, declaring, "It is known in all parts of the House—it is known to ministers—that a number of the leaders of the Arab disturbances in Palestine have been acting by the encouragement of German and Italian

The revolt began with an Arab mob attack in Jaffa against Jewish passersby in which nine Jews were killed and ten were injured.[13] It quickly spilled over against the British as well: British personnel were targeted, as were roads, bridges, telephone lines, the oil pipeline, and even police and army installations. By the end of October, when the Arabs temporarily suspended their revolt, the official casualty list numbered 312 killed, including 195 Arabs, 80 Jews, and 37 police and military personnel. The official list of the injured numbered over 1,300, including about 800 Arabs, 300 Jews, and 200 police officers and military servicemen.[14] The Arab community itself was not immune to Arab violence. Arabs who were accused of cooperating with the Jewish community or who refused to observe the strike were also vulnerable—of the 195 Arabs killed, 55 were killed by fellow Arabs.[15]

The British sent in a military force under the command of Lieutenant General John Dill to deal with the revolt, but the military was hobbled by the Palestine administration, which exonerated the grand mufti and the Arab Higher Committee and considered the armed Arab bands from inside and outside Palestine as spontaneous rioters for

---

agents. It is known that part of those disturbances, a large part, can be traced to German and Italian activities in that country. Suppose Herr Hitler is in power in ten years time and suppose Mussolini is in power—what is to stop them then still sending their agents to Palestine and working upon the Arab people in the way they have been doing—working for the persecution of the Jewish race, working for the disarmament of the Jewish race by the new government, working for the exclusion and persecution of the Jewish race in Palestine? What is to prevent them from doing that? As far as I can see, nothing, and about that possibility, the right hon. gentleman thinks nothing at all" (*Hansard*, House of Commons, Debates, vol. 347, cc.2140, May 23, 1939).

13. Michael Cohen, *Palestine: Retreat from the Mandate, the Making of British Policy 1936–45* (New York: Holmes & Meier, 1978), 10.
14. *The Peel Commission Report*, 105–106. The report suggested that the casualty figures may have been significantly underestimated.
15. Gilbert, *Exile and Return*, 164.

whom the leaders were not responsible. A military staff officer serving under Lieutenant General Dill noted in puzzlement:

> The connection between the Arab leaders in Palestine and the armed bands raised in Palestine, as well as those brought in from abroad, seems to be established. The civil authorities persisted in maintaining that there was no connection and persisted in trying to squeeze a public pronouncement against the use of armed force out of the mufti… they refused to act vigorously against the Arab leaders. Why that theory was fixed in their minds remains a mystery.[16]

The military command favored the declaration of martial law, but Wauchope was firmly opposed to this, and he recommended instead that yet another commission of inquiry be sent to Palestine. To appease the Arabs, Wauchope abandoned his earlier support for the Jewish national home and proposed, in the face of Hitler's persecution of the Jews, that immigration should be suspended until the commission of inquiry issued its recommendations.[17] Despite strong Zionist opposition to both proposals, the London government announced the appointment of a royal commission under the chairmanship of Lord Robert Peel on July 29, 1936, but it refused to send the commission to Palestine until the Arab Higher Committee

---

16. H. J. Simpson, *British Rule and Rebellion*, cited in Weizmann, *Trial and Error*, 382. Weizmann added, "The connection between the Arab Higher Committee and the rioting was clear enough. Fawzi Kawakji, the Syrian guerrilla fighter who came into Palestine to organize the bandits, was an old friend of the mufti's. The waylaying and murdering of Jewish travelers, the attacks on Jewish settlements, the burning of Jewish fields, the uprooting of Jewish trees spread over the entire country."
17. Cohen, *Palestine: Retreat from the Mandate*, 16. Wauchope also suggested that the government should intimate to the commission his recommendation to suspend Jewish immigration, but the Colonial Office rejected that suggestion, fearing that the members would not agree to serve under such government pressure.

agreed to abandon the strike and end the violence. It also withheld announcement of its decision on the suspension of Jewish immigration until after the commission went to Palestine. The grand mufti, on the other hand, believing that he held the upper hand, refused to call off the strike before the British announced their agreement to suspend immigration.

At the behest of the grand mufti, King Ibn Saud of Saudi Arabia raised the issue in London, thereby bringing the Foreign Office into play on the question of Palestine, which, since 1921, under Churchill, had been the responsibility of the Colonial Office alone. The Foreign Office accepted the Saudi offer of mediation, but when the Saudi minister, seconded by Yemen and Iraq, called for Britain's acceptance of the grand mufti's demands, it reversed course and turned down the Saudi offer.[18]

Wauchope, desperate to end the continuing Arab revolt in Palestine without resorting to force, now took the initiative to invite the intervention of the neighboring Arab states. In August 1936, he requested the foreign minister of Iraq, Nuri Said, to negotiate with the grand mufti's Arab Higher Committee. Nuri injected himself as bargaining agent for the Palestinian Arabs, demanding that Great Britain agree to meet all the Arab demands as a precondition for the Arabs calling off the strike and the violence. The cabinet rejected what it saw as a virtual Arab ultimatum, and in a Colonial Office statement of policy on September 7, 1936, the London government overrode Wauchope's objections and announced its intent to impose martial law, including a decision to send an extra division of troops to stop the violence.[19]

The threat of martial law proved effective. Convinced that there was no hope of extracting any further concessions, the grand mufti decided to end the strike. To save face, however, it was arranged,

---

18. For a detailed discussion of Britain's invitation to the Arab kings to intervene in the Palestinian Arab revolt, see Cohen, *Palestine: Retreat from the Mandate*, 20–31.
19. *The Peel Commission Report*, 101.

with British approval, to issue the announcement to end the strike in response to an appeal by the Arab kings of Transjordan, Iraq, and Saudi Arabia. This was done on October 11, 1936, and on November 5, 1936, the Colonial Office agreed to send the Peel Commission to Palestine. The government then declared that a suspension of Jewish immigration in the course of the Peel Commission's investigation would not be justifiable on economic grounds and might prejudice the work of the Peel Commission. At the same time, however, the colonial minister requested from the high commissioner the reduction of the estimate for Palestine's economic absorptive capacity for Jewish immigrants for the next half year by more than three-quarters, from about 8,000 to 1,850.[20] The compromise was protested by both the Jews and the Arabs. The Arab Higher Committee denounced the decision and refused to cooperate with the Peel Commission. It ended its boycott of the Peel Commission only in January 1937, less than two weeks before the end of the hearings in Jerusalem, and again arranged to save face by agreeing to do so only in response to a recommendation by the kings of Saudi Arabia and Iraq.[21]

In a letter dated October 31, 1936 addressed to General A. P. Wavell, Lieutenant General Dill wrote with remarkable insight as well as foresight:

> Arthur Wauchope loves every stone of this country, he has worked himself to the bone for it—and it has let him down… His forbearance knew no bounds, and for it he got no thanks—it was merely held to be weakness. He hated the idea of martial law. He felt its operation would leave a sullen people with rebellion in their hearts. He is delighted that peace has come without having to resort to stern measures. But the peace is only a truce.

---

20. United States Government, "Telegram from Ambassador Bingham in the United Kingdom to the US Secretary of State, November 6, 1936" in *Foreign Relations of the United States: Diplomatic Papers, 1936, vol. 2* (Washington DC, United States Government Publishing Office).
21. *The Peel Commission Report*, 102–103.

The whole Arab organization, under that arch-scoundrel the mufti, remains to renew rebellion when the result of the royal commission's labors proves distasteful to the Arab population. The fatal error was bringing the Arab kings into the party. From henceforth, they will consider themselves entitled to a say in Palestinian affairs. Moreover, they prevented the declaration of martial law, because we obviously could not act while the conversations, which we had encouraged, were going on. And so, the Arab leaders slipped out with honor and renown instead of being scattered to the four winds.[22]

As Lieutenant General Dill predicted, the Peel Commission's concessions to the Arab demands failed to satisfy the grand mufti, and in September 1937, two months after the release of the Peel Commission Report, he renewed the Arab revolt against the government, with the support of the Arab and Moslem worlds. About four hundred Arabs representing the surrounding Arab states, as well as Palestine, met in Syria in September 1937, where they declared Palestine "an integral part of the Arabian homeland," and added that Britain had to choose "between our friendship and the Jews." And the next month, Moslem members of the legislative councils from as far as British India protested British support for a Jewish state in any part of Palestine.

In October 1937, the new colonial minister, William Ormsby-Gore (1936–1938), finally overcame Wauchope's reluctance to use force and ordered firm countermeasures. The military disbanded the Arab Higher Committee, arrested five of its ten leaders, whom it expelled to the Seychelles Islands, and removed the grand mufti from his post as head of the Supreme Moslem Council. The grand mufti was not arrested, however. With the connivance of administration officials, he was permitted to escape to Syria, where, under the eyes of the French government, he continued to direct the Palestine revolt and to recruit Arabs for the task. The French administration, undoubtedly

---

22. John Connell, *Wavell, Scholar and Soldier to June 1941* (London: Collins, 1964), 188.

remembering the attempts of the Palestine military administration, during and after World War I, to "biff the French right out of Syria" (see Chapter 3), evidently now repaid the British administration in kind, seeing no reason to stop the grand mufti from attempting to "biff" the British right out of Palestine.

In August 1938, the grand mufti had built up such political power that according to the new high commissioner, Sir Harold MacMichael (1938–1944), it was "too strong even for a high commissioner." As MacMichael informed the new colonial minister, Malcolm MacDonald (1938–1940), "No Arab political leaders could come and discuss politics with him or me. It would put them in an exceedingly embarrassing position, and even in danger of foul play from terrorists afterwards." And MacMichael, unlike the Palestine administration and the Peel Commission, believed:

> Terrorism was not a national movement. The moderate Arab leaders were opposed to it, and the great majority of Arabs in the country disliked it and began to feel that it was fruitless. But the power of intimidation of the terrorists was so great and Arab politicians generally were so lacking in courage that there was no lead against the terrorists amongst Arabs. If the mufti were not sitting just across the border, other political leaders might arise; but whilst he is there, the Arabs could not believe that he would not soon return to Palestine.[23]

During the revolt, Arab bands terrorized Jewish and Arab towns, including Old Jerusalem. The British struck back with considerable force and inflicted considerable casualties upon the Arabs, but they failed to stop the revolt until the onset of World War II in September 1939. In 1938 alone, 292 Jews and 69 British were killed, but the Arabs are estimated to have suffered at least 1,600 dead.[24] Many of the Arab

---

23. Gilbert, *Exile and Return*, 205–206.
24. Nicholas Bethell, *The Palestine Triangle: The Struggle for the Holy Land* (New York: G. P. Putnam's Sons, 1979), 36.

casualties were at the hands of the Arab rebels, however—for the three-year period of the revolt before the outbreak of World War II, the Arab rebels are estimated to have killed more Arabs than Jews.[25]

The Haganah, the Jewish defense forces under Jewish Agency control, observed a policy of *havlagah*, or "self-restraint," acting only in self-defense but refraining from any reprisals against Arabs. Once again, as in so many instances regarding Israel's rebirth in its ancient homeland, Palestine's Jews came to benefit from a completely unexpected source. During this period, an exceptional British military officer, Captain Orde Wingate, arrived in Palestine and devoted himself (1936–May 1939) to providing the Haganah with highly effective military training. Like Colonel Richard Meinertzhagen, the other extraordinary British military official who had served in Palestine before him, Wingate was an ardent Christian Zionist. In addition to training Jewish settlements to protect themselves against the Arab terror, he transformed the Haganah into an effective military force, with outstanding military commanders who subsequently led Israel in its stunning victories in the wars with the Arabs.

The Irgun, a smaller rival organization to the Haganah, placed itself in 1937 under the authority of Vladimir Jabotinsky, who had resigned from the Zionist Executive after the issuance of the 1922 Churchill White Paper and subsequently formed the more militant Revisionist Party. In the face of the mounting Jewish casualties at the hands of the Arabs, the Irgun adopted a policy of reprisals against the Arabs. This policy was strongly condemned by the Jewish Agency, and about half of the Irgun membership left and rejoined the Haganah.

The Peel Commission

The Royal Peel Commission, which arrived in Palestine on November 11, 1936, heard evidence there until January 18, 1937 and returned to London for further meetings with British, Jewish, and Arab leaders, issuing its report on July 7, 1937. Chaim Weizmann,

---

25. Samuel Katz, *Days of Fire* (Garden City, NY: Doubleday, 1968), 8–9.

who testified several times, considered the Peel Commission "by far the most distinguished and ablest of the investigatory bodies ever sent out to Palestine."[26]

The Peel Commission's historical review of the Palestine problem and its analysis of the economic and social issues in Palestine were free of much of the anti-Zionist bias that characterized the reports of its predecessors. In contrast to Arab and Moslem propaganda today, which insists on describing Zionism only as a nineteenth-century racist, colonial, and imperial invasion of an alien people to Arab Palestine, a fiction supported by many UN governments and much of today's media, the Peel Commission devoted the first chapter of its report to an unbiased review of Jewish history from biblical times to its own day, which emphasizes the strong enduring ties of the Jewish people to Palestine, its ancient national homeland.

Turning to its consideration of World War I and the Mandate, the Peel Commission cited the testimony of Lloyd George, the prime minister responsible for the Balfour Declaration to facilitate the establishment of a Jewish national home in Palestine, that its aim had been to enlist the support of world Jewry at a time that the Allies were in a very critical position in World War I and the German government was doing all it could to win the Zionist movement over to its side. The Peel Commission added this telling comment on the almost universally ignored contribution which the Jews had made to Arab independence by providing the critical support needed for the Allied victory:

The facts that the Balfour Declaration was issued in 1917 in order to enlist Jewish support for the Allies and that this support was forthcoming are not sufficiently appreciated in Palestine. The Arabs do not appear to realize first that the present position of the Arab world as a whole is mainly due to the great sacrifices made by the Allied and associated powers in World War I, and second that in so far as the Balfour Declaration helped to bring about the Allies' victory, it

---

26. Weizmann, *Trial and Error*, 383.

helped to bring about the emancipation of all the Arab countries from Turkish rule.[27]

On the meaning of the term "Jewish national home" in the Balfour Declaration, the Peel Commission cited Prime Minister Lloyd George as testifying, "It was contemplated that…if the Jews had meanwhile responded to the opportunity afforded them by the idea of a national home and had become a definite majority of the national inhabitants, then Palestine would thus become a Jewish commonwealth." The Peel Commission added,

> Thus, His Majesty's Government evidently realized that a Jewish state might in course of time be established… The Zionist leaders, for their part, recognized that an ultimate Jewish state was not precluded by the terms of the [Balfour] Declaration, and so it was understood elsewhere.

The Peel Commission noted, in particular, that this was also the understanding of the American president, Woodrow Wilson, the author of the Mandate Policy of the Allied Powers, citing as evidence his statement on March 3, 1919, "I am persuaded that the Allied nations, with the fullest concurrence of our own government and people, are agreed that in Palestine shall be laid the foundations of a Jewish commonwealth." The Peel Commission added that the responsible British government leaders at the time—including Lord Robert Cecil in 1917, General Smuts (a member of the Imperial Cabinet when the Balfour Declaration was issued) in 1919, Herbert Samuel in 1919, and Winston Churchill in 1920—all "spoke or wrote in terms that could only mean that they contemplated the eventual establishment of a Jewish state."[28]

Even more significantly, the Peel Commission called attention to the agreement on January 3, 1919 between Chaim Weizmann and Emir Feisal, the representative of the Arabs at the Paris Peace

---

27. *The Peel Commission Report*, 24.
28. *The Peel Commission Report*, 24–25.

Conference after World War I, in which the two parties pledged cordial cooperation between the Arab state and the Jewish national home in Palestine.[29] In this agreement, which the Arabs and British anti-Zionists have long since chosen to forget, Feisal not only accepted the Balfour Declaration but specifically approved a policy calling for "all necessary measures...to encourage and stimulate the immigration of Jews into Palestine on a large scale and...to settle Jewish immigrants upon the land through closer settlement and intensive cultivation of the soil" (see Chapter 2). Thus, as the Peel Commission noted in its conclusion, the Arab statesmen at the time "had been willing to concede little Palestine to the Jews, provided that the rest of Arab Asia were free," a condition that as the Peel Commission emphasized, was "on the eve of fulfillment now"[30] and that has long since been totally fulfilled. It is also noteworthy that the Palestine the Arabs were willing to concede to the Jews at the time included Transjordan, since the Feisal–Weizmann agreement was written in 1919, three years before Churchill separated Transjordan for Feisal's brother, Emir Abdullah, as part of the Palestine Mandate, where the Balfour Declaration would not apply (see Chapter 5).

The Peel Commission also supported the Zionist position on the primary purpose of the Mandate. Previous official policy statements—dating back to Herbert Samuel, the first high commissioner of Palestine—saw in the Mandate only a thesis of "equal obligations" to the Jewish people and to the Arabs. The Peel Commission, however, after a detailed review of the text of the Mandate, concluded categorically, "Unquestionably, however, the primary purpose of the Mandate, *as expressed in its preamble and its articles* [emphasis in the original], is to promote the establishment of the Jewish national home."[31]

---

29. *The Peel Commission Report*, 26–27.
30. *The Peel Commission Report*, 395. Although the Arab proviso that it should gain the rest of the Middle East has long since been fulfilled, much of the Arab world today still contests Israel's right to exist, even in a limited portion of "little Palestine."
31. *The Peel Commission Report*, 39.

In its review of the history of immigration under the Mandate and its relation to the principle of economic absorptive capacity laid down in the 1922 Churchill White Paper, the Peel Commission also came to a conclusion that, in contrast to the Shaw Commission and Hope Simpson Report and the 1930 Passfield White Paper, was remarkably supportive of the Zionist position. After taking into account the notable increase in immigration that had taken place under Wauchope, the Peel Commission Report concluded:

> So far from reducing "economic absorptive capacity," immigration increased it. The more immigrants came in, the more work they created for local industries to meet their needs, especially in building—and more work meant more room for immigrants under the "labour schedule." Unless, therefore, the government adopted a more restrictive policy, or unless there were some economic or financial setbacks, there seemed no reason why the rate of immigration should not go on climbing up and up.

After citing the economic indices that showed the expansion in commercial and industrial activity in Palestine as well as the growth in government revenues associated with the increase in Jewish immigration, the Peel Commission Report added, "On the material side, indeed, most other countries at that time might well have envied Palestine."[32]

Turning to its review of Arab progress under the Mandate, the Peel Commission Report, again unlike its predecessors, emphasized that "the Arabs have shared to a considerable degree in the material benefits which Jewish immigration has brought to Palestine."[33] Most striking was the commission's difference to Hope Simpson's extraordinary conclusion in his report that Palestine had no absorptive capacity for even a single additional Jewish immigrant, without doing harm to the level of living of the Arab *fellaheen* ("landless tenants").

---

32. *The Peel Commission Report*, 85–86.
33. *The Peel Commission Report*, 130.

In contrast, the Peel Commission spelled out in some detail the economic and social benefits from which the Arab community benefitted because of Jewish immigration. In the economic area, it noted the expansion of Arab citriculture and Arab industry, both of which had been financed by the capital obtained from the sale of Arab land to Jews at very high, and even uneconomic, prices; the rise in Arab agricultural productivity; the enlarged markets for Arab agricultural products and industrial goods; the expanded Arab employment; and the rise in Arab wages to levels far above those prevailing in Egypt and Iraq. In the social area, the Peel Commission Report cited the improvements in public sanitation and health services; the resulting significant lowering of infant mortality; the consequent rise in the average lifespan; and the consequent explosive growth in Palestine's Arab population, which had hitherto been stagnant for centuries. All of these gains, economic and social, the Peel Commission recognized, were largely the result of Jewish immigration and Jewish capital under the Mandate. As the Peel Commission Report emphasized, the Arabs "could not deny that such public services as had in fact been provided had benefited their people; nor could they deny that the revenue available for those services had been largely provided by the Jews."[34]

In 1938, Malcolm MacDonald, the newly appointed colonial minister, was especially effusive in his comments in parliament on the remarkable effects of Jewish immigration on the Arab population:

> The Arabs cannot say that the Jews are driving them out of their country... If not a single Jew had come to Palestine after 1918, I believe the Arab population of Palestine today would still have been round about the six-hundred-thousand figure at which it had been stable under Turkish rule. It is because the Jews who have come to Palestine bring modern health services and other advantages that Arab men and women who would have been dead are alive today, that Arab children who would

---

34. *The Peel Commission Report*, 125–130.

never have drawn breath have been born and grown strong. It is not only the Jews who have benefited from the Balfour Declaration. They can deny it as much as they like, but materially, the Arabs in Palestine have gained very greatly from the Balfour Declaration."[35]

✡ ✡ ✡

But paradoxically, even though the Peel Commission's historical review of the Balfour Declaration and the Mandate as well as its analysis of the economic and social benefits to the Arabs stemming from the Jewish national home were both so highly supportive of the Zionist program, its recommendations of short-term measures for dealing with the Arab revolt were the most anti-Zionist of all the commissions. For the Peel Commission arrived at a paradoxical finding that was profoundly anti-Zionist, declaring,

> But there were two sides to the picture; and the brighter grew the one, the darker grew the other. With almost mathematical precision, the betterment of the economic situation in Palestine meant the deterioration of the political situation. As the national home expanded from 1933 onwards, so the Arab hate and fear of it increased.[36]

The Peel Commission accordingly asserted that the Arab hate and fear of the Jewish national home, linked with the Arab desire for national independence, were the two underlying causes of the Arab violence in every instance—in 1920, 1921, 1929, 1933, and 1936.

---

35. *Hansard*, House of Commons, Debates, vol. 341, cc1992, November 24, 1938. This assessment of the remarkable effects of Jewish immigration on the Arab population did not deter MacDonald from authoring the 1939 white paper, which, as discussed later in the text, repudiated the Balfour Declaration and the Mandate, in favor of establishing all Palestine as an Arab state.
36. *Peel Commission Report*, 86.

162 INDEPENDENCE

As a consequence of this paradoxical finding, the Peel Commission formulated a new criterion for controlling Jewish immigration that was most crippling to the prospects for the Jewish national home—and, as follows from the Peel Commission's own analysis, for Arab economic and social welfare. The Peel Commission declared that the criterion of economic absorptive capacity adopted in the 1922 Churchill White Paper for controlling the rate of Jewish immigration must be supplemented by the criterion of the political and psychological absorptive capacity of the existing population for Jewish immigration.[37]

To satisfy this political and psychological criterion, the Peel Commission recommended, without explanation, that the rate of immigration for the next five years should be restricted to a maximum of twelve thousand people per year.[38] This figure, the Peel Commission made clear, was to set only an upper limit—the Palestine administration should also retain the right to limit actual immigration below this number on the basis of its estimate of economic absorptive capacity. The maximum five-year total of sixty thousand recommended by the Peel Commission, it must be noted, was lower than the immigration of nearly 62,000 for the single year 1935, the year before the Peel

---

37. *Peel Commission Report*, 297–301. In addition to subjecting Jewish immigration to Arab psychological absorptive capacity, the Peel Commission proposed the enlargement of the Arab Committee to include representatives of the neighboring Arab countries—Transjordan, Iraq, Saudi Arabia, Syria, and perhaps Egypt, along with Palestinians. Such an agency, according to the report, would make the Arabs more willing to meet with the Jews in conferences, and the Jews would also benefit, because they "would find a body of responsible men with whom difficulties might be discussed and even possible compromises contemplated." The Peel Commission Report itself quickly fell victim to the strong objections of the Arab countries. (See, e.g., the statement by Iraq's prime minister quoted in footnote 47 below).

38. *The Peel Commission Report*, 306. The Peel Commission also recommended additional restrictions on land purchases beyond those already contemplated in the past, including the "definite prohibition of the sale of isolated and comparatively small plots of rural land to Jews" as well as of all land in Palestine's hill districts.

Commission's arrival in Palestine. The Peel Commission made this recommendation for the extreme cutback in Jewish immigration in the face of Chaim Weizmann's prescient warning:

> Almost six million Jews in that part of the world [Central, East and South-East Europe, excluding the Soviet Union] are doomed to be pent up in places where they are not wanted, and for whom the world is divided into places where they cannot live, and places into which they cannot enter.[39]

The Peel Commission's criterion of Arab psychological absorptive capacity was based on its conviction that the Arab violence was a spontaneous uprising of the Arab people at large. It attached little weight to the role of the Palestine administration in stoking the Arab hate and fear, even though, as Winston Churchill had noted as early as 1921, nine-tenths of their number were opposed to the Balfour Declaration and the Mandate under which they served and Britain legally governed. It discounted completely the evidence of the role of the Palestine military administration in the 1920 pogrom (documented in Chapter 3) and the role of the civilian administration in the 1929 massacres (documented in Chapter 6). Indeed, the Peel Commission itself called attention to multiple legitimate grievances of the Jews against the Palestine administration, of which the two most important were the administration's lack of sympathy for the Balfour Declaration incorporated in the Mandate and its failure to maintain law and order, both of which fed the Arab riots.

The Peel Commission similarly attached little weight to the grand mufti's role in fomenting the Arab uprising in contrast to members of the League of Nations Palestine Commission, who, in their review of the 1929 massacres, had maintained that they had been fomented by the grand mufti and his *effendi* associates. The fear and hatred of these Arab leaders involved no paradox—they feared the erosion of their feudal power over the poor, illiterate *fellaheen* from the economic and

---

39. Weisgal, *The Letters and Papers of Chaim Weizmann*, Series B, vol. 2, 100–102.

social revolution in Arab life generated by the growth of the Jewish national home. Limiting Jewish immigration to their psychological absorptive capacity—which they had made clear was nil—served only to strengthen their feudal power over the *fellaheen*, who were thereby condemned to ongoing economic and social stagnation.

The Peel Commission's Proposal for the Partition of Palestine

Unlike previous commissions, the Peel Commission recognized that its proposals for sharply cutting back Jewish immigration and land settlement were only palliatives and not long-term solutions. In Part III of its report, the commission therefore submitted its proposal for a long-term solution to the Palestinian problem.[40] After deciding that Zionist aspirations and Arab political demands were irreconcilable, the Peel Commission arrived at its far-reaching conclusion that the only long-term solution was to amend the Mandate to permit the partition of Palestine once again. In 1922, Winston Churchill had separated all of Transjordan (now named Jordan) for the Emir Abdullah as a purely Arab area of the Palestine Mandate, in which the Balfour Declaration and the Zionist provisions of the Mandate would not apply. The Peel Commission recommended that the remaining area of Palestine, west of the Jordan, should now also be partitioned to establish two states—a Jewish state and an Arab state. Jerusalem, however (together with the surrounding area and a corridor to the sea at Jaffa), should remain under British Mandatory rule, because of the special character of Jerusalem as holy to all three monotheistic faiths: Judaism, Christianity, and Islam.

The Jewish State was proposed to include the Galilee together with the Palestine coastal area running from the border with Lebanon to about twenty miles south of Tel Aviv (except for Jaffa)—the small area of Palestine where Jewish settlements had until then been concentrated—with Tel Aviv its main city. The Jews were not to be

---

40. *The Peel Commission Report,* 380–393.

given immediate control, however, of the four other major cities within this Jewish area. Haifa and Acre, which had mixed Arab and Jewish populations, as well as Safed and Tiberias, holy to the Jews, were to be kept for an unspecified period under Mandatory administration, even though they were included within the boundaries of the proposed Jewish State.

The rest of Palestine—including the entire Negev and the eastern side of the Sea of Galilee (the source of the Jewish supply of water) and excluding the Jerusalem area and a corridor to the Mediterranean—was proposed to become an Arab state, united with Transjordan, with Jaffa its main city. It is noteworthy that despite the Peel Commission's emphasis on the Arab demand for national independence as one of the two underlying causes of all the Arab violence since 1920, it refrained from recommending the establishment of an independent national state of Palestine. Instead, it proposed only "an Arab State, consisting of Transjordan united with that part of Palestine" that was to be assigned to the Palestinian Arabs.[41]

The Peel Commission did not flinch from dealing with the difficult problem that no borders could be drawn that would separate all Arabs and Arab-owned land from all Jews and Jewish-owned land. It asserted that sooner or later, "there should be a transfer of land and, as far as possible, an exchange of population."[42] For land transfers, it recommended that the governments of the states concerned should assume responsibility for the purchase of Jewish-owned land in the proposed Arab State and the purchase of Arab-owned land in the Jewish State, at a price to be fixed, if necessary, by the Mandatory administration. The more difficult problem, it realized, was that of the transfer of population. It estimated that in the area it allocated to the Arab State, there were at the time about 1,250 Jews, while in the area it assigned to the Jewish State, there were about 225,000 Arabs. Calling attention to the precedent of the compulsory exchange of

---

41. *The Peel Commission Report*, 381.
42. *The Peel Commission Report*, 389.

populations involving 1.3 million Greeks and some 400,000 Turks following the Greco–Turkish War of 1922, it recommended that the proposed Jewish and Arab states should agree to such a compulsory transfer of population. A program of development of farmland was proposed to be undertaken in the Arab State to absorb the incoming Arab population. The Peel Commission made no provision for dealing with the problem that would arise in case the Arabs rejected the proposal for a compulsory transfer of the 225,000 Arabs living in the Jewish State.

✡ ✡ ✡

Since it would take time to put the proposal for partition into effect, the Peel Commission recommended that to avoid adding to future difficulties, further restrictions on Jewish immigration and land settlement, going well beyond the 1930 Passfield White Paper restrictions, should be put into effect in the interim. Land purchases by Jews in the proposed Arab area (as well as by Arabs in the proposed Jewish area) should be prohibited. Jewish immigration into the area proposed for the Arab state should likewise be prohibited.[43]

Remarkably, the Peel Commission failed to recommend similar restrictions against Arabs moving into the proposed Jewish area during the transition period. It thus ignored both the Arab immigration from outside Palestine, for which the administration kept no data, and the internal migration of Arabs from their own lower-income areas into the more prosperous and progressive Jewish area. In the absence of reliable statistical data, the Peel Commission accepted the Palestine administration's thesis that despite the economic gains in agriculture, industry, employment, wages, and markets for Arab goods and despite the social gains in education, health, sanitation, infant mortality, and enhanced lifespans accruing to the Arabs from Jewish immigration—which the Peel Commission had itself documented—Arab immigration into the Jewish areas of settlement had been negligible

---

43. *The Peel Commission Report*, 291–292.

under the Mandate. And it evidently also ignored the internal Arab migration to the economically and socially more progressive Jewish areas. Such a thesis flies in the face of economic theory, historical experience (e.g., Hispanic immigration into the United States or Moslem immigration into Europe in recent decades), and common sense. The thesis was particularly absurd in regard to Palestine, where the residents of Transjordan were legally free to enter and where Arabs from all over the Middle East and Africa, in the administration's total disregard of the strict border controls it exercised against Jewish illegal immigration, had no difficulty in entering illegally.

Better-informed officials than the Peel Commission members were not taken in by the Palestine administration's biased thesis on Arab immigration. In the 1936 parliamentary debate on Wauchope's proposal for a Palestine legislative council, Mr. Thomas Williams stated, "I am informed the Arabs who have emigrated into Palestine number round about two hundred and fifty thousand. It may be including the natural increase, slightly more or slightly less, but the point remains just the same."[44] In the debate in the House of Commons on the 1939 White Paper,[45] Winston Churchill emphasized, "So far from being persecuted, the Arabs have crowded into this country and multiplied till their population has increased more than even all world Jewry could lift up the Jewish population."[46] And, in the United States, President Franklin Roosevelt wrote in a memorandum to his secretary of state on May 17, 1939, the day Britain issued its white paper repudiating the Balfour Declaration and the Mandate, "Arab immigration into Palestine since 1921 has vastly exceeded the total Jewish immigration during this whole period."[47]

---

44. *Hansard*, House of Commons, Debates, vol. 313, cc1331, June 19, 1936.
45. Malcolm MacDonald, *Palestine: Statement of Policy*, White Paper, CMD 6019 (London: His Majesty's Stationery Office, 1939) ("the 1939 White Paper").
46. *Hansard*, House of Commons, Debates, vol. 347, cc2178, May 23, 1939.
47. *Foreign Relations of the United States: Diplomatic Papers, 1939, vol. 1*, 5, Palestine, 757–758.

Parliament's Non-Committal Decision on Partition

Britain's cabinet was divided over the proposal for partition. On the one hand, the Foreign Office, headed at the time by Anthony Eden (December 1935–February 1938), had become adamantly opposed to the establishment of a Jewish state in any part of Palestine. It insisted, instead, that all of Palestine must evolve into an Arab state. Eden, preoccupied with the growing threat from Hitler and Mussolini as well as with the mounting problems with Communism in the Soviet Union and China left Palestinian policy to be directed by George Rendel, head of the Foreign Office's Eastern Department (1930–1938). Rendel, like all the key officials of his department and of the Palestine administration, was ardently pro-Arab, and he insisted on a policy of placating the Arabs. Otherwise, he warned, Britain would be faced with the opposition not only of the Arab world, particularly Saudi Arabia and Iraq, with their oil reserves, but also of the entire Moslem world, including even British India with its large Moslem population. He therefore urged that all Palestine must become another Arab state.

Colonial Minister Ormsby-Gore, on the other hand, supported the partition proposal. He was worried that Britain would arouse world Jewry's hostility if it were totally to repudiate its Mandate, particularly at a time of crisis for the Jewish people, and he was anxious, as well, about the potentially serious repercussions in British–American relations. Like the Peel Commission, he had laid stress on the Feisal–Weizmann Agreement in favor of the Balfour Declaration and his warm support for Zionist aspirations, and he believed the Arabs would accept a Jewish state in a small part of Palestine. And, like the Peel Commission, he also thought the Arabs would agree to the transfer of population, since the transfer would be only over a short distance to another part of the same country, among their own people, with the same religion, language, and history.

The cabinet decided to accommodate Ormsby-Gore's position by accompanying the release of the Peel Commission Report with a statement expressing its agreement in principle with the partition proposal but without any commitment on the specifics. In the meantime, the government adopted the Peel Commission's "palliative" restrictions against the Jewish national home. Land transactions that might prejudice the partition scheme were prohibited, and immigration was cut back to a maximum of eight thousand people for the period August 1937–March 1938, an average of a thousand per month.[48]

In the parliamentary debate on July 21, 1937, the cabinet's proposal for approval of partition in principle, submitted by Ormsby-Gore, found little support. Britain's pro-Zionists in parliament attacked partition as a violation of the Balfour Declaration and an abandonment of British responsibilities under the Mandate for a Jewish national home in all Palestine. A month before the Peel Commission Report was issued, Weizmann had discussed the rumored proposal for partition with several leading political supporters of the Zionist program, including, in particular, Winston Churchill and Clement Attlee, leader of the Labour Party. Weizmann had indicated that if the government refused to carry out the Mandate, he could see no other alternative but to accept partition. Churchill, however, emphatically disagreed, warning that the government was not trustworthy—that they were "a lot of lily-livered rabbits"—and would let the Jews down. "The Jewish State would not materialize," he emphasized with remarkable foresight of the events that followed. "The Arabs would immediately start trouble, and the government would run away again." Churchill added (concerning himself), "Of course, if Dr. Weizmann told him to shut up, he would shut up. He would stay at home, but he would be brokenhearted about it."[49]

Attlee, who, as post-war prime minister, vigorously supported the bitter anti-Zionist policy of his foreign minister, Ernest Bevin, had not yet shed his longstanding zealous support of the Balfour Declaration and was likewise in firm opposition to the proposal for partition. He told Weizmann:

---

48. Weisgal, *The Letters and Papers of Chaim Weizmann*, Series B, vol. 2, 271.
49. Weisgal, *The Letters and Papers of Chaim Weizmann*, Series B, vol. 2, 269–271.

He was shocked by the suggestion. The Jews had done a great work in Palestine. It was a great experiment which had proved very successful. Stripped of all verbiage, what was being proposed now was a concession to violence. Of course, if the Zionists agreed to the proposal, he would not fight it, but it seemed to him to put an end to a great experiment in cooperation between peoples; it represented a complete confession of failure in the working of the Mandate and would be a triumph for fascism, and he, Attlee, could not agree to the idea.[50]

In the parliamentary debate on partition Morgan Jones, speaking for the Labour Party, vigorously rejected the Peel Commission's proposal.[51] Emphasizing that the Jews had originally been promised a Jewish national home in Palestine,

> ...an area which comprised Transjordan, and that comprised 45,000 square miles. Transjordan was taken off, and that reduced it to 10,000 square miles. Now, you are taking the rest of Palestine off, and it is now less than 2,000 square miles. Is this the home? Is this the promise? ...You reduce this Jewish State to less than 2,000 miles, and then you say that inside that territory, not one single town shall remain wholly Jewish, except Tel Aviv. There will not be a town left in the State, because all the rest are under the Mandatory Power, except Tel Aviv... They are not even sure that they are going to have complete control of Tel Aviv as a port. Now, will the right hon. gentleman tell me what he means by flinging about this word "sovereignty"? You are abusing language when you use the word "sovereignty."

Citing the Peel Commission's own evidence of what he called the administration's "subtle and sustained opposition to the Mandate in Palestine," even failing to provide law and order and public security

---

50. Weisgal, *The Letters and Papers of Chaim Weizmann, Series B, vol. 2*, 269–271.
51. *Hansard,* House of Commons, Debates, vol. 326, cc2260–2261, July 21, 1937.

to the point where, "for an Arab to be suspected of a lukewarm adherence to the nationalist cause is to invite a visit from a body of 'gunmen,'" Jones declared that the root of the Palestine problem was not the Mandate but its maladministration, to a degree that could justifiably be called "sabotage."

Even if partition were necessary, Jones added, the Peel Commission's proposal for partition was "unthinkable"—"wholly unacceptable." The Peel Commission would divide Palestine into three Palestines, a Jewish state with a large Arab minority, an Arab state with a small Jewish minority, and a Mandatory state as a corridor between the Arab and Jewish states. Each of those states would reproduce the problems that prevail in the whole of Palestine. Jones noted:

> In the Jewish State, there would be, I gather, 225,000 Arabs and 258,000 Jews… If 1 million Arabs cannot live and work with 400,000 Jews, how can 225,000 Arabs live and work with 258,000 Jews? …You cannot guarantee that for all time, the Jews and Arabs in the Jewish State will agree, and you cannot guarantee that the Jews and Arabs on the Arab side will agree. Supposing there is trouble, who is to be called in? The Mandatory Power, and so, you will be called in one week when there is trouble here, and the next week when there is trouble there, and your last position will be worse than your first.

Sir Archibald Sinclair, the Liberal Party leader, noted, inter alia, that in the fulfillment of the McMahon pledge to the Arabs in return for their help during the war against the Ottoman Empire, Britain had carved out five Arab kingdoms—Hedjaz, Nejd (subsequently merged with Hedjaz by Ibn Saud to form Saudi Arabia), Yemen, Iraq, and Transjordan—and Syria was about to become another Arab state. But, reminding the House of Commons regarding the Balfour Declaration pledge to the Jews, he emphasized:

> No British statesman could have expected it to bring greater help to the Allied cause in its time of need as in fact it did. The

Jews fulfilled their part of the bargain without stint... The debt of the Arabs is not only to Britain and the Allied countries, as the secretary of state reminded us—the Arabs have a debt to the Jews, too. Is it just or reasonable to this powerful agent of Allied victory and of Arab emancipation, the Jewish people, that the provision of a national home for the 16 million in world Jewry should be whittled down to a territory the size of an English county?

After objections by other speakers along similar lines, the government dropped its call for approval of partition in principle, and parliament adopted instead a resolution calling for the Peel Commission Report to be submitted for consideration to the Permanent Mandates Commission of the League of Nations and for the government to submit a specific proposal, taking into account the Peel Commission's recommendations.[52]

The Cabinet Reverses Course, Rejecting Partition in Favor of All Palestine Becoming an Arab State

Parliament's decision to postpone action on partition pending examination by the League of Nations and the government's submission of a specific scheme gave the Foreign Office time to mobilize an effective opposition to the establishment of a Jewish state in any part of Palestine, no matter how small. Under Rendel's leadership, it embarked upon an intensive campaign to undo the cabinet's approval of the principle of partition and to adopt instead a decision to convert all of Palestine into an independent Arab state in which the Jews would be frozen as a permanent minority. The role newly granted to the surrounding Arab states for their involvement in Palestine affairs now proved to be a powerful Foreign Office tool for reversing the previous cabinet decision. The Foreign Office invited the Arab kings to submit their views on the subject, in the full knowledge that they

---

52. *Hansard*, House of Commons, Debates, vol. 326, cc2245–2361, July 21, 1937.

would be unanimous in rejecting partition.[53] Britain's ambassadors to the Arab and other Moslem countries were also invited to send in their dispatches—all of them, as expected, warning of the dire consequences for British imperial interests in all the Arab countries and in the entire Moslem world should partition be approved.

The campaign against partition came to a head on November 19, 1937, with Eden's memorandum to the cabinet, drafted by George Rendel. It declared, in the bluntest terms, that the Jews must not be permitted to become a majority in Palestine and must not be given sovereignty in any part of it. The memorandum read in part:

> The Arabs are not a mere handful of aborigines who can be disregarded by the "white colonizer." They have a latent force and vitality which is stirring into new activity. If any stimulus were required to their growing nationalism, it is hard to imagine any more effective method than the creation of a small dynamic state of hated foreign immigrants on the seaboard of the Arab

---

53. The Arab rulers were far from unanimous in private in their views on partition. The Christian Arabs ruling in Lebanon were pleased with the prospect of a Jewish state on their southern border that might serve as a counterweight to the potential threat from Syria's ambitions for a Greater Syria, with borders embracing both Palestine and Lebanon. The president of Lebanon, on learning of the Peel Commission's proposal, asked Weizmann in a private meeting to promise that its first treaty of friendship should be with Lebanon. Abdullah of Transjordan would naturally have been happy with the expansion of his kingdom envisaged in the Peel Commission Report, but he did not dare oppose the grand mufti or to ignore the warning of Iraq's prime minister, "Any person venturing to agree to act as head of such a state"— that is, an Arab State such as the government proposed to set up—"would be regarded as an outcast throughout the Arab world and would incur the wrath of Moslems all over the East. I declare, both as the head of an Arab government and as a private citizen, that I should always oppose any individual's right to stab the Arab race in the heart in order to secure the rulership of the proposed new state" (quoted by Sir Archibald Sinclair, *Hansard*, House of Commons, Debates, vol. 326, cc2270, July 21, 1937).

countries with a perpetual urge to extend its influence inland… Arab opposition in neighboring countries is even more serious [than in Palestine]… There is only one way in which we can now make our peace with the Arabs and avoid the dangers I have indicated above—that is, by giving the Arabs some assurance that the Jews will neither become a majority in Palestine nor be given any Palestinian territory in full sovereignty.[54]

Eden's memorandum to the cabinet won the day. The cabinet reversed its position and decided to reject outright the Peel Commission's recommendation for partition. The Jews would not be granted sovereignty in any part of Palestine. Instead, the whole of Palestine would evolve into an independent Arab state, with Jewish immigration restricted so as to ensure that the Jews would remain frozen as a permanent minority.

✡ ✡ ✡

Before announcing its new decision, the government resorted to its oft-repeated device of sending out yet another commission for further examination of the problem. In December 1937, Colonial Secretary Ormsby-Gore informed Palestine's High Commissioner Wauchope of the appointment of yet another commission, its ostensible purpose being "to consider the details and practical possibilities of a partition scheme." The Woodhead Commission, appointed on January 4, 1938, was given terms of reference:

> to recommend boundaries for the proposed Arab and Jewish states and the British enclaves, which would:
>
> (a) afford a reasonable prospect of the eventual establishment… of self-supporting Arab and Jewish states;
>
> (b) necessitate the inclusion of the fewest possible Arabs and Arab enterprises in the Jewish area and vice versa; and

---

54. Gilbert, *Exile and Return*, 192–193.

(c) enable the British government to carry out its Mandatory responsibilities.

But although the Woodhead Commission was appointed ostensibly to consider how to implement partition, it was intended, in fact, only as a screen for the decision the government had already made to abandon partition. Rendel obtained cabinet approval to amend the proposed terms of reference so as to suggest to the Woodhead Commission the government's belief that partition was impracticable. Ormsby-Gore, who had favored partition, was left with the humiliating task of sending Rendel's suggestion of the impracticability of partition to Sir John Woodhead, with the comment that if his commission concluded that partition was not practicable, it must say so.[55]

Chaim Weizmann, who learned of the government's plan to repudiate the Balfour Declaration and the Mandate and to establish all of Palestine as an independent Arab State, wrote in great bitterness on December 31, 1937 to the permanent undersecretary for the colonies, Sir John Shuckburgh:

> Jews are not going to Palestine to become, in their ancient home, "Arabs of the Mosaic faith," or to exchange their German or Polish ghetti for an Arab one. Whoever knows what Arab government looks like, what "minority status" signifies nowadays, and what a Jewish ghetto in an Arab state means—there are

---

55. Cohen, *Palestine: Retreat from the Mandate*, 38–45. Ormsby-Gore had originally proposed the inclusion of three clauses in the Woodhead Commission's terms of reference to ensure that it would not tamper with the government's initial decision in favor of the principle of partition. These clauses would have (a) limited the Woodhead Commission to consider only issues relevant to partition, (b) noted that offering the Jews permanent minority status in Palestine would be incompatible with the Balfour Declaration, and (c), declared it to be the government's intent to implement partition with or without cooperation by either side in Palestine. The cabinet decided in favor of the Foreign Office to delete these three clauses from the proposed terms of reference.

quite a number of precedents—will be able to form his own conclusions as to what would be in store for us if we accepted the position allotted to us in these "solutions." It is not for the purpose of subjecting the Jewish people, which still stands in the front rank of civilization, to the rule of a set of unscrupulous Levantine politicians that this supreme effort is being made in Palestine. All the labors and sacrifices here owe their inspiration to one thing alone: to the belief that this at last is going to mean freedom and the end of the ghetto. Could there be a more appalling fraud of the hopes of a martyred people than to reduce it to ghetto status in the very land where it was promised national freedom?[56]

The Woodhead Commission Report, published on November 9, 1938, declared, as the government had fully anticipated, that the Peel Commission scheme for partition, which it designated as "Plan A," could not be implemented.[57] One member favored another scheme, "Plan B," under which both the Galilee and a small area in the south would also have been excluded from the already cramped Jewish state proposed in Plan A. Two other members favored "Plan C," which would have greatly reduced both the Jewish and Arab boundaries, retaining under the British Mandate both the Galilee and the Negev as well as the Jerusalem enclave. A fourth member rejected all three plans. The Woodhead Commission concluded that it was "unable to recommend boundaries for the proposed areas which will afford a reasonable prospect of the eventual establishment of self-supporting Arab and Jewish states."[58] In considering the Woodhead Commission Report, the British government concluded in a statement of policy in November 1938, in full accordance with the scenario that had been

---

56. Weizmann, *Trial and Error*, 395.
57. John Woodhead, *Palestine Partition Commission Report*, CMD 5854 (London: His Majesty's Stationery Office, 1938) ("The Woodhead Commission Report").
58. *The Woodhead Commission Report*, cited in Weisgal, *The Letters and Papers of Chaim Weizmann*, Series B, vol. 2, paper 37, fn. 31, 330.

laid out by the Foreign Office, that "the political, administrative, and financial difficulties involved in the proposal to create Arab and Jewish states inside Palestine were so great that this solution of the problem is impracticable."[59] The nature of the financial difficulties in partitioning Palestine was spelled out in striking fashion by the new colonial secretary, Malcolm MacDonald, in his presentation to parliament.

> The Woodhead Commission Report makes it clear that partition, as proposed by the Peel Commission, is impracticable. That report makes it clear that if we were to divide Palestine into a Jewish state, and an Arab state, and a Mandated area, then the Jewish state would have a great surplus in its budget every year, but year after year, the budgets of the Arab State and the Mandated Territory would show great deficits. The commission therefore reported that under their terms of reference, they were unable to recommend boundaries for the proposed areas which would afford a reasonable prospect of the eventual establishment of self-supporting Arab and Jewish states. I think that is itself a remarkable tribute to the achievement of the Jews. It is impossible, without the continuous aid of the Jews, for the people living in Palestine beyond the Jewish settlements to maintain the standard of government and the social services to which they have become accustomed. But that state of affairs also kills the proposal for the dividing up of Palestine into two sovereign states, and His Majesty's Government lost no time in accepting the position. A part of Palestine is not to be handed over to control by the Jews, another part is not to be handed over to control by the Arabs…the government have declared that they will continue their responsibility for the government of the whole country.[60]

---

59. "British Statement of Policy, November 1938" in *The Israel–Arab Reader*, ed. Laqueur, Doc. 16, 62.
60. *Hansard*, House of Commons, Debates, vol. 341, cc1993–1994, November 24, 1938.

The government, in other words, "lost no time" in deciding that the Jews cannot have a state even in a small part of Palestine—despite having been promised under the Balfour Declaration that they could form a state in all of Palestine—not because a Jewish state would not be viable, but, on the contrary, because the Jews are needed instead to continue to serve as the "cash cow" to finance the budget deficits of both the Arab economy and the Mandatory government so as to enable Palestine's Arabs "to maintain the standard of government and the social services to which they have become accustomed." And, as MacDonald emphasized in the same speech, as had the Peel Commission and many members of parliament, Palestine's Arabs had become accustomed to that standard of government and social services only as a result of the financial, economic, and technological assistance that the Jewish national home provided.

MacDonald added that the government intended to hold discussions in London with the Arabs and the Jews in the hope that they could agree on some compromise solution to the Palestine problem but that if the discussions do not yield some kind of understanding within a reasonable period of time, "the government will itself take full responsibility, in the light of its examination of the question."

Parliament Approves the 1939 White Paper for Palestine as an Arab State

With its rejection of the plan for partition, the government was then in a position to adopt the Foreign Office program to repudiate the Balfour Declaration and to transform Palestine into an independent Arab state where the Jews would be limited to permanent minority status. Before announcing its new policy, however, the Foreign Office resorted to yet another screen for the decision it had already made, this time, a London Conference of Jewish Agency and Arab representatives, including representatives of the neighboring Arab states, whose purpose was to consider "future policy, including the question of immigration into Palestine."

The pious hope was expressed that the conference would help to promote agreement between the Arabs and the Jews, but knowing that no such agreement was possible, the government declared that "it had already given much thought to the problem," and:

> If the London discussions should not produce agreement within a reasonable period of time, they will take their own decision in the light of their examination of the problem and of the discussions in London and announce the policy which they propose to pursue.[61]

At the conference opening at the Palace of St. James on February 7, 1939, the Arabs refused, as had been anticipated, to meet jointly with the Jews, and the government met separately with each side. On February 15, the Colonial Minister, Malcolm MacDonald, suggested to the Jewish delegation that in order to facilitate an agreement with the Arabs, they should accept British restrictions on land sales in some areas and total prohibition in other areas. On February 21, the new foreign secretary, Lord Halifax (1938–1940), suggested to the Jews that they should agree to terminating immigration after ten years, unless the Arabs consent to further immigration. The Jewish delegation turned down both requests, as the government must also have surely anticipated. After arranging two informal meetings of Jews with Iraqi and Egyptian representatives, MacDonald proceeded to outline the government's own anti-Zionist proposals for Palestine. The Jews would be limited to a goal of no more than forty percent of the total population, and immigration would be restricted to ten thousand people annually for a period of five years, after which it would cease, unless the Arabs gave their consent. Palestine would evolve toward independence, with safeguards and a share in the government for the Jewish minority.[62]

---

61. "British Statement of Policy, November 1938" in *The Israel–Arab Reader*, ed. Laqueur, Doc. 16, 62–63.
62. Weisgal, *The Letters and Papers of Chaim Weizmann*, Series B, vol. 2, paper 40, February 16, 1939, 360–64.

Both the colonial minister and the foreign minister asked the Jews to agree to Britain's proposal, which amounted to a death sentence for their hope of re-establishing a Jewish state in their ancient national homeland as well as their hopes of providing a safe haven for hundreds of thousands of Jews desperately seeking to escape the death that awaited them in Nazi Europe. MacDonald threatened that if the Jews would not cooperate, Britain would abandon them to their fate.[63] And Lord Halifax told Weizmann that the time had come when expediency should take precedence over principle, pleading that "it would be desirable that you make an announcement of the great principles of the Zionist movement to which you adhere, and at the same time, renounce your rights under the Mandate and under the various instruments deriving from it."[64] The Arabs and the Jews each rejected MacDonald's proposal, albeit for opposite reasons, and on March 15, 1939, the conference ended in a complete stalemate.

Shortly before the government announced its decision, Weizmann cabled Prime Minister Neville Chamberlain from Palestine to warn that it would not pacify the country and that surrender to the terrorist demands would not produce peace—they would compel the government to use force against the Jews, who, having nothing to lose anywhere, would be driven to counsels of despair in Palestine. Weizmann's intervention, including a personal meeting with Chamberlain, proved fruitless. As he later wrote:

> [Chamberlain] was bent on appeasement of the Arabs, and nothing would change his course. What he gained by it is now a matter of history: the Raschid Ali revolt in Iraq, the mufti's services to Hitler, the famous "neutrality" of Egypt, the ill-concealed hostility of practically every Arab country.[65]

---

63. Walter Laqueur, *A History of Zionism* (London: Tauris Parke, 2003), 525.
64. Weizmann, *Trial and Error*, 403–404.
65. Weizmann, *Trial and Error*, 409–410.

The 1939 White Paper for Palestine as an Arab State 181

On May 17, 1939, Britain set forth the government's decision on Palestine in the 1939 White Paper.[66] Under the first of three headings, "The Constitution," Britain repudiated its obligation under the Balfour Declaration and the Palestine Mandate to facilitate the development of the Jewish national home. In its place, it declared, "The objective of His Majesty's Government is the establishment within ten years of an independent Palestine State." It sugarcoated this decision by adding, "The independent State should be one in which Arabs and Jews share in government in such a way as to ensure that the essential interests of each community are safeguarded." Unfortunately, the Jews were expected to take this assurance on faith—the white paper provided no indication of how the government would in fact ensure that an Arab state controlled by the grand mufti's *effendi* colleagues, who "feared and hated the Jewish national home," would safeguard the essential interests of the permanent Jewish minority.

Under the second heading, "Immigration," the white paper declared,

> The alternatives before His Majesty's Government are either (i) to seek to expand the Jewish national home indefinitely by immigration, against the strongly expressed will of the Arab people of the country or (ii) to permit further expansion of the Jewish national home by immigration only if the Arabs are prepared to acquiesce in it… His Majesty's Government… have decided that the time has come to adopt in principle the second of the alternatives…
>
> Jewish immigration during the next five years will be at a rate which, if economic absorptive capacity permits, will bring the Jewish population up to approximately one-third of the total population of the country… This would allow the admission, as from the beginning of April of this year, of some seventy-five thousand immigrants over the next five years. After the period

---

66. *The 1939 White Paper*, reproduced in J. C. Hurewitz, *The Middle East and North Africa in World Politics*, 531–538.

of five years, no further Jewish immigration will be allowed unless the Arabs are prepared to acquiesce in it.

The 1939 White Paper continued with the warning,

> His Majesty's Government are determined to check illegal immigration, and further preventive measures are being adopted. The numbers of any Jewish illegal immigrants who, despite these measures, may succeed in coming into the country and cannot be deported will be deducted from the yearly quotas.

Under the third heading, "Land," the white paper declared:

> There is now, in certain areas, no room for further transfer of Arab land, whilst in some other areas, such transfers of land must be restricted if Arab cultivators are to retain their existing standard of life and a considerable landless Arab population is not soon to be created. In these circumstances, the high commissioner will be given general powers to prohibit and regulate transfers of land.

Fearing the likely outbreak of war with Germany and Italy and anxious about a potential Arab threat to their interests in the Middle East, Great Britain had decided to appease the Arab leadership by abandoning its internationally legal obligations to the Jews under the Mandate for Palestine. There was no need to be concerned about any negative Jewish reaction, since the Jews would have no choice but to support Britain in a conflict with the Nazis. In 1936, Britain had stood by while Mussolini took over Ethiopia. In March 1938, Britain had again stood by while Germany annexed Austria and imposed the Nazi repression of the Jews in that country. In September 1938, Prime Minister Neville Chamberlain had made his infamous Munich Pact with Hitler, permitting him to seize Czechoslovakia. By May 1939, even Chamberlain had come to realize that Hitler's appetite was insatiable, and that despite all previous attempts at appeasement, war with Germany was inevitable. But although appeasement of Germany was ended, appeasement of the Arab leadership continued. In face of the Nazi persecution of the Jews in Europe, Britain had decided to surrender to the threat of Arab terror and to shut the doors to Jews seeking a safe haven in Palestine, where it was internationally mandated to facilitate the establishment of the Jewish national home. Palestine, which the Jews had been promised could evolve into a Jewish state, would evolve instead into an Arab state, where the Jews were to be frozen into a minority of one-third of the total population. Evidently, the Jews were expected to continue to enable Arab Palestine "to maintain the standard of government and the social services to which they have become accustomed," despite the total repudiation of the promise of the Jewish national home.

✡ ✡ ✡

In the Parliamentary debate of May 22–23, 1939, the 1939 White Paper was criticized by political leaders from the government's own Conservative Party as well as from the opposition.[67] Leopold Amery, a Conservative and a former colonial minister (1924–1929), referring to the 1922 Churchill White Paper, declared,

> The Jews were to be in Palestine as of right, and not on sufferance, and no other consideration was to be allowed to prevent their free entry and free settlement as long as that entry and that settlement did not inflict direct injury upon the existing community, Jew or Arab. That was the meaning, the only possible meaning, of the test of economic absorptive capacity. To the principle of that test, every British government since has been pledged… In the present white paper, the whole settlement of 1922 is thrown overboard. It is a direct reversal of principle and policy. It means that henceforth, after a brief interlude of drastic restriction, Jews will only be able to enter their national home on sufferance of the Arabs… What is the watchword now?… The watchword is, "appease the Arabs," appease the

---

67. *Hansard*, House of Commons, Debates, vol. 347, May 22–23, 1939.

mufti. Appease them at all costs. Appease them by abandoning the declared policy of every government for twenty years past. Appease them by breaking faith with the Jews. Appease them at the cost of sacrificing all the prestige which we might have gained from either Jews or Arabs by consistency, by firmness, by justice to both sides… I could never hold up my head again to either Jew or Arab if I voted tomorrow for what, in good faith, I repeatedly told both Jews and Arabs was inconceivable: namely, that any British government would ever go back upon the pledge given not only to Jews but the whole civilized world when it assumed the Mandate.

Churchill attacked the 1939 White Paper in ringing terms, declaring, "I should feel personally embarrassed in the most acute manner if I lent myself, by silence or inaction, to what I must regard as an act of repudiation." Calling the white paper, "the end of the vision, of the hope, of the dream, a confession of recoil" that would tempt the enemy to consider it "another Munich," Churchill warned the government:

> You are not going to found and forge the fabric of a grand alliance to resist aggression, except by showing continued examples of your firmness in carrying out, even under difficulties, and in the teeth of difficulties, the obligations into which you have entered…
>
> Yesterday, the minister responsible…descanted eloquently in glowing passages upon the magnificent work which the Jewish colonists have done. They have made the desert bloom. They have started a score of thriving industries, he said. They have founded a great city on the barren shore. They have harnessed the Jordan and spread its electricity throughout the land. So far from being persecuted, the Arabs have crowded into the country and multiplied till their population has increased more than even all world Jewry could lift up the Jewish population. Now, we are asked to decree that all this is to stop, and all this is to come to an end. We are now asked to submit—and this is what rankles most with me—to an agitation which is fed

with foreign money and ceaselessly inflamed by Nazi and by fascist propaganda.

Churchill concluded with a pointed reminder of the comments Chamberlain had himself made twenty years earlier in support of the Balfour Declaration, when he had said:

A great responsibility will rest upon the Zionists, who before long, will be proceeding, with joy in their hearts, to the ancient seat of their people. Theirs will be the task to build up a new prosperity and a new civilization in old Palestine, so long neglected and misruled.

Churchill continued, "Well, they have answered his call. They have fulfilled his hopes. How can he find it in his heart to strike them this mortal blow?"

The leaders of the opposition Labour Party attacked the white paper in no less powerful terms. Philip Noel-Baker objected:

The secretary of state's proposition is a euphemism for giving way to lawless force. It is a polite way of saying that we will surrender to the mufti and his gang, that in the hope of getting peace, we must do another Munich on the Jews…

This policy is bound to fail. It will fail because in the most tragic hour of Jewish history, the British people will not deny them their Promised Land.[68]

And Herbert Morrison, a minister in both the Churchill and the post-war Attlee cabinets, called the 1939 White Paper,

…a cynical breach of pledges given to the Jews and the world, including America, a thing which is dishonorable to our good name, which is discreditable to our capacity to govern, and which

---

68. *Hansard*, House of Commons, Debates, vol. 347, cc2044 and cc2047, May 22, 1939.

is dangerous to British security, to peace, and to the economic interest of the world in general and of our own country...

It ought to be known by the House that this breach of faith, which we regret, this breach of British honour, with its policy, with which we have no sympathy, is such that the least that can be said is that the government must not expect that this is going to be automatically binding upon their successors.[69]

Chamberlain's Conservative Government, however, had a solid majority in parliament, and the white paper was easily adopted by a vote of 268 to 179. When Britain submitted the 1939 White Paper to the League of Nations, its Mandates Commission declared, "The policy set out in the white paper is not in accordance with the interpretation which, in agreement with the Mandatory Power and the Council, the Commission has placed upon the Palestine Mandate."[70] The MacDonald Commission's finding was due to be taken up by the League of Nations Council, but, with the outbreak of World War II, the Council ceased to meet, and the Mandates Commission's decision remained the League's last official action on the issue. Britain proceeded to enforce the terms of the 1939 White Paper, however, in defiance of the decision of the Mandates Commission.

✡ ✡ ✡

As Weizmann had earlier warned, the repudiation of the Balfour Declaration generated a more militant spirit in the *Yishuv*. The Zionist Executive in Jerusalem, of which Ben-Gurion was Chairman, announced, "The pioneers of the land of Israel, who for three generations have shown their ability to revitalize a barren land, will display their courage in defending immigration, the national home, and the freedom of the Jewish people."[71] And, at the Twenty-First Zionist

---

69. *Hansard*, House of Commons, Debates, vol. 347, cc2142 and cc2144, May 23, 1939.
70. Quoted in Weizmann, *Trial and Error*, 414.
71. Ben-Gurion, *Israel: A Personal History*, 53–54.

Congress in Geneva in August 1939, shortly before the outbreak of World War II, Chaim Weizmann affirmed, "The Jews will stand united in defense of their rights in the land of Israel, rights based on international agreements and the eternal link between the people and their homeland."

Ben-Gurion set the World War II policy for Palestine's Jewish community with the slogan, "We must fight the war as if there was no white paper and fight the white paper as if there was no war." The underground Irgun, which had begun a series of counterattacks upon the Arabs during the Arab revolt of 1936–1939, decided at the outbreak of World War II to cease its attacks. In 1940, however, some members of the Irgun, dissatisfied with this decision, broke away and founded a more militant organization, known by its Hebrew acronym, Lehi, aimed at driving Britain out of Palestine and establishing a Jewish state. And, in 1944, when the Irgun came under the command of Menachem Begin, it too became more militant, embarking upon a policy of attacking the civilian administration, albeit not the military forces, to overthrow the Palestine regime. The Jewish Agency, led by Chaim Weizmann and Ben-Gurion, together with the Haganah under their control, were in firm opposition to the Irgun and Lehi, both of which insisted on maintaining their freedom of action before the State of Israel was established.

Who could have predicted in 1939, viewing Britain as it repudiated the Balfour Declaration and its Mandate, and shut Palestine's gates to the Jews in face of the Holocaust—all in the hope of protecting its imperial interests—that only one decade later, Great Britain would lose all its Empire, and the Jews would realize, against all the overwhelming odds, their two-thousand-year-old dream of the rebirth of their national state, Israel, on its ancient national homeland?

– 8 –

Churchill Keeps the 1939 White Paper in Force

WITH THE ERUPTION OF WORLD War II, the Chamberlain government began rigidly enforcing its 1939 White Paper policy, slamming shut Palestine's gates to Jews, who had no other means of escape from the Nazi horror, while rewarding the Arabs in its concern over military security. Indeed, Colonial Minister Malcolm MacDonald set forth a new policy to restrict Jewish immigration even more than the already-limited quotas set in the 1939 White Paper. He canceled 161 immigration certificates that had been issued before the outbreak of World War II on the grounds that the Jews, who were now under Nazi control, might be sent to Palestine to work for Germany, while their relatives were kept at home as hostages.[1] And two weeks after King Ibn Saud of Saudi Arabia protested that Jewish land purchases were still continuing, MacDonald published new land regulations to prohibit further purchases in much of Palestine.[2]

So closely did the Chamberlain government identify itself with Arab goals that it rejected Palestine Jewry's request to join the British army to fight Germany. In the course of the Arab revolt in 1936–1939, the Palestine administration had provided the Haganah with arms and had permitted Captain Wingate to provide military training for

---

1. For the details of the roles of British and American administrations in blocking avenues of escape for Jews seeking refuge from the Holocaust, see, in particular, David S. Wyman, *The Abandonment of the Jews* (New York: Garland Publishing, 1989–1991).
2. Bethell, *The Palestine Triangle*, 78–86.

the Jews to defend themselves against Arab attacks. But now, with the government having ended the Arab revolt, it transferred Wingate out of Palestine and prohibited the Jews once again from carrying arms. A platoon of the Haganah, including the future Israeli general, Moshe Dayan, which was observed marching in military formation, was arrested and sentenced to long prison terms.

Churchill, who had joined Chamberlain's war cabinet as first lord of the admiralty, protested the government's enforcement of the 1939 White Paper. He warned that Britain might lose the support of American Jewry and emphasized his disagreement with the notion that Britain could not win World War II without the help of the Arabs. But his cabinet colleagues failed to support him.

The Jews were greatly relieved in May 1940, when parliament rejected Chamberlain and his failed foreign and military policy and chose Winston Churchill as the new prime minister. At long last, they could hope for some amelioration of the 1939 White Paper's brutal restrictions on Jewish immigration and for the formation of a Jewish army to fight against Hitler. But they were to be bitterly disappointed on both grounds.

The Request for the Establishment of a Jewish Army Is Rejected

In August 1940, when it became apparent that World War II would spread to the Mediterranean, Weizmann proposed to Churchill the establishment of a Jewish Palestinian fighting force. Noting that it was impossible to say "what the strategic disposition of the British fleets and armies may be before victory is achieved," Weizmann warned: "Should it come to a temporary withdrawal from Palestine—a contingency which we hope will never arise—the Jews of Palestine would be exposed to wholesale massacre at the hands of the Arabs, encouraged and directed by the Nazis and fascists." Weizmann accordingly called for the recognition of "our elementary human right to bear arms, which should not morally be denied to the loyal citizens of a country at war."[3]

Churchill did favor the establishment of a Jewish army, but his Foreign Office, his Colonial Office, his War Office, his chiefs of staff, and his Palestine Administration, were all firmly opposed. They argued that (a) establishment of a Palestinian Jewish fighting force would serve as a provocation to the Arabs and (b) there was a danger that the Jews might turn their guns on the Arabs. Churchill tried to persuade Lord Lloyd, his newly appointed colonial secretary (May 1940–February 1941), to drop his opposition to a Jewish army.

> The failure of the policy which you favor…is proved by the very large numbers of sorely needed troops you have to keep in Palestine…probably more than twenty thousand men… If the Jews were properly armed, our forces would become available, and there would be no danger of the Jews attacking the Arabs, because they are entirely dependent upon us and upon our command of the sea. I think it is little less than a scandal that at a time when we are fighting for our lives, these very large forces should be immobilized in support of a policy which commends itself only to a section of the Conservative Party.[4]

But though Churchill proved to be one of the most outstanding political leaders in British history, in his extraordinary ability to mobilize the British people for victory against the military might of the enemy, he could not muster the strength to override the objections of the ministers of his own government. Churchill approved the establishment of a Jewish brigade in September 1940, but it was not formally established until four years later, in September 1944, when the defeat of Germany was already visible on the horizon.[5]

The government accepted Jews into British army units but did not release its Haganah, Irgun, and Lehi prisoners for war duty until 1941,

---

3. Weizmann, *Trial and Error*, 424.
4. Winston Churchill, *The Second World War*, vol. 2 (London: Cassell & Co., 1950–1955), 172–173.
5. Weizmann, *Trial and Error*, 424–425.

when Italy invaded North Africa and threatened to drive Britain out from Egypt and Palestine. In accordance with the call of Palestine's Zionist Executive upon the Jews to join Britain's armed forces, about 130,000 men and women out of a total population of some 500,000 volunteered to serve in the British military forces, and they made a powerful contribution to the Allied victory.[6] Of special significance was Palestinian Jewry's contribution to General Montgomery's remarkable victory in October 1942 over German Field Marshall Rommel at El-Alamein, Egypt, a victory that kept North Africa, the Suez Canal, and the Middle East in Allied hands and provided the key to the subsequent defeat of Mussolini and Hitler in Europe. On the significance of this contribution to the victory, the American journalist, Pierre van Paassen, wrote:

> Jewish Palestine contributed more effectively to the repulse of the Axis advance upon Syria, Iraq, Egypt, and the Suez Canal, to the triumph of British arms in Ethiopia, Eritrea, and Somaliland and to the final liberation of the Libyan and Tripolitanian coastal regions than the fifty-times-larger populations of the Arab countries combined.[7]

But despite the significance of the Jewish contribution to the Allied victory, Churchill's government not only continued to reject the request for establishment of a Jewish brigade, but it also avoided any public acknowledgement of the Jewish contribution.[8] Instead, the

---

6. Ben-Gurion, *Israel: A Personal History*, 54.
7. Van Paassen, *The Forgotten Ally*, 227.
8. Pierre van Paassen wrote this eloquent protest against the British attitude: "Never once was Jewish heroism mentioned. Not a word leaked out of that numerically small Jewish community standing like a rock in the smoldering hostile Arab world at the back of the British Army. As little as possible was said of Jewish soldiers standing side by side with Englishmen, Australians, and South Africans and facing fearful odds presented by Rommel's overwhelming superiority. And yet, the Near East swarmed with foreign correspondents from the beginning of the campaign to the end. Palestine

Palestine Administration took advantage of the victory to cease its cooperation with the Israeli underground forces. Underlying Britain's ungrateful attitude was its worry that a Jewish army would create a moral claim for government efforts to rescue Europe's Jews from the Nazi Holocaust and, possibly, even for reopening a debate on the 1939 White Paper's repudiation of the Balfour Declaration and the Mandate. As subsequent events demonstrated, the War Office and the Palestine administration were determined not to permit recognition of any such Jewish claims.

The Churchill Government Enforces the 1939 White Paper

Britain's ingratitude for Palestine Jewry's contribution to the war effort pales in significance in comparison to its behavior in enforcing the 1939 White Paper's restrictions on Jewish immigration into Palestine. In light of his magnificent parliamentary speech in 1939 against parliament's approval of the white paper, the Jews had hoped that one of Churchill's first acts in 1940 as prime minister would be its repudiation, or, at the very least, its temporary suspension. But despite Churchill's ringing condemnation of the white paper only a year earlier (see Chapter 7) as "the violation of the pledge...the end of the vision, of the hope, of the dream...another Munich"; despite his insistence upon the urgency of "firmness in carrying out, even under difficulties, in the teeth of difficulties, the obligations into which you have entered"; and despite his query of Chamberlain, "How [can he] find it in his heart to strike them this mortal blow?"—Churchill had the heart to strike the Jews that same mortal blow and to enforce the 1939 White Paper against the Jews with no more consideration of the Jewish plight than might have been expected had Chamberlain continued as prime minister.

Jewry's effort in the war must be considered the best-guarded military secret of all!" (*The Forgotten Ally*, 235–236).

At a cabinet meeting on June 12, 1940, only one week after the heroic rescue of the British army at Dunkirk, Churchill, together with Labour Party leader, Clement Attlee, and Liberal Party Leader, Archibald Sinclair, all declared their continued opposition to the 1939 White Paper. Two weeks later, however, they all agreed at another cabinet meeting that the policy could not be revised under the circumstances and would have to remain in effect.[9] Churchill did tell his cabinet in October 1940 of his intention to repudiate the 1939 White Paper, but his cabinet disagreed, and it was Churchill, rather than his cabinet, who yielded.[10]

The Churchill government continued the Chamberlain policy of exerting pressure on other governments to prevent refugee boats from setting sail, and it used up precious war resources to erect radar stations and patrol the oceans by boats and aircraft in order to detect and follow the movement of refugee ships from the moment they left the European ports. Naval forces were used to detain refugee boats that managed to elude detection at sea and to arrive at a port in Palestine, and its passengers were trans-shipped for detention in Mauritius and other colonies or even turned back to Europe to face extermination.

One of the major tragedies under the Churchill administration involved the Patria, a French liner the British had chartered to transship from offshore Haifa to Mauritius nearly 1,800 seized Jewish refugees in November 1940. It blew up and sank inside Haifa Bay, with a loss of about 260 lives, from explosives the Haganah had brought aboard to sabotage the engines and prevent the deportation. Colonial Minister Lord Lloyd, Anthony Eden, war minister at the time (11 May 1940–22 December 1940), and General Wavell, commander in

---

9. Bethell, *The Palestine Triangle*, 89.
10. Sir Harold Wilson, who served as the Labour prime minister a generation later, blamed Churchill's failure to carry out his decision to repudiate the infamous 1939 white paper on his administration rather than on Churchill himself. In his words, "Downing Street disposes, but before long, the rats get at it—in this case the Colonial Office, the military, and the Palestine Administration" (Wilson, *The Chariot of Israel*, 118).

chief of the Middle East military forces, all insisted upon continuing with the trans-shipment of the surviving refugees.[11] Only Churchill's personal intervention, protesting that to force the trans-shipment of refugees who had been subject to such peril and suffering would be inhumane and unworthy of British honor gained the refugees entry into Palestine, albeit only to Britain's detention camps.

The Jews were made to pay a price for the special compassion shown to the Patria refugees. On December 26, 1940, one month after the decision allowing these refugees to enter, Lord Lloyd, upset over having been overruled, suspended the quota for all legal immigration for three months—until March 1941. The suspension was extended another six months until September 1941 under his successor, Lord Moyne (February 1941–February 1942), costing the lives of thousands of Jewish refugees who were prevented from entering Palestine even within the restricted limits set out in the 1939 White Paper. And Shuckburgh, the colonial permanent undersecretary, after learning of Churchill's compassionate reaction in the Patria affair, decided not to inform him of the suspension of the quota. "Our object," he wrote, "is to keep the business as far as possible on the normal administrative plane and outside the realms of cabinet policy."[12]

The most traumatic tragedy stemming from Britain's callous, and even hostile, policy toward Jewish refugees involved the Struma, a little over a year after the Patria affair. The Struma was one of the "coffin boats" carrying 769 refugees from a Romanian Black Sea Port toward Palestine. Arriving in Istanbul, Turkey, in December 1941, the refugees sought entry into Palestine. Lord Moyne turned down the Jewish Agency's request for immigration certificates for these refugees, even within the existing quota, on the same security grounds Lloyd had previously introduced, namely that Jews from enemy countries might be Nazi agents. Turkey then turned the boat back into the Black Sea,

---

11. Foreign Minister Lord Halifax had yielded only after being stung by Weizmann's query about his Christian mercy.
12. Gilbert, *Exile and Return*, 250–255.

where it sank on February 24, 1942, with the loss of all but two of its 769 refugees. This bit of history is commemorated at Yad Vashem as part of Holocaust history.[13]

Additional opportunities for saving many thousands of Jewish lives were rejected by the Palestine administration. Toward the end of 1942, the Jewish Agency received a proposal to release 4,500 Bulgarian Jews for emigration to Palestine. Lord Moyne, newly appointed British governor of Middle East and Africa (August 1942–November 6, 1944), turned down the Jewish Agency's urgent request for their admission into Palestine within the existing immigration quotas—as he had done the previous year in the case of the Struma refugees—on the grounds they might be Nazi agents. Since virtually all would-be Jewish immigrants into Palestine originated in German-controlled territory, this policy effectively blocked all further immigration and rescue of European Jews, even within the 1939 White Paper quotas.

Security concerns were not the real reason, however, for Britain's refusal of legal immigration and rescue of Jews. The true reason emerged quite clearly in 1943 over the issue of an extraordinary offer by Romania to permit the emigration of around seventy thousand Jews to any place of Allied refuge, with Romania even offering to provide its ships for the voyage. Romania, originally asked about $130 per refugee, but it subsequently reduced the price to less than $2.50 per person. The necessary funds could be released only with the approval of both the United States and Great Britain. In the United States, the State Department, after many months of resistance, had finally been forced, through the exceptional efforts of Treasury Secretary Henry Morgenthau (urged on by a group of righteous officials in his financial division), to agree to the release of the necessary funds for the provision of the immigration licenses. Britain's foreign office, headed once again by Anthony Eden (22 December 1940–26 July 1945) rejected the proposal, however, with this cold-blooded explanation,

---

13. Cruise O'Brien, *The Siege*, 248.

> The Foreign Office are concerned with the difficulties of disposing of any considerable number of Jews should they be rescued from enemy-occupied territory... They foresee that it is likely to prove almost if not quite impossible to deal with anything like the number of seventy thousand refugees whose rescue is envisaged by the Riegner plan. For this reason, they are reluctant to agree to any approval being expressed even of the preliminary financial arrangements.[14]

The five-year quota of seventy-five thousand Jewish immigrants provided for in the 1939 White Paper had a scheduled expiration date of March 1, 1944. Although the government yielded to the public pressure to extend the expiration date, it never filled this immigration quota. In November 1945, months after the war's end, the United States Consul in Jerusalem reported that of the seventy-five thousand certificates under the white paper quota, the British government had deducted twenty thousand as an offset for their estimated number of illegal immigrants since 1939, and an additional three thousand certificates still remained to be issued.[15]

Japanese documentation suggests that some British officials even discouraged other governments from granting the Jews safe haven. In the summer of 1940, the year before Japan entered World War II, Chiune Sugihara, the Japanese consul general in Kaunas, Lithuania, a man of compassion and conscience, took it upon himself to rescue thousands of Polish Jews by providing them with transit visas to Japan in violation of his government's orders. Japanese government files on Sugihara reveal that instead of welcoming such activity, "Britain warned that these unwanted Jews would become a burden for Japan."[16]

---

14. For a detailed account of the Romanian offer and the remarkable efforts of the financial section in the United States Treasury Department to overcome the State Department's opposition to rescuing Jews from the Holocaust, see Wyman, *The Abandonment of the Jews*, 82–83, 182.
15. *Foreign Relations of the United States: Diplomatic Papers, 1945, vol. 8*, 815.
16. Hillel Levine, "Sugihara's List," *The New York Times*, September 20, 1994.

After World War II, Churchill sought to justify Britain's wartime enforcement of the 1939 White Paper on the basis of the need to concentrate single-mindedly on winning the war. In a speech in parliament on August 1, 1946, after losing the election to the Labour Party, Churchill repeated his support of Zionist policy, declaring,

> I have never altered my opinion that the white paper constituted a negation of Zionist policy, which, the House must remember, was an integral and indispensable condition of the Mandate. That is the view I hold today… Then came the war. After the fall of France and the attack upon us by Italy, when we stood utterly alone, we had a great need to concentrate our troops against the enemy and economize in our outlying garrisons and commitments.[17]

Churchill's excuse rings hollow, however. His government did not economize in its commitments to Zionist policy. Instead, it diverted substantial military manpower and equipment as well as financial resources in direct violation of its commitments to the Zionist policy, which as Churchill himself had emphasized, "was an integral and indispensable condition of the Mandate." The very resources the administration utilized to prevent Jews from entering Palestine and escaping the Holocaust could have been employed instead to facilitate their entry and save their lives. After the victory in October 1942 at El-Alamein, which ended the threat to the Middle East, even the excuse, however weak, of the Arab danger no longer existed. As Churchill himself noted in the very same speech before parliament, with the victory at El-Alamein, "This menace was removed at once and for ever."

---

17. *Hansard*, House of Commons, Debates, vol. 426, cc1248, August 1, 1946, reproduced in Robert Rhodes James, *Winston S. Churchill: His Complete Speeches, 1897–1963, vol. 7—1943–1949* (New York: Chelsea House Publishers, 1974), 7373.

Britain's extraordinary expenditure of diplomatic effort and military resources to keep Europe's Jews from escaping the Nazi Holocaust prompted Menachem Begin, leader of the Irgun and future Israeli prime minister, to make this embittered comment, unpleasant as it may be to contemplate, "One cannot say that those who shaped British Middle East policy at that time did not want to save the Jews. It would be more correct to say that they very eagerly wanted the Jews not to be saved."[18]

The Zionist Reaction: Demand for Palestine as a Jewish State

In face of the growing frustration over Churchill's enforcement of the 1939 White Paper, the Zionist movement came increasingly to believe that the problem of Jewish homelessness and helplessness could never be resolved under British rule in Palestine and that only an independent Jewish state could defend the persecuted Jews from destruction. What had until then been a minority position amongst Zionists, upheld by Jabotinsky and his followers in the Revisionist party, was now winning enough converts to achieve a majority within the Zionist movement, both in Palestine and America.

Even Chaim Weizmann, the leader of the "moderate" Zionists, who had always maintained that the British Mandate provided the only hope for the development of a Jewish national home, came to believe in the need for the establishment of an independent Jewish state. As early as March 1940, Colonel Meinertzhagen recorded in his diary that Weizmann had told him upon returning from the United States that it was his intention "to secure American cooperation and demand Jewish sovereignty." Meinertzhagen added, "This was the first occasion on which I found Weizmann inclined to go for the big thing and demand a Jewish sovereign state, a move I advocated in 1919."[19]

---

18. Menachem Begin, *The Revolt: Story of the Irgun* (Nash Publishing, 1977), 63.
19. Meinertzhagen, *Middle East Diary*, 183.

Weizmann went public with this view in January 1942, at the time the fate of the Struma was being decided by Lord Moyne in Britain's Colonial Office. In an article in *Foreign Affairs*, he wrote:

> The Arabs must...clearly be told that the Jews will be encouraged to settle in Palestine and will control their own immigration; that the Jews who so desire will be able to achieve their freedom and self-government by establishing a state of their own, and ceasing to be a minority dependent on the will and pleasure of other nations... A Jewish state in Palestine would be more than merely the necessary means of securing further Jewish immigration and development. It is a moral need and postulate, and it would be a decisive step toward normality and true emancipation.[20]

In May 1942, four months after the Nazi Wannsee Conference formally adopted Hitler's Final Solution to annihilate all European Jewry, the leaders of all Zionist organizations and parties, including Chaim Weizmann and David Ben-Gurion, met for the first United States Conference of the World Zionist Movement at the Biltmore Hotel in New York. Weizmann was living in the United States for the year, working at Roosevelt's request on his chemical project for development of synthetic rubber for the Allied war effort, but Ben-Gurion came from Israel for the meeting. At the urging of Ben-Gurion, the conference adopted what came to be known as the Biltmore Program, which declared that the Mandate could no longer be relied upon for the development of the Jewish National Homeland and called instead for Palestine to be established as an independent Jewish state.[21]

---

20. Quoted in Neumann, *In the Arena*, 169.
21. It was not by mere chance that the Zionist conference in May 1942 had been held in the United States rather than in Great Britain. In part, the venue reflected the change in numbers of Zionist membership—in the European countries, the membership was already being decimated by the Nazi killings, and in Britain, the Zionist membership numbers were much smaller than in the United States. More significantly, however, the decision

200 INDEPENDENCE

The Biltmore Conference declared:

> The new world order that will follow victory cannot be established on foundations of peace, justice, and equality unless the problem of Jewish homelessness is finally solved. The conference urges that the gates of Palestine be opened; that the Jewish Agency be vested with control of immigration into Palestine and with the necessary authority for upbuilding the country, including the development of its unoccupied and uncultivated lands; and that Palestine be established as a Jewish commonwealth integrated in the structure of the new democratic world.[22]

The Biltmore Program went beyond the call for a Jewish state in Palestine, requesting instead Palestine as a Jewish state. Nevertheless, unlike the Peel Commission's 1937 proposal for partition, it called not for transfer of the Arab population but for cooperation with the Arab peoples and states:

> In the new values thus created their Arab neighbors in Palestine have shared. The Jewish people in its own work of national redemption welcomes the economic, agricultural, and national development of the Arab peoples and states. The conference reaffirms the stand previously adopted at congresses of the World Zionist Organization, expressing the readiness and the desire of the Jewish people for full cooperation with their Arab neighbors.

---

marked the recognition by the world Zionist leaders that the United States would inevitably emerge as the major world power at the end of the war. As such, it would henceforth be the United States that would have the major voice in the political solution of the problem of Jewish homelessness and the establishment of a Jewish state.

22. *Declaration Adopted by the Extraordinary Zionist Conference at the Biltmore Hotel of New York City*, May 11, 1942, reproduced in *The Israel–Arab Reader*, ed. Laqueur, 77–79.

The Biltmore Program was presented to the Zionist General Council in Jerusalem on October 15, 1942, where it was adopted by a large majority as the official platform of the World Zionist Movement.[23] The moderate Zionists, in opposition, continued to believe that the focus of the Zionist effort should remain on persuading the Mandatory Power to abolish the white paper's restrictions on immigration and that the issue of Jewish statehood should be set aside. Interestingly enough, Weizmann remained on the side of the moderates rather than the activists. Although he had called for a Jewish state in his article in *Foreign Affairs* and had accepted the Biltmore Program at the conference in May of that year, he regarded the issue of Jewish statehood only as a long-term ideal rather than as a matter of immediate practical significance. It was on this issue that a split that could never be healed developed between Chaim Weizmann, the moderate Zionist leader on the world scene, and David Ben-Gurion, the activist leader of what became mainstream Zionism in Palestine.

The increasing acceptance of an activist position, rejecting reliance on Britain and the Mandate and favoring the establishment of a Jewish state, also marked a significant change in the United States, where the leadership within the Zionist movement gradually passed from Rabbi Stephen Wise, supporter of Weizmann, to Rabbi Abba Hillel Silver, who refused to settle for anything less than the establishment of an independent Jewish state. In the spring of 1943, Rabbi Silver was chosen as co-chairman with Rabbi Wise of the American Zionist Emergency Council, an organization that represented all Zionist agencies in America, and in the summer of 1945, he was elected president of the Zionist Organization of America.[24]

The change of leadership in World Zionism from Weizmann to Ben-Gurion and in American Zionism from Rabbi Wise to Rabbi Silver became particularly marked at the World Zionist Conference held in London in August 1945, after the end of World War II but

---

23. Jewish Agency for Israel, *Jewish Zionist Education*, vol. 7: *World War II*.
24. Neumann, *In the Arena*, 195–210.

just before the surrender of Japan. At that conference, Rabbi Judah Leib Fishman, leader of the religious Zionists, the Mizrachi, declared his hope of seeing Palestine established as a Jewish state. Weizmann dissociated himself from the rabbi's comments, shocking his listeners with the comment, "It is all very well for Rabbi Fishman to speak as he did, for he is a believer—a believing Jew; but what shall I do, who am not a believer and cannot associate myself with his words and expectations about a Jewish state?"[25] Ben-Gurion replied in anger, "Dr. Weizmann has expressed his own view—he did not speak for the Jewish people." The conference then proceeded to adopt a resolution, favored by Ben-Gurion and Rabbi Silver, even more explicit in its phrasing than the Biltmore resolution. It called for a Jewish state in Palestine—"undivided and undiminished."[26]

Palestinian Jewry's Reaction: Increased Militancy

Palestine Jewry's reaction to Britain's closing of Palestine's gates to Europe's Jews was a significant increase in its militancy. The Haganah, the Jewish defense arm under the control of the Jewish Agency headed by Ben-Gurion, did continue its longstanding policy of *havlagah*, "self-restraint," during World War II, limiting its operations to defending Jews in the case of Arab attack and not initiating any counterattacks. But although it continued to avoid attacks against the administration, it did adopt and carry out an active program of smuggling Jewish refugees into Palestine in defiance of British regulations against "illegal" Jewish immigration.

Unlike the Haganah, the Irgun actively harassed the civilian Palestine administration, attacking government property and seizing

---

25. Weizmann's profound pessimism in August 1945 may have reflected his deep disappointment over Churchill's response to his request on May 22, 1945, two weeks after VE Day, to permit the Jews still lingering in the Nazi concentration camps to immigrate to Palestine. Churchill shocked Weizmann with his reply that the question of Palestine must wait until the Allies were seated at the peace table.
26. Neumann, *In the Arena*, 210–211.

weapons, while seeking, as far as possible, to avoid the loss of innocent lives. In December 1943, when the Revisionist leader, Menachem Begin, became commander of the Irgun,[27] he began organizing a military revolt against Great Britain, with the goal of establishing Palestine as a Jewish state. Early in 1944, the Irgun published its call to revolt:

> Four years have passed since the war began, and all the hopes that beat in your hearts then have evaporated without a trace. We have not been accorded international status, no Jewish army has been set up, the gates of the country have not been opened. The British regime has sealed its shameful betrayal of the Jewish people, and there is no moral basis whatsoever for its presence in *Eretz Yisrael*... Our people is at war with this regime—war to the end. This war will demand many and heavy sacrifices, but we enter on it in the consciousness that we are being faithful to the children of our people who have been and are being slaughtered... This then is our demand: Immediate transfer of power in *Eretz Yisrael* to a provisional Hebrew government. We shall fight. Every Jew in the Homeland will fight. The God of Israel, the Lord of Hosts, will aid us. There will be no retreat. Freedom—or death.[28]

The third, and smallest, underground fighting force, Lehi, formed in June 1940 by members of the Irgun in protest at its decision at the outbreak of the war to cooperate with Britain, was even more militant. Led by Abraham Stern, the group continued its attacks on the Palestine administration during the war, even targeting key British officials for assassination, to avenge the deaths of thousands of Jewish refugees that their decisions had aided and abetted.

The Jewish Agency and the self-defense force under its control, the Haganah, were firmly opposed to both of the more militant organizations—in part, on political grounds, because the organizations

---

27. Begin arrived in Palestine with the Free Polish Army of the Polish government-in-exile in May 1942.
28. Begin, *The Revolt*, 80–81.

insisted upon operating independently, outside the discipline of the Jewish Agency of mainstream Zionism. In large part, however, the opposition was based on moral and ideological grounds, because the Jewish Agency regarded their wartime attacks against the British administration not only immoral but also harmful to the prospects for partition, which was then under renewed consideration in Britain. In mid-summer of 1944, Ben-Gurion's representative, Moshe Sneh, met with Begin in an attempt to persuade him to give up the Irgun's revolt against Great Britain, but Begin refused, explaining that he was opposed to partition, and, in any event, he could no longer put any trust in Great Britain. In the autumn of 1944, Eliyahu Golomb, head of the Haganah, accompanied by Moshe Sneh, again met with Begin to warn him to give up his "childish games" because they were endangering the prospects for a Jewish state that the London government was promising to Weizmann. Begin again refused and expressed the hope that one day they would be fighting the British together, to which Golomb angrily replied, "We shall step in and finish you."[29]

Churchill Re-Opens the Question of Long-Term Policy for Palestine

Although Churchill permitted the enforcement of the 1939 White Paper against Jewish immigration throughout World War II, he did not accept its long-term policy to convert Palestine into an Arab state. Resisting the pressure from his cabinet ministers, Churchill informed his colleagues on April 18, 1943, "I cannot agree that the white paper is 'the firmly established policy' of the present government. I have always regarded it as a gross breach of faith committed by the Chamberlain government in respect of obligations to which I personally was a party... it runs until it is superseded." Ten days later, on April 28, 1943, Churchill submitted a war cabinet memorandum in which he spelled out his views on the white paper, saying:

---

29. Begin, *The Revolt*, 192–201.

I cannot in any circumstances contemplate an absolute cessation of immigration into Palestine at the discretion of the Arab majority…

We have certainly treated the Arabs very well, having installed King Feisal and his descendants upon the throne of Iraq and maintained them there; having maintained the Emir Abdullah in Transjordania and having asserted the rights of self-government for the Arabs and other inhabitants of Syria. With the exception of Ibn Saud and the Emir Abdullah, both of whom have been good and faithful followers, the Arabs have been virtually of no use to us in the present war. They have taken no part in the fighting, except insofar as they were involved in the Iraq rebellion against us. They have created no new claims upon the Allies should we be victorious.[30]

The Foreign Office rejected Churchill's thesis, providing a more candid argument as the basis of its pro-Arab position, "The question is…not whether we owe the Arabs a debt of gratitude but whether we have important interests centering in the Arab world. The answer must be emphatically that we have—and in particular, our oil interests."[31] Churchill evidently did not agree that oil interests must trump Britain's commitments to the Jews under the Balfour Declaration and the Mandate. On May 5, 1943, only a week after the Churchill memorandum to his colleagues, United States Brigadier General Patrick Hurley, Roosevelt's personal representative in the Middle East, reported to the president that Churchill had been quoted as having said in a private conversation in Cairo, "I am committed to the establishment of a Jewish state in Palestine, and the president will accept nothing less."[32]

The cabinet took up the question of Palestine at the beginning of July 1943. After hearing Churchill repeat that the government was not

---

30. Cohen, *Palestine: Retreat from the Mandate*, 161–162 and 221 fn. 61–63 and 65.
31. Cohen, *Palestine: Retreat from the Mandate*, 163.
32. *Foreign Relations of the United States: Diplomatic Papers, 1943*, vol. 4, 780.

committed to the end goals of the white paper, the cabinet decided to set up a committee to consider and report to the war cabinet on the long-term policy for Palestine. The starting point for consideration was to be not the 1939 White Paper but the 1937 Peel Commission's plan for partition, and the committee was to consider whether that plan, or some variant of it, might be adopted. Churchill had now evidently abandoned as impractical the position he had taken in the 1922 Churchill White Paper that under the Mandate, the Jewish people were in all of Palestine as a matter of right and not of sufferance, subject only to Palestine's economic absorptive capacity. He was now evidently willing to settle for partition, a compromise policy he had firmly rejected in 1937, when he told Weizmann that he, Churchill, would be brokenhearted if Weizmann were to accept it.

Churchill set up the committee with members who had almost all voted in 1939 against the white paper's long-term policy for Palestine as an Arab state. He accepted Eden's appeal, however, for the Foreign Office parliamentary undersecretary to be added to the committee but rejected his request to remove Mr. Lowell Amery, the former colonial secretary, who shared Churchill's views in opposition to the white paper's long-term policy.[33]

The committee met in four sessions between early August and early December 1943. Except for the Foreign Office representative, all of its members—including the new colonial secretary, Colonel Oliver Stanley (November 1942–July 1945), who had voted in favor of the 1939 White Paper—were now in favor of partition, although differing on the area to be allotted to the Jewish state. Amery recommended that the area proposed by the Peel Commission for the Jewish state should be enlarged to extend its proposed coastal area down to the Egyptian border, including the Negev. The Arabs, in turn, would get all of the northern Galilee, which the Peel Commission had proposed for

---

33. See Cohen, *Palestine: Retreat from the Mandate*, 164–182 for a detailed discussion of the Churchill cabinet's consideration of partition as the long-term policy for Palestine.

the Jews. Herbert Morrison recommended even reopening the 1922 Churchill White Paper decision to separate Transjordan from the rest of the Palestine Mandate, declaring that the committee's consideration of the Palestine problem should be extended to include Transjordan.

On October 25, 1943, Churchill told Weizmann at a luncheon at which Clement Attlee was present that he was thinking of the partition of Palestine. He added that Attlee and the Labour Party were committed to it. Attlee, who, as prime minister of Great Britain less than two years later, was to demonstrate his bitter opposition to a Jewish state in any part of Palestine, nodded in agreement. Churchill added that after World War II, when Hitler had been defeated, the Jews would have to be established, "where they belong... I have had an inheritance left to me by Balfour and I am not going to change."[34]

At its third meeting in mid-November 1943, the committee decided in favor of Amery's proposal for partition, with the exception that the Negev should remain provisionally under the Mandate until its economic potential could be determined. In addition, the committee agreed provisionally to a proposal by Lord Moyne, the deputy minister of state in Cairo, that as in the Peel Commission proposal, the Palestinian area assigned to the Arabs should not become an independent state, but, unlike the Peel Commission's proposal, it should be united with Syria in a greater Syrian state rather than with Transjordan.[35]

The Foreign Office reacted strongly against the committee decision. It called partition a breach of good faith and a betrayal of Arab interests, as expressed in the 1939 White Paper, ignoring the fact, noted again by Churchill, that the 1939 White Paper was itself a breach of faith and a betrayal of internationally recognized commitments to

---

34. Abba Eban, *Tragedy and Triumph*, 267, cited in Laqueur, *A History of Zionism*, 541.
35. Presumably such a link of Palestine to a Greater Syria, an ambition entertained by Syrian Arabs and the British military establishment since the period of World War I, would serve as an instrument for eliminating French influence in Syria, when it gained independence after the war.

the Jewish people, embodied in the Balfour Declaration and the Palestine Mandate. At its fourth meeting in early December 1943, the committee overrode the Foreign Office objections, and it reaffirmed its recommendation of the previous meeting in favor of partition.

Churchill accepted the cabinet committee's recommendation. On January, 12, 1944, he wrote to Clement Attlee and Anthony Eden that "some form of partition is the only solution." On January 25, he sent a memorandum to his chief of staff, Lord Ismay, declaring, "There cannot be any great danger in our joining with the Jews to enforce the kind of proposals which are set forth in the ministerial paper... Obviously, we shall not proceed with any plan of partition which the Jews do not support."[36]

The cabinet gave its preliminary endorsement of the committee's report in favor of partition on the same day, January 25, 1944. It agreed, however, to Anthony Eden's request to delay a final decision in order to permit him to consult with his ambassadors in the Middle East. The cabinet also decided to keep the plan secret until after Germany was defeated, in keeping with Churchill's belief that no announcement on the subject should be made until after the end of the war in Europe.

✡ ✡ ✡

The cabinet did not resume consideration of the Palestine problem until August 1944, and the delay was to prove crucial to the final outcome.[37] Just as the 1937 delay had served to replace the preliminary decision for partition with the 1939 White Paper for all Palestine as an Arab state (see Chapter 7), so now the 1944 delay served to

---

36. Gilbert, *Exile and Return*, 268; Laqueur, *A History of Zionism*, 542.
37. Only Amery saw the danger of delay. In a memorandum to Churchill on January 22, 1944, he commented: "The one thing that can make a Solomon's judgment possible is the swift and clean cut. What we cannot afford to do is to saw slowly away at a squealing infant in the presence of two hysterical mothers and amid the ululations of a chorus of equally hysterical relatives in the Arab and Jewish world" (Cohen, *Palestine: Retreat from the Mandate*, 172).

prevent partition from being adopted and to keep the white paper in force for the remainder of Britain's rule in Palestine.

The ambassadors whom Eden consulted reacted as anticipated, and indeed as guided by the Foreign Office, all predicting firm Arab opposition from the rulers of the countries to which they were assigned.[38] One surprising convert to partition was Sir Harold MacMichael, who had succeeded Wauchope as high commissioner of Palestine and served in that capacity in the period 1938–1944. In a dispatch in July 1944, MacMichael, whose enforcement of the 1939 White Paper had made him an assassination target of both the Irgun and the Lehi, declared his support for partition as a second-best solution, because, he was convinced, the post-war pressure for Jewish immigration would be too great for the government to control. If uncontrollable immigration were to take place in an undivided Palestine, he argued, it would be disastrous for British imperial interests and for Middle East security.

At its August 1944 meeting, the cabinet requested of the Colonial Office and the Foreign Office their collaboration in preparation of a final scheme for partition, but no agreement between them proved possible. The Colonial Office submitted its recommendation, the following month, in favor of partition, along the lines previously adopted by the cabinet committee, with boundaries based on existing Jewish settlements. It proposed, however, one major revision of its earlier proposal in order to take account of recommendations made at a conference of the British Middle East representatives that Lord Moyne had called in Cairo. That conference had agreed with Lord Moyne's recommendation against setting up an independent state of

---

38. Anthony Eden wrote to his ambassadors that they "may be surprised that the committee, in the light of their past knowledge of the history of Palestine, should have recommended what is essentially a return to the Peel plan, which was responsible for so much opposition and bloodshed in the years before the war" (Cohen, *Palestine: Retreat from the Mandate*, 172). Eden had evidently forgotten that the Peel Commission had been appointed in 1937 in response to the Arab revolt that had begun the year before, in 1936.

Palestine, but instead of his Greater Syria plan, it recommended the creation of a Greater Transjordan, which should comprise Transjordan and Arab Palestine and should be named Southern Syria.[39] The Colonial Office recommended, therefore, that the Galilee should go to Transjordan rather than to Syria. It also added some further boundary modifications in favor of the Arabs.

The Foreign Office continued to insist, however, that partition would be resisted by the Arabs. Partition would permit unlimited immigration into the Jewish area and would remove the white paper limit restricting Jews to thirty-three percent of Palestine's total population. The Jews, it argued, would then use the Jewish state as a stepping-stone to expand their state so as to embrace all of Palestine and even Transjordan. Partition, therefore, would not solve the Palestine problem but would only transfer it from the Colonial Office to the Foreign Office. It recommended instead a proposal submitted earlier by Colonel Hoskins in President Roosevelt's name, calling for a binational Palestinian State to be governed by Britain under the authority of a newly proposed United Nations in lieu of the Mandate of the now-defunct League of Nations.

The cabinet resumed its discussions of the Palestine issue on September 19, 1944, and again at a session a week later on September 26, 1944, at which the ministers, except for Eden, reaffirmed their support for the principle of partition. They accepted the specific modifications by the Colonial Office from its previous recommendations, replacing the earlier proposed union of Arab Palestine with Syria by union with Transjordan. The new state, to be called Southern Syria, was to get the Galilee, and the future of the Negev was to remain open. The session also stressed the importance of Jerusalem, proposing that it was to be governed by Britain as the guardian of the city that is sacred to all three religions. Eden continued his objections, however, and no final decision was made.

---

39. The Middle East representatives were probably more confident about the prospects for continued British control of Transjordan than of Syria.

During the first week of October 1944, shortly after the cabinet meeting, Eden had his hand strengthened by a decision made by the neighboring Arab states, who, after considerable encouragement from the Foreign Office over a number of years, had decided to form the Arab League to serve as a united front on issues of joint interest. In a speech more than three years earlier, on May 29, 1941, Eden had suggested that it would be "both natural and right that the cultural and economic ties between the Arab countries, yes, and the political ties too, should be strengthened." He had then added, "His Majesty's Government for their part will give their full support to any scheme that commands general approval." Nearly two years later, on February 24, 1943, Eden had repeated, in a speech before parliament, his government's sympathy for "any movement among the Arabs to promote their economic, cultural, or political unity."[40] Now, in October 1944, the newly formed Arab League adopted a resolution declaring, "The rights of the Arabs could not be infringed in Palestine without danger to the peace and stability of the Arab world." Although the Arab states had rejected the white paper at the London Conference in 1939, the Arab League now defined as the "acquired rights" of the Arabs all the anti-Zionist provisions contained in that white paper. The cessation of Jewish immigration, the prohibition of sales of land to the Jews, and the preparation of Palestine for independence called for in the white paper were now claimed as Arab rights that could not be infringed without danger to peace and stability.[41] The rights of the Jews to a Jewish national home in Palestine, embodied in the Balfour Declaration and the League of Nations Mandate, were evidently to be ignored.

Evidently attaching little importance to the Arab League's resolution, Churchill met again with Weizmann on November 4, 1944 and informed him that a government committee had been set up to

---

40. *Hansard*, House of Commons, Debates, vol. 387, cc139, February 24, 1943.
41. Cohen, *Palestine: Retreat from the Mandate*, 146–150.

consider the future of Palestine. He advised Weizmann, "If you could get the whole of Palestine, it would be a good thing, but I feel that if it comes to a choice between the white paper and partition, you should take partition."[42] Churchill added that he was in favor of including the Negev in the future Jewish State and declared that he was in close touch with America concerning the Jewish National Home. Recognizing the intensity of opposition within his own Foreign Office and Britain's weakened economic and political condition as a result of World War II, he stressed that active United States participation would be needed to achieve the goal.[43]

The following month, on December 6, 1944, Wallace Murray, director of the Office of Near Eastern and African Affairs in the State Department, sent a memorandum to Secretary of State Hull concerning a recent Weizmann–Churchill conversation—presumably referring to their November 4 meeting. The highlights of the conversation were:

(a) The British government has not yet made a decision regarding the future of Palestine, and nothing will be decided until after the end of the war with Germany;

(b) Mr. Churchill (whose sympathy to Zionism is well known) frankly recognizes the opposition to Zionism within the cabinet but believes he can carry the day with the support of President Roosevelt. He stressed the need for American participation in the settlement;

(c) partition is under consideration, but no definite plan has evolved that will recognize the need, which Weizmann claims Churchill recognizes, for bringing one and one-half million Jews into Palestine for the next ten years; and

---

42. Abba Eban, *Tragedy and Triumph*, 274, quoted in Laqueur, *A History of Zionism*, 542.
43. Weizmann, *Trial and Error*, 436–437; Laqueur, *A History of Zionism*, 542.

(d) the prime minister was very critical of the opposition to Zionism advanced by certain American Jews, such as Bernard Baruch.[44]

Moyne's Assassination and Churchill's Withdrawal of Support for Zionism

Churchill had suggested to Weizmann that on his way to Palestine, he should stop off in Cairo to see Lord Moyne, who, he informed him, had become friendlier to the Jewish cause. Only two days later, on November 6, 1944, came the shattering news from Cairo of the assassination of Lord Moyne by two members of Lehi. Weizmann wrote to Churchill of his indignation and horror and assured him that the Jewish community would do its utmost to eradicate the evil from its midst. Churchill was so enraged by the assassination of his closest friend in political life, however, that he threatened to withdraw all further support of Zionism.

In a speech before parliament on November 17, 1944, eleven days after the assassination, Churchill pronounced, in inflamed rhetoric:

> This shameful crime has shocked the world. It has affected none more strongly than those like myself, who, in the past, have been consistent friends of the Jews and constant architects of their future. If our dreams for Zionism are to end in the smoke of assassins' pistols and our labors for its future to produce only a new set of gangsters worthy of Nazi Germany, many like myself will have to reconsider the position we have maintained so consistently and so long. If there is to be any hope of a peaceful and successful future for Zionism, these wicked activities must cease, and those responsible for them must be destroyed root and branch... I have received a letter from Dr. Weizmann, president of the World Zionist Organization—a very old friend of mine—who has arrived in Palestine, in which he assures me that

---

44. *Foreign Relations of the United States: Diplomatic Papers, 1944, vol. 5,* 642–643.

Palestine Jewry will go to the utmost limit of its power to cut out this evil from its midst. In Palestine, the executive of the Jewish Agency has called upon the Jewish community—and I quote their actual words: "to cast out the members of this destructive band, to deprive them of all refuge and shelter, to resist their threats, and to render all necessary assistance to the authorities in the prevention of terrorist acts, and in the eradication of the terrorist organization." These are strong words, but we must wait for these words to be translated into deeds.[45]

The irony in Churchill's demand for the Jews of Palestine to match words with deeds evidently escaped him. For Churchill, more than anyone else in British political life, was guilty of failing to translate words into deeds. After his magnificent pro-Zionist speeches in 1939 against the 1939 White Paper, Churchill had kept Palestine's doors shut to Jewish refugees seeking to escape the Nazi death camps. Churchill was decrying the shameful crime of the killing of one British official by two Lehi members, but that official, Lord Moyne, had presided over a policy—still being continued by the Churchill administration in full knowledge of the consequences—that was nothing less than aiding and abetting the Nazi Holocaust.

Churchill's fiery outburst over the killing of one British official was also in striking contrast to Britain's callous indifference regarding the 1929 Arab massacres of Jews, its officials insisting that the government must remain "neutral and impartial between quarrelling Arabs and Jews." And how much of a contrast it was to the attitude regarding those massacres shown by Lady Passfield, wife of Colonial Minister Lord Passfield (see Chapter 6): "I can't understand why the Jews make such a fuss over a few dozen of their people killed in Palestine. As many are killed every week in London in traffic accidents, and no one pays any attention."

---

45. *Hansard*, House of Commons, Debates, vol. 404, cc2242–2243, November 17, 1944, reproduced in James, *Winston S. Churchill: His Complete Speeches, 1897–1963, vol. 7—1943–1949*, 7034–7035.

Colonel Meinertzhagen, whom Churchill had appointed in 1921 as his chief military official in the colonial ministry (see Chapter 5), reacted most sharply to Churchill's anti-Zionist tirade. He wrote, inter alia:

> Churchill's denunciation is on a par with Hitler's reaction to the killing of one of his ministers in Paris a few years ago. Hitler blamed the whole of Jewry and increased his bloody persecution and slaughter. Churchill now threatens Zionism with the withdrawal of the support of [His Majesty's Government] unless they will eradicate this murderous element from their ranks. What hypocrisy!... Less sympathy with the Zionist movement could not have been extended to Jewry, so why pretend to withdraw what has never been given?... When the Arabs were murdering British officials in Palestine for years, were the Arabs as a nation held responsible, was such strong language used in the House of Commons deprecating their murderous activities, were they told that [His Majesty's Government] would withdraw support and sympathy for them if such actions continued? No—the Arabs, whatever they did, were condoned, even though murder, assassination, and violence were political weapons extolled by all Arab peoples... The Palestine administration and the policy of [His Majesty's Government] must shoulder the responsibility for the murder of Lord Moyne. Churchill's statement is an attempt to evade that responsibility.[46]

The Jewish Agency did in fact translate its words into deeds, even attempting to carry out its earlier threat to Begin to "step in and finish you." Ben-Gurion drafted a very far-reaching four-point plan for the liquidation of the terror activity of both organizations: 1. expulsion from his job or from school of anyone connected with the activities of either the Irgun or Lehi; (2) refusal of shelter or refuge to any of the participants; (3) rejection of threats from any of the gangs; and

---

46. Meinertzhagen, *Middle East Diary*, 193–194.

(4) collaboration with the British in the crushing of the terrorism. The Jewish Agency organized an active campaign carried out by the Haganah and nicknamed in the underground as "the season" to hunt down members of the Irgun and to hand them over to the British authorities.[47] Nevertheless, Churchill carried out his threat to withdraw any further Zionist support. In February 1945, Churchill decided to suspend further cabinet discussion of its provisional decision on partition. With this decision, and with Churchill's display in the House of Commons of his anger with Zionism, the push for partition in his cabinet collapsed.[48]

Sir Edward Grigg, the replacement for Lord Moyne in Cairo (November 21, 1944–July 27, 1945), was opposed to partition. Insisting that the Arab League's opposition had increased the danger of partition for Great Britain, he proposed the formation of a new international trusteeship for the whole of Palestine, with Britain retaining its control and administration of the country, but with immigration policy

---

47. Begin, *The Revolt*, 210–211.
48. Given Churchill's loss of interest in Zionism after Moyne's assassination, some doubt may be entertained whether, had he remained in office, he would in fact have carried out his proclaimed Zionist policies even after the war. As already noted in footnote 25, when Weizmann asked Churchill (immediately after the end of the war) for the immediate lifting of the 1939 white paper immigration restrictions, Churchill replied that the question of Palestine must wait until the Allies are seated at the peace table. In August 1946, when Churchill was no longer in power, he declared that for some years past, he had felt that "an unfair burden was being thrown upon Great Britain by our having to bear the whole weight of Zionist policy, while Arabs and Muslims, then so important to our Empire, were alarmed and estranged, and while the United States...and other countries sat on the sidelines and criticized our shortcomings with all the freedom of perfect detachment and irresponsibility." Had he returned to office, he had intended "to put it to our friends in America, from the very beginning of the postwar discussions, that either they should come in and help us in this Zionist problem...on even terms, share and share alike, or that we should resign our Mandate."

set by the international body. Essentially, as Colonel Oliver Stanley noted, Grigg's proposal amounted to the retention of the 1939 White Paper policy but with responsibility for immigration policy shared by an international body, including, in particular, the United States.

At the beginning of April 1945, at an economic conference in Cairo, Britain's Middle East ambassadors unanimously supported Grigg's criticism of partition and urged that every effort should be made to adhere to the 1939 White Paper policy. They emphasized that Palestine was the key to the strategic defense of the Middle East and must remain completely under British rule. Although the white paper called for Palestine to become an Arab state, Britain's Middle East representatives clearly intended for that state to remain under British control.[49]

✡ ✡ ✡

Before the Churchill cabinet could meet again to consider the question of Palestine, World War II officially ended on May 8, 1945, with Germany's unconditional surrender. Attlee withdrew his Labour Party from the wartime coalition government, and Churchill formed a new caretaker Conservative government to prepare for new parliamentary elections. Following a campaign that centered on Britain's future economic and social policy, Churchill lost the election despite his outstanding wartime leadership, and the 1939 White Paper continued in effect when he was succeeded on July 26, 1945 by Attlee and his Labour government.

---

49. Cohen, *Palestine: Retreat from the Mandate*, 180–181.

– 9 –

The US Supports Britain's 1939 White Paper Policy

With its entry into the war, the United States government became as actively involved as Great Britain in the Palestine question, and President Roosevelt, who, like Churchill, had been a firm pro-Zionist before the war, disappointed the wartime expectations of the Jewish people as much as did Churchill. Roosevelt presided over a wartime administration that was as firmly opposed to the Balfour Declaration and the Mandate for a Jewish national home in Palestine as was Churchill's administration.

Roosevelt's Personal Sympathy for Zionism and the State Department's Opposition

Before World War II, Roosevelt's attitude toward Zionism had been very positive. In 1938, when Britain was formulating its policy (crystallized in the 1939 White Paper), Roosevelt told his secretary of state, Cordell Hull, "I was at Versailles, and I know that the British made no secret of the fact they promised Palestine to the Jews. Why are they now reneging on their promise?"[1] Yet, despite his pro-Zionist leanings, Roosevelt often yielded to the pressure of his profoundly anti-Zionist State Department officials. Wallace Murray, the head of the Department's Office of Near East and African Affairs, cared nothing about the fate of European Jewry and was a determined opponent of the Jewish National Home in Palestine. His Division

---

1. Grose, *Israel in the Mind of America*, 134.

of Near Eastern Affairs, headed by Gordon Merriam, was staffed entirely by pro-Arab officers who, under a departmental regulation in effect almost since the division had been established, were required to have some experience of service in the Near East.[2] The officers identified with Arab culture—they spoke Arabic but knew no Hebrew or Yiddish, and they were concerned, like their counterparts in the British administration, with the country's oil interests as well as its educational, archaeological, and missionary interests in the Arab countries. Like so many in the British administration, they had no understanding or sympathy for the depth of the Jewish people's ties to their ancient national homeland, and they considered the Jews only as an alien colonial element imported into an Arab land. They also tended to worry that the Jews were likely to turn Palestine into a communist country.[3] In their Realpolitik approach to policy, they might have conceded that the Balfour Declaration may have been helpful in securing the support of world Jewry in World War I, but they believed that securing and maintaining the support of the Arabs in World War II required the repudiation of the Balfour Declaration and the League of Nations Mandate to facilitate the development of the Jewish National Home in Palestine.[4]

So powerful was Murray's grip on the US policy for Palestine that he took it upon himself to ignore Roosevelt's policy position, without being called to account, either by Secretary Hull or by the president. In April 1939, shortly before Britain's announcement of the 1939 White Paper, Roosevelt again expressed to the British Foreign Office his interest in Jewish immigration into Palestine. He followed this up on

---

2. Evan Wilson, *Decision on Palestine: How the US Came to Recognize Israel* (Stanford, CA: Hoover Institution Press, Stanford University), 6–7.
3. Murray told Chaim Weizmann he was opposed to Zionism because the Jews would convert Palestine into a Communist country. To this, Weizmann replied, "Since coming to this country… I have heard it claimed that the president of the United States is a communist" (Neumann, *In the Arena*, 157–158).
4. Grose, *Israel in the Mind of America*, 135–137.

May 10, with a written comment to Secretary Hull, "I still believe that any announcement about Palestine at this time by the British government is a mistake, and I think we should tell them that."[5] There is no record of the British being informed of Roosevelt's position. Instead, five days later, on May 15, 1939, Murray prepared a memorandum for Secretary Hull, summarizing the main features of the final British decisions on Palestine to be issued in its white paper two days later. Although the new British policy was designed to put an end to Jewish immigration in five years and to convert Palestine into an Arab state, Murray and his office reached the conclusion that "the final British decisions represent perhaps as reasonable a compromise between Jewish and Arab aspirations as it is practicable to attempt to effect at this time."[6] Murray proceeded accordingly to have his officers briefed by the British officials on the new policy adopted in the 1939 White Paper, ignoring Roosevelt's request that the British should be told that their announcement of a new policy on Palestine would be a mistake.[7]

Roosevelt was angered when he received the Murray memorandum in support of the British final decisions on Palestine. On May 17, 1939, the day the British government issued the white paper, and five days before it was adopted in parliament, Roosevelt wrote a remarkable memorandum to Cordell Hull rejecting Britain's rationale for its white paper:

> I have read with interest and a good deal of dismay the decisions of the British government regarding its Palestine policy... Frankly, I do not believe that the British are wholly correct in saying that that the framers of the Palestine Mandate "could not have intended that Palestine should be converted into a Jewish state against the will of the Arab population of the country." My recollection is that this way of putting it is deceptive for

---

5. *Foreign Relations of the United States: Diplomatic Papers, 1939, vol. 4*, 748.
6. *Foreign Relations of the United States: Diplomatic Papers, 1939, vol. 4*, 751–757.
7. Grose, *Israel in the Mind of America*, 138.

the reason that while the Palestine Mandate undoubtedly did not intend to take away the right of citizenship and of taking part in the government on the part of the Arab population, it nevertheless did intend to convert Palestine into a Jewish home which might very possibly become preponderantly Jewish within a comparatively short time. Certainly, that was the impression that was given to the whole world at the time of the Mandate.

Frankly, I do not see how the British government reads into the original Mandate or into the white paper of 1922 any policy that would limit Jewish immigration. The white paper is something that we cannot give approval to by the United States.

My offhand thought is that while there are some good ideas in regard to actual administration of government in this new white paper, it is something that we cannot give approval to by the United States.

Before we do anything formal about this, please talk with me.[8]

Roosevelt evidently added this last sentence as a warning to Hull against any further violation of his instructions.[9] Perhaps in view of Roosevelt's warning, Murray decided to take no action on the president's memorandum. As will be seen later, the failure to register Roosevelt's strong objections to the 1939 White Paper with the British government subsequently proved useful to the State Department in preparing one of its many "glosses"—reinterpretations of Roosevelt's pro-Zionist policy statements into pro-Arab policy positions.

Advisors' Opposition to Wartime Formation of Jewish Army

In addition to the regular State Department staff for Middle Eastern Affairs, Roosevelt employed two personal pro-Arab advisors

---

8. *Foreign Relations of the United States: Diplomatic Papers, 1939, vol. 4,* 757–758.
9. Grose, *Israel in the Mind of America,* 138.

on special missions to the Middle East. Lieutenant Colonel Harold Hoskins, who had been born in Beirut of American missionary parents, was officially on detail to the Near East Division of the State Department, but he had direct access to the president. In June 1942, he collaborated with Murray in urging the president to call for an end to the Zionist agitation for the formation of a Jewish army to fight under the United Nations banner. Like the officials in the Churchill administration, Murray and Hoskins regarded the formation of such a Jewish army as dangerous to the war effort.[10] Roosevelt turned down their request in a memorandum to Secretary Hull on July 7, 1942 in which he wrote:

> The more I think of it, the more I feel that we should say nothing about the Near East or Palestine or the Arabs at this time. If we pat either group on the back, we automatically stir up trouble at a critical moment.[11]

Hoskins did not cease his campaign, however. During a mission to the Middle East, he cabled back from Cairo on January 23, 1943 that if the complicated Arab-Jewish situation would be allowed to drift, "a very bloody conflict is in the making...that will inflame not simply Palestine but in varying degrees, all of [the] Moslem world from Casablanca to Calcutta." He therefore recommended that the United States should issue, preferably jointly with Great Britain, a statement "that would rule out in advance any Allied military support for the extreme positions of either Zionists or Arab nationalists." He further proposed that Emir Abdullah of Transjordan, together with five or six moderate Arab nationalists, be invited to America to present their case to the American public. Similarly, a group of Jewish leaders, including Dr. Judah Magnes, chancellor of Hebrew University

---

10. *Foreign Relations of the United States: Diplomatic Papers, 1942, vol. 4*, 538–540.
11. *Foreign Relations of the United States: Diplomatic Papers, 1942, vol. 4*, 543–544.

and head of *Brit Shalom*, who championed a bi-national Arab-Jewish state in Palestine, should be invited.[12] Undersecretary of State Sumner Welles turned down this suggestion, replying that "our present feeling is that that it would be inadvisable to bring groups of Arabs and Jews to this country for a discussion of the Palestine problem."[13]

Advisors' Opposition to a Post-War Jewish State in Palestine

In addition to Hoskins, Roosevelt had as his personal representative in the Middle East another pro-Arab advisor, Colonel Patrick J. Hurley. Like Hoskins, Hurley warned the president on the dangers that any pro-Zionist policy would pose for US relations with the Arabs. His concern in 1943 was with Churchill's announced rejection of the 1939 White Paper's long-term policy and his promotion of the post-war partition of Palestine (see Chapter 8). On May 5, 1943, Hurley reported to Roosevelt, "There is deep-seated Arab hostility to any immigration program intended to create a Jewish majority in Palestine and to the establishment of a Jewish sovereign state." After noting that during his visit to Cairo, Churchill was reported to have stated that he was "committed to the establishment of a Jewish state in Palestine and the president will accept nothing less," Hurley warned that the Arabs believed that "Washington has forced the British government to acquiesce in the establishment of a Jewish political state in Palestine."[14]

This belief had evidently been fostered by, among others, Sir Ronald Storrs, the first British governor of Jerusalem under both General Allenby and Herbert Samuel. Storrs, who had played a role in the British-inspired Arab riots of 1920 (see Chapter 3), revisited Palestine and several Arab states in 1943 and was apparently still doing

---

12. *Foreign Relations of the United States: Diplomatic Papers, 1943, vol. 4*, 747–751.
13. *Foreign Relations of the United States: Diplomatic Papers, 1943, vol. 4*, 751.
14. *Foreign Relations of the United States: Diplomatic Papers, 1943, vol. 4*, 780.

his bit to win Arab support for Great Britain, even if it would be at the expense of the United States. According to information received by US officials, Storrs had told the leader of the Arab Moslems in Palestine, "His Britannic Majesty's Government is opposed to the establishment of a Jewish political state in Palestine, but Washington is forcing British acquiescence in the establishment of a Jewish political state."[15]

On May 7, 1943, two days after Hurley's report, Secretary Hull transmitted to Roosevelt a copy of Hoskins's report to the State Department on his mission in the Middle East. In this report, Hoskins repeated his earlier warning of the danger of an outbreak of hostilities between Arabs and Jews in Palestine, a danger he attributed primarily to Arab fears engendered by Zionist propaganda for the establishment of a Jewish state. Hoskins proposed, therefore, that the United States, and preferably the four major powers, should issue a statement to relieve existing tensions and win the wartime support of the Arabs. The statement should declare that it would be helpful to the war effort if public discussions and activities relating to Palestine were to cease, and, Hoskins added, it should give assurances on two points: "1. that no final decisions regarding Palestine will be taken until after the war; 2. that any post-war decisions will be taken only after full consultation with both Arabs and Jews." An assurance of such full consultations before any decision was taken was, in reality, as Hoskins surely knew and undoubtedly intended, an assurance to the Arabs that no decision in favor of partition or any other pro-Jewish action would ever be undertaken. Hoskins went on to outline his own recommendation for a post-war solution according to which Palestine would become a bi-national state of Arabs and Jews within a proposed "Levant federation," uniting Lebanon, Syria, Palestine, and Transjordan.[16] It is not

---

15. *Foreign Relations of the United States: Diplomatic Papers, 1943, vol. 4,* 776–780.
16. *Foreign Relations of the United States: Diplomatic Papers, 1943, vol. 4,* 781–785.

difficult to imagine to what extent such a Levant federation would be protective of its Jewish minority's interests.

The messages from Roosevelt's two personal representatives, combined with similar messages from the regular State Department representatives in the field and the protests of Arab ambassadors in Washington, only reinforced the prevailing pro-Arab political campaign in the State Department's Near East Division. On March 16, 1943, nearly two months before the Hoskins report, William L. Parker of the Near East Division had already suggested the desirability of including Palestine in a yet-to-be-formed Arab federation. Referring to a speech by Anthony Eden on May 29, 1941, in which he had suggested that it would be "both natural and right that the cultural and economic ties between the Arab countries—yes, and the political ties, too—should be strengthened" (see Chapter 8), Parker suggested in a State Department memorandum "that Mr. Eden be asked whether the British government has considered the issuance of a statement... to the effect that the British government would view with favor any plan for an Arab federation upon which the Arab peoples themselves could agree." Mr. Parker added, "A statement of this kind would refer specifically to Palestine and would be based squarely on principles enunciated in the Atlantic Charter."[17] The Atlantic Charter, a more common name for a joint declaration of a set of peace principles for a better post-war world—prepared by Churchill and Roosevelt in August 1941, before the United States entered the World War—was adopted by the United Nations in 1942. Included among these principles is:

> [The United Kingdom and the United States] respect the right of all peoples to choose the form of government under which they will live, and they wish to see sovereign rights and self-government restored to those who have been forcibly deprived of them.

---

17. *Foreign Relations of the United States: Diplomatic Papers, 1943, vol. 4,* 763–764.

Mr. Parker failed to provide any explanation as to how including Palestine in an Arab federation and totally ignoring the rights of the Jewish people to a Jewish national homeland in Palestine, as embedded in the Balfour Declaration and the League of Nations Mandate, could be reconciled with—let alone be "based squarely" on—this principle of the Atlantic Charter, which pledges to "respect the right of all peoples to choose the form of government under which they will live."

Two weeks later, on March 29, 1943, Wallace Murray, head of the Near East and African staff, followed up Parker's proposal in a meeting with Eden's deputy undersecretary, whom he asked "whether the British government had considered the issuance of a statement, either by itself or jointly with the American government, for the purpose of putting an end to the current agitation for a Jewish state in Palestine." Murray pointed out that the agitation referred to:

> …was having dangerous repercussions in the Arab world and… the declaration, which would be based squarely on the principles of the Atlantic Charter, might go beyond Mr. Eden's statement of May 31, 1941, by referring specifically to Palestine.[18]

Thus, at the time that Churchill and Roosevelt, the authors of the Atlantic Charter, were promoting the post-war establishment of a Jewish state in Palestine, their staff members were working assiduously to prevent such an outcome and were promoting instead the establishment of an Arab federation including Palestine.

Roosevelt Reverses Course under State Department Pressure

The anti-Zionist activities of the president's two personal representatives in the Middle East, Colonel Hoskins and General Hurley,

---

18. *Foreign Relations of the United States: Diplomatic Papers, 1943, vol. 4*, 764–765.

along with those of Murray and his staff, proved quite successful. They stimulated a batch of communications from the leaders of the Arab countries, who were expressing their fears and worries over Palestine. On April 30, 1943, Ibn Saud, who only two weeks earlier had stated that he preferred to be silent so as not to embarrass the president, also wrote to Roosevelt to express his concern about Zionist aspirations in Palestine.[19] The flurry of letters from the Arab countries and the reports of his own officials had their intended impact upon the president. In his letter of reply to Ibn Saud on May 26, 1943, drafted for him by the State Department, the president included the far-reaching anti-Zionist assurance earlier proposed by Hoskins: "It is the view of the government of the United States that no decision altering the basic situation of Palestine should be reached without full consultation with both Arabs and Jews."[20] This assurance was given to Ibn Saud at a time when the Jewish community was desperately looking for help to rescue Jews from the Holocaust. It meant that there could be no change in the policy against Jewish immigration to Palestine laid down in Britain's 1939 White Paper. Bartley Crum, a member of the 1946 Anglo-American committee to recommend a solution to the Palestine problem who was shown the State Department records on Palestine, later commented on this letter:

> This, of course, implied that nothing would be done. It was a vitally important message, because at that moment, delicate negotiations were going on in Europe for the ransoming of Jews. Difficult though it is to say, this note may have helped send to death additional hundreds of thousands of European Jews.[21]

---

19. *Foreign Relations of the United States: Diplomatic Papers, 1943, vol. 4*, 768–771, 773–775.
20. *Foreign Relations of the United States: Diplomatic Papers, 1943, vol. 4*, 786–787.
21. Bartley Crum, *Behind the Silken Curtain: A Personal Account of Anglo-American Diplomacy in Palestine and the Middle East* (Port Washington, NY: Kennikat Press), 39.

The guarantee was also clearly designed to ensure that no Jewish state would ever arise in Palestine, since, as the State Department knew well, no Arab state would ever agree to such a decision. It became the cornerstone of American policy on Palestine, with the State Department making certain that this US government assurance would be repeatedly invoked in US government correspondence with every Arab state.[22]

In June 1943, Roosevelt sent Secretary of State Cordell Hull his approval for issuing a statement, either jointly with Great Britain or by the United Nations, along the lines earlier suggested by Hoskins and Murray, intended "to put an end to the current agitation for a Jewish state...with its dangerous repercussions in the Arab world." Eden stated his preference for a joint statement of the two governments, and he proposed some minor changes in the wording to strengthen the text. The revised text was again submitted to Roosevelt, who gave it his approval on July 19, 1943, and the declaration was scheduled for simultaneous publication in Washington and London on July 27, 1943.[23]

Despite all these preparations, the statement was not issued. Only after the text had been twice submitted to and approved by Roosevelt and only after the publication date had already been scheduled did Secretary Hull decide to consult Secretary of War Henry Stimson on the validity of the State Department's worries that the agitation on Palestine posed a serious danger to the war effort. Stimson replied that after investigation, they "had come to the conclusion that the security situation in Palestine was not so serious as to warrant any action from a military point of view and that the War Department did not propose to take the matter up." Under the circumstances, Hull had no choice but to abandon the joint proposal at the last moment, and he so informed Britain's Foreign Office on August 7, 1943. Both Foreign

---

22. Wilson, *Decision on Palestine*, 34.
23. *Foreign Relations of the United States: Diplomatic Papers, 1943, vol. 4*, 790–792, 797–801.

Secretary Eden and Colonial Minister Colonel Stanley expressed their great disappointment to US Ambassador John G. Winant.[24] At the Quebec Conference on August 21, 1943, the British again sought to have the US agree to issue the declaration. Hull sent a copy of the Quebec communication to Stimson for his comments, but Stimson replied that he saw no reason to change his view that the military situation does not warrant the issuance of the declaration.[25]

Hoskins was not content, however, to let the issue rest. On September 27, 1943, he once again returned to the issue in his conversation with the president, reminding him that both he and Britain had already approved the declaration. The president told him, however, that both governments had now withdrawn their support, and the statement would not be issued.[26]

Because of Hoskins' persistent anti-Zionist urgings, Roosevelt now came to change his position on the Jews and on Jewish immigration to Palestine to a level that seems difficult to believe. In a report to the State Department, Hoskins asserted that in his conversation with the president, Roosevelt had mentioned that he had been "receiving an increasing amount of information that indicated that many European Jews after the war would not care to migrate to Palestine but would prefer to return to their countries of origin."[27] Murray spelled out, in more callous language, the anti-Zionist policy implications behind the wishful thinking attributed to Roosevelt, adding a warning:

> As the Zionists wish for political reasons to place as many Jews in Palestine as possible, it will be necessary to see to it that European Jews are not dragooned [*sic*] into emigrating to

---

24. *Foreign Relations of the United States: Diplomatic Papers, 1943, vol. 4*, 802–804.
25. *Foreign Relations of the United States: Diplomatic Papers, 1943, vol. 4*, 804–805, 810–811.
26. *Foreign Relations of the United States: Diplomatic Papers, 1943, vol. 4*, 813.
27. *Foreign Relations of the United States: Diplomatic Papers, 1943, vol. 4*, 811–814.

Palestine in excess of the emigration that is absolutely required by their situation.[28]

According to Hoskins, the president had apparently now come to believe, as Murray claimed, that many Jewish survivors from Hitler's "Final Solution" would not care to emigrate to Palestine, to be embraced by their fellow Jews eagerly awaiting them, many of whom, indeed, were the parents, children, siblings, or other relatives of their own destroyed families. They would prefer instead to return to live among the mass murderers of their entire families and communities. And evidently, the good citizens of these countries would eagerly welcome them back, return the Jewish homes and property they had seized, and restore the Jewish survivors to their jobs and professions from which they had ousted them before shipping them off to the gas chambers.

Hoskins also reported that he had discussed with the president the issue of post-war policy for Palestine, emphasizing once again "that the establishment of a Jewish state in Palestine can only be imposed by force and can only be maintained by force." The president had then stated, according to Hoskins, "that his own thinking leaned toward a wider use of the idea of trusteeship for Palestine—of making Palestine a real Holy Land for all three religions, with a Jew, a Christian, and a Moslem as the three responsible trustees."[29] Originally, the president had insisted, like Churchill, that he would accept nothing less than a Jewish state in Palestine, but evidently, he had abandoned that idea by the fall of 1943. The State Department was very pleased to learn of Roosevelt's new thinking on Palestine. Murray proceeded to spell out a program for a trusteeship, completely rejecting any notion of a Jewish state. Murray's proposed trusteeship consisted, however, of three or six Christians, two Moslems, and only one Jew, instead of

---

28. *Foreign Relations of the United States: Diplomatic Papers, 1943, vol. 4,* 816–821.
29. *Foreign Relations of the United States: Diplomatic Papers, 1943, vol. 4,* 811–814.

the three equal trustees, as Roosevelt had suggested. For good measure, the appointment of the Jewish representative was to be rotated amongst a Zionist, a non-Zionist, and an anti-Zionist.[30] The Near East Division kept working on the new proposal for trusteeship, and with some refinements, this became the firmly held position of the State Department[31] until it finally had to be abandoned with President Truman's surprise recognition of the State of Israel in May 1948.

Roosevelt's Deceptive Assurances to the Zionist Leadership

Roosevelt's thinking on Palestine took yet another series of twists and turns in 1944. At the beginning of the year, an election year, bipartisan resolutions were introduced in both Houses of Congress in support of the Zionist goals for Palestine to become a Jewish state. The resolutions called upon the United States:

> ...use its good offices and take appropriate measures to the end that the doors of Palestine shall be opened for the free entry of Jews into that country...so that the Jewish people may ultimately reconstitute Palestine as a free and democratic Jewish commonwealth.[32]

The resolutions produced another flurry of communications from the rulers of the Arab countries, addressed to the US representatives stationed there, to the State Department, to the president, and to the senators involved. Britain's Foreign Office also expressed its unhappiness with the resolutions.[33]

---

30. *Foreign Relations of the United States: Diplomatic Papers, 1943, vol. 4*, 816–821.
31. Wilson, *Decision on Palestine*, 37.
32. *Foreign Relations of the United States: Diplomatic Papers, 1944, vol. 5*, 560–561.
33. The British undersecretary of state for foreign affairs denied that his government had anything to do with these Arab protests against the resolutions,

Roosevelt and his administration were opposed to the resolutions, but Roosevelt did not think it wise, especially in an election year, to go public with his opposition. Secretary of State Hull again sought the help of War Secretary Stimson in opposing these resolutions. With Roosevelt's approval, Stimson wrote in private to the chairmen of the Senate and the House Committees on Foreign Affairs, stating that the resolutions were prejudicial to the war effort. Hull then followed up with a letter that in view of the military considerations noted by Stimson, no further action would be advisable. When Congress still failed to shelve the resolutions, Roosevelt and Hull sought to have Stimson make his letters to Congress public, but Stimson objected. Congress shelved the resolutions on March 17, 1944, after General George Marshall, then chief of staff responsible for the conduct of the war, testified in private before Congress, and Stimson sent a second letter to the House Committee, which its chairman, Congressman Sol Bloom, made public.[34]

Although he was working behind the scenes to kill the resolutions in support of Jewish immigration and a Jewish state, Roosevelt evidently felt that he could not afford to be silent in an election year on an issue that was of such urgent concern to the entire Jewish community and on which, in the past, he himself had demonstrated a very favorable attitude. On March 9, 1944, therefore, Roosevelt invited the Zionist leaders, Rabbi Stephen Wise and Rabbi Abba Hillel Silver, to the White House in order to reassure American Jewry of his support for their cause. Although he could not go so far as to endorse the position taken in the congressional resolutions, which he was working to shelve, he did authorize the two rabbis to issue a more ambiguous but nevertheless positive statement in his name. Upon leaving his office, the two rabbis announced that the president had authorized them to state:

---

but reports to the contrary were received by US officials in the region (*Foreign Relations of the United States: Diplomatic Papers, 1944, vol. 5*, 603).

34. *Foreign Relations of the United States: Diplomatic Papers, 1944, vol. 5*, 563–591.

> The American government has never given its approval to the White Paper of 1939... When future decisions are reached, full justice will be done to those who seek a Jewish national home for which our government and American people have always had deepest sympathy—and today more than ever in view of [the] tragic plight of hundreds of thousands of homeless Jewish refugees."[35]

Even this statement of support for the Jewish goals on Palestine was too much for the State Department, and it persuaded the president to shift gears once again. Within the week, after warning Roosevelt of the Arab protests, the State Department received the president's approval for Hull to circulate a message to its representatives in the Arab countries that declared, "with some subtlety," as Evan Wilson, a former official of the Near East Division, subsequently described it:

> You should point out that the statement mentions a Jewish national home rather than a Jewish commonwealth... You should say that while it is true that the American government has never given its approval to the White Paper of 1939, it is also true that this government has never taken a position with regard to the White Paper.

The message added the assurance that US policy remains that no decision altering the basic situation of Palestine should be taken without full consultation with both Arabs and Jews.[36] How the promise that "full justice will be done to those who seek a Jewish national home" could be reconciled with the promise of no decision to be taken "without full consultation with both Arabs and Jews" was left unexplained.

It is difficult to know what to make of such double-talk by Roosevelt, promoted by the Near East Division of the State Department,

---

35. *Foreign Relations of the United States: Diplomatic Papers, 1944, vol. 5,* 588.
36. *Foreign Relations of the United States: Diplomatic Papers, 1944, vol. 5,* 590–591; Wilson, *Decision on Palestine,* 42–43.

especially in light of Roosevelt's firm memorandum to Secretary Hull in 1939 that spelled out his strong objections to the 1939 White Paper. Evan Wilson, writing thirty-five years after the event, remained quite pleased with his division's performance, in this as in other instances. In response to the criticism leveled by some writers against such tactics, Evan Wilson responded:

> Commenting in general on our attempts to put a gloss on presidential statements, the pro-Zionist author, Frank Manuel, has some rather harsh words to say about what he calls the "clever double-dealing" of the members of the Near East Division. He says that we might think we were practicing astute diplomacy when our efforts were only a "clumsy imitation of the British." I believe, on the other hand, that we did pretty well, here and elsewhere, in getting the president out of a tight situation.[37]

The second half of the year saw yet another sharp turn in Roosevelt's pronouncements on Palestine. On June 27, 1944, the Republican National Convention adopted a pro-Zionist plank in its platform, calling for unrestricted Jewish immigration and land ownership in Palestine "so that in accordance with the full intent and purpose of the Balfour Declaration of 1917 and the Resolution of a Republican Congress in 1922, Palestine may be constituted as a free and democratic commonwealth."[38] The Democratic National Convention followed suit on July 24, 1944, with a similar plank, calling for the establishment in Palestine of a "free and democratic Jewish commonwealth."[39]

As the presidential campaign neared its climax in the fall of 1944, Roosevelt evidently became concerned that he might be outbid on the Palestine issue by his Republican opponent, Governor Thomas Dewey of New York. This concern led him to make a complete

---

37. Wilson, *Decision on Palestine*, 42–43.
38. *Foreign Relations of the United States: Diplomatic Papers, 1944*, vol. 5, 605 fn.
39. *Foreign Relations of the United States: Diplomatic Papers, 1944*, vol. 5, 606 fn.

political somersault on the issue. Roosevelt now issued another public statement in which he explicitly and unequivocally endorsed the Democratic platform calling for free Jewish immigration into Palestine and the establishment there of a Jewish commonwealth. In a letter dated October 15, 1944 addressed to Senator Robert Wagner of New York, who was to attend the convention of the Zionist Organization of America, Roosevelt wrote:

> Please express my satisfaction that in accord with the traditional American policy and in keeping with the spirit of the "four freedoms," the Democratic Party at its July convention this year included the following plank in its platform: "We favor the opening of Palestine to unrestricted Jewish immigration and colonization and such a policy as to result in the establishment there of a free and democratic Jewish commonwealth."
>
> Efforts will be made to find appropriate ways and means of effectuating this policy as soon as practicable. I know how long and ardently the Jewish people have worked and prayed for the establishment of Palestine as a free and democratic Jewish commonwealth. I am convinced that the American people give their support to this aim, and if re-elected, I shall help to bring about its realization.[40]

Roosevelt's endorsement of the plank for the establishment of Palestine as a Jewish state was too explicit to be reinterpreted by any "subtle" State Department gloss. In his book, cited earlier, Evan Wilson does make an attempt at such a gloss by suggesting that "the pledge was so worded that it might be interpreted as having been given as a personal rather than official assurance."[41] But it is Evan Wilson's gloss that appears to have been "personal rather than official." The Near East Division prepared a series of memoranda calling attention to the Arab protests against the American support

---

40. *Foreign Relations of the United States: Diplomatic Papers, 1944, vol. 5,* 615–616.
41. Wilson, *Decision on Palestine,* 45.

for Zionism and emphasizing the risks to American interests in the Arab world. Murray urged the new undersecretary, Edward Stettinius, to bring the problem to the president's attention even in the midst of the election campaign.[42] Stettinius decided to wait until after the election. Roosevelt was easily re-elected to an unprecedented fourth term. It was estimated that he received over ninety percent of the American Jewish vote.[43]

The Murray memorandum, which Stettinius sent on December 13, 1944, warned the president:

> The recent pro-Zionist statements in this country...gave rise to a wave of shocked disillusionment and protest in the Near East... If this trend should continue, it would seriously prejudice our ability to afford protection to American interests, economic and commercial, cultural and philanthropic, throughout the area. It, of course, would have a very definite bearing upon the future of the immensely valuable American oil concession in Saudi Arabia.

The memorandum went on to introduce a new concern of the State Department regarding US interests in the Middle East. It emphasized that the political position of the US in the Near East *vis-à-vis* both Great Britain and Soviet Russia would also be weakened by American support of Zionism. The British, the memo noted, "naturally welcome any development which strengthens their own position with the Arabs," and the Russians, who were opposed to Zionism, were eager to expand their influence in the Arab world.[44]

The State Department warnings were not without effect. On October 10, 1944, five days before Roosevelt's letter to Senator Wagner endorsing the Democratic platform in favor of the establishment of

---

42. *Foreign Relations of the United States: Diplomatic Papers, 1944*, vol. 5, 624–6.
43. Grose, *Israel in the Mind of America*, 146.
44. *Foreign Relations of the United States: Diplomatic Papers, 1944*, vol. 5, 636 fn, 648–649.

a democratic Jewish commonwealth in Palestine, Secretary of War Stimson had written to Senator Taft that the War Department no longer had any objection to the Congressional resolutions in favor of Jewish immigration and a Jewish state in Palestine.[45] Congress had then decided to reopen the issue. However, Roosevelt and his newly appointed secretary of state, Edward R. Stettinius, considered this to be unwise. On December 6, 1944, a month after Roosevelt's re-election, Stettinius issued a statement opposing the passage of the resolutions "from the standpoint of the general international situation." Under the circumstances, Congress again withdrew the resolutions.[46] It was not until one year later, in December 1945, after Truman became president following the sudden death of President Roosevelt in April 1945, that Congress finally adopted its resolutions on this subject. The resolutions called for the free entry of Jews into Palestine to the maximum of its agricultural and economic potential so as to enable them "freely to proceed with the upbuilding of Palestine as the Jewish National Home" and to establish Palestine as a democratic Jewish commonwealth.[47]

Roosevelt's Meeting with Ibn Saud and His Confirmation of Pro-Arab Assurances

The final combination of twists in Roosevelt's Palestine policy came from a meeting with Ibn Saud on February 14, 1945 following the Yalta (Crimea) Conference (February 4–11, 1945) of the three main wartime leaders, Roosevelt, Churchill, and Stalin. Roosevelt had set up the meeting to persuade Ibn Saud to agree to a proposal for setting up a Jewish state in Palestine, but in fact, the subject was

---

45. *Foreign Relations of the United States: Diplomatic Papers, 1944, vol. 5*, 618 fn.
46. *Foreign Relations of the United States: Diplomatic Papers, 1944, vol. 5*, 641–646.
47. *Foreign Relations of the United States: Diplomatic Papers, 1945, vol. 8*, 841–842.

never broached, and the meeting only gave Ibn Saud an opportunity to vent his rage against the Jews.

The official memorandum of the conversation between Roosevelt and Ibn Saud, as signed by the president, begins with the statement, "The president asked His Majesty for his advice regarding the problem of Jewish refugees driven from their homes in Europe." Ibn Saud replied that the Jews should return to the homes from which they were driven or, if this were not feasible, that they should be given living space in the Axis countries that oppressed them. The president's reply was that since the Germans killed three million Polish Jews, there should be space in Poland for the resettlement of many homeless Jews. Only the president's grave illness at the time—the gravity of which was known only to those closest to him—could possibly account for such an unfeeling response that the Jewish survivors would be willing to return to Poland, where their entire families had been massacred and entre towns wiped out and for such a naïve belief that the Poles would be willing to give up the Jewish homes and properties they had appropriated and welcome back the Jews.

Ibn Saud then presented the Arab case for Palestine and stated that the Arabs and the Jews could never cooperate, neither in Palestine nor in any other country. The Arabs, he said, "would choose to die rather than yield their lands to the Jews." When Ibn Saud stated that the Arabs base their hopes upon the expectation that the United States would support them, Roosevelt responded with an extraordinary pledge, declaring that "he wished to assure His Majesty that he would do nothing to assist the Jews against the Arabs and would make no move hostile to the Arab people." It is impossible to see how Roosevelt could reconcile his pledge to Ibn Saud with the pledge he had given to the Jewish people in his public letter to Senator Wagner on October 15, 1944, only four months before his meeting with the king.[48]

---

48. Richard Crossman, a Labour member of parliament, who in 1946 served on the Anglo-American Committee of Inquiry on Palestine, reported that three of his committee colleagues who spoke with Ibn Saud in Saudi Arabia returned with the following report of the king's conversation with

Ibn Saud further suggested sending an Arab mission to America and England to expound the case of the Arabs and Palestine. The president replied he thought that this was a very good idea, because many people in America and England are misinformed. Ibn Saud replied that such a mission would be useful, "but more important to him was what the president had just told him concerning his own policy toward the Arab people."[49]

As Harry Hopkins, the president's closest adviser, described the meeting:

> It developed into a monologue by Ibn Saud: When the president asked Ibn Saud to admit some more Jews into Palestine, indicating that it was such a small percentage of the total population of the Arab world, he was greatly shocked when Ibn Saud said, "No." ... He stated plainly that the Arab world would not permit a further extension beyond the commitment already made for future Jewish settlement in Palestine. He clearly inferred that the Arabs would take up arms before they would consent to that, and he, as religious leader of the Arab world, must naturally support the Arabs in and about Palestine.[50]

On his return to the United States, Roosevelt appeared at a joint session of Congress on March 1, 1945 to report on the Yalta Conference. In the course of his speech, Roosevelt turned to his meeting with Ibn Saud, which occurred after the conference, and shocked his

---

Roosevelt: "I then said if you assure me that you are speaking man to man, I would ask you why you are so insistent on the immigration of the Jews into Palestine and on giving them domination there, contrary to justice." Roosevelt replied, "I tell you frankly that I neither ordered nor approved of the immigration of Jews to Palestine, nor is it possible that I should approve it" (Richard Crossman, *Palestine Mission* [New York: Arno Press, 1977], 165–166).

49. *Foreign Relations of the United States: Diplomatic Papers, 1945, vol. 8*, 2–3.
50. Robert E. Sherwood, *Roosevelt and Hopkins: An Intimate History* (New York: Enigma Books, 2001), 517–518.

listeners in and out of Congress with this comment: "On the problem of Arabia, I learned more about that whole problem, the Moslem problem, the Jewish problem, by talking with Ibn Saud for five minutes than I could have learned in the exchange of two or three dozens of letters."

Harry Hopkins later commented: "I gained the impression the president was overly impressed by what Ibn Saud said. And I never could reconcile the president's statement at a press conference later that he had learned more from Ibn Saud about Palestine in five minutes than he had learned in a lifetime—because the only thing he learned, which all people well acquainted with the Palestine cause know, is that the Arabs don't want any more Jews in Palestine."[51]

This was still not the end of Roosevelt's twists and turns on Palestine. Rabbi Wise, upon hearing Roosevelt's statement, asked for a meeting with the president. After seeing Roosevelt on March 16, 1945, Wise emerged to report that the president had authorized him to say that he stood by his pledge of October 15, 1944 to Senator Wagner to establish Palestine as a democratic Jewish commonwealth. According to *The New York Times* of March 17, Wise stated that he had been authorized to quote the president as saying, "I made my position on Zionism clear in October. That position I have not changed, and [I] shall continue to seek to bring about its earliest realization."[52]

This zig-zag naturally aroused Arab protests. After satisfying himself that Rabbi Wise had in fact quoted the president accurately, Murray warned that the Arab world would react with dismay and consternation. In his memorandum to the acting secretary of state, Murray warned, "The president's continued support of Zionism may thus lead to actual bloodshed in the Near East and even endanger the security of our immensely valuable oil concession in Saudi Arabia."[53]

---

51. Sherwood, *Roosevelt and Hopkins*, 518.
52. *Foreign Relations of the United States: Diplomatic Papers, 1945, vol. 8*, 693 fn.
53. *Foreign Relations of the United States: Diplomatic Papers, 1945, vol. 8*, 694–695.

The Near East Division then drafted another of its "glosses" on the president's comments, which Murray said he did not think would satisfy the Arabs, "but we think it is the only one which can be made in the circumstances."

With the president's approval, a telegram was sent to the United States representatives in the Near East, authorizing them to explain that the president's October 15 pledge (to seek to bring about the "earliest realization" of the establishment of Palestine as a democratic Jewish commonwealth) referred only to "possible action at some future time." The telegram added that "the president is, of course, keeping in mind the assurances which were communicated on a number of occasions...that in the view of this government, no decision altering the basic situation should be reached without full consultation with both Arabs and Jews."[54]

After his meeting with Roosevelt, Ibn Saud arranged for the Arab rulers of Iraq, Lebanon, Syria, Transjordan, and Yemen to join him in sending letters to the president on March 10, 1945, each of them affirming complete hostility to Jewish immigration and a Jewish national home in Palestine.[55] Roosevelt replied to Ibn Saud on April 5, 1945, a week before his death, in a letter drafted for him by the Near East Division in which he reiterated his previous assurances to the king, whom he addressed as his "great and good friend." The letter read:

> Your Majesty will recall that on previous occasions, I communicated to you the attitude of the American government toward Palestine and made clear our desire that no decision be taken with respect to the basic situation in that country without full consultation with both Arabs and Jews. Your Majesty will also doubtless recall that during our recent conversation, I assured

---

54. *Foreign Relations of the United States: Diplomatic Papers, 1945, vol. 8,* 696–697.
55. *Foreign Relations of the United States: Diplomatic Papers, 1945, vol. 8,* 691–693.

you that I would take no action, in my capacity as chief of the executive branch of this government, which might prove hostile to the Arab people.

It gives me pleasure to renew to Your Majesty the assurances which you have received regarding the attitude of my government and my own, as chief executive, with regard to the question of Palestine, and to inform you that the policy of this government in this respect is unchanged.[56]

The staff of the Near East Division evidently introduced the reference to Roosevelt as chief executive in the assurances to Ibn Saud as a basis for yet another one of its notable glosses on the president's comments. The staff noted that the reference to Roosevelt as chief executive in the letter to Ibn Saud and its absence in the letter to Senator Wagner could be interpreted to imply that whereas the pledge to Ibn Saud was made in an official capacity, the pledge to Senator Wagner was made only in a personal capacity. This bizarre gloss would have us understand that Roosevelt assures Ibn Saud that as president of the United States, he will take no action in Palestine in favor of the Jews, but that in his personal capacity he stands by his pledges to the Jews to seek to bring about the earliest realization of the establishment of a Jewish state in Palestine.

Given Roosevelt's contradictory pledges to Ibn Saud and to the Jews, both of which he reaffirmed orally and in writing to the parties involved, it is difficult to know where Roosevelt really stood on the subject of Palestine. Indeed, one is left wondering whether Roosevelt himself really knew.

On April 12, 1945, one week after signing his letter to Ibn Saud, Roosevelt died, and he was succeeded by his vice president, Harry S. Truman. In a conversation on October 19, 1945, Truman's Secretary of State James Byrnes, told British Ambassador Lord Halifax that Roosevelt must have signed the letter to Ibn Saud the day that he left Washington, when he, Byrnes, knew that Roosevelt "was in

---

56. *Foreign Relations of the United States: Diplomatic Papers, 1945, vol. 8,* 698.

no condition at all to be transacting business."[57] Letters similar to the one sent to Ibn Saud reiterating the pledge to him also went out to the regent of Iraq and to the president of Syria, with Roosevelt's signature, on April 12, 1945, the day of the president's death.[58]

Roosevelt evidently did not attach too much importance to the tragedy of the Jews or to the problem of Palestine, and he seems to have been ready to say whatever he thought his listeners would like to hear.[59] Walter Laqueur, in his *History of Zionism*, gave the following assessment of Roosevelt's performance:

> On the two most vital issues, on Palestine and the admission of refugees, Roosevelt said little and did less. Roosevelt was a consummate politician. He knew that a determined effort on behalf of the Jews would have reaped few tangible rewards, for the Jewish vote was in any case his. At the same time, it would

---

57. *Foreign Relations of the United States: Diplomatic Papers, 1945*, vol. 8, 778–779.
58. The State Department notified the newly installed President Harry Truman the following month of the exchange of letters between Roosevelt and the Arab rulers and presented a similar letter of reply for his signature. The State Department called Truman's attention to the fact that Roosevelt had signed his letter to Ibn Saud a week before his death. Truman felt obliged to sign, and the letter under his signature went out to King Abdullah of Transjordan on May 17, 1945. On June 4, a similar letter went out under his signature to the prime minister of Egypt (*Foreign Relations of the United States: Diplomatic Papers, 1945*, vol. 8, 703–704, 707–09). Byrnes told British Ambassador Halifax on October 19, 1945 that Truman was greatly disturbed and embarrassed about what had transpired and added that he would not sign such a letter "today."
59. Roosevelt's attitude is reminiscent of the story about the village judge settling a dispute between two villagers. After listening to the first party, he says, "You know, my good friend, you are right." He then hears his opponent, and replies, "My great and good friend, you are absolutely right." At this point, his wife, who has listened in on the case, inquires, "But how can they both be right?" The judge answers, "My dear wife, you too are right."

have caused a great many difficulties and complications both at home and abroad. Roosevelt's attitude towards the Jews was certainly not unfriendly: He was simply unwilling to go out of his way to help them...

The Zionists managed to create a climate of opinion favorable to Zionism among legislators, church dignitaries, journalists, and the public in general... But once the Zionists came up against the State Department, the Pentagon, and the White House, they faced interests and forces superior to their own, and references to the tragedy of the Jewish people did not cut much ice. The president himself, a curious mixture of patrician and popular tribune, of naïvety and sophistication, of honesty and duplicity, clearly regarded the whole issue as a minor nuisance.[60]

Walter Laqueur writes that David Niles, personal assistant to both presidents Roosevelt and Truman, wrote in 1962 that he seriously doubted whether Israel would have come into existence had Roosevelt lived.[61]

---

60. Laqueur, *A History of Zionism*, 553–556.
61. Laqueur, *A History of Zionism*, 554; Wilson, *Decision on Palestine*, 56. Undoubtedly, the most damning comment on Roosevelt was made by President Harry Truman when he was running for election in 1948. Of the president who had chosen him as his vice president in 1944 and of an earlier Roosevelt who had also been president, he wrote on his desk calendar on July 16, 1948, the day after his nomination by the Democratic convention: "I don't believe the USA wants any more fakers—Teddy and Franklin are enough. So I'm going to make a common-sense, intellectually honest campaign. It will be a novelty—and it will win" (Margaret Truman, *Harry S. Truman* [New York: William Morrow & Co, Inc., 1973], 15).

– 10 –

The Truman–Attlee Rift Over Immigration Policy

THE JEWS GREETED WITH HOPE, and many with optimism, the Labour Party's assumption of government power on July 26, 1945 upon its election victory under Clement Attlee's leadership. Despite all the disappointments with previous British administrations, including, in particular, the just-ended Churchill administration, Chaim Weizmann still retained his faith in the British government as the essential instrument for reestablishing the Jewish national home in Palestine.

The Labour Party's Promise and Performance

The Labour Party campaign platforms, approved at the annual political conferences, had remarkably strong pro-Zionist planks. At its 1943 conference, the Labour Party resolution read:

> The conference reaffirms the traditional policy of the British Labour Party in favor of building Palestine as the Jewish national home. It asks that the Jewish Agency be given authority to make the fullest use of the economic capacity of the country to absorb immigrants to develop the country, including the development of unoccupied and undeveloped lands.[1]

This resolution went beyond the Balfour Declaration in that it called for building Palestine as the Jewish national home rather than

---

1. The citations of the Labour Party platforms in this and the paragraphs that follow are from Wilson, *The Chariot of Israel*, 123–125.

for a Jewish national home in Palestine. And it asked for giving the Jewish Agency authority over immigration, even though the Churchill administration was continuing to enforce the 1939 White Paper to close Palestine's doors to the Jews.

At its December 1944 conference, only seven months before assuming government power, the Labour Party's resolution on Palestine was so far-reaching—going well beyond even the Zionist Biltmore Program (see Chapter 8)—that it stunned the Zionists themselves. Its resolution in favor of setting up Palestine as a state with a Jewish majority included an explicit call for a transfer of the Arab population from Palestine and even proposed extending Palestine's borders in agreement with Egypt, Syria, or Transjordan. It was Clement Attlee, as Labour Party leader, who made the motion for adoption of this resolution, which declared:

> There is surely neither hope nor meaning in a Jewish national home *unless we are prepared to let Jews, if they wish, enter this tiny land in such numbers as to become a majority.* There was a strong case for this before the war. There is an irresistible case now, after the unspeakable atrocities of the cold and calculated German Nazi plan to kill all Jews in Europe. Here, too, in Palestine, surely is a case on human grounds and to promote a stable settlement for [the] transfer of population.[2] *Let the*

---

2. Although any suggestion of population transfer has been rendered taboo as a result of the late Rabbi Meir Kahane's provocative approach to the subject, it is noteworthy that from 1937 until after World War II, the proposal of transfer—accompanied by some international program of finance and development—was still sufficiently respectable to be promoted as part of a stable settlement between Jews and Arabs, first by the Royal (Peel) Commission of 1937 and subsequently by Roosevelt, Churchill, and the British Labour Party, and, even more, remarkably, by the anti-Zionist H. St. John Philby, key British "adviser" to King Ibn Saud of Saudi Arabia, who—strange as it may seem—actively promoted for a time a plan for the transfer of Palestine's Arab population to Saudi Arabia for £20 million.

Arabs be encouraged to move out as the Jews move in. Let them be compensated handsomely for their land, and let their settlement elsewhere be carefully organized and generously financed. The Arabs have many wide territories of their own—they must not claim to exclude the Jews from this small area of Palestine, less than the size of Wales. Indeed, we should reexamine also the possibility of extending the present Palestinian boundaries by agreement with Egypt, Syria, or Transjordan. We should seek to win the full sympathy and support both of the American and Russian governments for the execution of this Palestinian policy [emphases in the original].

At its May 1945 conference, shortly before assuming government power, the Labour Party election campaign platform had included this extraordinary pronouncement:

It is morally wrong and politically indefensible to impose obstacles to the entry into Palestine now of any Jews who desire to go there. We consider Jewish immigration into Palestine should be permitted without the present limitations... Steps should be taken in consultation with these two governments [American and Soviet] to see whether we cannot get that common support for a policy which will give us a happy, free, and prosperous Jewish state in Palestine.

Reflecting on the Labour Party's 180-degree turnaround immediately after it assumed power, Harold Wilson, a junior Labour cabinet member in the Attlee government and future Labour prime minister during Israel's Six-Day War in 1967, commented in 1981:

It would not have been possible for a political party to be more committed to a national home for the Jews in Palestine than was Labour. In the election, the party had uncompromisingly demanded that the 1939 White Paper be rescinded. It pledged itself categorically not to prevent the Jews from achieving a majority in Palestine by immigration. This was not an election-eve manoeuvre. The party had supported the Jewish national home ever since the Balfour Declaration—indeed since 1917, when this theme had been incorporated in Labour's statement of war aims. It had been reiterated eleven times from then to May 1945. A generation of Labour [spokesmen] on foreign and colonial affairs was committed… Time after time, Labour's official team on the opposition front bench, denouncing Conservative support for "corrupt pashas and effendis," had committed the party, on taking power, to sweeping away all restrictions on immigration into Palestine.

The Mapai (the Jewish Workers' Party in Palestine), pinning its hopes on the new Labour government, congratulated the British Labour Party on its 1945 election victory:

Our hearty greetings at your brilliant victory. The workers of Palestine have followed your rise to the highest rung of national and international responsibility with friendship and trust. We are confident that in fulfilling your great plans, you will act at once for the salvation of the suffering remnants of our people and for the upbuilding of an independent Homeland.

Davar, the Mapai newspaper, declared: "The victory of the Labour Party, which raised the banner of undiluted Zionism during the election campaign, is therefore a clear victory for the demands of Zionism within British opinion."[3] And *The Jewish Frontier*, a Zionist journal, hailed the election "as an epoch-making event of worldwide significance which opened up hopeful new perspectives for Zionism."[4]

Interestingly enough, David Ben-Gurion, the leader of Mapai and future first prime minister of newly reborn Israel, was more far-seeing than many of his colleagues. At the first post-war Zionist conference, meeting in London in August 1945, Ben-Gurion commented:

---

3. Begin, *The Revolt*, 246–247.
4. Laqueur, *A History of Zionism*, 564.

The assumption that a party in power will fulfill the pledges it made while in opposition is a highly dubious one. We have no reason to be certain that a party reaching power will demand from itself what it previously demanded from others. In England, and perhaps in other countries as well, power does not reside solely in the hands of elected politicians. There is also a permanent civil service. Governments come, and governments go, but most of the civil service remains. This is true of England as a whole, and particularly in regard to matters affecting the British Empire. The great majority of the members of the colonial civil service are anti-Zionist, as they have been since the time of the Balfour Declaration, and they will remain in office. Let us not underestimate their influence on the Labour government.[5]

Ben-Gurion proceeded to call for resistance to the implementation of the white paper, having declared earlier, on the occasion of his visit to the United States, that if the British government intended to enforce the white paper, it could do so only through resort to "bloody terror." Rabbi Abba Hillel Silver, the new president of the American Zionist Organization, was equally skeptical, and he rejected Weizmann's policy of continuing Zionist cooperation with Great Britain, emphasizing, "The personal diplomatic approach of yesterday is totally inadequate today... It might be the height of statesmanship to be unstatesmanlike."[6]

No one was more skeptical than Menachem Begin, head of the underground Irgun, which had earlier declared open revolt against British rule in Palestine. The Irgun published the following declaration:

> In Britain, a Labour Party government has taken office. Before coming to power, this party undertook to restore the land of Israel to the people of Israel as a free state to which all the

---

5. Ben-Gurion, *Israel: A Personal History*, 56–57.
6. George Kirk, *The Middle East 1945–1950* (London: Oxford University Press, 1954), 191.

exiles of Zion and those who long for Zion could return. This in itself is no guarantee for the attainment of the national aim. The Jewish people, schooled in suffering, has learnt from experience. Men and parties in opposition…have for twenty-five years made many promises and undertaken clear obligations. But on coming to power, they have gone back on their word and perpetuated the policies of their predecessors. The consequence has been the robbery of our country and the destruction of our people. This experience, which has cost the Jewish people six million lives, teaches us that only the war of liberation, independent and purposeful, will set in motion political and international factors and bring salvation to our oppressed and decimated people.[7]

Even Begin, however, was willing to give the new Labour government a chance to prove whether it meant to carry out its promises. The Irgun declaration continued:

In view of the fact that all the members of the British government, as members of the Labour Party, subscribed to the program of mass repatriation to Zion and the establishment of the Jewish State, we consider it our duty, out of a sense of responsibility and of our own free will, to give them an opportunity of proving whether they mean to go the way of all their predecessors—the way of denial and betrayal—or whether they mean to fulfill their solemn undertakings without delay. In view of the known plight of our people, only a very short time—weeks and not months—is required in order to determine whether they mean to translate their words into deeds or whether to the many tragic illusions of the Jewish people is to be added yet another, perhaps the last illusion, which will be shattered only if we all rally—to war, war to the end, war till victory.[8]

---

7. Begin, *The Revolt*, 247–248.
8. Begin, *The Revolt*, 248.

The skepticism quickly proved to have been justified. As Harold Wilson commented on Labour's behavior, "There cannot have been in twentieth-century British history a greater contrast between promise and performance than was shown by the incoming government over Middle Eastern issues." No sooner was the Labour Party voted into office to replace Winston Churchill's wartime government than it abandoned its repeated pro-Zionist pledges issued every year since the 1917 Balfour Declaration. The Labour government immediately shifted course to adopt the most rabid anti-Zionist agenda of the government bureaucracies dealing with the Middle East.[9]

The Foreign Office Middle East Department, supported by Britain's ambassadors in the region, was as determined as ever to prevent the establishment of a Jewish state in any part of Palestine. It continued to adhere firmly to the 1939 White Paper policy. The Colonial Office abandoned the policy for the partition of Palestine, which the previous colonial ministers, Lowell Amery and even Colonel Oliver Stanley, had supported during Churchill's wartime review of post-war policy for Palestine. Under the new colonial minster, George Hall (August 3, 1945–October 4, 1946), the Colonial Office proposed instead to continue British rule in Palestine but with provisions for setting up autonomous Arab and Jewish provinces, a scheme quite similar to the cantonization plan that the Peel Commission had considered and rejected in 1937. And the military establishment looked upon Palestine as a strategic base for the protection of the British Empire, extending all the way to India.[10] Under the influence of these government departments, Attlee—immediately upon assuming power—abandoned his lifetime, public embrace of Zionism and adopted instead a thoroughgoing anti-Zionist position, rigidly enforcing the 1939 White Paper and refusing to open Palestine's gates even for the Holocaust survivors in the displaced persons camps.

---

9. Wilson, *The Chariot of Israel*, 125.
10. Cohen, *Palestine: Retreat from the Mandate*, 181–184.

The Earl Harrison Report and the Truman–Attlee Rift

In contrast to the cooperative relationship that had prevailed during the war between Roosevelt and Churchill, a serious rift quickly developed between their respective successors, President Harry Truman and Prime Minister Clement Attlee, over the issue of the immigration of Holocaust survivors into Palestine. Unlike Roosevelt, who had displayed shockingly callous indifference to the fate of Europe's Jews during the Holocaust, Truman upset his own State Department and opened a serious rift with the British government over his determined effort to alleviate the suffering of the surviving Jewish refugees. This difference between Roosevelt and Truman regarding their responses to Jewish suffering presents us with a remarkable paradox. Roosevelt, who was callously indifferent to the fate of the Jews in the Holocaust, does not seem to have harbored any anti-Semitic instincts. Meanwhile, Truman, according to recently revealed comments in his private diary and in letters to his family, did harbor anti-Semitic instincts—along with anti-black and anti-Oriental instincts.[11] Nevertheless, he fought both his own State Department and the British government soon after he succeeded Roosevelt to the presidency in the spring of 1945 on behalf of Jewish survivors seeking refuge in immigration to Palestine.

After receiving reports of the horrible conditions prevailing in the liberated concentration camps where the Holocaust survivors were being kept, Truman sent the former US commissioner of immigration and naturalization, Earl G. Harrison, to Europe on June 22, 1945 to investigate and submit his recommendations. On July 24, 1945, even before receiving Harrison's report and before the change in Britain's government, Truman appealed to Churchill during the Potsdam Conference of the three major Allied leaders (July 17–August 2, 1945):

---

11. See Michael J. Cohen, "A New Look at Truman and 'Exodus 1947,'" *The Israel Journal of Foreign Affairs* 3, no. 1 (2009): 93–100.

Knowing your deep and sympathetic interest in Jewish settlement in Palestine, I venture to express to you the hope that the British government may find it possible without delay to take steps to lift the restrictions of the White Paper on Jewish immigration into Palestine.[12]

A week later, it was the newly elected Labour prime minister, Clement Attlee, who replied in a two-sentence note dated July 31, 1945: "You will I am sure understand that I cannot give you any statement on policy until we have had time to consider the matter."[13] Evidently, Attlee had already totally forgotten the policy contained in his Labour Party resolution of December 1944, "to let Jews, if they wish, enter this tiny land in such numbers as to become a majority."

One month later, on August 31, 1945, Truman addressed a memo to Attlee, to be transmitted by hand, by his new secretary of state, James Byrnes, to which he attached a copy of Harrison's report on the problems and the needs of the Jewish refugees among the displaced persons. The Harrison report noted that the available certificates for immigration to Palestine would be exhausted in the near future, and recommended:

> The granting of an additional one hundred thousand such certificates would contribute greatly to a sound solution for the future of Jews still in Germany and Austria and for other Jewish refugees who do not wish to remain where they are or who for understandable reasons do not desire to return to their countries of origin.[14]

---

12. *Foreign Relations of the United States: Diplomatic Papers, 1945, vol. 8,* 716–717.
13. *Foreign Relations of the United States: Diplomatic Papers, 1945, vol. 8,* 719.
14. Harrison was also severely critical of the conditions in the displaced persons camps, writing that the Jews appear to be treated much as they had been under the Nazis, except that they were not being exterminated. Truman also sent a copy of Harrison's report to General Dwight Eisenhower and called for the situation to be remedied (United States National Archives,

Truman added that he concurred with Harrison's recommendation, and, in emphatic language, he urged upon Attlee the need to act on this recommendation without long delay:

> On the basis of this and other information which has come to me, I concur in the belief that no other single matter is so important for those who have known the horrors of concentration camps for over a decade as is the future of immigration possibilities into Palestine... No claim is more meritorious than that of the groups who for so many years have known persecution and enslavement. The main solution appears to lie in the quick evacuation of as many as possible of the non-repatriable Jews, who wish it, to Palestine. If it is to be effective, such action should not be long delayed.[15]

Attlee's two-part reply, dated September 14 and September 16, 1945, was a remarkable demonstration of the political distance he and his Labour Party had travelled from their annual passionate calls for unlimited Jewish immigration to enable the Jews to become a Jewish majority in Palestine and to establish a Jewish state. In his interim reply of September 14, Attlee warned Truman in blunt terms that if, as Secretary Byrnes had discussed with Foreign Minister Bevin that

---

"Letter to General Eisenhower Concerning Conditions Facing Displaced Persons in Germany" in *Public Papers of the Presidents*, September 29, 1945, no. 152).

15. *Foreign Relations of the United States: Diplomatic Papers, 1945*, vol. 8, 737–739. On the same date that the president called for the rapid immigration of as many Jews as possible to Palestine (August 31, 1945), Loy Henderson, the new director of the Office of Near East and African Affairs, transmitted a memorandum to the secretary of state recommending that "The United States should refrain from supporting a policy of large-scale immigration into Palestine during the interim period" and expressed the hope that the secretary would find the memo helpful should the British in London ask him about the United States attitude on the subject (*Foreign Relations of the United States: Diplomatic Papers, 1945*, vol. 8, 734–736).

same day, Truman were to publish his letter of August 31 with its request for the admission of an additional hundred thousand Jewish refugees into Palestine, "such action could not fail to do grievous harm to relations between our two countries."[16] Totally ignored was the Labour Party Resolution, even of only three months earlier, "It is morally wrong and politically indefensible to impose obstacles to the entry into Palestine now of any Jews who desire to go there. We consider Jewish immigration into Palestine should be permitted without the present limitations."

In his lengthier reply of September 16, Attlee warned Truman, in shockingly callous language, of the danger of giving the Jews any special consideration that would place them "in a special racial category at the head of the queue." He then added:

> In [the] case of Palestine, we have the Arabs to consider as well as the Jews, and there have been solemn undertakings, I understand, given by your predecessor, yourself and by Mr. Churchill, that before we come to a final decision and operate it, there would be consultation with the Arabs. It would be very unwise to break these solemn pledges and so set aflame the whole Middle East.

Attlee went on to complain that the Jews "have not taken up the 1,500 available [certificates] for this month which was offered them. Apparently, they are insisting upon the complete repudiation of the white paper and the immediate granting of a hundred thousand certificates quite regardless of the effect on the situation in the Middle East which this would have."[17] For good measure, Attlee then added that Britain must also consider how the Moslems in India—of whose

---

16. *Foreign Relations of the United States: Diplomatic Papers, 1945, vol. 8,* 739.
17. Bevin was less diplomatic in speaking to Chaim Weizmann, greeting him with these remarks: "What do you mean by refusing certificates? Are you trying to force my hand? If you want a fight, you can have it" (Weizmann, *Trial and Error,* 440).

existence he would seem to have become aware only now—might be inflamed by Jewish immigration into Palestine.[18] Taking all these considerations into account, Attlee concluded, "We have got this matter under urgent examination...and I shall be very happy to let you know as soon as I can what our intentions are in this matter."[19]

Truman replied the next day, saying he was aware of the difficulties that Attlee saw, but he also had difficulties. He expressed the hope that they could "work out a successful program that will provide for them [Jews and other displaced persons] some measure of relief at an early date" and added that he would take no further action in the matter until after Mr. Byrnes returned.[20]

The US State Department officials, like those in the British Foreign Office, were unhappy with Truman's request for the hundred thousand certificates, and they continued the practice of invoking pro-Arab "glosses" in communications to the Arab countries, such as they had employed so effectively under Roosevelt (see Chapter 9). In his request for the issuance of a hundred thousand certificates

---

18. General Sir Archibald Wavell, who, as commander in chief in the Middle East in the early years of the war, had strongly opposed Churchill's proposal for the formation of a Jewish army, had subsequently been appointed viceroy and governor general of India. In the latter capacity, he added the "Indian factor" in his attack on partition of Palestine, when it was still being considered by Churchill's cabinet committee in May 1945. He wrote: "India contains ninety million Muslims who would deeply, perhaps actively, resent a solution of the Palestine problem which was against the Arabs. Agitation on an external Muslim grievance of this kind can quickly become formidable" (Cohen, *Palestine: Retreat from the Mandate*, 181). In November 1945, when Bevin repeated in the House of Commons the argument that "Zionism is a matter of keen interest to ninety million Mohammedans in India," Meinertzhagen wrote, "Utter rubbish. Not one percent of Indians have ever heard of Palestine nor of Zionism" (Meinertzhagen, *Middle East Diary*, 199).
19. *Foreign Relations of the United States: Diplomatic Papers, 1945, vol. 8*, 739–741.
20. *Foreign Relations of the United States: Diplomatic Papers, 1945, vol. 8*, 741.

for Jewish immigration, Truman had stated, "No other single matter is so important for those who have known the horrors of concentration camps... No claim is more meritorious... The main solution appears to lie in the quick evacuation of as many as possible of the non-repatriable Jews, who wish it, to Palestine." The State Department, however, wired its representatives in the Arab countries to give the Arabs this watered-down message:

> During recent weeks, [the] president has been in exploratory correspondence with Prime Minister Attlee of Great Britain in an effort to find ways and means of alleviating the situation of the displaced Jews in Europe... The president has suggested that among other measures consideration be given to Palestine as possible haven for some of these homeless Jews.

The message naturally added the reassurance so meticulously invoked under President Roosevelt:

> In making this suggestion he of course kept in mind the well-known policy of the US with regard to Palestine as communicated on a number of occasions...no decision affecting the basic situation in Palestine will be made without full consultation with both Arabs and Jews.[21]

Attlee's Call for an Anglo-American Commission of Inquiry

On October 19, 1945, Lord Halifax, British ambassador to the US, brought a memorandum to Secretary Byrnes setting out his government's considered proposal for dealing with the problem of the surviving Jewish refugees. The proposal called for the establishment of yet another in the long series of ill-fated commissions of inquiry, this one to be a joint Anglo-American commission. The intent of the

---

21. *Foreign Relations of the United States: Diplomatic Papers, 1945, vol. 8,* 784–785.

proposal was evident from the suggested terms of reference, which simply omitted any reference to Palestine and mentioned only "to examine the possibility of relieving the position in Europe by immigration into other countries outside Europe." Britain also did not appear to be in any great hurry to find such a solution. The memorandum stated that "the commission would be invited to carry out their assignment with the utmost expedition," but noted that "if the investigation is to be thorough and effective, it must inevitably take time." And, afar had the Labour government now strayed from its repeated pledges of unlimited Jewish immigration to establish Palestine as a Jewish State—even including encouragement of a transfer of the Arab population—that its memorandum had reverted back to the anti-Zionist notion of the Mandate's so-called irreconcilable "dual obligations" to Arabs and Jews.[22]

President Truman understood Britain's proposal as a device to stall any action on his request for implementation of Harrison's recommendation for the hundred thousand immigration certificates. In his reply on October 24, 1945, Truman made it clear that he would be prepared to accept an invitation to participate in a joint Anglo-American committee only with terms of reference that focused on the issue of Jewish immigration into Palestine. In accepting such an invitation, his note added, the United States would not necessarily associate itself with the observations in Bevin's memorandum relating to his proposal. On the contrary, the reply emphasized that the president still adhered to the views he had expressed with regard to the migration of Jews from Europe to Palestine.[23] Only after extended negotiations, including one stage (on October 27–28, 1945) in which Truman felt obliged to withdraw entirely from the British proposal, did Bevin agree to accept sufficiently explicit terms of reference regarding

---

22. *Foreign Relations of the United States: Diplomatic Papers, 1945, vol. 8*, 771–775.
23. *Foreign Relations of the United States: Diplomatic Papers, 1945, vol. 8*, 785–786.

immigration into Palestine for Truman to be able to agree to a joint Anglo-American commission of inquiry.[24]

In parliament on November 13, 1945, Bevin announced the decision to set up a joint Anglo-American committee to examine the question of European Jewry and to review the Palestine problem in light of that examination. That no speedy resolution of the problem might be expected was evident from Bevin's explanation of the manner in which the government intended to proceed. It would deal with the issue in three stages. First, it would consult with the Arabs for an arrangement to ensure that in the interim, until the committee would submit its report, immigration into Palestine might be maintained at the current rate. Second, after considering the recommendations of the committee, it would explore with the parties concerned the possibility of devising other temporary arrangements until a permanent solution could be reached. Finally, it would prepare a permanent solution for submission to the United Nations.

In announcing the Labour government policy, Bevin made the rash declaration in parliament that he would be willing to stake his political future on finding a solution to the Palestine problem.[25]

President Truman also issued a statement the same day, November 13, 1945. Evidently angry over Britain's stand, he decided to make public his request of August 31, 1945 for the hundred thousand certificates, despite Attlee's warning, noted earlier, that "such action could not fail to do grievous harm to relations between our two countries."

---

24. See the extended exchanges on this subject between Great Britain and the United States in *Foreign Relations of the United States: Diplomatic Papers, 1945*, vol. 8, for October 19, 1945, 771–783; October 24, 1945, 785–786; October 25, 1945, 788–790; October 26, 1945, 794–799; October 27, 1945, 800; October 28, 1945, 800–801; November 5, 1945, 810–812; November 6, 1945, 812; November 7, 1945, 814; November 9, 1945, 815–816; November 13, 1947, 819–820; December 10, 1945, 839–840.
25. *Hansard*, House of Commons, Debates, vol. 415 cc1927–1935, November 13, 1945; *Foreign Relations of the United States: Diplomatic Papers, 1945*, vol. 8, 821.

The British government, he now added, had not been able to adopt his policy recommendation and had suggested instead the establishment of a joint Anglo-American committee of inquiry. To this he had acceded in the belief that "it will be of aid in finding a solution that is both humane and just."[26]

At a press conference following the announcement of the government policy, Bevin totally repudiated the Balfour Declaration embedded in the Mandate under which the League of Nations authorized Britain to govern Palestine, together with all the Labour Party's own previous pro-Zionist pledges. With the news of the Holocaust still fresh in everyone's mind, Bevin expressed himself in this brutal fashion:

> I am very anxious that Jews shall not in Europe overemphasize their racial position... If the Jews, with all their suffering, want to get too much at the head of the queue, you have the danger of another anti-Semitic reaction through it all.[27]

Richard Crossman, a Labour Party member of parliament who visited displaced persons camps as a member of the Anglo-American committee of inquiry, commented on Bevin's remark,

> That might go down in Britain; in Belsen, it sounded like the mouthing of a sadistic anti-Semite. Such an attitude had figured in Britain's rejection of every opportunity during the war for rescuing tens of thousands of would-be escapees from the gas chambers of the Nazi concentration camps.[28]

---

26. United States National Archives, "Statement by the President on the Problems of Jewish Refugees in Europe" in *Public Papers of the Presidents*, November 13, 1945, no. 187.
27. Kirk, *The Middle East 1945–1950*, 199–200. It may be noted that Bevin was only expressing in public and in rather more blunt language the thought that Attlee had already expressed to President Truman in private and in somewhat more diplomatic language in his communication of September 16, 1945, cited earlier.
28. Crossman, *Palestine Mission*, 85.

To the Zionists, Britain's announcement of its decision to reject President Truman's request for the hundred thousand immigration certificates and to set up instead yet another commission of inquiry came as a bitter disappointment. Weizmann's reaction is reflected in in his autobiography:

> It was on November 13, 1945 that the Labour government officially repudiated the promises of the Labour Party and offered us, instead of the abrogation of the white paper and relief for the Jews in the detention camps—a new commission of inquiry. The extraordinary spirit in which this was conceived may be understood from the opening. The British government "would not accept the view that the Jews should be driven out of Europe or that they should not be permitted to live again in these countries without discrimination, contributing their ability and talent toward rebuilding the prosperity of Europe."
>
> The British government, in other words, refused to accept the view that six million Jews had been done to death in Europe by various scientific methods and that European anti-Semitism was as viciously alive as ever. The British government wanted the Jews to stay and contribute their talents (as I afterward told the UN Special Committee on Palestine) toward the rebuilding of Germany so that the Germans might have another chance of destroying the last remnants of the Jewish people.[29]

The Christian Zionist who had been actively involved with Palestine since World War I, Colonel Richard Meinertzhagen, reacted with even greater bitterness, writing:

> The Labour Party had pledged themselves to reverse the white paper policy and included that pledge in the recent election propaganda, but like most election promises, it was a lie… For twenty-five years, successive British governments have failed to implement their pledge to the Jews and, having failed, they now

---

29. Weizmann, *Trial and Error*, 439–440.

have the temerity to say "every effort has been made," etc. On the contrary every effort has been made to sabotage Zionism and drive the Jews to desperation... I am utterly disgusted and depressed... The fact must be faced that the world is so inured to Jewish persecution and pogroms that all decent feelings towards these unhappy people are dulled. Only last week, several dozen Jews were murdered by fanatical Arabs in Tripoli, and hundreds of Jews were ill treated and several killed in Cairo only a few days ago—and all for no reason except anti-Semitism. No notice is taken of it. What would happen and what does happen if a single Arab is killed by a Jew? It is considered an outrage. The murder of Jews is just an incident of little import.[30]

Two issues still remained to be resolved before the Anglo-American committee could be appointed: 1. setting a time limit for the completion of the work and 2. agreeing on the size of the committee. Bevin was opposed to any definite time limit, but Truman insisted that the appointment of a committee would otherwise be seen only as a device for shelving the issue. Worried about the likelihood of an unfavorable bill being adopted in Congress, Bevin finally agreed to a time limit of 120 days.[31] On the issue of the size of the committee, Bevin proposed that each side appoint seven members, but the United States countered with a proposal for five, and a compromise was reached on six for each side.

The composition of the committee was announced by the two governments on December 10, 1945. Seven months had passed since the war had ended in Europe, and the Holocaust survivors were still languishing in the Allied displaced persons camps, their plight only now to be examined by a joint Anglo-American committee, whose report was not even due for another four months after beginning

---

30. Meinertzhagen, *Middle East Diary*, 199–201.
31. *Foreign Relations of the United States: Diplomatic Papers, 1945*, vol. 8, 827–828; November 20, 1945, 829; November 24, 1945, 830–831; November 25, 1945, 831–832; November 27, 1945, 833.

their investigation. Any action on their problem would have to wait still longer, until the two governments had examined the report and had consulted the Arabs and the Jews before reaching their decisions on how to respond.³²

The Jewish Revolt

The Labour government's repudiation of all the pro-Zionist promises the Labour Party had consistently made since 1917 led Palestine's Jewish community to open a new chapter of armed resistance to British rule. The Jewish Agency now reversed its policy of collaboration with the British government, under which it had been hunting down the dissident Jewish groups for arrest and exile by the British administration (see Chapter 8). Instead, it now gave its approval to the formation of a united underground resistance against British rule to be directed by the Haganah in agreement with both the Irgun and the Lehi. On September 23, Moshe Sneh, then the head of the Haganah, wired Ben-Gurion in London to request the Jewish Agency's approval for the commission of some act of violence as a warning to the British authorities.³³ Ben-Gurion replied a week later instructing him to undertake "sabotage and retaliation actions" that were "substantive and impressive" but to refrain from personal terror.³⁴ A month later, on the first of November, Sneh wired that the Haganah had come to a working arrangement with both the Irgun and Lehi, according to which they would be assigned certain tasks under the command of the Haganah, and he urged the Executive of the Jewish Agency to put the agreement into effect without delay. He also reported on the substantive and impressive actions that had already been taken on the previous night of October 31 by this new

---

32. *Foreign Relations of the United States: Diplomatic Papers, 1945, vol. 8,* November 19, 1945, 828; November 24, 1945, 831; December 6, 1945, 838; December 10, 1945, 839–840.
33. Begin, *The Revolt,* 243–265.
34. Cited in Jones, *Failure in Palestine,* 81–82.

United Resistance. The Haganah had sunk three naval craft and had cut the railway system all along the line, leading to a suspension of the railroad service from the Syrian coast to Gaza as well as inland from Haifa and Lydda. The Irgun had attacked the Lydda railway station and the Lehi had seriously damaged the Haifa oil refinery.[35]

On November 5, 1945, only days after the initial acts of the United Resistance, the British Defense Committee met to consider the developing Jewish violence in Palestine. After hearing from the colonial secretary that the illegal Jewish army, numbering about seventy thousand, "was dangerously strong and well organized," the Defense Committee considered the question of military measures to seize the illegal arms. The commanders in chief of the Middle East suggested that it would be necessary sooner or later to disarm the whole population of Palestine, both Arabs and Jews, but in order not to torpedo the upcoming Anglo-American inquiry, this was to be done only at some appropriate psychological moment, after a major terrorist provocation. On January 1, 1946, they added a new dimension, calling for the seizure of the leaders of the Haganah and its striking force, the Palmach. They noted that while the degree of success in seizing arms might be problematic, "seizure of leaders in order to break up the illegal organization is of primary importance, and seizure of the arms is secondary to this."[36] The cabinet accepted their advice to seize the leaders of the resistance and to disarm the Jews at some psychologically appropriate moment.

The Anglo-American Committee

The Anglo-American Committee began its hearings in Washington on January 7, 1946 and proceeded to London on January 18, 1946, for a week of hearings beginning January 25, 1946. In the month of February, the committee split up to visit Germany and other European countries, and at the beginning of March, the committee went

---

35. Begin, *The Revolt*, 254–255.
36. Jones, *Failure in Palestine*, 82–84.

on to Palestine, with a stopover in Cairo and with subcommittee visits in the neighboring countries. After a month of hearings in the region with the Jews and the Arabs, as well as with British officials, they proceeded to Lausanne, Switzerland, where they completed their report on April 20, well before the designated deadline of 120 days.[37]

Bevin had urged upon the United States the importance of appointing to the committee only persons who were impartial and uncommitted on the issue of Palestine.[38] Apparently, uncommitted did not necessarily mean unprejudiced, as Richard Crossman, the Labour member of parliament, who kept a diary of his experience as a member of the committee, indicated. He wrote:

> We start with a blankness towards the philosophy of Zionism which is virtually anti-Zionist. We have a feeling that the whole idea of a Jewish national home is a dead end out of which Britain must be extricated, that whereas it is obvious that Arab independence in the end must be granted, we have not a similar obligation to permit the Jews in Palestine the fulfillment of Zionism. So the tendency is to define the problem as one of finding homes somewhere for the surplus Jews in Europe in order to cut away the Zionist case for impossible immigration into Palestine.[39]

And Bartley Crum, appointed to the committee at the insistence of the president over the repeated objections of the State Department,[40]

---

37. *Foreign Relations of the United States: Diplomatic Papers, 1946, vol. 7*, January 17, 1946, 576–578; February 5, 1946, 579–580; March 1, 1946, 582; April 19, 1946, 584–585; April 30, 1946, 588, fn. 22.
38. *Foreign Relations of the United States: Diplomatic Papers, 1945, vol. 8*, 822–823.
39. Crossman, *Palestine Mission*, 25.
40. Bartley Crum wrote that the State Department "preferred not to have me on the committee. From other sources in government, I learned that the president himself had sent in my name but that it was rejected three times. Only through the insistence of Mr. Truman, who found it necessary to

noted that he felt most uncomfortable with what appeared to him to be the prejudgment of the case by the British members. On the Queen Elizabeth ship, on the way over to London:

> The British generally began to make it clear that they viewed Zionism with anything but favor. Sir Frederick referred repeatedly to Lessing Rosenwald's phrase, "the danger of Jewish nationalism." One British member spoke of Zionism as "Jewish fascism," another characterized it as "Communism in disguise" and told me, "Bear in mind that hundreds of thousands of these Jews have been behind the Russian lines for years. We simply cannot afford to have the Middle East go communistic."[41]

The anti-Zionist prejudices of the British committee members were nourished by Britain's expert staff, headed by Harold Beeley, Bevin's political adviser on Palestine, who, according to Crum, was so pro-Arab that he seemed to place the Arabs even ahead of the British Empire. Beeley told him on the boat to London:

> The Palestine issue must be seen in the framework of strong Soviet expansionism. The Soviet planned to move down into the Middle East.[42] The United States, therefore, would do well to join Britain in establishing a cordon sanitaire of Arab states. If Palestine were declared an Arab state, it would be a strong link in this chain.[43]

---

cable Mr. Byrnes in Moscow, was I finally appointed" (Crum, *Behind the Silken Curtain*, 4).

41. Crum, *Behind the Silken Curtain*, 42.
42. Beeley's argument about the need to consider the Soviet threat in connection with Palestine had already been sharply stated in a briefing by the new chief of the Near East Division, Loy Henderson, in Washington.
43. Crum, *Behind the Silken Curtain*, 33. Crum was not convinced of the wisdom of Beeley's proposal, given "the Arab position during the war" and "the elasticity of its loyalties." He wrote, "If the issues were as clear cut as Beeley saw them, the investigation we were making seemed hardly worth the effort" (*Behind the Silken Curtain*, 33).

Beeley's American counterpart was Evan Wilson from the State Department's Near East Division, an Arabist official like his colleagues in the division who shared the anti-Zionist views of the British civil servants in the Foreign Office and Colonial Office. Crum reported that Wilson had warned him on the boat to London, "If the committee reaches a decision which would be interpreted as too favorable to the Jews, an aroused Arab world might turn to the Soviet Union for support. This is a matter the committee must consider seriously."[44]

But despite the anti-Zionist prejudices entertained at the outset of the inquiry and the anti-Zionist coaching of the British and American staff, the members were sufficiently impressed by what they learned in the course of the hearings and their visits in Europe and Palestine that they were able to reach unanimous agreement on a compromise report that differed markedly from what Bevin and the British government had expected.[45]

✫ ✫ ✫

The committee hearings in the United States began with a meeting with President Truman, who emphasized that no problem concerned him more deeply. He stressed that the democracies had an obligation to give the survivors in the displaced persons camps a chance to rebuild their lives, expressed the hope that the committee would be able to conduct its investigations and make its recommendations within 120 days, and assured them that he and the US government would do everything in their power to carry out a solution.[46]

---

44. Crum, *Behind the Silken Curtain*, 31. Crum disagreed, writing, "Only a few days earlier, Winston Churchill, upon arrival in the United States, had stated that he had always been and still was a Zionist... Surely...if the situation were as grave in British eyes as Wilson indicated, Churchill would not have spoken as he did" (*Behind the Silken Curtain*, 32).
45. A summary of the recommendations of the committee appears in *Foreign Relations of the United States: Diplomatic Papers, 1946*, vol. 7, 585–587.
46. Crum, *Behind the Silken Curtain*, 7.

The committee hearings began with Earl Harrison presenting his report on the Jewish refugees in the displaced persons camps and his recommendation for the hundred thousand certificates for Jews to go to Palestine. More than a dozen Jewish, Christian, and Arab organizations then presented their views before the committee. The Arabs were unanimous in their opposition to opening the doors of Palestine to any Jewish refugees or to setting up a Jewish state in any part of Palestine. The Jewish spokesmen, however, represented a broad spectrum of views, including Zionist, non-Zionist, and even anti-Zionist ideology. The Zionist leaders, Rabbi Stephen Wise and Dr. Emanuel Neumann, declared the 1939 White Paper to be a violation of the Balfour Declaration and the League of Nations Mandate and presented the case for Zionism as the legal and practical solution to the problem of the Jewish refugees seeking entry into Palestine. Judge Joseph Proskauer, who headed the non-Zionist American Jewish Committee and was opposed to the Biltmore Program for Palestine as a Jewish state, nevertheless supported—on purely humanitarian grounds—opening Palestine's doors to the Jewish refugees. Lessing Rosenwald, president of the anti-Zionist American Council for Judaism, on the other hand, came to argue against a Jewish state. Like Edwin Montagu in Great Britain, who had opposed issuing the Balfour Declaration (see Chapter 1), he argued that Jews were not a people, that Judaism was only a religion and not a national concept, and that Zionism raised a question of dual allegiance.[47] It remained for an American non-Jew on the committee, Dr. James G. McDonald, to ask him whether he thought that men like Lloyd George, Churchill, and President Wilson, who were friends of the Jewish people, would have supported the Zionist program if it had implied, even remotely, divided loyalty.

The committee members were most disconcerted, however, by hearing from the renowned Albert Einstein, who had also come as a spokesman for the Jewish case, that he regarded the committee a

---

47. For a brief discussion of these issues, repeated in the founding PLO National Charter, see the Introduction to this book.

waste of time and only a smoke screen, because in the end, the Colonial Office would impose its own policy.[48] Although the committee was upset by Einstein's remarks, it was to learn—shortly after it had completed its work—that his prediction had proven to be correct.

The first shock for Crum came aboard ship on the way to London, when he read a summary of the State Department's secret file on Palestine, the existence of which, according to him, "apparently not even President Truman had known." Commenting on this summary, Crum wrote:

> According to this file, since September 15, 1938, each time a promise was made to American Jewry regarding Palestine, the State Department promptly sent messages to the Arab rulers discounting it and reassuring them, in effect, that regardless of what was promised publicly to the Jews, nothing would be done to change the situation in Palestine. This file confirmed the charges of double-dealing that had been hurled at both the United States and Great Britain... It revealed that steadily and successively, we had made public promises to the Zionists and private promises to the Arabs...[49]
>
> I think I ought to book passage home as soon as we arrive in Southampton. I don't see that there is any purpose in going on with our work.[50]

In London, the committee visit was notable for its luncheon meeting with the Foreign Minister, Ernest Bevin. As Richard Crossman later reported, Bevin, in the presence of cabinet ministers and other high-ranking officials, "stated slowly but emphatically that if we achieved a unanimous report, he would personally do everything

---

48. Crum, *Behind the Silken Curtain*, ch. 1.
49. For the practice of double-dealing during President Roosevelt's presidency, see Chapter 9. The State Department practice continued under President Truman as well, as in the "gloss," noted earlier in the text, on his urgent request to Attlee for the hundred thousand immigration certificates.
50. Crum, *Behind the Silken Curtain*, 36–37.

in his power to put it into effect." Bevin's remarks, Crossman noted, made an enormous impression on the committee, especially on its American members, who had been worried by Einstein's comments about the committee being a waste of time because Britain would not change its anti-Zionist policy in Palestine. The committee now felt that Bevin had an open mind and intended to follow the committee's advice if it was reached unanimously.[51]

The Colonial Office, concerned with guiding the committee in the direction of British policy, submitted its plan for the establishment of autonomous Arab and Jewish provinces in Palestine under continued British rule, the plan similar to the one that had already been considered and rejected by the Peel Commission in 1937. The Foreign Office submitted a paper, prepared by the chiefs of staff in London, emphasizing that trouble resulting from a decision acceptable to the Arabs but not to the Jews would be confined to Palestine, but a decision acceptable to the Jews but not to the Arabs would create trouble not only in Palestine but also in other Moslem countries. Implicit in the Foreign Office submission was its hope for the joint committee's endorsement of a policy along the lines of the 1939 White Paper for restrictions on Jewish immigration, for the prohibitions on land purchases by the Jews, and for the evolution of Palestine as an Arab state.[52]

In the same month, January 1946, Britain also decided to declare Transjordan an independent state—perhaps, as Colonel Meinertzhagen suggested, as a precaution against any possibly undesirable committee recommendation.[53] Although Transjordan had until then been part of the League of Nations Mandate for Palestine, Britain now decided that it had legal authority to act on its own, to establish it as an independent state outside the Palestine Mandate, without any need to secure the approval of the United Nations as the heir to the defunct League of Nations.

---

51. Crossman, *Palestine Mission*, 65–66.
52. Jones, *Failure in Palestine*, 76–77.
53. Meinertzhagen, *Middle East Diary*, 208.

In Palestine, the committee learned that the United Resistance, which had been formed the year before, was increasing its military activities against the administration, even while the committee was in session. In mid-January, after the British had intercepted a ship with 911 immigrants, the United Resistance attacked the central prison in Jerusalem. This was followed by attacks on military installations, the most serious taking place toward the end of February, when three Royal Air Force airfields were attacked, and many planes were destroyed.[54]

The Cairo military establishment echoed the views of the London military, and John Shaw, chief secretary of the Palestine Administration, echoed the position of the London government and the military establishments in both London and Cairo. He told the committee that the Jewish Agency must be dissolved or it will become the government of Palestine. He indicated that if the Jewish Agency were disbanded and the Haganah were disarmed, he would then be willing to recommend the admission of a hundred thousand Jews into Palestine over a period of three to four years.[55]

The committee received a completely different picture, however, from the two top British officials in Palestine, from Lieutenant General D'Arcy, the general officer commanding Palestine, and surprisingly enough, also from Sir Alan Cunningham, the new British high commissioner (November 21, 1945–May 14, 1948). D'Arcy informed the committee that from a military point of view, he could enforce a pro-Jewish solution without much difficulty and that the Haganah could be most helpful in enforcing such a solution. On the other hand, if a pro-Arab solution were to be imposed, he would have to contend with a highly efficient military organization, the Haganah, and Arab support would be of no military value. Moreover, he added, if British troops were withdrawn from Palestine, the Haganah would immediately take over all of Palestine. When asked if he believed that

---

54. Jones, *Failure in Palestine*, 83–84; Begin, *The Revolt*, 262–265.
55. Crum, *Behind the Silken Curtain*, 221.

the British government could not disarm the Haganah, he replied, "You cannot disarm a whole people. I rather think the world will not stand for another mass murder of Jews."[56]

Sir Alan Cunningham, asked by Bartley Crum whether American troops would be needed in Palestine if a hundred thousand Jews were admitted, replied, "No, sir. But I should not mind having a token squad of American troops to show everyone that the United States is behind Britain in such a solution." And when Crum asked if the Jewish Agency should be dissolved because of its failure to stop Jewish violence, Sir Alan replied, "No, I shouldn't want to see the Agency disbanded. I am not one of those who underestimate it. The Palestine government may not like it, but it cannot ignore it: It is a force to be reckoned with, and my own feeling in the matter is that it really cannot be destroyed—even if the government should wish to do so."[57]

After further hearings during the final week in Palestine, the committee began, at the end of March, 1946, to prepare its report in Lausanne, Switzerland. The preliminary report the Foreign Office received from its representatives on the committee staff was that the committee had been shocked to learn about the degree of armed preparedness of the Jews and their readiness to resort to violence as well as about the Jewish Agency's abuse of its authority. Consequently, the committee's preliminary recommendations were that there should be no Jewish state, that the Jewish paramilitary organizations should be disarmed, and that the Jewish Agency should be abolished or radically reconstituted. The chiefs of staff, delighted to learn of this development, set about on April 15 to prepare plans, in consultation with the commanders in chief for the Middle East, for speedy military action against the Jews, following the publication of the Anglo-American Committee Report.[58]

✡ ✡ ✡

---

56. Crum, *Behind the Silken Curtain*, 219–220
57. Crum, *Behind the Silken Curtain*, 225.
58. Jones, *Failure in Palestine*, 85–87.

On April 20, 1946, only five days after these British military consultations, the committee published its report. The report must have come as a rude shock to Prime Minister Attlee, to his Foreign Office, and to the military establishment. Although the committee did agree that there should be no Jewish state, it also decided against both the Foreign Office plan for Palestine to evolve into an Arab state as in the 1939 White Paper and the Colonial Office plan for Arab and Jewish provinces in Palestine under British rule. Instead, it adopted the position presented by Judah Magnes, president of Hebrew University and head of a small Jewish political group called Ihud, in favor of a unitary bi-national state of Arabs and Jews.

Richard Crossman regarded this view as completely unrealistic and utopian, writing,

> I felt all through that what he said represented nothing real in Palestine politics. Maybe twenty-five years ago, that was possible; it's too late for it now… His ideas would be all right if all the Jews were as patient and rational as he is; if the Arabs were not certain that the British are on their side; and if Mr. Bevin were able to replace all the key officials in the Middle East by men who believed in the national home and in helping Arabs and Jews to work together. But isn't that just utopia?[59]

Although Magnes had minimal support among Jews and none amongst Arabs, he favorably impressed the committee, and it accordingly recommended that Palestine should be neither a Jewish nor an Arab state. Instead, it should be retained under British Mandate, until it would be transferred under UN trusteeship, to promote its development into a unitary bi-national state.[60]

Weizmann and Ben-Gurion had privately informed Richard Crossman and Bartley Crum that the Zionists would support a program for

---

59. Crossman, *Palestine Mission*, 142–143.
60. Crossman, *Palestine Mission*, 189–192; Crum, *Behind the Silken Curtain*, 273–275.

the partition of Palestine, provided that Galilee and the Negev were included in the Jewish State.[61] Crossman and Crum argued strongly in favor of partition but were unable to persuade the rest of the committee, some of whom considered the proposal to be a "counsel of despair." In the interests of unanimity, both members agreed not to submit a minority report, but they received permission to express their personal views in speaking and writing, after the report was published.[62]

Far more upsetting to the Foreign Office and to the Attlee government were the committee's recommendations on the immigration and land purchase policies of the 1939 White Paper. Under the leadership of the American co-chairman, Hutcheson, the committee agreed unanimously that the 1939 White Paper was in violation of the League of Nations Mandate and was therefore illegal. Calling in effect for the abrogation of the 1939 White Paper, the committee recommended that immigration for the development of the Jewish national home should be facilitated and that the land transfer regulations should be amended to provide for freedom of sale, lease, and use of land without restriction on race, community, or creed.[63]

But it was the committee's recommendation on the immediate questions of the Jewish violence in Palestine and the issuance of a hundred thousand immigration certificates for the Jews in the displaced persons camps that the Foreign Office and the military establishment must have found most galling. The committee readily concluded 1. that the one hundred thousand refugees could not be kept in the

---

61. Crossman, *Palestine Mission*, 134–137, 163–165.
62. Crossman, *Palestine Mission*, 189–192; Crum, *Behind the Silken Curtain*, 273–275. One American member of the committee, Frank Buxton, editor of *The Boston Herald*, took a more pro-Zionist position, favoring a Jewish state in an undivided Palestine as in the Biltmore program, but he too yielded in the interests of unanimity (Crum, *Behind the Silken Curtain*, 270).
63. *Foreign Relations of the United States: Diplomatic Papers, 1946, vol. 7*, 585–587.

displaced persons camps indefinitely; 2. that after so much suffering in Europe, they had a strong desire to go to Palestine to live among their own people; 3. that Palestine could readily absorb the new immigrants; 4. that the means for their evacuation from the camps and for their transportation were readily available; and 5. that no destinations other than Palestine were available for their absorption.

The issue of the continuing Jewish revolt in Palestine, however, divided the members of the committee until the very last. Sir John Singleton, the British co-chairman of the committee, sided with the views of the British government and military officials who were opposed to additional significant Jewish immigration until the Haganah was disarmed and the Jewish Agency was "reorganized." His position was supported by the other British members of the committee, with the exception of Richard Crossman, who agreed with the views of General D'Arcy that it was neither desirable nor possible to disarm the Haganah nor to disband the Jewish Agency. As Crossman noted, what was necessary to end the violence in Palestine was to remove the cause of the violence. That cause was the 1939 White Paper, which continued to keep Palestine's doors closed to the Jewish survivors from the Holocaust. Only if the doors were opened to Jewish immigration would the violence end. In this position, Crossman was joined by all the American committee members such that, as Crossman noted to his British colleagues, unless they yielded, the division would range a British minority against a united American opinion.

Here, the promise Bevin had given them that if they arrived at a unanimous position in the report, he would do all in his power to implement their recommendations proved to be the decisive factor. With this promise in mind, the other British members soon joined Crossman and their American colleagues, leaving Singleton isolated. Judge Hutcheson, the American co-chairman of the committee, carried the day when he emphatically declared that he would not, "under any circumstances, be a party to any recommendation which would strip the Jews of Palestine of their right to defend their lives." In the end, the committee unanimously agreed to recommend the immediate issuance, without any conditions, of a hundred thousand certificates for the Jews in the displaced persons camps to immigrate into Palestine, as Truman had requested of Attlee shortly after the war's end.[64]

On April 20, 1946, the committee finished its report in a state of high excitement, happy that it had achieved unanimity. Believing that the report would be quickly implemented, they anticipated that the displaced Jews in Europe would be on boats to Palestine within a matter of weeks. Within hours of its completion, the two co-chairmen left by air for Washington and London to submit their report in person to President Truman and Prime Minister Attlee.[65]

✡ ✡ ✡

President Truman was delighted with the committee's report. His statement, issued on April 30, 1946, the day the report was released, declared:

> I am very happy that the request which I made for the immediate admission of one hundred thousand Jews into Palestine has been unanimously endorsed by the Anglo-American committee of inquiry. The transference of these unfortunate people should now be accomplished with the greatest dispatch. The protection and safeguarding of the Holy Places in Palestine sacred to Moslem, Christian, and Jew is adequately provided in the report. One of the significant features in the report is that it aims to insure complete protection to the Arab population of Palestine by guaranteeing their civil and religious rights and by recommending measures for the constant improvement in their cultural, educational, and economic position.
>
> I am also pleased that the committee recommends in effect the abrogation of the White Paper of 1939, including existing restrictions on immigration and land acquisition to permit the

---

64. See Crossman, *Palestine Mission*, 185–189; Crum, *Behind the Silken Curtain*, 271–273, 278–280.
65. Crossman, *Palestine Mission*, 191–193.

further development of the Jewish National Home. It is also gratifying that the report envisages the carrying out of large-scale economic development projects in Palestine which would facilitate further immigration and be of benefit to the entire population.

In addition to these immediate objectives, the report deals with many other questions of long-range political policies and questions of international law which require careful study and which I will take under advisement.[66]

Britain Rejects the Anglo-American Committee Report

In London, the report was received with dismay. At a meeting of the Defense Committee on April 24, chaired by Prime Minister Attlee, Bevin insisted that the Jews must first be disarmed, and until that was done, Britain could not agree to take in the one hundred thousand Jewish immigrants "who might swell the ranks of the illegal organizations." Attlee complained that the report recommended a policy that "would set both the Arabs and the Jews against us" and said he was not optimistic about US cooperation in Palestine. The cabinet, at its meeting on April 29, adopted the position that Britain should seek United States cooperation and assistance on Palestine and that the Jewish organizations must be disarmed before the recommendations of the Anglo-American committee could be adopted.[67]

On May 1, 1946, Prime Minister Attlee discussed in parliament the reasons for Britain's inability to approve the Anglo-American Committee Report, declaring:

> The report must be considered as a whole in all its implications. Its execution would entail very heavy immediate and long-term commitments. His Majesty's Government wish to

---

66. *Foreign Relations of the United States: Diplomatic Papers, 1946, vol. 7*, 588–589.
67. Jones, *Failure in Palestine*, 96–102.

be satisfied that they will not be called upon to implement a policy which would involve them single-handed in such commitments and in the course of joint examination, they will wish to ascertain to what extent the government of the US would be prepared to share the resulting additional military and financial responsibilities.

The report recommends that a hundred thousand certificates for the admission of Jews to Palestine should be awarded immediately, so far as possible in 1946, and that actual immigration should be pushed forward as rapidly as conditions permit. The practical difficulties involved in the immediate reception and absorption of so large a number would obviously be very great.

It is clear from the facts presented in the report regarding the illegal armies maintained in Palestine and their recent activities that it would not be possible for the government of Palestine to admit so large a body of immigrants unless and until these formations have been disbanded and their arms surrendered.[68]

✡ ✡ ✡

The Anglo-American committee was greatly disappointed and most of its members were angered that their unanimous recommendations had been summarily rejected, particularly in view of Bevin's assurance at the luncheon in London at the beginning of their inquiry that if the committee arrived at a unanimous report, he would do everything in his power to put their recommendations into effect. James McDonald, whom President Truman later appointed to serve as US special representative to a newly established Israel, wrote that upon meeting with Bevin in London to get a first-hand view of the British position before taking up his post, Bevin not only emphatically declared that he had given an unequivocal pledge that he would

---

68. *Foreign Relations of the United States: Diplomatic Papers, 1946, vol. 7,* 589–590.

accept the report if it were unanimous, but he also insisted that he had kept the pledge. "There were ten points in your program," he said, "I accepted all ten. President Truman accepted only one." McDonald's reaction was, "I was aghast. For the moment I felt as if I had heard the echo of Hitler's words about telling a big lie. For the truth in this matter was exactly the contrary. If any fact was beyond dispute, it was the fact that Bevin had rejected virtually all of them."[69]

Bartley Crum commented:

> Here was a unanimous report by a joint commission representing two great nations and set up at the invitation of the British government. The manner and the matter of that government's refusal to act in fulfillment of its recommendations were hardly such as to foster international amity or to give hope for a happy outcome of the Palestine problem. Not least disturbing were the cavalier references to the Jews. Never in her long history of empire, I believe, has Britain had more loyal friends than the Jewish community of Palestine and the Jews of America. I may say that I never dreamed that when we finally produced our report urging that the hundred thousand be allowed to enter—I never dreamed that after this slow and arduous day-by-day argument—our entire report would be so cavalierly discarded by Mr. Bevin and Mr. Attlee.[70]

Richard Crossman wrote of Attlee's statement in Parliament:

> The effect of this statement in Palestine was catastrophic. It destroyed the new atmosphere of conciliation. The extremists

---

69. James McDonald, *My Mission in Israel* (New York: Simon and Schuster, 1951), 23–24.
70. Crum reported that when he publicly charged Bevin with having broken his promise, the British Foreign Office answered that it had no record of it. Crum's reaction was, "There may be no record, for the press was excluded, but many members of the British cabinet were there and heard his words" (*Behind the Silken Curtain*, 61).

among the Jews and Arabs were exultant. They had always called the committee a "smoke screen" and predicted that the British cabinet would disregard the report. Now, the prime minister seemed to have justified their prediction. Everyone in Palestine knew that the disarming of the Haganah would involve full-scale military operations against the Jews and so precipitate the crisis which it had been the purpose of the report to prevent. After a few hours of eager hope, the moderates had once again been discredited by the British government.[71]

---

71. Crossman, *Palestine Mission,* 198. Colonel Richard Meinertzhagen's reaction, as recorded in his *Middle East Diary* for May 2, 1946 (210), was, "I think it is clear that [His Majesty's Government] has no intention of implementing this splendid report unless forced to do so by the USA."

– 11 –

The Bankruptcy of Britain's Palestine Policy

President Truman, seeking to salvage the Anglo-American committee recommendations in the face of Attlee's formal rejection of the report, proposed to Attlee on May 8, 1946 that the United States and Britain should proceed to the second stage of their original plan and initiate consultations with the Jews and the Arabs on the basis of the report. Stating that he intended to ask the two sides to submit their views within, say, two weeks, he suggested that Britain do likewise. He added:

> In view of the urgency surrounding the question of the admission to Palestine of the one hundred thousand Jews whose entry is recommended by the committee, I sincerely hope that it will be possible to initiate and complete the consultations with Arabs and Jews at the earliest possible moment.[1]

On May 13, Attlee accepted Truman's proposal but suggested it would be inconvenient to begin the consultations before May 20 and that the parties were likely to need a month, rather than two weeks, to prepare and submit their views.

---

1. *Foreign Relations of the United States: Diplomatic Papers, 1946, vol. 7,* 596–597.

Attlee Proposes a Joint Study of the Committee Report by Government Experts

Attlee added two considerations that would further delay any decision on the committee's recommendations. He proposed that provision should be made "for the study by expert officials of our two governments of the implications of the committee's report, with particular reference to the military and financial liabilities which would be involved in its adoption." In addition, as a final stage in the consultations, there should be a conference of the two governments with both the Arabs and the Jews to consider the entire question.[2]

President Truman, still eager to save the recommendation for the hundred thousand immigration certificates, accepted Attlee's proposal for a joint expert study of the recommendations and asked "if we might have as soon as possible some indication of subjects which your [government] thinks should form [the] basis of these discussions." On the issue of a conference with the Arabs and Jews, Truman was not prepared to commit himself, but he agreed that it should be considered.[3]

In response, Attlee submitted a list of over forty topics, an average of more than four items for each of the ten committee recommendations, "on which decisions would be required before the report could be implemented."[4] Truman replied on June 5, noting, "It will take considerable time to find satisfactory answers to all the problems which you have listed" and suggesting, therefore, "that we begin immediately [the] consideration of the question of the one hundred thousand Jews whose situation continues to cause great concern."[5] At the president's urging, Attlee finally agreed to hold preliminary

---

2. *Foreign Relations of the United States: Diplomatic Papers, 1946, vol. 7,* 606.
3. *Foreign Relations of the United States: Diplomatic Papers, 1946, vol. 7,* 607–608.
4. *Foreign Relations of the United States: Diplomatic Papers, 1946, vol. 7,* 612–615.
5. *Foreign Relations of the United States: Diplomatic Papers, 1946, vol. 7,* 617–618.

discussions on the issue of the one hundred thousand certificates but twice stressed that it would not be possible to reach any decision on this matter until agreement had been reached on all the issues raised by the report.[6] These preliminary discussions began in mid-June and were completed on June 27, 1946, but in accordance with Attlee's insistence, any action would have to await expert discussions and decisions on the Anglo-American committee's report as a whole.[7]

The Acceleration of the Jewish Revolt and the British Administration's Response

In Palestine, the Jews responded to Attlee's rejection of Truman's proposal for one hundred thousand immigration certificates with an intensification of attacks by the United Resistance, which had been formed in 1945 (see Chapter 10). The Haganah stepped up its activity against Britain's immigration policy, bringing in shiploads of Jewish refugees whom the British designated as illegal immigrants. Between July 1945 and the end of 1946, around thirty ships entered Palestine's waters, eighteen of which, carrying an average of a thousand refugees each, were intercepted by the British naval forces, and their passengers were forcibly transferred to detention camps in Palestine and Cyprus. Twelve smaller ships, carrying an average of about a hundred refugees each, managed, however, to evade the British patrols and to land their passengers to be readily absorbed within Palestine's Jewish community.[8] The Irgun also embarked upon an accelerated program of violence against the British administration. In March 1946, Britain captured two Irgun members in the course of a daring raid on the armory of a British airborne division and sentenced them to death.

---

6. *Foreign Relations of the United States: Diplomatic Papers, 1946, vol. 7*, "Truman to Attlee, June 5, 1946," 617–618; "Attlee to Truman, June 10, 1946," 623–624; "Truman to Attlee, June 14, 1946," 626; "Attlee to Truman, June 14, 1946," 627.
7. *Foreign Relations of the United States: Diplomatic Papers, 1946, vol. 7*, 626–627; 638–639.
8. Bethell, *The Palestine Triangle*, 313.

The Irgun retaliated by seizing six British officers on June 18, to be held as hostages, with the warning they would be executed if Britain carried out the death sentence against the Irgun captives. One of the hostages escaped, and the Haganah demanded the release of the others, but the Irgun, determined to save the lives of its two members, released only two of the British officers and insisted on keeping the other three hostage.[9] The threat proved successful. Only after the high commissioner announced in the beginning of July the reprieve of the death sentence against the two Irgun members did the Irgun release the British officers.[10]

With the intensification of the violence, Britain decided that it now had the needed justification for implementing its program of action against the Jewish Agency, on which their commanders-in-chief for the Middle East had earlier decided. On Friday evening, June 28, 1946, one day after the preliminary joint discussions with American experts on the one hundred thousand immigration certificates had been completed, Attlee sent Truman a top-secret telegram, notifying him:

> In view of the continuation of terrorist activity in Palestine culminating in the recent kidnapping of six British officers, His Majesty's Government have come to the conclusion that drastic action can no longer be postponed... It is proposed to raid the Jewish Agency and to occupy it for a period necessary to search for incriminating documents. At the same time, members of the Agency considered implicated directly or indirectly in Haganah

---

9. The Irgun's hostage-taking was too much even for Meinertzhagen, who demanded their immediate and unconditional release. He commented, "Jewish terrorism has once and for all refuted the taunt that Jews would not fight. They are in fact some of the toughest people in the world... The Jews have always fought well in a righteous cause, and their recent exploits in Palestine prove them to be as tough, as resourceful, and brave as any partisans anywhere. I admire them for it but cannot condone the kidnapping of officers as hostages" (*Middle East Diary*, 211).
10. Begin, *The Revolt*, 315–331.

outrages will be arrested. Similar action will be taken in the case of headquarters of illegal organizations.[11]

The British Army acted at 4:15 a.m. Saturday morning, only three hours after President Truman had been notified. As Menachem Begin described the British action:

> Tens of thousands of British soldiers fanned out over the whole country, imposed a curfew, and led thousands away to detention. The building of the Jewish Agency was occupied. The heads of the official institutions and active members of the Haganah were arrested in accordance with prepared lists... The blow to the Palmach was tremendous. Nearly half its members were arrested. The higher ranks of the Haganah were also severely affected.[12]

The arrests were carried out on the Jewish Sabbath, without regard for Jewish religious requirements. Even the secular Jewish community was angered that Rabbi Fishman, a leader of the religious Zionists, the Mizrachi, had been forcibly transported to Latrun prison in violation of the Sabbath.[13]

In retaliation against the arrest of the Jewish Agency Executive, the United Resistance leadership agreed on July 1, 1946 on an Irgun assault on government offices. The Haganah accordingly gave the Irgun written authorization to bomb the military headquarters and the government offices in Jerusalem's King David Hotel.[14] To avoid the loss of lives as far as possible, the Haganah instructions were that

---

11. *Foreign Relations of the United States: Diplomatic Papers, 1946,* vol. 7, 639-40.
12. Begin, *The Revolt,* 276. One hundred thousand British troops and ten thousand police officers were used in the hunt, and the number of Jews arrested the first day was 2,659 men and 59 women (Bethell, *The Palestine Triangle,* 249).
13. Neumann, *In the Arena,* 224.
14. Begin, *The Revolt,* ch. 15. For a detailed discussion of the King David affair, drawing on official British sources, Begin's book, and many personal

the attack should be made outside of office hours and that a warning to evacuate the hotel should be given thirty minutes in advance.[15] On July 6, however, Chaim Weizmann asked the Haganah to suspend its activity until after the sessions of Jewish Agency members still at liberty, scheduled for the following month in Paris. The Haganah then twice asked Begin orally to suspend the planned bombing, but Begin, claiming that it was too late and too dangerous to suspend the attack, decided to go ahead with the plan. The attack was carried out on July 22, but contrary to the original plan, it was decided to do it during office hours when access to the hotel would be easier.[16] The Irgun set the bomb's timing mechanism for thirty minutes and called in bomb warnings to the hotel, to *The Jerusalem Post*, and to the French Consulate, as had been originally agreed, but whether the threat was regarded as a hoax, whether those inside the hotel were distracted by two smaller explosions that had been set off outside the hotel, or because there was much general confusion—or perhaps for all three reasons—the hotel was not evacuated, and the casualties were heavy.[17]

---

    interviews with those involved on both sides of the affair, see Bethell, *The Palestine Triangle*, ch. 8, 240–268.

15. The warning time was held to thirty minutes in part to minimize the time available for locating and defusing the bomb and in part to keep the British from trying to save documents they had taken in their raid on the Jewish Agency. It was feared that Britain might use these documents to declare the Jewish Agency illegal, because they showed that some of its key officials were aware of the activities of the Haganah.
16. Bethell, *The Palestine Triangle*, 253–254.
17. Figures on the casualties vary. Begin listed the casualties as more than two hundred people killed or injured (*The Revolt*, 295). Bethel put the figure of killed at 91, comprising 41 Arabs, 28 Britons, 17 Jews, and 5 others (*The Palestine Triangle*, 263). Former US Secretary of State Dean Acheson, however, gave the casualties as 41 killed and 43 injured (Dean Acheson, *Present at the Creation: My Years in the State Department* [New York, W. W. Norton & Company, 1987], 174).

Angered by the attack, General Sir Evelyn Barker, the British commander in Palestine, issued an order to his troops, declaring:

> As from the receipt of this letter, all Jewish places of entertainment, cafés, restaurants, shops, and private houses are out of bounds. No British soldier will have contact with any Jew, and duty contacts will be made as short as possible and will be limited to the duty concerned. I understand that these measures will create difficulties for the troops, but I am certain that if my reasons are explained to them, they will understand their duty and will punish the Jews in the manner this race dislikes most: by hitting them in the pocket, which will demonstrate our disgust for them.

The *Yishuv* obtained a copy of this anti-Semitic order and published it immediately.[18]

The heavy casualties in the explosion shocked the Jewish community in Palestine. The Haganah dissociated itself from the attack, and Chaim Weizmann demanded that military operations against the British administration be stopped. When Moshe Sneh, the head of the Haganah, refused to give such an undertaking, Weizmann threatened to resign from his post as president of the Zionist Organization. The issue was brought before the meeting of the remaining members of

---

18. Begin, *The Revolt*, 296–297; David Horowitz, *State in the Making* (New York: Alfred A. Knopf, 1953), 118. Meinertzhagen's reaction to Barker's order was, "This is a most shameful and direct incentive to anti-Semitism, just at a time when it is least justified. We were not even asked to hold the Germans in contempt. If the Jews get Barker, he deserves all he gets; in any case, he should be removed from his command for such an inhuman order" (*Middle East Diary*, 214–215). The London government dissociated itself from his order, and on August 9, it was withdrawn. On October 5, 1946, the Jewish Agency, in its discussions with the British government, asked for the immediate removal of General Barker because of fears he would be assassinated. He was recalled in February 1947 (Kirk, *The Middle East 1945–1950*, 222–223, 230; *Foreign Relations of the United States: Diplomatic Papers, 1946, vol. 7*, 705).

the Jewish Agency Executive in Paris, where Ben-Gurion, who had authorized the formation of the United Resistance in 1945, supported Sneh at first but then changed his mind and sided with Weizmann. Sneh then resigned as chief of the Haganah, and the United Resistance was dissolved.[19] The Haganah ceased its military operations, except for its continued activity on behalf of "illegal" immigration, but the Irgun decided, in the face of resumed strong objections from the mainstream leadership, to intensify its violent resistance to the British occupation.

The Joint Government Expert Committee and the Morrison-Grady Plan

The second phase of the joint government discussions on the problems of implementation of the Anglo-American committee recommendations began on July 12, 1946, two weeks after Britain's attack on the Jewish Agency. Heading up the British expert delegation was Sir Norman Brook, secretary of the British cabinet, who had been in charge of the cabinet preparations on the Palestine question. He was assisted by experts from the Colonial Office and Foreign Office, including Harold Beeley, who had served as the secretary to the British members of the Anglo-American commission, and Douglas Harris, author of the Colonial Office's proposal for provincial autonomy that had already been rejected by the Anglo-American committee, but was now to be negotiated with the American delegation.

The American delegation, consisting of alternates to the secretaries of the State Department, the War Department, and the Treasury, with Ambassador Henry F. Grady, alternate to Secretary Byrnes, serving as chairman, was no match for its British counterpart. It had virtually no experience in dealing with Palestine, and its members received no significant briefings from their respective departments. As Richard Crossman, the British member of parliament on the Anglo-American committee, wrote, "Unfortunately, the three Americans knew virtually

---

19. Begin, *The Revolt*, 282–283.

nothing of Palestine and were singularly ill equipped to face the real experts of the British Colonial Office on the other side of the table." The proceedings, in Crossman's view, were accordingly "tragi-comic."[20]

The State Department did give a briefing paper to Grady, but the staff had its own agenda on Palestine in disagreement with Truman's endorsement of the Anglo-American committee's recommendations for immediate action, particularly for the issuance of the one hundred thousand immigration certificates. The State Department's brief stated only that "we should do our best" to get the British, "in a friendly and understanding way," to agree to the one hundred thousand certificates but warned, "We should not, however, exert pressure to force the British against their will to adopt a policy with regard to the one hundred thousand Jews alone, without reference to the remainder of the report."[21]

President Truman, continuing his attempt to save the Anglo-American committee recommendations, gave Ambassador Grady, on the day before he left for London, his approval to support the committee's report as a whole, including its recommendation for "no Jewish, no Arab state." In order to make the committee recommendation for the one hundred thousand certificates more palatable to Britain and to the Arabs, Truman added that he was willing to call for the enhancement of the United States' contribution to the broader solution of the refugee problem by 1. asking Congress to admit another fifty thousand non-quota victims of the Nazi persecution into the United States; 2. asking the appropriate United States lending agencies for substantial funds for the development of Middle Eastern countries, including Palestine; and 3. providing substantial financial aid for the immigration of the one hundred thousand Jews into Palestine.[22]

As strange as it may seem, Grady appears to have acted as if he had received no instructions and therefore had carte blanche to reject

---

20. Crossman, *Palestine Mission*, 205.
21. Jones, *Failure in Palestine*, 130.
22. *Foreign Relations of the United States: Diplomatic Papers, 1946*, vol. 7, 644–645.

the Anglo-American committee's entire report. He readily agreed to the British rejection of the committee recommendations and adopted in full the Colonial Office's plan for provincial autonomy approved by the British cabinet. And, instead of the unconditional immigration of the one hundred thousand Jews into Palestine, as recommended by the Anglo-American Committee and as repeatedly requested by Truman, Grady agreed to the British plan, under which the immigration was made contingent upon the highly improbable acceptance by both Arabs and Jews of Britain's constitutional proposal for Palestine.

According to that proposal, Palestine would continue to be ruled by the British but with provision for semi-autonomous Arab and Jewish provinces—the plan, quite similar, as already noted, to the cantonization plan considered and rejected by the Peel Commission in 1937 and again by the Anglo-American committee. Palestine—now defined as excluding Transjordan, which Britain had declared independent in January—was to be divided into four regions, of which Britain was to retain complete control in two: the Jerusalem district (including Bethlehem) and the district of the Negev, together comprising forty-three percent of Palestine. The Arab provincial autonomy area was to take up forty percent, and the similar Jewish area, seventeen percent of Palestine. Britain was to retain exclusive control of defense, foreign relations, customs and excise taxes, and, initially, the administration of law and order, transport and communication, and the Haifa harbor. Britain's high commissioner would appoint the councils of ministers of the Jewish and Arab provinces after consultation with their elected legislatures and would retain veto power over the legislature on matters concerning the rights of minorities. Jewish immigration into its province would be subject to the limits of economic absorptive capacity, with final control remaining, as before, with Great Britain.[23]

---

23. *Foreign Relations of the United States: Diplomatic Papers, 1946, vol. 7,* 652–667.

The Jews were being offered the restoration of the rights they had before the 1939 White Paper's betrayal of the Mandate, but the area in which those rights were now to prevail would be reduced to seventeen percent of the Palestine Mandate area—redefined to exclude Transjordan. Interestingly enough, although Britain maintained that implementation of the Anglo-American committee recommendations would involve a military and financial burden beyond its ability to bear, no such difficulty was envisaged for its own plan, even though the cabinet must surely have known that the plan would be rejected by the Arabs and intensely resisted by the Jews.

On July 19, 1946, only one week after the beginning of the expert discussions, Grady informed Secretary Byrnes of his acceptance of the British plan, explaining, "The plan seems to offer the only means now apparent of moving the one hundred thousand into Palestine in the near future. It is strongly backed by the British [government]." Noting that "The plan, as presented by the British, is almost a verbatim copy of the plan for provincial autonomy submitted anonymously to the Anglo-American committee in January by Sir Douglas Harris of the Colonial Office,"[24] he ignored the fact that this committee, after months of study of the Palestine problem, had rejected the plan. And Grady seemed equally oblivious to the fact that he had completely ignored the president's instructions in support of the report and had instead endorsed, in full, the plan submitted by the British delegation in rejection of that report. Five days later, on July 24, Grady cabled the text of the agreement he had reached with the British officials, and urged its "most expeditious consideration and acceptance." He also cabled the same day to Mr. Loy Henderson, the State Department's new director of the Office of Near Eastern and African Affairs, saying, "We have considered every phase of [the] problem and see no practical alternatives to our recommendations." Seemingly unaware of the irony inherent

---

24. *Foreign Relations of the United States: Diplomatic Papers, 1946, vol. 7*, 646--647.

in his comment, Grady added, "They [the British] have been most reasonable and completely cooperative."[25]

Two days later, on July 26, Secretary Byrnes, in a teletype conference, told Grady:

> After the stand that the president has taken, we do not see how we can enter into any arrangement which would prevent us from continuing to take the position that the one hundred thousand should move without awaiting for agreement on [the] part of Arabs and Jews. That agreement might be delayed for months or years, and we would have to be silent... [The] president's position has been that [the] one hundred thousand immigration was to start immediately and [as] he has stated so publicly, time and time again. [The] trouble with [the] British plan is [that] immigration never starts unless they get acquiescence of Jews and Arabs.[26]

Sir Norman Brook and his team, as well as Bevin and Attlee, must have been delighted with Grady's total acceptance of Britain's plan for limited provincial autonomy in Palestine, under which the

---

25. *Foreign Relations of the United States: Diplomatic Papers, 1946, vol. 7,* 651–667.
26. *Foreign Relations of the United States: Diplomatic Papers, 1946, vol. 7,* 670–671. Three days later, after meeting with Bevin at the Twenty-One-Nation Peace Conference in Paris, Byrnes changed his mind, cabling Truman a suggested draft statement in which the president would endorse the British plan (*Foreign Relations of the United States: Diplomatic Papers, 1946, vol. 7,* 671–673). Byrnes did not explain the reason for his change of heart, but very likely, as Richard Crossman suggested, it was because of his concern over the deadlock developing in Paris in the negotiations with the Soviet Union, a deadlock that was to evolve into the Cold War between the Soviet Union and the West that lasted until the demise of the Soviet Union. In view of that looming conflict, Byrnes may have come to feel that in the interest of having a joint Anglo-American policy to thwart Russian inroads in the Middle East, the United States should yield to Britain on Palestine (Crossman, *Palestine Mission,* 205).

issuance of the one hundred thousand immigration certificates was made contingent upon Arab and Jewish acceptance of Britain's plan. But Britain had overplayed its hand. Even some staff members on the Grady team had objected to his acceptance of the British plan, and it was leaked to the press, creating a storm in Zionist circles.[27] President Truman decided he could not approve the proposed plan, and he recalled Grady and his team for consultations. On July 30, Acting Secretary Dean Acheson requested the British ambassador in Washington to communicate the president's decision urgently to Prime Minister Attlee.[28]

Herbert Morrison, deputy prime minister, nevertheless, announced the plan in parliament the next day, July 31, 1946, as the plan approved by the American and British experts, and it thus came to be known as the Morrison-Grady Plan. Morrison—who, as spokesman for the Labour Party in parliament, had called the 1939 White Paper, "a cynical breach of pledges given to the Jews and the world, including America, a thing which is dishonorable to our good name, which is discreditable to our capacity to govern, and which is dangerous to British security, to peace, and to the economic interest of the world in general and of our own country" (see Chapter 7)—now emphasized that his government would allow the one hundred thousand Jewish refugees in Europe's displaced persons camps to enter Palestine only if both the Jews and the Arabs accepted Britain's provincial

---

27. Oscar Gass, a Washington economist and adviser to the Jewish Agency, reported from London on July 28 to the Jewish Agency representative in the United States, "The Americans were going about quietly to accept everything the British suggested... To say that Grady was acting as a British 'stooge' is a gross understatement. He was actually publicly reprimanding his staff for venturing to differ with the British even over secondary matters... It is impossible for you to go too far in emphasizing to our friends and to the press the complete abandonment of the president's declared program by Grady" (Jones, *Failure in Palestine*, 137).
28. *Foreign Relations of the United States: Diplomatic Papers, 1946*, vol. 7, 673–674.

autonomy plan for Palestine. Moreover, only refugees from Germany, Austria, and Italy would be permitted to enter—Jewish refugees from Poland, Romania, and other countries of Eastern Europe would not be given entry, except for orphan children. Morrison then added the qualification that full implementation of the experts' plan as a whole depends on the United States' cooperation. Expressing the hope that it would be forthcoming, he warned that if it did not, Britain would have to reconsider its position.[29]

Churchill's statement in the debate that followed demonstrated how far his position too had shifted in less than two years since the assassination of his friend Lord Moyne in 1944. The statesman—whose heart "had always throbbed with Zionism," who had declared in his 1922 White Paper that the Jews were in Palestine as a matter of right, not of sufferance, and who had condemned the 1939 White Paper in such ringing terms as "the end of the vision, of the hope, of the dream, a confession of recoil"—now declared, "The idea that the Jewish problem could be solved or even helped by a vast dumping of the Jews of Europe into Palestine is really too silly to consume our time in the House this afternoon." Turning to the King David Hotel bombing ten days earlier, Churchill added, "It is perfectly clear that Jewish warfare directed against the British in Palestine will, if protracted, automatically release us from all obligations to persevere as well as destroy the inclination to make further efforts in British hearts."[30]

Commenting on the Morrison-Grady Plan itself, Churchill declared, "Almost any solution in which the United States will join us could be made to work." He then made the historic recommendation that the government should declare, "If the United States will not come and share the burden of the Zionist cause, as defined or as agreed, we should now give notice that we will return our Mandate to [the

---

29. *Hansard*, House of Commons, Debates, vol. 426, cc970–971, July 31, 1946.
30. *Hansard*, House of Commons, Debates, vol. 426, cc1253–1254, August 1, 1946.

United Nations Organization] and that we will evacuate Palestine within a specified period."[31]

On August 7, Truman sent Attlee a preliminary note saying he could not in the present circumstances approve the Morrison-Grady Plan but that he was having the matter carefully reviewed.[32] Attlee replied two days later, expressing his great disappointment and informing Truman that he was proceeding with the arrangements for the proposed conference with Jews and Arabs at the end of the month. He added that it was his intention to present the Morrison-Grady Plan as the basis for the negotiations at the conference, but, in the absence of United States support, the plan will have to be modified with respect to "the tempo and extent of Jewish immigration."[33]

In the meantime, Jewish Agency Executive members, meeting in Paris, adopted a resolution on August 5, 1946, declaring the Morrison-Grady Plan unacceptable as a basis of discussion. Instead, they called for the immediate grant of one hundred thousand immigration certificates and the immediate beginning of the transportation of the hundred thousand Jews to Palestine. At the same time, however, they also departed from the Biltmore conference decision of 1942 for all Palestine to become a Jewish state. They were now prepared to accept the partition of Palestine for "a viable Jewish state in an adequate area of Palestine," and they called for the grant of immediate full autonomy, together with the right to control immigration in the area of Palestine to be designated to become a Jewish state.[34]

---

31. *Hansard*, House of Commons, Debates, vol. 426, cc1257, August 1, 1946. The League of Nations officially ended its existence in April 1946 and its authority and responsibilities were transferred to the United Nations.
32. *Foreign Relations of the United States: Diplomatic Papers, 1946, vol. 7*, 677.
33. *Foreign Relations of the United States: Diplomatic Papers, 1946, vol. 7*, 677–678.
34. *Foreign Relations of the United States: Diplomatic Papers, 1946, vol. 7*, 679–682. Neither Weizmann, who favored partition, nor Rabbi Silver, who was strongly opposed thereto, had attended the Jewish Agency's Paris meeting. Ben-Gurion, who convened the executive meeting, abstained (Laqueur, *A History of Zionism*, 572–573).

Dr. Nahum Goldmann, the American representative of the Jewish Agency in the United States, informed the State Department of the agency's Paris resolutions and added that the Jewish Agency Executive would accept a plan that would provide for: 1. the immediate partitioning of Palestine, with the Jewish area to include roughly the borders laid down by the Peel Commission plus the Negev; 2. the termination of the Mandate in the Jewish area and the establishment of a Jewish state there within a fixed period of no more than two or three years; 3. the Jews to set up their own administration, including considerable home rule in economic matters, pending establishment of the Jewish state; and 4. Jews to have full control of immigration into their area immediately upon the adoption of the plan.[35]

Before reaching his final answer on the Morrison-Grady Plan, Truman assigned Undersecretary of State Dean Acheson to chair a meeting between the American members of the Grady team and those of the Anglo-American committee. As Acheson described the session, the meeting was stormy, the members on the Anglo-American committee presenting their views…

> …with passion and at length. As they saw it, the [Morrison-Grady] report proposed a ghetto in attenuated form, a sellout—"very pretty, even grandiose, but a sellout, nevertheless." In Billy Phillips' more restrained diplomatic vocabulary, the plan was "entirely unacceptable"; he was not aware, he said, that the United States had become "the tail to the British kite."
> …The Judge [Hutcheson, American co-chairman of the Anglo-American committee] declared that the Morrison-Grady report violated the cabinet committee's instruction first by nullifying and not carrying out his own committee's earlier recommendations and secondly by violating the League of Nations Mandate by its recommendations for cantonization and restriction of movement in Palestine. Further, he argued,

---

35. *Foreign Relations of the United States: Diplomatic Papers, 1946, vol. 7, 1946,* 679–682.

the president had no power—for legal reasons—to agree to a change in the Mandate without the advice and consent of the Senate.[36]

After receiving Acheson's report, Truman notified Attlee on August 12, 1946 that he could not support the Morrison-Grady Plan. He called attention, instead, to the suggestions that had been made in Paris by the Zionist Executive in favor of partition and added that should the proposed London conference with Arab and Jews be broadened to consider these proposals:

> It is my earnest hope that conference may make possible decision by your [government] upon a course for which we can obtain necessary support in this country and in the Congress so we can give effective financial help and moral support.[37]

The London Conference

President Truman instructed the United States Embassy in London to discuss with Great Britain the Zionist leadership's proposals for partition, but the British government, while declaring its willingness to consider any counterproposals submitted by either side, insisted on the Morrison-Grady Plan as the basis of the discussion.[38] The Jewish Agency Executive members in Paris decided, however, that they could attend the London conference to negotiate only on the basis of their own compromise proposal for the establishment of a Jewish state in Palestine within a fixed time period and for the immediate Jewish control of immigration into Palestine in the area to be designated as the Jewish state. Negotiating on the basis of the Morrison-Grady Plan was unacceptable, because, at best, it could result only in some

---

36. Acheson, *Present at the Creation*, 175–176.
37. *Foreign Relations of the United States: Diplomatic Papers, 1946*, vol. 7, 682; Crossman, *Palestine Mission*, 206; Neumann, *In the Arena*, 223.
38. *Foreign Relations of the United States: Diplomatic Papers, 1946*, vol. 7, 682–687.

further compromise between that plan and their own proposal for partition, which constituted their minimum demand.[39]

The conference began in London on September 10, 1946 between Great Britain and the Arab states alone. Shortly before the opening, Jewish Agency Executive members in Paris suggested to Bevin that they were willing to attend the conference to state their views on the condition that the imprisoned members of the Jewish Agency in Palestine would be released and permitted to attend. Bevin refused the offer. At the conference with the Arabs, Great Britain tabled the Morrison-Grady Plan, and the Arabs rejected it. They submitted their counterproposals calling for the termination of the Mandate and the establishment of Palestine as an independent Arab state, with all Jewish immigration to stop immediately. On October 2, 1946, Britain stated it desired more time to consider the Arab proposals, and, in light of the need for many of the delegates to attend the UNGA sessions, it adjourned the conference until December 16, 1946.[40]

Truman was so frustrated by the decision to adjourn the conference for two and one-half months that he informed Attlee the very next day that he would issue a statement the following day, on October 4, the eve of Yom Kippur, expressing his deep regret. After reviewing the events since his first call in 1945 for admitting a hundred thousand Jewish survivors in the European displaced persons camps, he emphasized,

> In view of the fact that winter will come on before the conference can be resumed, I believe and urge that substantial immigration into Palestine cannot await a solution to the Palestine problem and that it should begin at once. Preparations for this

---

39. *Foreign Relations of the United States: Diplomatic Papers, 1946, vol. 7*, 692–693.
40. *Foreign Relations of the United States: Diplomatic Papers, 1946, vol. 7*, September 20, 1946, 697–698; September 23, 1946, 698–699; October 2, 1946, 700–701.

movement have already been made by this government and it is ready to lend its immediate assistance.

Truman's statement went on to lend support to the Jewish Agency Executive's proposal for partition, noting:

> Meanwhile, the Jewish Agency proposed a solution of the problem by means of the creation of a viable Jewish state in control of its own immigration and economic policies in an adequate area of Palestine instead of the whole of Palestine. It proposed furthermore the immediate issuance of certificates for a hundred thousand Jewish immigrants. The proposal received widespread attention in the United States, both in the press and in public forums. From the discussion which has ensued, it is my belief that a solution along these lines would command the support of public opinion in the United States. I cannot believe that the gap between the proposals which have been put forward is too great to be bridged by men of reason and goodwill. To such a solution, our government could give its support.[41]

Truman's appeal angered the Arabs, and it infuriated Attlee and Bevin.[42] Indeed, American officials in Arab countries were reporting that British officials there were "successfully conveying [the] impression that [the] recommendation for [the] entry of one hundred thousand Jews into Palestine was one of purely American origin against

---

41. *Foreign Relations of the United States: Diplomatic Papers, 1946, vol. 7*, 701–703.
42. Attlee addressed a note to the president that is notable for its undiplomatic language: "I have received with great regret your letter refusing even a few hours grace to the prime minister of the country which has the actual responsibility for the government of Palestine... I am astonished that you did not wait to acquaint yourself with the reasons for the suspension of the conference with the Arabs... I shall await with interest to learn what were the imperative reasons which compelled this precipitancy" (*Foreign Relations of the United States: Diplomatic Papers, 1946, vol. 7*, 704–705).

which British members struggled unsuccessfully."[43] President Truman's stand also generated a series of protests by the Arab governments, including a letter of protest on October 15, 1946 addressed to President Truman by King Ibn Saud of Saudi Arabia.

Truman replied to the king on October 25, 1946 confirming the United States support for Jewish immigration into Palestine on a humanitarian basis. After emphasizing the urgency of relieving the plight of the Jewish survivors in the displaced persons camps in Europe, Truman's letter went on to include the most unequivocal pro-Zionist stand of any president in a communication to an Arab head of state. The president declared:

> The government and people of the United States have given support to the concept of a Jewish national home in Palestine ever since the termination of the first World War, which resulted in the freeing of a large area of the Near East, including Palestine, and the establishment of a number of independent states which are now members of the United Nations… It is only natural, therefore, that my government should favor at this time the entry into Palestine of considerable numbers of displaced Jews in Europe—not only that they might find shelter there but also that they may contribute their talents and energies to the upbuilding of the Jewish National Home.

---

43. *Foreign Relations of the United States: Diplomatic Papers, 1946, vol. 7,* 595. When Secretary Byrnes expressed his concern to the British Embassy regarding these reports circulating in the Arab countries, the British denied any effort by its officials in the Arab countries to drive a wedge between the United States and Great Britain. Colonel Eddy, the State Department advisor on the Middle East, however, informed a staff member of the Division of Near Eastern Affairs, "Every British official who has recently talked to me in the Middle East has said officially that the British have been forced into their present stand on Palestine through the actions of the United States" (*Foreign Relations of the United States: Diplomatic Papers, 1946, vol. 7,* May 24, 1946, 611; June 7, 1946, 620–622 and fn. 64).

Turning next to Ibn Saud's protest that Truman's action was in contradiction to two United States promises—first given by President Roosevelt—not to take any action hostile to the Arab people and not to reach any decision on Palestine without consultations with both Arabs and Jews, Truman responded:

> I am at a loss to understand why Your Majesty seems to feel that this statement was in contradiction to previous promises or statements made by this government... I do not consider that my urging of the admittance of a considerable number of displaced Jews into Palestine or my statements with regard to the solution of the problem of Palestine in any sense represent an action hostile to the Arab people... I furthermore do not feel that my statements in any way represent a failure on the part of this government to live up to its assurance that in its view there should be no decision with respect to the basic situation in Palestine without consultation with both Arabs and Jews. During the current year, there have been a number of consultations with both Arabs and Jews.[44]

✡ ✡ ✡

Britain's decision to adjourn the London conference was motivated at least in part by its recognition that the conference was not likely to achieve any results as long as the Jews refused to participate, and it entered into negotiations in an attempt to reach an agreement to enable the Jewish Agency to participate. On November 5, 1946, the new colonial secretary, Arthur Creech Jones (October 4, 1946–February 28, 1950), announced in the House of Commons that in view of the condemnation of terrorism by the Jewish Agency on October 29, Britain had decided to release the Jewish leaders from detention. At the same time, the government also released the Palestinian Arabs who had been arrested for acts of violence. It expressed the hope that

---

44. *Foreign Relations of the United States: Diplomatic Papers, 1946*, vol. 7, 708–709, 714–717.

these actions would facilitate progress towards a general settlement of the Palestine problem at the resumed London conference.[45]

In December, the World Zionist Congress in Basel, Switzerland rejected the Morrison-Grady Plan—as had the Jewish Agency Executive before it—as "unacceptable, even as a basis for discussion." The congress was divided, however, between supporters of Weizmann, who favored continued cooperation with Great Britain, and followers of Rabbi Silver, who argued that continued reliance upon the goodwill of Great Britain was a policy of defeatism. Rabbi Silver rejected participation at the London conference "unless it was for the purpose of discussing the actual establishment of a Jewish state" and urged that the policy of active resistance adopted by the *Yishuv* should have the moral support of world Jewry. Weizmann, objecting to Rabbi Silver's position, however, announced that he would not be able to continue as president of the World Zionist Organization if the congress decided against participation at the London conference.

It was Rabbi Silver and his supporters who won in the vote. The congress resolved "that in the existing circumstances, the Zionist movement cannot participate in the London conference" but added, "If a change should take place in the situation, the General Council of the Zionist Organization shall consider the matter and decide whether to participate in the conference or not." This decision rendered Weizmann's reelection as president of World Zionist Congress impossible, and in deference to him, the post was left vacant. Ben-Gurion, as chairman of the Jewish Agency Executive, became the *de facto* head of world Zionism, and Rabbi Silver was elected the chairman of the American Section of the Executive of the World Zionist Congress, replacing Rabbi Stephen Wise, Weizmann's key American supporter.[46]

✡ ✡ ✡

---

45. *Foreign Relations of the United States: Diplomatic Papers, 1946, vol. 7,* 721-722.
46. Neumann, *In the Arena*, 228–235.

During the period of suspension of the conference session, the British government devoted considerable time to a further review of its Palestine policy. The Foreign Office continued its firm opposition to the proposal for partition favored by Truman, arguing that any borders that might reasonably be put forward would be objectionable to both Jews and Arabs. Instead, the Foreign Office now called for replacing the Morrison-Grady Plan by the Arab proposal to establish Palestine as an Arab state, modified only to allow for perhaps fifty or sixty thousand Jewish immigrants in the immediate future, and for some small, limited immigration thereafter.

The new colonial minister, Arthur Creech Jones, on the other hand, supported partition, maintaining that it ought to be possible to devise a scheme that would be sufficiently fair to Arabs and Jews to be acceptable to both or at least to win support in the UN. In this, he was relying upon the recommendation of Palestine's high commissioner, Sir Alan Cunningham, who favored partition and opposed the Morrison-Grady provincial autonomy plan, because it provided only an interim program but no solution to the Palestine problem. In addition, several other ministers in Attlee's cabinet, including Hugh Dalton, the chancellor of the exchequer, and Emanuel Shinwell, minister of fuel and power, also favored partition as a solution to the Palestine problem.[47]

The report that Creech Jones and several of his cabinet colleagues favored partition led the Zionist Organization Executive to decide that circumstances had changed sufficiently to enable it to participate informally in the resumed session of the London conference. At Bevin's prompting, however, the cabinet rejected the suggestion of placing the partition proposal before the conference. Instead, the conference was to replace the Morrison-Grady Plan with the Foreign Office proposal for Palestine to become an Arab state, as in the 1939 White Paper, but with allowance for Jewish immigration of four thousand people per month for a period of two years, to take into account Truman's demand for the one hundred thousand immigration certificates.

---

47. Jones, *Failure in Palestine*, 198–220, 239.

Britain's Decision to Take the Palestine Mandate to the United Nations

The London conference resumed its sessions with the Arab states and the Arab Higher Committee on January 27, 1947. Nine members of the Zionist Organization Executive, with Ben-Gurion at their head, joined in informal sessions with Great Britain two days later. The two separate sets of discussions proved to be fruitless. The Arabs demanded that the whole of Palestine be established as a unitary Arab State and that Jewish immigration must be stopped. Ben-Gurion put forward three alternative proposals: 1. Palestine should become a Jewish state or 2. Britain should return to the regime prevailing in Palestine under the British Mandate prior to the 1939 White Paper. If Britain rejected both of these alternatives, then (3) the Jewish Agency would be willing to consider partition, with adequate boundaries for the Jewish state, if Britain would offer such a proposal.

Creech Jones vehemently rejected the suggestion of continuing to administer Palestine under the Mandate regime, in effect, prior to the 1939 White Paper. Bevin, on the other hand, dismissed partition as being impractical, because, inter alia, 1. Palestine could not be divided into two viable states, 2. the Arab states would object, and 3. the UN would not approve it. Instead, in his meetings with the Jews on January 29 and with the Arabs the next day, Bevin asked them to consider the possibility of a bi-national central government with a large measure of local autonomy.

After a number of separate sessions with the Arabs and with the Jews during which the British concluded that no agreement between Arabs and Jews could be reached, the government submitted its own proposals on February 7, 1947.[48] These proposals called for the immediate establishment of a central government of Palestine, headed by Britain's high commissioner for Palestine but with a large measure of responsibility to be exercised by the Arab and Jewish communities

---

48. *Foreign Relations of the United States: Diplomatic Papers, 1947, vol. 5,* 1033–1035.

for local affairs. The government would function under a UN trusteeship agreement with the promise of complete independence after a period of transition for a fixed period of five years.[49] Jewish immigration would be permitted at the rate of four thousand immigrants per month for a period of two years, allowing for nearly a hundred thousand immigrants over the two-year period. For the remaining three years of the trusteeship, the continuance of immigration and its rate would be decided by the high commissioner, with due regard to the principle of economic absorptive capacity and the rights of the non-Jewish population of the country. In the case of disagreement, a UN arbitration tribunal would make the final decision. Control over land transfers would rest with the local authorities.

If the Foreign Office had entertained any hopes that by going as far as it had toward satisfying the Arab demand for an independent Arab Palestine, Britain would be able to preserve its strategic interests in the country, it was quickly disillusioned. On February 9, Bevin informed Truman's newly appointed secretary of state, George Marshall, that the initial reaction of the Arabs was sharply hostile and that he had no hopes for a better reception by the Jews. After further meetings with both the Arabs and the Jews, the British concluded on February 14, 1947 that the conference had reached an impasse, with both sides rejecting its proposals.[50]

Realizing that even a greatly expanded military force in Palestine was now incapable of dealing either with the Jewish resistance against British measures to prevent "illegal" immigration or with the intensification of Irgun violence against British facilities, Bevin recognized that Britain could not arrive at any solution for governing Palestine. Now at the end of his rope, Bevin informed Britain's House of Commons on February 18, 1947, four days after the close of the London

---

49. Under the trusteeship agreement, the Jewish Agency would also lose its position as the government's official channel of communication with Palestine's Jewish community that had been assigned to it under the Mandate.
50. *Foreign Relations of the United States: Diplomatic Papers, 1947, vol. 5*, 1035–1047.

conference, that he had decided to submit the Palestine problem to the UN. He declared that Britain would supply to the UN all the information and all the documents relating to the various proposals that had been considered but would not itself make any recommendations.

Colonial Minister Creech Jones explained Britain's purpose in going to the UN thus: "We are not going to the UN to surrender the Mandate. We are going to the UN setting out the problem and asking for advice as to how the Mandate can be administered."[51] Although much of the cabinet had grown weary of the burdens of Palestine, the military establishment continued to regard control of Palestine as a vital strategic necessity for Britain. And the Arabist officials in the Foreign Office evidently believed that the UN would be incapable of arriving at any solution, in which case, Britain would be free to impose its own policy in favor of establishing Palestine as an Arab state.

✡ ✡ ✡

The United States State Department was unhappy with Bevin's decision not to make any recommendations to the UN, and President Truman was deeply disappointed with the failure to make any progress on the one hundred thousand certificates that he had been urging upon Britain since the summer of 1945. On February 21, 1947, Secretary Marshall, taking note of the "difficult and delicate task" that the British government had been undertaking, wired to Bevin that the "transfer of [the] vexatious problem to [the] UN unfortunately does not render it any less complicated or difficult." In the meantime, he inquired, "Is it possible, without bringing about any marked deterioration of the situation in Palestine, to increase appreciably [the] number of displaced European Jews who might be admitted into Palestine between [the] present and final disposition of the problem by [the] UN?" Marshall added that such a decision "might make both Arabs and Jews more willing to look for [a] compromise solution."

---

51. *Hansard*, House of Commons, Debates, vol. 433, cc2007, February 25, 1947.

On February 24, the day before the opening of the parliamentary debate on Bevin's proposal, President Truman pledged his continuing efforts toward achieving his immigration goal.[52] Apparently, this was too much for Bevin. In the debate on Palestine that opened in parliament on February 25, 1947, he placed the blame for his failure to arrive at a solution of the Palestine problem on the president's pressure for the one hundred thousand certificates and insisted that while he had been criticized in the United States for not accepting the recommendations of the Anglo-American committee, the president had accepted none of the report either, except for the one point of the admission of one hundred thousand immigrants. Referring to Truman's Yom Kippur statement of the previous year in which the president had repeated his longstanding request for the hundred thousand certificates, Bevin declared, to cheers in parliament, "In international affairs, I cannot settle things if my problem is made the subject of local elections."[53]

Truman, in his statement issued simultaneously with the release of the Anglo-American Committee Report on April 20, 1946 and sent to Bevin in advance of its issuance, had, as noted earlier, accepted all of the committee's proposals that called for immediate action. These included, in addition to the one hundred thousand immigration certificates, the abrogation of the 1939 White Paper's restrictions on land purchases and immigration; the recommendations for large-scale economic development projects; and the proposed measures for the improvement of the cultural, educational, and economic position of the Arab population. Truman reserved judgment only on "questions of long-range political policies and questions of international law which require careful study and which I will take under advisement."

Truman did not issue a reply to Bevin's charge. What really angered him was Bevin's accusation that the president's position on

---

52. *Foreign Relations of the United States: Diplomatic Papers, 1947*, vol. 5, 1054-55, 1056 fn. 3.
53. *Hansard*, House of Commons, Debates, vol. 433, cc1908, February 25, 1947; *Foreign Relations of the United States: Diplomatic Papers, 1947*, vol. 5, 1056–1057.

the one hundred thousand immigration certificates was based on considerations relating to the pending presidential elections in the United States. In his *Memoirs*, Truman later wrote, "This was a very undiplomatic—almost hostile—statement for the foreign secretary of the British government to make about the president of the United States. He knew that this was my position all along." Truman added, "While I was outraged by Mr. Bevin's charge, I had Charlie Ross issue a very moderate, entirely impersonal statement from the White House that pointed out that the matter of getting one hundred thousand Jews into Palestine had been the cornerstone of our Palestine policy since my first letter to Attlee in August 1945."[54]

---

54. Harry S. Truman, *Memoirs, vol 2: Years of Trial and Hope* (New York, New American Library, 1965), 153–154. The text of the White House statement is reproduced in *Foreign Relations of the United States: Diplomatic Papers, 1947, vol. 5*, 1057–1058.

– 12 –

The United Nations Special Committee on Palestine

ON APRIL 2, 1947, BRITAIN formally requested of the United Nations a special session of the UNGA for "constituting and instructing a special committee to prepare for the consideration of the Palestine question at the second regular session of the General Assembly." At Britain's request, a special session of the UNGA was convened on April 28, 1947 to deal with the "Palestine question." The Arab members of the UN all called for the addition of a second item on the agenda of the special session, entitled, "The termination of the Mandate over Palestine and the declaration of its independence," but this proposal was rejected in the General Committee by a vote of one in favor, eight against, with five abstentions.[1]

The special session of the UNGA lasted until May 15, during which time neither the United States nor Great Britain announced any policy position regarding Palestine. Britain's ambassador, Alexander Cadogan, informed the UN on May 9, 1947 that Great Britain would not enforce any policy that did not have the agreement of both Arabs and Jews. Britain refrained, however, from making any policy statement on Palestine, because it did not wish to assume responsibility for the outcome of the committee's deliberations. And the United

---

1. United Nations General Assembly. Official Records of the 1st Special Session of the General Assembly: Volume 1, Plenary Meetings of the General Assembly, Verbatim Record, Document A/PV.68-79 (April 28–May 15, 1947). Accessed August 8, 2023. https://digitallibrary.un.org/record/3827201?ln=en.

States had not yet been able to formulate an agreed policy stand on the issues of Jewish immigration and the establishment of a Jewish state in Palestine in advance of the report and recommendations of the UNGA special committee.

The Soviet Union did declare its position on May 14, 1947, a day before the closing of the special session, and its position astonished the UNGA because of the sympathy it expressed for the legitimate interests of the Jews as well as the Arabs. In contrast to the delegates of the Arab member states that insisted, inter alia, that 1. the Jews are not a people; 2. Jews have no roots in Palestine; 3. Palestine is not the homeland of the Jews; and 4. Jews are not entitled to a state in any part of Palestine, the Soviet representative, Ambassador Andrei Gromyko, declared:

> It is essential to bear in mind the indisputable fact that the population of Palestine consists of two peoples, the Arabs and the Jews. Both have historical roots in Palestine. Palestine has become the homeland of both these peoples, each of which plays an important part in the economy and the cultural life of the country... An equitable solution can be reached only if sufficient consideration is given to the legitimate interests of both these peoples. All this leads the Soviet delegation to the conclusion that the legitimate interests of both the Jewish and Arab populations of Palestine can be duly safeguarded only through the establishment of an independent, dual, democratic, homogeneous Arab-Jewish State. Such a state must be based on equality of rights for the Jewish and the Arab populations, which might lay foundations of cooperation between these two peoples to their mutual interest and advantage.

Gromyko, added, however, this stunning fallback position:

> If this plan proved impossible to implement, in view of the deterioration in the relations between the Jews and the Arabs... it would be necessary to consider the second plan...which

provides for the partition of Palestine into two independent autonomous states, one Jewish and one Arab.[2]

Since the Soviet government had until then considered Zionism only a tool of British imperialism and Zionist activity a crime subject to years of punishment in Siberian prison, Gromyko's declaration of support for partition and a Jewish state astounded the UNGA delegations. Indeed, Great Britain and the United States as well as the Arab states remained convinced, despite Gromyko's statement, that in the regular UNGA session beginning in September, the Soviet Union would return to its pro-Arab, anti-Zionist position of the past and would vote against the establishment of a Jewish state in Palestine. Harold Beeley, Bevin's adviser on Palestine, had taunted David Horowitz of the Jewish Agency at the end of the London Conference, "You can only win a majority if the Eastern bloc and the United States join together and support the same resolution in the same terms. That has never happened, it cannot happen, and it will never happen!"[3]

On the last day of its special session, May 15, 1947, the UNGA adopted a resolution by a vote of forty-five to seven, establishing a UN Special Committee on Palestine, known by its initials as UNSCOP and consisting of the representatives of eleven UN member states. The committee was given the power to study all relevant questions and issues relating to the Palestine question and to make its

---

2. United Nations General Assembly, 1st Special Session: 77th Plenary Meeting, Held on Wednesday, May 14, 1947. Document A/PV.77 (May 14, 1947), accessed on August 8, 2023, online at https://digitallibrary.un.org/record/3829520?ln=en.
3. Horowitz, *State in the Making*, 143. The US shared Britain's opinion as late as September 22, 1947, when Loy Henderson, in a memorandum to Secretary Marshall, reported, "The embassy in Moscow and other observers are convinced that in the final showdown, the Soviet Union will support the Arab states" ("Henderson Memo to Marshall" in *Foreign Relations of the United States: Diplomatic Papers, 1947, vol. 5*, 1154–1158; "Memorandum Prepared in the State Department," 1169).

recommendations for a solution by September 1, 1947 in time for consideration by the next regular session of the UNGA.[4]

The Arab states all voted against the resolution establishing UNSCOP on the grounds that 1. its terms of reference "contained no mention of the independence of Palestine or the principles of the Charter"; 2. the "future government" of Palestine had been replaced by the vague term "problem" of Palestine; 3. the clause relating to the consideration of the interests of all the inhabitants of Palestine had been omitted; 4. the mandate to the special committee to conduct investigations wherever it deemed useful had been expressly intended to enable the committee to visit the displaced persons camps and bring about a connection between the two problems; and 5. the proposed terms of reference would not make for peace in the Middle East. They reserved the attitude of their governments on the question.[5]

The UNSCOP consisted of three representatives from Latin America—Guatemala, Peru, and Uruguay—and two each from the following four areas of UN membership: 1. the British Commonwealth—Australia and Canada; 2. Western Europe—The Netherlands and Sweden; 3. Eastern Europe—Czechoslovakia and Yugoslavia;, and 4. Asia—India and Iran. None of the major powers were represented on the committee.

The committee held its first meeting on May 26, 1947 at Lake Success, New York. At its second and third meetings on June 2–3, the committee adopted provisional rules for procedure, including a provision for the appointment of liaison officers to the committee by the Mandatory Power, the Arab Higher Committee, and the Jewish

---

4. United Nations General Assembly, 1st Special Session: 79th Plenary Meeting, Held on Thursday, May 15, 1947. Document A/PV.79 (May 15, 1947), accessed on August 8, 2023, online at https://www.un.org/unispal/document/auto-insert-178314.
5. United Nations General Assembly, Official Records of the 1st Special Session of the General Assembly: Volume 1, Plenary Meetings, Verbatim Record, Document A/PV.68-79 (April 28–May 15, 1947), accessed on August 8, 2023, online at https://digitallibrary.un.org/record/3827201?ln=en.

Agency for Palestine. The Arab Higher Committee, however, rejected the invitation to appear, informing the UN secretary-general:

> [The] Arab Higher Committee, Palestine desire [to] convey to United Nations that after thoroughly studying the deliberations and circumstances under which the Palestine fact-finding committee was formed and the discussion leading to terms of reference, they resolved that Palestine Arabs should abstain from collaboration and desist from appearing before said committee for [the] following main reasons. Firstly, United Nations' refusal [adopts the] natural course of inserting [the] termination mandate and declaration [of] independence in [the] agenda [of the] Special United Nations Session and in [the] terms of reference. Secondly, [there is a] failure [to] detach Jewish world refugees from [the] Palestine problem. Thirdly, [the committee is] replacing [the] interests [of] Palestine inhabitants by [the] insertion [of] world religious interests, although these are not [the] subject of contention. Furthermore, [the] Palestine Arabs' natural rights are self-evident and cannot continue to be subject to investigation but deserve to be recognized on the basis of [the] principles of [the] United Nations Charter.[6]

The UNSCOP members assembled in Palestine on June 16, 1947, where they spent a month in sessions to hear representatives of Britain's Palestine administration and the Jewish Agency. Members of UNSCOP visited Palestine's Jewish communities, where they received

---

6. According to the US Consul General in Jerusalem (memorandum to the secretary of state, June 11, 1947), Jamal Husseini explained that the Arab Higher Committee boycotted UNSCOP because 1. UNSCOP was a device for "policy procrastination through investigating committees well understood by Arabs"; 2. the provision for declaration of Palestine's independence was omitted from the terms of reference; 3. Palestine was connected to the displaced persons problem; 4. Eastern Europe was under-represented in UNSCOP; and 5. religious matters were included in the terms of reference to justify Britain's remaining in Palestine (*Foreign Relations of the United States: Diplomatic Papers, 1947, vol. 5,* 1102).

a very warm welcome, and Arab communities, where they received very cold receptions. At the end of its stay in Palestine, UNSCOP traveled to Beirut to hear the representatives of Egypt, Syria, Lebanon, Iraq, and Saudi Arabia and then to Amman to hear the views of Jordan's King Abdullah, all of whom wished to be heard, despite the Arab Higher Committee boycott. Then, UNSCOP visited the displaced persons camps in Germany and Austria at the beginning of August for a first-hand view of the state of the Jewish refugees there.

The British administration confined itself, by and large, to the presentation of information on Palestine rather than to urging any particular policy before the committee, although the administration's chief secretary, Sir Henry Gurney, stressed what Britain regarded as its problem of "dual obligation" to the Jews and the Arabs under the Mandate.

David Ben-Gurion, head of the Jewish Agency, rejected the Palestine administration's notion of dual obligation, emphasizing that the League of Nations Mandate called for the establishment in Palestine only of a Jewish national home. This was subject to two reservations, namely that the civil and religious rights of non-Jewish communities in Palestine and the status of Jews living elsewhere should not be prejudiced—reservations that did not imply any dual obligation to set up an Arab state in Palestine. Ben-Gurion maintained, therefore, that the Jews were entitled under the Mandate to the establishment of Palestine as a Jewish state, but he added that the Jewish Agency had informed Britain it would be willing to compromise and consider a Jewish state in a viable part of Palestine, if it were offered. When asked whether the Jews based their case on the Balfour Declaration, which the Arabs regarded as illegal, Ben-Gurion replied that the Jewish claim was three thousand years old and had only been confirmed by the 1917 Balfour Declaration.[7] More explicit in his support for

---

7. Ben-Gurion, although he was a secular rather than a religious Jew, had given the same explanation before the Peel Commission more than ten years earlier, on January 7, 1937, when he declared: "I say on behalf of the Jews that the Bible is our Mandate, the Bible which was written by us, in

partition was Chaim Weizmann, the elder statesman of the Zionist movement but no longer its head; he appealed for sweeping away the 1939 White Paper and for the partition of Palestine, with boundaries for the Jewish state to be approved along the lines recommended by the Peel Commission—but including the Negev.

Several committee members, together with UN representatives Assistant Secretary-General Victor Hoo and Director Ralph Bunche, heard in secret the Haganah High Command, which was continuing to bring Jewish refugees to Palestine in defiance of the British clampdown, pursuant to the 1939 White Paper, on such immigration. A newspaper report of the meeting of the chairman of the committee with the head of the Irgun, Menachem Begin, created a sensation in England, because Begin still had a price on his head for the revolt he was continuing to conduct against Great Britain, and the Palestine administration had been unable to find him despite repeated searches. Begin declared that the Irgun sought the removal of British rule in Palestine and the creation of the Jewish State. Since the government had refused to carry out its obligations under the Mandate under which it ruled Palestine, he considered Britain's rule to be illegal and the Jewish revolt against Britain to be legal. He added he would honor the UNGA's call for a truce during UNSCOP's inquiry only if Britain ceased its program of repression in Palestine, permitting the Jewish refugees to enter the country and halting its program of curfews, searches, and death sentences. He warned that if Britain executed members of the Irgun—whom he considered to be prisoners of war—the Irgun would capture and execute British soldiers.[8]

---

our own language, in Hebrew in this very country. That is our Mandate. It was only the *recognition* of this right which was expressed in the Balfour Declaration" (*Peel Commission Minutes*, cited in Cruise O'Brien, *The Siege*, 225).

8. Evidently, Begin made a positive impression on his interlocutors, since at the meeting's end, the UNSCOP chairman expressed his regret over the absence of other committee members, and the two UN officials made supportive comments. Victor Hoo commented, "*Au revoir* in an

316   Independence

On the very day of its arrival in Jerusalem, June 16, 1947, UNSCOP found itself caught up in the ongoing war between the Palestine administration and the Irgun. A British military court announced that day the death sentence for yet three more Irgun members, together with life imprisonment for two others who had been captured about a month earlier in an Irgun attack against the hitherto "impregnable" Acre fortress prison, which succeeded in freeing 251 Irgun and Lehi prisoners.[9] The Irgun, basing itself upon a clause in the UN resolution establishing UNSCOP, which called "upon all governments and peoples...to refrain, pending action by the General Assembly on the report of the special committee on Palestine, from the threat or use of force or any other action which might prove prejudicial to an early settlement," requested UNSCOP to intervene on behalf of the three prisoners whose death sentence had just been announced. In response, UNSCOP adopted a resolution notifying the secretary-general that "the majority of the members of the committee have expressed concern as to the possible unfavorable repercussions of the death sentences pronounced by the Military Court of Jerusalem on June 16th, the day on which the committee held its first meeting in Jerusalem, might have upon the fulfillment of [their] task."

Great Britain was annoyed by the committee's resolution. In its reply to the secretary-general, it declared that it interpreted the UN resolution as applying to action calculated to disturb the peace and it "cannot admit its relevance to normal processes of justice there." It

---

    independent Palestine," and Ralph Bunche shook Begin's hand and said, "I can understand you. I am also a member of a persecuted minority" (Begin, *The Revolt*, 386–394).

    According to David Horowitz (*State in the Making*, 204), Bunche replied to a question, raised by British MP Crossman in jest, whether he had already turned anti-Semitic from being immersed in the Jewish question: "That would be impossible, because I've been a negro for forty-two years. I know the flavor of racial prejudice and racial persecution. A wise negro can never be an anti-Semite."

9. Begin, *The Revolt*, 371–374.

added that the whole matter is still sub judice, that if the sentences were confirmed, the high commissioner has the power of granting pardon and that it was not the practice of the government to interfere with the high commissioner's discretion.[10]

Not expecting any British pardon, the Irgun seized two sergeants in British intelligence and announced that if its men were hanged, the Irgun would hang the two officers. The British carried out the death sentences on July 23, 1947, while UNSCOP was in Beirut for its hearings with the Arab states. The next day, the Irgun hanged the two British officers and booby-trapped the bodies, wounding the officer who came to recover the bodies. Thirty years later, when Begin had been elected prime minister of Israel, he justified this brutal retaliation, declaring:

> There is no doubt that had we not retaliated, avenues of gallows would have been set up in Palestine and a foreign power would be ruling in our country to this day. The grim act of retaliation forced upon us in Netanya not only saved scores of Jewish young men from the gallows but broke the back of British rule... This was confirmed in unambiguous terms by the chief assistant to the chief secretary of the British government in *Eretz Yisrael*, Colonel Arthur-Cust. In a lecture to the Royal Empire Society, he said: "The hanging of the two British sergeants did more than anything to get us out."[11]

---

10. *Foreign Relation of the United States: Diplomatic Papers, 1947, vol. 5,* 1117–1118.
11. Begin, *The Revolt,* 378–380. The Irgun harmed its case in the eyes of many pro-Zionists, including, in particular, Zionist mainstream Jewry, by the booby-trapping of the hanging bodies, injuring the officer who came to recover the bodies. Colonel Meinertzhagen's reaction to the hanging, however, was, "The real men responsible for the killing of those two sergeants are the politicians who sit in Downing Street, the government of this country and ultimately the British public. All my sympathy is with the Jews who have been driven by apathy, anti-Semitism, and broken promises into a

The mainstream Zionist leadership—in particular, Weizmann, Ben-Gurion, and the Jewish Agency's Haganah—vigorously opposed the Revisionists and their Irgun, insisting that their violence was both immoral and an impediment to the Zionist political efforts toward the establishment of the State of Israel. However, General Jan Smuts, a personal friend of Weizmann, who, as a member of Britain's War Cabinet, played a significant role in the issuance of the Balfour Declaration, emphatically disagreed. According to Smuts, it was the Jabotinsky Revisionists "who compelled Britain to admit defeat and gave Weizmann his opportunity...and when history comes to be written, [Jabotinsky] will be the patriot who made it possible to bring Israel into the world."[12]

UNSCOP was more actively involved in the dramatic episode of the Haganah-directed Exodus 1947 ship, which was carrying a boatload of Jewish refugees to Palestine. Determined to block the Exodus 1947 from picking up Jewish refugees in Europe for transport to Palestine, Britain had shadowed the boat from the time it had set sail from the United States. Despite the obstacles placed in its path by the British, the boat reached France, where it took on 4,500 refugees, even though it was built for less than a fifth of that number. Foreign Minister Bevin, who was in Paris at the time, warned the French not to permit the ship to set sail, but the Haganah captain managed to take it out of the harbor despite the warning. Although the reason for Bevin's trip to Paris was to discuss with the French the needed arrangements for handling the Marshall Plan (the European Recovery Program), the British found that they could, nevertheless, afford to send a fleet of six destroyers and a cruiser to shadow the boat's journey toward Palestine. When the Exodus 1947 came within seventeen miles of Haifa, two British ships rammed it and boarded it, killing its American chief mate and two refugees and wounding more

---

state of exasperation. If I were a Jew, I should be a terrorist, a violent one, and I would aim at Whitehall" (Meinertzhagen, *Middle East Diary*, 219).

12. Meinertzhagen, *Middle East Diary*, 244.

than a hundred passengers.[13] The British then escorted the boat to the port of Haifa, where they transferred the refugees to three British transports and caged them below deck.

UNSCOP was still in Palestine when the Exodus 1947 arrived in Haifa on July 18, 1947. Some committee members who were present in Haifa at the time personally witnessed the refugees being transferred into prison boats. In addition, the Guatemalan member of UNSCOP, Jorge García-Granados, received a full accounting of the events from the Reverend John Grauel of Worcester, Massachusetts, who had been so moved by the plight of the Jews in the displaced persons camps that he had enlisted as a cook on the Exodus 1947. The Reverend Grauel concluded his story of what had transpired with this comment:

> I would like to make only one statement, gentlemen. I have watched these people. I know what they are. And I tell you, the Jews in the European displaced persons camps insist on coming to Palestine, they will come to Palestine, and nothing short of open warfare and complete destruction will halt them.[14]

Bevin was still not satisfied that he had taught the refugees a sufficient lesson with this episode. Determined to make an example of the Exodus 1947, he decided that instead of interning these refugees in Cyprus, they must be sent back to France, where they had embarked. When the refugees refused to disembark in France, and the French refused the British request to remove them by force, Bevin ordered the ships sent to Germany, where the refugees were returned to a displaced persons camp.

---

13. Melvin Urofsky, *We Are One!: American Jewry and Israel* (Garden City, NY: Anchor Press, 1978), 136.
14. Jorge García-Granados, *The Birth of Israel: The Drama as I Saw It* (New York: A. A. Knopf, 1949), 172–182. The committee members were able to confirm this judgment for themselves later when they visited the displaced persons camps after leaving Palestine for Geneva to write their report.

The United States repeatedly expressed its concern to Britain's Foreign Office, warning of the negative impact this decision would have upon the British position in the United States, but Bevin remained unmoved.[15] Bevin was so determined to punish the Jewish refugees for daring to defy his orders that he was oblivious to the impact of his decision not only on the United States but also upon the UNSCOP members. The Guatemalan representative, García-Granados, called the forced return of the Exodus 1947 refugees to a displaced persons camp in Germany, "a British decision which must go down as one of the most heartless and stubborn ever made by a civilized government."[16] The committee was so shocked by the entire episode that it concluded unanimously to recommend the termination of Britain's Mandate for Palestine. The historian, and sometime Irish representative to the UN, Conor Cruise O'Brien, wrote that had Bevin worked in collusion with the Zionists, he could not have contrived an event so favorable to their cause.[17]

After concluding its investigations, UNSCOP moved to Geneva to prepare its report, which it completed precisely by its deadline date of August 31, 1947. The committee reached unanimous agreement on eleven recommendations, of which the first two were the key proposals that 1. Britain's Mandate should be terminated, and 2. Palestine should be granted independence at the earliest practicable date. The next two unanimous recommendations provided for 3. a short transitional period and 4. that the authority administering Palestine during the interim should be responsible to the United Nations.

---

15. *Foreign Relations of the United States: Diplomatic Papers, 1947, vol. 5,* 1138–1142.
16. García-Granados, *The Birth of Israel,* 182.
17. Cruise O'Brien, *The Siege,* 277. The Exodus 1947 appears to have been aptly named: Bevin's behavior in relation to this boat is reminiscent of the hardening of the heart of another tyrannical ruler more than three thousand years earlier—the Pharaoh of the Exodus of the Jews from Egypt. In both cases, the results were disastrous for the countries that they ruled.

The other unanimous recommendations provided for (5) the preservation of the sacred character of Palestine's holy places and the rights of the religious communities; (6) the UNGA to arrange for the problem of the Jewish refugees to be dealt with on an urgent basis; (7) the constitution of the new state or states to be based on democratic principles, providing for human rights, fundamental freedoms, and the protection of minority rights; (8) the constitutional provisions to incorporate the international obligations contained in the UN Charter for the peaceful settlement of disputes; (9) the economic unity of the independent Palestine to be preserved; (10) all states to renounce any special privileges and immunities in Palestine dating back to the capitulations and practices under the Ottoman Empire; and (11) the UNGA to call upon the peoples of Palestine to end the violence there and to cooperate with the UN in the settlement of the Palestine problem.

Although the committee was unanimous in rejecting Britain's plan in its 1939 White Paper to transform all Palestine into a unitary Arab state, it could not reach unanimous agreement on a long-term political solution for Palestine. A majority of seven members—consisting of the three representatives from Latin America, the two from Western Europe, and the representatives of Canada and Czechoslovakia—made the historic recommendation for the partition of Palestine, to provide for the establishment of two independent states, one Jewish and one Arab, with an economic union between them. Jerusalem and its environs, including Bethlehem, were not to be part of either the Jewish or the Arab state but were to be governed under an international trusteeship of the UN.

The proposed Arab state would include 1. Western Galilee, 2. the hill country of Samaria and Judea,[18] except for the city of Jerusalem,

---

18. What is known today as the West Bank was then still known, even by the Arabs and the UN, only by its biblical name, Judea and Samaria. The name "West Bank," in common use today, was given to the area only by Jordan in 1950, when it annexed the area shortly after seizing it in the 1948 Arab War against the newly formed State of Israel.

and 3. the coastal plain from Ashdod to the Egyptian border. The Jewish State would include the rest of Palestine—except for Jerusalem—comprising 1. Eastern Galilee, 2. the Esdraelon Plain/Jezreel Valley, 3. most of the coastal area, and 4. the Beer Sheva District, including the Negev. Both the Arab and Jewish states were to become independent after a two-year transition period from the beginning of September 1947. During the transition period, Britain was to continue its administration of Palestine, but it was to be under UN auspices, and it was to allow the immigration of 150,000 Jews into the area of the proposed Jewish State. The Arab and Jewish states were to form an economic union and to provide for other matters of common interest through a treaty arrangement.

Three members—the two Moslem representatives of India and Iran, along with the representative of Communist Yugoslavia—rejected the partition proposal and recommended, instead, that Palestine be established as a bi-national federal state. Jerusalem was to be the capital of the federal state. The representative of Australia endorsed neither plan and instead set out his reservations about both plans in an appendix to the committee's report.[19]

✡ ✡ ✡

The reaction of the Arab states to the UNSCOP report was uncompromisingly negative. According to the US ambassador to the United Kingdom, the Iraqi foreign minister said before he departed for the regular UNGA session, that the report "proves Arab wisdom in boycotting UNSCOP" and that both the majority and the minority reports were "ridiculous." The Iraqi foreign minister added the warning that if the UN adopted the UNSCOP recommendations, the Arab states would leave the UN, and there would be a bloody

---

19. United Nations Special Committee on Palestine, Report of the United Nations Special Committee on Palestine, vol. 2: Report to the General Assembly, Document A/364 (September 3, 1947), accessed on August 8, 2023, online at https://digitallibrary.un.org/record/563036?ln=en.

uprising "first against Jews as invaders and second against British troops if these interfered."[20]

In contrast to the Arabs, the Jews reacted positively to the UNSCOP majority recommendation for partition. Under the leadership of Ben-Gurion, the Jewish Agency, despite having serious misgivings about the failure to include the Western Galilee—especially, Jewish Jerusalem—within the boundaries for the Jewish State, saw the UNSCOP proposal as a practical compromise with the Arabs that would finally provide for an independent Jewish state and Jewish control of immigration into its state. Chaim Weizmann had been among the first to express his acceptance of partition,[21] and even Rabbi Abba Hillel Silver, the leader of American Zionism, who had long held out against compromise, now came to support the UNSCOP proposal.[22]

---

20. *Foreign Relations of the United States: Diplomatic Papers, 1947, vol. 5*, 1144–1145.
21. In a statement to the press on March 25, 1948, Chaim Weizmann summarized his support for partition as follows: "The plan worked out by the General Assembly was the result of a long and careful process of deliberation in which the conflicting claims of the various parties were judged in the light of international equity. In order to achieve a compromise between Jewish and Arab national claims, the Jews were asked to be content with one eighth of the original area of the Palestine Mandate. They were called upon to co-operate in a settlement for Jerusalem which set that city's international associations above its predominantly Jewish character. We accepted these limitations only because they were decreed by the supreme authority of international judgment, and because in the small area allotted to us, we would be free to bring in our people and enjoy the indispensable boon of sovereignty—a privilege conferred upon the Arabs in vast territories" (Weizmann, *Trial and Error*, 473).
22. Rabbi Abba Hillel Silver, chairman of the American section of the Jewish Agency, who, like Begin, had earlier championed the cause of a Jewish state in all of Palestine, declared at the UN (see Chapter 13) that while partition was a very heavy sacrifice for the Jews, they would accept it. At a meeting of the American Zionist Emergency Committee in December 1947, shortly after the UN adopted its resolution on partition, Rabbi Silver explained the gains of the resolution, namely: "statehood, recognition of

Only the Irgun and the even smaller Lehi opposed the UNSCOP proposal, declaring partition to be illegal and invalid and calling for the entire Israel to be restored to the Jewish people, with Jerusalem as its capital. Menachem Begin, the head of the Irgun, warned that nothing was to be gained by compromise, because the Arabs would fight just as hard against partition as against Jewish rule of the entire country.[23]

British Preparations for the United Nations Debate on the Special Committee on Palestine Report

Given the debates in parliament prior to the decision to send the Palestine problem to the UN, the responsible agencies of the British government differed significantly in their response to the UNSCOP report. The Colonial Office, on the one hand, considered partition a workable solution, provided the area for the Jewish State recommended in the majority plan would be reduced so as to keep the number of Arabs in the Jewish State to a minimum. The Colonial Office presented a paper to Bevin on September 16 recommending that Britain accept UNSCOP's unanimous recommendations, remain neutral on its majority plan for partition, and suggest a date for withdrawal. In contrast to the military joint planning staff, it suggested that such a solution would not only be workable and avoid an Arab revolt but that it might even also enable Britain to retain the use of military facilities in the region. This optimistic assessment was based in part on the assessment of the Palestine administration, which welcomed the UNSCOP report and informed the colonial secretary on September

---

the Jewish nation as a nation on Earth, and this marked the end of *galut* [exile] for our people. With this comes the great opportunity for us to ingather all the dispersed of our people…and a possibility in a very short time of emptying the displaced persons camps of Europe and giving a home at last to hundreds of thousands of our people. The UN decision is therefore of incalculable significance for our people and for the history of mankind."

23. Begin, *The Revolt*, 433–434.

8, that a Jewish state could be established within six months. The Arab reaction, it believed, could be contained by martial law until it was ameliorated by the prospect of independence.

The military joint planning staff, on the other hand, adhered to its earlier views concerning Palestine's strategic importance as a British security asset, and, in a paper to the cabinet on September 18, 1947, it warned that the implementation of the majority plan would be "at the immediate and lasting expense of our overriding strategic requirement of retaining Arab goodwill." Since the Arabs would probably reject the minority plan as well, the only other option was Britain's withdrawal from Palestine, and that, too, would present considerable military difficulties.

The Foreign Office, like the military establishment and in opposition to the Colonial Office, rejected both the majority and the minority plans of the UNSCOP report. Although Great Britain had ruled Palestine under a League of Nations Mandate to facilitate the development of the Jewish National Home, and although the 1922 Churchill White Paper had declared that the Jews were in Palestine as a matter of right, not of sufferance—with Jewish immigration in all Palestine subject only to economic capacity, even if this led to a Jewish majority—the Foreign Office regarded the majority plan for partition as so unfair to the Arabs that it was difficult to see "how we could reconcile it with our conscience." The Foreign Office warned that an Arab uprising against partition appeared likely, and, in any event, the plan would earn for Great Britain the everlasting hostility of the Arabs. The Foreign Office likewise rejected the minority plan for a bi-national federal state in Palestine, because that plan would require Arab-Jewish cooperation, which was unattainable. The only solution the Office continued to consider acceptable was to establish Palestine as an independent Arab state, but that solution had been rejected by UNSCOP.

Bevin recommended, therefore, that Britain should abstain in the UN vote on the UNSCOP report. If the UNGA were to approve some plan like the majority proposal for partition, Britain could not accept responsibility for its implementation, and it would have to withdraw completely from Palestine. Britain's cabinet, in a decision on September 20, 1947, adopted Bevin's proposal. In supporting the decision, Prime Minister Clement Attlee added his directive that in its statement to the UNGA, Britain should avoid any commitment to cooperate with other nations in implementation of the UN decision on Palestine.[24]

American Preparations for the UN Debate on the Special Committee on Palestine Report

With Britain's refusal to help implement any UN decision that did not have the agreement of both Arabs and Jews, the major responsibility for formulating policy on Palestine naturally shifted to the United States, where President Truman, who had already expressed his support for partition to the British, faced powerful opposition by the key officials of both the Military Department and the State Department. James Forrestal, the crusading secretary of defense, together with the chiefs of staff of the Armed Forces as well as the CIA, all argued that support of a Jewish state in Palestine would 1. harm United States' relations with the British, 2. jeopardize US interests in the Arab world, 3. risk the loss of the supply of oil to the West, and 4. endanger the security of the United States and Europe. The US State Department opposed the establishment of a Jewish state as vigorously as did Britain's Foreign Secretary Bevin and his Foreign Office. Looming large in their calculations, in addition to all the considerations raised by the military, was the importance of safeguarding the United States' educational, cultural, and church interests built up in Arab countries.

Not quite a week after Truman had succeeded Roosevelt as president of the United States, Secretary of State Edward Stettinius sent him a memorandum prepared by the Division of Near Eastern Affairs, warning him:

---

24. See Jones, *Failure in Palestine*, 282–296 for a detailed review of the British position on the UNSCOP report.

It is very likely that efforts will be made by some of the Zionist leaders to obtain from you at an early date some commitments in favor of the Zionist program which is pressing for unlimited Jewish immigration into Palestine and the establishment there of a Jewish state. As you are aware, the government and the people of the United States have every sympathy for the persecuted Jews of Europe and are doing all in their power to relieve their suffering. The question of Palestine, is, however, a highly complex one and involves questions which go beyond the plight of the Jews in Europe.

The memorandum concluded with the following comment:

There is continual tenseness in the situation in the Middle East, largely as a result of the Palestine question, and, as we have interests in the area which are vital to the United States, we feel that the whole subject is one that should be handled with the greatest care and with a view to the long-range interests of the country.[25]

Truman, who had been brought up on the Bible at home and was a lifelong student of history, had a special interest in Palestine. Having familiarized himself with the history of the question of a Jewish homeland in Palestine and with the positions of the British and the Arabs as well as of the Roosevelt administration, he was irritated by the State Department memorandum. In his *Memoirs*, Truman wrote:

I was skeptical, as I read over the whole record up to date, about some of the views and attitudes assumed by the "striped-pants boys" in the State Department. It seemed to me that they didn't care enough about what happened to the thousands of displaced persons who were involved. It was my feeling that it would

---

25. *Foreign Relations of the United States: Diplomatic Papers, 1945, vol. 8*, reproduced in Harry S. Truman, *Memoirs, vol. 1: Year of Decisions* (New York: Doubleday, 1955), 69.

be possible for us to watch out for the long-range interests of our country while at the same time helping these unfortunate victims of persecution to find a home.[26]

In his *Memoirs*, Truman added this comment about the State Department officials: "I am sorry to say there were some among them who were also inclined to be anti-Semitic."[27]

✡ ✡ ✡

In preparation for the regular session of the UNGA, the State Department, in an exchange of memoranda with Senator Warren Austin, head of the US delegation to the UN, made clear that it was opposed to partition, and it recommended instead that Palestine be set up as a single independent state.[28] Until such an independent state was established, Palestine should be governed under a UN trusteeship agreement, administered either by the UN Trusteeship Council or by one or more members of the UN. The State Department proposed that immigration for the first two years of the agreement should be kept to a maximum of 2.5% of the total population on January 1, 1947, but in the following years, it should be limited to no more than 0.5%. About 45,000 immigrants per annum would thus have been allowed for the first two years, and only about 9,000 per annum thereafter. The State Department, like the British Foreign Office but in opposition to President Truman, thus sought to condemn the Jewish population to a permanent minority status in an independent Palestinian state, dependent upon the goodwill of

---

26. Truman, *Memoirs*, vol. 1, 69.
27. Truman, *Memoirs*, vol. 2, 164.
28. *Foreign Relations of the United States: Diplomatic Papers, 1947*, vol. 5, 1086–1088, 1096–1101. The State Department's proposal for a single independent Palestinian state ignored President Truman's earlier support of the Zionist compromise proposal for partition made during the London Conference (see Chapter 11).

an Arab ruling majority that was firmly insisting upon stopping all further Jewish immigration.[29]

In July 1947, Loy Henderson presented to Secretary of State George Marshall a memorandum prepared by his Office, containing the outlines of four plans for Palestine: 1. a uni-national Palestinian state; 2. a bi-national Palestinian state; 3. partition with the Negev allocated to the Arab State; and 4. partition with the Negev going to the Jewish State. The plans were presented in order of preference, Henderson making it clear that plan number one would be "preferable from the point of view of the international position of the government." Regarding the other three plans, Henderson stated, "It appears probable that it will not be possible, except through the use of force, to continue mass Jewish immigration to Palestine or to establish a workable Jewish state in the whole or in a part of Palestine."

Conscious, however, of the support for partition in the White House and among the public at large, Henderson recommended that the United States not take any public position on the issue until after UNSCOP had presented its report to the UN and only after Britain and the representatives of the Jews and Arabs had stated their views on the report. At the same time, Henderson sought to acquire control over the US delegation to the UN on the Palestine issue. In the

---

29. The State Department, like the British Foreign Office, had gutted the meaning of the Jewish National Home in the Balfour Declaration and the League of Nations Mandate so as to eliminate any right to a Jewish state in Palestine and to refer only to Jewish spiritual and cultural rights—rights that they, like all citizens, enjoy in democratic countries. In this redefinition, they cast away Britain's definition of the Jewish National Home when it issued the Balfour Declaration and the League of Nations' definition of the Mandate for the British rule of Palestine. The State Department likewise ignored the position taken by President Woodrow Wilson and the US Congress in approving the Mandate (see Chapter 5), as well as by President Roosevelt in his interpretation of the Mandate (see Chapter 9), along with Truman in his approval of partition, all of whom repeatedly endorsed the Jewish National Home as intended to provide for a Jewish state in Palestine.

same memorandum to Secretary Marshall, he proposed that one of the US representatives to the UN be given exclusive responsibility for the Palestine problem, "receiving his direct orders from the president or the State Department" and that for this purpose, he be given a separate staff, distinct from the regular staff of the US delegation. Henderson failed to achieve this objective, owing to the resistance of the US delegation, but he did succeed in placing on the delegation the US ambassador to Iraq, George Wadsworth, a confirmed pro-Arab diplomat like himself, who had the complete confidence of the Arab states.[30]

Henderson's strategy might well have been decisive for the outcome of the US position on Palestine had it not been countered by a suggestion to the president from his assistant for minority relations, David Niles. He recommended that in order to ensure the US delegation to the UN would carry out the president's policy on Palestine, Truman should add the assistant secretary of state for the occupied territories, General John Hilldring.[31] Hilldring had shown his compassion for the Jews in the displaced persons camps in 1946

---

30. *Foreign Relations of the United States: Diplomatic Papers, 1947, vol. 5,* 1120–1123.
31. On July 29, 1947, Niles sent a memorandum to Truman, recalling, "There was much unfavorable comment last April from certain sources about the alleged failure of the United States Delegation to the Special Session of the United Nations to carry out your policy on Palestine." Niles noted that the fault lay not with the policy nor with the delegation but with the advisers to the delegation. Similar trouble, he added, might be expected at the regular session of the UNGA opening in September, because the key advisers on Palestine to the US delegation will be Loy Henderson and George Wadsworth, both of whom "are widely regarded as unsympathetic to the Jewish viewpoint." Niles added, "On the basis of their past behavior and attitudes, I frankly doubt that they will vigorously carry out your policy. But your administration, not they, will be held responsible." Niles then went on to recommend that Truman appoint General Hilldring, the assistant secretary of state for the occupied territories, to serve as an advisor to the US delegation, in order "to insure that [Truman's] viewpoint

by urging the immediate implementation of the Anglo-American committee's recommendation for the issuance of the one hundred thousand immigration certificates for Palestine. As Niles commented, he fitted the bill completely for the need to appoint an adviser who would be "a vigorous and well-informed individual in whom you, the members of the US delegation, and American Jewry have complete confidence." On September 10, 1947, Truman appointed Hilldring as an alternate representative on the US delegation, to serve as the liaison between the delegation and the White House.

On September 15, 1947, Secretary Marshall and Loy Henderson met in New York with the US delegation to the UN to discuss the US position on Palestine. Marshall recognized that there was popular desire for US support of the UNSCOP majority report in favor of partition and that the delegation would be accused of "pussyfooting" if it failed to take a clear stand. He noted, however, that adoption of the majority report would lead to a very violent Arab reaction, and he was concerned that the announcement of US support for the majority report would arouse the Arabs and precipitate their rapprochement with the Soviet Union. Moreover, he added, Henderson was particularly concerned that if the delegation committed itself in favor of the majority report, the US would be obligated to take part in implementing any action agreed upon by the UNGA, and Arab reaction to such action would be hostile. Undersecretary Robert Lovett and Loy Henderson had therefore prepared for Warren Austin a non-committal, opening statement to deliver in the UNGA in which he would express the hope that the UN would find a definite solution to the problem of Palestine, with general agreement being reached after study of the UNSCOP report.

General Hilldring responded that the proposed statement would be a disappointment to American Jews and to Jews everywhere and that the United States should go further and accept the majority

---

is effectively expressed" (Zvi Ganin, *Truman, American Jewry, and Israel, 1945–1948* [New York, Holmes & Meier, 1979], 126–128).

report. He recognized, however, that there was disagreement in the United States government on this issue and that it may therefore be necessary to inform the representatives of the Jews that this was not yet the time for the United States to take a definite position.

Like General Hilldring, Eleanor Roosevelt, the former first lady whom President Truman had appointed as a member of the US delegation, spoke in favor of supporting the majority report. First, she raised the question of whether it was really evident that the USSR would be opposed to the majority report. Secretary Marshall replied that this was the assumption, since this case provided the Soviet Union with a fine opportunity to carry out their goal regarding the Arabs. Evidently, everyone discounted Soviet Ambassador Gromyko's statement at the UNGA special session that the Soviet Union would favor partition if a bi-national state was not workable. They took it for granted instead that in the final vote in the regular UNGA session, the Soviet Union would side with the Arabs and ignore what Gromyko had called the legitimate rights of the Jews.

Mrs. Roosevelt added, as another consideration, the necessity to support a report submitted by a UN committee in order to promote the success of the UN and to strengthen it in the minds of the American people. Secretary Marshall then commented that he had been surprised by the quality of the UNSCOP report and by the extent of agreement that had been reached on such an extraordinarily difficult matter. Loy Henderson intervened to emphasize that the majority report, if accepted, would have to be implemented by force. Only the great powers could provide such force, and since Britain, France, and the Soviet Union would be unwilling to contribute, the burden would fall entirely upon the United States. Evidently anxious regarding the support that had been expressed for the UNSCOP report, Henderson went on to attack the report as full of sophistry and not based on any principle, but only on expediency.

Henderson's intervention apparently failed to persuade the US delegation. Ambassador Warren Austin did agree that troops would be necessary to carry out the majority report but nevertheless maintained that if the United States was going to support the majority report, it was best to announce that position in an opening statement by Secretary Marshall before the UNGA. That statement, he argued, "should be as clear as possible—the United States then would stand before the world as courageous and wise, and by creating a determined effect early, would prevent the situation from flaring up—since the Arabs would not get the idea that they would yet convince the delegation."[32]

The views of the delegation evidently made their impact upon Secretary Marshall, who decided that his opening statement to the UNGA on September 17, 1947 should be less open to the charge of "pussyfooting" and should indicate instead the United States's receptivity to the UNSCOP majority proposal for partition.

---

32. *Foreign Relations of the United States: Diplomatic Papers, 1947, vol. 5,* 1147–1151.

– 13 –

The UN General Assembly Votes for Partition

UNSCOP's RECOMMENDATION FOR PARTITION WAS only the first act in the UN drama surrounding Israel's rebirth. The UNSCOP Report, with its majority and minority recommendations, went to the UNGA at its regular session in September 1947, where US Secretary of State George Marshall expressed US support of the report in the plenary session on September 17, 1947 in accordance with his decision two days earlier in his meeting with the US delegation (see Chapter 12). After commending the committee for the progress it had made in agreeing unanimously on eleven recommendations for Palestine, even though it had not been able to reach unanimous agreement on partition, Marshall concluded,

> While the final decision of this assembly must properly await the detailed consideration of the report, the government of the United States gives great weight not only to the recommendations which have met with the unanimous approval of the special committee but also to those which have been approved by the majority of the committee.[1]

Establishment of an Ad-Hoc Committee to Consider the Special Committee on Palestine Report

In view of the importance of the Palestine question, the UNGA bypassed its standing committee on political and security affairs (the

---
1. *Foreign Relations of the United States: Diplomatic Papers, 1947, vol. 5,* 1151.

First Committee) and established instead an ad-hoc committee of the entire UNGA membership to devote itself exclusively to the Palestine issues on its agenda and to report its recommendations to the UNGA for further action at its subsequent plenary session. Three items were placed on the ad-hoc committee's agenda: 1. "the Palestine question," as requested by the United Kingdom, 2. "the Report of UNSCOP," and 3. "termination of the Mandate over Palestine and the recognition of its independence as one state," as requested by Saudi Arabia and Iraq. The committee held its first session on September 25, 1947 to elect its officers, and invited both the Arab Higher Committee of Palestine and the Jewish Agency to be represented at all its meetings.[2]

After UNSCOP's chairman, Judge Sandstrom, presented the report of his committee, the ad-hoc committee heard the representatives of the three major parties directly involved in the question of Palestine: the United Kingdom, the Arab Higher Committee, and the Jewish Agency. On September 26, 1947, Britain's colonial minister, Arthur Creech Jones, restated the position of his government on the Palestine question. The UK government agreed with UNSCOP's unanimous recommendations that the Mandate should be terminated and that Palestine should become independent, but placed the UNGA on notice that it would take no measures to enforce any resolution that did not have the agreement of both the Arabs and the Jews. The British government argued that when adopting any resolution on Palestine, the UNGA must therefore also provide for its enforcement, and the willingness of the UK to share in such enforcement would depend on its judgment as to the justice of the decision and the degree of force that might be required. Creech Jones added that in the absence of a plan approved by both Arabs and Jews, Britain would have to plan

---

2. For a summary of the UNGA sessions dealing with Palestine, see "Section 9: The Question of Palestine" in United Nations, *Yearbook of the United Nations, 1947–1948* (New York: United Nations Department of Public Information, 1948).

for an early withdrawal of its forces from, and of its administration of, Palestine.[3]

Jamal Husseini, speaking on September 29, 1947 on behalf of the Arab Higher Committee,[4] declared invalid both the Balfour Declaration and the League of Nations Mandate for Palestine; rejected both UNSCOP's majority recommendation for partition and its minority recommendation for a federal state of Palestine; and insisted instead that all of Palestine must be established as a unitary Arab state. A Palestinian Arab state, Jamal Husseini assured the UN, "would respect human rights and fundamental freedoms" and "would protect the legitimate rights and interests of all minorities, whilst guaranteeing freedom of worship and access to the Holy Places." The credibility of this assurance might have been greater but for the fact that in Palestine, even under the Mandate, no Jew was permitted to visit the holiest Jewish sites—Jerusalem's Temple Mount and Hebron's Cave of the Biblical Patriarchs and Matriarchs—and (on the Jewish High Holidays) Jewish services at the Western Wall of the Temple Mount were policed against even the minutest infraction of the Ottoman restrictions on Jewish services (see Chapters 4 and 6). In conclusion,

---

3. United Nations General Assembly, Ad-Hoc Committee/General Debate, Document GA/PAL/2 (September 26, 1947), accessed on August 8, 2023, https://www.un.org/unispal/wp-content/uploads/1947/09/ecb5eae2e1d29ed08525686d00529256_gapal02.pdf.

4. Jamal Husseini was vice president of the Arab Higher Committee, and his brother, Grand Mufti Haj Amin al-Husseini, founding father of the committee (established in 1936), was its president. The grand mufti had spent World War II in Germany as an ally of Hitler and Mussolini, where he plotted the introduction of Hitler's Final Solution to "the Jewish problem" into Palestine and the Arab Middle East. At the end of the war, Britain and Yugoslavia requested his extradition as a war criminal, but the French rejected their request and arranged for his transfer to Egypt, where he was protected from extradition. From his base in Egypt, he directed the Arab guerilla war against the Jews and the State of Israel in 1947–1948, but he could not represent the Arab Higher Committee before the United Nations, from which all Axis allies were excluded.

Husseini warned, "The Arabs of Palestine [are] determined to oppose with all the means at their disposal any scheme that [provides] for segregation or partition or that would give to a minority special and preferential status."[5]

Rabbi Abba Hillel Silver, the Jewish Agency representative, speaking on October 2, 1947, declared unacceptable UNSCOP's minority recommendation for a federal state of Palestine, because although it referred to two "states," it would in fact establish only an Arab state with two Jewish enclaves. The Jewish Agency was prepared, however, to recommend the acceptance of UNSCOP's majority proposal for partition, subject to further discussion of several constitutional and territorial provisions that involved heavy sacrifices of Jewish interests. In particular, Rabbi Silver was critical of the provisions for giving Western Galilee to the Arab state and especially for internationalizing the whole of Jerusalem, including even the Jewish section of modern Jerusalem. If this was the unavoidable requirement for the immediate re-establishment of the Jewish State, however, the Jewish Agency was prepared to accept even this heavy sacrifice. The Jewish Agency also accepted UNSCOP's proposal for an economic union with the Arab state in spite of the heavy economic costs this would involve. The Jews of Palestine, Rabbi Silver concluded, wanted to be good neighbors of the Palestinian Arabs and of all the Arab States, but he warned that if their offer of peace and friendship were rejected, the Jews would defend their rights to a Jewish state. They had built a

---

5. United Nations General Assembly, Ad-Hoc Committee/General Debate, Document GA/PAL/3 (September 29, 1947), accessed on August 8, 2023, https://www.un.org/unispal/wp-content/uploads/1947/09/a8c17f-ca1b8cf5338525691b0063f769_gapal03.pdf. On October 2, 1947, the Arab Higher Committee notified the US consul general in Jerusalem that the Arabs of Palestine had declared a general strike in protest against the UNSCOP recommendation for partition and earnestly draw the attention of the US government to the serious situation that would arise in Palestine if their demands for all Palestine to become an Arab state would not be implemented (*Foreign Relations of the United States: Diplomatic Papers, 1947, vol. 5*, 1107–1112).

nation in Palestine that demanded its independence and would fight any effort to dislodge it or deprive it of its national status.[6]

✧ ✧ ✧

When the general debate began in the ad-hoc committee on October 3, 1947, any rational probability calculation would have ruled out any prospect for a favorable UN vote for the partition of Palestine and the establishment of a Jewish state. According to the UN system, committee resolutions for recommendations to the UNGA require only a simple majority of those voting for or against the resolution, but in the UNGA itself, adoption of a resolution on a substantive issue requires a majority of two-thirds of those voting for or against—i.e., there must be two votes in favor for every vote against—with abstentions not taken into account.

Of the fifty-seven UN member states in the 1947 UNGA, six were Arab countries—Egypt, Iraq, Lebanon, Saudi Arabia, Syria, and Yemen—and four were other Moslem countries—Afghanistan, Iran, Pakistan, and Turkey—all firmly opposed to partition.[7] In addition, India and China had large Moslem populations, and European countries such as France and the Netherlands also had significant Moslem concerns as colonial powers ruling over large Moslem empires. The Soviet Union, with its own three votes in the UNGA,[8] included a number of Moslem Soviet republics in Asia, and in addition, it was ideologically anti-Zionist and widely expected to oppose the

---

6. United Nations General Assembly, Ad-Hoc Committee/General Debate, Document GA/PAL/4 (October 2, 1947), accessed on August 8, 2023, https://www.un.org/unispal/wp-content/uploads/1947/10/a62f2fe8807066038525691b00658f74_gapal04.pdf.
7. Pakistan and Yemen were admitted as UN member states on September 30, 1947.
8. President Roosevelt had agreed with Stalin for the Soviet Union to have three votes in the UNGA through the admission of the two Soviet republics, Belarus and Ukraine, as UN Charter member states of the UN, along with the Soviet Union itself.

establishment of a Jewish state. And the three Eastern-European member countries—Czechoslovakia, Poland, and Yugoslavia—being either wholly or partially in the Soviet sphere of influence,[9] were expected not to deviate from the Soviet Union's opposition to partition. These twenty countries constituted more than one-third of the fifty-seven-member UNGA, and their combined opposition would have rendered impossible the adoption of a UNGA resolution for partition, even if all the remaining thirty-seven countries were to vote in favor. In fact, however, several more countries were expected to abstain or vote against partition: The UK had emphasized it would abstain in the vote; a number of Latin American countries with large Catholic populations were heavily influenced by the Vatican's ideological opposition at the time to the formation of a Jewish state; and some countries had already entered into deals to vote against partition in return for Arab support for their election to other UN councils or commissions.[10]

Even US support for partition was far from certain, despite Secretary Marshall's public statement that the US gave great weight to UNSCOP's majority report in favor of partition. The State Department remained as opposed to the establishment of a Jewish state as were

---

9. Communist Yugoslavia under Tito was not completely subservient to the Soviet Union, with Tito occasionally voting differently from the Soviet Union. But there was every reason to expect Yugoslavia not to vote in favor of partition, since it had a large Moslem population, and its representative in UNSCOP had allied himself with India and Iran in the preparation of UNSCOP's minority proposal for a federal state of Palestine.
10. The same calculations about the improbability of the UN voting for partition that may have given the British Foreign Office confidence in submitting the Palestine problem to the UN had also produced a great deal of worry within the Jewish Agency. As noted in Chapter 11, both Ben-Gurion and Rabbi Silver had indicated to Bevin that they would prefer to have Britain remain as the Mandatory Power, provided that it would agree to lift the restrictions on immigration. Bevin, however, refused the proposal, informing the British Cabinet that he had made his decision to submit the problem of Palestine to the UN.

the UK Foreign Office ministers and the Arabs, and it continued its agitation against partition. On September 22, 1947, five days after Marshall's statement in the UNGA, Henderson sent an anguished memorandum to him, arguing, "It would not be in the national interests of the United States for it to advocate any kind of plan at this time for the partitioning of Palestine or for the setting up of a Jewish state in Palestine."[11] The memorandum warned against American support for such a proposal, because 1. it "would be certain to undermine our relations with the Arab, and to a lesser extent, with the Moslem world," whose friendship and cooperation the Western world needed; 2. the US would "certainly be expected to make major contributions in force, materials, and money" to implement partition; 3. any plan for partition would be unworkable; and (4) partition "would guarantee that the Palestine problem would be permanent and still more complicated in the future."

The memorandum added another argument, pressed by all the Arab delegations: (5) The UNSCOP plan for partition and the establishment of a Jewish state "are not only not based on any principles of an international character" but were rather in contravention to the principles of the UN Charter and to American concepts of government.[12] Henderson was in effect charging that President Woodrow Wilson and the US Congress—without whose endorsement (noted

---

11. *Foreign Relations of the United States: Diplomatic Papers, 1947, vol. 5,* 1153–1158.
12. Henderson seems to have forgotten his own comments two months earlier, on July 7, 1947, when he had written to Secretary Marshall, "An examination of the various statements and resolutions emanating from executive and legislative officials during the last twenty-five years would indicate that in general, this government has taken the position that the mandate for Palestine, which incorporates the substance of the Balfour Declaration, is recognized by us as an international commitment; that the United States government favors mass Jewish immigration to Palestine; and that it might look with favor upon some arrangement providing for a partition of Palestine, provided such an arrangement gave promise of being workable."

in earlier chapters) the Balfour Declaration and the League of Nations Mandate would not have been issued—as well as President Truman and President Roosevelt, all of whom interpreted the Mandate as providing an opportunity for a Jewish state in Palestine, had all those years acted in contravention to the principles embodied in the UN Charter and to American concepts of government.

The Henderson memorandum went on to propose, therefore, that the US should concentrate on the goal of setting up a trusteeship for a period of years that "would be instructed to function in such a neutral manner as not to favor either partition or a single state." As for Marshall's statement at the opening session of the UNGA that the government gave great weight to the majority proposals for partition, Henderson proposed a "gloss" of the type that had served his State Department so well in the past in rendering President Roosevelt's pro-Zionist pledges meaningless (see Chapter 9). He proposed:

> On an early occasion, we should repeat that statement, making it clear at the same time that our minds are by no means closed and that we shall also give due weight to the views of other nations and particularly of the interested parties.

Marshall had the courage and integrity to reject Henderson's proposed "gloss," and on September 24, 1947 in a meeting with General Hilldring and Mrs. Roosevelt—attended by Loy Henderson, Dean Rusk, and State Department Counselor Charles Bohlen—he declared, undoubtedly to the dismay and frustration of all his advisers in his State Department and in military and intelligence officialdom, that the US "should embrace support of the majority report of UNSCOP" including "the provisions for partition and large-scale immigration."

Marshall added two significant qualifications, however. The first was that US support for partition should include provisions for "such amendments as are now believed by the United States government to be wise and essential to a workable plan." The second was that the US should prepare a tentative draft of a switch position in case it appeared that partition did not command the support of the two-thirds majority of the member states, required for the UN adoption of any substantive resolution.[13]

Marshall's qualifications provided Henderson with an opportunity to plan for partition to fail even with a US vote in its favor. On September 30, Henderson responded with a memorandum, proposing "to implement the United States position on the Palestine question... by methods best calculated to safeguard the strategic, economic, and political interests of the United States in the Near East." The memorandum proposed, first, that "the US should give support to the majority plan in principle, with a view to perfecting the plan in certain of its features." The principal modifications to be sought were: 1. The city of Jaffa, adjoining Tel Aviv, should be assigned to the Arab state as an enclave; 2. the eastern boundary of Western Galilee should be extended to include Safad in the Arab state; 3. the Gaza district should be extended to include a larger area within the Arab state, and finally, 4. the Negev should be allocated to the Arab state instead of the Jewish State, as UNSCOP had recommended.

Turning to Marshall's request for a US switch position, Henderson recommended that in the case that the UN failed to approve the majority plan, the minority plan should then be put to a vote. If, as anticipated, an impasse was then reached, the US should call for the establishment of a subcommittee to formulate a new plan that would combine the best features of the two plans "or any other workable and just plan which stands a reasonable chance of adoption."

In this context, Henderson noted, on the one hand, that "The embassy in Moscow and other observers are convinced that in the final showdown, the Soviet Union will support the Arab states" and that "concerted opposition of the Soviet bloc and the Arab League states and their Moslem supporters could defeat any proposal which did not command almost unanimous support of the other members

---

13. *Foreign Relations of the United States: Diplomatic Papers, 1947*, vol. 5, 1162–1163.

of the United Nations." He warned, on the other hand, that the Arab states will probably "reject any solution that creates a Jewish state or province or permits further Jewish immigration into Palestine" and that "it is possible that they will withdraw from the United Nations in case any such solution is adopted." After again emphasizing the importance of maintaining the Moslem world's goodwill toward the US as a primary foreign-policy goal, Henderson concluded that the US should not press other countries to support partition and that any plan for partition that the UNGA might adopt must be "a United Nations solution and not a United States solution."[14]

On October 3, 1947, the opening date of the general debate in the UNGA ad-hoc committee, Secretary Marshall met in Washington, DC with key members of the US delegation to the UN, where, according to a memorandum prepared by a State Department official, the proposal that the US should support partition in principle but with pro-Arab modifications of territory was accepted. Henderson's recommendation that "the US should not attempt to persuade members of the General Assembly to vote for the majority plan" also "seemed to win general support," even though it was also generally recognized that "in all probability, the majority plan does not obtain a two-thirds majority at present."[15] With this "seeming" general support, Henderson now had reason to hope that the defeatist strategy he had devised had significantly reduced the prospects for the UN adoption of a resolution for partition and the establishment of a Jewish state, even with a US vote in its favor.

The same day, October 3, Dr. Jamali of Iraq and Emir Feisal of Saudi Arabia met with Ambassador Wadsworth in New York to deliver a démarche on behalf of all six Arab delegations to the UN that unless the US government gave them assurance that it would not support partition and the establishment of a Jewish state, they would make a

---

14. *Foreign Relations of the United States: Diplomatic Papers, 1947, vol. 5*, 1166–1170.
15. *Foreign Relations of the United States: Diplomatic Papers, 1947, vol. 5*, 1173–1174.

deal with the USSR—six votes for six votes—to support any issue of importance to the Soviet Union in exchange for Soviet support of the Arab position on Palestine. This support, the Arab delegations made clear, would extend even to the Greek question and to the Korean issue—the two most inflamed theatres, at the time, of the Soviet–American Cold War.[16]

The General Debate in the Ad-Hoc Committee

The ad-hoc committee devoted the period of October 3–16, 1947 to a general debate on its three interrelated agenda items: the Palestine Question, the UNSCOP Report, and the Arab request to terminate the Mandate and establish Palestine as a unitary Arab state. In this debate, the Arab delegations repeated their arguments that both the Balfour Declaration and the League of Nations Mandate to facilitate building a Jewish national home in Palestine had no legal validity, that the Jews had no roots in Palestine, that the problem of the Jewish refugees was an international problem and had nothing to do with Palestine, that the UNSCOP majority proposal for the partition of Palestine violated the UN Charter, and that the only legitimate solution was to establish Palestine as a unitary independent Arab state to which the Jews had no rights of immigration. They repeatedly warned that any decision to set up a Jewish state in any part of Palestine would lead to much bloodshed, because the Arabs would defend by force their exclusive right to all Palestine.[17]

On October 26, 1947, King Ibn Saud of Saudi Arabia reinforced these Arab warnings in a letter cautioning President Truman, "The Arabs have definitely decided to oppose establishment of a Jewish state in any part of the Arab world. The dispute between the Arab

---

16. *Foreign Relations of the United States: Diplomatic Papers, 1947, vol. 5,* 1171–1172.
17. United Nations General Assembly, Ad-Hoc Committee/General Debate, Document GA/PAL/5 (October 3, 1947), accessed on August 8, 2023, https://www.un.org/unispal/wp-content/uploads/1947/10/4d434db-66697dc3f85256929006d26c5_gapal05.pdf.

and Jew will be violent and long-lasting and without doubt will lead to more shedding of blood."[18]

Truman Approves the US Announcement of Support for Partition

On October 9, 1947, President Truman gave final approval to a statement negotiated between the State Department, the US delegation to the UN, and the White House, announcing the US government's support for partition. His decision had the support of the US delegation to the UN and, remarkably, also of Secretary Marshall, but it was reached in the face of the fundamental opposition of the key diplomatic, military, and intelligence advisers in the State Department, the Defense Department, and the newly organized Central Intelligence Agency. Had Roosevelt lived to serve his full term as president until the end of 1948, it is doubtful, in light of his erratic record during World War II on the question of Palestine (see Chapter 9), that he would have been able to withstand their combined pressure against the UNSCOP proposal for partition and the establishment of a Jewish state.

Truman's historic decision seems to have been motivated by three key factors. First, as he wrote in his memoirs, "The Balfour Declaration, promising the Jews the opportunity to re-establish a homeland in Palestine, had always seemed to me to go hand in hand with the noble policies of Woodrow Wilson, especially the principle of self-determination."[19] Second, like Eleanor Roosevelt, he believed that it was essential for the US to give its support to the UN, which had been formally established in 1945, shortly after he had succeeded to the US presidency. In addition, Truman, like General Hilldring, had been profoundly affected by the plight of the Jewish survivors of the Holocaust who were still languishing in displaced persons camps two years after the end of World War II. Truman came to the conclusion, therefore, that the US was obligated to support the majority proposal

---

18. *Foreign Relations of the United States: Diplomatic Papers, 1947, vol. 5*, 1212.
19. Truman, *Memoirs, vol. 2*, 133.

of UNSCOP to permit the Jews of Palestine to set up their own state that would absorb the Jewish refugees.[20]

It was the Arab belligerency against partition and the establishment of a Jewish state that apparently precipitated Truman's announcement of his decision. As the president explained in his memoirs:

> The Arabs' reaction [to the partition plan] was quite plain. They did not like it. They made it clear that partition would not be carried out except over their forceful opposition. On October 9, I was informed that the Arab League Council had instructed the governments of its member states to move troops to the Palestine border, ready for later use, and the public statements of the Arab leaders were belligerent and defiant. I instructed the State Department to support the partition plan.[21]

On October 11, 1947, Ambassador Herschel Johnson accordingly announced in the UNGA ad-hoc committee that the US government supported the basic principles of the unanimous recommendations of UNSCOP together with its majority plan for partition and for Jewish immigration. The US government was prepared to participate in a UN program to implement partition by providing financial aid and assistance and by sharing in a UN volunteer police force for the maintenance of law and order, if needed, in the transition from the British Mandate to partition.[22]

---

20. Truman's critics, notably Foreign Minister Ernest Bevin and his staff in the British Foreign Office as well as key officials in the State Department and other anti-Zionists more generally, maintained that Truman's decision was determined primarily, if not entirely, by domestic political considerations. While the timing of some of his actions may have been influenced by such considerations, it would have been altogether out of character for Truman to take any action in foreign-policy matters that he did not believe to be in the best interests of the US.
21. Truman, *Memoirs, vol. 2*, 155.
22. United Nations General Assembly, Ad-Hoc Committee/General Debate, Document GA/PAL/12 (October 11, 1947), accessed on August

The Soviet Union's Surprise Announcement of Its Support for Partition

Undoubtedly the most improbable and most astonishing aspect of the general debate in the ad-hoc committee was the Soviet Union's announcement of its firm support for partition. When Bevin had called for a special session of the UNGA to consider the problem of the Palestine Mandate, he certainly did not anticipate such a decision from the Soviet Union. Marxist–Leninist doctrine had always opposed Zionism: the notion that Jews are a people entitled to a state of their own. In the Marxist demonology, Zionism was only a deviationist, *petit-bourgeois* form of nationalism, allied with Western imperialism.[23] Moreover, the two superpowers were then in the deep freeze of the Cold War, and they had not been able to agree on any international-policy issues. And, as noted in Chapter 12, Harold Beeley, Bevin's adviser on Palestine, firmly believed that for a majority of the Eastern bloc and the US to join together and support the same resolution in the same terms "has never happened—it cannot happen, and it will never happen!"[24]

Britain's assumption that the Soviet Union would reject any proposal for the establishment of a Jewish state was fully shared by the US. On May 10, 1947, four days before Gromyko's surprising announcement in the special session of UNGA, the US embassy in

---

8, 2023, https://www.un.org/unispal/wp-content/uploads/1947/10/7b-33678fe44b8dac85256929006e1e9e_gapal12.pdf.

23. In April 1941, the Soviet Union sentenced Menachem Begin—a Polish Zionist leader (at the time) who had fled to Russia—to eight years of hard labor on the charge that Zionism served the cause of British imperialism.

24. Horowitz, *State in the Making*, 143. Soviet support of a Jewish state was in fact short lived. For four decades, from around 1951 until its collapse in 1991, the Soviet Union was in the forefront of the UN in its opposition to Zionism and to Israel. It supported all the Arab wars against Israel after 1948, and it led the pro-Arab, anti-Israel campaigns in the UN, including the successful campaign for the adoption of the infamous 1975 UN resolution that equated Zionism with racism.

Moscow cabled the State Department that the Soviet policy would be in "opposition to formation in all or part of Palestine of [a] Jewish state, which [the] USSR would regard as [a] Zionist tool of [the] West, inevitably hostile to [the] Soviet Union."[25] The State Department did not change its assessment even after Gromyko's statement that it would regard partition as reasonable if a bi-national state proved unfeasible. Even as late as September 22, 1947, after the UNGA regular session had already begun, Loy Henderson sent Secretary Marshall a memorandum, stating, "The embassy in Moscow and other observers are convinced that in the final showdown, the Soviet Union will support the Arab states."[26]

The Arabs were likewise convinced that the Soviet Union, with its intense opposition to Zionism as a tool of British imperialism, could not possibly support the establishment of a Jewish state in Palestine and would cast its vote in the plenary session against partition. It was in this belief that the Arab Higher Committee had listed as one of the reasons for their boycott of UNSCOP "the inadequate representation" of the Eastern-European countries in UNSCOP. And, as already noted, the leaders of the Arab delegations warned in a démarche on October 3, 1947 to US Ambassador George Wadsworth that if the US did not give them assurance it would oppose partition, they would make a deal with the Soviet Union, which had made overtures of support to them.[27]

And yet, at the decisive moment, Stalin overcame his Marxist anti-Zionism and considerations related to the Cold War, and to everyone's utter astonishment, he had the Soviet Union representative declare in the ad-hoc committee on October 13, 1947, two days after the US announcement, that the Jews were a people with roots

---

25. *Foreign Relations of the United States: Diplomatic Papers, 1947, vol. 5,* 1081, 1088–1089.
26. *Foreign Relations of the United States: Diplomatic Papers, 1947, vol. 5,* 1154–1158, 1169.
27. *Foreign Relations of the United States: Diplomatic Papers, 1947, vol. 5,* 1171–1173, 1175–1176.

in Palestine and with legitimate rights to statehood in Palestine that must be taken into account equally with the legitimate rights of the Arabs. The Soviet Union would therefore vote in favor of partition and of the establishment of both a Jewish state and an Arab state in Palestine.[28] What "has never happened," what "cannot happen," and what "will never happen" happened!

Britain was unhappy with the US and Soviet announcements. Having gone to the UN to seek its advice on administering the Mandate, it had decided to surrender the Mandate rather than risk losing Arab goodwill. On October 16, the last day of the general debate, Colonial Minister Creech Jones repeated before the ad-hoc committee that Britain would continue to administer Palestine only if the Jews and Arabs agreed on a plan for Palestine. If UNGA, however, recommended a plan to which the Arabs or Jews did not agree, Britain would refuse to continue to administer the Mandate. It would also not cooperate with other countries to implement any plan that did not have the agreement of both Arabs and Jews.[29]

---

28. United Nations General Assembly, Ad-Hoc Committee/General Debate, Document A/AC.14/SR.12 (October 13, 1947), accessed on August 8, 2023, https://www.un.org/unispal/document/auto-insert-205565.

    Both the UK and the US were mystified by the Soviet announcement. In a memorandum of his conversation with the British ambassador on October 15, 1947, Undersecretary Robert Lovett reported, "The ambassador said that he had been greatly surprised at the position taken by the Soviet government with respect to the majority report. He frankly failed to see what they would gain by it. In fact, assuming that their desire was to stir up trouble, it would seem that it would be better if they were to back up the Arabs as the Arabs had felt they were going to do. I said that we too were mystified as to the reasons for the Soviet position" (*Foreign Relations of the United States: Diplomatic Papers, 1947, vol. 5,* 1183).

29. Arthur Koestler aptly described the British position at this point: "From here onward, British policy can no longer be qualified as muddled, short sighted, or pseudo-Machiavellian—it became plainly surrealistic. Six months earlier, Mr. Bevin had asserted that he had no right to impose immigration on Palestine 'by force,' but he had taken for granted that he had the right to exclude immigration by force. Britain had rejected

The State Department Strategy to Defeat the Resolution on Partition

The State Department, even while being obliged by President Truman's instructions in support of partition, immediately began implementing its plan to ensure that if a plan for partition would be approved, it would be considered a UN plan and not a US plan. Its strategy quickly became public knowledge. A week after Ambassador Johnson's announcement in favor of partition, two New York newspapers carried reports that although the US had declared its support for partition, the State Department was privately informing other delegations that it did not really favor it.

The US delegation was disturbed by these reports, and on October 18, an adviser to the delegation suggested that it would be helpful to have Dean Rusk, the director of the State Department's Division for UN Affairs, come to New York to discuss the difference of opinion that seemed to exist between the delegation and the State Department. Robert McClintock, Dean Rusk's special assistant, who visited the delegation on his behalf, wrote on October 20 to Undersecretary Robert Lovett that he was convinced that they "must take a more decisive line with regard to Palestine." The partition plan had already become identified as a US plan, McClintock warned, and,

---

the Anglo-American and the United Nations committees' recommendations on the grounds that she could not carry them out alone—now that international assistance was offered, she refused even to take her share along with others. Six months earlier, the foreign secretary had renounced Britain's Mandate on the grounds that the claims of Jews and Arabs were irreconcilable and agreement between them impossible; from now onward, British spokesmen kept repeating that Britain would only support a solution which conciliated Jewish and Arab claims and was based on agreement between the two. To appeal for the judgment of an international body in order to stop two parties from quarrelling and then to reject the judgment because it meant enforcing peace between them was no longer diplomacy but sheer Harpo Marx logics" (Arthur Koestler, *Promise and Fulfillment: Palestine 1917–1949* [New York: Macmillan, 1949], 143).

"If the partition plan fails of acceptance at this assembly, we shall be involved in a most unpleasant mess." McClintock therefore recommended, in opposition to the general position of the State Department, that the only course available to the US was "firmly to support the majority plan for partition of Palestine and to see that it is passed at this assembly."[30]

Lovett sent McClintock's memorandum for comment to Loy Henderson, who, in a memorandum on October 22, dismissed its recommendations out of hand. If the US were to "carry the flag" for partition, he argued, it would "inescapably be saddled with the major if not the sole responsibility for administration and enforcement, which, we gather, neither the Congress nor the American people are willing to undertake." His office and important departments of the government, Henderson added, were "unwilling and unprepared to accept the losses to the US position in the Middle East which would be bound to follow an aggressive partition policy." He agreed that "under our present policy for supporting partition without waving the flag…partition will probably fail of a two-thirds vote." But, unlike McClintock, he did not see such failure as a problem. Either some compromise plan might be proposed, which would receive a

---

30. "Memorandum by Mr. Robert McClintock to the Undersecretary of State (Lovett)" in *Foreign Relations of the United States: Diplomatic Papers, 1947*, vol. 5, 1188–1192. To mollify the Arabs, McClintock proposed to amend the UNSCOP recommendation through territorial adjustments in favor of the Arabs and to make "a constructive effort to help the Arabs." In this regard, he called attention to two proposals suggested by the pro-Arab ambassador to Iraq, George Wadsworth. The first was to support the "Greater Syria" scheme, under which the Palestine area that was to be assigned to the Arabs would become part of Syria. Alternatively, if a proposed irrigation project materialized in Iraq, Wadsworth suggested that Iraq could then offer land to the Palestinian Arabs "infinitely richer and more attractive than the stony hills of Judea on which they now scrabble for existence." Once again, as in the case of the adviser to Ibn Saud, H. St. John Philby, a suggestion for "population transfer" of the Palestinian Arabs originated with one of the most ardent Arab supporters in the diplomatic arena.

two-thirds vote, or failing that, "It would be in order to propose a temporary trusteeship with fairly substantial immigration, ending in a plebiscite in Palestine."[31]

McClintock's and Henderson's memoranda were both sent to the assistant secretary of state for political affairs, Norman Armour, who agreed with Henderson that the US should not attempt to influence other delegations and should not assume active leadership in favor of partition. He decided that there was no reason to trouble anyone higher up with the matter.[32] The State Department had thus firmly committed itself to a program of action under which it knew that the president was likely to go down in defeat in his support for partition, without finding it necessary to consult or inform him of its decision.

The Appointment of Sub-Committees to Prepare Detailed Plans

On October 21, 1947, the ad-hoc committee, after hearing again from the Jewish Agency and the Arab Higher Committee, decided to set up two sub-committees to spell out specific detailed plans in preparation for the voting in the ad-hoc committee: Sub-Committee I for the implementation of the UNSCOP majority recommendations for partition and Sub-Committee II for the establishment of Palestine as a unitary Arab state. The two sub-committees, whose members the committee chairman appointed the next day, were asked to report on their plans to the committee a week later, but they were granted extensions of time and submitted their plans to the ad-hoc committee only a month later—on Wednesday, November 19, 1947.

---

31. *Foreign Relations of the United States: Diplomatic Papers, 1947, vol. 5*, 1195–1196. Henderson must surely have realized that even after substantial Jewish immigration, the Jews would still be a minority, and a plebiscite would only result in a vote in favor of the Arab proposal for a unitary Arab state.
32. *Foreign Relations of the United Nations: Diplomatic Papers, 1947, vol. 5*, 1196, fn. 3.

On November 12, as Sub-Committee I was completing its report on a detailed resolution for partition, Secretary Marshall wrote to Ambassador Austin that the US delegation should continue its strong stand in the UN to modify the proposal so as to transfer the Negev to the proposed Arab state. Ambassadors Johnson and Hilldring replied to Marshall on November 18, 1947 that Sub-Committee I was opposed to the US position on the Negev—that "it would be a mistake to carry the issue of the Negev farther" and that the US "should accept the boundary recommendations," which Sub-Committee I would be transmitting to the ad-hoc committee. If the department's proposal would be introduced in the ad-hoc committee, they explained, "It will be vigorously opposed by the Jewish Agency and probably by all the friends of partition in the United Nations," and only the Arab states would actively support the US position. In that case, should partition fail to pass in UNGA, "The blame for it will unquestionably be placed upon the US for raising this major doubt as to the justice of the partition plan."[33]

The State Department disagreed, however. Undersecretary Lovett, acting secretary of state in Marshall's absence, instructed ambassadors Johnson and Hilldring the next morning, November 19, 1947, that the delegation "should not yield to the demand" of the Jewish Agency and should call for a vote in the ad-hoc committee for the transfer of the Negev to the proposed Arab state. Lovett added, "We realize that our position on the Negeb might not be accepted by the ad-hoc committee." In that case, he agreed, the US should vote for the partition proposal as recommended by Sub-Committee I, but "making it clear that in so doing, we defer to the will of the majority."[34]

Ambassador Johnson was unhappy with Lovett's instruction. He stated as his firm conviction that if the US were to carry the issue of the Negev to the ad-hoc committee, many states would abstain in

---

33. *Foreign Relations of the United States: Diplomatic Papers, 1947, vol. 5*, 1266–1268.
34. *Foreign Relations of the United States: Diplomatic Papers, 1947, vol. 5*, 1269–1270.

the vote on partition, and it might fail to receive even a simple majority in the committee. Johnson therefore requested authorization to maintain the US position on the Negev only during the debate in the sub-committee, "And then, if we were beaten in the vote in the sub-committee, gracefully to announce our readiness to be guided by the will of the majority." The State Department yielded, undoubtedly not without considerable reluctance, to Johnson's request.[35]

Once again, another of the so many improbable turns of events in the history of Israel's rebirth intervened in support of the Jewish position. On the morning of November 19, 1947, the day of the sub-committee's final meeting, US Ambassador Johnson was meeting in New York with Moshe Shertok, the Jewish Agency representative to the UN, for the purpose of informing him of the US decision to propose in the sub-committee the re-allocation of the Negev to the proposed Arab state. On that same morning, however, Chaim Weizmann had been granted a meeting with President Truman to try to persuade him to keep the UNSCOP recommendation that the Negev should go to the Jewish State. The Negev, he emphasized, could only be developed through comprehensive irrigation schemes, and it would remain useless desert to the Arabs as it had been throughout the centuries. Only the Jews, for whom the area was a vital necessity for development, would invest the necessary energy and resources to redeem the land, and, in fact, they were already growing potatoes, carrots, and bananas there, where not even a blade of grass had grown for two thousand years.

President Truman, with his farming background and his intimate familiarity with the Bible, appreciated Weizmann's argument, and he agreed that the Negev should go to the Jewish State as recommended by UNSCOP. Herschel Johnson was already meeting with Shertok but had not yet informed him of the US intention when the president personally phoned to say that nothing should be done "to upset the apple cart" on the Negev. After taking the president's call, in private, Johnson returned to tell Shertok that this meeting was to inform him

---

35. *Foreign Relations of the United States: Diplomatic Papers, 1947*, vol. 5, 1270.

there was no change in the US position in support of the UNSCOP majority recommendation on the Negev.[36] Johnson and Hilldring decided accordingly that the delegation would remain silent in the sub-committee and permit its report to go to the ad-hoc committee as a unanimous report.[37]

In its report, Sub-Committee I accepted the UNSCOP recommendations for the termination of the Palestine Mandate and for the partition of Palestine to establish two independent states—a Jewish state and an Arab state—with an economic union between them, but with Jerusalem and its environment to be governed separately under a UN trusteeship.

The sub-committee recommended the reallocation of Jaffa to the proposed Arab state so as to reduce the number of Arabs in the Jewish State, together with some minor territorial modifications for administrative reasons. The major difference from the UNSCOP report, however, was the addition of provisions for administering Palestine during the transition period between the termination of the Mandate and the establishment of the two independent states. In recognition of Britain's determination to withdraw its troops from Palestine and to do nothing to implement a UN decision that was not acceptable to both Jews and Arabs, the sub-committee report called for the establishment of a commission of representatives of five governments to which Britain should turn over its authority in each of the areas as they were progressively vacated by its troops. The commission would in turn hand over responsibility for the maintenance of law and order during the transition period to the local authorities. The report also

---

36. For a vivid description of the meeting between Johnson and Shertok and the effect of the president's call, see Horowitz, *State in the Making*, 267–270.
37. *Foreign Relations of the United States: Diplomatic Papers, 1947, vol. 5*, 1271–1272. The US noted it had some reservations regarding the Negev, but Johnson withdrew these reservations in the ad-hoc committee on November 22 in light of a concession by the Jewish Agency allowing for a bridge between the Negev and Egypt (*Foreign Relations of the United States: Diplomatic Papers, 1947, vol. 5*, 1278–1280).

called upon Britain to provide a seaport by February 1, 1948 in the area to be assigned to the Jewish State so as to permit the commencement of free Jewish immigration into its area. It called upon the new commission to assist Britain in the process of evacuating its troops and upon Britain, in turn, to cooperate with the commission in the discharge of its responsibilities during the transition.[38]

The Vote in the Ad-Hoc Committee

In the ad-hoc committee's session on Thursday, November 20, 1947, Ambassador Cadogan made it clear that the UK would retain exclusive control of Palestine prior to its termination of the Mandate and would not cooperate with the newly proposed commission for the implementation of partition, because partition was not acceptable, neither to Arabs nor to Jews. The committee's provisions for implementation would therefore have to be revised.[39]

On Saturday morning, November 22, 1947, the chairman of Sub-Committee I for partition presented a set of revised provisions for implementation necessitated by Cadogan's explanation of the UK government's position. The Arab representatives again objected that partition was illegal, with Dr. Jamali, the Iraqi representative, calling partition "an act of conquest by the United Nations. If the sub-committee considered this legally, morally, or humanly justifiable, he warned, then it should prepare for an army to back it up, for the Arabs would be bound to fight against such an act of conquest."[40]

---

38. United Nations General Assembly, Ad-Hoc Committee/General Debate, Document GA/PAL/73 (November 19, 1947), accessed on August 8, 2023, https://www.un.org/unispal/document/auto-insert-214178 and Document GA/PAL/74 (November 19, 1947) accessed on August 8, 2023, https://www.un.org/unispal/document/auto-insert-214134.
39. United Nations General Assembly, Ad-Hoc Committee/General Debate, Document GA/PAL/76 (November 20, 1947), accessed on August 8, 2023, https://www.un.org/unispal/document/auto-insert-214132.
40. United Nations General Assembly. Ad-Hoc Committee/General Debate. Document GA/PAL/80 (November 22, 1947), accessed on August 8,

At the afternoon session the same day, Ambassador Johnson made a strong speech in support of the partition plan recommended by Sub-Committee I. "There is no present plan before the General Assembly of the United Nations…and none which has been presented or suggested that could possibly meet" the requirement that it would have the approval of both the Arabs and Jews. Partition was the most practicable and most just solution to the Palestine problem, and the US government stood ready to share responsibility with the other UN members for its enforcement should the situation develop into a threat to peace. Johnson even went public with strong criticism of the British government for its refusal to cooperate with the UN, thereby rendering the committee's task more difficult.[41]

Loy Henderson, still as adamantly opposed to partition as ever, was shocked by Johnson's speech. On Monday, November 24, the final day of the general debate in the ad-hoc committee, he wrote to Undersecretary Lovett:

> I feel it again to be my duty to point out that it seems to me and all the members of my Office acquainted with the Middle East that the policy which we are following in New York at the present time is contrary to the interests of the United States… The Arabs are losing confidence in the integrity of the United States and the sincerity of our many pronouncements that our foreign policies are based on the principles of the Charter of the United Nations… It is extremely unfortunate that we should be criticizing the British for following the only policy which, it seems to me, they can follow if they are to remain in the Middle East.

2023, https://www.un.org/unispal/document/auto-insert-214186.

41. *Foreign Relations of the United States: Diplomatic Papers, 1947, vol. 5*, 1280–1281; United Nations General Assembly, Ad-Hoc Committee/General Debate, Document GA/PAL/81 (November 22, 1947), accessed on August 8, 2023, https://www.un.org/unispal/document/auto-insert-214177.

Henderson added that he wondered whether the president realized that under the plan being supported by the US, wide-scale violence was bound to erupt in Palestine, and he warned that this would lead to the introduction of American forces and, even more serious, Soviet military forces into the Middle East.[42] Lovett took Henderson's memorandum to the president and explained that the State Department regarded this as a serious matter and believed the president should know of the probable attempts to get the US committed militarily in Palestine.

Truman did not alter his decision for the US to vote in favor of the pending resolution on partition; indeed, as noted earlier, his decision had in fact been precipitated by the Arab belligerence and the Arab League's decision to resort to force against partition. Nevertheless, Truman did agree now to the State Department's proposal against the use of "improper pressure" on other delegations to vote for the resolution. Lovett accordingly phoned Ambassador Johnson and General Hilldring at the UN to inform them, "The president did not wish the United States delegation to use threats or improper pressure of any kind on other delegations to vote for the majority report favoring [the] partition of Palestine." Lovett added his own interpretation that within the president's orders also lay "the general requirement that the United States was not to be an 'advocate' for the majority report."[43] Henderson must have been pleased with the president's alleged objection to "advocacy." In the absence of US advocacy for

---

42. *Foreign Relations of the United States: Diplomatic Papers, 1947, vol. 5,* 1281–1282.
43. *Foreign Relations of the United States: Diplomatic Papers, 1947, vol. 5,* 1283–1284. The State Department's qualms about "waving the flag" and "advocacy" applied only to proposals to which it was opposed. When, in 1948, the State Department decided to reject partition and to propose trusteeship instead, it did not hesitate to wave the flag and to "advocate." In *The Birth of Israel,* 273–278, García-Granados describes in some detail the discussion at a luncheon that Senator Austin, the head of the US delegation to the UN, gave for the chiefs of all 20 Latin-American delegations "to lobby for votes, to impress upon us the necessity for a trusteeship over

its position, Henderson fully expected partition to fail in the plenary session of UNGA in spite of the announcements of both the US and the Soviet Union that they favored partition. The door would then be open for his proposal to place Palestine under a trusteeship, and the US would safeguard its goodwill among the Arabs.

✡ ✡ ✡

The ad-hoc committee began voting on the reports of its two sub-committees at the evening session of Monday, November 24, 1947. That evening, it rejected by a vote of 29 to 12, with 14 abstentions, the draft resolution of Sub-Committee II for the establishment of Palestine as a unitary Arab state. The next day, Tuesday, November 25, 1947, the ad-hoc committee approved the draft resolution of Sub-Committee I based on UNSCOP's majority recommendations in favor of partition by a vote of 25 to 13, with 17 abstentions (plus 2 absent: Paraguay and the Philippines). The resolution, one vote shy of the required two-thirds majority for UNGA adoption, was sent for a final vote in the plenary session scheduled for the following day, Wednesday, November 26, 1947.

The prospects for a favorable two-thirds majority vote in the UNGA plenary session on Wednesday, November 26, 1947 were far bleaker than might be suggested by the vote in the committee the previous day. In addition to the thirteen nations that had voted against the resolution in the committee, three—Greece and Haiti, which had abstained in the committee vote the day before, together with the Philippines, which had been absent—announced in the plenary session on Wednesday that they would be voting against the resolution.[44] The total negative vote would now be sixteen, and

---

Palestine, and to get as many of us as possible to place our countries behind the American proposal."

44. United Nations General Assembly, 124th Plenary Meeting, Held in the General Assembly Hall at Flushing Meadow, New York on Wednesday, November 26, 1947, Document A/PV.124 (November 26, 1947), accessed on August 8, 2023, https://digitallibrary.un.org/record/734598?ln=en;

at least thirty-two votes—seven more favorable votes than in the ad-hoc committee the previous day—would therefore be needed for the resolution to be adopted in UNGA.

Even this was still not the full extent of the difficulties that would be faced on the day that the final vote was scheduled to take place. The fact that Greece, Haiti, and the Philippines—all dependent upon the US for economic support—had declared their intention to vote against partition indicated to other delegations that the US was not really interested in getting partition approved. Several more votes were thus placed in jeopardy: Liberia and Ethiopia, both of which had also abstained in the committee vote, now indicated that they were also leaning toward a negative vote, and Paraguay, which had been absent in the committee, had not yet received its instructions on the vote. If these three countries were also to cast negative votes, the total votes against partition would be nineteen, and the resolution would be doomed. For the resolution to be approved, all the remaining thirty-eight UN member countries, including the UK, would have to vote in favor of partition, and the UK had categorically refused to take any action that had not been approved by both the Arabs and the Jews.

Even some votes that had been cast in favor of partition in the committee could not be taken for granted in the final vote in UNGA, because the Arabs were exerting considerable pressure on other UN member countries, particularly among the Latin-American delegations, to vote against the resolution. The Syrian delegate told García-Granados that if he refused to change his vote, he might have been forced to resign, because the Arabs were working very hard on the government of Guatemala to instruct him to vote against partition. And the Costa-Rican delegate told García-Granados that the Arabs had pressured his government, offering to support Costa Rica in its bid for

---

United Nations General Assembly, 125th Plenary Meeting, Held in the General Assembly Hall at Flushing Meadow, New York on Wednesday, November 26, 1947, Document A/PV.125 (November 26, 1947), accessed on August 8, 2023, https://digitallibrary.un.org/record/734600?ln=en.

membership of the Trusteeship Council, provided it would change its pro-partition vote.[45] As it turned out, Chile, which had voted in favor of the resolution in the committee, did abstain in the final vote in the UNGA plenary session as a result of the Arab pressure.[46] And Greece, which had abstained in the committee, did vote against the resolution in the plenary session as a result of a deal it was offered whereby Greece would receive in return Moslem support for all Greek issues in any organ of the UN.[47]

The supporters of partition were thus faced with two important tasks: on the one hand, to persuade as many countries as possible that had abstained in the committee the day before to now vote favorably in the plenary session, and on the other hand, to persuade the wavering countries that had abstained or been absent in the committee not to go through with their plans to cast a negative vote in the plenary session. The enormity of these tasks rendered impossible their accomplishment in the short hours that remained before the expected vote in the plenary session on Wednesday afternoon.

---

45. García-Granados, *The Birth of Israel*, 263–268; Horowitz, *State in the Making*, 297–304.
46. After Chile's vote in favor of partition in the ad-hoc committee, the Saudi-Arabian delegation to the UN complained to the State Department that Chile had intended to vote against partition but had been persuaded to vote in favor as a result of pressure by the US government. In response to Lovett's inquiry on November 28, the US embassy in Chile replied on December 2 that the president of Chile and members of his government were personally sympathetic to the Jewish cause, and the Chilean delegate had therefore been instructed to vote in favor of partition in the committee. Arab pressure had, however, led the government to change its instruction and to abstain in the final vote in the plenary session (*Foreign Relations of the United States: Diplomatic Papers, 1947, vol. 5*, 1290).
47. *Foreign Relations of the United States: Diplomatic Papers, 1947, vol. 5*, 1307, fn.

The United Nations General Assembly Adopts Partition

Nineteen countries, of which the Arab countries numbered five, were still registered to speak in the UNGA plenary session that opened on the afternoon of Wednesday, November 26, 1947, after which the General Committee resolution for partition was scheduled to come to a vote. The Arab countries made strong appeals and issued strong warnings against approving partition, with the Saudi representative arguing, for example, that a vote for partition would "tear the Charter to pieces" and that the choice was between "the establishment of peace and security in the Middle East" and "the fomentation of disturbances and bloodshed." The Syrian delegate argued, "This organization cannot trample on its own Charter" and warned, "We will never recognize this proposed partition, and we reserve the right to act accordingly."[48]

Had the vote actually taken place at that session, the resolution would have failed to pass, because with the announcements made by Greece, Haiti, and the Philippines that they would vote against partition in the plenary session, the two-thirds majority that would be necessary to overcome sixteen votes against partition was nowhere in sight. But then a completely unexpected reversal of the situation began to unfold. That Wednesday, November 26, 1947 was the day before the US Thanksgiving holiday. After eight delegates had spoken, the president of UNGA, Oswald Aranha of Brazil, announced that eleven delegates remained on the list of speakers; reminded UNGA of the series of procedures required for it to vote on the resolution and to formally close the session; and called for a vote on a proposal to hold a night session. However, UNGA rejected the proposal, and Aranha then recessed the session for Thanksgiving, scheduling the

---

48. United Nations General Assembly. 125th Plenary Meeting, Held in the General Assembly Hall at Flushing Meadow, New York on Wednesday, November 26, 1947. Document A/PV.125 (November 26, 1947). Accessed August 8, 2023. https://digitallibrary.un.org/record/734600?ln=en.

next session for Friday morning. This recess opened a narrow window for the supporters of partition to organize a last-minute lobbying blitz to line up the vitally needed support for the resolution. The window was widened at the Friday afternoon session, when at the close of the general debate, France formally proposed to postpone the final vote to the next day, and the proposal was adopted by a vote of twenty-five to fifteen. President Aranha then scheduled the next meeting for Saturday afternoon.

The most plausible candidates for persuasion in the four days between the committee vote on Tuesday, November 25 and the plenary session vote on Saturday, November 29, 1947 were the four European countries—Belgium, France, Luxembourg, and the Netherlands—and the British Commonwealth country of New Zealand, all five of which had abstained in the committee vote. Belgium, a largely Catholic country, was concerned about the Vatican's opposition to a Jewish state, France was additionally concerned for its colonial interests in Arab North Africa, and the Netherlands was the colonial power in the Moslem East Indies, now known as Indonesia. Nevertheless, these countries, except for France, whose position continued to remain doubtful, were the first to be persuaded to change their position and to vote in favor of partition in the plenary session on Saturday.

Even if French approval could in the end also be secured, however, yet another two new favorable votes would be needed for the resolution to be adopted. In addition, supporters of the resolution were faced with the problem of Ethiopia and Liberia, which had abstained in the committee vote but had since shown signs of wavering.

Greece was beyond persuasion by the supporters of partition, but the Jewish Agency representatives at the UN and the Zionist leadership in the US worked feverishly to mobilize support everywhere else. Two Supreme Court justices, Felix Frankfurter and Frank Murphy, together with leading US senators, were enlisted to persuade the Philippines to reverse its plan to vote against the resolution in the plenary session. General Carlos Romulo, a powerful political figure in the Philippines who had announced on the eve of Thanksgiving that his country would vote against partition in the plenary session, suddenly returned home, and the Philippines instructed his replacement to vote, instead, in favor of partition.[49]

Remarkably, even two former senior State Department officials seem to have been overpowered by some mysterious need to share in the epic event of the rebirth of a Jewish state in the ancient Jewish national homeland. Edward Stettinius, a former secretary of state, had, like his predecessors and successors, not been known for any pro-Zionist sentiments. In December 1944, Stettinius had warned President Roosevelt that if he should continue with his recent pro-Zionist pronouncements, "It would seriously prejudice our ability to afford protection to American interests, economic and commercial, cultural and philanthropic, throughout the area." And only five days after Truman became president, Stettinius had irritated him with his memorandum (see Chapter 12) warning, "This whole subject is one which should be handled with the greatest care." Yet it was this same Stettinius, now once again a private citizen, who in this crucial Thanksgiving period of 1947, surprisingly responded to the needs of the hour and enlisted to help with Liberia. The Liberian representative had abstained in the committee vote on Tuesday and had indicated in the plenary session on Wednesday his intention to oppose partition, but Stettinius successfully intervened and persuaded President Tubman of Liberia to cast Liberia's vote on Saturday for the partition of Palestine and the establishment of a Jewish state.[50]

In Haiti, Adolf A. Berle, assistant secretary of state under President Roosevelt, is another example of a surprise intervention in the establishment of a Jewish state by a former senior State Department official who was not previously known to harbor pro-Zionist sentiments. Berle had earlier advised the Zionists:

---

49. *Foreign Relations of the United States: Diplomatic Papers, 1947, vol. 5,* 1305–1307; James Forrestal, *Forrestal Diaries* (New York: Viking Press, 1966), 357–358 (reporting on Henderson's comments at lunch on January 9, 1948).
50. Grose, *Israel in the Mind of America,* 252.

[They] ought to make a deal with Ibn Saud to renounce political claims in Palestine and move a large part of the *Yishuv* to Kenya for the duration of the war. In return, they would receive a Vatican city in Palestine after the hostilities, as well as real territory, worthy of a nation, some place in Africa, such as Abyssinia.[51]

Now, over this Thanksgiving period in 1947, Adolf Berle, responding to Nahum Goldman's plea, cabled the president of Haiti to persuade him to vote for partition. Haiti's president had already changed his mind several times, and his delegation had already announced in the plenary session on Wednesday that it would vote against partition after having abstained in the committee vote. But Berle's intervention was successful, and the president cabled back, instructing Haiti to vote in favor of partition on Saturday.[52]

Equally extraordinary was the fact that among those Jews who now exerted their influence on behalf of partition and the birth of a Jewish state were several who only a few years earlier had been either non-Zionist or even anti-Zionist. Bernard Baruch, probably the most prominent among assimilated American Jews at the time, was so far removed from Zionism that Justice Brandeis had once remarked to President Roosevelt, "Baruch would be more likely to consider colonization of Jews on some undiscovered planet than Palestine."[53] Yet it was this same Baruch who was now moved during the Thanksgiving recess in 1947 to persuade the French to vote in favor of partition instead of abstaining, as they had done in the committee vote.[54]

Just as striking was the influence exerted on behalf of partition by Judge Joseph Proskauer, the president of the American Jewish Committee. In June 1942, when his predecessor as president of the American Jewish Committee had shown interest in collaborating with

---

51. Neumann, *In the Arena*, 158–159.
52. Grose, *Israel in the Mind of America*, 252.
53. Grose, *Israel in the Mind of America*, 110.
54. Grose, *Israel in the Mind of America*, 253.

the Zionist leadership, Judge Proskauer had declared, "The time has come when the American Jewish Committee has got to fish or cut bait on Zionism... I find there is a rising tide, not of non-Zionism, but of anti-Zionism, and it has got to have expression." Believing that a Jewish state would adversely affect Jewish rights in the US and elsewhere, Judge Proskauer had threatened to bolt the American Jewish Committee and take his fellow anti-Zionists with him.[55] In 1943, Judge Proskauer withdrew his American Jewish Committee from an American Jewish conference on Palestine and postwar problems, because the conference had approved the Biltmore Program for a Jewish state in Palestine. Yet now, in November 1947, when the fate of partition was in the balance, Judge Proskauer was among those who led the effort to win support for a favorable vote to bring the Jewish State into being.[56]

✡ ✡ ✡

Given the determined State Department opposition to US "advocacy" for partition, however, it is doubtful whether the Jewish Agency representatives would have been so successful in mobilizing all this support if the efforts to secure the vote had not won the last-minute support of the White House. Truman's role in the mobilization of support for the UN resolution has been obscured by his public statements in opposition to the exercise of improper pressure on other

---

55. Urofsky, *We Are One*, 20.
56. Urofsky, *We Are One*, 144. Commenting on the efforts made by the American Jewish community on behalf of the establishment of the Jewish State, David Horowitz, the first governor of the Bank of Israel, who was a Jewish Agency representative to the UN at the time, wrote, "One potent factor, which excelled all others operating on our behalf, was the strong action and pressure exerted by American Jewry. This great community, from the Zionists to the American Jewish Committee led by Judge Joseph Proskauer of New York, rallied massively to help in the political struggle waged by the Jewish Agency representatives at Lake Success" (Horowitz, *State in the Making*, 254).

delegations. In his memoirs, Truman wrote that he was opposed to using government pressure on other nations, and he complained, "Not only were there pressure movements around the UN unlike anything that had been there before, but...the White House too was subjected to a constant barrage." Truman added that he had raised the subject in his meeting with Weizmann on November 19 and that Weizmann had written him a few days later to assure him that concerning the representatives of the Jewish Agency, "At no time have they gone beyond the limits of legitimate and moderate persuasion."[57] And as already noted, the president had, as late as November 24, told Mr. Lovett that "he did not wish the US delegation to use threats or improper pressure of any kind on other delegations to vote for the majority report favoring partition of Palestine."

It seems, however, that, at the last moment, the White House did decide to gain support from the nations that were wavering. This is attested to by a number of sources who were close to the scene of activity during the hectic hours between Thanksgiving Day, November 27, and the day of the vote, Saturday, November 29, 1947. David Horowitz, a representative at the time of the Jewish Agency at the UN, wrote of the sudden change in the US attitude:

> America's line of action had swung in a new direction. As a result of instructions from the president...the US exerted the weight of its influence almost at the last hour, and the way the final vote turned out must be ascribed to this fact.[58]

Rabbi Abba Hillel Silver similarly wrote:

> During this time, we marshaled our forces: Jewish and non-Jewish opinion, leaders and masses alike, converged on the government and induced the president to assert the authority of his administration to overcome the negative attitude of the State

---

57. Truman, *Memoirs, vol. 2*, 158.
58. Horowitz, *State in the Making*, 301.

Department which persisted to the end and persists today. The result was that our government made its intense desire for the adoption of the partition plan known to the wavering governments.[59]

Similar evidence is available from US government officials close to the scene. Truman's special counsel, Clark Clifford, wrote in a memorandum to the president on March 8, 1948, "We crossed the Rubicon on this matter, when the partition resolution was adopted by the Assembly—largely at your insistence."[60] The most emphatic statement on the influence exerted by the president on behalf of partition is to be found in a statement by Sumner Welles, former undersecretary of state under President Roosevelt, who, unique among senior State Department officials, was pro-Zionist. In a book published in 1948 to counter the State Department's attempted reversal of the president's policy, Welles wrote:

> In the light of later events, it is important that there be no misunderstanding of the position that the United States assumed at that juncture. By direct order of the White House, every form of pressure, direct and indirect, was brought to bear by American officials upon those countries outside of the Moslem world that were known to be either uncertain or opposed to partition. Representatives or intermediaries were employed by the White House to make sure that the necessary majority would at length be secured.[61]

On the Saturday after the Thanksgiving holiday, the day on which the vote on partition had been scheduled by UNGA, the needed support for the UN resolution had been lined up. Many votes had been

---

59. "Minutes of the American Zionist Emergency Committee, December 11, 1947," quoted in Ganin, *Truman, American Jewry, and Israel*, 145.
60. *Foreign Relations of the United States: Diplomatic Papers, 1948, vol. 5*, 694.
61. Sumner Welles, *We Need Not Fail* (Boston, MA: Houghton Mifflin Co., 1948), 63.

gained in favor of partition and the establishment of a Jewish state, and only two losses had been suffered. Chile, which had voted in favor of partition in the committee vote, had decided to abstain instead in the UNGA plenary session. Its loss was, however, more than offset by a gain of nine votes in favor of partition, seven from among those who had abstained and two from Paraguay and the Philippines, which had been absent from the committee vote. This raised the total votes in favor of partition from twenty-five in the committee on Tuesday to thirty-three in the UNGA plenary session on Saturday.

Greece, which had abstained in the committee vote, did vote against partition in the plenary session, as it had announced the day before Thanksgiving, but remarkably, even this switch did not add to the total vote against partition. The loss of Greece was offset by a completely unexpected change in the approach of the government of Siam (Thailand), which had voted against partition in the committee vote. Over the Thanksgiving holiday, a coup took place in Siam, leaving that country without a vote in UNGA. The total vote against partition in the plenary session, therefore, remained thirteen, as it had been in the committee vote.

The historic UNGA Resolution 181(II) "Concerning the Future Government of Palestine"[62] for the partition of Palestine to provide for the establishment of a Jewish state in Palestine, the ancient Land of Israel, after nearly two thousand years of exile, was formally adopted on Saturday, November 29, 1947, by a vote of thirty-three in favor to thirteen against, with ten abstentions.

---

62. For pertinent excerpts from UNGA Resolution 181(II), see Appendix 1.

– 14 –

The Battles against the Creation of the Jewish State

The Jewish people received with great jubilation UNGA Resolution 181(II) of November 29, 1947 for the partition of Palestine which would establish an independent Jewish state and an independent Arab state in Palestine. It is true that the UNSCOP majority proposal on which it was based had been met with mixed emotions in the *Yishuv*. The proposal involved a second partition of the Mandate for Palestine, which reduced the area of the Holy Land left for the Jewish State to only one-eighth of the land that had been included in the original Mandate for Palestine. What was especially rankling was the proposal for a UN trusteeship of all Jerusalem, despite its religious, cultural, and historical significance for the Jewish people for nearly three thousand years. The Jews had constituted the city's majority population for the last half-century of the Ottoman rule and was, at the time of the resolution for partition, a thriving community of a hundred thousand Jews populated modern Jerusalem.

The resolution's proposed boundaries also left the new Jewish State extremely vulnerable to Arab attacks. The Jewish State would get the Negev, the eastern Galilee, and a strip on the coast, including Tel Aviv and Haifa, where the main Jewish population was concentrated. This coastal strip would be separated from the rest of the State, however, both at the northern and southern ends, except for a "kissing point" at each end. The Jewish State would thus have the shape of two hourglasses instead of being truly contiguous. And there were also serious concerns about the substantial economic burden that the resolution's proposal for an economic union would place on the Jewish State.

Despite all these concerns, the Jewish reaction to the adoption of the UN resolution for partition was overwhelmingly favorable, for it meant the realization of the Jewish people's two-thousand-year-old dream of finally ending its exile and national homelessness and restoring its sovereignty within its ancient national home. Dov Joseph, a member of the Jewish Agency delegation to the UN, wrote of the Jewish reaction in Palestine:

> The streets were filled with singing and dancing: Even British soldiers, remembering Old Testament readings, were moved by the sanctity of the moment and joined in the celebration. The synagogues were packed to the doors. Rams' horns were sounded... Even the most agnostic confessed at that moment they felt the hand of God was upon them.[1]

Hoping for a bright future to be ushered in by the rebirth of the Jewish State in its ancient national homeland, the Jews issued a call to the Arabs for peace and brotherhood. On Sunday morning, November 30, 1947, the day after the UN resolution's passage, the Jewish Agency declared, "The main theme behind the spontaneous celebrations we are witnessing today is the *Yishuv*'s desire to seek peace and its determination to achieve full cooperation with the Arabs."[2] In an address to the Jewish people the same day, David Ben-Gurion, Israel's first prime minister, referred to the UN decision as:

> ...a challenge to all the communities of Israel...for the development of our wasteland and the creation of an independent

---

1. Dov Joseph cites the Psalmist in reaction to the UN vote in UNGA: "When the Lord brought about the Redemption of Zion, we were like those in a dream. Our mouths were filled with laughter, and our tongues with a joyful shout" (Psalm 126). He was moved to add: "There is no way in which men can express the utterly overflowing gladness of the heart. The whole of one's being becomes a prayer" (Dov Joseph, *The Faithful City: The Siege of Jerusalem, 1948* (London: Hogarth Press, 1962), 14–15).
2. Joseph, *The Faithful City*, 15–16.

Jewish society which will express the great ideals of the prophets of Israel—human brotherhood, social justice, and peace among the nations.

The Arab Guerrilla War against the Creation of a Jewish State

But the calls of the *Yishuv* for peace were met by the Arabs' call to arms. The Palestinian Arab Higher Committee and the Arab states all categorically rejected UNGA Resolution 181(II) for the partition of Palestine as a Jewish state and an Arab state. Their reaction to the resolution was to launch a holy war to prevent the establishment of the Jewish State. They had repeatedly argued, at every stage of the UN general debate on partition, that the Balfour Declaration and the League of Nations Mandate to facilitate a Jewish national homeland were invalid and illegal; that Jews are not a people entitled to a state; that Jews have no roots in Palestine and no legally valid claims in Palestine; and that the partition of Palestine to include a Jewish state violated the UN Charter. They had all insisted that the establishment of a Jewish state in any part of Palestine was an act of aggression against the Arabs, and they had all declared their readiness to defend Arab rights to all Palestine by all the means at their disposal (see Chapter 13).

The Arab warnings were solemnly repeated at the close of the UNGA session on Saturday, November 29, 1947, immediately after the passage of the UN resolution for partition. Saudi Arabia's Amir Feisal warned UNGA:

> Today's resolution has destroyed the Charter and all the covenants preceding it... The government of Saudi Arabia registers, on this historic occasion, the fact that it does not consider itself bound by the resolution adopted today by the General Assembly. Furthermore, it reserves to itself the full right to act freely in whatever way it deems fit.

Jamali of Iraq, likewise, warned:

> We believe that the decision which we have now taken is a very serious one. It is one that undermines peace, justice, and democracy. In the name of my government, I wish to state that it feels that this decision is antidemocratic, illegal, impractical, and contrary to the Charter. It contradicts the spirit and letter of the Charter. Therefore, in the name of my government, I wish to put on record that Iraq does not recognize the validity of this decision, will reserve freedom of action towards its implementation, and holds those who were influential in passing it against the free conscience of mankind responsible for the consequences.

And Syria's Amir Arslan similarly proclaimed:

> Gentlemen, the Charter is dead. But it did not die a natural death; it was murdered, and you all know who is guilty. My country will never recognize such a decision. It will never agree to be responsible for it. Let the consequences be on the heads of others, not on ours.[3]

The bellicose Arab statements in the course of the debate in 1947 on the UN resolution for partition were quickly followed by militant Arab action, even before the passage of the resolution in November. In mid-September, two weeks after the issuance of the UNSCOP report, the political committee of the Arab League met in Sofar, Lebanon, where they sought to arouse Palestine's Arabs to join the imminent war against the establishment of a Jewish state in Palestine, proclaiming, "They—the Palestinian Arabs—will launch a relentless

---

3. United Nations General Assembly, Resolution 181(II)—Future Government of Palestine, Documents A/PV.128 and A/RES/181(II)[A] (November 29, 1947), accessed on August 8, 2023, https://digitallibrary.un.org/record/671195?ln=en and https://digitallibrary.un.org/record/667160?ln=en.

war to repel this attack on their country, especially so as they know that all the Arab countries will back and assist them, supplying them with men, funds, and ammunition."[4] The league's secretary-general, Azzam Pasha, spelled out the league's war plan in more bloodcurdling terms in the Egyptian press on October 11, 1947, the day Ambassador Herschel Johnson announced US support for the UN resolution. Azzam Pasha's definition was, "This war will be a war of extermination and a momentous massacre which will be spoken of like the Mongol massacres and the Crusades."[5]

The Arab League wasted no time after the passage of the UN resolution to recruit, train, and equip guerrilla armies from the Arab countries for infiltration into Palestine to prevent the establishment of a Jewish state. Invasion with the regular armies of the Arab states would wait until the end of the British Mandate in Palestine. On December 17, 1947, at the end of more than a week of meetings in Cairo that had begun on December 8, the Arab League adopted a resolution asserting, "The Arab League is resolved to prevent the creation of a Jewish state in Palestine and to conserve Palestine as a united, independent state."[6] In order to be able to start the guerrilla operations in Palestine immediately, they committed themselves to furnish three thousand volunteers, ten thousand rifles, and GBP 1 million.[7]

---

4. al-Ahram, Cairo, September 21, 1947, cited in United Nations General Assembly and United Nations Palestine Commission, Memorandum from the Jewish Agency: Acts of Aggression by Arab States, Document A/AC.21/JA/12 (February 2, 1948), accessed on August 9, 2023, https://www.un.org/unispal/document/auto-insert-211102.

5. Akhbar Al-Yom, October 11, 1947, cited in United Nations General Assembly and United Nations Palestine Commission, Memorandum from the Jewish Agency: Acts of Aggression by Arab States, Document A/AC.21/JA/12 (February 2, 1948), accessed on August 9, 2023, https://www.un.org/unispal/document/auto-insert-211102.

6. Larry Collins and Dominique Lapierre, O Jerusalem! (New York: Simon & Schuster, 2007), 81–82.

7. Collins and Lapierre, O Jerusalem!, 82.

The Arab rulers competed with one another in promoting the war against the creation of a Jewish state. Lebanon's prime minister declared on December 15, "We will never sleep until we save Palestine as an independent unitary Arab state. We promise you we will supply Palestine with...weapons, equipment, and men." Saudi Arabia's foreign minister proclaimed even more passionately, "We promise you to save Palestine by our soul, money, and sons... I am depending on God and you to maintain Palestine as an Arab independent state." And Syria's prime minister summed up, "The time for speeches is past, and the stage for action is at hand. We should all be determined to liberate Palestine by our might and money."[8]

The Arab unanimity, it should be noted, extended only to preventing the creation of a Jewish state in Palestine and not to Arab plans for Palestine in the absence of a Jewish state. The Arabs paid lip service to the concept of a unitary state of Palestine, but the states neighboring Palestine, particularly Syria, Egypt, and Transjordan, had their own designs on at least some part of Palestine. Indeed, after the Mandate's end on May 15, 1948, Egypt took Gaza, and Transjordan seized Judea and Samaria—as the area was then still called since biblical times—along with east Jerusalem, and they maintained control of these areas until they lost them to Israel in the Six-Day War in June 1967. Transjordan went on to annex the area in April 1950, renaming it the West Bank of a newly named Hashemite Kingdom of Jordan, and the Palestinian people not only failed to rise up against

---

8. Associated Press, Cairo, December 15, 1947, cited in United Nations General Assembly and United Nations Palestine Commission, Memorandum from the Jewish Agency: Acts of Aggression by Arab States, Document A/AC.21/JA/12 (February 2, 1948), accessed on August 9, 2023, https://www.un.org/unispal/document/auto-insert-211102. In light of this ample record of the zealous Arab enlistment in their war to prevent the creation of a Jewish state immediately upon the passage of the UN resolution for partition, it is strange to read in Abbas's op-ed column the claim: "Zionist forces expelled Palestinian Arabs to ensure a decisive Jewish majority in the future state of Israel, and Arab armies intervened" (Abbas, "The Long Overdue Palestinian State," *The New York Times*, May 17, 2011).

the annexation, but they even overwhelmingly approved it in a referendum, with Amman, rather than Jerusalem, as its capital. Evidently, their goal was not Palestinian independence but rather the prevention of the creation of a Jewish state in Palestine.

Violent Palestinian attacks against Jews, encouraged by the Arab states, broke out the day after the resolution's passage in Jerusalem, Jaffa, Haifa, and in isolated Jewish settlements surrounded by Arab villages. On New Year's Eve, the Arabs placed a massive roadblock at Jaffa Gate in the Old City of Jerusalem, placing its Jews there under siege. In response, PA, shrugging aside its basic duty under the Mandate to maintain law and order, proposed the "ethnic cleansing" of Jerusalem's Old City and asked the Jewish Agency to evacuate the Old City's ancient Jewish Quarter. The Jewish Agency refused, and only at the end of January—a month after the blockade had been put in place—did PA agree to provide partial relief, providing an escort for three convoys weekly through the Zion Gate, into the Jewish Quarter.

At its December 1947 meetings in Cairo, the Arab League resolved to establish an "Arab Liberation Army" for Palestine, based in Syria, with Fawzi al-Qawuqji, a leader of the 1936–1939 Arab revolt, in command. Syria was placed in charge of recruiting volunteers from all Arab countries and of providing them with the necessary military training, equipment, and financing to infiltrate Palestine via the Syrian, Lebanese, and Jordanian borders to carry out attacks against Jewish communities in the north and in the Galilee. The US mission in Damascus provided full details of the program launched by the Syrian government, reporting crossings of Arab army units into Palestine on December 20, 22, and 28, 1947 and on January 3, 12, and 15, 1948. In its dispatch on January 15, it proposed:

> [The State Department] might consider cautioning the Syrian government that its participation in recruiting, arming, training, financing, and transporting the "irregulars" to the frontier

in Syrian army trucks is contrary to the word and spirit of the UN Charter and the [UNGA] resolution on partition.⁹

The US government repeatedly urged restraint upon the Arab governments, expressing its hope that:

> ...in their disappointment and resentment at the decision of the UNGA, the governments of the Arab countries will not attempt by armed force, or will not encourage the use of armed force, to prevent the carrying out of that decision.¹⁰

---

9. A memorandum of the US State Department, undated but presumably prepared between January 24 and January 26, 1948, declared, "Reports from the US mission at Damascus indicate that Syria is the center of recruitment and training of the so-called 'irregulars' which are intended for infiltration over the Palestine border and subsequent guerilla work in Palestine. There is evidence that such forces have already proceeded across the border to a considerable extent… Active recruiting of 'irregulars' under Fawzi Kauqji [al-Qawuqji] has been carried on in Syria. The total recruited by January 1, 1948 was estimated at approximately 16,000… Syria appears to be the training center for recruits from Palestine, Egypt, and Iraq. The Liberation Army chief of staff is reported to be Taha [al-]Hashimi and the field commander to be Kaukji [al-Qawuqji]… Sizeable bands of the volunteer 'irregulars' have crossed the border from Syria into Palestine." The memorandum refers to reports of such crossings in dispatches from Damascus on December 20, 22, and 28, 1947 and on January 3, 12, and 15, 1948 (*Foreign Relations of the United States: Diplomatic Papers, 1948, vol. 5, pt. 2*, 555–556).
10. Such messages went forward to Egypt on December 26, 1947 (*Foreign Relations of the United States: Diplomatic Papers, 1947, vol. 5*, 1319–1321), to Pakistan on January 28, 1948 (*Foreign Relations of the United States: Diplomatic Papers, 1948, vol. 5, pt. 2*, 569–571), to Saudi Arabia on February 6, 1948 (*Foreign Relations of the United States: Diplomatic Papers, 1948, vol. 5, pt. 2*, 603–604), and to Iraq and Lebanon on February 10, 1948 (*Foreign Relations of the United States: Diplomatic Papers, 1948, vol. 5, pt. 2*, 616–617). The Arab states all rejected these suggestions.

And in mid-February 1948, President Truman published an appeal to the Arab leaders "to preserve the peace and practice moderation." But, as Truman reported in his memoirs, "They rejected it flatly."[11]

Grand Mufti Haj Amin al-Husseini, seeking to take control of the Arab guerrilla war, established his "Army of the Holy War in Palestine" and assigned the command to his relative, Abd al-Qadir al-Husseini, the most able and charismatic Arab leader of the 1936–1939 Arab revolt.[12] In command, al-Qadir focused his military campaign on modern Jewish Jerusalem, terrorizing its hundred-thousand Jews with spectacular bombing exploits in the center of the city and laying siege to the city by seizing control of the roads leading to and from Jerusalem. His attempt to seize Kfar Etzion on the road south of Jerusalem was repulsed, though at the cost of considerable Jewish casualties and loss of equipment, but his guerrilla army seized control of Latrun, north of Jerusalem, with its water-pumping station, the major source of the water flow to the city. It also occupied the Arab village of Kastel, a major choke point on the road from Tel Aviv to Jerusalem, and interdicted the essential source of supplies of food and fuel to the city. Until April 1948, al-Qadir's siege of Jerusalem threatened its Jewish population with death from starvation and thirst.

The tide began to turn in favor of the Jews in the first week of April 1948, with the Haganah's launch of Operation Nachshon, named after the biblical Nachshon, chief of the tribe of Judah,[13] who, according to an ancient *midrash* (rabbinic interpretation), jumped into the Red Sea before it miraculously split. In several days of fierce fighting around

---

11. Truman, *Memoirs, vol. 2*, 159.
12. Collins and Lapierre, *O Jerusalem!*, 82–83. Abd al-Qadir had helped the grand mufti in the pro-Axis coup in Iraq during World War II. Fawzi al-Qutub, whom al-Qadir put in charge of the Jerusalem bombings, had been associated with the grand mufti in Nazi Germany during World War II, plotting the extension of Hitler's Holocaust to the Jewish communities of Palestine and the Middle East after the anticipated Nazi victory (Collins and Lapierre, *O Jerusalem!*, 567–570).
13. Numbers 1:7.

the village of Kastel, where all but one of the Jewish commanders lost their lives, Abd al-Qadir also met his death on April 9, 1948, and the Jews seized Kastel, which the Arabs had unexpectedly abandoned. This enabled the Jews to send through three large convoys of essential food supplies to Jerusalem, including kosher-for-Passover food supplies only four days before the holiday.[14] After this third convoy, the Arabs retook Kastel, and no further supplies could reach Jerusalem until after the State of Israel was established on May 15, 1948.[15]

As the Mandate's termination drew near, the Arab states were bound to be disappointed, however, with the results of the guerrilla war they had launched against UNGA Resolution 181(II) and the creation of a Jewish state. The Jews had been able to make significant territorial gains, albeit at the cost of serious casualties in deaths and wounded. They did suffer the loss of the Etzion bloc to Jordan's Arab Legion two days before the end of the Mandate, but they had captured four cities with mixed Arab and Jewish populations—Haifa, Jaffa, Safed, and Tiberias—and the fall of Acre would take place only a few days later. All of the Galilee, both western and eastern, was now in Jewish hands, along with many Arab villages in the area that the UN had assigned to the Arab state.[16]

A Jewish state would be established at the termination of the Mandate, but as the Arab rulers had made abundantly clear, it would be faced, upon its birth, with the invasion of the regular armies of all the neighboring Arab states to annihilate the Jewish State whose creation their guerrilla armies had failed to prevent.

---

14. Joseph, *The Faithful City*, 99–105. This convoy was attacked at Bab el-Wad, the middle of three choke points on the road to Jerusalem, resulting in three deaths and many wounded, and several trucks were lost. The trucks were left by the side of the road to commemorate the battle to save Jerusalem.
15. Dov Joseph assumed responsibility for feeding Jerusalem's population during the months of siege, and he introduced a stringent rationing system to ensure that the city could sustain itself during the war.
16. Netanel Lorch, *Israel's War of Independence 1947–1949* (Hartford, CT: Hartmore House, 1968), 149–150.

In light of this well-documented UN record, it seems strange to read the comments of the president of the PA, Mahmoud Abbas, on the events following the UN's decision in favor of partition. In a *New York Times* op-ed article in May 2011, he referred to the vote in the UNGA on November 29, 1947 in favor of partitioning Palestine into two states and lamented: "Minutes after the State of Israel was established on May 14, 1948, the United States granted it recognition. Our Palestinian state, however, remains a promise unfulfilled."[17]

This lament should be directed first and foremost to the Palestinian Arab Higher Committee and all the rulers of Arab states who so fiercely opposed the UN resolution—before, during, and after its passage in 1947. No Palestinian leader and no Arab ruler dared agree to fulfill the resolution's promise of an Arab state limited to only part of Palestine alongside the creation of a Jewish state. Such an act—as they had repeatedly made clear—would have been considered a treasonous betrayal of the claimed Arab rights to all of Palestine. Had the Arab leadership accepted the UN resolution for partition into an Arab state and a Jewish state in 1947 and proceeded accordingly to establish an Arab state in the part of Palestine allocated to the Arabs, there would have been no war, no Arab or Jewish casualties, and no Arab or Jewish refugees. Instead of commemorating the Nakba ("Catastrophe," referring to the events surrounding the establishment of the Jewish State as they affected the Palestinian Arabs), the Palestinian Arabs, like the Jews, would have been celebrating the sixty-fourth birthday of their state on May 15, 2012, the sixty-fourth anniversary of the termination of the Mandate.

Many reasons have been advanced for Arab–Israel peace remaining so elusive, but the basic reason is surely that the Palestinian leadership refuses to accept the key element of the UN resolution, namely the partition of Palestine into a Jewish state alongside an Arab state. Even now, Abbas and the PA, who claim to accept the 1947 UNGA

---

17. Abbas, "The Long Overdue Palestinian State," *The New York Times*, May 17, 2011.

resolution for partition and Israel's right to peaceful existence in accordance with UNSC Resolution 242 (1967), continue to insist that they do not and will not ever accept Israel as a Jewish state. If so, then, in fact, their two-state solution is not the partition of Palestine as a Jewish state and an Arab state called for in UNGA Resolution 181(II). A partition that does not accept Israel as a Jewish state would yield only two Arab states—one a Palestinian state that is *"Judenfrei,"* as the PA demands for its Palestinian state, and a second state that would also become governed by Arabs in which the Jewish population of Israel would become a minority through the claimed "right of return" to Israel rather than to the Palestinian state of over five million Palestinian Arabs defined by the United Nations Relief and Works Agency (UNRWA) as refugees.

But even if the PA were finally to agree to give up their claimed "right of return" and accept Israel as a Jewish state, as proposed in UNGA Resolution 181(II), there would still remain the formidable problem of the militant/terrorist organization Hamas, which now rules Gaza and may one day win a majority in the West Bank. It does not seek peace with Israel but totally rejects the UN resolution for partition of Palestine into two states: its *raison d'être* is to preserve all Palestine, which they consider to include all Israel, as a unitary Islamic state in which there is no room for Jews.

Britain as an Arab Ally in the War against the Creation of the Jewish State

Britain's public rationale for refusing to cooperate with the UN in its implementation of the UN resolution for partition was that it could not cooperate with any policy that did not have the support of both Arabs and Jews, but in reality, its policies, both political and military, were consistently in support of the Arab war against the creation of a Jewish state. García-Granados, the Guatemalan representative to the UN and member of the UNSCOP majority group, took the floor even before the vote on the UN resolution, to warn:

The United Kingdom's plan and behavior will lead only to bloodshed in Palestine. I warn you that there will be torrents of blood, and I tell you now, before it is too late, that the party responsible for that blood will be the United Kingdom.[18]

The UN resolution for partition had provided for a Palestine commission of five member nations to which Great Britain was required to turn over the administration of each area progressively as it withdrew its armed forces. It also required that "the mandatory power shall, to the fullest possible extent, coordinate its plans for withdrawal with the plans of the commission to take over and administer areas which have been evacuated" and that "the mandatory power shall not take any action to prevent, obstruct, or delay the implementation by the commission of the measures recommended by the General Assembly."[19] Great Britain decided, however, not to abide by the resolution, and in January 1948 it informed the commission that it would not be permitted to enter Palestine until two weeks before the termination of the Mandate, which it set for May 15, 1948. As the commission noted in its first special report to UNSC on February 16, 1948, Britain's decisions made the commission's task of taking over and administering evacuated areas impossible to fulfill.[20]

---

18. García-Granados, *The Birth of Israel*, 257.
19. United Nations General Assembly. Future Government of Palestine—Resolution 181(II) Adopted by the General Assembly. Documents A/PV.128 and A/RES/181(II)[A] (November 29, 1947). Accessed August 9, 2023. https://digitallibrary.un.org/record/671195?ln=en and https://digitallibrary.un.org/record/667160?ln=en.
20. United Nations Palestine Commission, First Special Report to the Security Council: The Problem of Security in Palestine, Document A/C.21/9 (February 16, 1948), accessed on August 9, 2023, https://unispal.un.org/pdfs/AAC21R9.pdf. Great Britain did request the commission's secretariat to send four of its staff members to Palestine, but Ralph Bunche, the UN director who had served with UNSCOP, told US Representative Austin that this was "a British maneuver to enable them to say to the [Security Council] that although the commission itself has not gone to Palestine,

384   INDEPENDENCE

Sir Alexander Cadogan, the British representative to the UN, also informed the commission that no British subjects would be seconded to the Arab or Jewish governments, and any British member of the Palestine Administrative Service accepting employment with the new states would forfeit all pension rights. His government held that to allow British nationals to serve the new states would violate its neutrality. He warned the commission, therefore, that it must plan to recruit a civil administration ready to take over after Britain left. When he was asked how that could be done in the short two weeks Britain allotted to the commission, Cadogan replied that he did not know.[21]

The US consul general in Jerusalem reported to the secretary of state on February 9, 1948:

> The British continue to be adamant in their refusal to assist in any shape or fashion the implementation of the partition recommendation. Their officials, generally speaking, cannot

---

as a substitute, there is a secretariat advance party." As Austin informed Secretary Marshall on February 19, 1948, "Bunche was derisive as to how much four men could do in the present situation" (*Foreign Relations of the United States: Diplomatic Papers, 1948, vol. 5, pt. 2,* 615). Pablo de Azcárate, a Spanish diplomat who headed the team of four UN officers and two secretaries sent to Palestine in response to the British request, described in *Mission in Palestine 1948–1952* (Washington, DC: Middle East Institute, 1966), the humiliating treatment he received at the hands of the British administration. A British second lieutenant who met him at the airport brought him to Jerusalem in an army truck, where he was obliged to lie on the floor for his own "protection." In Jerusalem, he and his staff were assigned to rooms on the ground floor of a small two-story house across the street from the King David Hotel. When Azcárate entered the building, he found a plumber installing their toilet, the electric current off, and a pair of workmen knocking a hole in the wall. There were no supplies, not even ink or writing paper. The Arabs, the only servants whom the British allowed inside their security zone, refused to have anything to do with them, and they had to fetch their meals under guard from the nearby YMCA.

21. *Foreign Relations of the United States: Diplomatic Papers, 1948, vol. 5, pt. 2,* 544–545.

get out of Palestine too soon. The police have no sympathy for the Jews and state freely their opinion that the latter will "collect a packet" from the Arabs once the British relinquish the mandate. Many police add that in their opinion the Jews have "asked for it."[22]

The UN resolution inter alia called upon Great Britain "to ensure that an area situated in the territory of the Jewish State, including a seaport and hinterland adequate to provide facilities for a substantial immigration, shall be evacuated at the earliest possible date and in any event not later than 1 February 1948." Britain rejected this UN decision, however, and until May 15, 1948, when the Mandate ended, it continued to enforce the naval blockade begun under its 1939 White Paper.[23] On December 6, 1947, Secretary of State Marshall wired Undersecretary Lovett from London concerning Bevin's pressure for US support:

> Bevin laid particular stress on the importance of stopping any further illegal immigration. It was bound to lead to bloodshed, since the Arabs would undoubtedly be incited to massacre the Jews, and the situation might then require the use of force. The US government might then find themselves required to provide forces, and the Soviet Government might press to provide a force. Would the US government like this? I admitted that the greatest fear of the US military authorities in regard to the question was the presence of a Russian force in Palestine. Bevin, continuing, said that if on the other hand, Jewish immigration ceased until they were ready to hand over the administration to the UN commission in May, it would be

---

22. *Foreign Relations of the United States: Diplomatic Papers, 1948, vol. 5*, 611–612. The US consul general added in his report to the secretary of state, "However, high-ranking British officials have expressed the belief that Jews and Arabs will eventually fight to a standstill and then come to an agreement which will not be based on partition."
23. *Foreign Relations of the United States: Diplomatic Papers, 1948, vol. 5*, 612.

possible to proceed in an orderly way. They should then hope to be able to introduce into Palestine the illegal immigrants now in Cyprus, numbering nearly thirty thousand, and they might also be able to provide a port on the Palestine coast for the introduction of the legal immigrants after the taking over by the UN commission.[24]

Perhaps the most striking feature of Britain's sabotage of the UN resolution for partition was its bias in discharging its responsibility under the Mandate for the maintenance of law and order in Palestine. According to Dov Joseph:

> [The] Haganah was illegal and underground until the end of the Mandate. From 1946, when an ultimate showdown was seen as inevitable by both Jews and British, our efforts to build its strength had been matched by British searches for arms and arrests of Haganah leaders... These problems were worst of all in Jerusalem, where British troops searched Jews coming in and out of each Jewish quarter. At vital points on highways, they established checkpoints to search Jewish convoys for arms... Before organized fighting began, these Haganah forces took over the job of patrolling the streets of Jerusalem...trying to protect Jewish life and property... It was dangerous work.

The Arabs, however...

> ...had at all times the passive and sometimes the active help of the British. No effort was made to check their movements across the frontiers. Arab desertions, with weapons, from the police force were not checked. The border police, which was

---

24. *Foreign Relations of the United States: Diplomatic Papers, 1947, vol. 5*, 1301–1302. Contrary to Bevin's proposal to Marshall, Britain never made a port available for Jewish immigration into Palestine, and it did not release the Jews from Cyprus in 1948, permitting them to enter Israel only after armistice negotiations were concluded between Israel and the Arabs in 1949.

ninety-five per cent Arab, was dissolved and allowed to join the armed bands with full equipment. Some of the deserters were British—on March 10, a British spokesman stated that 233 British soldiers and police had deserted since January 1. Nearly all of these men are believed to have joined the Arab gangs.[25]

✡ ✡ ✡

Britain went well beyond passive support of the Arab armies, however, while claiming a policy of neutrality in the UN; in fact, it served as an active military ally of the Arabs in their war against the creation of a Jewish state. Its Foreign Office and its Middle East embassies were busily negotiating agreements with the Arab states in support of their plans. On January 9, 1948, shortly after the Arab League had decided in Cairo to invade Palestine upon the termination of the Mandate, Britain signed a major contract with Iraq for the sale of arms. Included in that contract was a secret codicil authorizing the use of the arms "to discharge Iraq's responsibilities vis-à-vis the Arab League." The military responsibilities Iraq had to the Arab League were for the invasion of Israel in a united attempt to destroy the Jewish State upon its birth.[26]

In Cairo, Britain was also busy negotiating the terms on which it would assist Egypt in the invasion of Israel. Less than a month before the Palestine Mandate was due to expire, the British ambassador, Sir Ronald Campbell, met with Egypt's prime minister, Nokrashi Pasha. The prime minister was still reluctant to commit the Egyptian forces to the invasion of the Jewish State, even though King Farouk had ordered him, on threat of dismissal from his post, to ask the Egyptian parliament for a declaration of war.[27] Sir Ronald told Nokrashi Pasha:

---

25. Joseph, *The Faithful City*, 29–31.
26. Collins and Lapierre, *O Jerusalem!*, 151.
27. On May 11, 1948, four days before the Mandate's end and Israel's rebirth, Nokrashi Pasha obtained a declaration of war in the Egyptian parliament, with only one dissenting voice (Collins and Lapierre, *O Jerusalem!*, 387–388).

> Should it be Egypt's decision to enter the war, Great Britain would not oppose her efforts nor hinder the movement of her forces... Should Egypt decide to go to war and find herself in need of armaments, His Majesty's Government was prepared to allow the Egyptian army access to her Suez Canal supply depots on two conditions. The first was discretion. The second was that the two nations continue satisfactory progress toward a solution to the problem which most concerned them: the Sudan.[28]

In the spring of 1948, Transjordan received approval for invasion of Palestine directly from Foreign Minister Bevin. Transjordan's prime minister, Taufiq Pasha, accompanied by Glubb Pasha, the British commander in chief of the country's Arab Legion, held a secret meeting in the British Foreign Office with Bevin. As reported by Glubb Pasha, Transjordan's prime minister told Bevin:

> The Jews had prepared a government which would be able to assume power as soon as the Mandate was terminated on May 15th. But the Palestine Arabs had made no preparations to govern themselves. They had no leaders in the country capable of organizing an administration... If the situation were left as it was, one of two things would happen. Either the Jews would neglect the UN partition plan and would seize the whole of Palestine up to the River Jordan, or else the [grand] mufti would return and endeavor to make himself ruler of Arab Palestine. Neither of these alternatives would suit either Britain or Transjordan. The grand mufti was the bitterest enemy of Britain and had spent the war with Hitler in Berlin. He was also an irreconcilable enemy of Transjordan and considered himself to be the personal rival of King Abdullah.[29]

---

28. Collins and Lapierre, *O Jerusalem!*, 341–343 and 684 fn., based on interviews with key Egyptian officials.
29. Sir John Bagot Glubb, *A Soldier with the Arabs* (New York: Harper, 1957), 63.

During recent weeks, King Abdullah and the government of Transjordan had received and were still receiving many requests and petitions from Palestinian Arab notables. In all these communications, the Palestinians begged for the help and protection of the Arab Legion as soon as the British forces withdrew. The Transjordanian government accordingly proposed to send the Arab Legion across the Jordan when the British Mandate ended and to occupy that part of Palestine awarded to the Arabs that was contiguous with the frontier of Transjordan.[30]

Taufiq Pasha added that he was consulting Mr. Bevin in accordance with the Anglo–Transjordanian treaty calling for consultations between the two countries whenever a critical situation threatened to arise. Bevin interrupted him to give his approval of Transjordan's proposal, saying, "It seems the obvious thing to do." When Taufiq Pasha concluded, Mr. Bevin repeated, "It seems the obvious thing to do" and added, "but do not go and invade the areas allotted to the Jews."[31]

As a result of this meeting, Britain increased its subsidy to Transjordan's Arab Legion threefold.[32] With this increased subsidy, Glubb Pasha was able to expand the Arab Legion to more than three times its previous size, from a force of two thousand men to one of seven thousand. The British government officially agreed to give the Arab Legion enough arms for a thirty-day war, but Glubb Pasha arranged to obtain, in addition, British spare ammunition in Palestine that had been scheduled to be dumped in the Dead Sea.[33]

In Amman, the British ambassador, Sir Alexander Kirkbride, worked closely with Glubb Pasha in implementing the policy approved by Bevin for Transjordan's invasion of Palestine. Kirkbride was the most senior British diplomat in the Middle East, his experience there dating back to World War I, when he had served as a colleague of Lawrence of Arabia in the Cairo Intelligence Office of the British

---

30. Glubb, *A Soldier with the Arabs*, 63.
31. Glubb, *A Soldier with the Arabs*, 63–66.
32. Collins and Lapierre, *O Jerusalem!*, 211–212 and 678 fn.
33. Collins and Lapierre, *O Jerusalem!*, 390.

army. Now, Kirkbride was a friend of a second Lawrence of Arabia, Glubb Pasha, British commander in chief of the Arab Legion of Transjordan.[34] On the same day that Britain had signed its arms agreement with Iraq authorizing the use of the arms for Palestine—January 9, 1948—it was Kirkbride who had agreed with Glubb Pasha to provide Arab Legion guards to escort the Syrian Liberation Army to Transjordan's border for crossing into Palestine. The crossing was made at night to permit Britain to deny any knowledge of it.[35]

What the Palestinian Arabs and the volunteer armies from abroad could not achieve despite several attempts—the destruction of Kfar Etzion on the road to Jerusalem—Britain helped Sir John Bagot Glubb and the Arab Legion of Transjordan (manned, trained, equipped, and financed by the British) to accomplish before the Mandate's termination on May 15, 1948.[36] It was this Arab Legion, newly supplied by the British with military equipment from its depot in the Suez Canal zone, which, on May 13, 1948, only two days before the end of the British Mandate in Palestine, destroyed the four Jewish settlements of the Etzion bloc on the road between Hebron and Jerusalem and allowed its Jewish population to be massacred.

Glubb Pasha himself described the role of Britain and of his Arab Legion in the destruction and massacre at Kfar Etzion:

> Throughout 1947 and until immediately before the end of the Mandate in 1948, the Arab Legion had a garrison company in

---

34. In *A Soldier with the Arabs* (37), Glubb Pasha wrote, "I went to the Arab countries in 1920 as an ordinary regimental officer in the British army. I stayed there for thirty-six years, because I loved them." When he accepted his post as commander of the Arab Legion, he told King Abdullah, "Sir, I give you my word of honour. From now onwards, I am a Transjordanian, except under the conditions you mentioned [should it ever come to fighting between Transjordan and the English] and which I pray God may never come" (*A Soldier with the Arabs*, 19)."
35. Dan Kurzman, *Genesis 1948: The First Arab–Israeli War* (New York: Da Capo Press, 1992), 60–61.
36. Glubb, *A Soldier with the Arabs*, 71.

Gaza and Rafah. The line of communication of this company lay through Beer Sheba and Hebron to Jerusalem and thence to Amman. In addition, the Arab Legion was still drawing stores from the Suez Canal zone from the British army… In the first half of May—the last fortnight before the end of the Mandate—the British instructed us to draw a quantity of stores and vehicles from Egypt. It was our last chance to do so… Meanwhile, however, [Kfar] Etzion was in a position completely to block the road… We accordingly decided to remove the [Kfar] Etzion colonies before they could destroy our convoy and cut us off from Hebron. Two days before the end of the Mandate, the Arab Legion attacked [Kfar] Etzion with two companies, supported by four three-inch mortars… Eventually, all four colonies were captured and their garrisons transferred to Transjordan. The Arab Legion treated all Jews as prisoners of war. As soon as the Arab Legion withdrew, the villagers of the Hebron district looted the Jewish colonies, leaving not one stone upon another. These colonies had been so aggressive that they had deliberately compelled Arab retaliation.[37]

Here is a most striking example of Britain's so-called policy of neutrality toward the very end of its Mandate in Palestine. While Britain continued to disarm the Haganah, it instructed the British general of the Arab Legion to draw a quantity of stores and vehicles from the British army at the Suez Canal zone, which he used—as he himself reported without any sense of guilt or fear of possible reprimand—to attack and destroy Jewish settlements. All this was done while he and his army were still serving in Palestine under Britain's general command to help maintain law and order under the Mandate.[38]

---

37. Glubb, *A Soldier with the Arabs*, 77–78. Glubb did not explain the nature of Kfar Etzion's aggressiveness that "deliberately compelled" the brutal Arab retaliation.

38. It was only on May 30, two weeks after the end of the British Mandate, when the British, responding to heavy American pressure, finally agreed to order British officers seconded from the British army to withdraw from

It is difficult to escape the conclusions reached by the Guatemalan representative, García-Granados, on Britain's role during the months before the termination of the Palestine Mandate:

> Britain actually allowed—even facilitated—both strife within Palestine and a methodical invasion from without. It was invasion by consent. The Mandatory government ruled Palestine, was charged with maintaining law and order in Palestine, yet allowed thousands of uniformed, armed Arabs to enter from Syria, Iraq, and Transjordan. Great Britain, whose navy in the darkness of night could detect a tiny refugee ship on the high seas far from the shores of Palestine, found herself unable to see long convoys of military vehicles and marching troops crossing the Palestine borders in the light of day.
>
> Politically, she obstructed partition by completely upsetting the UN timetable... She was to have consulted the Palestine commission before announcing the date on which she would end the Mandate; instead, on January 30, without consultation, she announced that the Mandate would terminate on May 15. This Commission...was to have gone to Palestine immediately after November 29 to prepare for the complicated task of taking over the government on May 15 and setting up the provisional Jewish and Arab councils. But Britain refused to allow it to enter Palestine until May 1, only two weeks before the

---

the Arab Legion. Glubb Pasha, who remained in command of the Arab Legion, complained bitterly of having been let down in the midst of the war against Israel, writing, "The withdrawal of the British officers was a shattering blow. They included all operational staff officers, both the brigade commanders and the commanding officers of three out of the four infantry regiments—and all the trained artillery officers. The artillery having only been raised three months before, none of the Jordanian officers were yet really competent to direct the fire of the guns... The British regular officers were therefore the keystone to the whole edifice in 1948" (Glubb, *A Soldier with the Arabs*, 134). Glubb Pasha himself was not affected by the British order, because he left the British army and joined the Arab Legion in his own capacity.

Mandate's end... She refused to transfer authority progressively... She refused to evacuate a Jewish seaport for immigration on February 1, 1948... She refused to allow the commission to organize and train local militias to maintain law and order after May 15, nor would she cooperate with the commission in any administrative or financial matters... In effect, the British by negative action and the Arabs by positive action had joined in a combined attack upon the UN.[39]

The United States State Department Campaign to Undo the United Nations Resolution for Partition

The State Department supported Britain's policy of sabotaging the UN resolution for partition and even reinforced it by imposing an embargo on the shipment of arms to Palestine early in December 1947, even though Britain did not hesitate to continue to ship arms to the Arab states.[40] Eleanor Roosevelt, along with many in and out of Congress, protested this policy, writing to Marshall in January 1948, "The quicker we remove the embargo and see that the Jews and any UN police force are equipped with modern armaments...the better it will be for the whole situation." Marshall, refusing to distinguish between supporters and violators of the UN resolution, replied that the shipment of American arms to Palestine and neighboring states "would only facilitate further violence."[41] Had it not been for the arms smuggled into the *Yishuv* in violation of the US embargo, this combination of British and American peculiar "neutrality" policies might well have given the Arab states the expected victory in their war to prevent Jewish national independence.[42]

---

39. García-Granados, *The Birth of Israel*, 270–271.
40. *Foreign Relations of the United States: Diplomatic Papers, 1947, vol. 5*, 1249.
41. *Foreign Relations of the United States: Diplomatic Papers, 1948, vol. 5, pt. 2*, 629.
42. The US continued its embargo on arms shipments even after Israel was established, and it was only the arms smuggling and military equipment that Czechoslovakia provided at a crucial period in 1948 that enabled

But the State Department did far more than reinforce Britain's policy of sabotaging partition—it launched its own relentless campaign to overturn the resolution for partition.[43] On December 12, 1947, not quite two weeks after the UN vote for partition was cast, the State Department's campaign went into high gear in response to a US National Security Council request for a draft report on the US position regarding the Palestine problem. Its preliminary report, prepared in Loy Henderson's office and dated December 17, 1947, maintained that partition was "impossible of implementation" but that the US was not yet ready to make such a declaration.[44] On January 19, 1948, George Kennan, director of the State Department's policy planning staff, recommended that the US should declare that "it is impracticable and undesirable for the international community to attempt to enforce any form of partition," and it should call instead for the whole matter to be reopened in UNGA. In the absence of an agreed decision, the UN should be requested to investigate the possibilities of any other solution "such as a federal state or trusteeship, which would not require outside armed force for implementation."[45]

Neither Henderson nor Kennan ever explained why a policy of trusteeship, which both Arabs and Jews opposed, could be implemented without unacceptable outside force, whereas partition, which only the Arabs opposed, would require such outside force. The absence of any explanation is all the more striking, since except for a change in

---

Israel to defend itself against the official invasion of all its neighboring Arab states immediately after the State's rebirth. For a vivid history of the arms-smuggling operation and the Czech military assistance, see Leonard Slater, *The Pledge* (New York: Pocket Books, 1971).

43. The State Department had the full support of Secretary of Defense Forrestal, who worried the UN decision "was fraught with great danger for the future security of this country" (James V. Forrestal, *Forrestal Diaries*, December 1, 1947, 346).

44. *Foreign Relations of the United States: Diplomatic Papers, 1947*, vol. 5, "Editorial Notes," 1283, 1313.

45. *Foreign Relations of the United States, Diplomatic Papers, 1948*, vol. 5, pt. 2, 553–554.

auspices, a trusteeship would be virtually the same as the League of Nations Mandate that Britain had finally surrendered, because even its hundred thousand troops (and more) in Palestine were unable to maintain law and order in the face of the opposition.

In a memorandum to Lovett a week later, on January 26, 1948, Dean Rusk, the State Department's director for UN affairs, posed a series of searching questions on the Kennan paper:

> What events have occurred which create a "new situation" with respect to the action taken by the UNGA on Palestine? Were not the considerations discussed in the attached paper known at the time of the decision to support the plan of the UNSCOP majority? At what point or points can it be reasonably concluded that the situation in Palestine will render impossible the implementation of the UNGA resolution?
>
> What has been done thus far by the Department of State, either within or outside the UN, to increase the chances of success for the solution approved by us and by the UNGA?
>
> What steps could now be taken by the Department of State, either within or outside the UN, to ensure maximum opportunity for the successful execution of the UNGA recommendation on Palestine? Are such steps of such a serious character as to require us to reconsider our Palestine policy as being prohibitively costly?

Rusk went on to suggest a number of steps the State Department could take to assist in the implementation of partition, such as bilateral talks with Great Britain to secure its cooperation and multilateral talks with Arab and other Moslem governments to persuade them not to frustrate the UNGA resolution. He concluded with the comments, "Armed intervention by the Arab states would clearly be aggression" and "The [UNSC] may be required to use such powers as it has under the Charter to bring such aggression to a close."[46]

---

46. *Foreign Relations of the United States: Diplomatic Papers, 1948, vol. 5, pt. 2*, 556–562.

Rusk's comment gave Loy Henderson an opportunity to question the legal validity of the UN resolution for partition, even though the US government had so vigorously promoted it only months earlier in 1947 under President Truman's direction. In a memorandum on February 6, 1948, Henderson questioned whether armed intervention by the Arab states would even be considered aggression: "Would this be aggression against the Mandatory power?" Henderson wondered, "and if so, would not we be in an anomalous position if the Mandatory power denied that there was aggression?" Henderson then went on to question, "Supposing after the termination of the Mandate of May 15th, the Arab population of Palestine invited the Arab states into Palestine, would this be aggression?"[47]

The UNGA resolution for partition included a request that "The [UNSC] determine as a threat to the peace, breach of the peace, or act of aggression... any attempt to alter by force the settlement envisaged by the resolution." Henderson, however, was now arguing that an invasion by the Arab states against the Jewish State, established under this UN resolution, could not be considered aggression. In contrast with presidents Wilson, Roosevelt, and Truman, along with the US Congress, who had all firmly supported the Balfour Declaration and the League of Nations Mandate, Henderson evidently agreed with the Arab position that they were both invalid, and the UN resolution for partition and the creation of a Jewish state was illegal.

The State Department's Strategy Shift to a New Position on Palestine

Despite Rusk's very pertinent questions on Kennan's paper, it did not take long for him to be won over and indeed to take the leading role in putting the Kennan–Henderson policy recommendations against partition into effect. On February 11, 1948, only two weeks after expressing his reservations on the Kennan paper, Dean Rusk

---

47. *Foreign Relations of the United States: Diplomatic Papers, 1948, vol. 5, pt. 2,* 600–603.

sent a memorandum to Undersecretary Lovett entitled "Shift to New Position on Palestine." There he laid down a very peculiar legal argument significantly gutting the UNSC's enforcement powers, which provided the State Department with its public rationale for the US to retreat from partition. Rusk contended that although "The UN Charter clearly empowers the UNSC to use force to resist aggression and keep international peace," it "does not authorize force to be applied within a state to compel a political settlement. The purpose of the UN is to keep peace, not to make war." Since partition could be implemented only with the use of outside force, and according to Rusk, UNSC could not employ force if it would implement a UN decision, it followed that the UN had to abandon its decision in favor of partition. He recommended, therefore, as had Kennan and Henderson before him, that the US should propose to UNSC that the whole problem of Palestine be reviewed by a special session of UNGA. In the meantime, UNSC should call on Britain to continue to uphold its responsibility for law and order in Palestine pending further recommendations from the special session of UNGA.[48]

The Palestine commission's first special report to UNSC on February 16, 1948 provided the State Department with the opportunity to bring to fruition its plan to overturn the UN decision in favor of partition. The report stated that owing to Arab violence in Palestine aimed at nullifying the UNGA resolution and given the progressive liquidation of the British administration in Palestine, the commission must request UNSC to provide an adequate non-Palestinian armed force in order to carry out the recommendations of the UNGA resolution of November 29, 1947.[49]

---

48. *Foreign Relations of the United States: Diplomatic Papers, 1948, vol. 5, pt. 2*, February 11, 1948, 617–618.
49. United Nations Palestine Commission. First Special Report to the Security Council: The Problem of Security in Palestine. Document A/C.21/9 (February 16, 1948). Accessed August 9, 2023. https://unispal.un.org/pdfs/AAC21R9.pdf.

UN Secretary-General Trygve Lie supported the commission's request, explaining in a book he later wrote:

> The stand of the Palestine commission was unquestionably sound. It was responsive to the fact then dominating the scene: that the Arab states were making open preparations to invade Palestine and overthrow a UN decision. Any invasion would be aggression, in flagrant violation of the Charter. Its unlawfulness would be compounded by its design to upset the specific will of the UN.[50]

Faced with this commission report, which called so unambiguously for the implementation of the UNGA resolution through the use of international force, the State Department decided it must act urgently to counter the request. On February 21, 1948, it submitted a top-secret message to the president containing a working draft of a basic position paper for US Ambassador Warren Austin to present at the UNSC session scheduled for February 24. Paragraph 9 of this draft incorporated Rusk's peculiar limitation on UNSC's enforcement powers:

> UNSC, under the Charter, is empowered to take action to prevent aggression from outside. UNSC is also empowered to take action to prevent a threat to international peace and security from inside Palestine. This enforcement action must be directed solely to the maintenance or restoration of international peace. UNSC is not authorized by the Charter, however, to employ enforcement measures to give effect to recommendations either of UNGA or of UNSC itself. This applies to the UNGA resolution on Palestine.[51]

---

50. Lie, *In the Cause of Peace*, 166.
51. *Foreign Relations of the United States: Diplomatic Papers, 1948, vol. 5,* 637–640.

Although the State Department had decided on language intended to "knock the plan for partition in the head,"[52] it was concerned that it would be unwise to retreat publicly from the support the US had given to partition throughout 1947. It therefore deferred public US abandonment of partition to a subsequent stage, when the onus for it could be placed on UNSC rather than on the US government. The draft position paper submitted to the president included, therefore, three paragraphs "for the president's consideration and approval in relation to future development of the problem," even though the paragraphs would not be used in Austin's speech at the session of February 24, 1948. The first paragraph recommended that if UNSC could not implement partition without enforcement measures and could not develop an alternative solution acceptable to both Arabs and Jews, then the matter should be referred back to a special session of UNGA. The second paragraph proposed that since reaching a peaceful solution under UNSC auspices may take time, it may be necessary for UNSC to ask the Mandatory power to retain the Mandate, pending further UN consideration of the problem. The third paragraph declared that the State Department "plans to take vigorous diplomatic action" with all the parties concerned "to bring about an immediate cessation of violence and illegal acts of all kinds which are contributing to the present disorders."[53]

President Truman evidently had some concerns about the State Department draft, but he seems to have failed to understand its full intent to "knock partition in the head." He informed Secretary Marshall the next day, February 22, 1948, that he approved in principle the basic position in the working draft, but added the warning: "I want to make it clear, however, that nothing should be presented to UNSC that could be interpreted as a recession on our part from the position we took in UNGA" on November 29, 1947 in support of

---

52. *Foreign Relations of the United States: Diplomatic Papers, 1948*, vol. 5, pt. 2, 648–649, fn. 1.
53. *Foreign Relations of the United States: Diplomatic Papers, 1948*, vol. 5, pt. 2, 639–640.

the resolution for partition of Palestine into Jewish and Arab states. The president also requested that the final draft of Austin's statement to UNSC be sent to him for his consideration.[54]

The following day, February 23, 1948, Secretary Marshall sent the president the final draft of the statement to be made by Ambassador Austin before UNSC, together with a reply to Truman's warning against any recession from the US position in favor of partition. In light of the memoranda by Kennan, Henderson, Rusk, and McClintock cited earlier and of the State Department's plan to ensure UNSC would reject partition without having the onus placed on the US, Marshall's reply to the president was most extraordinary:

> Austin's speech does not represent recession in any way from position taken by us in UNGA. In fact, it is stronger with regard to threats to the peace which have developed since [the] UNGA discussion. Those who may construe this as recession hold the incorrect view that [the] Charter authorizes UNSC to impose recommendations by force.[55]

This reply to the president's warning apparently misled Truman into believing that the State Department was still truly supporting the UNGA resolution for partition. With this reassurance, the president approved the State Department's draft of the speech rejecting

---

54. *Foreign Relations of the United States: Diplomatic Papers, 1948, vol. 5, pt. 2,* 645.
55. *Foreign Relations of the United States: Diplomatic Papers, 1948, vol. 5, pt. 2,* 648–649. How Secretary Marshall approved the text of the reply he sent to Truman in response to the president's warning is as puzzling as Truman's approval of the accompanying text of Austin's speech. Marshall surely understood that Austin's speech, in the words of McClintock, "in effect knocks the plan for the partition of Palestine in the head." While it is not uncommon for busy political officials to sign large batches of memoranda and letters daily without reading them, relying upon aides for pre-screening them, it is difficult to believe that memoranda to the president were not separated out for Marshall's special attention.

UNSC's power to enforce partition for Austin's delivery in UNSC the next day.⁵⁶

At the UNSC session on February 24, 1948, not quite three months after the US vote in UNGA in favor of partition, Ambassador Warren Austin presented the official US legal position that UNSC may act to keep the peace but does not have the power under the UN Charter "to enforce a political settlement, whether it is pursuant to a recommendation of UNGA or of UNSC itself." Thus, UNSC may act to keep the peace but may not enforce partition. He did not yet call for a special session of UNGA but proposed instead that a committee of the five permanent members of UNSC should look into the issue of the possible threats to the peace arising from the Palestine situation and should consult all the interested parties concerning the implementation of the UNGA resolution.⁵⁷

Although the State Department thus continued to maintain publicly that it stood behind partition, Truman was apparently the only one who believed this to be true. Austin's speech was recognized, by supporters and opponents of partition alike, as the State Department's opening salvo toward moving UNSC to abandon the UN's decision in favor of partition. The Egyptian foreign minister told the US ambassador in Cairo that he had read Austin's speech with "considerable relief." Similar "cautiously favorable" reactions were reported by the leaders of the other Arab states, including Syria, Lebanon, Iraq, and Saudi Arabia. ⁵⁸ On the other hand, the Soviet newspaper *Trud* carried a headline reading, "USA Sabotages UN Decision on Palestine." UN Secretary-General Trygve Lie was extremely upset, recording later that with Ambassador Austin's statement:

---

56. *Foreign Relations of the United States: Diplomatic Papers, 1948, vol. 5, pt. 2,* 651.
57. *Foreign Relations of the United States: Diplomatic Papers, 1948, vol. 5, pt. 2,* 651–654.
58. *Foreign Relations of the United States: Diplomatic Papers, 1948, vol. 5, pt. 2,* 677–678, fn. 3.

Washington took the heart out of any support which UNSC might have mobilized to enforce peace and maintain the decision on partition. This attitude, I feared, would prejudice fundamentally the powers of the organization in addition to damaging its prestige. I was opposed in principle, as well as on practical grounds.[59]

When the Palestine commission requested an opinion from the legal division of the UN on the rights of UNSC regarding Palestine, Lie submitted an official document in which he publicly took issue with the US position announced by Austin.

The Zionist reactions to the State Department's plans were naturally far sharper than Trygve Lie's. The plans had become the subject of widespread rumors even before Austin delivered his speech in UNSC, and Rabbi Abba Hillel Silver, head of the American Zionist movement, attacked both the State Department and President Truman for their betrayal of the 1947 US policy for partition. Moshe Shertok, in charge of foreign affairs for the Jewish Agency, wrote to Undersecretary Lovett on February 22, two days before Austin's speech, to express his alarm about "the rumors now afloat that a move is about to be made calling for the 'freezing' of the Palestine situation, so that a new effort of conciliation might be undertaken." Such a move, he protested, would tend to undermine the UNGA resolution, would come as a reward for Arab violence, and would shatter Jewish confidence in the UN. "Far from serving the interests of peace," he warned, "it would only prolong and intensify the present strife." Shertok added that the Jews "would view with the greatest anxiety any attempt to prevail upon the British government to prolong their Mandate over Palestine." Given "the progressive disintegration of the British governmental machine in Palestine, its failure to maintain law and order, and the distrust and suspicion which its every action and inaction evokes," any such attempt "is tantamount to courting disaster." He appealed instead for the "speediest possible

---

59. Lie, *In the Cause of Peace*, 168.

establishment of a provisional council of government for the Jewish State, the immediate preparation of a properly armed Jewish State militia, and if at all possible, the setting up of an international force adequate in composition and size."[60] The State Department cast aside Shertok's appeal and continued with its plan to have UNSC overturn the UNGA decision in favor of partition.

Austin Calls for a Special Session of the United Nations General Assembly

On February 25, 1948, the day after his speech to UNSC, Austin submitted the State Department's draft resolution containing two paragraphs in which UNSC would resolve:

> to accept the requests on partition which the UNGA addressed to UNSC in the UNGA resolution of November 29, 1947 and
>
> to set up a mechanism for UNSC's five permanent members
>
> to consider the situation in Palestine and to make recommendations for guidance and instructions to the Palestine commission;
>
> to consider whether there is a threat to international peace and security in Palestine and make recommendations for appropriate UNSC action; and
>
> to consult with the Palestine commission and representatives of the Arab and Jewish communities of Palestine concerning the implementation of the UNGA resolution of November 29, 1947.

As Undersecretary Lovett noted the next day in explaining the US strategy underlying the submission of its draft resolution, "The basic question now confronting UNSC was whether or not to accept the responsibilities which UNGA sought to impose on it by the resolution

---

60. *State of Israel Political and Diplomatic Documents No. 220*, February 22, 1948, 368–372, reproduced in *Foreign Relations of the United States: Diplomatic Papers, 1948*, vol. 5, pt. 2, 645–648.

of November 29, 1947," as proposed in Paragraph 1 of the US draft. "If it decided not to accept, then there was justification to call a special session [of UNGA] to consider what to do next."[61] This was the strategy Austin followed in a statement before UNSC on March 2, in which he declared that the US government stood behind partition and noted, "A vote for Paragraph 1 would be a vote for partition as a solution of the Palestine question." Having already undermined the US government's support for partition, however, through Austin's speech of February 24 gutting UNSC's enforcement powers in relation to partition, the State Department had already made it certain that UNSC would vote to reject the first paragraph of the department's draft resolution.

In UN Resolution 42 (1948) of March 5, UNSC rejected, as anticipated, the first paragraph of the State Department's draft resolution and retained only paragraph 2(a) of the draft to arrange for consultations of the permanent UNSC members, but it added a call for "recommendations to it regarding the guidance and instructions which the council might usefully give to the Palestine commission with a view to implementing the resolution of UNGA." The council had thus rejected enforcement but was still calling for recommendations for the implementation of partition. The five permanent UNSC members were requested to report back to UNSC within ten days.

Despite UNSC's request for guidance on the implementation of partition, the State Department kept to its position that UNSC's rejection of the first paragraph of the US draft resolution constituted UNSC's rejection of partition. It was therefore appropriate to propose moving immediately to the second stage of its strategy to call for a special session of UNGA to establish a trusteeship of Palestine. Austin objected that the US government should at least wait until the UNSC's committee of permanent members reported on the results of its consultations, and Marshall agreed to be guided by Austin's

---

61. *Foreign Relations of the United States: Diplomatic Papers, 1948, vol. 5, pt. 2,* 660.

opinion that the process would lead to the inevitable conclusion that partition had to be abandoned. Waiting for the committee's report also had its advantages, as Marshall noted, because the procedure now to be followed "would indicate that we were impressed by the facts reported by the conciliation committee but would not force us to go on record as voting against partition."[62]

In collaboration with Ambassador Austin, the State Department prepared a statement for him to make before UNSC after the completion of the ten-day consultation process of the five permanent members of UNSC. This statement—approved by Secretary Marshall on March 5, the day of the UNSC vote for Resolution 42 calling for the consultation process to begin—took for granted the expected results of the consultations. Declaring, "UNSC now has before it clear evidence that the Jews and Arabs of Palestine and the Mandatory power are not prepared to implement the UNGA plan of partition through peaceful means," it warned, "The announced determination of the Mandatory power to terminate the Mandate on May 15, 1948, if carried out by the UK, would clearly result... in chaos and heavy fighting in Palestine."[63] It therefore proposed that UNSC should, inter alia:

> request of the secretary-general the immediate convocation of a special session of UNGA to consider further the question of Palestine;
>
> consider the recommendation to the special session of UNGA that until the people of Palestine were ready for self-government, they should be placed under the trusteeship system of the UN; and

---

62. *Foreign Relations of the United States: Diplomatic Papers, 1948, vol. 5, pt. 2,* 679–680.
63. On March 2, the British colonial minister, Arthur Creech Jones, announced in UNSC that the UK government would under no circumstances alter its decision to terminate its Mandate on May 15, 1948.

instruct the Palestine commission to suspend its activities pending further recommendations by UNGA.[64]

At a cabinet meeting on the same day, March 5, 1948, Marshall informed the president and the cabinet:

> Without endeavoring to prophesy, the future trend seems to be that UNSC will find itself unable to proceed with partition and that it will refer the Palestine problem to an immediate special session of UNGA for fresh consideration.[65]

Marshall and Austin could confidently make this prediction because, as UN Secretary-General Trygve Lie later wrote:

> From the start, the consultations were a frustrating affair. Only the Soviet Union seemed to be seriously intent upon implementing partition; the US clearly was not. Rumors were flying that the US was seeking to moderate the Arab stand even at the price of abandoning partition, and in such an atmosphere, firm action by UNSC or its permanent members was out of the question.[66]

The text for Austin's statement to UNSC, as approved by Secretary Marshall, was submitted to President Truman on March 8, and Marshall informed Austin that the president had approved the draft statement of March 5, together with the draft recommendations that had been included for use if and when necessary.[67]

The president was warned by members of his staff that State Department officials were working to undermine his policy on partition.

---

64. *Foreign Relations of the United States: Diplomatic Papers, 1948, vol. 5, pt. 2*, 682–685.
65. *Foreign Relations of the United States: Diplomatic Papers, 1948, vol. 5, pt. 2*, 678–679.
66. Lie, *In the Cause of Peace*, 169.
67. *Foreign Relations of the United States: Diplomatic Papers, 1948, vol. 5, pt. 2*, 697.

Among these staff members, the key role in 1948 was played by Clark Clifford, who succeeded Judge Samuel Rosenman as the president's counsel and who headed the president's 1948 re-election campaign. On March 8, 1948, the same day on which Marshall informed Austin that the president had approved his statement for delivery in UNSC, Clifford sent the president a memorandum recommending the strongest possible support for implementing the UN resolution of November 29, 1947, accompanied by a warning that State Department officials were working to kill partition.[68] Knowing the president's sensitivity to charges from anti-Zionists, even in his own State Department, that his Palestine policy was motivated by election concerns, Clifford began by stating that his views had nothing to do with the election but were concerned only with what was best for the US.

Clifford then proceeded to demolish the State Department's case for the abandonment of partition. The president's support for partition, enabling the Jews to set up their state in Palestine, he emphasized, was in complete conformity with the policy of support for the Balfour Declaration that had been approved by President Wilson and had since been restated in substance by every president, including Truman himself. It was also in harmony with national interests, because it was "the best hope of a permanent solution of the Palestine problem that may avoid war." He warned that a retreat on Palestine would be a body blow to the UN and added, "We 'crossed the Rubicon' on this matter when the partition resolution was adopted by UNGA—largely at your insistence." Clifford added that abandonment of partition would also be a blow to US foreign policy, because countries "would justifiably discount the value of any commitments we might propose to make in the face of our repudiation of a commitment we only made last November."

Clifford took up the other State Department arguments against partition, including the risk of losing Arab oil, the bogey of potential

---

68. *Foreign Relations of the United States: Diplomatic Papers, 1948, vol. 5, pt. 2*, 690–696.

communist influence in a Jewish state, and the claimed non-workability of partition. Arabian oil supplies, he explained, will not be imperiled by US support of the UN decision, because "political and economic self-preservation will compel the Arabs to sell their oil to the US. Their need of the US is greater than our need of them." As for fear of Communist influence, he noted that Jewish Palestine was strongly oriented toward the US and away from Soviet Russia. Finally, he dismissed the State Department's claim that partition is not workable by noting that this claim "comes from those who never wanted partition to succeed and who have been determined to sabotage it. If anything has been omitted that could help kill partition," he added, "I do not know what it would be."

After rejecting the State Department's arguments against partition, Clifford presented a program of action for the implementation of the UNGA resolution for partition that must have left the State Department officials shaking their heads in disbelief. The US, he recommended, should exert every pressure it can bring to bear upon the Arab states to accept partition. If they continue with their violent resistance, it should urge UNSC to declare Arab action a threat to peace. The US should also call upon UNSC to require Great Britain to comply with the UNGA resolution—to refrain from taking any action to prevent, obstruct, or delay the implementation by the Palestine commission of the measures recommended by UNGA. In particular, Britain should be required to permit the immediate entry of the UN commission into Palestine and to set aside Tel Aviv as a port for Jewish immigration in compliance with the UNGA resolution.

Clifford also spelled out in some detail his recommendations for the use of force in Palestine to preserve the peace. The US, he said, should call upon UNSC to create the Arab and Jewish militias recommended in the UNGA resolution and to provide the means for them to procure the necessary arms. It should immediately lift its unilateral embargo on arms to the Middle East and withdraw its instructions to lift the passports of American citizens who volunteer to serve in the militias approved by the UN. Finally, the US should cooperate with the UNGA Palestine commission in its plan to establish an international security force in Palestine. The force should consist of volunteers drawn from countries other than the major powers or from nations directly involved in the Middle East.[69]

But despite Clifford's warning that the State Department was doing everything possible to sabotage the UN decision on partition, the president retained full confidence in Secretary Marshall, insisting, "I know how Marshall feels, and he knows how I feel."[70] The president's confidence that he knew how Marshall felt on partition seems, however, to have been badly misplaced.

On March 16, just before the committee of UNSC's permanent members reported on their consultations, Marshall sent another telegram to Austin, warning that the situation in Palestine "grows daily more fraught with danger to international peace" and urging the need to act without delay, in accordance with the statement that, as he reminded Austin, had been approved by the president on March 8 for use if and when necessary.[71] Ambassador Austin was unhappy with Secretary Marshall's instructions to act without delay on the request for a special session of UNGA, and at one point, he was intent upon taking up with the president his differences with the State Department. After further persuasion by Dean Rusk in New

---

69. *Foreign Relations of the United States: Diplomatic Papers, 1948*, vol. 5, pt. 2, 687–689. Clifford added that if Russia were to veto the exclusion of volunteers from the major powers, the US should agree but should limit the total number of volunteers from the major powers to fifty percent and the number from any one major power to ten percent. If the competent military authorities estimated that it would not be possible to meet the needs with volunteers alone, the US should agree to calling upon the member nations to provide troops under the same limitations as those proposed for the volunteer forces.
70. Jonathan Daniels, *The Man of Independence* (London: Victor Gollancz Ltd, 1951), 318.
71. *Foreign Relations of the United States: Diplomatic Papers, 1948*, vol. 5, pt. 2, "The Secretary of State to the United States Representative at the United Nations," March 16, 1948, 728–729.

York, however, he dropped his opposition and agreed to carry out Marshall's instructions.[72]

Austin carried out his instructions on March 19, 1948 in the UNSC session dealing with the report on the consultations of the committee of permanent members, where he declared that there was general agreement that the UNGA plan could not be carried out by peaceful means. He then presented the State Department's well-prepared proposal that UNSC should therefore request of the secretary-general the convocation of a special session of UNGA with a recommendation to UNGA and the Mandatory power to establish a trusteeship for Palestine. It should also instruct the UN Palestine commission to suspend its efforts to implement partition.[73]

✡ ✡ ✡

The general reaction of the Arab states to Ambassador Austin's statement was naturally favorable, even if it was marked by some notes of caution. The Syrian government expressed its "gratitude" for America's rejection of partition, the Saudi Arabian government was "pleased", and the Egyptian government "universally welcomed" the US action.[74] In Jerusalem, however, the US consul general reported to the Secretary of State that the Jewish reaction to Austin's statement "was one of consternation, disillusion, despair, and determination. Most feel [the US] has betrayed Jews in [the] interest [of] Middle Eastern oil and for fear [of] Russian designs." The consul general added that "most observers feel bloodshed will now increase tremendously, with Jews desperate and Arabs feeling new strength."[75]

---

72. *Foreign Relations of the United States: Diplomatic Papers, 1948, vol. 5, pt. 2,* March 17, 1948, p. 730.
73. *Foreign Relations of the United States: Diplomatic Papers, 1948, vol. 5, pt. 2,* 742–744.
74. *Foreign Relations of the United States: Diplomatic Papers, 1948, vol. 5, pt. 2,* 753, fn. 2.
75. *Foreign Relations of the United States: Diplomatic Papers, 1948, vol. 5, pt. 2,* March 22, 1948, 753.

The State Department had rejected partition because it could not be implemented peacefully only to propose in its stead a plan that, as its representative in Palestine reported, was expected to lead to a tremendous increase in bloodshed.

On March 25, the UN published the text of a US statement called "Truman's Trusteeship Proposal," presumably submitted by the State Department in justification of its proposed amendments to the UNGA resolution for partition. It emphasized,

> The US has proposed to UNSC a temporary UN trusteeship for Palestine to provide a government to keep the peace. Such trusteeship was proposed only after we had exhausted every effort to find a way to carry out partition by peaceful means. Trusteeship is not proposed as a substitute for the partition plan but as an effort to fill the vacuum soon to be created by the termination of the Mandate on May 15. The trusteeship does not prejudice the character of the final political settlement. It would establish the conditions of order which are essential to a peaceful solution.

In the UN, the US proposal came as a bombshell. It sabotaged a hard-fought decision of UNGA for which, less than four months earlier, the US had voted and had in the end worked vigorously to support with votes from other UN member states. Eleanor Roosevelt, a strong supporter of the UN who had also become a firm pro-Zionist, was so upset with the US State Department's proposal for a Palestine trusteeship that she submitted her resignation as a member of the US delegation to the UN. Only following the president's personal plea did she withdraw her resignation.[76]

More remarkable was the attitude of Secretary-General Trygve Lie. As he pointed out with some irony,

> The US would in effect repudiate partition on the very day, March 19, when the committee of permanent members reported on its recommendations for implementing partition…

---

76. Truman, *Harry S. Truman*, 389.

The American reversal was a blow to the UN and showed a profoundly disheartening disregard for its effectiveness and standing. I could not help asking myself what the future of the UN would be if this was the measure of support it could expect from the US.

Trygve Lie proposed to Ambassador Austin that they should both resign their posts in public protest, but Austin expressed surprise that Lie should feel so passionately about the matter and dissuaded him from resigning.[77]

David Ben-Gurion, soon to become prime minister of the State of Israel, commented forcefully on the same day:

> The American announcement does more harm to the UN—in standing and authority—than it does to us. The change in the American position indicates that the US has surrendered to Arab terror. But this does not basically change the situation here or impede the establishment of a Jewish state... We have laid the foundations for the establishment of a Jewish state, and we will establish it. We will not agree to a trusteeship—temporary or permanent. We will no longer accept foreign rule in whatever form, and we will devote ourselves even more intensely to defending ourselves.[78]

Four days later, on March 23, the Jewish Agency and the Vaad Haleumi (the Jewish National Council) declared, "Upon termination of the Mandatory administration, and not later than May 16 next, a provisional Jewish government will commence to function... in Palestine."[79]

---

77. Lie, *In the Cause of Peace*, 169–171.
78. Ben-Gurion, *Israel: A Personal History*, 72.
79. *State of Israel Political and Diplomatic Documents*, No. 302, "Cable from Ben-Gurion and Remez to Shertok, March 23, 1948," 493–494, reproduced in *Foreign Relations of the United States: Diplomatic Papers, 1948, vol. 5, pt. 2*.

Even Chaim Weizmann, who had always been the voice for moderation in the Zionist movement, gave this decision his full support. In a statement to the press on March 25, he commented:

> The Jews of Palestine will have the support of Jews the world over in those steps which they will deem necessary to assure their survival and national freedom when the Mandate ends. I would now urge the Jewish people to redouble its efforts to secure the defense and freedom of the Jewish State.[80]

---

80. Weizmann, *Trial and Error*, 473.

– 15 –

The Drama of the Rebirth of the Jewish State: Israel

As surprising as it may seem, the person most stunned and angered by Austin's speech on March 19, 1948 to UNSC proposing abandonment of the partition of Palestine and the convocation of a UNGA special session to establish a Palestine trusteeship was President Truman. Despite Secretary Marshall's statements on March 8 and again on March 16 that the president had approved the text of Ambassador Austin's March 19, 1948 speech (see Chapter 14), Truman was completely shocked that he had been betrayed. As Margaret Truman later revealed in her biography of her father, the president wrote in his diary the next day, March 20, 1948:

> The State Department pulled the rug from under me today. I didn't expect that it would happen. In Key West or en route there from St. Croix, I approved the speech and statement of policy by Senator Austin [for the] UN meeting. This morning, I find that the State Department has reversed my Palestine policy. The first I know about it is what I see in the papers! Isn't that hell? I am now in the position of a liar and a double-crosser. I've never felt so in my life.
>
> There are people on the third and fourth levels of the State Department who have always wanted to cut my throat. They've succeeded in doing it: Marshall's in California and Lovett's in Florida.[1]

---

1. Truman, *Harry S. Truman*, 388.

President Truman's outrage was all the greater, because, as his daughter noted, Austin's speech followed on the heels of a meeting Truman had granted (most reluctantly)[2] to Chaim Weizmann the previous day:

> The two men talked for about three-quarters of an hour. Once more, Dr. Weizmann begged Dad to support the inclusion of the Negev in any Jewish state. My father assured him that this idea had his full support. He also made it clear that the US still backed the idea of partition and wished to see it achieved as soon as possible. In fact, he told Dr. Weizmann that Warren Austin, the head of our UN delegation, would make an important statement to this effect the following day. Warren Austin did make an important statement in the UN the following day. But it was not the statement Dad expected him to make—in support of partition. Instead, Ambassador Austin announced that the US was *abandoning* [emphasis in original] partition and now supported a UN trusteeship to replace the British Mandate.[3]

If, as noted in the preceding chapter, UN Secretary-General Trygve Lie and the former first lady, Eleanor Roosevelt, were ready to resign in protest against Austin's announcement, one can readily imagine what the reactions of the Zionists were to Austin's speech. As Margaret Truman wrote in the biography of her father:

---

2. Truman was so angered by the renewal of the fierce Zionist attacks against him and by the State Department for its reversal of the US position on partition that he instructed his staff he "did not want to be approached by any more spokesmen for the extreme Zionist cause" (Truman, *Memoirs*, vol. 2, 160). He refused to see even Chaim Weizmann, and as Truman described in vivid detail in his *Memoirs* and in Merle Miller's oral biography of him, Truman agreed to see Weizmann only after the tearful plea of Eddie Jacobson, Truman's good friend and business partner from the World War I days (Truman, *Memoirs*, vol. 2, 160–161; Merle Miller, *Plain Speaking: An Oral Biography of Harry S. Truman* [New York: Tess Press, 2004], 217).
3. Truman, *Harry S. Truman*, 388.

Headlines and Zionists exploded across the country and the world. My father was called a traitor, a liar, and a lot of other unjustified names. Dr. Weizmann was one of the few Jewish spokesmen who remained silent. He knew that Dad had been double crossed.[4]

Concerned that Weizmann should not believe ill of him, the president took the opportunity the following morning, when his former counsel, Judge Samuel Rosenman, came to see him on another matter, to ask him "to see Dr. Weizmann and tell him there was not and would not be any change in the long policy he and I had talked about."[5]

Deeply disturbed over Austin's announcement, Truman called his counsel, Clark Clifford, at 7:30 a.m. that Saturday morning telling him, "There is a story in the papers on Palestine, and I don't understand

---

4. Truman, *Harry S. Truman*, 388.
5. Truman, *Memoirs, vol. 2*, 161–162. Truman also assured Weizmann, under a request of strict secrecy, that when they spoke, the president had been unaware of what Austin would say at the UN. Fortified by the president's secret message to him, Weizmann was able to resist the pressures of the State Department and the US delegation to enlist his help to discourage the Jews from establishing the Jewish State upon the termination of the Mandate. Ambassadors Warren Austin and Philip Jessup met with Weizmann at his hotel shortly after the reversal of US policy in the UN to warn him how dangerous it would be for peace if the Jews of Palestine were to proclaim a state at the Mandate's end. Weizmann, who had always been a "moderate," was on this occasion uncompromising. In his autobiography, Weizmann wrote, "I must have astonished as well as disappointed them, for I declared bluntly that I put no stock in the legend of Arab military might and that I considered the intention of Palestine Jewry to proclaim its independence the day the Mandate ended thoroughly justified and eminently realistic" (*Trial and Error*, 475). Abba Eban quotes Weizmann as having replied that in his view, "Palestine Jewry would be off its head if it postponed statehood for anything so foolish as the American trusteeship proposal" (Abba Eban, "Tragedy and Triumph," in Meyer Wolfe Weisgal, Joel Carmichael, and David Ben-Gurion (eds.), *Chaim Weizmann: A Biography by Several Hands* [New York: Atheneum, 1963], 308–309).

what has happened." When Clifford arrived, Truman asked, in "bewilderment and consternation, 'How could this have happened? I assured Chaim Weizmann that we were for partition and would stick to it. He must think I am a plain liar. Find out how this could have happened.'" Truman also asked Clifford to ascertain whether Marshall had foreknowledge of the State Department's decision to abandon partition.[6]

In response to Clifford's investigation, Undersecretary Lovett explained on March 22 that he and Secretary Marshall had discussed the situation with Truman on March 8, and Lovett had told the president that on March 5, UNSC had rejected the first paragraph of the US draft resolution of February 25, 1948 calling upon it to accept the UNGA request concerning the implementation of partition (see Chapter 14). Lovett had added that while he did not regard this decision as a complete rejection of partition, he did not believe that there were enough votes in UNSC to approve partition. An alternative solution would therefore be required: namely, the proposal for trusteeship contained in the State Department draft the president had been shown. According to Lovett, "The president then said we were to go through and attempt to get approval for the implementation of the UNGA resolution [for partition], but if we did not get it, we could take the alternative step."[7] Marshall and Lovett evidently made no attempt to secure such UNSC approval of partition; instead, convinced that UNSC would not approve partition, Marshall informed Austin that the president had approved the draft statement calling for a special session of UNGA for the establishment of a trusteeship and urged him to proceed accordingly.

To contain the damage that Austin's call for a special session had done, Truman now had Marshall issue a statement justifying the trusteeship proposal as only a temporary provision to prevent total

---

6. Clark Clifford, "Recognizing Israel," *American Heritage* 28, no. 3 (April 1977): 7; Daniels, *The Man of Independence*, 318.
7. *Foreign Relations of the United States: Diplomatic Papers, 1948*, vol. 5, pt. 2, 749.

chaos at the Mandate's termination, a statement reproduced in the files of UNISPAL on March 25 as "Truman's Trusteeship Proposal" (see Chapter 14). The justification was met with total skepticism in the UN.

In 1977, nearly thirty years after Austin's speech, Clifford made public, in an article in *American Heritage*, the results of his investigation, according to which, "Both Marshall and Undersecretary Robert Lovett had known in advance of the *de facto* reversal of the president's policy." Clifford wrote that Truman had approved the State Department draft subject to three qualifications, which the State Department had ignored in its instructions to Austin to make his statement:

The conciliatory machinery of UNSC must be completely exhausted,

the council must vote to reject partition altogether, and

the council itself must then vote to propose an alternative to partition.[8]

---

8. Clifford, "Recognizing Israel," 7. Clifford added that an inspection of State Department files had also revealed that Dean Rusk's thesis that UNSC had no power to enforce partition had not won unanimous support in the State Department. Lawyers in the State Department's legal office had rejected Rusk's thesis, declaring instead, "The authority of UNSC subsisted regardless of the consideration that the council's authority...to maintain or restore peace and security might facilitate implementation of UNGA's partition plan." The same search also revealed that there was also a division of opinion within the State Department concerning the issue of assisting the establishment of a Jewish state in accordance with the UNGA resolution for partition. The Division of International Security Affairs recommended "the imposition of the arms embargo against certain Arab states and the arming of a Jewish militia in Palestine. Going further... [it] similarly contended that there were indeed military, economic, and diplomatic measures that the US could initiate through the UN body to facilitate the implementation of partition." Yet this dissenting view, like that of the legal adviser, Clifford added, was to his knowledge never presented to Secretary Marshall—let alone to the White House.

Marshall mentioned none of these qualifications to Austin on March 8 and March 16, informing him only that the president had approved the draft statement for delivery in UNSC.

Harold Wilson, a later prime minister of Britain, aptly commented on the State Department's behavior in its conduct of US foreign policy on Palestine:

> The Washington traditional private enterprise system continued to function in the State Department there, busily organizing their own declaration of independence of the president. They stuck to their trusteeship fetish as though Truman did not exist... The State Department ground out their resolutions as though the White House was untenanted: The Mandate should be continued, on a multinational—not specifically British—basis.[9]

The United Nations Security Council, meeting on April 1, 1948 in response to Austin's call for a special session of UNGA, adopted two US-sponsored resolutions: 1. Resolution 43, calling for a cessation of violence by armed Arab and Jewish groups as well as asking the Jewish Agency and the Arab Higher Committee to make their representatives available to UNSC for arranging a truce between the Arab and Jewish communities and 2. Resolution 44, requesting the secretary-general to convoke a special session of UNGA to consider further the question of the future government of Palestine.

The Special Session of the United Nations General Assembly

The UNGA special session, which opened on April 16, 1948—only one month before the Mandate's end—had before it a report from the UN Palestine commission setting out the reasons why it could not perform its functions for implementing UNGA Resolution 181(II) for partition:

---

9. Wilson, *The Chariot of Israel*, 226–227.

The Commission... has the duty to report to UNGA that the armed hostility of both Palestinian and non-Palestinian Arab elements, the lack of cooperation from the Mandatory Power, the disintegrating security situation in Palestine, and the fact that UNSC did not furnish the commission with the necessary armed assistance are the factors which have made it impossible for the commission to implement UNGA's resolution.

In the absence of forces adequate to restore and maintain law and order in Palestine following the termination of the Mandate, there will be administrative chaos, starvation, widespread strife, violence, and bloodshed in Palestine, including Jerusalem. These calamitous results for the people of Palestine will be intensified unless specific arrangements are made regarding the urgent matters outlined above well in advance of 15 May 1948.[10]

The United Nations General Assembly referred the question to its standing Committee for Political and Security Affairs, the First Committee, where general debate began on April 20, 1948. In preparation for the debate, Ambassador Austin, at an informal meeting of UNSC members on April 5, 1948, presented a working paper setting out fifteen general principles for inclusion in a UN trusteeship agreement for Palestine.[11]

In contrast to its earlier insistence that UNSC had no authority to enforce the UNGA resolution for partition, the State Department maintained that UNSC could enforce a resolution for trusteeship, because it would be acting as a government under the authority of trusteeship. The US, Austin noted, would also be ready to collaborate with the UN in enforcing the trusteeship. To avoid opening the door for the Soviet Union to follow suit—a risk it had so feared in connection with partition—the US draft agreement provided that the governor general, who would lead Palestine under the trusteeship,

---

10. "Section 9: The Question of Palestine," in United Nations, *Yearbook, 1947–1948*.
11. *Foreign Relations of the United States: Diplomatic Papers, 1948*, vol. 5, 801.

"should be authorized to call upon such states as would be specified in the agreement to assist in the maintenance of security in Palestine." Despite the British Foreign Office's repeated refusal to continue any further involvement in Palestine after its termination of the Mandate, the State Department remained hopeful that Britain could still be persuaded to change its mind. It also believed that France too should be called upon to contribute some forces, despite Arab bitterness over past French rule in Syria.

Although the proposed trusteeship was labeled temporary, the draft agreement provided for it to be of indefinite duration—to be terminated only when the Arab and Jewish communities of Palestine agreed upon the future government of the country. Since Britain had been unable to achieve any such agreement between the two communities in the course of the three decades of its rule of Palestine under the Mandate, the State Department could hardly have been under any illusions that a UN trusteeship might be of short duration. It remains a puzzle how the State Department had convinced itself that the UN could succeed where Britain had failed so completely that it was now determined to surrender its Mandate, even at the cost of leaving Palestine in a state of complete chaos.

Britain's Foreign Office no longer shared any such illusions. On April 9, a week before the scheduled special session, British Ambassador Alexander Cadogan left an *aide-memoire* with the US delegation that punctured all the State Department's illusions regarding trusteeship. It emphasized, instead:

> There was little reason to suppose that the Arab and Jewish communities in Palestine would come to an understanding on a plan for self-government;
>
> the trusteeship would prove to be an interim one in name only;
>
> the Jews would object to the provisions proposed for terminating the trusteeship, because they rule out any possibility of partitioning Palestine;

the Arabs would oppose the trusteeship agreement in that it postponed independence indefinitely and empowered the Jews to veto the constitution of an independent unitary state; and,

the Arabs would not agree to the proposed immigration and land transfer provisions.[12]

On April 20, 1948, Austin opened the debate in the UNGA First Committee with a statement of the US position, calling for a military truce and for the establishment of a trusteeship in Palestine. At the same time, he submitted as a working draft of the proposed trusteeship agreement that he had earlier discussed informally with the UNSC delegations. The UK delegation told UNGA, however, that in light of the difficulties it had experienced in administering Palestine under the Mandate, the US call for a trusteeship seemed overly ambitious, and it would be better to aim at a more modest goal of establishing a truce in Palestine.[13]

The State Department did not give up easily. Ambassador Douglas in London, despite having already been repeatedly rebuffed by Bevin and the Foreign Office for the week prior to the opening of the UN special session, continued during the special session to press Bevin repeatedly for a second week to accept joint responsibility with the US and with France for the maintenance of security in Palestine under a trusteeship. Douglas met with Bevin on April 16, 20, and 21 and again twice on April 22, 1948, when he cabled Secretary Marshall twice that Bevin would not yield.[14] The following day, April 23, even Loy Henderson, who had written Lovett the previous day to urge Secretary Marshall to take personal charge of mobilizing support for partition, began to resign himself to the prospect of defeat, now

---

12. *Foreign Relations of the United States: Diplomatic Papers, 1948, vol. 5*, 767–769.
13. "Section 9: The Question of Palestine," in United Nations, *Yearbook, 1947–1948*.
14. *Foreign Relations of the United States: Diplomatic Papers, 1948, vol. 5*, 839–840, 847, 850–851.

writing to Lovett that it was uncertain whether UNGA would approve a trusteeship or whether it would do anything at all.[15]

In fact, the trusteeship proposal won almost no support in the First Committee. As Secretary-General Trygve Lie noted, the US had rejected the UN decision of November 29, 1947 on the grounds that partition could not be implemented peacefully. Yet it was now requesting the UN to take enforcement action against that very partition decision for which the US had itself voted and that was now already being implemented *de facto*, concurrently with the dissolution of British authority.[16] No country was prepared to follow the State Department's lead and contribute any forces on behalf of a Palestine trusteeship.

Many UN members, most notably the representatives of the Soviet Union and of Poland—who had surprised the world by voting for the UN resolution of November 29, 1947—as well as García-Granados of Guatemala and Professor Fabregat of Uruguay—both of whom had become champions of partition since serving as members of UNSCOP—argued forcefully against the abandonment of the UN decision for partition. And Sir Carl Berendsen of New Zealand spoke so movingly against capitulating to threats and violence in Palestine and abandoning partition as to impel Trygve Lie to report, "Berendsen so well expressed the thoughts and feelings closest to my heart that—the first time I ever did such a thing for a speech—I sent him an admiring bouquet of roses." Sir Carl told UNGA that partition was the right solution in November, and it was the right solution in April. New Zealand, for its part, would continue to support enforcing

---

15. In light of the uncertainty whether UNGA would support a trusteeship for Palestine, Henderson proposed that the US should submit a separate plan for a trusteeship for the Jerusalem area, which under the UN resolution of November 29, 1947 was to go neither to the Jewish nor to the Arab state (*Foreign Relations of the United States: Diplomatic Papers, 1948, vol. 5*, 840–845, 853–855).
16. Lie, *In the Cause of Peace*, 172.

partition. He concluded with the ringing statement, "What the world needs today is not resolutions—it is resolution."[17]

The debate on the US trusteeship proposal concluded in the First Committee on May 5, 1948, with a decision to set up a sub-committee (Sub-Committee 9) with terms of reference to "formulate and report to the committee a proposal for a provisional regime for Palestine," taking into account "whether it is likely that such proposal will commend itself to the Jewish and Arab communities of Palestine; whether it is possible to implement this proposal and make it workable; and the approximate cost of such proposal."[18]

The United States' Proposal for a Political Standstill

Recognizing the lack of support for a Palestine trusteeship, the US shifted the focus of its attention to the imposition of a political and military standstill as the means of preventing the establishment of a Jewish state. Already on April 17, 1948, UNSC had upgraded its Resolution 43 of April 1, 1948 for a military truce by adopting Resolution 46, which, in addition to strengthening the provisions for a military truce, added a call for a political truce. On April 23, UNSC adopted, in addition, Resolution 48, which established a truce commission for Palestine to "assist UNSC in supervising the implementation by the parties of its Resolution 46 (1948)." In accordance with a formula devised to exclude the Soviet Union from membership, the commission was composed of "representatives of those members of UNSC which have career consular officers in Jerusalem."[19]

On April 28, Dean Rusk's deputy, Mr. McClintock, after consultations with the Jewish Agency's Moshe Shertok and with representatives of the Arab League at the UN, transmitted to Undersecretary

---

17. Lie, *In the Cause of Peace*, 172.
18. "Section 9: The Question of Palestine," in United Nations, *Yearbook, 1947–1948*.
19. Syria, which qualified for membership under this formula, had to be persuaded to agree not to serve.

Lovett for relay to the Jewish Agency in Jerusalem the text of fourteen articles of an informal politico-military truce proposal that called upon the Arab and Jewish authorities to take no steps to proclaim a sovereign state during the truce. In the hope of winning the support of the Jewish Agency, the draft provided for the entry of four thousand Jewish displaced persons per month during the truce. At the insistence of both the Arab and Jewish negotiators in New York, the proposal provided for the truce to be effective—not for an indefinite period as the US had desired but only for three months, after which either party could terminate it upon thirty days' notice of termination to the truce commission.[20]

The next day, Moshe Shertok wrote to Secretary Marshall of his very serious objections to the proposed truce, emphasizing that it "entails the deferment of statehood and renders its attainment in the future most uncertain," thereby prejudicing Jewish rights under UNGA Resolution 181(II). In addition, the truce would involve the use of considerable force in Palestine, raising the suspicion that the truce was intended to continue British authority in Palestine. The military truce would likewise put the Jewish community of Palestine at a gross disadvantage. The Arab states would be free to build up their military strength for later use in Palestine, and the Palestinian Arabs would be free to train in the neighboring countries. The Jews, however, had no such outside resources for the acquisition of weapons or for large-scale military training.[21]

The State Department nevertheless intensified its pressure on the Jewish Agency to agree to its politico-military truce proposal. On May 5, John Ross, US alternate delegate to the special session, met with Moshe Shertok and Rabbi Abba Hillel Silver in a further attempt to persuade them to accept the US truce proposal. He warned them that

---

20. *Foreign Relations of the United States: Diplomatic Papers, 1948, vol. 5,* 858–859, 864, 866–868.
21. *State of Israel Political and Diplomatic Documents, No. 428,* December 1947–May 1948, 695–696, reproduced in *Foreign Relations of the United States: Diplomatic Papers, 1948, vol. 5,* 874–875 and fns.

in the absence of such a truce, the Jews would run the serious risk of not being able to establish their state and of losing much of the gains they had made over the past years. Rabbi Silver replied that the Jews were willing to accept an immediate and unconditional ceasefire, but he objected to the political truce in the same vein as Shertok had already written to Secretary Marshall a week earlier. Under Ross's pressure, however, he did make a significant concession: If the Jews could establish a provisional government, he would be willing to forego the establishment of a sovereign state on May 15, provided there was a guarantee that they could do so at the end of the truce period, including a guarantee that the US would prevent aggression by the neighboring Arab states. Ross found this suggestion interesting but noted that it came with "impractical conditions attached."[22]

The following day, May 6, the State Department submitted to the president for his approval its latest draft articles for a political truce, and the president approved, despite his pledge to Weizmann on his support for partition and probably in deference to Secretary Marshall. The draft articles required that no steps should be taken during the truce period to proclaim a sovereign state, including the establishment of a provisional government in the area under its control. Instead, the Jews would have to agree to function only as a "temporary truce regime," thereby signing away their right to set up a state granted them under the UN resolution of November 29, 1947 for partition. On the other hand, the original provision for Jewish immigration at a rate of four thousand people per month had been seriously eroded in the new draft. The Arab states had rejected any increase in immigration above the 1939 White Paper level of one thousand five hundred people per month, and no provision was made for any separate letter of understanding for any further increase in immigration.[23]

---

22. *Foreign Relations of the United States: Diplomatic Papers, 1948, vol. 5,* 917–920.

23. *Foreign Relations of the United States: Diplomatic Papers, 1948, vol. 5,* 927–929. Rusk added only the consideration that both the Jews and the Arabs were aware of the British determination to evacuate the eighteen

Despite the one-sided character of the final draft truce, Rusk noted in his memorandum to Marshall that they had already impressed upon Mr. Shertok, "The US government considers the articles of truce as now drawn to be fair and equitable and is prepared to back these articles in every appropriate way." With this came the explicit warning,

> If a truce is not agreed, we believe that the situation with respect to Palestine will constitute a threat to international peace and will urge UNSC to take the necessary action to remove that threat... The US will direct its own policies and conduct in support of UNSC decisions.[24]

Shertok met with Secretary Marshall, Undersecretary Lovett, and Dean Rusk on May 8, 1948, before flying off for consultations in Palestine, to restate the Jewish objections to the truce articles and to add an anguished appeal:

> We had fought alone and unaided. We had asked the US government for arms, but they were not forthcoming. We asked for military expert advice, and even that was withheld. There was an occasion when we asked for the release of armor plate to protect passenger buses against attack, and even that was refused. Not having helped us, why should the US government now try to prevent us from attaining what was so imminently within our reach?[25]

Shertok went on to note that even Britain had come to accept partition. In a conversation with the British colonial minister, Creech

---

to twenty thousand Jews from the camps in Cyprus to Palestine. This "would give the Arabs a chance to accept a status quo in principle and to submit to the British evacuation of Cyprus," and "It would give the Jews from four to six thousand immigrants per month during the course of the truce" (*Foreign Relations of the United States: Diplomatic Papers, 1948, vol. 5*, 932–933).

24. *Foreign Relations of the United States: Diplomatic Papers, 1948, vol. 5*, 934.
25. *State of Israel Political and Diplomatic Documents*, No. 483, 757–769.

Jones predicted that the Jews would have their state on May 15 and added that King Abdullah of Transjordan would move his Arab Legion only into the area assigned to the Arabs and not into the area proposed for the Jewish State. Why could the US not support this new British position, he asked, now that it seemed clear that the trusteeship proposal did not have the support of the UN? Shertok concluded his appeal with the comment, "Apparently, the determination of the Jewish people to achieve statehood was not fully realized—that determination was unshakeable."[26]

Shertok failed to persuade either Lovett or Marshall. According to Shertok's report to the Jewish Agency, Lovett replied, "The truce was a better course...to safeguard the interests of the Jewish State of the future than the continuation of warfare." Lovett also disagreed with Shertok's reference to the absence of UNSC support for trusteeship, asserting that US officials...

...had so far not taken any determined steps to secure the acceptance of their trusteeship proposals, but their information was to the effect that the necessary majority would be forthcoming if it was made clear that this was their definite policy.

Lovett added the clear threat that the US had, for the time being, left public opinion alone, but "If they would explain properly how they viewed the position, public opinion would undergo a marked change to our detriment." And in a veiled threat to cut off contributions of American Jews to the Jewish cause in Palestine, Shertok commented that Lovett "had figured out that the operation of the Haganah must be costing us [the Jewish Agency] several million dollars a month."

Secretary Marshall complained, in addition, about the difficulties they had experienced with American Zionists and bluntly warned that the State Department's files "were full of...all the political pressure, the blustering, the misleading assurances, etc., etc." Moreover, the Jewish Agency had been most unhelpful about illegal immigration,

---

26. *State of Israel, Political and Diplomatic Documents*, No. 483, 757–769.

such that while the US government was trying to impress a certain course of action upon Great Britain, it "was all the time throwing back into their face this charge that they were aiding and abetting in illegal immigration." But his main point was to warn against rejecting the truce. As a military man, Marshall wanted…

> …to warn us [the Jewish Agency] against relying on the advice of our military people. He indicated that flushed by victory, their counsel was liable to be misleading. If we succeed, well and good. He would be quite happy—he wished us well. But what if we failed? He did not want to put any pressure on us. It was our responsibility, and it was for us to face it. We were completely free to take our decision, but he hoped we would do so in full realization of the very grave risks involved. He said again and again that if we succeeded in setting up a Jewish state and maintaining it, he would be only too happy, but, etc., etc.[27]

The next day, May 9, the State Department instructed its consul general in Jerusalem to deliver the draft truce proposals to his colleagues on the truce commission for their approval, and on May 11, it asked him to arrange for the submission of the draft to the representatives of the Jewish Agency, the Arab Higher Committee, and the Arab League. The consul general reported back the same day, however, that the Truce Commission was having difficulty finding any representative Arabs, because they had apparently fled or gone underground. In his opinion, therefore, the truce talks for all of Palestine had only a very slight chance of success. Indeed, even for Jerusalem itself, the British High Commissioner for Palestine reported on May 12 that neither side had replied to the terms of truce proposed by the government of Palestine, and he was therefore turning over the responsibility for further truce talks on Jerusalem to the UN Truce Commission.[28]

---

27. *State of Israel Political and Diplomatic Documents*, No. 483, 765–769.
28. *Foreign Relations of the United States: Diplomatic Papers, 1948, vol. 5*, May 7, 1948, 927–929; May 9, 1948, 944–945; May 11 and 12, 1948, "Secretary

The Drama at the White House

While the State Department was acting out its anti-partition drama in the UNGA special session, President Truman opened up a pro-partition drama of his own in the White House. With the Jews putting the partition of Palestine into effect, and with even Loy Henderson coming to doubt whether the UN would go along with the US State Department's attempt to undo partition, Truman decided he had to make amends to Weizmann for the announcement of the abandonment of partition on March 19, the day after the president assured Weizmann—in a face-to-face meeting—of his support for partition. On April 23, 1948, he called once again upon his former counsel, Judge Rosenman, to transmit to Weizmann a secret personal pledge from the president.

Abba Eban, in his contribution to a biography of Chaim Weizmann, painted a dramatic picture of the circumstances surrounding the communication of the president's pledge.[29] Friday, April 23, 1948 was the eve of Passover, and Weizmann was due to celebrate the Seder that night at the house of his friends. Before leaving his hotel that evening, Weizmann received an urgent request to visit Judge Rosenman at the Essex House Hotel, where the judge was immobilized by a leg injury. Weizmann stopped off to visit Rosenman before going to the Seder and spent an hour closeted with him. The judge told him in the strictest confidence that the president had told him, "I have Dr. Weizmann on my conscience." He had not realized when he had spoken to Weizmann on March 18 that the State Department had gone so far in its attempts to abandon the UN decision on partition. And now, the president would like to revert US policy in favor of the UN resolution for partition. If UNGA would not reverse the decision on partition, and the Jews declared their State in Palestine, the

---

of State to Consul General," 969; "Consul General to Secretary of State," 971–972.
29. Abba Eban, "Tragedy & Triumph," in Weisgal, Carmichael, and Ben-Gurion, eds., *Chaim Weizmann: A Biography by Several Hands*, 309–310.

president would recognize it immediately. Truman laid down one absolute condition: He was still so enraged by the criticism other Zionist leaders had heaped upon him that Weizmann would be the only Zionist leader with whom the president would liaise. Weizmann understood, therefore, that should this extraordinary story leak, there would be no deal.[30]

The Truman–Marshall Meeting to Consider the United States' Recognition of the Jewish State

Truman's close advisers—Clark Clifford, David Niles, and Max Lowenthal—were aware of the president's furious reaction to the State Department's March 19 betrayal of his policy on partition. When it became clear that the Jewish community in Palestine would establish a Jewish state at the termination of the Mandate, they urged Truman

---

30. The president's secret communication to Weizmann played a significant role in the Jewish Agency's final decision to establish the State of Israel immediately upon the termination of the Mandate. Even Ben-Gurion, who had long championed the establishment of a Jewish state, hesitated before knowing whether it would meet with Weizmann's approval. And now, it was the moderate Weizmann, who, without being able to reveal the news about the president's communication, strengthened the resolve of the other leaders. On May 8, when Shertok left for Israel after his meeting with Marshall and Lovett, Weizmann asked him to take a personal message to Ben-Gurion and his colleagues, "Moshe, don't let them weaken, don't let them swerve, don't let them spoil the victory—the Jewish State, nothing less." Shertok's flight was diverted, however, and he was delayed in arriving in Israel. Ben-Gurion then asked Meyer Weisgal, a close associate of Weizmann, to contact him and discover his attitude towards the proclamation of the Jewish State. When Weisgal phoned Weizmann from a stopover in Nice, Weizmann cried out impatiently to him in Yiddish, "What are they waiting for?" Weisgal then cabled Ben-Gurion, "The answer is yes." Ben-Gurion immediately called a meeting of the Jewish Agency and the National Council to proclaim the Jewish State (Vera Weizmann and David Tutaev, *The Impossible Takes Longer: The Memoirs of Vera Weizmann, Wife of Israel's First President* [New York: Harper & Row, 1967], 231–232).

to give immediate recognition to the new state. On May 7, the day after Truman had approved the State Department's draft truce proposal, Clifford gave Truman a draft of a public statement in which he proposed that at his next press conference scheduled for May 13, the president should announce his intention to recognize the Jewish state. Truman was sympathetic, but he phoned Marshall to get his reaction. Marshall, as expected, objected to the proposed statement, and the president asked him and Lovett to come to the White House the following week to discuss the question. The president then told Clifford that he believed Marshall would continue to take a very strong position, and he wanted Clifford to make the case in favor of recognition. Clifford quotes Truman as having said:

> You know how I feel. I want you to present it just as though you were making an argument before the Supreme Court of the US. Consider it carefully, Clark—organize it logically. I want you to be as persuasive as you can possibly be.[31]

As Clifford much later described Truman's attitude, five factors dominated the president's thinking on the establishment of a Jewish state in Palestine: 1. Truman had always detested intolerance and discrimination; 2. he had been deeply affected by the plight of the Jewish refugees from World War II, who, alone among all the homeless, had no homeland of their own to which they could return; 3. he was horrified by the Holocaust, as its full dimensions were made known after the war; 4. he believed that the Balfour Declaration committed the UK and, by implication, the US, to the creation of the Jewish state in Palestine; and finally, 5. as a long-time student of and believer in the Bible, he felt the Jews had a legitimate historical right to Palestine.[32]

The meeting between Marshall, Lovett, and the president took place on Wednesday, May 12 at 4:00 p.m., only fifty hours before the

---

31. Clark Clifford, *Counsel to the President: A Memoir* (New York: Anchor Books, 1992), ch. 1, 5.
32. Clifford, *Counsel to the President*, ch. 1, 7–8.

termination of the Mandate, when the Jewish State would be established. The State Department had prepared a position paper for the president, setting out the rationale for its proposals in the UNGA session for a Palestine trusteeship and for a political and military truce. In addition, it brought for the president's approval a draft resolution for yet a third proposal in the hope of preventing partition: the appointment of a UN commissioner to serve as a mediator in Palestine.

Lovett began the State Department's presentation with a lengthy summary of the situation, calling particular attention to the meeting on May 8 when Moshe Shertok had called upon the secretary of state and himself. Shertok had informed them of the statement made to him by the British minister for colonial affairs, Sir Arthur Creech Jones, that King Abdullah of Transjordan might enter the Arab portions of Palestine, but his Arab Legion would make no attempt to take the Jewish areas. A similar message had been received earlier by the Jewish Agency in Palestine from Colonel Goldy of the Arab Legion. This intelligence, Lovett noted, had produced a hardening of the Jewish Agency's position. Only a week before, Lovett claimed, Shertok and other representatives of the Jewish Agency had seemed seriously interested in the US truce proposals. But since then, they had shifted position:

> They seemed confident, on the basis of their recent military successes and the prospect of a "behind the barn" deal with Abdullah, that they could establish their sovereign state without any necessity for a truce with the Arabs of Palestine.

Marshall intervened to recall the strong objections to the behavior of the Jewish Agency he had expressed at that meeting and the emphatic military warning he had addressed to Shertok:

> I had stressed that it was extremely dangerous to base long-range policy on temporary military success. There was no doubt that the Jewish army had gained such temporary success, but there was no assurance whatever that in the long range, the tide might

not turn against them. I told Mr. Shertok they were taking a gamble. If the tide did turn adversely and they came running to us for help, they should be placed clearly on notice now that there was no warrant to expect help from the US, which had warned them of the grave risk which they were running.

After Lovett resumed and concluded his summary of the situation, the president invited Clifford to speak. Clifford began by expressing his objection to the State Department's truce proposal, emphasizing, "There has been no truce in Palestine, and there almost certainly will not be one." He reminded everyone of Dean Rusk's statement at a meeting chaired by the president on March 24 that a truce could be negotiated within two weeks, but that goal, he noted, was still not in sight. Second, Clifford maintained, the State Department's trusteeship proposal presupposes a single Palestine, and that too was unrealistic, because the partition of Palestine had already taken place.

Bearing in mind that the president had requested him to present his case as forcefully as he could, Clifford went on to state his third and main point: "Mr. President, I strongly urge you to give prompt recognition to the Jewish State immediately after the termination of the British Mandate on May 14." And in full awareness that Marshall and Lovett would be annoyed by the implication that the State Department had embarrassed the president by reversing the American policy with Austin's call on March 19 for a special session of UNGA, Clifford deliberately added, "This would have the distinct value of restoring the president's firm position in support of the partition of Palestine. Such a move should be taken quickly, before the Soviet Union or any other nation recognizes the Jewish State."

Clifford continued with his fourth point, proposing that the president should announce his intention of recognizing the Jewish State at his press conference the next day. He then circulated a draft press statement in which the president would add that he had asked the Secretary of State to have the US take this matter up in the UN "with a view toward urging early recognition of the Jewish State by the other members of the UN."

Clifford ended his statement with three broad arguments in support of his proposals. First, he referred to the Balfour Declaration, noting that the Jews all over the world have been waiting for thirty years to have the promise of a homeland of their own to be fulfilled, and there was no reason to wait any longer. Trusteeship, he stated, would postpone that promise indefinitely. Second, he urged that the US had a great moral obligation to seize the opportunity to bring the ancient injustices to the Jewish people to an end. Giving the Jews their own homeland and lifting them to the status of other peoples who have their own country, he said, "would help atone, in some small way, for the atrocities so vast as to stupefy the human mind that occurred during the Holocaust." Finally, Clifford maintained, recognition of the Jewish State would be in the best strategic interests of the US:

> In an area as unstable as the Middle East, where there is not now and never has been any tradition of democratic government, it is important for the long-range security of our country, and indeed the world, that a nation committed to the democratic system be established there, one on which we can rely. The new Jewish State can be such a place. We should strengthen it in its infancy by prompt recognition.[33]

Clifford's pointed criticism of the State Department hit home. More than forty years later, in describing this meeting in his memoirs, he still recalled that Marshall's face reddened with suppressed anger during his presentation and that as soon as the meeting ended, Marshall exploded in protest against his very presence at the meeting. "Mr. President," he protested, "I thought this meeting was called to consider an important and complicated problem in foreign policy. I don't even know why Clifford is here. He is a domestic adviser, and this is a foreign policy matter." Despite Truman's admiration for Marshall, which bordered on hero worship, Marshall's comment was too

---

33. Clifford, *Counsel to the President*, 11–12.

much for the president to pass up without a response: "Well, general, he's here because I asked him to be here."

Marshall still could not contain his anger. Brushing aside the foreign policy issues Clifford had raised in support of recognition of the Jewish state, he insisted that Clifford was concerned only with political considerations. "These considerations," Clifford quotes him as responding in scarcely concealed ire, "have nothing to do with the issue. I fear that the only reason Clifford is here is that he is pressing a political consideration with regard to this issue. I don't think politics should play any part in this."[34]

After Marshall's outburst, Lovett began the detailed rebuttal for the State Department. Replying to Clifford's objection to the article on the truce in the State Department's draft resolution calling for a commissioner to serve as mediator, Lovett noted that in light of the US promotion of its truce proposals at the special session of UNGA, it would be unbecoming for it now to fail to express its support for UNSC's efforts to secure a truce. Lovett's main criticism, however, was directed against Clifford's proposal for the president to announce in advance his intention to recognize the Jewish State before it even came into existence. Such premature recognition, he declared, would be highly injurious to the UN, which had been called into special session at the request of the US and was still considering the question of the future government of Palestine. Then, explicitly spelling out the basis of Marshall's anger, he added that "such a move would also be injurious to the prestige of the president," because "it was a very transparent attempt to win the Jewish vote," which in his opinion, "would lose more votes than it would gain."

Finally, he claimed, to recognize the Jewish State prematurely "would be buying a pig in a poke." He asked further: "How [do] we know what kind of Jewish State would be set up?" He then read excerpts from intelligence telegrams and reports, according to which Soviet agents were allegedly being sent to Palestine under the cover

---

34. Clifford, *Counsel to the President*, 12.

of Jewish immigration.[35] Lovett also saw no urgency for the US to rush to recognize the Jewish State ahead of the Soviets.[36]

When Lovett concluded, Marshall repeated his objection to Clifford's proposal, insisting, as had Lovett, that it was only a political scheme. He remarked:

> Speaking objectively, I could not help but think that the suggestions made by Mr. Clifford were wrong. I thought that to adopt these suggestions would have precisely the opposite effect from that intended by Mr. Clifford. The transparent dodge to win a few votes would not in fact achieve this purpose. The great dignity of the office of the president would be seriously diminished. The counsel offered by Mr. Clifford was based on domestic political considerations, while the problem which confronted us was international.

Still furious over Clifford's advice and indeed over his very presence at the meeting, Marshall then went on to add an extraordinary threat, which, equally remarkably, he decided to include in the official records of the State Department in less than diplomatic language: "I said bluntly that if the president were to follow Mr. Clifford's advice, and if in the elections I were to vote, I would vote against the president."[37]

---

35. During World War II, one of the excuses given by the British Foreign Office and the US State Department for impeding the escape of European Jews from the Holocaust was that the Nazis were infiltrating their agents among the Jewish refugees. Now, after the war, one of the excuses given by these same offices against the establishment of a Jewish state was that the Soviet Union was infiltrating its agents among the Jewish refugees. Both arguments were patently absurd, and there was not a shred of evidence to support them. Clifford later wrote that he found the intelligence reports read by Lovett to be "ridiculous, and no evidence ever turned up to support them. In fact, Jews were fleeing communism throughout Eastern Europe at that very moment" (Clifford, *Counsel to the President*, 12).
36. *Foreign Relations of the United States: Diplomatic Papers, 1948*, vol. 5, 975.
37. *Foreign Relations of the United States: Diplomatic Papers, 1948*, vol. 5, 975.

Marshall's outburst left everyone stunned. The president admired Marshall as the greatest living American, and he was relying upon him to build the postwar western alliance to confront the growing threat from the Soviet Iron Curtain. Marshall's threatened open break with the president would not only be personally painful for Truman and jeopardize any prospects he might have for re-election, but it would also threaten the collapse of the key elements of the president's foreign policy, including, in particular, both the Marshall Plan for Europe's postwar economic recovery and reconstruction and the Truman Doctrine for the "containment" of the Soviet Union.

Everyone realized that the meeting needed to be adjourned before any further damage was done. Clifford and Lovett each made a conciliatory gesture: Clifford withdrew his proposal for announcing the intent to recognize the new Jewish State before it was established, and Lovett promised to send over immediately a paper by the State Department's legal adviser on the legal aspects of recognition. Truman then initialed the State Department's draft resolution for the appointment of a commissioner to serve as mediator in Palestine, and he adjourned the meeting with the comment that he was fully aware of the difficulties and dangers involved in the situation.[38]

The Clifford–Lovett Negotiations on Recognition of the Jewish State

In light of the crisis created by Marshall's outburst, Truman must surely have been left wondering how he could possibly fulfill his personal pledge to Weizmann to recognize the Jewish State as soon as it was established. Apparently, he did not completely give up hope. He told Clifford that it would be best to "let the dust settle a little—then

---

38. Clifford, *Counsel to the President*, 13; *Foreign Relations of the United States: Diplomatic Papers, 1948*, vol. 5, 975–976. Clifford wrote that he considered the State Department proposal for a mediator to be a clever way of avoiding recognition of the Jewish State, but he believed the president would approve it anyhow out of respect for Marshall.

you can get into it again and see if we can get this thing turned around." Truman added that he still wanted to do it, but he could not afford to lose Marshall.[39]

And now, when the prospects for the US recognition of a Jewish state seemed to have disappeared, a startling reversal of the situation began to unfold. After returning to his office from the meeting, Clifford received a phone call from Lovett, saying that he had been deeply disturbed ever since the meeting in the president's office and that it would be a great tragedy if Marshall and the president were to break over the issue of recognition of the Jewish State. Lovett asked Clifford to drop by his house for a drink on his way home that night to talk about the problem.

Lovett opened the discussion that evening on the note that a break between the president and General Marshall would have unacceptable consequences for the conduct of American foreign policy: A split in the ranks in the midst of the Cold War with the Soviet Union would be catastrophic. If Clifford were to present some modification of the State Department's views that Truman could accept, Lovett asked, might the president be persuaded to moderate his position and work something out with General Marshall to get past the crisis?

Clifford replied that there was no chance that Truman would change his mind on the basic issue of recognition and that his own presentation that afternoon had been made at the president's instruction; therefore, it represented the president's views. The president was determined to recognize the Jewish State, so if anyone were going to yield, it would have to be Marshall. Clifford left the house somewhat encouraged by Lovett's reply that in that case, he would see what could be done in the State Department. Lovett, Clifford knew, had great influence with Marshall, with whom he had served in the War Department during World War II and whose appointment as undersecretary of state Marshall had made a condition of his own appointment as secretary of state.

---

39. Clifford, *Counsel to the President*, 15.

When Clifford reported to the president the next morning on his meeting with Lovett, Truman, pleased that the process of "letting the dust settle" had begun, told Clifford to keep encouraging Lovett to work on the general. In the middle of the day, Lovett called Clifford, suggesting that a formal decision to recognize the new Jewish State should be made but that announcing or implementing it should be delayed for an unspecified time period. Clifford turned this proposal down, saying this was "a nothing approach," that he had talked with the president, and that Truman was rock solid on recognition and would not budge an inch. Lovett then suggested recognizing the new Jewish State *de facto* instead of *de jure*. Clifford, believing that this was not a critical issue at the moment and that the nature of recognition could be upgraded later, yielded on this point. Nevertheless, Thursday, May 13 ended without any resolution of the crisis between Marshall and the president. Only hours remained before the Mandate would terminate and the Jewish State was to come into existence on Friday, May 14 at 6:00 p.m. Washington, DC time (midnight May 15 British time).

Early Friday morning, when Clifford called, he found that Lovett and Marshall were still opposed to recognition of the Jewish State, but that Lovett was still trying to find some minimum suggestion that might satisfy the president. Clifford said that the president understood that Marshall would not make any retraction and support president on recognition. All the president would need was assurance that Marshall would not oppose him on the issue. Lovett agreed to see what he could do.

At 10:00 a.m., even though Lovett had still not sent word on the matter, and the president had not yet made his decision on recognition, Clifford decided to set the process in motion so that recognition could take place immediately after the Jewish State was established, in case the president made such a decision. Clifford called Eliahu Epstein, the Jewish Agency representative in Washington, DC, asking him to send an official letter to President Truman before noon, formally requesting of the US government its recognition of the new Jewish State. A copy of the letter was also to be sent directly to Secretary Marshall.

A few minutes later, Epstein called back to ask Clifford for help with composing the letter, because the Jewish Agency lacked experience in the preparation of such a letter. Epstein also got in touch with two highly experienced lawyers in Washington, DC, David Ginsburg and Benjamin Cohen, who were sympathetic to the Zionist cause and had advised Chaim Weizmann and members of the Jewish Agency on other issues in the past year. With Clifford's help, they drafted the Jewish Agency's request for state recognition, and Epstein sent it to Clifford for submission to the president. Epstein did not yet know the name of the new Jewish State for which recognition was being requested, so he used only the phrase, "the Jewish State." But while his press aide was still on the way to Clifford with the letter, Epstein learned by way of his shortwave radio that the new Jewish State had just been proclaimed at 10:00 a.m. Washington, DC time (4.00 p.m. Israel time), and it had been given its ancient name: Israel. He quickly sent another messenger to intercept his press aide with this information, and the press aide crossed out the words "the Jewish State" and substituted the word "Israel." The letter with this penned correction was then handed to Clifford.[40]

Not yet having received an answer from Lovett, Clifford called him late that morning to insist that the issue be resolved. Lovett suggested they meet for lunch in a small private club near the White House to which he belonged. At lunch, even though the two were still far apart on whether recognition should be granted, Lovett willingly reviewed with Clifford the technical aspects of the US government's recognition of the Jewish State. Although less than four hours now remained before the Jewish State would be established, Lovett continued to argue against "indecent haste" in recognizing Israel and begged Clifford to get the president to delay for a day or so. The objections he raised, however, were directed against recognition *per se* more than against indecent haste. Lovett argued that there would

---

40. Clifford, *Counsel to the President*, 15–20. The president's signed statement of recognition had also been typed with the term "the Jewish State," and this too was crossed out, with the name "Israel" substituted by pen.

be a tremendous reaction in the Arab world; that the effects of many years of hard work with the Arabs might be lost; that the US position with the Arab leaders would be jeopardized; and finally that the diplomatic missions and consular representatives would be placed in personal jeopardy.

Clifford replied that both he and the president had been impressed by Lovett's argument at the Wednesday meeting in the White House against announcing the US government's intention to recognize the new state before it had been established. By 6:00 p.m. that evening, however, the Mandate would be terminated, and there would then be no internationally recognized government or authority in Palestine unless the president acted. The president wished to avoid this situation by taking urgent action on recognition of the Jewish State. Clifford added that "speed was also essential to preempt the Russians," reminding Lovett that he and Marshall had been greatly concerned that indecision on the part of the US government might give the Soviet Union an opportunity to gain a toehold in the region. And, Clifford concluded, "A one-day delay will become two days, three days, and so on."

The luncheon ended with a vague indication that Lovett might be ready to yield. Lovett protested rather weakly that it would be impossible to inform all the diplomatic offices in time, since it was still not known when the president would make his final decision. Clifford replied that the president would make his final decision that afternoon.

At 4:00 p.m., with only two hours remaining before the State of Israel would officially come into existence upon the Mandate's end, Clifford finally received the word from Lovett that he had been so anxiously awaiting. Lovett reported that General Marshall could not support the president's position, but "He has agreed that he will not oppose it." Thrilled with the message, Clifford thanked Lovett for his efforts and asked him if he could get Marshall to call the president directly with the news. Lovett agreed to try, but Marshall evidently found it too painful to do so, and it was Lovett who called the president instead to confirm Marshall's position.

About 5:30 p.m., with only a half hour remaining, when Clifford assumed everything had been finally settled, Lovett called once again to ask whether the president would delay his announcement until UNGA had ended its session at about 10:00 p.m. that evening. Clifford said he would check with the president, but after waiting for about three minutes, he called back to say any further delay was out of the question. The president would announce the US government's recognition of the Jewish State immediately after it was established.[41]

The Remaining United Nations Issues in the Two Days Prior to the Mandate's End

Two issues still remained to be decided in the UN in the final two days, May 13 and 14, before the termination of the Mandate for Palestine at 6:00 p.m. Washington, DC time on Friday, May 14. The first issue, on which everyone seemed to agree, was the need for further consideration of the disposition of Jerusalem, which, under the 1947 UNGA resolution for partition, was to be a separate entity, belonging neither to the Arab state nor to the Jewish one. The United Nations General Assembly adopted Resolution 187(II) on May 6, calling upon the Mandatory power to appoint before May 15, 1948 a special municipal commissioner "to carry out the functions hitherto performed by the municipal commission." This resolution also instructed the First Committee to give urgent attention to the question of further measures for the protection of the city of Jerusalem and its inhabitants, for which purpose the First Committee had set up Sub-Committee 10 on May 11: to consider such further measures and to submit its recommendations to the First Committee as promptly as possible.[42] Sub-Committee 10 had before it a proposal submitted jointly by the US and France for a temporary international trusteeship regime for

---

41. Clifford, *Counsel to the President*, 20–22; *Foreign Relations of the United States: Diplomatic Papers, 1948, vol. 5*, 1005–1007.
42. "Section 9: The Question of Palestine" in United Nations, *Yearbook, 1947–1948*.

Jerusalem. The sub-committee amended the proposal, and on May 13, it approved the amended proposal for a temporary trusteeship in Jerusalem, to be administered by a UN commissioner, operating under the authority of the Trusteeship Council. The trusteeship would terminate in December 1948 unless UNGA decided otherwise. The sub-committee submitted its report to the First Committee at 4:15 p.m. on May 13 and adjourned its final meeting.

The second issue, on which there were significant differences of opinion in UNGA, was the disposition of Palestine. The State Department had put aside its proposals both for a trusteeship and for a political standstill for which it had requested a special session of UNGA, and it now opted for the appointment of a UN commissioner to serve as a mediator for Palestine, the proposal that the president had quickly approved at the meeting with Marshall and Lovett the previous day, May 12. The US draft resolution submitted to the First Committee's Sub-Committee 9 would 1. strongly affirm its support for the efforts of UNSC to secure a truce in Palestine and 2. empower a UN commissioner for Palestine, working as a mediator in cooperation with UNSC's Truce Commission, to use his good offices with the local and community authorities to promote agreement on the future government of Palestine. The draft also provided for the discharge of the UN Palestine commission, which had been set up under the 1947 UNGA resolution, from further exercise of responsibilities.[43]

The US draft resolution was significantly amended in Sub-Committee 9 to reduce the status and authority of the appointee before being reported back to the parent First Committee. Instead of a commissioner, the amended resolution called for the appointment of a mediator, and their responsibility to use their good offices with the local and community authorities in Palestine was reduced from promoting "agreement on the future government of Palestine" to promoting "a peaceful adjustment of the future situation of Palestine."

---

43. *Foreign Relations of the United States: Diplomatic Papers, 1948, vol. 5,* 978–980, 986–987, 994–995.

The Jewish Agency representatives were opposed to the amended proposal for a mediator, as they had been to the original US proposal for a commissioner. They feared that the enemies of partition might interpret the proposal to prohibit the Jews from proclaiming their state under the resolution for partition, as the Jews planned to do. Indeed, the delegates of Poland and the Soviet Union charged that this resolution was in fact a veiled attempt to undo UNGA's decision in favor of partition of November 29, 1947. Sub-Committee 9, however, adopted the resolution in its amended form at its final session in the afternoon of May 13 and sent its report to the First Committee shortly after Sub-Committee 10 had submitted its report on Jerusalem to the committee.

Given the urgent need to make decisions concerning the proposals of the two sub-committees before the expiration of the Mandate the next day, the First Committee met to consider the reports almost immediately after receiving them. After several delegates objected that they had not been given the time to study the reports, the First Committee decided to hold an evening session on the report of Sub-Committee 9 to permit those delegations that were ready to discuss the report for a Palestine mediator to speak.[44] US Ambassador Jessup spoke late that night in the First Committee on behalf of the mediator proposal, declaring that the US trusteeship proposal had the support of many members but that neither the Arabs nor the Jews had agreed to it, and that in the absence of such agreement, armed force would be essential to enforce any trusteeship. The US had offered to contribute a share of the needed armed forces, but other governments had not been ready to participate. The US had also sought to achieve a military and political truce in Palestine, but this proposal had been rejected by all the parties involved in the Palestine dispute. In light of these developments, the US had now decided to propose the plan for the appointment of a mediator as approved in Sub-Committee 9

---

44. "Section 9: The Question of Palestine" in United Nations, *Yearbook, 1947–1948*.

on Palestine. After 10:00 p.m., Ambassador Gromyko of the Soviet Union said he wished to discuss the proposal the next day, and the chairman decided to adjourn the session at 10:35 p.m.

The next day, May 14, the US delegation carefully worked out its plan to close the debate in the hope of securing the approval of the mediator proposal in the First Committee and its adoption in the plenary session of UNGA before the expiration of the Mandate at 6:00 p.m.[45] According to the UNGA Rules of Procedure, a representative may at any time move the closure of the debate. Permission to speak on that motion is then given only to two speakers, one for and one against the motion, after which the motion must immediately be put to a vote. In accordance with the US delegation's plan, the chairman recognized the Cuban delegate, who moved the closure of the debate, and the representatives of Iran, who spoke for closure, and the representatives of Thailand, who spoke briefly against closure. The motion for closure was then put to the vote, and it was approved. The draft resolution for the appointment of a mediator was almost immediately put to a vote in the First Committee, and it was approved by a vote of thirty-five to six, with ten abstentions.

The First Committee still had to deal with the report of Sub-Committee 10 on Jerusalem. García-Granados of Guatemala emphasized the importance of coming to a vote on this report in the plenary session before 6:00 p.m., when the Mandate would expire, because after that hour, there would be no basis in international law for making any special arrangements for Jerusalem. As the First Committee debate on this item continued after 3:00 p.m. and threatened to jeopardize any vote in plenary before the 6:00 p.m. deadline, Ambassador Jessup moved that the sub-committee report be sent directly to plenary without a vote in the First Committee. His motion carried, and the First Committee adjourned at 3:45 p.m.

---

45. For a first-hand account of the US delegation's attempt to have the resolution for the appointment of a mediator adopted before the expiration of the Mandate at 6:00 p.m., see Philip C. Jessup, *The Birth of Nations* (New York: Colombia University Press, 1974), 274–279.

The UNGA plenary session opened almost an hour later at 4:40 p.m.[46] The US delegate called for consideration of the report of Sub-Committee 10 on Jerusalem first, because it was already almost 5:00 p.m., only one hour before the expiration of the Mandate for Palestine. During the debate in the plenary session, the resolution was amended before being voted on as a whole. When the final vote was taken, the amended draft resolution failed to obtain the necessary two-thirds majority for adoption, the vote being twenty in favor to fifteen against, with nineteen abstentions.[47] The only action regarding Jerusalem taken by the UNGA special session was thus the adoption on May 6, 1948 of Resolution 187, which had the limited purpose of appointing a commissioner for the protection of Jerusalem and its inhabitants.

It was now after 6:00 p.m., and the First Committee's draft resolution for the appointment of a mediator for Palestine had not yet been taken up in the plenary session. The Mandate for Palestine had already expired, and the State Department had failed to get the special session of UNGA to undo partition by imposing either a Palestine trusteeship or a political standstill, and even a decision in favor of the appointment of a mediator for Palestine had not been made. The only action UNGA had taken prior to the expiration of the Mandate was the adoption of Resolution 187 on May 6, 1948 for the appointment

---

46. The permanent UN headquarters in Manhattan had not yet been built in 1948, and the UN was housed at the time in temporary headquarters in the former Sperry Plant at Lake Success, nearly an hour's drive to midtown Manhattan, where most UN delegations had their offices. The committees of UNGA met at the Lake Success building, but UNGA met in its plenary sessions in Flushing Meadows, Queens, in a building remaining from the 1939 World's Fair. The interval of nearly an hour between the close of the First Committee and the opening of the plenary session of UNGA was due to the fact that many delegates had to rush in their cars from the committee session in Lake Success to the plenary session in Flushing Meadows, Queens.
47. "Section 9: The Question of Palestine" in United Nations, *Yearbook, 1947–1948*.

of a commissioner for the protection of the people of Jerusalem and its Holy Places.

The Jewish State, Israel, Is Reborn

Britain's Mandate for Palestine had thus come to an end on May 14 at 6:00 p.m. Eastern Standard Time (midnight May 15, 1948 London time) without the adoption of any UNGA decision to rescind or amend its Resolution 181(II) of November 29, 1947 in favor of partition. As Secretary-General Trygve Lie confirmed, "The assembly did *not* [emphasis in original] rescind or amend its resolution of November 29, 1947. The partition decision remained and remains valid."[48]

On Friday, May 14, 1948, at 4:00 p.m. Tel Aviv time (10:00 a.m. New York time), the Jewish National Council met in Tel Aviv under the leadership of David Ben-Gurion and had proclaimed the establishment of the Jewish State, to which it gave the state's ancient historical name: Israel. The Jewish National Council could not wait until the termination of Britain's Mandate at midnight because the Jewish Sabbath would begin at sundown on Friday. The Jews thus formally proclaimed the State of Israel's independence just before the beginning of the Sabbath on May 14, 1948, the fifth day of the month of Iyar in the year 5708 of the Jewish calendar.

Israel's Declaration of Independence reviewed the historical basis of Israel's rebirth, emphasizing the following points:

> the spiritual, religious, and national ties of the Jewish people to the land of Israel;
>
> the Jewish people's striving throughout the centuries to return to the Land of Israel and to regain statehood;
>
> the Jewish immigrants, who, coming to the Land of Israel even in defiance of restrictive legislation, made deserts bloom,

---

48. Lie, *In the Cause of Peace*, 172–173.

revived the Hebrew language, built villages and towns, and created a thriving community that controlled its own economy and culture;

the Balfour Declaration of 1917 and the League of Nations Mandate, which recognized the right of the Jewish people to reconstitute their national home in the Land of Israel;

the Nazi Holocaust that engulfed millions of Jews in Europe, which proved anew the urgency of the re-establishment of the Jewish State to solve the problem of Jewish homelessness;

the contribution made by the Jewish people of Palestine against the Nazi evils during World War II; and

the UNGA resolution of November 29, 1947 for the establishment of an independent Jewish state in Palestine.

The members of the Jewish National Council, representing the Jewish people, accordingly proclaimed the establishment of the Jewish State in Palestine, to be called Israel, with the Jewish National Council constituting the provisional government of the State of Israel.

The Declaration of Independence affirmed that Israel would:

be open to the immigration of Jews from all countries of their dispersion;

promote the development of the country for the benefit of all its inhabitants;

be based on the precepts of liberty, justice, and peace taught by the Hebrew Prophets;

uphold the full social and political equality of all its citizens, without distinction of race, creed, or sex;

Guarantee full freedom of conscience, worship, education, and culture;

safeguard the sanctity and inviolability of the shrines and Holy Places of all religions; and

dedicate itself to the principles of the UN Charter.

The declaration called upon the Arabs in the State of Israel to return to the ways of peace. It offered "peace and unity to all the neighboring states and their peoples" and invited them "to cooperate with the independent Jewish nation for the common good of all." It added that the State of Israel would be "prepared to make its contribution in a concerted effort for the advancement of the entire Middle East."

The Drama at the United Nations Concerning Truman's Recognition of Israel

Lovett had failed to alert Dean Rusk or the US delegation at the UN about the series of meetings and telephone discussions he had been holding with Clifford over the president's plan to grant immediate recognition to the Jewish State after it came into existence. It was only at 5:45 p.m., just fifteen minutes before the end of the Mandate, that Clifford apprised Dean Rusk of the president's decision. After the last hurdle to recognition had finally been cleared away at 5:40 p.m., Clifford called him with the information and asked him to inform Ambassador Austin at the UN that the White House would announce the US government's recognition of Israel immediately after it officially came into being at 6:00 p.m. Rusk could hardly believe what he was hearing. As he vividly recalled in a letter to the US government's historical office, he protested, "But this cuts across what our delegation has been trying to accomplish in UNGA under instructions, and we already have a large majority for that approach." "Nevertheless," Clifford replied, "Dean, this is what the president wishes you to do."[49]

Rusk then called Ambassador Austin, who had to leave the UNGA hall to take the call. Austin reacted to the news by leaving for his hotel instead of returning to the UNGA floor, leaving Ambassador Sayre and

---

49. *Foreign Relations of the United States: Diplomatic Papers, 1948, vol. 5,* 993.

Ambassador Jessup, who were still on the UNGA floor, completely in the dark about the president's decision. Apparently, Austin decided to take this action in order to make it clear that his delegation had no responsibility for this reversal of US policy and that it had not been playing a hypocritical game with the other delegations at the UN. The US delegation thus continued until the very last minute to press the State Department's proposals in the UN in complete ignorance of the president's decision.

At 6:11 p.m. New York time, eleven minutes after the British Mandate ended in Palestine and the State of Israel came legally into being, President Truman astonished the world with his announcement of the US government's *de facto* recognition of the provisional government of the State of Israel. Three days later, the USSR became the first country to grant *de jure* recognition to Israel, and within the first five days of its existence, Israel was recognized by seven more countries whose representatives had ardently championed the cause of the Jewish State in the UN, including Guatemala, Uruguay, and the members of the Soviet bloc.[50]

Truman's immediate recognition of Israel came as a bombshell in UNGA, which was still in session at the time. Even the US delegation to UNGA and nearly all of the senior staff dealing with the problem of Palestine in Washington, DC were caught completely unawares by the announcement. Rumors of President Truman's recognition of Israel swept through the UNGA hall and stunned the delegates—just before UNGA opened its debate on the US resolution for a mediator at its final meeting of the special session. The delegate of Colombia rose to ask whether the US delegation could confirm the information given to the press regarding the US government's recognition of the government of the Jewish State.[51] Ambassador Sayre had to reply that

---

50. Even Yugoslavia, which had abstained in the November 29, 1947 UNGA vote on partition, firmly supported partition in the 1948 special session, and it recognized Israel within the first five days of its establishment.
51. "Section 9: The Question of Palestine" in United Nations, *Yearbook, 1947–1948*.

for the time being, the US delegation had no information about any new developments.

As Ambassador Jessup subsequently described the amazing turn of events, he instructed an aide "to bring me a copy of the ticker tape—and fast!"[52] In the meantime, the debate in UNGA on the mediation proposal began. The Soviet and the Polish ambassadors welcomed the establishment of the Jewish State, with Katz-Suchy of Poland saying that the US government's recognition of the State of Israel showed that the US government agreed with him that the resolution on mediation that had been approved in the First Committee only three hours earlier was already obsolete.

Ambassador Belt of Cuba, with whom the US delegation had arranged to move for closure of the debate in the First Committee, said he was surprised to hear Ambassador Sayre say he had no information regarding the US government's recognition of the new Jewish State; evidently, the Soviet and Polish representatives were better informed on events in Washington, DC. The Syrian delegate charged that the US had given priority in the UNGA vote to the report on Jerusalem so that the US could first recognize the Jewish State.[53]

While Jessup was still speaking, the US aide returned with a crumpled piece of ticker tape that she had been able to fish out from the waste basket of the secretary-general, who had already left the premises. Jessup then unrolled the crumpled paper and read out to UNGA the following statement from the White House, signed by President Truman on May 14, 1948 at 6:11 p.m.:

> This government has been informed that a Jewish state has been proclaimed in Palestine, and recognition has been requested by the provisional government thereof.

---

52. Jessup, *The Birth of Nations*, 280.
53. "Section 9: The Question of Palestine" in United Nations, *Yearbook, 1947–1948*.

The United States recognizes the provisional government as the *de facto* authority of the new State of Israel.[54]

The United Nations General Assembly, which the State Department had arranged to be called into special session in order to nullify the 1947 resolution for partition and to put in its place a trusteeship for Palestine, turned out instead to be the forum where, to its complete amazement and profound embarrassment, the US delegation had to announce that the newly established Jewish State had immediately been recognized by the president of the US.[55] Truman was determined, as he later wrote in his memoirs, "to make it plain that the president of the US and not the second or third echelon in the State Department is responsible for making foreign policy, and

---

54. Jessup, *The Birth of Nations*, 279–281; *Foreign Relations of the United States: Diplomatic Papers, 1948, vol. 5*, 992. When Israel applied for admission to the UN on November 29, 1948, the anniversary of the UNGA resolution for partition, one of the arguments used by the Arab states against the US support for Israel's admission was that the US had granted it only *de facto* recognition—not *de jure* recognition. On that occasion, it was Ambassador Jessup who came to the support of Israel's admission to the UN, explaining that to the State of Israel, the US had extended *de jure* recognition—total and unconditional. It was only to Israel's provisional government that the recognition was *de facto* (Jessup, *The Birth of Nations*, 294–295). The US extended complete *de jure* recognition on January 31, 1949 after a regular government had been elected on January 25, 1949 to replace Israel's provisional government.

55. Writing to the historical office later, Dean Rusk described the pandemonium in UNGA when the news of Truman's recognition of Israel was learned: "When I use the word 'pandemonium,' I think I am not exaggerating. I was later told that one of our US mission staff men literally sat on the lap of the Cuban delegate to keep him from going to the podium to withdraw Cuba from the UN. In any event, about 6:15 [p.m.], I got a call from Secretary Marshall, who said, 'Rusk, get up to New York and prevent the US delegation from resigning *en masse*.' Whether it was necessary or not, I scurried to New York and found that tempers had cooled sufficiently so that my mission was unnecessary."

furthermore, that no one in any department can sabotage the president's policy."[56] Aware that "some of the State Department 'experts' would want to block recognition of a Jewish state," Truman evidently decided to keep his intentions of doing so to himself until almost the very last minute.[57]

✡ ✡ ✡

Clifford summarized his thoughts on Truman's decision for immediate recognition of the Jewish State as follows:

> Never once have I wavered in the conviction that what Harry Truman did was correct... I believed in the advice we gave the president, but it was he who made the decision... The charge that domestic politics determined our policy on Palestine angered President Truman for the rest of his life. The president's policy rested on the realities of the situation in the region; on America's moral, ethical, and humanitarian values; on the costs and risks inherent in any other course; and—of course—on America's national interests.[58]

---

56. Truman's stand was not simply a matter of personal pique but rather reflected his strong conviction about the proper role of career officials in government. Truman added the following comment: "The difficulty with many career officials in the government is that they regard themselves as the men who really make policy and run the government. They look upon the elected officials as just temporary occupants. Every president in our history has been faced with this problem: how to prevent career men from circumventing presidential policy. Too often, career men seek to impose their own views instead of carrying out the established policy of the administration... The civil servant, the general or admiral, the foreign service officer has no authority to make policy. They act only as servants of the government, and therefore, they must remain in line with the government policy that is established by those who have been chosen by the people to set that policy."
57. Truman, *Memoirs, vol. 2*, 164–165.
58. Clifford, *Counsel to the President*, 24.

What would have happened if President Truman had not acted as he did? History does not allow us to test alternatives, but in my view, American recognition and the support that followed was vital in helping Israel. Israel's condition at birth would have been infinitely more precarious, and in the war that followed, the Israelis would have been at an additional disadvantage. Emboldened by less American support for Israel, the Arabs might have been more successful in their war against the Jews. If that had happened, the US might have faced a far more difficult decision within a year: either offer the Israelis massive American military support or risk watching the Arabs drive the Israelis into the sea.[59]

Truman's decisive role in the destinies of the Jewish people and of Israel was well stated by Prime Minister Ben-Gurion in a message to President Truman expressing the Jewish people's profound gratitude and appreciation for his prompt recognition:

> Your consistent and wise advocacy of justice of our cause in national and international councils, your insistence on admission to Palestine of large numbers of survivors of Nazi oppression in Europe, your direction of the US policy giving [the] US delegation leadership at [the] November session of [UNGA] in favor of [the] creation [of the] Jewish state in Palestine, and finally, your lead to [the] whole world making the US the first power in history to recognise [the] State of Israel have been decisive in shaping [the] destinies of [the] Holy Land and Jewish people.[60]

On the first anniversary of the UN resolution for partition, November 29, 1948, President Truman summed up his own feelings toward the Jewish people and the State of Israel in a reply to a letter of congratulations on his re-election sent to him on November 5 by Chaim Weizmann as President of Israel. Truman wrote:

---

59. Clifford, *Counsel to the President*, 24–25.
60. *Foreign Relations of the United States: Diplomatic Papers, 1948*, vol. 5, 1004.

I was struck by the common experience you and I have recently shared. We had both been abandoned by the so-called realistic experts to our supposedly forlorn cause. Yet we both kept pressing for what we were sure was right—and we were proven to be right... In closing, I want to tell you how happy and impressed I have been at the remarkable progress made by the new State of Israel. What you have received at the hands of the world has been far less than was your due. But you have more than made the most of what you have received, and I admire you for it.[61]

The significance of the restoration of Israel's independence after nearly two thousand years of national homelessness was aptly recorded by several political leaders who had played key roles in bringing this historic event to fruition. Ambassador Jorge García-Granados, the Guatemalan member of UNSCOP and delegate to UNGA, who had been a key player in persuading fellow Latin-American delegates to vote for partition, wrote of his feelings on the evening of Israel's rebirth:

Many thoughts flooded my mind. We had seen the inevitable climax of a unique and strange national history this day. The sorrows of long exile marked by poignant human suffering were now to give way to the building of the world's newest nation. We of the UN, both big and small, had played our role, for to that historic consummation we had brought the authority of international agreement... I did not underestimate what the Jewish people themselves had done: Their success was due to their magnificent resolution, their patience, their courage, their discipline. By their almost predestined action, they had implemented one of the major parts of our plan for the future of the Holy Land which had been accepted by the majority of the nations of the world. We, who had considered the needs and

---

61. Truman, *Memoirs, vol. 2,* 168–169.

problems of Palestine and its people, knew that Israel would live. It must live![62]

Winston Churchill, whose "heart had throbbed with Zionism" for most of his political life but whose Zionism had weakened during his term of office as wartime prime minister, regained his former Zionist ardor when the State of Israel came into being. He had this to say in the House of Commons during its January 26, 1949 debate on the question of Britain's recognition of the State of Israel:

> The coming into being of a Jewish state in Palestine is an event in world history to be viewed in the perspective not of a generation or a century but in the perspective of a thousand, two thousand, or even three thousand years. That is a standard of temporal values or time values which seems very much out of accord with the perpetual click-clack of our rapidly changing moods and of the age in which we live. This is an event in world history.[63]

And Colonel Richard Meinertzhagen, the lifelong Christian supporter of Zionism who, ever since Britain had proclaimed the Balfour Declaration, had been a zealous protector of the Jewish national homeland against the fierce anti-Zionist opposition of his colleagues in Britain's military establishment as well as in the Colonial Office and Foreign Office, wrote:

> Thank God I have lived to see the birth of Israel. It is one of the greatest historical events of the last two thousand years, and thank God, I have been privileged to assist, in a small way, this great event, which, I am convinced, will bring benefit to mankind. The only constructive element which emerged from the wreckage of 1914–1918 was the principle of a home for

---

62. García-Granados, *The Birth of Israel*, 290–291.
63. Rhodes James, *Winston S. Churchill: His Complete Speeches*, 7777.

the Jews in Palestine, and the only worthwhile dividend of 1939–1945 is Israel.[64]

---

64. Meinertzhagen, *Middle East Diary*, 241.

– 16 –

The War to Liquidate the Newly Reborn Israel

THE JEWS WERE NOT GIVEN any time to celebrate the rebirth of Israel. Immediately after the Mandate for Palestine's end on Saturday, May 15, 1948, all the neighboring Arab states invaded Israel with their regular armies. Egypt, after bombing Tel Aviv, crossed into the Negev, laying siege to a number of Jewish settlements in the northern Negev. Syria and Lebanon attacked Israel in the Galilee area and on the coastal plain. Iraq crossed into Samaria, menacing the Jewish-populated coastal plain as far as Tel Aviv, while Transjordan's Arab Legion crossed into Judea and attacked Jerusalem.[1] The invading Arab armies were assisted by troops from other Arab countries, particularly from nearby Saudi Arabia and Yemen but also including support even from far-away Algeria.

Britain confidently expected that the Arab states would quickly defeat the new Jewish State. Already in December 1947, less than one month after the UN voted in favor of partition, Bevin had told Secretary Marshall he expected the Jews to get their "throats cut." In April 1948, General Sir Gordon Macmillan, commander of the British forces still in Palestine, predicted that the Arab armies "would have no difficulty in taking over the whole country."[2] And Prime Minister Attlee's biographer wrote, "The Foreign Office and the British Chief

---

1. Judea and Samaria, known only by their biblical names until 1950, became known as the West Bank only from 1950 when Transjordan annexed them and renamed them "the West Bank of the Hashemite Kingdom of Jordan."
2. Sachar, *A History of Israel*, 297.

of Staff reported categorically: The Arabs would 'throw the Jews into the sea.'"[3]

Britain's confidence in their anticipated outcome was based in large part on the fact that Transjordan's Arab Legion was virtually a British mercenary army in the war against Israel, with Britain significantly increasing the Arab Legion's finance, military equipment, and training for the invasion of Israel as well as furnishing all its key military officers, including the commander of the army, Glubb Pasha (see Chapter 14). Britain had simultaneously entered into secret agreements with Egypt and Iraq to provide them with British military equipment for the invasion of Israel. Harold Beeley, chief strategist for Bevin's Palestine policy, considerably underplayed Britain's role—and his own—as an Arab ally in the war against Israel, when two decades later, he noted in an interview:

> We were not trying to warn the Arabs off going to war, but we were cautious. It would be correct to say that if we did not encourage the Arab states to go to war in Palestine, we did not discourage them either.

Ambassador Kirkbride, Britain's advisor to King Abdullah and Glubb Pasha in Transjordan, was more candid, when he recalled, "We were waving the green flag at the Arabs."[4]

And despite Britain's role in promoting the invasion of Israel, Bevin warned the US that if it were to lift its arms embargo against Israel, "The unfortunate position will then be reached of one side being largely armed by the Americans and the other by the British." It was not until May 27, 1948, nearly two weeks after the Arab invasion of Israel, that Bevin agreed to suspend further British arms shipments to the Arab countries if the US would agree to support

---

3. Cruise O'Brien, *The Siege*, 290.
4. Collins and Lapierre, *O Jerusalem!*, 394.

the UK resolution on Palestine in the UN.[5]

UN Secretary-General Trygve Lie reacted to the comprehensive Arab invasion of Israel in anguish:

> During the next hours and days, events crowded upon us. The Arab states launched their invasion of Palestine with the end of the Mandate. This was armed defiance of the UN, and they openly proclaimed their aggression by telegraphing news of it to UN headquarters. The United Nations Security Council, when it met on the afternoon of May 15, had before it a cable from the Egyptian minister of foreign affairs, which brazenly announced, "Egyptian armed forces have started to enter Palestine to establish security and order."[6] The invasion of Palestine by the Arab states was the first armed aggression that the world had seen since the end of [World War II]. The United Nations could not permit that aggression to succeed and at the same time survive as an influential force for peaceful settlement, collective security, and meaningful international law. This was my view, and I acted upon it.[7]

The UNGA resolution for partition adopted on November 29, 1947 had included a request that UNSC should "determine as a threat to the peace, breach of the peace, or act of aggression, in accordance with Article 39 of the charter, any attempt to alter by force the settlement envisaged by this resolution." Nevertheless, as the profoundly disheartened Trygve Lie, wrote,

> At the UNSC meeting in the afternoon of Saturday, May 15, the day of the Arab invasion, the US did not say a word, and in UNSC as a whole (with the exception of the Soviet member), there seemed to be a conspiracy of silence reminiscent

---

5. *Foreign Relations of the United States: Diplomatic Papers, 1948, vol. 5, pt. 2,* 1064–1065.
6. Lie, *In the Cause of Peace,* 173.
7. Lie, *In the Cause of Peace,* 174.

of the most disheartening head-in-the-sand moments of the Chamberlain appeasement era.[8]

Writing urgently to the permanent members of UNSC, Trygve Lie warned:

> I consider it my duty…to emphasize to you that this is the first time since the adoption of the [UN] Charter that member states have openly declared that they have engaged in armed intervention outside their own territory. Moreover, this armed intervention has taken place in a territory which has been the special concern of the UN. A truce commission appointed by UNSC has been active in Palestine for some time, and it is only a matter of hours since UNGA adopted a resolution establishing a UN mediator with the mandate of seeking agreement of the parties to a peaceful adjustment of the situation in Palestine. The very first of the purposes of the UN is to maintain international peace and security. In Article 24 of the [UN] Charter, the members conferred on UNSC primary responsibilities for the maintenance of peace and security "in order to ensure prompt and effective action by the UN." A failure of UNSC to act under these circumstances can only result in the most serious injury to the prestige of the UN and the hopes for its future effectiveness in keeping the peace elsewhere in the world. Moreover, it may undermine the progress already made by UNSC in other security problems with which it is now dealing… Take account of the extreme seriousness of the situation which now faces the UN and of the necessity for prompt action at this crucial moment.[9]

Trygve Lie's intervention bore significant fruit in the US. Both Secretary Marshall and Undersecretary Lovett concluded that in view of the president's formal recognition of the State of Israel, the US could

---

8. Lie, *In the Cause of Peace*, 174.
9. Lie, *In the Cause of Peace*, 178–179.

no longer continue to question Israel's legitimacy, and it therefore had to meaningfully oppose the Arab invasion of Israel. Remarkably, they did so in the face of the continuing vigorous objections of their key State Department staff leader, George Kennan, who still questioned the legitimacy of Israel's existence, regarded the UN resolution for partition as invalid, and refused to consider the Arab invasion of Israel as aggression (see Chapter 14). Nevertheless, Marshall met with President Truman the same day, Monday, May 17, 1948, to receive his approval for Ambassador Austin to submit a forceful draft resolution in UNSC according to which UNSC was asked to:

> …[determine] that the situation in Palestine constitutes a threat to the peace and a breach of the peace within the meaning of Article 39 of the [UN] Charter; [order] all governments and authorities to cease and desist from any hostile military action and to that end to issue a ceasefire and steadfast order to their military and paramilitary forces to become effective within thirty-six hours after the adoption of this resolution; [direct] the Truce Commission established by [UNSC] by its resolution of 23 April, 1948 to report to [UNSC] on the compliance with these orders.

Bevin continued to reject Lie and Marshall's position, however, and on Wednesday, May 19, his ambassador to the UN, Sir Alexander Cadogan, submitted a redraft of the US resolution, according to which the problem of Palestine would be treated not under Chapter 7 of the UN Charter, which deals with threats to the peace and gives UNSC enforcement authority, but rather under Chapter 6, which is concerned only with measures for pacific settlement of disputes.[10]

Lie reacted to Britain's draft resolution with undisguised anxiety, recording:

---

10. *Foreign Relations of the United States: Diplomatic Papers, 1948, vol. 5,* 1016, fn. 2.

In [UNSC], Britain had again reverted to legalistic procedures, asking whether the invasion of Palestine was really aggression... On the battlefield, officers of British nationality were leading Jordan's Arab Legion, and British arms were used by the Arab armies.[11]

Lie's anxiety would have been far more intense had he known the extent of Britain's secret role in promoting the Arab invasion to destroy Israel at its rebirth (see Chapter 14). Bevin told King Abdullah not to invade the area the UN resolution for partition had allotted to the Jews, but this prohibition did not cover Jerusalem, which, under the resolution, was to become a separate international entity. King Abdullah—taking advantage of Britain's enlarged subsidy and the increase in military equipment to his Arab Legion as well as the substantial funds the Arab League was making available[12]—decided to seize all Jerusalem in addition to the entire area that had been allotted to the Arabs.

Glubb Pasha accordingly invaded Jerusalem's Old City on May 17, 1948, and in heavy house-to-house fighting during the next ten days, he defeated the greatly outnumbered and outgunned Jewish forces defending the elderly, totally unarmed, Old City Jews, all of them pacific—non-Zionist and even anti-Zionist—Jews who spent their days studying Torah. Glubb Pasha drove out the limited Israeli forces available, expelled its entire Jewish population, and demolished all its synagogues, making the Old City *Judenrein*. Transjordan's "Arabization" of the Old City's Jewish Quarter in 1948 was met without objection by UNGA, a striking contrast to the nearly universal condemnation of Israel's reintegration of Jerusalem in 1967. Since 1948, the world has been educated to forget that the Jews had already been

---

11. Lie, *In the Cause of Peace*, 182.
12. Azzam Pasha, secretary-general of the Arab League, told Glubb Pasha, "We need not worry about money... He said we could count on him for anything up to £3 million. As an earnest of his desire to help, he made us an immediate payment of £250,000" (Glubb, *A Soldier with the Arabs*, 85).

a majority of the Old City's total population prior to the onset of the political Zionist immigration—at least since around 1875. The world has accordingly been educated to designate even the Old City's Jewish quarter "Arab East Jerusalem," making the outcry of "Judaizing Arab East Jerusalem" a most powerful anti-Israel political slogan.

The Arab Legion had sought to drive on and conquer also modern Jewish Jerusalem, but its tanks had been stopped at the so-called Mandlebaum Gate, which came to define the dividing line between Jewish-held and Arab-held Jerusalem.[13] Glubb Pasha met the very next day, May 18, 1948, in Amman with Britain's Kirkbride for strategic advice on seizing all of Jerusalem. After looking over Glubb Pasha's map, Kirkbride advised him, "What happens in Jerusalem will be decided in Latrun. You'll have to go down there."[14] Latrun controlled both the main Tel Aviv–Jerusalem road, on which Jewish Jerusalem depended for its vital food supplies, and the pumping station that served as Jerusalem's source of external water supply. Glubb Pasha, following Kirkbride's advice, seized control of Latrun and laid siege to modern Jerusalem, threatening its hundred-thousand Jews with death from starvation and thirst.

Bevin, annoyed with the US over its disagreement with his policy, instructed his diplomat in Washington, DC, Sir John Balfour, to convey his views to the State Department. At a meeting on Friday, May 21, 1948 with Lovett, Loy Henderson, and Dean Rusk, Balfour presented the following briefing:

> Mr. Bevin is particularly anxious that over Palestine as over other matters, the British and the Americans should not drift apart, and it would obviously be dangerous if the situation were

---

13. Following the destruction of all the synagogues and Jewish institutions in the Old City, Transjordan proceeded to wipe out all evidence of Jewish life in the Old City. The ancient Jewish cemetery on the Mount of Olives overlooking the Temple Mount was desecrated, and access to the *Kotel*, the Western Wall of the Temple Mount, was closed off to the Jews.
14. Collins and Lapierre, *O Jerusalem!*, 497–498.

to develop in such a way that the Americans were giving increased support to one party and the British to the other. Nonetheless, there are certain points of policy concerning Palestine from which Mr. Bevin cannot deviate. He does not intend in the near future to recognize the Jewish State nor to support any proposal that it should become a member of the UN. Mr. Bevin also hopes that the US government will feel able to maintain its arms embargo. If this is raised, [His Majesty's Government] will almost certainly be obliged to raise their own embargo on the export of arms to certain Arab states, and the unfortunate position will then be reached of one side being largely armed by the Americans and the other by the British. Mr. Bevin cannot agree to any action under Article 39 of the UN Charter at least at this stage, since the situation is so confused that an impartial assessment of the true position is needed before any such drastic action is taken, the effect of which would be to place the blame upon one party only.[15]

The same day, May 21, 1948, George Kennan submitted a memorandum addressed to Secretary Marshall noting that his policy-planning staff wished:

...to record once more its deep apprehensions over the trend of US policy. Staff Paper No. 19 of January 19, 1948 and the supplement of January 29 made clear the view of the staff that this government should not take any action which would lead us to the assumption of major responsibility for the maintenance and security of a Jewish state in Palestine or bring us into a conflict with the British over the Palestine issue. The second of these documents specifically warned, in section 4, against our acceptance of the thesis that armed interference in Palestine by the Arab states would constitute aggression, which this government would be bound, as a member of the UN, to

---

15. *Foreign Relations of the United States: Diplomatic Papers, 1948, vol. 5,* 1019–1021.

join in opposing. The course of action we are now embarking on in the UN leads us in the direction of all these situations. It thereby threatens not only to place in jeopardy some of our most vital interests in the Middle East and the Mediterranean but also to disrupt the unity of the Western world and to undermine our entire policy toward the Soviet Union. This is not to mention the possibility that it may initiate a process of disintegration in the UN itself.[16]

Lovett forwarded Kennan's memorandum to Marshall but added his own comments, rejecting Kennan's theses:

I am unable, however, to join the policy-planning staff in the views expressed in their January 19 and January 29 papers on this subject insofar as they state that "This government should not take any action which would bring us into conflict with the British over the Palestine issue." I would gladly agree if the policy were to join the British when they are right and oppose them when they are wrong. I cannot believe that the US should give the British an implied warrant to take any course of action they may choose—however irresponsible, provocative, or unjust. I feel that this government should endeavor to cooperate fully and loyally with the British and that it should try to reach agreement on a parallel course of action whenever possible, but I think that it is of at least equal importance that this government pursue a course which it feels to be just and in keeping with the obligations we have undertaken as a member of the UN. If this brings us into conflict with the British, I think we should face up to this fact and not join them in actions we feel to be improper merely to avoid the conflict. It is hard for me to follow a line of reasoning which suggests, by implication at least, that "a process of disintegration in the UN" is initiated by the UN carrying out its primary functions—to maintain international peace and security. It would seem to me to be

---

16. *Foreign Relations of the United States: Diplomatic Papers, 1948, vol. 5, pt. 2,* 1020–1021.

equally logical to suggest that if the UN does not exercise its appropriate functions in the preservation of international peace and security, it seals its own doom.

Marshall, after reading both memoranda, noted his agreement with Lovett.[17]

The next day, Saturday, May 22, one week after Israel's rebirth, UNSC met to vote on the US draft resolution and the UK's proposed amendments to it. The US was able to muster only four supporting votes—those of Columbia, France, the Soviet Union, and the Ukraine. The other six member countries abstained. Ambassador Austin had already reported to Secretary Marshall, soon after Truman's stunning recognition of Israel, that many UN delegations had lost confidence in the integrity of the US. They doubted that the US would be willing to follow up a declaration of a threat to the peace with sanctions as would be required if the Arabs were to continue their invasion.

Before the final vote, Austin declared that the amended draft resolution "was not wholly adequate to accomplish what is required in Palestine," adding, "The US will vote for this amended resolution solely as it contains a call made to the parties to issue a ceasefire order within thirty-six hours after the stated time." He concluded that UNSC would have to consider further action if the parties did not promptly comply with the call.[18]

Thus, UNSC Resolution 49 of May 22, 1948 was as weak as those that had already been passed in previous months: UNSC *called upon* rather than *ordered* all involved to cease and desist from any hostile military action. Even more significantly, Britain succeeded in carrying over into this resolution, a week after Israel's birth, the phrase, "without prejudice to their rights, claims, and positions," thereby placing

---

17. *Foreign Relations of the United States: Diplomatic Papers, 1948, vol. 5, pt. 2,* 1021–1022.
18. *Foreign Relations of the United States: Diplomatic Papers, 1948, vol. 5, pt. 2,* 1028–1029.

on a par the rights and claims of the Arab states invading Israel in defiance of UNGA Resolution 181(II) of November 29, 1947 with those of Israel, which was born in accordance with that resolution.

Bevin, still upset with the US disagreement with his policy, decided to give US Ambassador Douglas in London a detailed briefing on Britain's view of Palestine's unique strategic significance. Lord Tedder of the Air Ministry, in a meeting on May 25 with Bevin and Prime Minister Attlee as well as key military officials and ministers of the Foreign Office, set forth the strategic military and political importance of Palestine to the UK, the US, and all Western Europe in terms reminiscent of the ancient Midrashic view of Jerusalem as the focal point of the world. He warned:

> Re strategic implications…Palestine is not [a] problem of Arabs vs. Jews but one of geography, since Palestine is not only part of [the] Middle East bridge between East and West but also between Asia and Africa. British chiefs of staff believe [the] Middle East is [the] "other foot" of [the] defense of [the] UK and Western Europe and that this is also true with regard to [the US government] vis-à-vis USSR, because [the] trans-polar route is "inadequate" and not likely [to] be decisive.[19]

Furthermore, UNSC Resolution 49 also included a paragraph calling upon all parties concerned to facilitate—by all means in their power—the task of the UN mediator appointed in the execution of UNGA Resolution 186 (S-2) of May 14, 1948. Remarkably, UNGA had been able to resume its session on Friday evening, May 14, after the pandemonium caused by the news of President Truman's immediate recognition of the State of Israel at 6:11 p.m. had subsided. The US delegation had then proposed that it would still be useful to appoint a commissioner for Palestine, approved earlier in the evening by the UNGA First Committee (see Chapter 14).

---

19. *Foreign Relations of the United States: Diplomatic Papers, 1948, vol. 5, pt. 2,* 1047–1050.

Adopted that evening, UNGA Resolution 186 (S-2) amended the original US proposal to downgrade the position from commissioner to mediator and to reduce their authority from their charge to "promote agreement on the future government of Palestine" to a requirement to "promote a peaceful adjustment of the Palestine situation."

Israel and the Soviet bloc were opposed even to this weakened resolution for a mediator, fearing that Israel's enemies might use it one day to seek to undo the UNGA resolution for partition of 1947, but it was adopted by a vote of thirty-one to seven, with sixteen abstentions.[20] The resolution provided for the appointment of a mediator by a committee consisting of the five permanent members of UNSC: China, France, the UK, the US, and the USSR.

On May 20, 1948, UNSC's five permanent members, acting on Trygve Lie's recommendation, appointed as the mediator Count Folke Bernadotte, president of the Swedish Red Cross and nephew of the King of Sweden. Lie knew Bernadotte as a fellow Scandinavian who "had led a life of devotion to other people's well-being."[21]

Bernadotte left Sweden for the Middle East on Tuesday, May 25, 1948, stopping in Paris, where he met the staff members Lie had appointed to assist him. Ralph Bunche, director of the UN Trusteeship Department who had served as a key adviser to UNSCOP in 1947 and was at this time designated as the secretary-general's personal representative, brought Bernadotte up to date regarding UN events.

---

20. Jessup, *The Birth of Nations*, 279–283.
21. Lie, *In the Cause of Peace*, 185. Toward the end of World War II, in March–April 1945, when the impending German defeat was already evident to the Nazis, Bernadotte negotiated with the head of the Nazi *gestapo*, Heinrich Himmler, the release of over seven thousand Scandinavians, including four hundred Danish Jews, and several thousand Jews from other countries. In answer to some criticism of his conferences with Himmler, Bernadotte noted that he had saved the lives of about ten thousand Jews (Folke Bernadotte, *To Jerusalem* [Westport, CT: Hyperion Press, 1976], 70–71).

Unfortunately, Bernadotte proved to be fundamentally flawed on a mediator's two basic requisites: He had no prior experience with or knowledge of the Palestine problem, and he had an incredibly biased attitude regarding the two sides, recording in his diary his being charmed by every Arab leader he met but annoyed with every Israeli leader.

Ashley Clarke, a British diplomat in Paris, briefed Bernadotte candidly on Britain's position on the Palestine problem:

> The British government was not prepared for the time being to take any steps against the Arabs—Britain was still continuing to supply arms to the Arabs. British officers who had joined the Arab forces as instructors were also taking an active part in the war. Nor were official British circles anxious to accept the American proposal that the Arab action should be regarded as provocation and a flagrant breach of the UN Charter.[22]

Bernadotte, before having arrived in the Middle East, instantly adopted the British policy that the UN resolution for partition of 1947 was not binding; that the Arab claim to all of Palestine was at least as strong as that of the Jews—despite the partition resolution—as the Jewish claim to national statehood in a part of Palestine; and that the Arab invasion of Israel cannot be considered aggression.

Bernadotte arrived at his first stop in the Middle East, Cairo, on Friday, May 28, 1928, where he met with Egypt's foreign minister, Ahmed Pasha. In striking contrast to Trygve Lie's bristling language on Egypt's invasion of Israel, "This was armed defiance of the UN... brazenly announced," Count Bernadotte found the foreign minister "correct and charming throughout the half-hour our conversation lasted, and [he] wished me all success in my mission... He even offered to arrange an audience for me with His Majesty."[23]

---

22. Bernadotte, *To Jerusalem*, 6–7.
23. Bernadotte, *To Jerusalem*, 19.

The next day, Saturday, May 29, 1948, UNSC adopted Resolution 50 to significantly strengthen its call for an Arab–Israeli truce and to make it more balanced than Resolution 49 between Arabs and Jews in multiple ways. Resolution 50 replaced the term "the two parties" throughout all the clauses by "all governments and authorities" so as to restrict the UK's behavior to the same degree as the two parties. It called for a truce limited to four weeks in place of the truce of indefinite duration in Resolution 49. It called upon all governments and authorities, including the UK, to "undertake that they will not introduce fighting personnel or military equipment during the ceasefire, not only into Palestine but also into Egypt, Iraq, Lebanon, Saudi Arabia, Syria, Transjordan, and Yemen." And it distinguished between the fighting and non-fighting personnel of military age, treating them in two separate paragraphs: Fighting personnel could not be introduced into the region during the truce period, but non-fighting personnel could continue to immigrate, provided the governments and authorities involved undertook not to mobilize them or submit them to military training during the ceasefire.

The following day, Sunday, May 30, Bernadotte met with Azzam Pasha, the secretary-general of the Arab League, who told him, "The UN is responsible for the war, because it forced through the unfortunate partition solution contrary to the will of the Arabs." Azzam Pasha had coordinated the war policy of the Arab States against Israel. Immediately after the November 29, 1947 UNGA resolution for partition, at an Arab League meeting in Cairo, they made the decisions to launch immediate guerilla operations against Palestine's Jews and to prepare for the coordinated invasion of Israel with their regular armies as soon as the British Mandate expired.

On May 15, 1948, the date of Israel's rebirth and the launching of the Arab war, Azzam Pasha had publicly repeated in an interview with the BBC the Arab war goals he had already placed on record in *Akhbar Al-Yom* (see Chapter 14, footnote 5) as early as October 11, 1947: "This will be a war of extermination and a momentous massacre which will be spoken of like the Mongolian massacre and the Crusades."[24]

But Bernadotte was excited over his meeting with Azzam Pasha:

> A most interesting experience. The secretary of the Arab League attracted me strongly I felt an instinctive liking for him... Azzam Pasha wished me every possible success in my work... I left this interesting man, firstly hoping that I should soon see him again, secondly with a feeling that I had in him a friend who would help me in every way with my difficult task.[25]

So full was Bernadotte of his feeling that Azzam Pasha would be a very helpful friend that incredible though it seems, he violated a mediator's fundamental requisite and confided in him the decision he had already made before meeting a single Israeli leader: "I was not bound by the UN resolution of 29 November, 1947—I had a free hand as far as putting forward new proposals for the future of Palestine was concerned."[26]

Bernadotte's enchantment with the Arab leaders continued in Amman, where he met on Tuesday, June 1 with Britain's Kirkbride, who put him in touch with Transjordan's foreign minister. Bernadotte found him to be "as charming as could be." He then met King Abdullah, to whom he "was anxious at all costs to pay [his] respects." Later, he "also had an opportunity to speak to the regent of Iraq," whom he found to be "an elegant and attractive young prince."[27]

Bernadotte had met in Israel with Prime Minister David Ben-Gurion and Foreign Minister Moshe Shertok the previous day, Monday, May 31. Ben-Gurion, he wrote, "showed a very bitter spirit." He complained that the Jews had previously twice accepted a truce, but the Arabs had turned it down both times, and UNSC had done nothing. He also complained that it would be considerably more

---

24. Collins and Lapierre, *O Jerusalem!*, 456–457 and 688, fn.
25. Bernadotte, *To Jerusalem*, 34–35.
26. Bernadotte, *To Jerusalem*, 33.
27. Bernadotte, *To Jerusalem*, 41–43.

difficult to impose an effective frontier control against the entry of fighting personnel and arms into the Arab countries than into Israel. Finally, he objected to the Arab aggressors being treated in the same category as Israel, their victim. Bernadotte felt no need to provide Ben-Gurion with any reassurances—his only comment was to warn that if the Jews rejected the truce, they would be placing themselves in an untenable position, going on to threaten, "You can hardly take the risk of UNSC finding itself obliged to take sanctions measures against the Israeli government."[28]

Both the Israeli provisional government and the Arab League (through Egypt's foreign minister) notified UNSC the next day, Tuesday, June 1, that they accepted UNSC's request in its resolution 50 of May 29 for a ceasefire of four weeks. Both parties accompanied their acceptances with statements of understanding. Israel based its acceptance on five assumptions of which a key assumption was that "the ban on the entrance of military forces under no circumstances implies a ban on Jewish immigrants of any age."[29] It added the required undertaking, "We agree that if immigrants of military age arrive during the four weeks, they will not be given military training during that period." The Arabs accompanied their acceptance with the assumption that the ultimate solution to the Palestine problem would ensure political unity for Palestine—liquidation of the State of Israel.[30]

---

28. Bernadotte, *To Jerusalem*, 37–39.
29. Ben-Gurion, *Israel: A Personal History*, 134–135. The Israeli government's four additional assumptions were: 1. a halt to the Egyptian naval blockade of Israel's shores; 2. that measures would be taken to supply Jerusalem with food and to protect people who were traveling on the roads; 3. a military status quo would be maintained in all areas that had been conquered before the truce; and 4. that the prohibition on the shipment of weapons to the neighboring Arab countries implied that weapons inside those countries belonging to a foreign power cannot be turned over to the local authorities.
30. United Nations Security Council, Resolution 50 (1948), Document S/801 (May 29, 1948), accessed on August 20, 2023, https://documents-dds-ny.

The following day, June 2, UNSC announced that Resolution 50 of May 29, 1948 had been accepted unconditionally and that the comments made by the parties were not considered to be setting conditions. Trygve Lie informed Bernadotte of UNSC's decision the next day and added that UNSC "had decided to authorize the mediator, in accordance with his suggestion contained in his telegram of 2 June, to fix the effective date for the ceasefire in consultation with the two parties and the Truce Commission."

Bernadotte adopted the UK's objection to immigration into Israel of non-fighting males of military age, providing a total replay of the earlier issue surrounding the validity of the UN resolution for partition of 1947. The Arabs opposed all Jewish immigration into any part of Palestine, including Israel, the right of which to exist they continued to reject. The UK agreed with the Arabs, rejecting any differentiation between fighting and non-fighting personnel, even though UNSC had officially voted down the UK's position in its Resolution 50. And Bernadotte adopted the UK–Arab rejection of any immigration of Jewish non-fighting personnel.

The UK pressure to persuade the US to adopt its position now was reminiscent of its pressure concerning the 1947 resolution for partition. On May 31, 1948, US Ambassador Douglas in London cabled the State Department that in response to Egypt's expression of concern that it would be difficult to check whether Jews of military age were being mobilized or given military training after reaching Palestine, Bevin had assured the Egyptian ambassador that he would continue to hold the Jews in Cyprus and would request from the Italian government and any other governments in a similar situation the prevention of departure of ships with Jews of military age that were ready to depart. Bevin hoped that the US would take similar action.[31]

---

un.org/doc/RESOLUTION/GEN/NR0/047/75/PDF/NR004775.pdf?OpenElement.
31. *Foreign Relations of the United States: Diplomatic Papers, 1948, vol. 5*, 1078–1079.

Lovett initially seemed to waffle somewhat, but in the end, he approved the following interpretation of the two paragraphs as guidance for the US mission to the UN:

> Paragraphs 3 and 4 do not preclude the admission of men of military age for exclusively civilian purposes provided this is carried out in good faith in light of the acceptance of the obligations of these paragraphs by the parties and under the supervision of the UN mediator.[32]

And Bernadotte again ignored the mediator's basic requisites in an echo of his behavior concerning the UNGA 1947 resolution for partition. On June 3, he met in Amman with Transjordan's foreign minister:

> ...[who] wanted to know my attitude towards the Jewish requirement that immigration into Palestine should continue during the truce... I answered by stating that I did not consider that any immigration should be allowed to take place and that I intended to say so most emphatically to the Jews.[33]

The mediator was to learn otherwise immediately upon his arrival in Haifa, recording in his diary:

> When I began my two-hour conference in Haifa with the Jewish foreign minister, Shertok (who was accompanied at our meeting by a representative of the prime minister), it turned out, however, that the Jewish representatives were very unwilling to agree to any compromise—above all on the question of continued Jewish immigration into Palestine during the truce. They maintained that the Jewish interpretation of certain expressions in the UNSC resolution was correct (which it probably was) and that consequently, "fighting personnel" must mean armed

---

32. *Foreign Relations of the United States: Diplomatic Papers, 1948, vol. 5*, 1087, fn. 2.
33. Bernadotte, *To Jerusalem*, 50.

personnel, whereas "men of military age" must mean men of military age who did not carry arms. The Jewish government wished accordingly to allow the immigration, which had begun as early as 15 May, 1948, to continue, but promised firstly that no arms should be imported, secondly that men of military age should be assembled in camps under my supervision—a guarantee against these men receiving either military training or arms. It also promised that I myself or my representatives on the Control Commission should be informed of the times at which ships would arrive; particulars would be given at the same time as to the various age groups and other categories to which the passengers belonged. Finally, the Jewish representatives promised me that immigration should not begin until the control apparatus had entered into operation; exceptions must, however, be made in the case of a few ships which were expected to reach Jewish ports within a few days.[34]

But although Bernadotte grudgingly recognized that Israel's interpretation of the resolution was "probably correct," and it was willing to place all non-fighting personnel of military age under his supervision, he seemed psychologically incapable of considering Israel as an independent state, a member of the UN. Instead, he constantly referred only to Jewish representatives as if they were representatives of some private Jewish organization having nothing to do with statehood and UN membership. Reluctantly, he decided he had to accept the principle of the immigration of non-fighting personnel, but he did so only with the imposition of a strict limit of about five hundred Jews.[35]

Shertok found Bernadotte's limits on its sovereign rights in the area of its highest priority especially galling, in part because UNSC Resolution 50 had not imposed any limits, but, far more significantly, because his imposition of a limit flew in the face of the sympathetic pro-immigration policy embedded in UNGA Resolution 181(II) of

---
34. Bernadotte, *To Jerusalem*, 51.
35. Bernadotte, *To Jerusalem*, 56.

November 29, 1947 for partition. The resolution for partition called upon Britain—still the Mandatory power at the time—to evacuate "at the earliest possible date and, in any event, not later than 1 February, 1948," a port and adequate hinterland so as to provide facilities for substantial Jewish immigration. And now, Bernadotte was replacing the oppositionist British rule and was imposing his own restrictions on Jewish immigration in the name of the UN. The US State Department had even followed suit and had also made the release of men of military age from its DP camps subject to Bernadotte's advance approval.[36]

Bernadotte was far from sympathetic to Shertok's objections, writing:

> In the end, I lost patience. I told him straight out—without mincing matters—that I had the impression that the Israeli government did not want a truce at all and that he, in any case, had no confidence whatever in me as mediator. If the Jewish government rejected my proposals, I continued, it would be my duty, in connection with the publication of the Israeli reply, to reveal what Shertok had just said to me: that one of the reasons for its rejection was that the Jewish side refused to accept the views put forward by the president of UNSC on the grounds that he happened for the moment to be a Syrian. Such an announcement, I pointed out in conclusion, would hardly benefit the Jewish cause either in UNSC or in the eyes of world opinion.[37]

---

36. *Foreign Relations of the United States: Diplomatic Papers, 1948, vol. 5,* 1348–1349, 1371.
37. In 1991, incidentally, Saudi Arabia's president of UNGA had no hesitation in distinguishing between his position as Arab representative and his role as president, and he absented himself from the rostrum when the foreign minister of Israel was to address UNGA. Neither UNGA nor world public opinion saw anything amiss.

Bernadotte's threat worked. Israel did not dare ignore his threat to turn both UNSC and world public opinion against it unless it accepted the notion that Syria's delegate, Faris al-Khouri, had interpreted Resolution 50 not as the conflicted representative of Syria but as the neutral president of UNSC. Remarkably, the world seems to be unaware of, or as with Bernadotte in this instance, shrugs aside, the 180-degree difference between the constitutional systems at the national level and the constitutional system prevailing within the UN and its associated agencies, such as UNESCO or the World Labor Organization. In Bernadotte's Sweden, as in all national constitutional systems, a judge who has a conflict of interest is required to recuse himself. Within the UN's constitutional system, however, a representative of an Arab country that is a party to a dispute may chair UNGA or any of its councils, including UNSC, and is fully authorized to guide its direction.

Bernadotte sent his formal proposal to Israel and to the Arab states on Tuesday, June 8, for a truce to take effect on June 11. Both sides informed him on Wednesday, June 9 that they accepted, and the four-week truce came into effect on Friday, June 11, 1948.

Bernadotte's Proposal for the Future Government of Palestine

Bernadotte had submitted his plan for governing Palestine to Israel and the Arabs, even before the first truce began on June 11:

> The UN resolution of 29 November, 1947 could hardly be regarded as a happy one. This resolution was bound, in my view, automatically to lead to the very situation in which we now found ourselves. The Arabs had, moreover, announced quite clearly and definitely that a solution of the kind adopted in 1947 must result in their resorting to military measures... It seemed clear to me now that I, in working out my own proposal, could not follow the resolution of 29 November, 1947 but that some modification must be found. Against this there

was, indeed, the circumstance that a number of countries, including the US and Russia, had already recognized Israel as an independent state and that it would certainly be very difficult to induce these states to alter their attitude on this question of principle. On the other hand, it might conceivably be possible for Israel to retain her position as an independent state and at the same time be associated in some sort of union with the Arabic part of Palestine.[38]

If this plan had truly originated with Bernadotte, as he records in his diary, it would have reflected his unbounded ego. He admitted he had been totally ignorant of Palestine's problems before taking on his appointment,[39] yet he was already confident on June 27, 1948, only one month after arriving in the Middle East, that his plan was preferable to—and should supplant—the decision arrived at by a majority of more than two-thirds of the UN member states, following UNSCOP's intensive consideration of the issues as summarized in its report to UNGA. But, in truth, Bernadotte did not author the plan but had again simply adopted the UK's plan, whose true author most likely was Harold Beeley, Bevin's key Middle East adviser.

Bernadotte accompanied his presentation of the plan to Israel and the Arabs with a warning that if it was rejected as a basis for negotiation with his assistance, he would feel free to submit his own conclusions to UNSC. According to his plan, even the right of unlimited Jewish immigration, which was enshrined as Israel's first priority in its Declaration of Independence, would be severely restricted. Immigration would be free only for the first two years but thereafter would

---

38. Bernadotte, *To Jerusalem*, 94.
39. "On one occasion," he recorded in his diary, "I thought I had found a solution that was both simple and acceptable. When I placed it before Dr. Bunche, he laughed and informed me that it was actually identical from beginning to end with a plan that had been discussed more than a year before but that for various reasons did not stand a chance of either gaining the support of UNSC or being accepted by the conflicting parties" (Bernadotte, *To Jerusalem*, 111).

be subject to Transjordan's approval. If the two parties could not agree, the conflict would go to the UN Economic and Social Council in order to obtain a binding decision. The council's decision, the mediator proposed, should be based on the principle of economic absorptive capacity, a principle that as discussed in earlier chapters of the present work, Britain had interpreted in the past to restrict and even halt Jewish immigration.

The most extraordinary feature of Bernadotte's plan was that modern Jerusalem, with its population of about a hundred thousand Jews, was to be transferred to Transjordan instead of to Israel or to become an international entity, as provided for in the UN resolution for partition.[40]

Fortunately for Israel, even the Arabs rejected the plan. Transjordan's King Abdullah would naturally have been happy to accept it, although even he understood that a federation of Transjordan with Israel was no longer feasible.[41] For the other Arab States, however, any enhancement of King Abdullah's power, given his undisguised ambitions at the time to rule over a Greater Syria that would merge Syria, Iraq, and Palestine with Transjordan, was a reason for rejecting

---

40. Bernadotte, *To Jerusalem*, 125–132.
41. On July 25, Mr. Wells Stabler, the US vice consul in Jerusalem, reported to the secretary of state that in a conversation with the king of Jordan that morning, King Abdullah had suggested that a final settlement would have to be imposed on both parties by UNSC. In such a settlement, he said, "Arab areas of Palestine should be attached to Transjordan, and these areas should also include [the Negev], Jaffa, and parts of Western Galilee." King Abdullah added, "Arabs and Jews could not share Palestine, and it would be necessary [to] have separate Jewish and Arab areas." Like Secretary Marshall, King Abdullah too believed that "shifts of population should take place to eliminate minority problems." Stabler added that the king made "usual uncomplimentary remarks about the Arab League and also referred to his Greater Syria scheme as the one hope of Arabs" (*Foreign Relations of the United States: Diplomatic Papers, 1948, vol. 5*, 1237–1238).

the plan.[42] In the face of their decision, King Abdullah had no choice but to reject it as well.

Harold Beeley, as early as June 6, 1948, five days before the four-week truce of June 11, had already proposed the UK's plan for circumscribing Israel's independence and sovereignty through a federation with Transjordan. He had informed the State Department's Loy Henderson that "The British government would not easily give up the idea of a federal state, which they regarded as the most practical solution." Even Loy Henderson, who had earlier fought so hard for a special UNGA session to undo the UNGA resolution for partition of 1947, now cautioned that the US government "could not support any measure which did not provide for the establishment of a Jewish state substantially along the lines envisaged in the November 29 resolution. The Jews had in fact a state, and we had recognized it." Beeley had also called for the transfer of the Negev to King Abdullah, noting that it "would be of definite strategic value, because of the possible port development at Gaza. As things stood at present, the British had no land connection from the sea to Transjordan." Again, Loy Henderson responded, "Modifications would have to be acquiesced in by the Jews."[43]

Ben-Gurion, upon receiving Bernadotte's proposals for governing Palestine, wrote, "Those who suspect that he is a Bevin agent are not too far off the mark."[44] He found practically all elements of the plan unacceptable, but the three key sticking points were Israel's sovereignty, Jewish immigration, and the status of Jerusalem. Having won the right to an independent state, which they had immediately brought into existence, and having thus far successfully defended themselves against the Arab invasion, Israel would "under no circumstances consider any proposal" that it should now agree to diminish

---

42. *Foreign Relations of the United States: Diplomatic Papers, 1947, vol. 5*, 738–759.
43. *Foreign Relations of the United States: Diplomatic Papers, 1948, vol. 5*, 1099–1101.
44. Ben-Gurion, *Israel: A Personal History*, 185.

its sovereignty in a union with Transjordan. Similarly, after having proclaimed the state as a haven for any Jew wishing to live there, Israel would not consider any proposal to restore a foreign authority to oversee immigration. And although the Jews had reluctantly accepted the internationalization of Jerusalem, they would not consider any proposal that envisioned "placing Jerusalem *in any way at all* under an Arab regime [emphasis in the original]."[45]

Israel's formal reply, as submitted by Moshe Shertok, spelled out the horror with which Israel greeted Bernadotte's proposal for King Abdullah to become ruler over Jerusalem:

> The provisional government was deeply wounded by your suggestion concerning the future of the city of Jerusalem, which it regards as disastrous. The idea that the relegation of Jerusalem to Arab rule might form part of a peaceful settlement could be conceived only in utter disregard of history and of the fundamental facts of the problem: the historic association of Judaism with the Holy City; the unique place occupied by Jerusalem in Jewish history and present-day Jewish life; the Jewish inhabitants—two-thirds majority in the city before the commencement of Arab aggression—a majority greatly increased since then as a result of Arab evacuation; the fact that the whole of Jerusalem, with only a few minor exceptions, is now in Jewish hands; and not least, the fact that after an exhaustive study of the problem and as a result of the overwhelming consensus of Christian opinion in its midst, UNGA resolved that Jerusalem be placed under an international regime. The provisional government must make it clear that the Jewish people will never acquiesce in the imposition of Arab domination over Jerusalem, no matter what formal municipal autonomy and right of access to the Holy Places of Jerusalem the Jews of Jerusalem might be allowed to enjoy. They will resist any such imposition with all the force at their command. The provisional government regrets to have to say that your startling suggestion regarding

---

45. Ben-Gurion, *Israel: A Personal History*, 199.

Jerusalem, by encouraging false Arab hopes and wounding Jewish feelings, is likely to achieve the reverse of the pacifying effect which you undoubtedly had in mind.[46]

At Lake Success, where the mediator went to present his proposals in person to UNSC, Abba Eban, then Israel's representative to the UN, bluntly told him that his proposals had caused Israel to lose faith in him. For his mission to succeed, he would have to aim instead at creating treaty relations between sovereign states.[47]

Ben-Gurion was firmly opposed to the June 11, 1948 truce and was even ready to risk the political consequences of its rejection.[48] In the four weeks since the Arab states had launched their war on Israel on May 15, 1948, Egypt's army had seized the Negev, and it now threatened to drive up the coastal plain to take Tel Aviv. Transjordan's Arab Legion was threatening Jerusalem and its one hundred thousand Jews with death from hunger and thirst. Iraq, together with Transjordan, had invaded Samaria and Judea, from which they threatened Israel's main population centers on the coastal plain. In comparison, Israel's gains in the Galilee paled in significance.

The provisional government had overruled Ben-Gurion and had agreed to the truce only because of the hunger that was again prevailing in Jerusalem. The reserve stocks of food and other essentials that had been replenished by the convoys that had entered the city just before Passover (see Chapter 14), were now depleted, and Jerusalem's Jews were again suffering from hunger and thirst. The truce would provide the city with some badly needed food supplies (and, hopefully, water), even if these would be strictly limited by the mediator and the Truce Commission to prevent any military advantage to the Jews upon the termination of the truce.

The need to haggle with the Truce Commission members over the quantities of essential food to be permitted to enter Jerusalem via the

---

46. Bernadotte, *To Jerusalem*, 151–152.
47. Ben-Gurion, *Israel: A Personal History*, 223.
48. Ben-Gurion, *Israel: A Personal History*, 138–145.

Tel Aviv–Jerusalem road generated profound bitterness. According to Jerusalem's military governor, Dov Joseph:

> The toughest problems were those created by the mediator and the Truce Commission. It seems a savage irony that these UN officials, appointed for humanitarian purposes, should have devoted so much of their time and energies to trying to make sure that the people of Jerusalem should find themselves close to the starvation level when the truce ended. But this is what actually took place. It was the logical result of Count Bernadotte's determination that "stocks of essential supplies shall not be substantially greater or less at the end of the truce than at the beginning." I contended one could not deal with the Jews of Jerusalem as if we were refugees in a camp where every calorie of food was weighed. During the truce, we were entitled to normal rations.
>
> The fiercest opposition to normal rations came from the US State Department member of the Truce Commission, John Macdonald, and his alternate, William C. Burdett Jr. John Macdonald produced a pamphlet on Jerusalem nutrition, which pointed to undernourishment in 1943 to 1946. He said that in China, there were millions of people who lived in a state of starvation. I replied that we preferred to model ourselves on the US rather than on China. The Jews of Jerusalem were not inmates of a concentration camp nor objects of charity being fed at the expense of the UN. This tussle over calories was only the first round. It was followed by altercations over how many people were in Jerusalem at the time of the truce… Then, we fought over the weight of packaging, which the commission had not allowed for in fixing permissible tonnages of food to be brought in… It was not just food that the commission had under its parsimonious and unhumanitarian pedantic eye. It also cut down the quantities of clothing and shoes we had asked for from 700 to 150 tons. Even children's clothing was not allowed into Jerusalem without the Truce Commission's prior approval.

I wondered at the time whether clothing too was a weapon dangerous to the peace.[49]

Only a seemingly miraculous discovery of a narrow dirt path that wound its way over hills and wadis between Jerusalem and Tel Aviv as well as bypassed the road in the blockaded Latrun area provided much-needed relief from the rigors of Bernadotte's truce enforcement. Through extraordinary efforts under the direction of the volunteer US Colonel David (Micky) Marcus, who outranked all Israeli military officers, the Jews succeeded—just one day before the UN truce came into effect—in widening the path into a transport-usable road, free from the mediator's controls.[50] Israel named this road its "Burma Road" in honor of the Burma Road to China that the US heroically built in 1937–1938 in its war with Japan.

But Transjordan's blocking of Jerusalem's normal water source via the Latrun pumping station continued. King Abdullah initially informed the mediator cold-bloodedly, "As to Jerusalem, I cannot allow that a single drop of water or a single pound of provisions should be taken into the city during the truce." Bernadotte replied, "Your Majesty must understand…that as [the] head of a humanitarian organization like the Red Cross, I cannot share Your Majesty's view that the starving Arabs and Jews in Jerusalem should not receive any humanitarian aid." King Abdullah yielded and agreed to Bernadotte's request.[51]

Despite this agreement, however, the Arab Legion in control of Latrun refused, using one pretext after another, to permit the resumption of the flow of water to Jerusalem. Dov Joseph's repeated complaints to both Bernadotte and the Truce Commission were of no avail, and Jerusalem never received a drop of water from its pumping station.

---

49. Joseph, *The Faithful City*, 231–233.
50. Collins and Lapierre, *O Jerusalem!*, 593–599.
51. Bernadotte, *To Jerusalem*, 62.

Both sides used the truce period to provide military training for new recruits, which was permissible under the regulations, but not for the training of newly arrived immigrants. More significantly, Ben-Gurion decided to transform Israel's military structure during the truce by insisting that the separate organizational militias of the Haganah, the Irgun, and Lehi must be incorporated within the State of Israel's national defense force—regardless of the costs involved. Menachem Begin, then head of the Irgun, brought in a ship named the Altalena loaded with military cargo, and when he refused to comply with the order to surrender the cargo, Ben-Gurion ordered Israel Defense Forces (IDF) units to fire at the ship, causing significant losses of lives both on the ship and on the shore, and to confiscate the cargo.

The Arabs likewise engaged in smuggling in weapons—though with less success than Israel, and they also reinforced their troops on all fronts. According to Glubb Pasha's estimates, admittedly unreliable, the Arab states had about 56,000 soldiers in Palestine on October 1 compared to 21,500 on May 15, 1948.[52]

Following both the Arab and Israeli rejections of his government plan, Bernadotte called for prolonging the truce, which was due to expire on July 9, 1948. When the Arabs turned him down, Bernadotte wired UNSC, which responded on July 7 with Resolution 53 addressing an urgent appeal to the interested parties "to accept in principle the prolongation of the truce for such period as may be decided upon in consultation with the mediator." Once again, Israel agreed, despite some serious misgivings, but the Arabs refused, and the truce expired on July 9, 1948.

When the Arabs rejected even Bevin's advice to accept UNSC's appeal, he finally agreed to the US proposal to have UNSC declare the situation a threat to the peace and to impose a truce under Chapter 7 of the UN Charter, with UNSC holding enforcement authority. On July 15, 1948, UNSC adopted Resolution 54, which took into consideration that Israel's government had indicated its agreement

---

52. Glubb, *A Soldier with the Arabs*, 94, 195.

to an extension of the truce but that the Arab states had rejected the successive appeals of the mediator and of UNSC for any prolongation. It declared the situation a threat to the peace and ordered the cessation of any further military action to take effect at a time determined by the mediator—but not more than three days later. The Arabs now also agreed to a ceasefire, which Bernadotte ordered to come into effect on July 18, 1948.

This second ceasefire, subject to UNSC enforcement under Chapter 7 of the UN Charter, was to remain in effect until a peaceful adjustment of the future situation in Palestine was reached. In addition to ordering the ceasefire, Resolution 54 also instructed the mediator to continue his efforts to bring about the demilitarization of Jerusalem.

The IDF became a much more powerful military force during the ten-day hiatus. In addition to having manufactured more light weapons for equipping its army, Israel had purchased heavy military equipment, including warplanes, that it had been unable to import during the truce period. In the removal of any prohibition during the ten-day hiatus, Israel was able to import this equipment, including three American Flying Fortresses flown in from Miami by way of Czechoslovakia.[53]

In the ensuing battles during the hiatus, Israel gained the upper hand. It seized three major Arab towns—Lydda, Ramla, and Nazareth—widening its control of the areas overlooking Tel Aviv and Beer

---

53. Ben-Gurion, *Israel: A Personal History*, 219; Slater, *The Pledge*, 311–312. Czechoslovakia was a key supplier of military equipment to the State of Israel in 1948, and its supplies helped Israel to turn the tables against the Arabs. The Arab states were also busy buying military equipment in European countries, including Czechoslovakia, which sold weaponry to the Arabs as well as to Israel. Israeli intelligence sank one boatload of such weapons that was destined for the Arabs before it was able to set sail from an Italian port. When the Arabs salvaged the weapons and transferred them to another boat, the *Haganah* seized it at sea and transferred the arms to Israel (Collins and Lapierre, *O Jerusalem!*, 295–299, 632–633; Slater, *The Pledge*, 239, fn.).

Sheva.⁵⁴ Its dislodging of the Iraqis from Rosh Ha'ayin, the source of the Yarkon River, would later prove to have special significance.⁵⁵

Two failures, however, still haunted the Israeli provisional government. It had not been able to gain free access to its settlements encircled by Egypt in the Negev or to dislodge the Arab Legion from Latrun. Nevertheless, as Bernadotte wrote, it was now quite clear even to the Arabs that their dream of destroying the Jewish State militarily had been crushed.⁵⁶ Evidently, the Arabs, the UK, and now Bernadotte as well had come to realize that their confidence at the outset of the Arab invasion that Israel would be easily crushed had been misplaced. They would now have to rely primarily on diplomatic weapons for liquidating Israel.

Ben-Gurion, who had been opposed even to the four-week truce of June 11, considered the multiple costs of the July 18 truce of indefinite duration totally unbearable. As he spelled out these costs in his report to the government on the first of August:

> An undeclared war is under way in the south. The Egyptians have apparently decided to take the entire Negev. They are grabbing areas all the time, since they are not under surveillance. In our case, the more we gain, the more trouble we have. We have captured additional areas, and now, we must hold onto them. If our army is forced to remain indefinitely—or even for a month or two—in the filthy, insect-ridden places that it has captured, without the possibility of rest, reorganization, or training, it is liable to fall apart. We have no way of knowing how long this truce will last... The UN has time; this matter

---

54. The Arabs refused to believe that Glubb Pasha had been unable to spare troops from Latrun to come to the defense of Lydda and Ramla and attacked him in the Arab press as a traitor. They charged that Glubb Pasha had accepted secret orders from British Foreign Minister Bevin to surrender the two towns to the Jews in order to put pressure upon the Arabs to accept the prolongation of the truce (Glubb, *A Soldier with the Arabs*, 164–165).
55. Ben-Gurion, *Israel: A Personal History*, 232.
56. Bernadotte, *To Jerusalem*, 201.

can drag on for months. It is unlikely that we can accept such a situation, if only for financial reasons.

Meanwhile, a new status quo is created, and the world learns to accept it. We are not a nation like all other nations. We are under supervision. There are supervisors here who do not even require our visas. The world is getting used to the idea that Israel is a dubious, problematical country... If the present situation continues for an indefinite period, our international position will worsen. Our military strength may decrease, and our economic strength may be undermined. There is no reason why we should accept a truce of unlimited duration. We must inform our friends, to the extent that they exist, as well as world public opinion that such a situation cannot be allowed to continue indefinitely. The invaders must be forced to leave the country or to make peace. Otherwise, we will drive them out ourselves. There is no political justice or wisdom in making us accept a state of affairs in which we suffer all the disadvantages of war and do not enjoy any of the benefits of peace, stability, independence, and tranquility.

The [United Nations] Security Council did not decide on a truce of unlimited duration. It simply decided not to set a specific time limit. The council will continue to discuss the question. We have the legal right to demand an end to the truce. If we do not succeed in persuading UNSC to fix a date, we will act on our own, explaining that we cannot accept the continued presence of foreign invaders on our soil in violation of the UN Charter. We must drive them out. We have less to fear from sanctions than from a continuation of the present condition... The truce must conclude by the end of August, or at the least, the middle of September. We must announce to the UN that if the foreign invaders do not leave the country by then, we will throw them out.[57]

---

57. Ben-Gurion, *Israel: A Personal History*, 232–234.

The Arab defiance of the second truce, via its control of the Latrun water pumping station, was so egregious that it threatened the very survival of Jerusalem and its hundred thousand Jews. The first truce had come and gone, and the second truce was now well under way, but the Arab Legion had not yet permitted a drop of water to flow into Jerusalem. Toward the end of July, the mediator finally concluded an agreement with the Arab Legion to place the pumping station under his supervision. On August 12, however, came the shattering news that the Arabs had blown up the pumping station.

Fortunately, as in the case of the earlier food blockage that Israel overcame by the near miraculous building of its "Burma Road," so now, through the seemingly miraculous building of a new water pipeline from Rosh Ha'ayin, the source of the Yarkon River, which it had seized during the ten-day hiatus, Israel was able to overcome the Arab-planned water disaster. Israel immediately began to lay an alternative pipeline to Jerusalem along its "Burma Road" from the Rosh Ha'ayin pumping station, which it completed on August 11, only the day before the Arabs blew up the Latrun pipeline on August 12, and thereby avoided the mediator's regulations and another catastrophe for Jerusalem.[58]

On August 16, President Truman's appointee as the US special representative to Israel, James McDonald (not to be confused with John Macdonald, the US consul in Jerusalem who served as the American member of the Truce Commission), wrote to Secretary Marshall that the destruction of the Latrun pumping station provided additional proof of the futility of the truce and of the dangerous optimism of the mediator. He concluded that he was personally convinced the truce was not increasing the chances for peace but rather the opposite, and he agreed with Israel that the situation called for efforts to secure real peace negotiations with the Arabs.[59]

---

58. Joseph, *The Faithful City*, 230.
59. *Foreign Relations of the United States: Diplomatic Papers, 1948*, vol. 5, 1315–1316.

Bernadotte Returns to the Long-Term Issues

Once the second truce was in place, Bernadotte again turned to the two issues of the demilitarization of Jerusalem and the refugee problem, for which he submitted his proposals on July 22. The government of Israel received his proposal for the demilitarization of Jerusalem "with incredulous astonishment." According to Bernadotte's plan, the Truce Commission would take complete control of Jerusalem and would decide who could live there or enter there and who could not. Men of military age who did not normally reside in Jerusalem could live in or enter the city only with the permission of the Truce Commission. Residents of Jerusalem who had served in military or defense forces would require special permission of the Truce Commission to live in or enter Jerusalem. About twenty thousand male members of the Haganah living in Jerusalem could thus be forced to leave their homes and families. Even men of non-military age as well as women and children who did not normally reside in Jerusalem would require permission to live in or enter Jerusalem. As Abba Eban protested to the US delegation to the UN, "In accepting the principle of demilitarization, the government of Israel never imagined that a ring of steel would be put around the city, barring access or residence to all but the aged and the infirm."[60]

The UNGA resolution for partition of 1947 had combined its call for the demilitarization of Jerusalem with its call for the city's internationalization. But at the outset of the Arab war on Israel, Transjordan's Arab Legion had seized the Old City, and Israel had taken control of modern Jerusalem. Bernadotte had recognized that under the existing political circumstances, internationalization was not practicable, but he had recommended that the whole of Jerusalem be turned over instead to Transjordan. This recommendation, as Israel had already made clear, was totally unacceptable.

---

60. *Foreign Relations of the United States: Diplomatic Papers, 1948, vol. 5*, "Report by Ambassador Jessup to Secretary Marshall, July 29, 1948," enclosing the text of a communication by Abba Eban, 1257–1258.

Shertok now countered Bernadotte's query as to whether the Jews accepted the demilitarization of Jerusalem with Israel's proposal that Jerusalem should be included in the Jewish State, and he hoped that the UN could be convinced of the justice of this proposal. The mediator simply repeated his question, "Do you accept the principle of demilitarization?" to which Shertok replied that the government had decided, "We cannot under any circumstances agree to the principle of demilitarization." Bernadotte, clearly disappointed, asked, "Does that mean that you reject it?" and insisted he had to have an answer "if not today, then tomorrow or the day after tomorrow."

The next day, Bernadotte sent a written inquiry to Israel as to whether it accepted the principle of the demilitarization of Jerusalem. The provisional government then sent him the following reply:

> The provisional government reiterates its absolute rejection of the demilitarization proposal presented to it by the mediator on July 22, 1948. The provisional government's attitude to the mediator's plan is inevitably influenced by his suggestion—never retracted—that in the final analysis, Jerusalem should be put under an Arab regime. The provisional government is ready, as it always has been, to discuss any reasonable plan to save Jerusalem from further destruction, if fighting should begin all over the country; any plan, to be acceptable, must safeguard the vital interests of the Jewish people in Jerusalem.[61]

Although Bernadotte was pressuring Israel to accept Jerusalem's demilitarization, he actually had serious doubts about his ability to police any such agreement. On July 20, two days after the second truce came into effect, Bernadotte had asked the US government to make available to him a Marine combat battalion to police the demilitarization agreement for Mount Scopus, which had been reached during the previous four-week truce. He noted that acceptance of the proposal for demilitarization of Jerusalem depended largely upon the

---

61. Ben-Gurion, *Israel: A Personal History*, 231–232.

UN's demonstration of its ability to discharge its obligations in regard to the Mount Scopus agreement. On July 28, Secretary Marshall cabled the consul general in Jerusalem, John Macdonald, to inform the mediator that it was not possible for the US to agree to his request and recommended instead that the mediator try to employ Arab and Jewish police.[62]

Macdonald reported back to the State Department on August 1 that the mediator had complained to him about the apparently uncooperative attitude of the US, noting that it was impossible for him to supervise the observance of the truce without sufficient staff and equipment. He had therefore asked Macdonald to inform Secretary Marshall: "I am not prepared to continue under such conditions, and unless the required personnel and equipment are forthcoming at once, I shall feel forced to resign as mediator."[63]

Bernadotte did not carry out his threat to resign, and despite the absence of any force to supervise demilitarization, he continued his pressure for the Arabs and Jews to agree to it. He spent the first three days of August in conferences with the Israeli prime minister and defense minister as well as with Glubb Pasha and Dov Joseph, and on August 5, he returned to the issue a second time with Shertok. His reaction, as he recorded in his diary, was as follows:

> Twist and turn the question as I might, I could get no definite answer out of Shertok. In the end, we agreed to define the Jewish attitude as being that it was the wish of the Israeli government that Jerusalem should not be involved in any military action if the war should flare up again.[64]

---

62. *Foreign Relations of the United States: Diplomatic Papers, 1948, vol. 5*, 1231, 1251.
63. *Foreign Relations of the United States: Diplomatic Papers, 1948, vol. 5*, 1264–1266.
64. Bernadotte, *To Jerusalem*, 204.

The Refugee Problem

Bernadotte also raised the refugee problem at his August 5 meeting with Shertok. Unlike the demilitarization of Jerusalem, which is now bygone history, the refugee problem is still very much with us, and indeed, remains at the very heart of the Arab–Israeli conflict.

Bernadotte had already raised the refugee problem on July 26 both with Shertok and at the UNGA, insisting that the Arab refugees, which he then estimated at 300,000 to 350,000, should be granted unrestricted right of return to their homes in Israel.[65] The Arabs charged that Israel was to blame for the existence of the refugees, claiming that the Jews expelled the Arabs from their homes to make room for Jewish immigration. Not surprisingly, the mediator echoed the Arab claim.

Michael Comay, Israel's representative to the UN, categorically denied the charge. In a letter to the US delegation to the UN on July 27, Comay maintained:

> The government of Israel must disclaim any responsibility for the creation of this problem. The charge that these Arabs were forcibly driven out by Israel authorities is wholly false; on the contrary, everything possible was done to prevent an exodus which was a direct result of the folly of the Arab states in organizing and launching a war of aggression against Israel. The impulse of the Arab civilian population to migrate from war areas, in order to avoid being involved in the hostilities, was deliberately fostered by Arab leaders for political motives. They did not wish the Arab population to continue to lead a peaceful existence in Jewish areas, and they wished to exploit the exodus as a propaganda weapon in surrounding Arab countries and

---

65. Bernadotte, *To Jerusalem*, 188–189. This estimate included the large number of refugees from the Arab cities of Lydda and Ramla, which the Jews had taken ten days earlier during the hiatus between truces. Bevin's estimate of the number of refugees was lower than Bernadotte's—he cited it as "not less than 250,000."

in the outside world. This inhuman policy has now faced the governments concerned with practical problems for which they must assume full responsibility.[66]

In his natural sympathy for the plight of the refugees, shared by Jews and Arabs alike, Count Bernadotte ignored the risk to Israel's security from the unrestricted admission of refugees, who could form a fifth column against the Jewish State. On June 15, four days into the June 11 truce, Moshe Shertok had told Bernadotte that the return of any Arab refugees must be contingent upon their acceptance of full citizenship of the State of Israel, with acknowledgment of its authority and sovereignty.[67] At their July 26 meeting, however, Shertok had declared, "There was no possibility of admitting the refugees during the war period." The Arab states, he maintained, "were trying to force us to accept the refugees, because they regarded them as a weapon to be used against us, a fifth column to destroy Israel from within."[68]

Bernadotte, in a meeting with Secretary Ireland of the US embassy in Egypt on August 7, 1948, increased his estimate of the number of Arab refugees to a range of 300,000 to 400,000.[69] Nonetheless, the mediator, who was so adamant about limiting Jewish immigration into Israel to about five hundred people so as to prevent Israel from gaining any advantage at the end of the truce, was psychologically incapable of taking into account any security risk to Israel from the unlimited return of several hundred thousand refugees, a risk whose reality Azzam Pasha himself later avowed. Bernadotte himself recorded on September 6 that Azzam Pasha, the Arab League's secretary-general, had told him, "It should be easy, among the hundreds of thousands of Arab refugees from Palestine, to form an irregular army that would

---

66. *Foreign Relations of the United States: Diplomatic Papers, 1948, vol. 5*, 1248.
67. *Foreign Relations of the United States: Diplomatic Papers, 1948, vol. 5*, 1151.
68. Ben-Gurion, *Israel: A Personal History*, 232.
69. *Foreign Relations of the United States: Diplomatic Papers, 1948, vol. 5*, 1295.

be in a position to cause a great deal of inconvenience to the Jews by acts of sabotage."[70]

The Arab claim that Israel is responsible for the refugees because Israel expelled them to make room for Jewish immigrants, a claim echoed by Bernadotte and reechoed later by Israeli Jewish revisionist historians who have devoted so much energy to digging through files of statements by Jewish officials, is sheer fiction. In fact, the refugees, like in all wars, fled of their own accord to escape the war dangers, actual or potential, even if, as during all wars, the military had to expel a small minority of residents or encourage them to flee in order to meet urgent war needs. If the Jewish revisionist historians still need irrefutable confirmation that wars—not political plotting—create grave refugee problems, it is now available in the UN report issued on Tuesday, November 13, 2012 that the civil war in Syria has already given rise to 2.5 million Syrian refugees and to the sequel published the next day that the UN expects the total number to rise to 4 million by early 2013.

What was truly unique in this war was the Palestinian Arab leadership's role in enhancing the flight of its own people. Followers of the grand mufti, Haj Amin al-Husseini, actively promoted Arab flight—in some cases, as in the striking example of Haifa, even against the wishes of the Jews. When the Jews seized the city on April 22, 1948, after the British evacuated it, US officials in Haifa wired to the State Department:

> Local grand mufti-dominated Arab leaders urged all Arabs to leave the city, and large numbers did so, the British providing convoy escorts to Lebanon and sea transport to Acre. By April 26, some six thousand to seven thousand Arabs had fled from Haifa, the [grand mufti-led] Arab Higher Committee reportedly ordering all Arabs to leave. The Jews wanted the Arabs to remain for political reasons to show democratic treatment—they

---

70. Bernadotte, *To Jerusalem*, 228.

will also need them for labor, although the Jews claim latter not essential.[71]

Difficult as it may be to believe, the grand mufti-led Arab Higher Committee was even opposed to the return of Arab refugees to their homes in Jewish areas. On August 12, 1948, at the same time that the mediator was pressuring Israel to agree to the return of the refugees, US Minister James Keeley (in Syria) transmitted to Secretary Marshall a copy of the Palestine Arab Higher Committee's "Note to the Arab League on the Refugee Situation," in which it "categorically [rejected] proposals that Arab refugees be returned to Jewish controlled areas," because "to do so would constitute a recognition of the imaginary Jewish state; place the refugees at the mercy of the Jews as virtual hostages; permit the Jews to exploit the refugees in a political sense, possibly winning their votes in a likely plebiscite; and place the refugees on the marginal fringe of the Jewish economy."[72]

In agreeing with the Arab charge against the Jews and insisting on the return of the Arab refugees to Israel (instead of calling for them to be integrated into the surrounding Arab states or within the Transjordan-held and quickly annexed West Bank), Bernadotte took no account of the fact that had the Arabs agreed to set up their own state in Palestine alongside the Jewish State, as provided for in UNGA Resolution 181(II) of November 29, 1947 for partition, there would have been no war, no casualties, and no refugees—Arab or Jewish. But the Arab League had chosen war instead, confident of an easy victory over Israel, leading to enormous war costs and excessive suffering for both sides. Around six thousand Israelis had died during the war—an almost unbelievable one percent of the total Israeli population at the time, far exceeding the corresponding percentage of the Palestinian

---

71. *Foreign Relations of the United States: Diplomatic Papers, 1948, vol. 5*, 838, "Telegram 40, April 22 and Telegram 44, April 26 from Haifa," in State Department files under 867N.01.
72. *Foreign Relations of the United States: Diplomatic Papers, 1948, vol. 5*, 1307–1308.

Arabs who had died. And the expulsion of the Jews by all the Middle East and North African Arab countries in sympathy with the Arab war against Israel—estimated at about 600,000—was far higher than the Arab refugee numbers cited by Bernadotte.

It is the difference between the Israeli and the Arab treatment of their brethren refugees that is most striking. Israel welcomed the Jewish refugees, even though the Jewish refugees all came from afar, except for those from Jerusalem's Old City. The Arabs, on the other hand, refused to permit their Arab brethren refugees to be integrated into their own states or even into the Palestinian communities in which more than forty percent of them had relocated. Indeed, the Arabs even refused to permit their refugee brethren to engage in any work programs for which the UNRWA was established in order to keep the refugees helpless and serve as a political weapon for Israel's destruction. Even a simple UNRWA project for the refugees to earn their living through chicken and egg breeding had to be abandoned, because of the Arab insistence that the refugees must be kept only on relief.

This Arab political weapon against Israel has now backfired on the Arabs themselves. The Arabs, along with the rest of the world, are now faced with the monstrous problem of a dwindling number of surviving original refugees, together with their children, grandchildren, and even great-grandchildren, now totaling about five million people, who are bottled up in refugee camps and living on international welfare—nurtured for nearly sixty-five years on an impossible dream that some day Israel will be their home. Surprisingly, even the US, which decided some years ago to reform and replace its own welfare structure with a work and education program, has continued to support rather than reform this international welfare structure that keeps generations and generations of Arab refugees helpless and hopeless only to serve as a political weapon against Israel.

The Arabs rest their political dream on UNGA Resolution 194(III) of December 11, 1948, which they have interpreted as providing an absolute "right of return" of the Arab refugees to Israel. In truth, however, this resolution provides no such "right of return." The resolution contains fifteen clauses, of which only clause 11 deals with the refugee problem, and it establishes no absolute "right of return" for Arab refugees.

Clause 1 expresses its appreciation for the work of the late mediator, Bernadotte, and gives its thanks to the acting mediator, Ralph Bunche. Clause 2 establishes a conciliation commission of three member countries to take over the functions of the mediator. Clause 3 decides that UNSC's permanent members should nominate the names of the three member countries for appointment to the Conciliation Commission. They nominated, and UNSC approved, France, Turkey, and the US as members of the Conciliation Commission. Clause 4 instructs the Conciliation Commission to begin its functions immediately. Clause 5 calls upon the governments concerned to begin negotiations, either through the Conciliation Commission or directly, to settle all outstanding problems between them. Clause 6 instructs the Conciliation Commission to assist the governments to settle the problems outstanding between them.

Clause 7 calls for the protection of the Holy Places of Israel and for the freest access to them. Clause 8 calls for the extended Jerusalem area to be established as a separate entity under effective UN control. Clause 9 resolves that pending further detailed arrangements, the freest access to the Jerusalem area should be provided by road, rail, or air. Clause 10 instructs the Conciliation Commission to seek arrangements relating to the economic development of the Jerusalem area, including access to ports, airfields, and the use of transportation and communication facilities.

Only clause 11 deals with the refugee problem, and it reads as follows:

> [The United Nations General Assembly] resolves that the refugees wishing to return to their homes and live at peace with their neighbors should be permitted to do so at the earliest practicable date and that compensation should be paid for

the property of those choosing not to return and for loss of or damage to property, which under principles of international law or in equity should be made good by the governments or authorities responsible.

The second paragraph of clause 11 reads:

> [The United Nations General Assembly] instructs the Conciliation Commission to facilitate the repatriation resettlement and economic and social rehabilitation of the refugees and the payment of compensation and to maintain close relations with the director of the United Nations Relief for Palestine Refugees and through him with the appropriate organs and agencies of the United Nations.[73]

This clause cannot be reconciled with the proposed two-state solution to the Arab–Israeli conflict that the Abbas-led PA claims it desires and that even the Netanyahu government has since endorsed. No solution to the Arab–Israeli conflict can be envisaged until the Arab world is ready to drop its impossible dream of an imaginary right of return and agrees that the millions of Arab refugees must be resettled within the Arab world, including, in particular, the future State of Palestine, where about forty percent of the total has lived since 1948.

Bernadotte, frustrated with his inability to get Shertok at the August 5 meeting to agree to his proposals on either of the two long-term issues, asked to have a private conversation with him. The foreign minister invited him to a private lunch at his home in Jerusalem in the second week of August. Reporting on this lunch, Bernadotte wrote:

> I had made up my mind to talk with him quite openly. I said that the government had expressed itself on various occasions in

---

73. United Nations General Assembly, Resolution 194(III)—Palestine: Progress Report of the United Nations Mediator, Document A/RES/194(III) (December 11, 1948), accessed on August 9, 2023, https://digitallibrary.un.org/record/210025?ln=en.

such a way that it was well on the way towards losing its head. It was my definite impression—I continued—that the Jews now felt they had two enemies. The Arabs were still Enemy No. 1. But I and the UN observers ran them a close second. I could not understand—I went on—why the Jewish government should adopt an attitude of such arrogance and hostility towards the UN representatives.

I thought I could see that what I said made a certain impression on Shertok. He admitted that his government's attitude had hardened after the military successes of the ten days [of] war. He admitted, too, that I and the UN observers in a way were regarded as "enemies." The Jews looked at the matter in this way: They had at last got free from the British Mandate. But they felt they were not yet completely free. They had only come under a fresh control—the control exercised by the UN. The truce was not limited to any given time, and so, it was impossible to say how long this state of affairs might continue—a circumstance which contributed to make the Jews still more bitter.

Shertok's reply evidently made some impression upon Bernadotte, who temporarily softened his tone to some extent. Thus, he wrote:

> From the purely psychological point of view, I could understand his line of argument very well. But I asked him, for the sake of the good cause and in order that we might eventually reach a solution, to try to mitigate the hostility that I and my staff met with on every side, not so much perhaps from the leading Jewish authorities as from the minor officials.

Several days after his meeting with Shertok, Count Bernadotte left for a Red Cross conference in Stockholm. There, he wrote he had a feeling that his negotiations had reached a deadlock: "The Jews had shown a blatant unwillingness for real cooperation. And the Arabs had asked me to leave them in peace for a few weeks."[74]

---

74. Bernadotte, *To Jerusalem*, 219.

While in Stockholm, the mediator received reports that approximately three thousand Jews of military age had entered Palestine since the beginning of the second truce:

> I was forced to the conclusion that this immigration must stop for a time, as otherwise, the military position of the Jews would obviously be improved... This aroused great indignation on the part of the Jewish government. It declared that I had been guilty of interfering with its right, in its capacity as representative of an autonomous state, to regulate immigration itself. I for my part considered it my duty to see to it that neither side obtained any military advantages during the truce.[75]

Evidently, Bernadotte could not accept the reality that it was equally his duty to prevent any military advantage to the Arabs from the entry of his estimated three thousand to four thousand Arab refugees into Israel, as it was his duty to prevent any advantage to the Jews from the entry of three thousand Jews of military age into Israel.

---

75. Bernadotte, *To Jerusalem*, 221.

– 17 –

The Mediator's Revised Peace Plan

Upon returning from Stockholm at the beginning of September, the mediator wrote in his diary: "I felt that I held a strong hand when I left Paris on 2 September to continue my journey." This feeling was apparently reinforced after an intermediate landing in Rome, where he had…

> …learnt from reliable sources that the Israeli government had requested the Vatican State to recognize the Jewish State—a request that had, however, been refused. Recognition by the Pope would, of course, have been a great triumph for the Jews. It would presumably have meant that a number of Catholic countries would have followed the Pope's example. Once again, however, Shertok had played altogether too high. I hoped that the next time I met him, I should find him more inclined than he had previously been to moderate his tone.[1]

Israel's request for recognition from Vatican City was, in his mind, such a piece of arrogance that the Pope's refusal gave him ground to hope that it would have chastened Foreign Minister Shertok.

Following talks with Arab leaders in Alexandria and Amman as well as with Jewish leaders in Tel Aviv from September 6–9, the mediator concluded that at least for the time being, there was "no prospect of voluntary agreement between the disputants, nor any willingness on the part of Arabs to negotiate with the Jews—either directly or through the mediator." He noted that Israel had extended

---

1. Bernadotte, *To Jerusalem*, 223.

an offer through him for direct negotiations, and he was convinced the offer was sincere, since he had recently learned that they had also extended the offer directly to the Arabs. Declaring that for his part, he would welcome such negotiations, he added that he "was well aware that at this particular time, such an offer was probably premature." Nevertheless, he wrote, he sensed "a more moderate and reasonable atmosphere in all quarters and a tendency to discuss—more realistically—the basic problems." He proposed, therefore, that "hostilities should be pronounced formally ended either by mutual agreement of the parties or, failing that, by the UN." In view of his belief that there was "no prospect of voluntary agreement between the disputants," this proposal really amounted to a recommendation that the UN should pronounce an end to hostilities. As the basis for such a pronouncement, he cited the fact that "UNSC, under pain of Chapter 7 sanctions, has forbidden further employment of military action in Palestine as a means of settling the dispute." But having dismissed any prospects for direct negotiations between the Arabs and the Jews as a means of achieving peace in Palestine, the only solution he had left was a recommendation for the UNGA to incorporate—in another resolution—his new proposals for a peaceful adjustment of the future situation in Palestine.

The new UNGA resolution, he conceded, would not readily win the willing approval of both parties. He was convinced, however, that:

> It is possible at this stage to formulate a proposal which, if firmly approved and strongly backed by UNGA, would not be forcibly resisted by either side—confident as I am, of course, that UNSC stands firm in its resolution of 15 July that military action shall not be employed by either party in the Palestine dispute.[2]

---

2. "Progress Report of the United Nations Mediator on Palestine, September 16, 1948" in United Nations, *Yearbook, 1947–1948*.

With this firm conviction, he set out his revised set of proposals for the peaceful adjustment of the future situation in Palestine.

The Mediator's Revised Plan for Peaceful Adjustment

In his explanation of the basic revisions to his previous proposals, the mediator noted in his diary that his consultations in UNSC in mid-July "had left me with the decided impression that it was the sheerest wishful thinking to imagine that UNSC or UNGA would ever abandon the principle of the resolution of 29 November 1947."[3] With the failure of the Arab and British dream to destroy Israel's existence, Bernadotte was evidently also prepared now to give up his own wishful thinking and to offer a plan representing a less radical departure from the 1947 UNGA resolution for partition. In this revised plan, submitted to the UN on September 16, 1948, the two major previously proposed reversals of the 1947 UNGA resolution for partition—the proposed federation of Israel with Transjordan and the transfer of Jerusalem to Transjordan—were abandoned. Under the new proposals, Israel would continue to exist as an independent state, and Jerusalem would become an international city under a UN trusteeship, as proposed in the 1947 UNGA resolution for partition.

The revised plan also qualified the original proposal for giving Transjordan the area of Palestine assigned to the Arabs in the 1947 UNGA resolution for partition. Taking into account the opposition of the other Arab states to his previous recommendation, Bernadotte now proposed that the matter…

> …should be left to the governments of the Arab states in full consultation with the Arab inhabitants of Palestine, with the recommendation, however, that in view of the historical connection and common interests of Transjordan and Palestine, there

---

3. Bernadotte, *To Jerusalem*, 184.

would be compelling reasons for merging the Arab territory of Palestine with the territory of Transjordan.[4]

Turning to the issue of the boundaries of the Jewish and Arab states, he declared that in the absence of agreement between the Jews and the Arabs, Israel's final boundaries would have to be fixed by the UN. For this purpose, he recommended a number of revisions to the boundaries established in the 1947 UNGA resolution. Continuing his opposition to its decision to assign the Negev to Israel, he insisted that it should be transferred to the Arabs. Lydda and Ramla, which the Israeli forces had taken in the hiatus between truces, should be returned to the Arabs. In addition, the port of Haifa should be declared a free port and the airport at Lydda a free airport. Western Galilee, which the 1947 UNGA resolution had awarded to the Arabs, would be offered to the Jewish State as compensation.

The mediator was emphatic concerning the need for the UN to affirm the right of the Arab refugees to return to their homes in Israel at the earliest possible date.[5] Among the seven basic premises on which he based his mediation recommendations, he listed as his fifth premise:

> The right of innocent people, uprooted from their homes by the present terror and ravages of war, to return to their homes should be affirmed and made effective, with assurance of adequate compensation for the property of those who may choose not to return.

---

4. Bernadotte, *To Jerusalem*, 235–244; "Progress Report of the United Nations Mediator on Palestine" in United Nations, *Yearbook, 1947–1948*.
5. The importance Bernadotte attached to the problem of the refugees is indicated by the structure of his progress report to the UN. That report was divided into three parts: Part 1 covered his mediation proposals, Part 2 covered his supervision of the two truces, and Part 3 covered the issue of assistance to the refugees.

He estimated that some 360,000 Arabs and some 7,000 Jews had become refugees as a result of hostilities in Palestine. The 7,000 Jews included refugees from Jerusalem's Old City and Jews from other Arab-occupied areas who had been expelled to Jewish-held areas. About sixty percent of the Arab refugees were dispersed in the neighboring Arab countries, but according to Bernadotte's estimate, 145,000 Arab refugees—or more than forty percent of the total—had not left Palestine and had found shelter instead in other parts of Arab-occupied Palestine.[6]

Although he included estimates of the number of Jewish refugees, and although his basic premise referred to the "right of innocent people…to return to their homes," without limiting this premise to Arab refugees only, Bernadotte failed to include the Jewish refugees in his recommendation for the affirmation of the rights of refugees. He limited his call for UNGA action only regarding Arab refugees, declaring:

> The right of the Arab refugees to return to their homes in Jewish-controlled territory at the earliest possible date should be affirmed by the UN, and their repatriation, resettlement, and economic and social rehabilitation, and payment of adequate compensation for the property of those choosing not to return, should be supervised and assisted by the UN conciliation commission.[7]

---

6. The mediator's progress report, submitted on September 16, 1948, provided these "confirmed estimates" of the Arab refugees: 3,000 sought refuge in Iraq, 50,000 in Lebanon, 70,000 in Syria, 50,000 in Transjordan, 145,000 in various parts of Arab Palestine, and 12,000 in Egypt—a total of 330,000. The remaining 30,000 were scattered along access roads or distributed in tiny isolated communities or hiding places over a wide area. Approximately, 50,000 Arabs remained in Jewish-controlled territory.

7. Although Bernadotte failed to mention the rights of the Jewish refugees to repatriation and compensation, he did include the Jewish refugees along with the Arab refugees in his conclusions regarding the need for assistance for a minimum period of one year. In Part III of his report

While noting that his proposal had been rejected by the provisional government of Israel on security grounds, he emphasized that it was his firm view "that the right of the refugees to return to their homes at the earliest practicable date should be affirmed."[8] Despite Azzam Pasha's statement to him that the returning refugees could be expected to form a fifth column to undermine the State of Israel from within, he ignored the condition laid down by Shertok in July that the return of the refugees must be contingent on their willingness to become Israeli citizens, accepting Israel's authority and sovereignty.

The mediator's recognition that Israel exists and that there was no reason to assume that it would not continue to do so did not mean that he was willing for it to be free of UN controls, like any other sovereign state. Instead, he proposed that the UN should establish a Palestine Conciliation Commission that would employ its good offices to recommend to the parties or to the UN and to take such steps as it considered appropriate to ensure "the continuation of the peaceful adjustment of the situation in Palestine." In addition to thus taking over his function as mediator, the commission would also have the responsibility to supervise the observance of the boundary arrangements as well as arrangements regarding rights to the roads, railroad, free port, and airport, together with supervision of minority rights and other arrangements as may be determined by the UN. The commission would, as noted above, also assist and supervise the repatriation, resettlement, and economic and social rehabilitation of

---

dealing with assistance to the refugees, he wrote: "(a) As a result of the conflict in Palestine, there are approximately 360,000 Arab refugees and 7,000 Jewish refugees requiring aid in that country and adjacent States. (b) Large numbers of these are infants, children, pregnant women, and nursing mothers. Their condition is one of destitution and they are 'vulnerable groups' in the medical and social sense. (c) The destruction of their property and the loss of their assets will render most of them a charge upon the communities in which they have sought refuge for a minimum period of one year (through this winter and until the end of the 1949 harvest)."

8. "Progress Report of the United Nations Mediator on Palestine," in United Nations, *Yearbook, 1947–1948*.

the Arab refugees, as well as the payment of adequate compensation for the property of those choosing not to return.[9] In effect, instead of being a truly sovereign state, Israel would be subject to a virtual UN trusteeship according to these mediation proposals. It was to this virtual trusteeship and with a major reduction in the territory assigned to the Jewish area that the mediator had convinced himself that Israel would be willing to give at least its tacit acceptance if it were firmly approved by UNGA.

The Roles of the UK and the US in the Formulation of Bernadotte's Plan

There is no indication in the mediator's report of any "guidance" that had been provided to him by either the UK or the US in making his proposals. Official US State Department documents show, however, that he indeed received such guidance in significant measure from both countries. On August 2, 1948, US Ambassador Douglas in London reported to Secretary of State Marshall the British government's belief that once the US and UK could agree on a lasting settlement, they might clarify to the mediator the similarity of their views. Secretary Marshall replied on August 12 that the department believed that "[an] informal US–UK approach to [the] mediator [is] desirable, informing him of our agreed views concerning settlement."[10]

On August 13, Secretary Marshall cabled Ambassador Douglas that Ralph Bunche, the secretary-general's personal representative on Bernadotte's team, had called on August 9 to present the mediator's tentative notions regarding the long-term settlement of the Palestine problem. Bernadotte, Secretary Marshall added, was "not eager to offer suggestions until he is assured that [the] US and UK [governments] are in agreement on [the] general lines of an equitable settlement."

---

9. "Progress Report of the United Nations Mediator on Palestine" in United Nations, *Yearbook, 1947–1948*.
10. *Foreign Relations of the United States: Diplomatic Papers, 1948, vol. 5*, 1268–1269, 1305.

On August 24, 1948, Marshall cabled the US embassy in Sweden to inform the mediator—who was still in Stockholm at the time—that they were "endeavoring to concert a common line of Palestine policy with [the] UK and hope, once these conversations have borne fruit, to discuss our views with the mediator."[11]

On August 27, 1948, Ambassador Douglas cabled Secretary Marshall an outline of the settlement approved by the British cabinet. It suggested that it would be convenient for the mediator to agree to sponsor the proposals. Recognizing that the Arabs no longer had any prospect of destroying the State of Israel, the outline abandoned the earlier Bevin policy of a federation of Israel with Transjordan, and it implicitly accepted the existence of the independent Jewish State. This acceptance of the principle of partition as embodied in the UN 1947 resolution for partition represented a major departure from the policy to which Britain had stubbornly adhered ever since the publication of its 1939 White Paper. It was also a major break with the Arab states, which remained adamant in their opposition to the existence of the Jewish State. The British cabinet outline proposed that given the incompatible claims of the Arabs and Jews, "No further attempt should be made to negotiate with the two sides about the general principles" for a peaceful solution; rather, "A permanent frontier line should be laid down on the ground as quickly as possible." It was proposed that the frontier line should be established by the mediator, if he would be willing to accept the responsibility, and failure to respect this line should be regarded as a breach of the truce to be dealt with by UNSC within its enforcement powers.

The British cabinet outline then proceeded to suggest the territorial lines that were later included in Bernadotte's report. While agreeing to the principle of partition, Britain was determined to confine Israel to the small area of the coast and the Galilee. In particular, the outline proposed that the entire Negev should be given to the Arabs,

---

11. *Foreign Relations of the United States: Diplomatic Papers, 1948, vol. 5*, 1309, 1341.

with the Jews receiving Western Galilee and Jaffa in exchange. It was proposed that Jerusalem would be a separate area under a governor responsible to the UN. A free port would be established in Haifa. The Arab area of Palestine was to go to Transjordan, the rationale being that the UNGA 1947 resolution calling for an independent Palestinian Arab state had been based on a recommendation—which had since proven unfeasible—for an economic union between the Arab and Jewish states. It concluded, "Without such a union, the Arab areas do not form a viable administrative or economic unit by themselves. It would not be a permanent solution to set up an independent Arab state covering this territory. The territory should therefore be incorporated in Transjordan."[12]

On September 1, Ambassador Douglas cabled Secretary Marshall a timetable suggested by the UK Foreign Office first, for reaching an agreement between the US and the UK on the substance of the mediator's statement, and second, for presenting these agreed views to him.[13]

On the same date, Secretary Marshall received President Truman's approval concerning a cable he proposed to send to James McDonald, the US special representative to Israel, concerning American views on Palestine. Included in the text was a statement on the suggested boundaries for the State of Israel. Although the State Department knew of Truman's personal, last-minute intervention to save the entire Negev for Israel in the UNGA 1947 resolution for partition, it now proposed: "Israel might expand into the rich area of Galilee, which it now holds in military occupation, in return for relinquishing a large portion of the Negev to Transjordan."[14] This differed from the UK proposal only in that it would permit Israel to retain a small portion in the northern part of the Negev, where there were a number of Jewish

---

12. *Foreign Relations of the United States: Diplomatic Papers, 1948, vol. 5,* 1354–1357.
13. *Foreign Relations of the United States: Diplomatic Papers, 1948, vol. 5,* 1365.
14. *Foreign Relations of the United States: Diplomatic Papers, 1948, vol. 5,* 1363–1364, 1368.

settlements, whereas the UK Foreign Office's proposal insisted on Israel's relinquishment of the entire Negev, including its settlements.

Truman, his mind undoubtedly distracted by the ardors of his campaign for reelection, gave his approval. Evidently, he failed to realize that it violated his promise to Weizmann a year earlier on the Negev and that it also conflicted with the Democratic platform on which he was running. That platform assured Israel that the new state would not be required to accept any changes in the territory that had been allotted to it in the UNGA 1947 resolution without the approval of Israel's provisional government.

Immediately upon receiving Truman's approval, Secretary Marshall cabled the US government's views concerning Palestine to James McDonald in Israel. At the same time, a copy of the cable was sent to Ambassador Douglas in the UK for him to show to Bevin. In this cable, Marshall commented, "You perceive from this instruction to McDonald that our views on [the] possible territorial settlement in Palestine are practically identical with those suggested in British working paper."[15]

On September 3, Ambassador Douglas cabled Secretary Marshall the concerns of the British Foreign Office about the dangers of a possible leak of the US government's views in Tel Aviv. It therefore perceived a need to speed up the timetable to inform the mediator of the agreed US and UK views. The cable pointed out:

> Officials feel it is important that from [the] moment [the] proposals become known, they should carry as [their] label "Mediator—made in Sweden." Since [the] Foreign Office has cabinet authority to approach [the] mediator with [the] proposals, officials suggest that [the] timetable…be speeded up and [the] US–UK proposals placed in [the] hands of [the] mediator by [the] US and [the] UK at [the] earliest possible moment.

---

15. *Foreign Relations of the United States: Diplomatic Papers, 1948, vol. 5,* 1366–1369.

As put by one official, "Now [the] cat is half out of [the] bag, [the] quicker [the] bag is handed to [the] mediator, the better."[16]

Marshall informed the US embassy in the UK on September 8 of his agreement concerning the need to place the US–UK proposals in the hands of the mediator at the earliest possible moment. On September 10, Secretary Marshall directed Robert McClintock as follows:

> …to proceed at the earliest possible opportunity to consult with the UN mediator Count Bernadotte, who, pursuant to the UNGA resolution of May 14, 1948, is endeavoring to arrange a peaceful adjustment of the situation in Palestine. You are authorized to inform Count Bernadotte of the views of this government with respect to such a peaceful adjustment of the situation of Palestine. In communicating this government's views to the mediator, you will be guided by the suggestions set forth in the [State] Department's telegram to Tel Aviv (No. 72) of September 1, which was approved by the president on that date. It is understood that your conversations with Count Bernadotte will be concurrent with, but not necessarily a joint representation of, similar conversations to be had with the mediator by representatives of the UK.[17]

On the same date, the State Department cabled the US embassy in Cairo as follows:

> With [the] utmost secrecy, inform Bernadotte and Bunche [of] McClintock's impending arrival and [the] nature [of the] conversations he [is] authorized [to] undertake. We re-emphasize [the] need for absolute secrecy. In response [to] chance inquiry from outsiders, it can be said that [the] purpose [of] McClintock's flight [to the] Near East is to study [the] Arab refugee

---

16. *Foreign Relations of the United States: Diplomatic Papers, 1948, vol. 5*, 1373.
17. *Foreign Relations of the United States: Diplomatic Papers, 1948, vol. 5*, 1382, 1387.

problem, in which [the] secretary [of state] has expressed deep personal interest.[18]

The day before the mediator submitted his report to the UN (on September 16), McClintock cabled to Secretary Marshall from Cairo the results of the consultations he and a representative of the UK government had held with Bernadotte on what was to be called "the Bernadotte plan." Two days had been devoted to a discussion of the substance of the report, and the morning of September 15 was devoted to tactics and timing. The mediator had already prepared a first draft of his report. Evidently, he was already well informed of the US and UK governments' views before the arrival of the two representatives. McClintock noted: "[The] principal matter of substance upon which [the] views of Bernadotte and [the] UK were at variance with our own was whether Israel should be given even a token salient into [the] Negev." The US favored such a salient, but the British were opposed, and they found firm support from the mediator. According to McClintock,

> Bernadotte said the responsibility was to propose terms founded on strict justice. If [the] Jews were to receive all of [the] rich Galilee in return for giving up [the] Negev to [the] Arabs, to whom it would ever remain a worthless desert, Jews should not in his opinion have any salient to that area.[19]

McClintock replied that he would recommend that the State Department should support the mediator's proposals in their entirety but that this recommendation would not be binding on the US government. He added, however, that in view of its political importance

---

18. *Foreign Relations of the United States: Diplomatic Papers, 1948, vol. 5*, 1387, fn. 2.
19. The mediator's argument was not quite precise. His proposal offered Israel only Western Galilee in return for giving up all of the Negev. The rest of Galilee had already been allotted to Israel under the UNGA 1947 resolution together with all of the Negev.

to the Jews, it might eventually be a good idea "to give Israel a token holding in the area."[20]

In their discussion of tactics and timing, the mediator insisted that the Palestine problem should be immediately placed on the agenda of UNGA. McClintock replied that the State Department had hoped to avoid another UNGA debate on Palestine, but if the issue had to be brought before UNGA once again, the matter should be dealt with expeditiously, "And 'the Bernadotte plan' should be rushed through, if possible, almost by acclamation." The mediator agreed.[21]

Assassination of the Mediator

By this time, Mediator Bernadotte had unfortunately aroused so much animosity in Israel over his plans to diminish Israel's sovereignty, independence, and boundaries that a small group of extremists decided to assassinate him. The mediator submitted his plan to the UN on September 16, and the very next day, September 17, 1948, he was assassinated in Jerusalem on his way to an appointment with the military governor, Dov Joseph. It was widely assumed that the assassins belonged to the outlawed Lehi. The provisional government of Israel condemned the assassination, and, acting to eliminate any further extremist activities, it ordered the arrest of all Lehi members. On September 20, it also dissolved the Irgun, commanding its members of military age to lay down their arms and to join as individuals in the IDF.[22] Thereafter, UNSC appointed Ralph Bunche as acting mediator. Bunche's experience in dealing with the problems of Palestine dated back to his service in 1947 with UNSCOP, whose majority report set the stage for the November 29, 1947 UNGA resolution in favor of partition.

---

20. *Foreign Relations of the United States: Diplomatic Papers, 1948, vol. 5,* 1398–1401.
21. *Foreign Relations of the United States: Diplomatic Papers, 1948, vol. 5,* 1400.
22. Ben-Gurion, *Israel: A Personal History,* 262–266.

Immediately after the British government received the conclusions of the mediator's report, Bevin called upon US Ambassador Douglas to urge the publication of the report as early as September 20. In addition, the US should issue a statement on September 21, followed by the UK on September 22, declaring: first, that the Bernadotte plan offered a fair and equitable basis for a settlement, and second, that the two governments were giving their fullest support to the Bernadotte plan as a whole.[23] Although the Bernadotte plan followed the UK government's proposal to give the entire Negev to Transjordan and was inconsistent with the proposal that President Truman had approved on September 1 for Israel to retain a salient in the northern Negev, the State Department agreed to Bevin's suggestions for the US and UK governments' statements.[24] On September 21, Secretary Marshall released a statement in Paris (where he was attending the UNGA session) declaring:

> The US considers that the conclusions contained in the final report of Count Bernadotte offer a generally fair basis for settlement of the Palestine question. My government is of the opinion that the conclusions are sound and strongly urges the parties and UNGA to accept them in their entirety as the best possible basis for bringing peace to a distracted land.[25]

Letters were sent to the US officials in the Middle East the next day, requesting that they urge the governments involved to approve the Bernadotte plan in its entirety.

---

23. *Foreign Relations of the United States: Diplomatic Papers, 1948, vol. 5,* 1409–1412.
24. On September 18, the State Department sent a message to the president, who was then on the campaign trail for reelection, informing him of Marshall's proposed statement—but no reply was received (*Foreign Relations of the United States: Diplomatic Papers, 1948, vol. 5,* 1431).
25. *Foreign Relations of the United States: Diplomatic Papers, 1948, vol. 5,* 1415–1416.

Bevin made a similar statement in support of the Bernadotte plan on September 22, and the Foreign Office requested its officials in the Middle East to urge the acquiescence of the Arab governments in the plan. To make such acquiescence more palatable, the Foreign Office also gave the Arab governments assurances that unprovoked Israeli violations of Arab frontiers would be considered an act of war against Great Britain, which would put into operation the existing Anglo–Arab treaties.[26]

The Objections of the Arabs, the Israelis, and the White House to the Bernadotte Plan

Despite the urgings of the US and UK governments, both the Arab states and Israel rejected the revised Bernadotte plan—as they had rejected his first set of proposals. Except for Transjordan, the Arab states would not agree to any plan that recognized the existence of the State of Israel. Amir Faisal, chief of the Saudi Arabian delegation to the UN, told the US delegation that the Palestine problem would never be solved as long as the State of Israel existed. The foreign minister of Lebanon declared that the Arab states would not recognize the State of Israel and would organize a boycott of Israel that would also extend secondarily to anyone engaging in trade with it.[27]

---

26. It is of interest to note that even though Syria, along with the other Arab states, had invaded Israel's frontiers, and Israel had invaded no Arab frontiers, the US minister in Syria sought the State Department's permission to inform the Syrian government that these British assurances were made with the full knowledge and approval of the US government and that while, for constitutional reasons, the US could not provide similar assurances, "It was bound by [the] UN Charter in concert with other UN members to take effective collective measures for the suppression of acts of aggression." The State Department replied that it was unable "at present" to authorize him to make such a statement (*Foreign Relations of the United States: Diplomatic Papers, 1948, vol. 5,* 1421–1422).

27. *Foreign Relations of the United States: Diplomatic Papers, 1948, vol. 5,* pp. 1416-1417. The Arab boycott against Israel, both primary and secondary, was maintained for decades, but after the Oslo Peace Agreement in

The Arab states, with Egypt in the lead, would also not agree to the Bernadotte plan for giving Arab Palestine and the Negev to Transjordan, despite being urgently pressed to do so by Great Britain. At the beginning of October, Egypt announced the establishment of a government of Arab Palestine in Gaza, which was to exercise its authority over all Palestine within the boundaries that had prevailed under the British Mandate.[28] With the exception of Transjordan, all the Arab states extended recognition to this Arab government.[29] Neither the UK nor the US, however, would recognize such a Palestinian government, particularly since it was to rely on the supporters of the grand mufti, and the Egyptian plan collapsed soon after it had been announced. Given the rejection of the Bernadotte plan by the other Arab states, King Abdullah of Transjordan, who would have gained the most from the plan and would personally have been willing to give his acquiescence if the plan had been adopted by the UN, had no choice but to reject it as well.

The provisional government of Israel likewise rejected the new plan. Although pleased that the mediator had come to accept Israel's existence as an established fact, it could not accept the limitations on its sovereignty implicit in the plan for a conciliation commission that would supervise many areas of activity and exercise governmental powers within the country. The proposal to remove the Negev from Israel and to transfer it to the Arabs, contrary to the UNGA 1947 resolution, was particularly objectionable.[30] On October 6, 1948,

---

September 1993 between Israel's Prime Minister Yitzchak Rabin and PA President Yasser Arafat, it was lifted in some Arab countries and was not effectively enforced in others. The boycott was revived and strengthened, however, as the Oslo Peace Agreement crumbled and gave way to the Arab intifada.

28. *Foreign Relations of the United States: Diplomatic Papers, 1948, vol. 5*, 1447–1448.
29. *Foreign Relations of the United States: Diplomatic Papers, 1948, vol. 5*, 1476–1477, fn. 1.
30. Ben-Gurion, *Israel: A Personal History*, 269–275.

the US special representative in Israel, James McDonald, wrote to the US president and to Acting Secretary of State Lovett in support of Israel's position on the Negev, noting, "Although [the] adoption of [the] Negev [suggestion in] Bernadotte's proposals might serve British strategic interest, it would disproportionately entangle this situation and sow dangerous seeds of bitterness."[31]

Secretary Marshall's announcement at the UNGA session in Paris of his full support for the Bernadotte plan in its entirety also created a furor within the Jewish community in the US, since the proposed transfer of the Negev to the Arabs not only contradicted the UNGA 1947 resolution but also violated the 1948 Democratic platform, which declared that no change in Israel's boundaries should be made without Israel's approval. In response to this furor, Clark Clifford informed Acting Secretary of State Lovett on September 29 that President Truman proposed to issue a statement on October 1 disavowing Secretary Marshall's position on the Negev. The statement would declare that Truman's position endorsing the boundaries set by UNGA in November 1947 and affirmed in the Democratic platform had not changed. Lovett urged Clifford to dissuade the president from taking this action, saying that such a reversal of a program the president had approved on September 1 would place Secretary Marshall in an intolerable position. Moreover, since agreements had been made with other countries in light of the agreed program, it would label the US as having violated its agreements and as completely untrustworthy in international matters. It was decided, therefore, that the president would instead send a reply to a telegram from Rabbi Stephen Wise stating that he hoped it would be possible to find a peaceful settlement in Palestine that could be accepted with honor by all interested parties and that he believed that the Bernadotte plan offered "a basis for continuing efforts to secure a just settlement."[32]

---

31. *Foreign Relations of the United States: Diplomatic Papers, 1948, vol. 5*, 1450–1451.
32. *Foreign Relations of the United States: Diplomatic Papers, 1948, vol. 5*, 1430–1432, 1437–1439.

The pressure against the State Department's support for the proposal to remove all of the Negev from Israel and give it to the Arabs prompted some State Department officials to suggest that some modifications to the Bernadotte plan should be made on the basis of negotiations between the parties. On October 10, Secretary Marshall submitted to Truman for his approval a draft statement for Lovett's use at a press conference, in which the State Department would note that the Arabs and the Israelis were far apart in their respective views on Palestine, with the Arabs refusing to recognize Israel's existence and Israel strongly objecting to the transfer of the Negev, which had been allotted to it in the UNGA 1947 resolution. While the draft did not explicitly propose a specific compromise on the Negev, it concluded with the statement that the Bernadotte plan provided "a sound basis for adjustment of their differences before the UN" and for reaching an agreement. The president approved the draft, but his political advisers turned it down, saying they "preferred to say nothing at all than to give this statement."[33]

Bevin, who was also shown Marshall's draft, informed US Ambassador Douglas that he was unhappy with the public mention of any modification to the Bernadotte proposals. If, however, there were compelling reasons for the US to mention modifications, he would want to add a sentence in order to emphasize the need for equilibrium as well as to remove any hint that the two sides might reach an agreement between themselves without the intervention of the UN. The sentence was proposed to read: "It should not be too difficult to reach a solution even though the UN may find it wise to make minor modifications which do not disturb the equilibrium provided for in the Bernadotte recommendations."[34] Bevin was still intent upon removing the Negev from Israel, and he was determined to resist any bilateral peace negotiations between the Arabs and Israel for fear

---

33. *Foreign Relations of the United States: Diplomatic Papers, 1948, vol. 5,* 1439, 1459–1460, 1466.
34. *Foreign Relations of the United States: Diplomatic Papers, 1948, vol. 5,* 1469–1470 and fn.

that in such negotiations, the Arabs might agree to let Israel retain the Negev. Although the Negev was of strategic importance to the British, it was of little significance to the Arabs—as Bernadotte had recognized.

Largely as a result of Arab opposition to the Bernadotte plan, UNGA had delayed taking up the Palestine issue until October 15, by which time the support the plan had garnered out of sympathy for the assassinated mediator had largely dissipated. And the US delegation to the UN, worried that any statement in support of the Bernadotte plan would inflame the political situation in the US in the remaining weeks of the election campaign, decided not to participate in any substantive discussion on the Palestine problem on October 15 and 16, after which time UNGA again postponed debate on the issue.[35]

After further discussions both within the US delegation, which itself was divided on the issue of the Negev, and with the British in London and Paris as well as with Acting Mediator Ralph Bunche, Secretary Marshall, on October 16, submitted to the president for his approval an agreed draft resolution on Palestine for UNGA. That draft would, inter alia, instruct the conciliation commission proposed by Bernadotte to appoint a technical boundaries commission "to assist in delimiting the frontiers in Palestine based on the specific conclusions of the UN mediator...subject to such adjustment as may promote agreement between the Arabs and the Jews."[36]

Rather than approving the draft resolution submitted by Marshall, however, the president insisted to Acting Secretary of State Lovett on Sunday, October 17 that the US delegation should "use [the] utmost efforts to have [a] debate on [the] mediator's plan deferred until after [the] elections, if possible" and instructed Lovett to ask Marshall "to use every effort to avoid having the US delegation drawn into the debate." That same evening, Truman issued an order "that no

---

35. *Foreign Relations of the United States: Diplomatic Papers, 1948, vol. 5,* 1470–1471 and fn.
36. *Foreign Relations of the United States: Diplomatic Papers, 1948, vol. 5,* 1470–1471, 1474–1476, 1481–1483.

statement be made or no action be taken on the subject of Palestine by any member of our delegation in Paris without obtaining specific authority from me and clearing the text of any statement."[37] On October 23, UNGA decided to postpone discussion of the Palestine problem for another week. As Dean Rusk informed Lovett, since the opening days of the debate would be devoted to procedural matters, it would not be necessary for the US delegation to speak before the middle or latter part of the week beginning November 1, when the US elections would finally be over.[38]

The Truce Gives Way to Armed Conflict in the Negev

On October 6, Ben-Gurion met with his cabinet to debate his proposal for military action to open the road to the Negev. Behind the Egyptian lines in the Negev, Israel had twenty-six settlements that required the replenishment of their food supplies and other essential goods. The mediator had decided that according the truce provisions, Israel had the right to pass through the Egyptian lines to provide the Jewish settlements with their essential requirements. The Egyptians had refused permission for Israel to do so, however, and the mediator had been unable to enforce his decision. Ben-Gurion had long since concluded that it would be futile to rely upon a favorable UN political decision, because the Arabs refused to accept the existence of Israel, and the UN was unable to enforce its political decisions by military means. He again warned of the dangers posed by the continuation of a truce that the UN was unable to enforce and that permitted the Egyptians to seize new military positions from time to time. Israel, he maintained, would need to undertake opening the road to the Negev even if the UN were not considering the Bernadotte plan to transfer the Negev from Israel to the Arabs.

---

37. *Foreign Relations of the United States: Diplomatic Papers, 1948, vol. 5,* 1489–1490.
38. *Foreign Relations of the United States: Diplomatic Papers, 1948, vol. 5,* 1511.

The Israeli provisional government decided that a convoy should be sent to the settlements during the hours approved by the UN and that if the Egyptians refused passage, Israel's military forces should break through the Egyptian lines. In the fighting that would ensue, Israel should attempt to defeat the Egyptian army and to take control of the Negev. Foreign Minister Shertok was consulted in Paris regarding the impact of such a campaign upon Israel's position in the UN. He approved the plan on October 10, 1948, and the operation was scheduled for Thursday, October 14, the day after Yom Kippur.[39]

Because of a delay in organizing the military force to follow the convoy, the Israeli operation began on Friday, October 15, the day on which UNGA briefly opened its debate on Palestine. The Egyptians, as expected, refused to give permission for the convoy to pass, and the Israelis then began a general attack against the Egyptian army. The next day, the UN observers ordered the two sides to halt operations and to return to the positions held on October 1. Both sides rejected the demand, and the fighting continued. On October 19, UNSC adopted a decision calling for an immediate and effective ceasefire as an "indispensable condition to a restoration of the situation." It then set out three conditions as a basis for further negotiations as insurance against similar outbreaks in the future: 1. withdrawal of both parties from any positions not occupied at the time of the outbreak of the armed conflict, 2. acceptance by both parties of the terms set by the Central Truce Supervision Board regarding convoys, and 3. agreement by both parties to negotiate concerning the outstanding problems in the Negev.[40]

---

39. Ben-Gurion, *Israel: A Personal History*, 275–280.
40. This council decision bears no UNSC resolution number—it was adopted as an amended version of the text submitted by Acting Mediator Ralph Bunche. United Nations Security Council Resolution 59, adopted the same day (October 19, 1948), deals with the assassination of Bernadotte and calls upon the governments and authorities concerned to cooperate with the acting mediator and the representatives of the Truce Commission (United Nations Security Council, Resolution 59 (1948), Document

The request for an immediate and unconditional ceasefire in accordance with the UNSC decision was transmitted by Bunche's personal representative on October 20. Ben-Gurion met with his cabinet in a special session that day and informed Bunche the next morning that his government had issued a ceasefire order to be put into effect twelve hours after an announcement by the acting mediator that the Egyptian government was abiding by the UNSC decision. The ceasefire went into effect the next day, October 22. During the seven days of fighting, the IDF had wrested control of the northern Negev from the Egyptian army. Indeed, the military situation had therefore been completely reversed. Instead of the Jewish settlements being held hostage by the Egyptian army, it was now the Egyptian troops in the northern Negev who had been bottled up, and Egypt had no means of supplying them with their food requirements. Israel had also captured Beer Sheva.[41]

The Israeli victory in the northern Negev was a bitter pill for Bevin, who continued to entertain the hope that he might be able, by means of the Bernadotte plan, to wrest all of the Negev from Israel and have it transferred to Transjordan. On the same day as the ceasefire in the Negev came into effect, Bevin suffered yet another blow to his hopes regarding the Negev, this time as a result of the election campaign in the US. In a letter on October 22 to Dean Alfange, the chairman of the American Christian Palestine Committee, Governor Thomas E. Dewey of New York, the Republican candidate for president, repudiated the State Department's policy in support of the Bernadotte plan. Instead, he reaffirmed his "wholehearted support of the Republican platform," including the Palestine plank, which pledged full recognition of Israel with its boundaries as sanctioned by the UN. In the circumstances, President Truman felt he had no choice but to issue a statement two days later declaring that he stood squarely on the

---

S/1045 [October 19, 1948], accessed on August 20, 2023, https://documents-dds-ny.un.org/doc/RESOLUTION/GEN/NR0/047/84/PDF/NR004784.pdf?OpenElement).
41. Ben-Gurion, *Israel: A Personal History*, 280–285.

provisions covering Israel in the Democratic platform. After recalling that he had promptly recognized the State of Israel on May 14, 1948, extending *de facto* recognition to its provisional government, he promised that when a permanent government would be elected in Israel, it would promptly be given *de jure* recognition. He then noted:

> The Democratic platform states that we approve the claims of Israel to the boundaries set forth in the UN resolution of November 29, 1947 and consider that modifications thereof should be made only if [they are] fully acceptable to the State of Israel. This has been and is now my position.[42]

Once again, President Truman had overruled the State Department on the Negev, this time in a public statement that he would support no changes to Israeli territory that did not have the approval of the Israeli provisional government. Nevertheless, to avoid embarrassing Secretary Marshall, Truman did not explicitly disavow the Bernadotte plan. Instead, he referred to the plan as providing a basis for a renewed effort in the UN to bring about a peaceful adjustment and expressed the hope that by using this plan as a basis for negotiations, the conflicting claims of the parties could be settled.

Israel's victories in the northern Negev marked the beginning of a major turning point in its War of Independence. On October 22, the last day of the fighting in the Negev, Kaukji, the leader of the irregular Arab forces in northern Israel, launched an attack against Israel in the Galilee. With the ending of the battles in the Negev, Israel decided to engage Kaukji with the purpose of destroying his Arab Liberation Army. When the fighting ended on October 31, the Arab Liberation Army had been driven out, and Israel had taken control of all Galilee.[43]

Israel's victories in the Negev also marked a major turning point in the attitude of the Arab states regarding the wisdom of continuing

---

42. *Foreign Relations of the United States: Diplomatic Papers, 1948, vol. 5,* 1512–1514.
43. Ben-Gurion, *Israel: A Personal History,* 285–287.

their war to destroy the State of Israel. On October 21, the day before the ceasefire came into effect in the Negev, King Abdullah of Transjordan informed Wells Stabler, the US vice consul in Jerusalem, that he was most anxious for the Jews to be informed: "He now desires restoration [of] peace and understanding with the Jews, with whom he believes he could have close relations."[44] And at a meeting of the Israeli cabinet on November 4, Foreign Minister Shertok announced that the Egyptian government had put out official feelers about a settlement, prompted by the fact that its army had been hit so hard in the Negev without having received any assistance from other Arab armies.[45]

Attempts to Restore the Status Quo Ante in the Negev

Acting Mediator Ralph Bunche was not yet ready to accept the new military situation in the Negev. In accordance with the UNSC decision of October 19 calling for withdrawal from any positions not occupied at the time of the outbreak of hostilities, Bunche ordered Israel and Egypt on October 25 to return to the military positions they had occupied on October 14. On October 28, the UK government, still determined to transfer the Negev to the Arabs, submitted a joint draft resolution with China proposing UNSC's endorsement of the acting mediator's order for withdrawal to the military positions occupied on October 14. Additionally, it was proposed that UNSC should also establish a committee to urgently examine and recommend what sanctions UNSC might impose under article 41 of the UN Charter if either party—or both parties—failed to comply with the order.[46]

---

44. *Foreign Relations of the United States: Diplomatic Papers, 1948, vol. 5,* 1501–1502.
45. Ben-Gurion, *Israel: A Personal History,* 293.
46. Under article 41 of the UN Charter, UNSC "may decide what measures not involving the use of force are to be employed to give effect to its decisions and may call upon members of the UN to apply such measures. These may include complete or partial interruption of economic relations and of rail,

Israel resisted the acting mediator's order and was opposed to the UK–China draft resolution. On October 29, Shertok cabled Secretary Marshall that the proposed withdrawal in the draft resolution would amount to an act of suicide to which Israel could not agree. He noted that Egypt's crushing defeat was the result of its own aggression, first in invading Palestine and second in violating the truce by cutting off the Negev settlements from contact with Israel and by refusing to let Israel's convoys pass to its settlements. Restoration of the situation of October 14 would recreate unjust and intolerable conditions to which Israel could not agree.[47]

The US special representative in Israel, James McDonald, cabled the State Department the same day in support of the Israeli position, adding that it was evident that Egypt had begun to realize that adjustment was inevitable and that Ben-Gurion appeared to have offered to negotiate a separate peace with Egypt. The Israeli victory, he said, had clarified the situation in the Negev and had raised some hope of settlement. To undo the new situation by demanding a return to the *status quo ante* under threat of sanctions would only lead to disillusionment in Israel about both the UN and the US, from which only Russia would gain. McDonald warned, moreover, that Israel would not yield to threats, and it would in fact be necessary to employ economic or more punitive sanctions to force its surrender.[48]

The UK government, however, exerted forceful pressure upon the US on behalf of its draft resolution in UNSC. On October 29, the day after Britain submitted its draft resolution, Ambassador Douglas in London reported that the British chiefs of staff considered holding the Middle East essential for offensive purposes in the event of war with the USSR. And Foreign Minister Bevin sent a personal message to

---

sea, air, postal, telegraphic, radio, and other means of communication, and the severance of diplomatic relations."
47. *Foreign Relations of the United States: Diplomatic Papers, 1948*, vol. 5, 1526–1527.
48. *Foreign Relations of the United States: Diplomatic Papers, 1948*, vol. 5, 1525–1526.

Secretary Marshall "asking him to make certain that [the US delegation] voted for [the] Palestine resolution, since US abstention would imperil [the] outcome."[49] At a meeting with Marshall the following day, Bevin added a warning that in light of Israel's military successes, it might be necessary for him to consider the delivery of ammunition and arms to the Arab Legion. This warning was issued in full knowledge of the fact that such action would be an open violation of the UNSC resolution against supplying arms to both parties and that it would place irresistible pressure upon the US to lift its boycott on providing arms to Israel. Bevin added, however, that he would take no action before the following Wednesday, November 4, evidently in deference to the American presidential election, which was to take place on Tuesday, November 3, 1948.[50]

The US delegation to the UN was deeply divided over the issue of supporting sanctions against Israel because of its refusal to withdraw to its original position in the Negev. While State Department officials were prepared to vote for Britain's draft resolution, three key delegation officials—Ben Cohen, John Foster Dulles, and former First Lady Eleanor Roosevelt—were firmly opposed to the imposition of sanctions against Israel in a war that the Arabs had launched with the openly declared purpose of eliminating the State of Israel.[51] The US

---

49. *Foreign Relations of the United States: Diplomatic Papers, 1948, vol. 5,* 1529–1533.
50. *Foreign Relations of the United States: Diplomatic Papers, 1948, vol. 5,* 1534–1535.
51. *Foreign Relations of the United States: Diplomatic Papers, 1948, vol. 5,* 1534–1535, 1540. Ben Cohen had played a leading role as assistant to President Franklin Roosevelt in formulating Roosevelt's New Deal policy. He had also helped in the exchange of documents requesting and granting recognition of the State of Israel. John Foster Dulles, a lawyer close to the Republican candidate for president, Governor Thomas E. Dewey, had been appointed to the US delegation by President Truman in order to provide for continuity in the US delegation to the UN in the event that Dewey would win the presidential election. Dulles served as secretary of state under President Dwight Eisenhower, who succeeded President Truman.

delegation was particularly embarrassed when Israeli representative Abba Eban informed them the day before the UNSC vote that British Minister Hector McNeil had told him very candidly that Britain was pressing for Israel's withdrawal from the Negev because otherwise, it would not be possible to implement the Bernadotte plan. This meant using UNSC not to restore peace but rather as a means of achieving a final settlement that ran counter to the president's commitment to the State of Israel.[52]

The US delegation consequently decided to propose softening the draft resolution in several respects. First, the resolution would "take note of" rather than "endorse" the mediator's proposal. Second, to answer the charge that UNSC would be imposing a final settlement in the guise of enforcing the truce, the resolution would specify that the call upon the interested governments for withdrawal was "without prejudice to their rights, claims, or position with regard to a peaceful adjustment of the future situation or to the position which members of UNSC may wish to take in UNGA on such peaceful adjustment." Finally, the committee to be appointed by UNSC would be asked to report on measures to be taken under the more general heading of Chapter 7 of the UN Charter, which relates to "action with respect to threats to the peace" instead of specifically under article 41 of that chapter, which spells out the range of sanctions that might be employed.[53] On November 4, the day after Truman's reelection as US president, UNSC adopted Resolution 61 (1948) for the withdrawal

---

52. As Abba Eban cabled Shertok, McNeil had told him, "Israel's presence in the Negev was harmful primarily in the political sphere." Abba Eban replied that McNeil's arguments "were not likely to convince us to withdraw from the Negev. In point of fact…the government and people of Israel were united in their opposition for just such reasons… We would lose politically by withdrawing from the Negev; this would settle the outcome of the political struggle in advance" (Ben-Gurion, *Israel: A Personal History*, 295).
53. *Foreign Relations of the United States: Diplomatic Papers, 1948, vol. 5*, 1543–1544.

of Egyptian and Israeli forces from the Negev, as amended by the US.[54]

Israel was unwilling to accede to the request of UNSC, however. On the day of the vote, Foreign Minister Shertok informed Secretary Marshall that Israel was unwilling to withdraw its troops from the area they now held in the Negev, even if the area were to be neutralized and the Egyptian troops were not to be permitted to return. Neutralization would prejudice the final settlement against Israel. The concern of UNSC was with the cessation of hostilities, a result that had already been achieved. Shertok argued that UNSC, therefore, should not take action that would prejudice the UNGA debate on the final disposition of the Negev. Both Transjordan and Egypt had expressed serious interest in opening negotiations, and the UNSC resolution would only serve to impair them. Instead, UNSC should summon both parties to negotiate, either directly or through the mediator, on all outstanding questions.[55]

The following day, November 5, Israel's President Weizmann, in a warm letter of congratulations to President Truman on his reelection, appealed to him not to permit the UK to carry out its plan to detach the Negev from Israel. It was most important, he emphasized, that "the unreal and untenable truce be brought to an end and be supplanted by a speedy and enduring peace… We have no aggressive design against anyone, and we are at any moment ready to negotiate a peace settlement." In the strongest language against the UK he had ever employed in public, Weizmann added:

> We have successfully withstood the onslaught of the Arab states, who were sent against us by the British, almost like a pack of hired assassins… Having failed in her efforts to wipe out our young commonwealth, she now appears bent on detaching the Negev from our state.

---

54. For the text of UNSC Resolution 61, see Appendix 2.
55. *Foreign Relations of the United States: Diplomatic Papers, 1948, vol. 5*, 1544–1545.

Recalling the effective role the president had played in ensuring that the Negev would go to Israel in the UNGA resolution of November 1947, Weizmann urged Truman to intervene once again and to issue firm instructions to the US delegation in Paris in order to prevent this plan from succeeding.[56]

Not all State Department officials were yet convinced that Truman meant to carry out his campaign promise not to approve any change in boundaries from the UNGA 1947 resolution that were not fully acceptable to Israel. On November 5, two days after President Truman's reelection, Robert McClintock sent a memorandum to Acting Secretary of State Lovett in which he declared that it was urgently necessary to review US policy concerning Palestine and to ascertain the president's desires. Summarizing the various positions the president had taken on Palestine, he concluded that the State Department "could fairly recommend to the president" that the US delegation in Paris should:

> …[seek] to secure most of the considerations of the Bernadotte plan, with the important modification that Israel should be permitted to expand its southern frontiers into that portion of the northern Negev, where most of the twenty-three Jewish settlements are situated.[57]

Ambassador Douglas also continued to champion the British cause of using the UN to wrest most, if not all, of the Negev from Israel and transfer it to the Arabs. As late as November 18, Ambassador Douglas urged in a memorandum to Secretary Marshall that the decision on boundaries should not be left to the parties to negotiate but should rather be decided by a UN boundaries commission to be

---

56. Weisgal, *The Letters and Papers of Chaim Weizmann, Series A: Letters*, "Letter 269, November 5, 1948" in *Foreign Relations of the United States: Diplomatic Papers, 1948, vol. 5*, 1549–1551.
57. *Foreign Relations of the United States: Diplomatic Papers, 1948, vol. 5*, 1551–1553.

set up in accordance with the Bernadotte plan. He added that while he was fully cognizant of the president's commitment to Israel in his campaign pledge of October 24, he believed that events that had since occurred in Palestine justified "in all good conscience and without infidelity to campaign utterances, a reevaluation by the president of the statement he then made."[58]

President Truman, however, had no intention of ignoring his campaign pledge after his reelection. On November 10, Acting Secretary of State Lovett transmitted to Secretary Marshall the president's instructions for the US delegation to the UN to act in accordance with his campaign pledge that he would approve no changes in boundaries from the UNGA 1947 resolution that were not acceptable to Israel. In a warm letter of reply on November 29, 1948—the first anniversary of the UNGA 1947 resolution in favor of partition—to Chaim Weizmann's letter of November 5 congratulating the president on his reelection, Truman reiterated his position on the Negev:

> I remember well our conversation about the Negev, to which you refer in your letter. I agree fully with your estimate of the importance of that area to Israel, and I deplore any attempt to take it away from Israel. I had thought that my position would have been clear to all the world, particularly in the light of the specific wording of the Democratic Party platform. But there were those who did not take this seriously, regarding it as "just another campaign promise" to be forgotten after the election. I believe they have recently realized their error. I have interpreted my reelection as a mandate from the American people to carry out the Democratic platform—including, of course, the plank on Israel. I intend to do so.[59]

---

58. *Foreign Relations of the United States: Diplomatic Papers, 1948, vol. 5*, 1610–1613.
59. As noted in Chapter 15, President Truman ended his letter with the comment, "In closing, I want to tell you how happy and impressed I have been at the remarkable progress made by the new State of Israel. What you have received at the hands of the world has been far less than was your due.

– 18 –

Armistice and Admission of Israel to UN

No sooner had UNSC adopted Resolution 61 of November 4, 1948 calling for withdrawal of Egyptian and Israeli forces to their October 14 positions in the Negev (subject to threat of enforcement under Chapter 7 of the UN Charter) than Acting Mediator Ralph Bunche realized that the resolution would prove futile. In the absence of armistice negotiations, Israel would continue to refuse to withdraw, and UNSC would be incapable of enforcing its resolution. On November 6, only two days after UNSC adopted Resolution 61, Bunche took the decisive step—a step that Bernadotte on September 16 had considered premature—of calling for negotiations between the parties, as Israel had requested. He recommended a draft resolution according to which UNSC would recognize that the truce must be considered as a first stage in the effort to restore peace, and it would call upon the parties to the conflict to undertake to begin negotiations immediately, either directly or through the acting mediator for the UN.[1]

The United Nations Security Council's Call for the Negotiation of Armistice Agreements

The UK government was vigorously opposed to Bunche's initiative, arguing that his proposal would in effect supersede the UNSC

But you have more than made the most of what you have received, and I admire you for it" (Truman, *Memoirs*, vol. 2, 168–169 in *Foreign Relations of the United States: Diplomatic Papers, 1948, vol. 5*, 1633–1634).

1. *Foreign Relations of the United States: Diplomatic Papers, 1948, vol. 5*, 1555–1556.

resolution of November 4, 1948 with its call for Israeli withdrawal from the Negev. Instead, Britain proposed to extend the scope of the November 4 resolution to include a demand for Israel's withdrawal from positions it had gained in the Galilee as well as in the Negev. France and Canada, however, strongly favored the Bunche initiative, maintaining that the November 4 resolution had been a mistake, because Israel would not comply in the absence of negotiations and UNSC would not be able to follow through with its threat of enforcement under Chapter 7. The US likewise supported the Bunche initiative, and it persuaded Britain to drop its proposal to extend the scope of the November 4 resolution. That resolution had served its purpose, the US argued, and to push it further would court disaster in UNSC. In an important concession to the UK, however, the US proposed the addition of a preambular clause to Bunche's draft resolution, stating that UNSC's call for negotiations was without prejudice to action of the acting mediator in their implementation of the UNSC resolution of November 4, 1948.[2] In light of this concession, the UK yielded.

On November 16, UNSC, giving effect to the Bunche initiative, adopted Resolution 62, in which it decided that an armistice would be established in all sectors of Palestine. The resolution called upon the parties to enter negotiations immediately either directly or through the acting mediator, with the goal of immediately establishing the armistice. Included in the negotiations would be the delineation of permanent armistice demarcation lines beyond which the armed forces should not move and such withdrawal and reduction of the armed forces as would ensure the maintenance of the armistice during the transition to permanent peace.[3]

---

2. *Foreign Relations of the United States: Diplomatic Papers, 1948, vol. 5,* 1559–1560, 1574–1577, 1582–1583.
3. United Nations Security Council, Resolution 62, Document S/1080(1948) (November 16, 1948), accessed on August 19, 2023, https://documents-dds-ny.un.org/doc/RESOLUTION/GEN/NR0/047/87/PDF/NR004787.pdf?OpenElement.

Israel heartily welcomed this turning point in UNSC's deliberations. In light of the call for armistice negotiations, Israel announced on November 19 its agreement to Bunche's earlier request, made under UNSC Resolution 61 of November 4, for their withdrawal to their previous positions of those troops that had entered the Negev after October 14. In accordance with its understanding of the acting mediator's order, troops who had been in the Negev before October 14 would remain, however. At the same time, Israel urged the acting mediator to announce the time and place of a meeting with the authorized representatives of the Arab governments for the purpose of opening direct negotiations.[4] Bunche declared himself satisfied and considered Israel's action to be statesmanlike.[5]

Britain's Continued Insistence on Transferring the Negev to the Arabs

Great Britain's acceptance of UNSC Resolution 62 calling for negotiations between the parties did not mean that it was ready to give up its campaign concerning the Negev. On the contrary, the UK sought UNGA approval of the Bernadotte plan for detachment of the Negev from Israel and the transfer thereof to the Arabs, preferably to Transjordan. On November 18, only two days after UNSC adopted Resolution 62, Great Britain submitted a draft resolution jointly with China according to which UNGA would endorse the specific conclusions of the Bernadotte plan and establish a conciliation commission to carry out the functions assigned to it in the resolution in accordance with that plan. The proposed conciliation commission would be instructed to appoint a technical boundaries commission to assist the parties in delimiting the boundaries in Palestine based on the conclusions in the Bernadotte plan.

---

4. Ben-Gurion, *Israel: A Personal History*, 309–311.
5. *Foreign Relations of the United States: Diplomatic Papers, 1948, vol. 5,* 1614–1616.

The UK–China draft resolution ran counter to the position that President Truman had directed the US delegation to follow. When Britain rejected the US suggestions to drop its insistence upon implementation of the Bernadotte plan, the US delegation was compelled to make public its differences with Great Britain.[6] In a speech to the UNGA First (Political and Security) Committee on November 20, 1948, US Ambassador Philip Jessup declared, in accordance with the president's instructions, that Israel was entitled to the boundaries established in the UN resolution of November 29, 1947; that any changes to those boundaries could be made only if they were acceptable to Israel; and that if Israel desired additional territory, it must offer an appropriate exchange through negotiations. Britain's Foreign Office called the US speech worse than it had expected.[7]

The UK–China draft resolution encountered fierce opposition from the Arab states no less than from Israel. The Arab states were as opposed to the Bernadotte plan for its recognition of the existence of the State of Israel, and Israel was opposed to it because of its proposed transfer of the Negev to the Arabs. On November 30, Great Britain reluctantly agreed to a compromise proposal of the US, dropping its insistence upon UNGA's explicit endorsement of the Bernadotte plan and upon instructing the conciliation commission to act in accordance with that plan. Instead, the revised draft called for the proposed conciliation commission to consider certain modifications to the territorial arrangements of the UNGA November 29, 1947 resolution, taking into account the recommendation of the Bernadotte plan in relation to the Negev.

The Arabs were opposed to this draft as well, and on December 4, the revised British draft passed in the UNGA First Committee by a vote of only twenty-five to twenty-one, with nine abstentions. This margin was insufficient for adoption in the UNGA plenary session, which requires a two-thirds majority for the approval of a substantive

---

6. *Foreign Relations of the United States: Diplomatic Papers, 1948, vol. 5,* 1603–1610.
7. *Foreign Relations of the United States: Diplomatic Papers, 1948, vol. 5,* 1617.

resolution. On December 11, UNGA adopted instead Resolution 194(III), which eliminated all references both to the Bernadotte plan and to the original plan for partition contained in the UNGA 1947 resolution. Resolution 194(III) provided for the establishment of a conciliation commission to take over the functions that had been assigned to the mediator by UNGA Resolution 186(S-2) of May 14, 1948. The mediator's office was to be terminated upon UNSC action similar to UNGA's action to transfer its assignments from the mediator to the proposed conciliation commission. The resolution called upon the parties to negotiate agreements, either directly or through the conciliation commission, to reach a final settlement concerning all outstanding questions. As in UNGA Resolution 181(II) for partition, a separate international regime was to be established for Jerusalem but with provision for maximum local autonomy. And unlike the Bernadotte plan, which had called for the right of Arab refugees to return to their homes without regard to Israel's concerns for its security, the resolution limited this right to refugees who wish "to live at peace with their neighbors."[8] In addition, unlike the Bernadotte plan, which provided only for Arab refugees, this resolution provided for all refugees, without any differentiation between Arabs and Jews. Jews expelled from the Arab areas of Palestine and from all Arab lands as

---

8. The entire Arab bloc of UN members of UNGA at the time voted against UNGA Resolution 194(III). Nevertheless, the Palestinian Arabs and their supporters have since adopted its paragraph on refugees as their key weapon to undermine the State of Israel by insisting that the resolution establishes an unlimited right of return of Arab refugees to Israel. On the one hand, they ignore the resolution's limitation for repatriation to refugees who wish to live at peace with their neighbors, and on the other hand, they insist that the right of return includes millions of descendants and other relatives who never lived in Israel. Even many of the Arabs who did live in Israel were not permanent residents there but had rather gone there to take up jobs created by Israeli development of the country. The UN refugee organization, UNRWA, includes as refugees anyone who lived in Israel for two years.

a result of the war could therefore presumably claim the same rights as Arab refugees from the area that is now Israel.[9]

Even the defeat of Britain's proposal in UNGA failed to persuade it to abandon its campaign for detachment of the Negev from Israel. It continued, instead, to discourage negotiations between Israel and the Arabs, and it supported Egypt's demand for Israel's complete withdrawal from the Negev under UNSC Resolution 61 of November 4. Bunche had informed the Arab governments on November 26, in accordance with UNSC Resolution 62 of November 16, of Israel's willingness to open peace negotiations. Egypt refused to negotiate, however, insisting instead that Israel should relinquish its gains from its victory in the Negev by freeing the Egyptian army that it had bottled up and by permitting an Egyptian military governor to return to rule Beer Sheva. Israel informed the acting mediator that it rejected any return to the *status quo ante*, and in the absence of negotiations, it refused to free the Egyptian forces.

On December 1, Egypt called for a UNSC session to force Israel to accede to its demand. Egypt's hopes to gain the Negev for itself suffered a severe blow the same day, however, at a Palestine Arab conference held in Jericho and attended by the mayors of major Arab cities in Palestine. The conference adopted a resolution declaring that the Palestine Arabs desired the immediate annexation of Arab Palestine to Transjordan, the recognition of Abdullah of Transjordan as their king, and the proclamation of Abdullah as king of the new territory.[10] On December 13, 1948, the resolution was approved by Transjordan's parliament, and the necessary modification of the constitution was passed into law, the combined area being named the Hashemite Kingdom of Jordan. The area formerly called Transjordan

---

9. United Nations General Assembly, Resolution 194(III)—Palestine: Progress Report of the United Nations Mediator, Document A/RES/194(III) (December 11, 1948), accessed on August 9, 2023, https://digitallibrary.un.org/record/670969?ln=en.
10. *Foreign Relations of the United Nations: Diplomatic Papers, 1948, vol. 5*, 1645–1646.

became East Jordan, and Arab Palestine—which until then even the Arabs had called by their biblical names, Judea and Samaria—was renamed the West Bank.[11]

Glubb Pasha, the commander of Jordan's Arab Legion, maintained that the unification of Arab Palestine with Transjordan was not a plot by King Abdullah but rather was the "spontaneous and genuine desire of the Palestinian people," because "Without a government or an army of their own, they had no alternative but to join another government, the army of which was already defending their country." He noted, "In spite of the opposition of all the other Arab countries, the Arabs of Palestine have never shown the least inclination to reverse their decision of December 1, 1948."[12]

Egypt, however, was convinced that King Abdullah would not have dared permit such a conference to be held and such a resolution to be adopted unless he was confident of Britain's support for his ambitions. The Jericho resolution thus placed Egypt at odds with Great Britain as well as with Transjordan. Like Egypt, the Arab League, Syria, Saudi Arabia, and Yemen, all declared their opposition to King Abdullah's bid to take over Arab Palestine.[13] Despite its pro-Arab, anti-Israel policy, Britain had now incurred the ill will of virtually all the Arab states—except for Transjordan—which had invaded Israel.

On November 29, 1948, the first anniversary of the UNGA 1947 resolution for the partition of Palestine, Israel submitted its application for membership in the UN. Despite US support for Israeli membership, the UK, on December 8, doomed the prospects for UNSC approval when it called for an emergency session of UNSC in order to force Israel's compliance, under threat of sanctions, with

---

11. See Glubb, *A Soldier with the Arabs*, 216–217, 237, and the map on 144.
12. Glubb, *A Soldier with the Arabs*, 217. The situation changed with Israel's conquest of the West Bank in 1967. Since then, the Palestinian Arabs have demanded an independent state of their own, a demand to which the government of Israel has now agreed in principle.
13. *Foreign Relations of the United States: Diplomatic Papers, 1948, vol. 5*, 1667–1668, fn. 1.

the Egyptian demand for their withdrawal from the Negev. The US delegation again had to take a public stand in opposition to Britain. It proposed that with the assistance of the acting mediator, it should be possible to reach an agreement involving the simultaneous implementation of the November 4 resolution for withdrawal and the November 16 resolution for negotiations with a view to establishing an armistice. There would, then, be no need for UNSC to consider the matter further.[14]

As James McDonald, the US special representative to Israel, cabled President Truman's Special Counsel Clark Clifford two days later, the UK's call for an emergency session was a "dangerous maneuver to embarrass the US and other countries" that were urging the approval of Israel's admission as a UN member. The central fact remained, he warned, that "the UK must desire peace and convince [the] Arab states of such desire before any peace becomes possible."[15]

Britain's Conservative Party finally broke sharply with the Labour government's Palestine policy, arguing that it was driving a dangerous wedge between the US and the UK at a time when the UK was financially dependent upon the US Marshall Plan for economic recovery from the effects of World War II. In the parliamentary debate on December 9 and 10, 1948, both Winston Churchill and his former foreign secretary, Anthony Eden, declared their firm opposition to the government's Palestine policy. Charging that Bevin's blundering Palestine policy had harmed the country's relations with the US, Eden demanded that Britain should give *de facto* recognition to Israel. Churchill followed the next day with a speech supporting Eden's demand, noting that in the last election, the Labour Party had gained votes by promises of concessions to the Jews on Palestine issues but that "when they came into office, they turned their backs on it all, raising bitter feelings of disappointment and anger." Declaring Bevin's

---

14. *Foreign Relations of the United States: Diplomatic Papers, 1948, vol. 5,* 1654–1655.
15. *Foreign Relations of the United States: Diplomatic Papers, 1948, vol. 5,* 1658–1659.

treatment of the Palestine problem a "lamentable tale of prejudice and incapacity," he warned that Israel "cannot be ignored and treated as if it did not exist."[16]

Bevin still refused to budge. On December 17, UNSC rejected Israel's application for membership in the UN by a vote of five in favor to one against (Syria), with five abstentions (the UK, Belgium, Canada, China, and France). Since the draft resolution fell short of the required seven affirmative UNSC votes, Israel's application for membership failed. Despite Bevin's repeated insistence on the need to formulate an agreed US–UK policy on Palestine, the UK Foreign Office blocked the adoption of a UNSC resolution that the US had strongly favored.

Three days later, on December 20, Bevin held another of his recurrent meetings with US Ambassador Douglas, to which he invited British chiefs of staff and key Foreign Office officials, in order to renew his government's appeal for US support for his Palestine policy. The chiefs of staff emphasized once again, as they had in past meetings, the importance of Britain's strategic requirements in the Negev and the need to have the Negev safe in Arab hands in order to safeguard British interests. Bevin complained that he had banked on US support for the Bernadotte plan to transfer the Negev to the Arabs, but the US had urged postponement of the UN's consideration of the Palestine issue until after the US elections, only to announce subsequently that it would not support the proposals. He maintained that it was essential for the Negev to be safely in Arab hands because the prospects in the foreseeable future for the UK to obtain its strategic requirements in the Negev from Israel were poor. Instead, he claimed that the possibility must be faced that "within five years," Israel may become Communist, because most of its immigrants were emigrating to Israel from countries behind the Iron Curtain, where they had been exposed to Communist philosophy. In fact, the risk of Communism in Israel was probably smaller at the time than it was in war-shattered

---

16. Rhodes James, *Winston S. Churchill: His Complete Speeches*, 7766–7767.

Britain—the Jewish immigrants who had lived under Communist rule had always been among its most passionate opponents.

Bevin did make one concession—he was now willing for Israel to keep the northern Negev area, but he continued to insist that the rest of the Negev, including Beer Sheva, must be in Arab hands. He proposed that the US and the UK should reach an understanding concerning the location of Israel's boundaries in the Negev and should ensure that the conciliation commission to be set up under UNGA Resolution 194(III) of December 11 would, within the next ninety days, achieve a settlement that would establish those boundaries.[17]

The Routing of Egypt in the Negev and Britain's War Threats against Israel

In view of Egypt's refusal to negotiate and Bevin's insistence on transferring the Negev to the Arabs, Ben-Gurion decided that military action was necessary to force the Egyptian army out of all the Negev. On December 22, after UNSC's rejection of Israel's application for UN membership and following several local Egyptian attacks on Israeli forces, Israel launched its attack. In a short while, Israel succeeded in driving Egypt completely out of the Negev. Indeed, within a few days, Israeli forces crossed into Egypt in hot pursuit of the enemy.

Anxious over the risk of complete defeat, Britain notified the State Department on December 26 of its intention to submit a draft resolution calling upon UNSC to reaffirm its resolutions of November 4 and 16 and to consider possible action under Chapter 7 of the UN Charter. The State Department rejected the UK's request for US support, seeing no point in reaffirming resolutions that had already been violated.[18] The UK nevertheless submitted its draft resolution to UNSC, and on December 29, UNSC adopted Resolution 66 (1948)

---

17. *Foreign Relations of the United States: Diplomatic Papers, 1948, vol. 5,* 1680–1685.
18. *Foreign Relations of the United States: Diplomatic Papers, 1948, vol. 5,* 1691–1692.

calling upon the Israeli and Egyptian governments to order an immediate ceasefire and to implement—without further delay—the UNSC resolution of November 4 concerning withdrawal. It also instructed the UNSC committee appointed under its November 4 resolution to report by January 7, 1949 on the extent of the Israeli and Egyptian governments' compliance with the present resolution and with the UNSC resolutions of November 4 and 16. The UNSC resolution was adopted by a vote of eight to none, with the US abstaining along with the Soviet Union and the Ukraine. Again, Britain had forced an open policy split with the US.

Alarmed by the magnitude of the developing Israeli victory in the Negev, Britain submitted a *note verbale* to Acting Secretary of State Lovett on December 30, 1948 in which it threatened to defend Egypt in accordance with the Anglo–Egyptian Treaty of 1936. The State Department asked UK Ambassador Sir Oliver Franks whether this treaty would be invoked by the UK or by Egypt, particularly in light of the fact that Egypt had sought in 1947 to have UNSC declare the treaty invalid.[19] The ambassador was unable to give a definite answer. Sir Franks also charged that King Abdullah had received a message from the Jews that the time for armistice negotiations had passed, that

---

19. Great Britain had maintained troops in Egypt under the Anglo–Egyptian Treaty of 1936. On July 8, 1947, the prime minister of Egypt addressed a letter to the secretary-general of the UN declaring that the British troops were being maintained in Egypt against the unanimous will of the Egyptian people and that their presence was a violation of the UN Charter. He asked UNSC to order the immediate evacuation of the troops from Egypt, including the Sudan, along with the termination of the administrative regime in the Sudan. (Sudan had not yet received its independence at the time but rather was administered jointly by Egypt and the UK, even though Egypt claimed it as Egyptian territory). At the opening of the UNSC debate on August 5, 1947, Egypt's prime minister argued that the 1936 Anglo–Egyptian treaty was no longer valid, because it had been signed under duress and was contrary to the UN Charter. Although UNSC discussed the issue in several sessions during the year, it did not adopt any of the draft resolutions that had been submitted.

the Jews were now interested only in negotiating peace, and that if it was not to be peace, it would be war. Britain accordingly felt bound to take the necessary steps to protect its own troops and installations in Transjordan. It would then proceed to move equipment into Transjordan and would no longer be able to refuse to carry out British contracts to arm the Arab countries.[20]

Lovett warned Sir Franks against renewing arms shipments to the Arabs, emphasizing that this would be a clear violation of UNSC's arms embargo and that it would also subject the US to pressure to lift its own arms embargo. President Truman, with whom Lovett discussed the UK's *note verbale* at 12:30 p.m. the same day (December 30, 1948), instructed him to cable the president's special representative in Israel, James McDonald, that the president was directing him to see Foreign Minister Shertok and Prime Minister Ben-Gurion immediately (as well as, at his discretion, President Weizmann) to inform Israel of Britain's threat regarding Israel's reported invasion of Egyptian territory. He was instructed to add the warning that the US would have to reconsider its own attitude toward Israel, including admission of Israel as a UN member state, unless Israel withdrew its forces from Egypt. McDonald was to add a similar warning in case the UK's report of Israel's threatening attitude toward Transjordan was confirmed.[21]

Israel was upset with the tone of the US protest, with Ben-Gurion commenting that it could have been written by Bevin.[22] Even Weizmann sent a personal letter of protest to Truman. While expressing his deep appreciation for the president's great contributions to the solution to the problem in his refusal to follow ill-advised British policies, he declared that he was unable to square the US warning concerning its support of Israel's membership in the UN with US

---

20. *Foreign Relations of the United States: Diplomatic Papers, 1948, vol. 5,* 1701–1703.
21. *Foreign Relations of the United States: Diplomatic Papers, 1948, vol. 5,* 1704.
22. *Foreign Relations of the United States: Diplomatic Papers, 1949, vol. 6,* 594–595.

sponsorship of Egypt's election to UNSC (beginning in January 1949). Egypt had acted as an aggressor in invading and attacking Israel, whereas Israel had acted only in self-defense.[23]

Israel assured the US that its forces had crossed into Egypt only in hot pursuit, that it had no designs on Egyptian territory, that its forces would speedily withdraw from Egypt, and that it stood ready to begin negotiations with Egypt. Together with this assurance, Israel expressed its resentment that the UK, which had encouraged the invasion of Palestine by Egypt and the other Arab states and had consistently defended this aggression in defiance of the UN Charter, was now coming to the defense of the aggressor in order to prevent its ejection from territory where it had no right to be.

Israel also noted that the reported threat against Transjordan was wholly without foundation and that on the contrary, the provisional Israeli government was in fact actively engaged in secret negotiations with Transjordan precisely with the aim of achieving an armistice agreement.[24] As McDonald reported on January 2, 1949, secret preliminary armistice negotiations between Israel and Transjordan had begun on December 25, 1948 in a cordial atmosphere, and a second meeting had been held on December 30, 1948.[25] The secrecy was intended to avoid possible embarrassment to King Abdullah and to prevent British interference.[26]

McDonald had also cabled President Truman and Acting Secretary of State Lovett on New Year's Day that the US representations had been interpreted in Israeli quarters as an indication of a reversal of US support in favor of the old British line. He also noted that at approximately 2:30 a.m. that morning, two Egyptian warships had

---

23. *Foreign Relations of the United States: Diplomatic Papers, 1949, vol. 6,* 594–595, 600–601.
24. *Foreign Relations of the United Nations: Diplomatic Papers, 1949, vol. 6,* 605–606.
25. Additional secret meetings were held on January 5 and 10, 1949.
26. *Foreign Relations of the United States: Diplomatic Papers, 1949, vol. 6,* 598–599.

approached off the coast to attack Tel Aviv and that Tel Aviv batteries had responded to the attack fire. While there were no hits and no casualties, Tel Aviv had issued a warning that if Egypt would repeat its attacks against Israeli civilians, Israel would take appropriate countermeasures against Egypt, including, in particular, the Egyptian capital, Cairo. McDonald added a warning of his own: that in forcing Israel to withdraw from Egyptian territory, the US had assumed a serious responsibility in case the withdrawal would again jeopardize Israeli forces in the Negev and would encourage Egypt to continue its attacks on Israeli territory.[27]

McDonald's cables apparently had their effect on the State Department. On January 2, Lovett asked the British embassy in Washington, DC to inform the British Foreign Office that in view of Israel's decision to withdraw all its forces from Egyptian territory, the State Department strongly believed that the UK should impress upon the Egyptians the necessity of refraining from further attacks such as the one on Tel Aviv. Otherwise, it would set off a chain of reprisals that would jeopardize any progress toward a final settlement.[28] Significantly, Lovett cabled the US embassy in Egypt the next day, January 3, to seek an immediate audience with King Farouk. The king was to be informed of the US representations to Israel against any invasion of Egypt and of Israel's assurances of the withdrawal of its forces from Egyptian territory. In the same friendly spirit, the US felt it necessary to express its concern that Egypt should comply with UNSC Resolution 62 of November 16 and promptly undertake negotiations with the goal of an armistice. Lovett added that in light of Israel's assurances of the withdrawal of its forces from Egyptian territory, the US could expect no less from Egypt than a policy of wise restraint with respect to further hostilities against Israel, such as the attack on Tel Aviv by two Egyptian ships and a reported bombing of Jerusalem. Lovett concluded with the following statement:

27. *Foreign Relations of the United States: Diplomatic Papers, 1949, vol. 6,* 595–596.
28. *Foreign Relations of the United States: Diplomatic Papers, 1949, vol. 6,* 596.

It should be urged upon [the] king in [the] most serious terms that [the] American government and people feel [the] time has come to make peace in Palestine. It is essential that hostilities should cease and that statesmanship should be employed to establish lasting peace.[29]

As the Egyptian public learned the news of the complete rout of its army in the Negev, enraged Moslem fundamentalists set off riots and assassinated the Egyptian prime minister. Egypt at last came to realize that its war in the Negev served only Britain's strategic interests, and the new Egyptian government turned down the British offer to invoke the Anglo–Egyptian Treaty of 1936.[30] It decided instead to enter armistice arrangements with Israel, as the US had urged. On January 5, 1949, the Egyptian government declared its readiness to begin armistice negotiations with Israel, and Israel agreed. On January 6, Bunche informed the president of UNSC that Israel and Egypt had unconditionally accepted his proposal for a ceasefire to come into effect on January 7, 1949. The ceasefire was to be followed immediately by direct negotiations between the two parties, under UN chairmanship, on the implementation of the UNSC resolutions of November 4 and 16. In accordance with this announcement, the armistice negotiations opened in Rhodes, Greece on January 13, 1949 under Bunche's chairmanship.

Bevin was still not willing to permit the negotiations between Israel and the Arabs to go ahead without hindrance. Still determined to detach the Negev from Israel, he instructed UK Ambassador Sir Franks on January 3, 1949 "to urge that the US and UK come to very firm conclusions and fix definite boundaries and thus arrive at [a] final settlement which will save [the] Middle East."

On January 4, the US embassy in the UK cabled the US secretary of state the information it had received from the UK Foreign Office:

---

29. *Foreign Relations of the United States: Diplomatic Papers, 1949, vol. 6*, 602–603.
30. Kirk, *The Middle East 1945–1950*, 292–293.

that Britain had advised King Abdullah not to finalize any agreement with Israel before the arrival of the Conciliation Commission. It had also counseled that it regarded a reasonable settlement with Israel to run along the lines it had previously discussed with the US, setting Israel's boundaries to the north of the Gaza–Beer Sheva road held by Egypt before Israel's seizure of the area in October 1948.[31]

At his meeting with Lovett on January 5, 1949, Sir Franks urged the US to exert pressure on the provisional Israeli government to withdraw to the lines in the Negev set by Bunche following UNSC Resolution 61 of November 4, 1948. Lovett firmly turned down this request, noting it would not be proper for the US to take on the responsibility of UNSC in applying its resolutions unilaterally. The ambassador then asked if the US could instruct the American representative on the Conciliation Commission to use his good influence to further this objective. Lovett replied that the American representative would naturally follow the main lines of US policy, which had already been made public by Ambassador Jessup in UNGA on November 20, 1948. According to this policy, he reminded Sir Franks, Israel was entitled to the boundaries set forth in the UNGA 1947 resolution. If it wished, however, to retain additional territory that it had since gained, such as western Galilee, it would have to offer compensation in some part of the Negev.

Sir Franks added that he had received permission to inform the US that the UK would shortly send a force to occupy Aqaba. Lovett replied that the US did not wish to receive this information officially and that such movement of British troops into Transjordan would be construed as a violation of UNSC Resolution 50 of May 29, 1948, which explicitly prohibited the movement of military personnel into Palestine or the neighboring countries. Despite Britain's insistence on Israel's observance of UNSC resolutions under threat of sanctions, Britain did not hesitate to occupy Aqaba on January 8, 1949, claiming that it was acceding to a request from Transjordan under the terms of

---

31. *Foreign Relations of the United States: Diplomatic Papers, 1949, vol. 6*, 607.

the Anglo–Transjordanian Treaty of March 1948.[32] This unprovoked action in violation of the UNSC Resolution 50 was evidently a show of force in the face of the official armistice negotiations that were about to take place between Israel and Egypt as well as of the private negotiations that were being held between Israel and Transjordan.

Adding yet another obstacle to the armistice negotiations, Britain sent out Royal Air Force planes on January 7, 1949 on two armed reconnaissance missions on the border between Israel and Egypt to check on Israeli compliance with the ceasefire order, which Acting Mediator Bunche had announced would take effect that day. As the planes crossed into Israeli air space, the new Israeli air force shot down four of the planes from the first British mission and one plane from the second mission, without suffering any casualties of its own.

On January 10, McDonald cabled President Truman and Acting Secretary of State Lovett that all his key staff believed that British actions in sending Royal Air Force reconnaissance flights over battle areas and the subsequent landing of British troops in Aqaba appeared to be determined efforts to forestall direct negotiations both between Israel and Egypt as well as between Israel and Transjordan—and these actions were destroying the opportunities for peace. McDonald urged the US to continue, as it had been doing since the turn of the year, to press London and the countries in the Middle East on the need to proceed with direct armistice negotiations.[33]

In a letter dated January 11, Israel filed a complaint with UNSC "against the menacing attitude adopted by the UK towards the State of Israel." The letter warned:

> The military, naval, aerial, and political measures which the UK has taken in recent days appear likely to endanger the maintenance of international peace and security and to widen the

---

32. *Foreign Relations of the United States: Diplomatic Papers, 1949, vol. 6*, 611–613 and fns.
33. *Foreign Relations of the United States: Diplomatic Papers, 1949, vol. 6*, 639–640.

limits of a local conflict which might otherwise respond to the processes of unprejudiced negotiations.[34]

The following day, Eliahu Epstein and Abba Eban, Israel's representatives to the US and UN, respectively, discussed Israel's concerns about the UK's actions with Acting Secretary of State Lovett. Eban said that the Israeli public feared that Britain might send troops into Palestine and thought that some UNSC action might be desirable to avert this possibility. Lovett replied that it was highly unlikely that Britain had any such aggressive plans and urged Israel not to aggravate the situation by a call for UNSC action. What the situation required, Lovett advised, was the highest degree of restraint and statesmanship to avoid extending the scope of the conflict in Palestine. It was necessary, instead, to proceed with the armistice negotiations in Rhodes.[35]

That same afternoon, January 12, Bevin made a final attempt to persuade the US to support his two objectives of wresting the Negev from Israel and resuming the UK's shipment of arms to the Arabs. Acting under Bevin's personal instructions, UK Ambassador Sir Franks transmitted two telegrams to Lovett, the first urging, yet again, US support on strategic grounds for pushing Israel's boundaries in the Negev back to the north of the Gaza–Beer Sheva road and the second repeating once more the threat to resume shipment of arms and war material to the Arab states. The following day, Sir Franks took up Bevin's request with President Truman. In what Sir Franks regarded as a friendly—but firm and frank—manner, Lovett and the president turned down Bevin's requests for US support for his plans for Palestine.

To Bevin's query about the US attitude concerning the strategic road in the Negev, Lovett replied that the importance of this strategic

---

34. *Foreign Relations of the United States: Diplomatic Papers, 1949, vol. 6*, 643, fn. 1.
35. *Foreign Relations of the United States: Diplomatic Papers, 1949, vol. 6*, 645–647.

road had been mentioned very late in the day and that ever since the autumn of 1947, the president and other officials had reiterated that Israel was entitled to all of the Negev as assigned to it in the UN 1947 resolution. To Sir Franks' comment that the British government's concern over its strategic interests in the Negev stemmed from Britain's lack of confidence in Israel's attitude, Lovett replied that real strategic security lay in encouraging a westward outlook in Israel. "Confining Israel in a straitjacket" and surrounding it "with a circle of weak Arab enemies kept in ring only by British armed assistance," Lovett declared, would inevitably result in creation of a hostile Israel. "Real security, therefore, lay not in any particular road in [the] Negev but in [the] attitude of Israel, which would be conditioned by [the] attitude of [the] Great Powers."

To Bevin's query whether the US supported UNSC Resolution 61 of November 4, 1948 and Resolution 66 of December 29, 1948 calling for Israel's withdrawal from the Negev, Lovett pointed out that Bevin was apparently visualizing technical truce lines as constituting the terms for the final political settlement. The US position, however, was that UNSC resolutions were valid only in their limited application to the momentary military situation but not to set out a final political settlement. That was left to the Palestine Conciliation Commission under UNGA Resolution 194(III) of December 11, 1948. The US position on the final settlement, Lovett again reminded Sir Franks, had been stated by Ambassador Jessup at the UN on November 20, 1948, according to which Israel was entitled to all of the Negev under UNGA Resolution 181(II) of November 29, 1947 but that if it insisted on retaining Arab areas since gained, such as western Galilee, Israel should offer compensation elsewhere, such as in part of the Negev. It was difficult to understand why the UK foreign secretary, who had remained silent in 1947 when the UN awarded all of the Negev to Israel, displayed such excitement now, when Israel might have to relinquish part of the area.

Lovett's response was exceptionally candid in regard to Bevin's urging that the two governments should get together and "do something" about the Palestine situation. The US, he stated, had been doing a great deal, getting Israel to withdraw from Egypt as well as influencing Egypt to accept a ceasefire and to open armistice negotiations with Israel under UN auspices. The UK, on the other hand, had perhaps been doing too much in a non-constructive sense. Sending troops to Aqaba, deploying Royal Air Force planes over the battlefield, and threatening naval movements in the Mediterranean certainly did not encourage the Israelis to believe that the UK was moving for peace. If Israel were to bring its charges against the UK before UNSC, Lovett added, "It could present [an] eloquent case which would do neither [the] US nor [the] UK any good." Israel's representative had been in to see him that same afternoon, and he had had to do his utmost to persuade the Israeli provisional government not to bring its differences with the UK before UNSC.[36]

Finally, Lovett warned yet again that Bevin's resumed threat to send arms to the Arab states would arouse considerable animosity in Israel, would place Britain in violation of the UNSC resolution despite Bevin's insistence on Israeli compliance with UNSC resolutions, and would force the US to lift its embargo against arms shipments to Israel. This would have the unhappy consequence of Britain arming the Arabs and the US arming Israel.

State Department records do not contain the president's response to Bevin's intervention. According to the first secretary of the UK embassy, the president responded in terms almost identical to those used by Acting Secretary of State Lovett.[37] James McDonald later wrote that Truman was reported to have told Sir Franks that the UK's reconnaissance flight over the battlefield and the landing of British troops in Aqaba were unwarranted and badly conceived; that Israel's prompt withdrawal from Egypt and its agreement to a ceasefire were proof of its good intentions; and that Anglo–American cooperation

---

36. *Foreign Relations of the United States: Diplomatic Papers, 1949*, vol. 6, 658–661.
37. *Foreign Relations of the United States: Diplomatic Papers, 1949*, vol. 6, 652.

was essential, but the US should be consulted, and its advice should be taken or seriously considered.[38]

Bevin's Surprise Reversal of the United Kingdom's Anti-Israel Policy

The president's and Lovett's frank responses to the UK ambassador, coming upon the heels of the attack in parliament by Churchill and Eden on Bevin's Palestine policy as well as of Egypt's rejection of Bevin's proposal to invoke the Anglo–Egyptian Treaty, evidently had their effect. Even officials within the Labour government, as well as public opinion, had finally come to realize the bankruptcy of Britain's anti-Israel policy. That policy had only infuriated the Jews and gained the ill will of the Arabs, and it was undermining relations between the UK and the US at a time when the UK was dependent upon the US Marshall Plan for assistance with its economic recovery and reconstruction after World War II. On January 13, the day after Lovett's meeting with Sir Franks, the UK embassy's First Secretary Bromley informed Robert McClintock that orders had been issued to the Royal Air Force in Egypt to refrain from further reconnaissance flights. He added that he personally felt that the views expressed by Lovett were completely right.[39]

On January 18, Sir Franks met again with Lovett to report that the conversations with Lovett "had had a material effect on the British government." He thought that Bevin was now "resolutely setting [a] new course." Worried about the accusation from Eden and Churchill that by his blundering policy over Palestine, he had managed to harm US–UK relations, Bevin instructed Sir Franks to leave an *aide memoire* with Lovett, asking for an agreed statement to be released declaring that there was an understanding between the two governments regarding the Middle East. At the same time, he proposed a startling

---

38. McDonald, *My Mission in Israel*, 126.
39. *Foreign Relations of the United States: Diplomatic Papers, 1949, vol. 6,* 651–652.

reversal of British policy. If the US would recognize Transjordan, even *de facto*, this would make it possible for the British government simultaneously to extend *de facto* recognition to the government of Israel. Sir Franks added that Britain intended to announce on Friday, January 21, 1949, the release of the Jewish prisoners in Cyprus.

Lovett replied that the US intended to extend *de jure* recognition to Transjordan as well as to Israel immediately after the elections scheduled to take place in Israel on January 25, 1949, provided, as was hoped, that the government established by the elections would be a moderate government worthy of *de jure* recognition. Lovett also suggested that provided Bevin did not revert to the line he had taken with the US the preceding week, it might be possible either for the president or the new secretary of state (Dean Acheson) to issue a statement to indicate that the two governments were in complete agreement in pursuing a policy designed to restore peace in the Middle East as quickly as possible. Such a statement might be issued in connection with the announcement of the British decision to release the Jews being held prisoner in Cyprus.[40]

A draft statement was prepared in the State Department on January 24 declaring that while there had been differences between Washington, DC and London concerning how best to deal with the problems of Palestine, there had been no difference whatsoever in their main objectives to increase economic well-being and security in the Middle East as well as to accelerate the return of lasting peace in Palestine. Issuance of this statement was premised on the fact that France had extended *de facto* recognition to Israel that day and that Britain was expected to announce a similar decision the same day. However, issuance of the statement had to be delayed, because Bevin decided that morning to postpone announcement of recognition until after British Commonwealth consultations. The Asian Commonwealth members—Pakistan, India and Ceylon (now Sri Lanka)—objected

---

40. *Foreign Relations of the United States: Diplomatic Papers, 1949*, vol. 6, 671–679 and fns, 674, 679.

to recognition of Israel, while Commonwealth members Australia and New Zealand both requested a delay of several days so that they might announce recognition simultaneously with Britain after a scheduled cabinet meeting on January 27, 1949.[41]

In the debate in the House of Commons on January 26, 1949, Bevin attempted to put the best face on his foreign policy, emphasizing the unity between the UK and the US on the basic objectives of achieving peace and security in Palestine as well as improving economic well-being in the region. Churchill responded, however, with a blistering attack on the "right hon. gentleman's astounding mishandling of the Palestine problem," declaring that "no one ever made such sweeping declarations of confidence in himself in dealing with the Palestine problem," and "no one has been proved by events to be more consistently wrong on every turning point and at every moment than he." Britain's misguided policy on Palestine was due, Churchill declared, "not only to mental inertia or lack of grip on the part of the ministers concerned but also, I am afraid, to the very strong and direct streak of bias and prejudice on the part of the foreign secretary."[42]

Recalling Bevin's brushing aside his call six weeks earlier for *de facto* recognition of Israel, Churchill asked what he was going to do now and expressed his regret that "he has not had the manliness to tell us in plain terms tonight and that he preferred to retire under a cloud of inky water and vapour, like a cuttlefish, to some obscure retreat." Churchill then added (as quoted earlier in Chapter 15):

---

41. *Foreign Relations of the United States: Diplomatic Papers, 1949, vol. 6,* 691–696.
42. Churchill added: "I do not feel any great confidence that he has not got a prejudice against the Jews in Palestine. I am sure that he thought the Arab League was stronger and that it would win if fighting broke out… The course he took led inevitably and directly to a trial of strength, and the result was opposite to what I believe he expected it to be."

The coming into being of a Jewish state in Palestine is an event in world history to be viewed in the perspective not of a generation or a century but in the perspective of a thousand, two thousand, or even three thousand years. That is a standard of temporal values or time values which seems very much out of accord with the perpetual click-clack of our rapidly changing moods and of the age in which we live. This is an event in world history.[43]

The die was now cast. In a stunning reversal of its persistent anti-Israel policy, Britain announced its *de facto* recognition of the State of Israel on January 29, 1949.[44]

On January 31, less than a week after the first elections for a government in Israel, the US granted *de jure* recognition to Israel. At the same time, the US granted *de jure* recognition to Transjordan.

The Signing of the Armistice Agreements

Now that Israel had defeated the Arab forces, Acting Mediator Ralph Bunche discarded the Bernadotte plan and focused his attention instead on the essential task of arranging armistice agreements between Israel and the Arab states. In this he was successful, and he won the Nobel Peace Prize for his efforts. Following his guidance, Israel signed armistice agreements in succession with Egypt, Lebanon, Transjordan, and Syria. Iraq withdrew its forces from Palestine unilaterally in March 1949, and Transjordan's armistice agreement with Israel covered the Iraqi forces as well as its own. The Saudi Arabian forces in Palestine had been under Egyptian command and were covered by the terms of the armistice agreement between Israel and

---

43. Rhodes James, *Winston S. Churchill: His Complete Speeches*, 7776–7777.
44. This was the Jewish Sabbath day, and the new ambassador decided, as a representative of the State of Israel, to go on foot—an hour's walk from his office—to present his credentials to Bevin. Kurzman, *Genesis 1948*, 685–687.

Egypt. Yemen supplied no military forces in the war with Israel, and no armistice agreement was therefore required with that country.

The first of the armistice agreements was signed between Israel and Egypt on February 24, 1949, with the armistice lines drawn at the border that had existed under the Mandate for Palestine, except for the Gaza strip, which Israel allowed Egypt to retain under its control. In return for Egypt's agreement to Israel's retention of the Negev, Israel agreed to permit the Egyptian forces bottled up in the Negev to return home with their weapons.

The armistice agreement between Israel and Lebanon was signed the next month, on March 23, 1949, with the armistice lines drawn along the border that had existed under the Mandate for Palestine. Israel agreed to withdraw its forces from the Lebanese villages that it had seized during the war in pursuit of the Lebanese invading forces. Unlike the other Arab countries, Lebanon did not insist on including a cause disclaiming the armistice lines as the permanent border, such that this border came to be treated as a border *de jure*.

Israel and Transjordan signed an armistice agreement eleven days later, on April 3, 1949, according to which Transjordan's forces were permitted to remain in Old Jerusalem and the West Bank. In return for Transjordan's agreement to withdraw its forces from a strip on the front line in the West Bank, which Israel required for its security, Israel agreed to permit Transjordan to take over the West Bank area that Iraq had previously held.

The agreement between Israel and Syria was signed on July 20, 1949, according to which Syria agreed to withdraw from the area it had taken west of the border that had existed under the Mandate for Palestine. That area was not given to Israel but rather was to be demilitarized.

All the armistice agreements were intended to lead to negotiations concerning permanent peace treaties. They incorporated language by which the parties declared that "with a view to promoting the return to permanent peace in Palestine," both parties affirmed the following principles, which would be fully observed by them:

The injunction of the Security Council against resort to military force in the settlement of the Palestine question shall henceforth be scrupulously respected by both Parties.

No aggressive action by the armed forces—land, sea, or air—of either Party shall be undertaken, planned, or threatened against the people or the armed forces of the other; it being understood that the use of the term "planned" in this context has no bearing on normal staff planning as generally practiced in military organizations.

The right of each Party to its security and freedom from fear of attack by the armed forces of the other shall be fully respected.

The establishment of an armistice between the armed forces of the two Parties is accepted as an indispensable step toward the liquidation of armed conflict and the restoration of peace in Palestine.[45]

In summarizing the armistice negotiations on July 21, 1949, the day after the signing of the Israeli–Syrian armistice agreement, Ralph Bunche emphasized in his final report to UNSC as acting mediator that:

The armistice agreements provide for a definitive end to the fighting in Palestine. Each agreement incorporates what amounts to a non-aggression pact between the parties and provides for withdrawal and reduction of forces. The agreements have all been negotiated at the governmental level and signed for and on behalf of their respective governments by delegations carrying credentials in good order. They are agreements voluntarily entered into by the parties, and any breach of their terms would involve a most serious act of bad faith.[46]

---

45. United Nations Security Council, Egyptian-Israeli General Armistice Agreement, Document S/1264/Rev. 1, Dee. 13 (February 24, 1949), *The Avalon Project*, accessed on July 10, 2023, https://avalon.law.yale.edu/20th_century/arm01.asp.
46. "The War of Independence: Letter from Dr. Bunche to the President of the Security Council, July 21, 1949," *Jewish Virtual Library*, accessed on July

On August 11, 1949, UNSC, in establishing Resolution 73 having noted with satisfaction the conclusion of the armistice agreements, expressed the hope that the parties would, at an early date, "achieve agreement on the final settlement of all questions outstanding between them" and declared that "the armistice agreements constitute an important step toward the establishment of permanent peace in Palestine."

Israel's Admission as a Member State of the United Nations

On March 4, 1949, eight days after the signing of the Israeli–Egyptian Armistice Agreement 1949, UNSC, having received and considered Israel's application for UN membership, decided in Resolution 69 that in its judgment, "Israel is a peace-loving state and is able and willing to carry out the obligations contained in the [UN] Charter." It accordingly recommended to UNGA that it admit Israel as a UN member state. The resolution was adopted by a vote of nine in favor to one—with Egypt voting against and the UK abstaining.

On May 11, 1949, almost on the first anniversary of Israel's rebirth as a state, UNGA, noting UNSC's recommendation in Resolution 69 and Israel's declaration that it "unreservedly [accepted] the obligations of the UN Charter," adopted Resolution 273(III) to admit Israel as a UN member state. The vote, thirty-seven in favor to twelve against, with nine abstentions, was even more favorable than the vote of thirty-three to thirteen, with ten abstentions, for the adoption on November 29, 1947 of UNGA Resolution 181(II) for the partition of Palestine and the establishment of the State of Israel. Despite all the odds in the long journey from the Balfour Declaration of 1917, the State of Israel had finally been accepted as a full member of the world community of nations a year after its rebirth in May 1948.

10, 2023, http://www.jewishvirtuallibrary.org/jsource/History/bunchlet.html.

– 19 –

The Suez War of 1956

The Arab states continued to be unwilling to accept the existence of the State of Israel, even though the 1949 armistice agreements they had signed with Israel included firm pledges against the renewal of hostilities, "with a view to promoting the return to permanent peace in Palestine." Despite the armistice agreements, Arab hostilities against Israel continued.

The Arab League, which had organized a boycott of Jewish goods and services in Mandatory Palestine in 1945, formalized its boycott of the newly established State of Israel in 1948. The Arab boycott—still in effect to this day, even if it has very much weakened—extends beyond the primary boycott of Israel to companies doing business with Israel (the secondary boycott) and to companies that do business with such companies (the tertiary boycott).[1]

Egypt continued to restrict international trade with Israel through the Suez Canal, claiming its right to the "visit, search, and seizure" of ships trading with Israel by virtue of the fact that the Israeli–Egyptian Armistice Agreement 1949 did not terminate the state of war between Egypt and Israel. In his report to UNSC in June 1951, the chief of staff of the UN Truce Supervision Organization declared that Egyptian interference with the passage of goods to Israel through the Suez Canal was an aggressive and hostile act and was contrary to the

---

1. For a study of the Arab boycott and of the US anti-boycott legislation and activities, see Martin A. Weiss, "Arab League Boycott of Israel," *Congressional Research Service*, accessed on July 10, 2023, https://crsreports.congress.gov/product/details?prodcode=RL33961.

spirit of the 1949 Armistice Agreement.[2] He believed, however, that the UN Mixed Armistice Commission was not competent to deal with the matter and that the issue should be referred to a higher body such as UNSC or the International Court of Justice. In July 1951, Israel brought the issue before UNSC, charging that the Egyptian action was in contravention of both the 1949 Armistice Agreement and the 1888 Constantinople Convention governing the operation of the Suez Canal. The 1949 Armistice Agreement included firm pledges against any further acts of hostility between the parties, and the 1888 Constantinople Convention prohibited any interference with the "free use of the [Suez] Canal, in time of war as in time of peace."[3] On September 1, 1951, UNSC agreed with Israel and adopted Resolution 95 (1951) in which it declared that under the armistice agreements, "Neither party can reasonably assert that it is actively a belligerent," and it called upon Egypt "to terminate the restrictions on the passage of international commercial shipping and goods through the Suez Canal, wherever bound." The resolution, co-sponsored by France, the UK, and the US, was approved by a vote of eight in favor, with none voting against and with three abstaining (China, India, and the USSR).[4] Egypt refused, however, to abide by the resolution, and its restrictions against international trade with Israel through the Suez Canal remained in effect.

Syria interfered with Israel's project for draining the malaria-infested Israeli Huleh marshes in the demilitarized zone between Syria and

---

2. For UNSC's consideration of the disputes in 1951 between Israel and the Arab countries at its borders—Egypt, Syria, Jordan, and Lebanon—see United Nations, *Yearbook, 1951*.
3. For the 1888 Constantinople Convention, see "Constantinople Convention, 1888," *Department of Political Science, San Diego State University*, accessed on August 7, 2023, https://loveman.sdsu.edu/docs/1888ConstantinopleConventionon.pdf.
4. For UNSC resolutions, see United Nations Security Council, *Resolutions*, accessed on August 9, 2023, https://www.un.org/securitycouncil/content/resolutions-0.

Israel, which was intended to turn the region into fertile agricultural land. In 1951, Israel complained to UNSC that Syrian soldiers and paramilitary units had attacked Israeli civilians engaged in work in and around the demilitarized zone, killing seven Israeli police officers on routine patrol in one such attack. Syria denied that its forces were involved in the attacks, but the UN Truce Supervision Organization's chief of staff confirmed Israel's charge when the *Syrian Official Gazette* of July 19, 1951 announced the awards of decorations to members of the Syrian armed forces who had participated in the war operations against Israel. The chief of staff agreed that Israel's civilian work in the demilitarized zone was not in violation of the Israeli–Syrian Armistice Agreement of 1949, but he asked Israel to suspend the work on Arab-owned land until an agreement could be reached with the owners. His request was endorsed by UNSC, and Israel sought to buy the Arab land, but when some Arab farmers adamantly refused to sell, lease, or exchange their small plots of land, Israel informed the UN that it could not permit a project of such vital national importance to be held hostage by Syria because of seven acres of land.

Israel also had to cope with continual Palestinian fedayeen terrorist attacks on civilians in towns and villages along all its borders. As casualties mounted and tensions reached an explosive stage, Israelis would retaliate in force against the Arab villages from which the attacks originated. The acts of retaliation that, as in the case of Qibya in Jordan, the Israeli government itself declared a tragic breakdown of restraint, earned Israel repeated resolutions of condemnation by UNSC, which, though it noted the Arab violations, failed to condemn them.[5]

---

5. See United Nations Security Council Resolution 101, November 24, 1953, which "expresses the strongest censure" of Israel's retaliatory action in Qibya against Jordan; Resolution 106, March 29, 1955, which "condemns" Israel's attack against Egypt in the Gaza Strip; and Resolution 111 of January 19, 1956, which "condemns" Israel's retaliatory action against Syria.

The Failure of Attempted Conciliation

The Conciliation Commission, set up under UNGA Resolution 194(III) of December 11, 1948 "to assist the governments and authorities concerned to achieve a final settlement of all questions outstanding between them (Article 6)," worked long and hard but met with no success. In November 1951, after three conferences—in Lausanne in 1949, in Geneva in 1950, and in Paris in 1951—the Conciliation Commission submitted its report to UNGA in which it declared its inability to move the parties toward a final settlement of the outstanding questions between them:

> The Arab states insisted upon a prior solution of the refugee question, at least in principle, before agreeing to discuss other outstanding issues. In their opinion, a solution of the refugee problem could be reached only as a result of unconditional acceptance by Israel of the right of refugees to be repatriated. Israel, on the other hand, has maintained that no solution of the refugee question involving repatriation could be envisaged outside the framework of an overall settlement.
>
> [The Arab parties] evinced no readiness to arrive at such a peace settlement with the government of Israel."[6]

Insisting on what they declared to be the inalienable right of repatriation of the Arab refugees to their previous homes in Israel, the Arab states refused to integrate the Palestinian Arab refugees into their own national economies. Citing UNGA Resolution 194(III)—against which they had cast their votes in 1948—as if it recognized an inalienable right of return, they insisted that Israel must agree to the repatriation of all the Arab refugees. "There could

---

6. United Nations Conciliation Commission for Palestine, Progress Report of the United Nations Conciliation Commission for Palestine to the Sixth Session of the United Nations General Assembly, Document A/1985 (January 23–November 19, 1951), accessed on August 9, 2023, https://www.un.org/unispal/document/auto-insert-186738.

be no limitations on the return of the refugees," the Arabs declared before the Conciliation Commission, adding, "As long as Israel [refuses] to allow the return of the refugees, there could be no peace in the Middle East." Israel, however, rejected mass repatriation, noting that UNGA Resolution 194(III) did not recognize any inalienable, unlimited, right of return for the refugees. It provided only for the return of refugees wishing to "live at peace with their neighbours," and the Arabs showed no willingness to live at peace with Israel. As Israeli Foreign Minister Moshe Sharett declared on June 15, 1949, a month before Syria signed the last of the Arab Armistice Agreements with Israel on July 20, 1949, "A mass repatriation of refugees without peace with the neighbouring countries would thus be an act of suicide on the part of Israel. No state in the world placed in our position would think of doing anything of the sort." Sharett added that owing to the influx of Jewish immigrants and the significant transformation of the Israeli economy that had already taken place, Israel would be able to absorb only a limited number of Arab refugees, even after the Arab states would agree to live in peace with Israel. The solution to the refugee problem lay in an international program for the resettlement of refugees to which Israel was ready to make its contribution.[7]

After the Lausanne Conference in 1949, the Conciliation Commission set up an Economic Survey Mission for the Middle East led by Gordon Clapp, chairman of the US Tennessee Valley Authority. Pursuant to the mission's recommendation in its initial 1949 report, UNGA, in Resolution 302(IV), established UNRWA in December 1949 to add a works program to the relief program that UNGA had originally implemented for the Palestinian refugees.[8] In its final 1949 report, the Economic Survey Mission drew up plans for several national

---

7. "Statement to the Knesset by Foreign Minister Sharett, 15 June 1949," *Israeli Ministry of Foreign Affairs*, accessed July 10, 2023, https://www.gov.il/en/Departments/General/2-statement-to-the-knesset-by-fm-sharett-15-june-1949.
8. For UNGA resolutions, see United Nations General Assembly, *Resolutions*, accessed on August 9, 2023, https://research.un.org/en/docs/ga/quick/regular/77.

development projects to provide work for and ultimate resettlement of the Palestinian refugees in Lebanon, Syria, the Sinai Peninsula, and Jordan.[9] In addition to the national development projects, the mission prepared a draft plan for a regional water development project for the mutual benefit of Israel and three Arab neighbors—Jordan, Lebanon, and Syria—sharing the waters of the Jordan–Yarmouk River system. In October 1953, US President Dwight Eisenhower (1953–1960) appointed Eric Johnston as his personal representative to negotiate such a scheme with Israel and Arab countries and offered to fund two-thirds of the development costs of an agreed regional plan. After negotiations over a three-year period, 1953–1955, Johnston achieved complete agreement between the Israeli and Arab representatives at the technical and legal levels for a specific plan, according to which the waters of the Jordan River and its tributaries in the four countries that were annually going to waste in the Dead Sea would be channeled for regional irrigation. The Arab countries would get sixty-nine percent of the total planned water allocation, and Israel would receive thirty-one percent.[10] The former grand mufti, Haj Amin al-Husseini, living in exile in Egypt and still the head of the Arab Higher Committee for Palestine, called upon the Arab states, however, to reject the plan, denouncing it as an imperialist and Zionist scheme.[11] The Arab League agreed with the grand mufti and rejected the plan, refusing to countenance any benefit to Israel, even though the rejection meant

---

9. United Nations Conciliation Commission for Palestine, Final Report of the United Nations Economic Survey Mission for the Middle East, Document A/AC.25/6 (December 28, 1949), accessed on August 9, 2023, https://digitallibrary.un.org/record/1640579?ln=en.
10. Aaron T. Wolf, "Hydropolitics along the Jordan River: Scarce Water and Its Impact on the Arab–Israeli Conflict," *United Nations University*, accessed on July 10, 2023, https://collections.unu.edu/view/UNU:8714.
11. "Letter from the Arab Higher Committee for Palestine concerning the Eric Johnston Scheme, 18 August 1955," *Israeli Ministry of Foreign Affairs*, accessed on July 10, 2023, https://www.gov.il/en/Departments/General/9-letter-from-the-arab-higher-committee-for-palestine-concerning-the-johnston-scheme-18-august-1955.

foregoing the far greater gains that would have accrued to them. In Jordan, the regional water plan would have provided for the resettlement of an estimated two hundred thousand Palestinian refugees on unused land that the plan would have rendered arable.[12]

The Arab states and the refugees themselves continued to refuse any solution involving the resettlement and reintegration of the Palestinian refugees into any Arab country, even into the Arab-populated West Bank of Mandatory Palestine. Instead, they kept the refugees unproductive in refugee camps, sustained permanently by international relief rather than meaningful work programs in order to preserve their claim to unlimited repatriation to the State of Israel. With the US as the primary contributor, the world has continued to this day to provide such relief—without work rehabilitation—to masses of Palestinian Arabs, now covering a span of as many as four generations in addition to the refugees themselves. The long-term maintenance of UNRWA as a pure relief program only, with any meaningful work program cast aside by the Arabs, has helped create a Palestinian nationality that is largely defined by a culture of frustration, bitterness, and anger; of hatred of Israel; and of virulent anti-Semitism, which has spread from Palestinians to parts of the Arab and Moslem worlds. It has thereby contributed to the emergence of a vicious culture of terror, directed against men, women, and children, that embraces the rite of suicide bombing propagated even among children in elementary schools. Regrettably, such amoral values, justified in the name of "liberating occupied territories" and employing slogans like "One man's terrorist is the next man's freedom fighter" have even found wide support in many political and intellectual circles in the Western world.

---

12. "The Johnston Mission Fails: Summaries by Ambassador Johnston and General Burns," *Israeli Ministry of Foreign Affairs*, accessed on July 10, 2023, https://www.gov.il/en/Departments/General/10-the-johnston-mission-fails-summaries-by-amb-johnston-and-gen-burns-19-october-1958.

Events Leading to the Suez Canal Crisis

Following the overthrow of the Egyptian monarchy in 1952 and the assumption of power in 1954 by the leader of the revolt, Gamal Abdel Nasser (1954–1970)—a charismatic, nationalist leader who came to be widely recognized as the leader of the Arab world—both Egypt and Syria intensified their belligerence against Israel. Both countries were encouraged in their belligerence by the Soviet Union's reversal of its earlier support of Israel, support that had been a key factor in the UNGA 1947 resolution in favor of the establishment of the State of Israel. The Soviet Union's policy appears to have turned against Israel after Israel disappointed Soviet hopes by aligning its foreign policy with the US and Western Europe in the Cold War with the Soviet Union, a war that flared up in 1950 with communist North Korea's invasion of US-supported South Korea. In a report dated May 12, 1952, the USSR legation in Israel concluded, "In 1951, Israel lost its independence in domestic and foreign policy to the US." After discussing Israel's "hostile attitude towards the USSR," the legation recommended "refraining from giving Israel political support in the UN."[13]

The reversal of Soviet policy toward Israel became abundantly clear in 1954 when it vetoed two draft resolutions in UNSC in support of

---

13. In February 1953, the Soviet Union severed diplomatic relations with Israel over a bomb that had been thrown into the grounds of the Soviet embassy in Tel Aviv in protest against the Soviet announcement concerning a planned trial charging Jewish doctors with a plot to poison Stalin. Stalin died less than a month later, and the following month, the Soviet Union retracted the blatant anti-Semitic charges against the doctors. In July 1953, the Soviet Union restored diplomatic relations with Israel, but Soviet policy remained oriented against the State of Israel. See Israeli Ministry of Foreign Affairs, The Foreign Ministry of the Russian Federation, The Israel State Archives, The Russian Federal Archives, The Cummings Center for Russian Studies at Tel Aviv University, the Oriental Institute, the Russian Academy of Sciences, eds., *Documents on Soviet–Israeli Relations 1941–1953*, accessed on July 10, 2023, abstracts published at http://www.tau.ac.il/~russia/series/book10.html.

Israel. In January 1954, the Soviet Union vetoed a draft resolution proposed by France, the UK, and the US that called for the UN Truce Supervision Organization's chief of staff to seek to reconcile the Israeli and Syrian interests involved in the dispute that had developed in 1953 over Israel's diversion of Jordan waters at Banat Yaqub in the demilitarized zone.[14] In March 1954, UNSC dealt once again, at Israel's urgent request, with the issue of Egypt's restrictions of international trade with Israel through the Suez Canal. Venezuela submitted a draft resolution that called upon Egypt to comply with UNSC Resolution 95 (1951). It was not adopted, however, because the Soviet Union, instead of abstaining as it had in the 1951 vote, exercised its right of veto in 1954.[15] The Soviet Union had come to consider the Arab–Israeli conflict as a major theater in the Cold War with the US, and it turned into the prime promoter of the endless Arab political attacks and resolutions against Israel in the UN as well as the chief military supplier to the Arabs in their war to destroy Israel.

In September 1955, Nasser entered an agreement with the Soviet Union for an arms deal, via Czechoslovakia, of USD 200 million in exchange for Egypt's cotton. The deal, as announced in Cairo, covered the Soviet Union's most advanced military hardware, including two hundred Soviet MIG fighters, fifty Ilyushin bombers, and significant numbers of tanks and half-tracks.[16] Israel applied to the US in the following month and again in January 1956 to purchase arms to restore the military balance in the Middle East. Despite the danger to Israel from the Soviet–Egyptian arms deal, the US State Department

---

14. United Nations Security Council, Water Works in Demilitarized Zone—Vetoed Draft Resolution, Document S/3151/Rev.2 (January 22, 1954), accessed August 9, 2023, https://digitallibrary.un.org/record/539477?ln=en.
15. United Nations, *Yearbook, 1954*.
16. The actual military shipments turned out to be even larger than the deal that had been announced in Cairo. See John P. C. Matthews, "John Foster Dulles and the Suez Crisis of 1956," *American Diplomacy* (2006). *Gale Academic OneFile*, accessed July 10, 2023, https://link.gale.com/apps/doc/A152745459/AONE?u=anon~fd8d4d89&sid=bookmark-AONE&xid=deee403c.

turned down Israel's request, with Secretary of State John Foster Dulles (1953–1959) informing the North Atlantic Treaty Organization (NATO) in May 1956 that in order to avoid a US–USSR confrontation in the Middle East, the US would not sell arms directly to Israel. Israel was then able, however, with the tacit approval of the US, to enter into a secret arms deal with France to restore the military balance with the Arab states.[17] France, it may be noted, had its own political reason for entering this deal: its grievance against Nasser, who was supplying arms to Algeria in its War of Independence (1954–1962) from France.[18]

Worried about the impact of the Soviet–Egyptian arms agreement on the USSR's developing political role in Egypt and the Middle East, Dulles offered Nasser a deal in October 1955 for financing the construction of the Aswan Dam, Nasser's revolutionary development project to modernize the Egyptian economy and reduce Egyptian poverty. The estimated foreign currency cost of the project was USD 400 million, in addition to more than double that amount in local currency that would be Egypt's responsibility. According to Dulles' proposal, the World Bank would loan Egypt USD 200 million, contingent upon agreement by the US and the UK to provide the balance. The US would provide USD 56 million and the UK would provide USD 14 million at the start of the project, with the remainder to be made available as the work progressed.

By 1956, however, both US Secretary of State Dulles and UK Prime Minister Anthony Eden (1955–1957) had second thoughts about financing the Aswan Dam.[19] Eden considered Nasser another

---

17. "Highlights of Main Events, 1947–1974," *Israeli Ministry of Foreign Affairs*, accessed July 10, 2023, https://www.gov.il/en/Departments/General/highlights-of-main-events-1947-1974.
18. France became Israel's main military supplier until the Six-Day War in June 1967, when it cited Israel's preemptive attack as its reason for imposing an arms embargo.
19. For a detailed study on Dulles's role in the Suez crisis, see Matthews, "John Foster Dulles and the Suez Crisis of 1956," https://link.gale.com/

Mussolini and a Soviet puppet, and although Dulles was less critical, he too found Nasser's strident attacks against Western colonialism and imperialism disturbing. Both Dulles and Eden had ample reason to be upset with Nasser as early as 1955, months before they had proposed financing the Aswan Dam. On February 24, 1955, the UK together with four Moslem countries that were friendly to the West at the time—Turkey, Iraq, Iran, and Pakistan—had established the Baghdad Pact, a security agreement promoted by the US with the aim of blocking Soviet expansion in the Middle East. The US and the UK urged Egypt, Syria, and Jordan to join, but Nasser vehemently opposed the pact, and the three countries did not join. Two months later, in April 1955, Nasser further angered Dulles and Eden when he played a major role in the Bandung Conference, sponsored by leading Asian and African rulers that were unfriendly to the West, including Indonesia's President Sukarno, China's Premier Zhou Enlai, India's Prime Minister Nehru, and Ghana's President Nkrumah. The conference leaders preached the virtues of maintaining neutrality in the Cold War between the Soviet Union and the US, but they were liberal in their denouncement of Western colonialism and imperialism while carefully avoiding criticism of the Soviet Union. As the champion of pan-Arab nationalism, Nasser also supported the liberation movement in Algeria against the French and worked to undermine Anglo–American influence everywhere in the Middle East. Nasser's decision on May 4, 1956 to grant formal recognition to Communist China may have been more than Dulles could abide, and he decided to renege on his offer to finance the Aswan Dam. In a meeting with the Egyptian ambassador to the US on July 19, 1956, Dulles withdrew this offer. The UK and the World Bank followed suit the next day.

With this decision, Dulles facilitated the emergence of the Soviet Union as the key power in the Middle East in competition with the US, the opposite policy to that which he had hoped to achieve

---

apps/doc/A152745459/AONE?u=anon~fd8d4d89&sid=bookmark-AONE&xid=deee403c.

through the Baghdad Pact. Nasser immediately turned to the Soviet Union to undertake the Aswan Dam project, and in 1958, he signed an agreement for the dam's construction under Soviet direction and using Soviet expertise, technicians, and equipment, with the Soviet Union assuming about one-third of the total cost.

One week after the withdrawal of the US offer, Nasser stunned the Western world with his announcement on July 26, 1956 of his decision to nationalize the Suez Canal Company,[20] which had become necessary, he explained, to finance the Aswan Dam project. The UK and France, with the support of the US, responded by setting up the Suez Canal Users Association to operate the canal and collect the user fees, but Nasser called their act a provocation of war. Following the failure of negotiations outside the UN framework, Egypt, France, and the UK brought the issue of Egyptian sovereignty versus international control of the canal before UNSC.[21] After a general debate in the last week of September, followed by private exploratory sessions to bridge the gap between the parties, France and the UK submitted a draft resolution to UNSC on October 13, 1956, on which UNSC

---

20. The Suez Canal, which links the Mediterranean Sea with the Indian Ocean by way of the Red Sea, was built over a period of eleven years (1859–1869) according to a concession obtained by a French diplomat, Ferdinand de Lesseps, from the viceroy of Egypt to construct a maritime canal that would be open to ships of all nations. The Universal Suez Canal Company, with Egypt and France as the major shareholders, was to operate the canal under a lease of ninety-nine years from the date of its opening for navigation in November 1869. In 1875, UK Prime Minister Benjamin Disraeli (1868; 1874–1880) purchased Egypt's shares, making the UK the major company shareholder. In 1882, the UK intervened in a civil war in Egypt and moved in troops to take *de facto* control of the Suez Canal. According to the Anglo–Egyptian Treaty 1936, the UK granted Egypt its independence but insisted on retaining control of the Suez Canal and the right to maintain troops in the canal area. In 1951, Egypt repudiated the 1936 treaty, and in 1954, the UK agreed to remove its troops.
21. For a detailed report on the UN debates and resolutions regarding the Suez Canal in 1956, see United Nations, *Yearbook, 1956*.

decided to vote in two parts. The first part set out six requirements for settlement of the Suez Canal issue, including 1. free and open transit through the canal without discrimination, 2. respect for Egyptian sovereignty, and 3. insulation of the canal's operation from the politics of any country. Thus, UNSC unanimously adopted this part of the draft as Resolution 118 (1956).[22] The second part of the draft resolution proposed that until Egypt presented a plan that would meet the six requirements listed in the first part, the newly formed Suez Canal Users Association should cooperate with the Egyptian authorities in the operation of the canal. The Soviet Union vetoed this part of the Anglo–French draft resolution.

At the same time at which he nationalized the Suez Canal, Nasser blockaded the Tiran Straits, seeking to strangle Israel's economy by cutting off its oil imports from the Shah's then-friendly Iran and the developing trade of Israel with Asian and African countries through the Gulf of Aqaba. To Israel's dismay, UNSC failed to approve its request to participate in the discussion concerning the Suez Canal problem, and it did not challenge Nasser's blockade of Israel's international trade. In addition, UNSC neither followed up nor even took note of its earlier Resolution 95 (1951) that had called upon Egypt, as noted earlier, "to terminate the restrictions on the passage of international commercial shipping and goods through the Suez Canal wherever bound and to cease all interference with such shipping."

The Suez Canal Crisis and Its Aftereffects

Only eight years after the UK had aided and abetted the Arab War to destroy the State of Israel upon its rebirth in 1948, it now joined with France and Israel in a secret pact to undo Egypt's blockade of Israel and its nationalization of the Suez Canal. In accordance with this pact, Israel launched a strike against Egypt on October 29, 1956

---

22. For the text of United Nations Security Council Resolution 118 (1956), see United Nations Security Council, *Resolutions*, accessed August 9, 2023, https://www.un.org/securitycouncil/content/resolutions-0.

with the aim of lifting Nasser's control of the Tiran Straits and the Suez Canal. The IDF quickly swept through the Egyptian-held Gaza Strip and the Sinai Peninsula, all the way to the Suez Canal. France and the UK followed suit two days later by invading the Suez Canal Zone, ostensibly to order the separation of the Israeli and Egyptian armies on either side of the canal but in fact to seize the Suez Canal and reverse Nasser's nationalization. To prevent Britain and France from taking over the Suez Canal's operation, however, Nasser immediately rendered the Suez Canal inoperable by ordering all ships in the Suez Canal to be sunk.

The well-coordinated Anglo–French–Israeli plan was doomed from the day it began, because President Eisenhower immediately condemned the Israeli attack and called for an urgent meeting of UNSC. At the UNSC meeting the next day, October 30, the US submitted a draft resolution to the effect that (as subsequently amended) called for an immediate ceasefire and for immediate Israeli withdrawal behind the demarcations of the Israeli–Egyptian Armistice Agreement 1949. At the end of four sessions of heated debate, after the Anglo–French invasion was also underway, the US draft resolution went down in defeat when France exercised its right of veto in the UNSC vote. Angered over the decision of the UK and France to deceive him regarding their plan to attack Egypt and concerned that the attack would enhance the Soviet Union's influence in the Arab world, Eisenhower decided to split with his close allies and to press them, along with Israel, to withdraw. The US response to the veto of its draft resolution in UNSC was to call upon the UN to convene an emergency special session of UNGA to consider the issue, which had been left undecided in UNSC.

Thus, UNGA opened its first emergency special session on November 1, 1956, the day after the UK and France invaded the Suez Canal Zone. The following day, UNGA adopted, as Resolution 997 (ES-I), a US draft resolution that urged, inter alia, 1. an immediate ceasefire of all forces involved in the hostilities, 2. prompt withdrawal of the forces to the 1949 armistice lines, and 3. steps to re-open the

Suez Canal to freedom of navigation.[23] To ensure acceptance of the ceasefire, Eisenhower withheld US approval for an emergency loan from the International Monetary Fund in support of the British pound until Britain agreed to withdraw. Faced with the threat of financial collapse, Britain quickly yielded and withdrew its forces, with France following suit.

Israel agreed to withdraw only after the UN put in place arrangements for lifting Egypt's blockade of Israel's international trade and ending the fedayeen incursions from Egypt and Gaza and only after having received President Eisenhower's firm assurance of US support for preserving its freedom of navigation through the Tiran Straits and the Gulf of Aqaba. On November 4, 1956, UNGA adopted, as Resolution 998 (ES-I), a draft proposal submitted by Canada, asking the UN secretary-general to prepare a plan for the placement of a UN Emergency Force (UNEF), with the consent of the parties, to secure and supervise the cessation of hostilities in accordance with the terms of Resolution 997 (ES-I). The next day, UNGA adopted Resolution 1000 (ES-I) to approve the secretary-general's plan for the establishment of UNEF. Two days later, November 7, 1956, it adopted Resolution 1001 (ES-I) to approve the guiding principles for the organization and the functioning of UNEF. The resolution also established an advisory committee to advise the secretary-general on all UNEF issues, including any potential Egyptian request for withdrawal of UNEF.

Israel completed its withdrawal in March 1957, after Secretary-General Dag Hammarskjöld (1953–1961) negotiated a secret agreement with Nasser in accordance with Resolutions 1000 and 1001 for the placement of UNEF on Egyptian borders. The agreed task of UNEF was to re-open international shipping to and from Israel through the Gulf of Aqaba and to provide security against further

---

23. United Nations General Assembly, Resolutions Adopted by the General Assembly during Its 1st Emergency Special Session, Document A/3354 (November 1–10, 1956), accessed on August 9, 2023, https://digitallibrary.un.org/record/228961?ln=en.

Palestinian fedayeen incursions from Egypt into Israel. Over seven hours of negotiation, Dag Hammarskjöld received Nasser's agreement to a draft text, stating that any decision by Egypt to withdraw UNEF before its task was completed would be in violation of its agreement with the UN and would require the secretary-general to bring the matter before UNGA at once.[24] Lester Pearson, the Canadian delegate who authored the plan for creating UNEF as a peacekeeping instrument, won the 1957 Nobel Peace Prize for his efforts. The Suez Canal was cleared for shipping in April 1957, a month after Israel had removed its forces.

The Suez Canal crisis significantly altered the international political landscape. The forced withdrawal of the UK and France from the Suez Canal put an end to their historic role as the major powers in the Middle East. The US replaced them in that role, but it now had the Soviet Union with which to contend in a Middle East that became a key theater in the Cold War. The entry of the Soviet Union as a major power in the Middle East led to an intensification of the polarization between states such as Egypt and Syria that were increasingly moving into the Soviet camp as well as between states such as Saudi Arabia and Jordan that continued to depend upon the US for support. Egypt credited the Soviet Union rather than the US with the Anglo–French withdrawal. The Suez Canal crisis had coincided with a Hungarian uprising against the Soviet Union, which the successor to Stalin as Soviet leader, Nikita Khrushchev (1953–1964), brutally suppressed. To insert himself more firmly into the Middle East while distracting world attention from the Soviet invasion of Hungary, Khrushchev threatened London and Paris with rocket attacks unless the UK and France immediately withdrew their troops from Egyptian territory. Many Arabs believed that it was this Soviet threat, not US pressure, that had forced the UK and the French to withdraw, and several Arab

---

24. "Memorandum by Secretary-General Hammarskjold, August 1957," *Israeli Ministry of Foreign Affairs*, accessed on July 10, 2023, https://www.gov.il/en/Departments/General/35-memorandum-by-sec-gen-hammarskjold-1-august-1957.

states—with Nasser's Egypt in the lead—turned increasingly against the West and instead aligned themselves with the Soviet Union.

Nasser's success in nationalizing the Suez Canal and defying the UK and France made him an outstanding leader in the Arab world, and it boosted his campaign of pan-Arab nationalism against Western imperialism and colonialism. So intense was this spirit of pan-Arab nationalism aroused by Nasser's achievement that it inspired the Syrian government to propose to Nasser a complete merger of Syria with Egypt to form a single Arab nation. The union, under the name United Arab Republic (UAR), came into being in February 1958, with Nasser as its president. King Hussein of Jordan, considering the formation of UAR a grave threat to his regime, proposed to his cousin, King Faisal II of Iraq, a federation of Jordan and Iraq. The federation came into being the same month in which UAR was formed (February 1958), but in July 1958, King Faisal II was killed in a military coup, and the federation was dissolved. The new Republic of Iraq, inspired by Nasser's pan-Arab nationalism, threw its support to UAR.[25]

Lebanon too was faced with a rebellion by Moslem pro-Nasser forces seeking to topple Christian President Camille Chamoun's pro-Western government and to merge the country with UAR. On May 23, 1958, Lebanon lodged a complaint with UNSC, charging that UAR was interfering in its internal affairs in support of the subversive forces in the country. Following the violent overthrow of the pro-Western Iraqi monarchy on July 14, 1958, Jordan also filed a complaint of UAR interference in its domestic affairs, and both Lebanon and Jordan called upon the US and the UK for military help

---

25. The Syrian government that came to power in a military coup in 1961 dissolved UAR and made Syria independent once again, with its own seat restored in the UN under its original name, Syria, but Egypt retained the name UAR as its official name until 1971. The government of Yemen decided in 1958 to join UAR in a loose confederation named the United Arab States (UAS). The confederation also dissolved in 1961.

and protection.[26] The US dispatched Marines to Lebanon, and the United Kingdom sent troops into Jordan, with the US and the UK both informing UNSC of their intention to remove their troops as soon as UNSC was able to take over the protection of the countries. The US intervention was in accordance with the Eisenhower Doctrine, promulgated by the president in an address to the US Congress on January 5, 1957 in which he requested approval for a program of providing financial and military assistance, including intervention with troops, to states in the Middle East that request protection against subversion by international Communism.[27]

Supported by the USSR, UAR denied the Jordanian and Lebanese charges and accused the US and the UK of interference in the internal affairs of the Arab states. On July 18, 1958, the USSR vetoed a US draft resolution that inter alia, 1. called for the immediate cessation of all Soviet interference in Lebanese affairs and 2. asked the secretary-general to arrange for "measures necessary to protect the territorial integrity and independence of Lebanon." On July 22, the USSR vetoed a Japanese draft resolution that asked the secretary-general to arrange for measures to "ensure the territorial integrity and political independence of Lebanon, so as to make possible the withdrawal of US force from Lebanon."[28]

---

26. For the UN's consideration of the Lebanese and Jordanian complaints of UAR interference in their domestic affairs, see United Nations, *Yearbook, 1958*.
27. See "Special Message to the Congress on the Middle East Situation, January 5, 1957," *The American Presidency Project*, accessed on July 10, 2023, https://www.presidency.ucsb.edu/documents/special-message-the-congress-the-situation-the-middle-east.
28. United Nations Security Council, Revised Draft Resolution [on Complaint by Lebanon in Respect of a Situation Arising from Interference of the United Arab Republic (Egypt) in the Internal Affairs of Lebanon, Document S/4050/Rev.1 (July 18, 1958), accessed on August 9, 2023, https://digitallibrary.un.org/record/536919?ln=en.

United Nations Security Council, Revised Draft Resolution [on Complaint by Lebanon in Respect of a Situation Arising from Interference of

In accordance with a request from the US, endorsed by UNSC, the secretary-general convened a third emergency special session of UNGA on Friday, August 8, 1958 to deal with the questions that remained undecided by virtue of the vetoes in UNSC. At a private meeting of the Arab member states of the UN, Lebanon, Jordan, and UAR agreed to settle their disputes, and on August 21, 1958, Sudan submitted a draft resolution on their behalf, which UNGA unanimously adopted the same day as Resolution 1237 (ES-III). This resolution declared that inter alia:

[UNGA...]

1. welcomes the renewed assurances given by the Arab states to observe the provision of article 8 of the Pact of the League of Arab States that each member state shall respect the systems of government established in the other member states...and that each shall pledge to abstain from any action calculated to change established systems of government and

2. calls upon all states members of the UN to act strictly in accordance with the principles of mutual respect for each other's territorial integrity and sovereignty, of non-aggression, of strict non-interference in each other's internal affairs, and of equal and mutual benefit, and to ensure that their conduct by word and deed conforms to these principles.[29]

Pursuant to this resolution, the US and the UK withdrew their troops, with the US completing its withdrawal from Lebanon on October 25 and the UK its withdrawal from Jordan on November 2,

---

the United Arab Republic (Egypt) in the Internal Affairs of Lebanon, Document S/4055/Rev.1 (July 22, 1958), accessed on August 9, 2023, https://digitallibrary.un.org/record/536964?ln=en.

29. United Nations General Assembly, Resolution 1237 (E-S III)—Questions Considered by the Security Council at Its 838th Meeting, Document A/Res/1237 (E-S III) (August 21, 1958), accessed on August 9, 2023, https://digitallibrary.un.org/record/207462?ln=en.

1958. The Lebanese parliament's election of General Fuad Chehab to succeed Camille Chamoun as president of Lebanon facilitated the resolution of the dispute. The general, who had maintained strict neutrality between the government and the rebels in order to keep the Lebanese army from splitting up between its Moslem and its Christian elements, was acceptable to both sides in Lebanon as well as to Nasser. On November 16, 1958, Lebanon's foreign minister, declaring that close relations between Lebanon and UAR had resumed their normal course, asked UNSC to delete the Lebanese complaint from its agenda. Lebanon, he added, intended to further strengthen its cooperation with UAR and other Arab states. Nasser's success in spreading to a wider Arab world his policy of national liberation, with its slogan of opposition to imperialism, colonialism, and Zionism, was accompanied by a corresponding spread of Soviet influence and contraction of US influence in the Middle East.

– 20 –

The Six-Day War

ARAB HOSTILITIES AGAINST ISRAEL INTENSIFIED following Syria's merger with Egypt in 1958 to form UAR, together with the overthrow of the pro-Western monarchy in Iraq the same year. In addition to the continuing hostilities—the Arab boycott; the Syrian attacks against Israeli civilian activity in the demilitarized zone; the Egyptian policy of the visit, search, and seizure of ships trading with Israel through the Suez Canal; and the fedayeen incursions into Israel—a major new area of hostilities developed concerning Israel's utilization of the Jordan River for irrigation.

Following the Arab League's official rejection in October 1955 of the agreement that Arab–Israeli negotiators had reached at the technical and legal levels on Eric Johnston's regional water plan, Israel and Jordan each developed national plans for diversion of the waters of the Jordan–Yarmouk River system within the allotments provided under the Johnston regional plan. The US supported these national plans as representing the best use of the river system for the benefit of all parties. The US government guaranteed a USD 15 million loan for Israel's national diversion plan, called the National Water Carrier (NWC), as well as a grant to Jordan for its national diversion project, the East Ghor Canal.[1] Israel's NWC was to become operational in 1964 and to carry about 320 million cubic meters (MCM) of water, four-fifths of Israel's thirty-one percent share of the 400 MCM designated

---

1. Ofira Seliktar, "Turning Water into Fire: The Jordan River as the Hidden Factor in the Six-Day War," *The Middle East Review of International Affairs* 9, no. 4 (June 2005).

under the Johnston plan.[2] Presidents John F. Kennedy (1961–1963) and Lyndon B. Johnson (1963–1968), like President Eisenhower before them, supported Israel's NWC plan.[3]

Despite the division of the Arab states between the pro-Soviet and pro-American camps, they remained united in their opposition to the existence of the State of Israel. The Arab League, which, in spite of Arab approval at the technical and legal levels, had rejected the Johnston plan in 1955 because it refused to countenance Israel's receipt of a share in the Jordan River's waters, was determined to frustrate Israel's implementation of its national plan that it had formulated within the limits of the Johnston plan. In 1960, an Arab League expert committee prepared a plan for the diversion of the Syrian and Lebanese headwaters of the Jordan in order to deprive Israel of its share of the Jordan River's water under the Johnston plan. In 1962, the Arab League's political committee approved the expert committee's plan.[4] The US opposed the Arab League's diversion plan, with the US ambassador to Egypt, John S. Badeau, warning Nasser in the beginning of 1964:

---

2. See Wolf, "Hydropolitics along the Jordan River."
3. In *Palestine Peace, Not Apartheid* (London: Simon & Schuster, 2008), 28, former President Jimmy Carter is implicitly critical of Israel's diversion of the water from the Jordan River, writing, "We were amazed to find that that it [the Jordan River] was not as large as the small creeks that flow through our own farm. We learned that much of the water was being diverted from the stream to irrigate Israeli crops—then one of the prime causes of the animosity between Israel and its eastern neighbors." Carter fails to mention any of the significant facts cited in the text above showing that Israel's water diversion plan had been approved by the US as representing the best use of the river system according to a plan prepared by President Eisenhower's personal representative, Eric Johnston. The US even provided financial assistance in the form of a guaranteed loan for the project. Moreover, Jordan, in accordance with the same Johnston plan, was also diverting a share of the Jordan's River water system under its East Ghor Canal project, for which it received a US grant.
4. Seliktar, "Turning Water into Fire."

Plans to divert [the] headwaters of Jordan, as speculated upon in [the] Cairo press, [were]...unrealistic and dangerous. Whatever legal rights or wrongs of such a move, any riparian state whose chief water supply is thus cut off would have no recourse but to fight. If in course of an Ethiopian-UAR dispute, Ethiopia diverted Blue Nile, Egypt would certainly move to stop this...[5] Israel...would do [the] same and would win [a] large measure of sympathy and support in [the] international community.[6]

---

5. Nasser responded that the withdrawal of Nile waters was based on agreement between the countries concerned, and no such agreement had been made between the Arab states and Israel. US Ambassador Badeau noted, however, that the Johnston plan "had evoked a technical 'meeting of minds' by all parties concerned, and on this basis, [the US] government believed progress in utilizing [the] potential of [the] Jordan waters for [the] benefit of all parties could be made." When Nasser asked, "Do you mean if we were to divert headwaters of [the] Jordan, we would be subject to Israeli aggression?" Badeau "objected to [the] use of [the] word 'aggression,' saying water was such [a] vital interest [that] any state would move to protect it, and this could scarcely be called 'aggression'" (*Foreign Relations of the United States: Diplomatic Papers, 1964–1968, vol. 18*).

6. Former President Jimmy Carter is not among those in the international community who have shown sympathy and support for Israel's water project. In his *Palestine Peace, Not Apartheid*, 58, Carter wrote with apparent sympathy for the Arab summit meeting against Israel's water project: "The Palestinians and individual Arab leaders continued their vehement objections to the increasing Israeli encroachments on what they considered to be their lands and rights. However, it was not until the announcement of Israel's plans to divert water from the Sea of Galilee and the Jordan River to irrigate western Israel and the Negev desert that the first summit meeting of Arab leaders took place early in 1964 and the PLO was formally organized." Carter failed to note that the Arab summit plan was not to protect the Jordan River's waters but rather to divert the Syrian and Lebanese headwaters of the Jordan River in order to deprive Israel of its main water supply, which the US ambassador to Egypt had warned Nasser was "unrealistic and dangerous." Despite "having studied Bible lessons since early childhood and taught them for twenty years" (22), Carter also took no notice of the PLO Charter's contempt for the

The US opposition to the Arab water diversion plans failed to perturb Nasser. On January 13–17, 1964, he hosted the first Arab League summit in Cairo, where the kings and heads of the thirteen Arab League member states officially decided to implement the Arab League's Jordan River project. The official communiqué of the summit did not spell out the specific decisions taken, declaring only that the member states at the summit:

> …having discussed Israel's new and aggressive plan to divert the course of the River Jordan, thereby grievously endangering the riparian rights of the Arabs with the object of realizing Zionist designs for expansion through immigration…
> …[have] therefore adopted the practical resolutions essential to ward off the imminent Zionist menace, whether in the defensive or the technical domains in the field of organizing the Palestinian people to enable them to play their part in the liberation of their country and attain self-determination.[7]

The measures adopted included the creation of a joint Arab force in anticipation of an Israeli military response to the project. The force, called the United Arab Command, comprised armed forces from Egypt, Syria, Jordan, and Lebanon, with Egypt in command.[8]

At its second summit on September 5–11, 1964 in Alexandria, Egypt, the council of kings and heads of state adopted resolutions, inter alia, to "[embark] on immediate work on projects for the exploitation

---

Bible in denying any claim of the Jewish people to any historical roots in Palestine (article 18).

7. "Arab Summit Decides to Divert Headwaters, Statement of the Council of the Kings and Heads of State of the Arab League Member Countries on its First Session, Cairo, 13–17 January 1964," *Israeli Ministry of Foreign Affairs*, accessed on July 10, 2023, https://www.gov.il/en/Departments/General/11-arab-summit-decides-to-divert-headwaters-13-january-1964.
8. "The Disaster of 1967," *Jordan History*, accessed on July 10, 2023, http://www.kinghussein.gov.jo/his_periods3.html.

of the waters of the River Jordan and its tributaries."[9] The Arab Headwater Diversion Plan, technically difficult and expensive, would have deprived Israel of about thirty-five percent of its water from its planned NWC, or about eleven percent of its total annual water supply.[10] Israel declared that it would regard such diversion as an infringement of its sovereign rights. Work on the Arab Headwater Diversion Plan began in 1965, and Israel hit the works in a series of military strikes, culminating in April 1967 in air strikes deep inside Syria.[11]

Nasser's motivation in hosting the first Arab League Summit in Cairo in January 1964 far exceeded the immediate Arab goal of sabotaging Israel's NWC project. His objectives were to promote Arab unity under his leadership and "to organize the Palestinian people and to enable them to take their role in the liberation of their homeland," a euphemism for the liquidation of the State of Israel. Following a summit decision, the Arab League, meeting in Jerusalem in May 1964 at the first Palestinian conference, established the PLO, an umbrella movement embracing various Palestinian Arab groupings intent upon

---

9. United Nations Security Council, Letter Dated 6 October 1964 Addressed to the President of the Security Council by the Representatives of Algeria, Iraq, Jordan, Kuwait, Lebanon, Libya, Morocco, Saudi Arabia, Sudan, Syrian Arab Republic, Tunisia, United Arab Republic, and the Arab Republic of Yemen, Document S/6003 (October 8, 1964), accessed August 9, 2023, https://digitallibrary.un.org/record/539894?ln=zh_CN ("Declaration Issued by the Council of Kings and Heads of State of the Arab League 1964").

10. "Appendix C: Historical Review of the Political Riparian Issues in the Development of the Jordan River and Basin Management" in Masahiro Murakami, *Managing Water for Peace in the Middle East: Alternative Strategies* (Tokyo: United Nations University Press, 1995), accessed on July 10, 2023, http://www.unu.edu/wwf/UNUwater-publications.html.

11. Students of international water problems consider the increase in Arab hostility over the Israeli NWC project to have been a major factor that led to the June 1967 war. See Seliktar, "Turning Water into Fire" and Murakami, "Appendix C: Historical Review of the Political Riparian Issues in the Development of the Jordan River and Basin Management."

liquidating the State of Israel. The PLO adopted a national charter to amass the forces of the Palestinian Arab people, "who believe in its Arabism and in its right to regain its homeland…to continue its struggle…on the path of holy war (al-jihad) until complete and final victory has been attained" (preamble). It declared, "The liberation of Palestine, from an Arab viewpoint, is a national duty," whose "responsibilities fall upon the entire Arab nation, governments, and peoples, the Palestinian peoples being in the forefront" (article 14). It pronounced the partitioning of Palestine in 1947 and the establishment of Israel illegal and therefore null and void (article 17). It considered the Balfour Declaration, the Mandate for Palestine, and everything based on them null and void (article 18). In a shocking display of contempt for the Bible and for centuries of Jewish and world history, article 18 added, "The claims of historic and spiritual ties between Jews and Palestine are not in agreement with the facts of history," as if to assert that the Jewish biblical Holy Land was some unknown land located somewhere on another planet. The PLO's assertion is especially shocking because the Quran recognizes the Hebrew Bible as a holy book, speaks with respect of biblical King Solomon (the builder of Israel's First Holy Temple on Jerusalem's Temple Mount), and reveres the prophets of Israel's biblical Holy Land. The PLO Charter, however, proceeds from its denial of Jewish historic and spiritual ties to Palestine to an attack on Zionism, which it defines as "a colonialist movement in its inception, aggressive and expansionist in its goal, racist in its configurations, and fascist in its means and aims" (article 19). It demands from all nations, in the cause of peace, security, and justice, that they "consider Zionism an illegal movement and outlaw its presence and activities" (article 20).[12]

In line with Nasser's pan-Arabism, the 1964 PLO Charter is remarkable in that it contains no provision for an independent sovereign

---

12. See Palestine Liberation Organization, "Palestine National Charter of 1964," *Israeli Ministry of Foreign Affairs*, accessed on August 9, 2023, https://www.gov.il/en/Departments/General/11-national-covenant-of-the-palestine-liberation-organization-28-may-1964.

Palestinian state to be governed by Palestinians. Although it declares, "Palestine, with its boundaries at the time of the British Mandate, is an indivisible territorial unit" (article 2) and "The Palestinian Arab people has the legitimate right to its homeland" (article 3), it does not propose a role for an independent Palestinian government in the areas of Palestine that were then under Jordanian, Egyptian, and Syrian rule. Before 1967, the West Bank was part of the Hashemite Kingdom of Jordan, Egypt occupied Gaza, and Israel's Himmah area was under Syria's rule. The PLO Charter explicitly declares that the PLO "does not exercise any territorial sovereignty over the West Bank in the Hashemite Kingdom of Jordan, in the Gaza Strip, or in the Himmah area" (article 24).[13] The PLO Charter's call for the liberation of the Palestinian homeland was thus a call for the liquidation of Israel within its 1949 Armistice Agreement borders and not for the establishment of a sovereign state of Palestine governed by the Palestinian people.

The Council of Arab Kings and Heads of State in attendance at the second summit welcomed the establishment of the PLO and approved its decision to establish a Palestine Liberation Army. It also welcomed the signing of the Joint Arab Defense Pact by all member states and declared that the council would consider an attack on any Arab state as an attack on all the Arab states.[14] Not surprisingly, the more militant Palestinian guerrilla organizations—including, in particular, the largest group, the Fatah, founded by Yasser Arafat in 1959—remained outside this Nasser-dominated PLO. It was not until after the defeat of the Arab states in 1967 that Arafat joined and took charge of the PLO under a revised charter that eliminated the 1964 clause denying Palestinian sovereignty in the West Bank and Gaza.

From his position as the major Arab world leader, idolized by many and feared by others, Nasser quickly rose to a major leadership

---

13. See Palestine Liberation Organization, "Palestine National Charter of 1964."
14. "Declaration Issued by the Council of Kings and Heads of State of the Arab League 1964."

role in the entire developing world of Africa and Asia. In that role, Nasser promoted a program of opposition to the existence of the State of Israel as only another manifestation of Western imperialism and colonialism. In 1961, Nasser had helped found, together with Tito of Yugoslavia and Nehru of India, the Non-Aligned Movement (NAM), and in October 1964, he hosted the second summit of NAM in Cairo. The NAM, which largely consisted, though not exclusively, of Afro-Asian developing countries that had recently gained their independence from European colonial powers, was intended to represent the Third World in international affairs and to avoid entanglement in the Cold War between the Communist world (led by the Soviet Union) and the capitalist, developed world (led by the US). Like the 1955 Bandung Conference, where the concept of NAM originated, NAM defined itself as "non-aligned." Its purpose, as stated in the Havana Declaration 1979, is "to ensure the national independence, sovereignty, territorial integrity, and security of non-aligned countries in their struggle against imperialism, colonialism, neo-colonialism, apartheid, racism, including Zionism and any forms of foreign aggression, occupation, domination, interference, and hegemony as well as against great power and bloc politics."[15] Nevertheless, despite its official policy of non-alignment, many of the its sponsors closely aligned themselves with the Soviet Union, and even Fidel Castro's Cuba, a Communist, Soviet satellite country, was one of NAM's founding members.

In 1963, Nasser also helped found the Organization of African Unity (OAU) to promote the solidarity of the North-African Arab states with the non-Arab Sub-Saharan states. The principles of the OAU Charter, adopted in Addis Ababa, included, in addition to "dedication to the total emancipation of the African territories which are still dependent," the "affirmation of a policy of non-alignment with

---

15. See "6th Summit Conference of Heads of State or Government of the Non-Aligned Movement," *Middlebury Institute of International Studies at Monterey*, accessed on August 7, 2023, http://cns.miis.edu/nam/documents/Official_Document/6th_Summit_FD_Havana_Declaration_1979_Whole.pdf.

regard to all blocs."[16] Initially, Israel had won many friends among the newly independent Sub-Saharan African states—including many Moslem states—owing to the outstanding technical assistance programs it offered the African states based on its highly relevant experience with the economic development of its own country after so many centuries of desolation.

The Arab states, however, strove to distance the non-Arab African countries from Israel by promoting the charge that "neo-colonialism is using Israel as a tool to realize its ambitions in the developing countries against their aspirations to attain progress, strength, and unity."[17] They promoted instead the concept of African unity and solidarity based on geographic ties and common history as former colonies of Western Europe and, in the case of the Moslem countries, emphasizing also the concept of pan-Islamic unity.

The Council of Arab Kings and Heads of State, declaring that Arab-African cooperation was a foundation of Arab policy, offered its support to the African countries in their political struggles, both for independence from the rule of European colonial powers and against domination by white minority regimes. To win support for the Arab cause, the council resorted to more than political measures alone—it also decided to regulate Arab relations with other countries "in accordance with their position regarding the Palestine question and other Arab causes."[18] By means of the oil weapon, the Arab countries achieved considerable success in turning all Africa against Israel in the aftermath of the Six-Day War in 1967.[19]

---

16. "Charter of the Organization of African Unity, September 13, 1963," *African Union*, accessed on July 11, 2023, https://au.int/sites/default/files/treaties/7759-file-oau_charter_1963.pdf.
17. Declaration Issued by the Council of Kings and Heads of State of the Arab League 1964.
18. Declaration Issued by the Council of Kings and Heads of State of the Arab League 1964.
19. After the 1973 Yom Kippur War against Israel, all Africa severed diplomatic relations with Israel in accordance with a resolution to this effect, adopted

In 1964, the Arab campaign against Israel came to benefit significantly from the establishment of yet another international organization, named the Group of 77 (G-77), which combined the Afro-Asian countries with those of Latin America and the Caribbean into an organization representing all the world's developing countries. The G-77 was established on July 15, 1964, in Geneva, Switzerland, by the seventy-seven developing states of the UN under the leadership of Raul Prebisch, the charismatic secretary-general of the UN Conference on Trade and Development.[20] It decided permanently to retain its original name, the G-77, even though its membership has grown each year as additional territories have gained independence and membership in the UN. In 2007, when the UN member states numbered 192, the G-77 had 132 members. The Arab countries have increasingly cultivated the support of the Latin American and Caribbean countries in the G-77 for their campaign against Israel in exchange for their support of Latin American pressure on the developed countries for concessions in international trade.[21] Over time, the Arab states came to enjoy the frequently unanimous political support of the G-77—accounting for the two-thirds of the UN membership that is required for the adoption of UNGA resolutions—for their unrelenting campaign against Israel in the entire UN system. Since the mid-1970s, this support and sponsorship from the G-77 has subjected Israel to an annual flood of anti-Israeli resolutions—many of them repeated year after year—in UNGA and in the international organizations affiliated with the UN.

---

by OAU under political and economic pressure from the Arab oil-exporting countries.

20. See "The Group of Seventy-Seven at the United Nations," *The Group of 77 at the United Nations*, accessed on July 11, 2023, http://www.g77.org.
21. In September 1969, yet another international organization, the Organization of the Islamic Conference (OIC), was formed with the aim of promoting Islamic solidarity between Arab and non-Arab Moslem countries against Israel.

The Soviet Anti-Israel Campaign

The most powerful international support the Arab countries received in the 1960s was the military and political backing of the Soviet Union, which championed their cause as part of the Cold War against the US and the West. After the 1956 Suez Canal crisis and especially after Syria's 1958 merger with Egypt and the pro-Nasser 1958 revolution in Iraq, the Soviet Union accelerated its supply of tanks and combat planes to Israel's Arab enemies, significantly upsetting the military balance in the Middle East. To restore the balance, President John F. Kennedy (1961–1963) decided in 1962 to lift President Truman's embargo against US direct sales of military equipment to Israel, which President Eisenhower had continued in force, and he agreed to provide Israel with Hawk anti-aircraft missiles against the Soviet Union's long-range bombers that had been supplied to the Arab states. As the Soviet Union continued to pump more combat equipment into the Arab states, President Lyndon B. Johnson (1963–1968) continued Kennedy's arms policies, supplying Israel in 1966 with Patton tanks and Skyhawk jet bombers.

Although these 1966 arms sales increased Israel's offensive capability, the US policy was not to provide Israel with a strategic military advantage but only to counter, in part, the massive, most advanced arms the Soviet Union was continuing to supply to Egypt, Syria, and Iraq. From 1956 to 1967, the Soviet Union equipped Egypt with nearly 1,000 tanks and 360 jets; transferred 400 tanks and 125 jets to Iraq; and sold Syria 350 tanks and 125 jets. According to a CIA estimate, the six Arab states—Egypt, Syria, Iraq, Lebanon, Jordan, and Saudi Arabia—most likely to be involved in major hostilities against Israel had significant numerical superiority over Israel in military equipment in 1966: a two-to-one ratio in the number of tanks, a three-to-one ratio in the number of major naval units, and a ten-to-one ratio in the number of bombers.[22] In its concern to main-

---

22. *Foreign Relations of the United States: Diplomatic Papers, 1964–1968*, vol. 18.

tain an even-handed policy, the US accompanied its sales to Israel with arms sales to Arab countries that were not then part of Nasser's pro-Soviet national liberation camp, including Saudi Arabia, Jordan, Lebanon, Libya (before Qaddafi seized power in September 1969), Morocco, and Tunisia.[23] For much of the period, the US even supplied significant food aid to Egypt to keep its people from starving and to keep Nasser from accepting complete Soviet control of Egyptian policy. Nasser's military build-up, together with his proxy war with Saudi Arabia in Yemen from 1962 to 1967,[24] came at the expense of Egypt's much-needed agricultural development and kept its people in permanent poverty.

In addition to its military aid, the Soviet Union gave political encouragement to the Arabs to intensify their hostilities against Israel. By its exercise of the right of veto, the Soviet Union provided the Arabs with assurance that no matter how much they provoked Israel, they would not suffer condemnation in UNSC. Israel, on the other hand, faced condemnation when Arab provocations led it to retaliate. In August 1963, UNSC considered a complaint by Israel

---

23. See Mitchell G. Bard, "US–Israel Strategic Cooperation: The 1968 Sale of Phantom Jets to Israel," *Jewish Virtual Library*, accessed on July 11, 2023, http://www.jewishvirtuallibrary.org/jsource/US-Israel/phantom.html. During the Six-Day War in June 1967, the Johnson administration re-imposed an arms embargo on the Middle East but lifted it shortly thereafter in response to the massive Soviet arms supplies to Syria and Egypt as well as to pressures from Israel and Jordan for renewed sales.
24. In 1962, a group of Yemenite officers who had received military training in Egypt rebelled against the royal ruler of Yemen and set up its own Yemen Arab Republic. Nasser supported the rebels and dispatched troops for their defense, while Saudi Arabia and Jordan supported the royal ruler. The Soviet Union supported Nasser in this war, whereas the UK and the US supported Saudi Arabia. The war proved to be such a serious drain on Egypt's resources—it had more than fifty thousand troops tied up in Yemen—that it came to be considered as Egypt's Vietnam War. Nasser finally withdrew from Yemen in 1967, after which time the Yemen Arab Republic soon fell.

that a group of armed Syrians had crossed into Israeli territory and had killed two Israeli farmers in Almagor, a village in the Galilee. The chief of staff of the UNTSO supported the validity of the Israeli claim. The Israeli representative reported to UNSC that this was only the latest in a series of Syrian border attacks on Israel and submitted a list of ninety-eight such incidents since December 1962. Eight of the eleven-member UNSC approved a draft resolution submitted by the US and the UK that condemned the attack, but the resolution was not adopted, because the Soviet Union exercised its right of veto in UNSC.[25]

From 1965, Yasser Arafat and his Fatah organization, encouraged by the founding of the PLO in 1964 and the Arab summit's call for the liberation of Palestine, stepped up their violent raids into Israel from a base they had established in Syria. In February 1966, a group of Syrian army officers conducted a military coup within the governing Baath party and established a radical socialist government in Syria. Not surprisingly, the new government, which vied with Nasser for the role of champion of Arab national liberation, assisted Fatah and gave it free reign to attack Israel via incursions from Lebanon, Jordan, and Syria. Fatah then embarked upon a chain of terrorist attacks in Israel, in crossings from Syria, Lebanon, and especially Jordan, that resulted in the killing and wounding of many Israeli civilians. On October 11, 1966, after a series of attacks in Israel—including Galilee, Jerusalem, and the area bordering Hebron—Israel asked the US to warn Syria against giving Fatah free reign to attack Israel and to urge Jordan to strengthen its controls against Fatah, because the Israeli government was under severe pressure to counterattack. The State Department, hoping to deter Israel from retaliating, advised it to bring the issue before UNSC.[26] The next day, Israel requested an urgent meeting of

---

25. The vote was eight in favor, with two opposing the resolution (Morocco, USSR) and one abstaining (Venezuela). See United Nations, *Yearbook, 1963*.
26. See *Foreign Relations of the United States: Diplomatic Papers, 1964–1968*, vol. 18.

UNSC to consider its complaints against Syria concerning 1. acts of aggression committed by armed groups operating from Syrian territory and 2. Syria's open threats of war against Israel's territorial integrity and political independence. Following the failure of UNSC to reach a consensus, a group of six powers submitted a mildly worded draft resolution to UNSC on November 3, 1966, whereby UNSC would, inter alia, 1. deplore the incidents that had been the subject of the debate as well as the loss of human life and casualties caused by them and 2. invite the government of Syria to strengthen its measures for preventing incidents that constitute a violation of the general Armistice Agreements of 1949.

Even the implicit suggestion in the resolution that Syria was not doing enough to deter Fatah's attacks against Israel was too much for the Soviet Union to accept. Although the vote of the newly enlarged UNSC of fifteen members[27] was ten in favor, four opposed (Communist Bulgaria, Arab Jordan, Moslem Mali, and USSR), and one that abstained (China), it was not adopted, because the Soviet Union exercised its right of veto.[28] The Soviet Union's exercise of its veto against any hint of criticism of any Arab action enabled the Arab states to continue to counter all Israeli complaints against Arab aggression with the boast that UNSC had never condemned any Arab state for aggression but had so condemned Israel many times.

Israel indeed received another such one-sided UNSC condemnation the following month. In response to a number of Fatah raids, culminating in an attack that killed three and wounded six, Israel—frustrated over UNSC's inability to deter terrorist raids because of the automatic exercise of the Soviet veto—launched a retaliatory attack on the West Bank border village of Samu, from which the terrorists had crossed into Israel. Although Israel had intended to conduct only a local operation, it grew out of bounds, because a Jordanian armored

---

27. The UN amended its charter on August 31, 1965 to enlarge UNSC from eleven to fifteen members by the addition of four states as non-permanent members of UNSC.
28. See United Nations, *Yearbook, 1966*, reproduced online on UNISPAL.

column hastened to repel the attack, and it suffered an overwhelming defeat with heavy casualties. The defeat led to Palestinian riots in major Jordanian cities and resulted in such severe political attacks by Egypt, Syria, and Iraq that King Hussein's throne was put in jeopardy. The US, angered by Israel's retaliation and the resulting harm to US interests—and, as it emphasized, even to Israel's interests—in preserving the stability of King Hussein's regime, decided to vote in favor of a harsh, one-sided draft resolution submitted by Nigeria and Mali to censure Israel and warn it against further such acts of retaliation. On November 25, 1966, UNSC adopted the draft resolution by a vote of fourteen in favor of the resolution, zero opposing it, and one abstaining (New Zealand) as its Resolution 228 (1966). According to this resolution, UNSC, inter alia,

> censures Israel for this large-scale military action in violation of the UN Charter and of the general Armistice Agreement between Israel and Jordan [and]

> emphasizes to Israel that actions of military reprisal cannot be tolerated and that if they are repeated, the UNSC will have to consider further and more effective steps as envisaged in the charter to ensure against the repetition of such acts.

The resolution failed to condemn the continuing Arab raids into Israel that prompted Israel's act of retaliation. The Arab attacks were noted vaguely only in the preamble, which read, "…recalling the repeated resolutions of UNSC asking for the cessation of violent incidents across the demarcation line and not overlooking past incidents of this nature."[29] Although many delegates expressed themselves in the same vein as New Zealand in the course of UNSC debate, only New Zealand decided to abstain in the vote, because, as its delegate declared in debate:

---

29. United Nations Security Council, Resolution 228, On Israeli Military Actions against Jordan, Document S/RES/228(1966) (November 25, 1966), accessed on August 9, 2023, https://digitallibrary.un.org/record/90503?ln=en.

If the matter were to be dealt with in a manner which fulfills the responsibilities of UNSC, such censure, however merited, should be accompanied by fair acknowledgement of the total situation within which the act of retaliation took place and by constructive proposals aimed at providing the means whereby the recurrence of violence might most effectively be checked.[30]

Instead of deterring Arab violence and encouraging the parties to seek to resolve the issues outstanding between them, the one-sided resolution only encouraged Syria, Fatah, and other guerrilla organizations, including the PLO, to intensify their hostilities against Israel.

Following the establishment of the radical socialist Baath regime in Syria on February 23, 1966, the Soviet Union adopted an even more protective position toward Syria and Egypt as well as a highly aggressive stance against Israel as part of the Cold War with the US and the West. The Soviet Union looked upon Israel only as a tool of the imperialist and colonialist powers, especially the US, encouraged by them to overthrow the Arab national liberation movements promoted by Syria and Egypt and championed by the Soviet Union. On April 18, the Soviet Government flew the new prime minister and defense minister of Syria to Moscow, where the two governments signed a treaty on May 2, 1966. On May 10–18, during his visit to Cairo, Soviet Prime Minister Alexei Kosygin (1964–1980) promoted the desirability of a mutual defense pact between Egypt and Syria, to be guaranteed by Moscow, and on May 17, 1966, he addressed the Egyptian National Assembly, where he stressed Egypt's role in the Arab struggle for a solution to the Palestinian question.[31] Kosygin's promotion of an Egyptian–Syrian defense pact bore fruit on November

---

30. United Nations Security Council, Attack on As Samu—SecCo Action/The Palestine Question (Last Consideration of Item)—SecCo Verbatim Record, Document S/PV.1328 (OR) (November 11, 1966), accessed on August 9, 2023, https://www.un.org/unispal/document/auto-insert-180759.
31. Isabella Ginor, "The Cold War's Longest Cover-Up: How and Why the USSR Instigated the 1967 War," *Middle East Review of International Affairs* 7, no. 3 (September 2003): 44.

4, 1966, when Nasser and the Syrian premier signed a defense pact in Cairo.[32]

The Soviet shift toward a more aggressive stance against Israel, including a series of patently false charges, began in the same month as Kosygin's visit to Cairo. On May 8, 1966, an article in the official Soviet government newspaper, *Izvestia*, claimed for the first time that Syria had become "a central object of military blackmail and provocation by Israel." On the same day, a cable in the official Soviet news agency, TASS, sent from Syria, mentioned for the first time "a suspicious concentration and movement of Israeli troops sighted lately on the border with Syria." On May 21, 1966, upon Kosygin's return from Cairo, the widely circulated national newspaper, *Sovietskaya Rossiya*, published the blatantly false charge that "about a third of the Israeli army, after marching to music through the streets of Haifa, was immediately following the parade transferred to the Syrian border." Four days later, the Soviet Union delivered the first official protest regarding the alleged troop concentrations to Israel's ambassador in Moscow.[33]

The Soviet charges echoed those of Syria and Egypt, both of whom falsely claimed that Israel was amassing its forces at the Syrian border as a prelude to an attack to overthrow the Baath regime. In August 1966, the US transmitted to Israel a message from Jordan containing a report from Syria that Israeli troops were amassing on the Syrian border and that in case of an outbreak of hostilities, the United Arab Command had ordered Jordan to attack Israel. Jordan feared that if it implemented the order, its forces "would be cut to pieces," but if it did not, Jordan would be accused of treason to the Arab cause. Israel replied that the report was baseless, and the US embassy confirmed that all the evidence available to it indicated that the report was without foundation.[34] In October 1966, rumors spread on

---

32. See *Foreign Relations of the United States: Diplomatic Papers, 1964–1968*, vol. 18, fn. 4.
33. Ginor, "The Cold War's Longest Cover-Up", 45.
34. See *Foreign Relations of the United States: Diplomatic Papers, 1964–1968*, vol. 18.

Egyptian radio and television of plots by Saudi Arabia, Jordan, Great Britain, the CIA, and Israel to topple the Baath government in Syria. In a conversation on October 7 with the Egyptian foreign minister, US Secretary of State Dean Rusk categorically denied the charges of CIA involvement and of any US involvement.[35]

On October 17, 1966, Israeli Prime Minister Levi Eshkol (1963–1969), in an address to the Knesset (Israeli parliament), after having charged Syria with training, financing, and supplying Fatah with weapons to launch its attacks on Israel, rejected the charge that Israel was planning to attack Syria and was concentrating forces on its borders. This charge, he declared, "is as baseless as the claim that Syria is innocent of the responsibility for the acts of sabotage on Israeli territory." In order to refute the falsehood, he added, "We have agreed with the chief of the UN Observers that an investigation shall be carried out to make it plain that there are no Israeli troop concentrations on the border." As for the charge that Israel has joined with imperialist forces to overthrow the "progressive" regime in Damascus, Eshkol emphasized, "We have repeatedly declared that Israel does not interfere with the regimes and the internal affairs of other countries… Israel's policy is absolutely independent and is not dictated by any foreign factor." Turning next to the Soviet role, Eshkol declared, "To my regret, I cannot ignore, in this discussion, the regrettable fact that

---

35. *Foreign Relations of the United States: Diplomatic Papers, 1964–1968, vol. 18*. Three days later, on October 10, 1966, in a meeting with the Syrian representative, US State Department officials expressed their concern and bewilderment over Syrian charges that the US was plotting to overthrow the Baath regime in Syria and categorically denied those charges. In November 1966, Nasser told a visiting American that he had "indisputable evidence that within the last several months agents of the CIA had entered into a conspiracy with Egyptians aimed at his assassination and violent overthrow of his government." Nasser added that he would be prepared to disclose the evidence and to discuss the matter with any representative of the US government. The US denied the authenticity of the report, and the US ambassador to Egypt pressed Nasser to make the evidence available, but Nasser produced no evidence and sought to change the subject.

a world power with which Israel desires to have sincere friendship is giving international currency to the foolish charge that Israel is planning an attack against Syria as part of an international plot against the Damascus regime. By this attitude, the Soviet Union encourages Syria and, to our regret, confuses the local tension between Israel and Syria with the question of the general international tension."[36]

Bolstered by its treaties with the Soviet Union and with Egypt as well as by their circulation of the false charges of a planned Israeli attempt to overthrow the Syrian regime, Syria intensified its hostilities against Israel in 1967. In five successive letters from January 8–17, 1967, Israel complained to UNSC of a serious intensification by Syria of acts of aggression along the border with Israel, including acts of sabotage by terrorists crossing from Syria, using mines and explosives. Such gross violations of the Armistice Agreement 1949, Israel warned, inflamed the tension along the border and endangered the peace of the whole area. Syria rejected the charges, claiming—as it had in the past—that Israel's aim was to increase tension in order to justify subsequent large-scale aggression against Syria.[37] Eshkol, still smarting from the political price Israel had paid for its attack on Samu in October 1966, decided against retaliation but rather informed President Johnson that Israel's patience with Syria was running out.[38] UN Secretary-General U Thant (1961–1971), successor to Dag Hammarskjöld (who had died in an airplane crash on a UN mission to the Congo in September 1961), urged restraint and invited Israel and Syria to an emergency meeting of the Israel–Syria Mixed Armistice Commission. Both sides accepted, but after several sessions, they reached an impasse. On April 7, 1967, a serious clash erupted in the demilitarized zone, involving artillery, tanks, and planes, and

---

36. "Statement to the Knesset by Prime Minister Eshkol, October 17, 1966," *Israeli Ministry of Foreign Affairs*, accessed on July 11, 2023, https://www.gov.il/en/Departments/General/5-statement-to-the-knesset-by-pm-eshkol-23-may-1967.
37. United Nations, *Yearbook, 1967*.
38. *Foreign Relations of the United States: Diplomatic Papers, 1964–1968*, vol. 18.

Israeli planes shot down six Syrian MiG aircrafts, two of them close to Damascus.[39]

The Unfolding of the Crisis in May 1967

The Soviet Union's role in the crisis leading to the Six-Day War has been a subject of continuing debate among scholars: Some believe that the Soviet Union deliberately instigated the war, some argue that they stumbled into the war, and yet others claim that their intent was to prevent the war. There seems to be little doubt, however, that Soviet action helped to trigger the war. In his report to the Central Committee of the Communist Party on June 20, 1967, General Secretary Leonid Brezhnev (1964–1982), successor to Nikita Khruschev, emphasized that in May 1967, the Soviet Union politburo adopted a decision to warn both Egypt and Syria that Israel was preparing a military attack against Syria and other Arab countries.[40] The Soviet Union employed multiple channels to deliver these warnings. According to Mohamed Heikal, the political analyst and confidante of both Nasser and his successor, Anwar Sadat, Soviet President Nikolai Podgorny (1965–1977) gave Sadat, during a stopover in Moscow, a message for Nasser, warning him of Israel's intent to deploy between nine and eleven battalions on the Syrian border.[41] Simultaneously, the Soviet intelligence "resident" in Cairo transmitted a similar message to

---

39. Michael K. Carroll, "From Peace (Keeping) to War: The United Nations and the Withdrawal of UNEF," *Middle East Review of International Affairs* 9, no. 2 (June 2005): 73.
40. "On Soviet Policy Following the Israeli Aggression in the Middle East—Report by Comrade L. I. Brezhnev to the Plenum of the Central Committee of the Soviet Communist Party, held on 20 June 1967," *Woodrow Wilson International Center for Scholars, Virtual Archive*, accessed on August 7, 2023, https://digitalarchive.wilsoncenter.org/document/soviet-policy-following-israeli-aggression-middle-east.
41. Youssef Aboul-Enein, "The Heikal Papers: A Discourse on Politics and the 1967 Arab–Israeli War with Egyptian President Gamal Abdel Nasser," *Strategic Insights* 4, no. 4 (April 2005).

Egyptian intelligence, and on May 12, the Soviet ambassador to Egypt passed on a similar message to the Egyptian authorities, "advising the Egyptian government to take the necessary steps."[42] The same week, Egypt's ambassador to Syria sent an urgent cable to Cairo warning of an imminent Israeli attack on Syria from May 22–26, 1967. Nasser sent General Mohammed Fawzi to the Syrian front to investigate, and he reported there was no Israeli build-up.[43] Nasser decided, however, to act in accordance with the disinformation that had been sent to him by the Soviet Union. Both Syria and Egypt informed the Soviet Union that they were taking the necessary steps and that their armed forces had been put on full alert.[44]

On May 16, 1967, Nasser reacted to the Soviet disinformation by moving his forces into the Sinai Peninsula and requesting the withdrawal of UNEF, ostensibly in order to facilitate Egypt's coming to the defense of Syria against the allegedly planned Israeli attack. Nasser's request was in violation of his 1957 agreement with UN Secretary-General Dag Hammarskjöld for UNEF to remain in place as long as it was required as an international buffer on the border with Israel. Secretary-General U Thant decided to comply immediately, before consulting the UN Advisory Committee on UNEF, and without bringing the matter to UNGA per the agreement Hammarskjöld had reached with Nasser for Israel's withdrawal from the Suez Canal after the 1956 crisis.[45] Nasser then proceeded to remilitarize the Sinai Peninsula. Three days later, on May 19, 1967, U Thant sent a special

---

42. Ginor, "The Cold War's Longest Cover-Up", 35–36.
43. According to Nadav Safran (*From War to War: The Arab–Israeli Confrontation 1948–1967* [New York: Pegasus, 1969], 274–275, fn. 8, Fawzi believed, "The Russians must have been having hallucinations," cited in Carroll, "From Peace (Keeping) to War", 73, fn. 10.
44. "On Soviet Policy Following the Israeli Aggression in the Middle East," *Woodrow Wilson International Center for Scholars.*
45. For the Hammarskjöld-Nasser Agreement, see Chapter 19. For a detailed study of U Thant's controversial response to Nasser's demand for the withdrawal of UNEF, see Carroll, "From Peace (Keeping) to War", 73.

report to UNSC concerning the dangerous tensions between Israel and the Arab countries, and he warned that the situation had reached the most menacing level since autumn 1956.

The crisis rose to explosive levels three days later, on May 22, when Nasser renewed his open challenge to Israel by announcing once again the closure of the Tiran Straits, a move that Israel had warned it would consider an act of war.[46] On May 23, U Thant proceeded to Cairo for discussions with Nasser on measures that might allow the explosive Israeli–Arab tensions to subside. On May 24, 1967, during U Thant's visit to Cairo, UNSC met at the request of Canada and Denmark in an urgent session to consider the grave situation in the Middle East. The two countries submitted a draft resolution whereby UNSC would:

> …1. express full support for the efforts of the secretary-general to pacify the situation, 2. request all member states to refrain from any steps which might worsen the situation, and 3. invite the secretary-general to report to UNSC upon his return to enable it to continue its consideration of the matter.[47]

The representatives of the US, the UK, France, and Japan spoke in support of the draft resolution, but the Egyptian representative objected. He questioned the motives of the draft's sponsors in calling for the UNSC session, arguing that they had ignored Israel's provocative actions and maintaining that Egypt was acting in self-defense. Supporting the position of the Arab nations, the Soviet Union's representative

---

46. In his report to the Central Committee of the Communist Party on June 20, 1967, Brezhnev faulted Nasser both for his call for withdrawal of UNEF and for his closure of the Tiran Straits, declaring that he had acted without consulting the Soviet Union ("On Soviet Policy Following the Israeli Aggression in the Middle East," *Woodrow Wilson International Center for Scholars*).
47. For the UN report on the 1967 debates and resolutions in UNSC and UNGA regarding the Arab–Israeli conflict, see United Nations, *Yearbook, 1967*.

also declared he saw no reason for the hasty convocation of UNSC. After repeating the false accusation against Israel of having mobilized its forces along the Syrian border in a plan to attack Syria, he claimed—in typical Cold-War phraseology—that Israel could not have behaved so threateningly "without encouragement from certain imperialist circles which sought to restore colonial oppression." Instead of acceding to the request for all member states to refrain from any steps that might worsen the situation, he threatened, "Any aggression in the Middle East would be met not only with the united strength of the Arab countries but also with strong opposition from the USSR and all peace-loving states."

Upon his return from Cairo, the secretary-general submitted a report to UNSC on May 26 in which, after having noted the heightened tensions following Nasser's decision to close the Tiran Straits, he called for a "breathing spell" to "allow tension to subside from its present explosive level." He urged all the parties concerned "to exercise special restraint, to forgo belligerence, and to avoid all other actions which could increase tension in order to allow UNSC to deal with the underlying causes of the crisis and to seek solutions."

Over four UNSC meetings, from May 29 to June 3, UNSC was unable to agree on a resolution in support of the secretary-general's recommendation. Instead, the Arab countries continued to insist—with the vigorous support of the Soviet Union—that the Arabs were acting only in self-defense against Israeli aggression and that UNSC must condemn that aggression. The Egyptian representative also claimed that Egypt was within its rights to bar enemy vessels in the Gulf of Aqaba, because the Arabs were in a state of war with Israel, a claim that UNSC had rejected in Resolution 95 of 1951. Nasser's decision to remove UNEF from Egypt's borders, he further argued, was a defensive act, made to enable Egypt to come to Syria's defense in face of what he charged, in accordance with the earlier Soviet warnings, was Israel's concentration and movement of troops for a planned attack against Syria. The Israeli representative denied that any such Israeli movement of forces had taken place, and Secretary-General U Thant had indeed confirmed in his report to UNSC ten days earlier that UNTSO observers had seen no Israeli concentration or movement of forces near the Syrian border. The blockade in the Gulf of Aqaba, the Israeli representative added, was an act of aggression against Israel, and Egypt's justification of its policy of continued belligerence had made an empty shell of the armistice agreements of 1949.[48]

Israel called for 1. an end to inflammatory threats against the territorial integrity and political independence of all states; 2. acceptance of the UN Charter's obligation of non-belligerence; 3. withdrawal of armed forces to their positions as of the beginning of the month; and 4. an end to sabotage, terrorism, and interference with shipping in the Gulf of Aqaba. The Soviet Union's representative, however, again placed the blame for the dangerous tensions in the Middle East on what he charged was Israel's aggressive action against the Arabs—taken, he added, with the support of "certain imperialist circles"—and he insisted on the need for UNSC to condemn Israel for its provocations and threats. The Soviet Union, together with the Arab countries, thus rejected not only Israel's recommendations for an end to the multiple Arab threats to its existence but also the secretary-general's call to exercise restraint, forgo belligerence, and avoid all actions that could increase tensions.

The danger to Israel was aggravated still further on May 30, when Jordan's King Hussein, fearing an outbreak of civil war from his majority Palestinian population if he failed to join forces with Egypt, rejected repeated calls from Israel against entering the battle and

---

48. As noted earlier, the UNSC had declared in its Resolution 95 (see the following citation), that under the armistice agreements, "neither party can reasonably assert that it is actively a belligerent," and it had called upon Egypt "to terminate the restrictions on the passage of international commercial shipping and goods through the Suez Canal": United Nations Security Council, Resolution 95, The Palestine Question, Document S/RES/95 (1951) (September 1, 1951), accessed on August 9, 2023, https://documents-dds-ny.un.org/doc/RESOLUTION/GEN/NR0/072/14/PDF/NR007214.pdf?OpenElement.

signed a defense pact with Nasser, turning his armed forces over to the Egyptian command. Iraq quickly followed suit in joining the war effort, and other Arab nations, including countries as distant as Algeria and Kuwait, offered significant military support. In his report on June 20, 1967, Brezhnev summarized the balance of forces on the eve of the war as follows:

> The armed forces of the UAR, Syria, Algeria, and Iraq were almost one hundred percent equipped with modern weapons, produced and supplied by us and by other socialist countries. The USSR had supplied, on favorable terms and reduced prices, its Arab allies with considerable amounts of aircraft, tanks, firearms, mine-throwers, AA guns, ground-to-air missiles, military vessels, and other modern weapon systems. A large number of Arab experts received military training in the USSR… Due to this generous aid rendered by the USSR and other countries, Arab countries were indisputably superior to Israel in weapons and military personnel prior to the outbreak of hostilities. The armed forces of the UAR, Syria, and Iraq had at least one-and-a-half times more tanks and airplanes than the IDF.[49]

Israel was therefore completely surrounded by Arab countries with well-trained and heavily equipped military forces at its land borders, while being subjected to a blockade by sea and to repeated Arab threats to "demolish the Zionist state," to "wipe Israel off the map," and to "throw Israel into the sea."

Given the evident inability of UNSC to deal with the multiple threats to Israel's existence, Israel sent Foreign Minister Abba Eban to Paris, London, and Washington, DC to discover if they were prepared to act to open the Tiran Straits to Israeli shipping in accordance with President Eisenhower's 1957 commitment. French President de Gaulle, who had decided—once France had granted independence to Algeria and to its other African colonies—to chart a new

---

49. "On Soviet Policy Following the Israeli Aggression in the Middle East," *Woodrow Wilson International Center for Scholars*.

international role as a champion of the developing world, was now distinctly cool to Israel. Britain's Prime Minister Harold Wilson and US President Johnson were supportive of Israel, but Johnson, caught up in the morass of the Vietnam War, was unable to carry out the US government's commitment to organize an international program for lifting Nasser's blockade against Israel in the Tiran Straits.

The Six-Day War

War between Israel and the Arab countries—with Israel's survival at stake and with Jews all over the world fearful of a second Holocaust about to befall their people—broke out on the Egyptian and Syrian fronts and in Jerusalem on June 5, 1967. At the beginning of the fighting, Israeli Prime Minister Levi Eshkol sought to ward off war with Jordan by notifying King Hussein, "We shall not engage ourselves in any action against Jordan unless Jordan attacks us. Should Jordan attack Israel, we shall go against her with all our might."[50] King Hussein failed to heed the warning, and—responding to Egypt's call and to its false reports of Egyptian air victories on the opening day of the war—launched an attack against Jewish Jerusalem. Israel, as Eshkol had warned, replied in force, with the aims of capturing the West Bank and the Old City of Jerusalem as well as of eliminating Jordan's standing threat to Israel by driving it back across the Jordan River within its Mandatory boundaries. At the end of the very first day of fighting, Israel's friends were exhilarated and Israel's enemies aggrieved to hear the astounding news reports that the Israeli air force had already succeeded, in a stunning series of air attacks, in destroying Egypt's air force as well as half of Syria's air force and Jordan's small number of planes.

The United Nations Security Council met in an emergency session on June 5 to receive the secretary-general's report on the fighting

---

50. "Message from Prime Minister Eshkol to King Hussein, 5 June 1967," *Israeli Ministry of Foreign Affairs*, accessed on July 11, 2023, https://www.gov.il/en/Departments/General/16-message-from-pm-eshkol-to-king-hussein-5-june-1967.

that had erupted that day between Israel and the Arab countries. The following day, June 6, UNSC unanimously adopted as Resolution 233 (1967) its president's draft text proposal in which UNSC 1. called for "as a first step...an immediate ceasefire and for a cessation of all military activities" and 2. asked the secretary-general "to keep UNSC promptly and currently informed on the situation."[51]

Israel's representative welcomed UNSC's call for a ceasefire, but the Arab representatives, with the support of the Soviet Union, rejected it and insisted rather that UNSC should condemn Israel as the aggressor and require its immediate and unconditional withdrawal to the 1949 Armistice Agreement lines. The Syrian representative, evidently believing it impossible for Israel's air force to have achieved, all by itself, such a stunning success against all the Arab air forces, charged the US and the UK with having joined in the Israeli air attacks and with having provided air cover for the IDF.

The same morning of June 6, 1967, at 7:40 a.m., Radio Cairo announced the charge of the US and the UK's participation in the attack on Egypt's air force. The US and the UK categorically denied the charges, for which the Arabs had produced no evidence, and declared their readiness to have the UN investigate the charges. Nevertheless, the Syrian representative announced that Algeria, Egypt, and had severed diplomatic relations with the US.[52] At the same time, Algeria and Iraq instituted a boycott of oil shipments to the US and the UK, and the other Arab oil-exporting countries, not wishing to appear anti-US and anti-UK, closed down their oil production entirely. The oil boycott remained in effect until an agreement was reached at an Arab summit meeting in Khartoum, Sudan in September to resume oil exports and use the proceeds as a weapon against Israel by assisting in the recovery of the economies of Egypt and Jordan from the losses they suffered in the war.

---

51. For the full texts of the 1967 UNSC resolutions, see United Nations Security Council, *Resolutions*, accessed on August 9, 2023, https://www.un.org/securitycouncil/content/resolutions-0.
52. United Nations, *Yearbook, 1967*.

Nasser was still rather optimistic at 8:00 a.m. on June 6 in his conversation with the Soviet ambassador to Cairo, stating, according to Brezhnev, "The situation on the front doesn't seem as bad for the UAR, as Western propaganda has tried to portray." At 6 p.m., however, Field Marshal Amer conveyed an urgent message from Nasser, declaring, "The situation is very dangerous and critical, and…it would further deteriorate tonight." At midnight, Field Marshal Amer met again with the Soviet ambassador to inform him that the situation on the front was grave and asked the Soviet government to reach a ceasefire agreement with Israel within the next five hours. The Soviet Union, now in a state of extreme anxiety over the magnitude of the Arab losses and concerned that the IDF might proceed to occupy Cairo and Damascus, requested an urgent meeting of UNSC early that morning, to which it submitted a draft resolution for a ceasefire.[53] This resolution set the time for the ceasefire to take effect at 8:00 p.m. GMT on June 7, 1967. In its anxiety over the Arab military losses, the Soviet Union omitted from its draft proposal its previous demands for the condemnation of Israel and for the immediate withdrawal of Israel's troops. Thus, UNSC unanimously adopted the Soviet draft text at a second session the same day, June 7, 1967, as Resolution 234 (1967).[54]

Israel accepted UNSC's call for a ceasefire subject to acceptance by the Arab parties. When Egypt and Syria failed to accept the ceasefire that day, both the US and the USSR requested, the following day, June 8, another urgent meeting of UNSC. Both Egypt and Jordan then notified the secretary-general that they had decided to accept UNSC's ceasefire resolution on the condition that the other party ceased fire. Israel also accepted, and the fighting ceased on those fronts.

Syria, however, still did not accept the ceasefire. On June 9, UNSC unanimously adopted as Resolution 235 (1967) its president's

---

[53] "On Soviet Policy Following the Israeli Aggression in the Middle East," *Woodrow Wilson International Center for Scholars*.

[54] See *Foreign Relations of the United States: Diplomatic Papers, 1964–1968*, vol. 34.

proposals 1. confirming its previous resolutions for an immediate ceasefire and 2. asking the secretary-general (a) to arrange for immediate compliance and (b) to report to UNSC within two hours. The fighting continued, however, and on June 10, UNSC held a pre-dawn emergency meeting at the request of the Syrian representative, who charged Israeli forces with moving toward Damascus. The Israeli representative accused Syria, in turn, of having continued to shell Israeli villages for twenty-six hours after having accepted the ceasefire and declared that the only Israeli activity was against those Syrian gun emplacements. The USSR representative informed UNSC that his government had notified Israel that if it did not forthwith end its military activities, "The USSR, together with all peace-loving states," would have to apply sanctions against Israel. The USSR also severed diplomatic relations with Israel, and all the countries of the Soviet bloc followed suit. It was not until October 1991, when the Soviet Union was already in a state of collapse, that Russia, under President Boris Yeltsin, restored diplomatic relations with Israel.[55]

On the evening of June 11, the secretary-general informed UNSC that both Israel and Syria had accepted the UN's arrangements for the cessation of all firing and of troop movements, effective as of 4:30 p.m. GMT on June 10. After a brief recess, UNSC resumed its session and unanimously adopted as Resolution 236 (1967) its president's proposals, calling, inter alia, for 1. the prompt return of troops to the ceasefire positions of 4:30 p.m. GMT on June 10, 1967 and 2. full cooperation with UN staff in implementing the ceasefire.

When the Six-Day War ended on June 10, 1967, the grave Arab threat to Israel's survival had been lifted. Israel had won a stunning victory over all the Arab states that had arrayed against it in their campaign to wipe it off the map. It had captured the Golan Heights from Syria, the Sinai Peninsula from Egypt, and all of the territory of

---

55. "PM Olmert's Remarks Following his Meeting with Russian President Putin, October 18, 2006," Prime Minister's Office, accessed on August 7, 2023, http://www.pmo.gov.il/PMOEng/Communication/EventsDiary/eventputin181006.htm.

Mandatory Palestine that Egypt and Jordan had taken in 1948: from Egypt, the Gaza Strip, and from Jordan, the West Bank and the Old City of Jerusalem, including the Temple Mount. For the first time in nearly two thousand years, the Jewish people were reunited with all their biblical Holy Land and with a united Jerusalem re-established as its capital.

In a statement to the Knesset on June 12, Israel's Prime Minister Levi Eshkol called upon the Arab states to begin negotiations with Israel for a peaceful settlement, to move from the existing ceasefire to a state of peace and security for all states in the region.[56] Foreign Minister Abba Eban, in a statement to UNGA on June 19, reiterated Israel's call for peace negotiations and held out a vision of the mutual benefits to Israel and the Arabs from the economic, social, and scientific development that peaceful cooperation in all spheres of life would generate.[57] The Arab states remained no less adamant in their opposition to Israel's existence, however, than they had been during the previous two decades following the establishment of the State of Israel. Israel's seemingly miraculous victory accordingly came with an enormous cost, because the large Palestinian population living within its new ceasefire boundaries quickly turned far more nationalist and far more militant than it had theretofore been. The burden of ruling over such a large Arab population gradually eroded much world support for Israel, despite the openly declared Palestinian goal of liberating all of Palestine—a euphemism for liquidating the State of Israel.

---

56. "Statement to the Knesset by Prime Minister Eshkol, 12 June 1967," *Israeli Ministry of Foreign Affairs*, accessed on July 11, 2023, https://www.gov.il/en/Departments/General/23-statement-to-the-knesset-by-pm-eshkol-12-june-1967.

57. "Statement to the General Assembly by Foreign Minister Eban, 19 June 1967," *Israeli Ministry of Foreign Affairs*, accessed on July 11, 2023, https://www.gov.il/en/Departments/General/25-statement-to-the-general-assembly-by-fm-eban-19-june-1967.

Israel's Reunification of Jerusalem

According to the Israeli historian, Michael Oren, Eshkol wrote to King Hussein before Israel captured the Old City of Jerusalem to inform him that if Hussein retook control of his army, accepted an unconditional ceasefire, and agreed to peace talks, Israel would not take the Old City of Jerusalem. "Levi Eshkol was within a hand's grasp of realizing a millennial Jewish vision and was willing to forfeit it," Oren stated, "in return for a peace process with Jordan. The letter was never answered."[58]

After it had captured the Old City, however, Israel was determined never to permit Jerusalem to be divided again. It tore down the barbed wire that had divided Jerusalem in two since Jordan had seized the Old City in 1948, and Jews were once again able to pray at the Temple Mount's Western Wall, as they had done for the nearly two millennia since the Roman destruction of the Holy Temple. Israel's Moslems were likewise free for the first time since 1948 to worship at the Dome of the Rock and the Al-Aqsa Mosque. Israel left the Christian and Moslem religious authorities in charge of all their own holy sites, retaining the Waqf, the Moslem organization responsible for the Temple Mount. Partly out of sensitivity to Moslem religious feelings, Israel also decided not to permit Jews to engage in communal prayer on the Temple Mount or even to ascend the Temple Mount in large numbers. It imposed these restrictions even though the Temple Mount is the most sacred site in Judaism, dating back to a millennium before the birth of Christianity and a millennium and a half before the birth of Mohammad.

On June 27, 1967, Israel announced the administrative reunification of the city of Jerusalem. Israeli secular law, covering municipal

---

58. Michael Oren, "The Unwanted War That Made the Middle East" (California: June 24, 2002), Commonwealth Club of California Records, *Hoover Institution Library & Archives*, ID 2003c87_a_0001136, Record 2003C87.2862, accessed July 11, 2023, https://digitalcollections.hoover.org/objects/3173/1967-the-unwanted-war-that-made-the-middle-east?ctx=473ba4dd-e459-41e1-96b2-79b35acf8b68&idx=3.

matters such as the provision of water supply; sanitation facilities and services; compulsory education; and welfare programs would henceforth apply equally to the Arabs and Jews of all Jerusalem—Old and New. The Israeli Knesset formally annexed the Old City to Israel only in 1980 under the former head of the Irgun, Menachem Begin, who served as prime minister of Israel from 1977–1983, but all Israeli governments of all political persuasions have, since 1967, proclaimed Jerusalem as the eternal, indivisible capital of Israel.[59] They have encouraged the restoration of the traditional Jewish Quarter of the Old City from which Jordan's Arab Legion had expelled the Jewish people in 1948 and the expansion of Jewish neighborhoods in the unpopulated outskirts of the Old City.

The overwhelming majority of UN member countries opposed Israel's administrative reunification of Jerusalem, considering it the same as annexation. On July 4, 1967, UNGA, at its fifth emergency special session, adopted a resolution opposing Israel's actions on Jerusalem. By a vote of ninety-nine to zero, with twenty abstentions, UNGA approved Resolution 2253 (ES-V), confirming:

[UNGA...]

1. considers Israel's action to change the status of Jerusalem to be invalid and

2. calls upon it to rescind all measures already taken and to desist from taking any further measures to change the status of the city.[60]

---

59. During the Camp David negotiations with Yasser Arafat, hosted by President Bill Clinton in 2000, Prime Minister Ehud Barak made an historic offer to share Jerusalem as the capital of both an Israeli state and a Palestinian state.
60. United Nations General Assembly, 5th Emergency Special Session: 1545th Plenary Meeting, Document A/PV.1545 (July 3, 1967), accessed on August 10, 2023, https://digitallibrary.un.org/record/718801.

Israel called the resolution unacceptable, because it violated the unity of Jerusalem and advocated a return to religious discrimination. On July 10, 1967, Abba Eban summarized the changes Israel had introduced in Jerusalem as follows:

> Where there was hostile separation, there is now harmonious civic union. Where there was a constant threat of violence, there is now peace. Where there was once an assertion of exclusive and unilateral control over the Holy Places, exercised in sacrilegious discrimination, there is now a willingness to work out arrangements with the world's religious bodies—Christian, Moslem, and Jewish—which will ensure the universal religious character of the Holy Places.[61]

However, UNGA remained firmly opposed to Israel's rule over the Old City. At its resumed emergency special session after a week's recess, on July 14 it adopted Resolution 2254 (ES-V) in which it deplored Israel's failure to comply with its previous resolution on Jerusalem and repeated its call against changing the status of Jerusalem. The US abstained in the vote on both UNGA resolutions but noted that it did not accept or recognize Israel's administrative measures as having altered the status of Jerusalem.[62]

In contrast to the resolutions passed in 1967 and the many others the UN adopted in subsequent years to deplore, censure, or condemn Israel's actions on Jerusalem, the UN, it may be noted, had raised no objections to Jordan's actions in Jerusalem's Old City, even though Jordan's measures were considerably more far reaching. In 1948, Jordan's Arab Legion engaged in the ethnic cleansing of the Old City, removing its entire Jewish population and destroying the Old City's Jewish synagogues and religious schools. Jordan desecrated

---

61. United Nations Security Council, Report of the Secretary-General on Measures Taken by Israel to Change the Status of the City of Jerusalem, Document S/8052 (July 10, 1967), accessed on August 10, 2023, https://digitallibrary.un.org/record/520093?ln=en.
62. See United Nations, *Yearbook, 1967*.

the ancient Jewish cemetery on the Mount of Olives and denied the Jews access to the Western Wall. In April 1950, it formally annexed the Old City, cutting the city of Jerusalem into two separate cities that were totally segregated from one another. At no time did the UN pass a resolution to consider invalid Jordan's measures to change the status of Jerusalem. It did not call upon Jordan to rescind those measures and it did not deplore, censure, or condemn its measures to deny to the Jewish people their historic access to the Western Wall of the Temple Mount, a never-abandoned sacred site whose Jewish roots predate those of Christianity and Islam in the Old City by time measured in millennia.

– 21 –

The United Nations' Principles for Peace

ISRAEL'S STUNNING VICTORY IN THE Six-Day War left it militarily stronger, but it failed to mitigate the refusal of the Arab states to accept the existence of the State of Israel and to begin peace negotiations. Shaken by the humiliating Arab defeat, Nasser offered his immediate resignation, but the Egyptians rejected his offer, and he remained the unchallenged leader of pan-Arab nationalism, in continued opposition to Israel's existence. The Soviet Union, worried that Nasser's defeat threatened its own political gains in the Middle East since 1956, encouraged Nasser to remain in his post and sent its top leaders to Egypt, Syria, and Algeria to provide reassurance of continued Soviet support for their cause. To keep the Arab defeat from becoming a disaster, the Soviet leadership embarked on a dual course: a costly military program to mitigate the Egyptian and Syrian military losses in the Six-Day War and a political campaign in the UN to push Israel back to its 1949 Armistice Agreement borders—without any peace negotiations. In return for this assistance, the Soviet Union posed a series of conditions to the Arabs, emphasizing, in particular, the essential need to maintain Arab unity in the campaign against Israel and the US.[1]

---

1. In a conversation with a Polish politburo member, the Soviet leader, Leonid Brezhnev said, inter alia, "The events shook up the Arabs, but at the same time, they made them sober. This was a unique shock for the Arabs. We undertook all possible precautions [measures] so this defeat would not be considered a disaster. We undertook many different steps. I directed a personal letter to Nasser so he should not resign from his post. We sent our comrades to the Arab nations. Cde. [Soviet President Nikolai

In a political speech in July 1970, Nasser reported most thankfully on the help the USSR had provided immediately following the Six-Day War. He stated:

> The leaders of the Soviet Union—Brezhnev, Kosygin, and Podgorny—sent me a message telling me not to despair, that the USSR would help us in every way and would supply us with arms to replace those lost in the battles in the Sinai... The arms from the USSR arrived immediately... The Egyptian people, all the peoples of the Arab nation, decided not to accept defeat. But we needed arms for our forces. So when we say we are deeply grateful to the USSR, it is because we remember that... the Soviet Union delivered planes, tanks, cannons, and arms to us within days of the defeat. In return, we offered the hope that we would resist and, with God's help, triumph...that we would build first a defensive army, then an offensive army which would enable us to liberate the territories usurped from us.[2]

V.] Podgorny went to Egypt [on June 21–24, 1967]. Cde. [Chief of the General Staff, Marshal Matvei V.] Zakharov went to Syria. We hosted [Algerian Prime Minister Houari] Boumedienne [in Moscow on June 12–13, 1967]... We posed a series of conditions before him, or rather principles, by which they should be guided. First, they must maintain Arab unity. Second, they must maintain friendly relations between progressive Arab leaders. The Arabs must unite, because only in this way will they be able to resist the aggression of imperialism... We must continue our work, continue to maintain our personal contacts and to give assistance. We have transferred many airplanes, tanks, and food to Egypt and other Arab nations. Among other things, we sent them ten thousand tons of sugar, butter, pasta, medicine, etc.

See "Record of Conversation between Polish Politburo Member Zenon Kliszko and Soviet Leader Leonid Brezhnev, Moscow, June 24, 1967," *Woodrow Wilson International Center for Scholars, Virtual Archive*, accessed on July 11, 2023, https://digitalarchive.wilsoncenter.org/document/record-conversation-between-polish-politburo-member-zenon-kliszko-and-soviet-leader-leonid.

2. Gamal Abdel Nasser, "A Political Testimony, July 23, 1970," *Pan-African Perspective*, accessed on August 10, 2023, https://www.

Nasser was so grateful for the Soviet help that he even declared his desire to forsake NAM, which had been the capstone of his political career. He told Podgorny during the latter's visit to Egypt in June, shortly after the end of the Six-Day War, that the policy of non-alignment with any blocs "does not work for Egypt" and that "we want to be with you forever." Brezhnev noted that the Soviet Union must give careful thought to this change in Nasser's attitude and respond appropriately.[3]

The Soviet Union's Anti-Israel Activities in the United Nations

In addition to re-arming Egypt and Syria, the Soviet Union repeatedly pressed the UN to force Israel's immediate and unconditional withdrawal to the 1949 Armistice Agreement lines. On June 13, three days after the Six-Day War's end, the USSR called again for an urgent meeting of UNSC at which its representative insisted that UNSC must now take additional measures going beyond its ceasefire resolutions. He submitted a draft proposal whereby UNSC would 1. vigorously condemn Israel's aggressive activities and continued occupation of territory of the Arab States and 2. demand that Israel immediately and unconditionally withdraw its troops behind the 1949 Armistice Agreement lines.[4]

Justice Arthur Goldberg, whom President Johnson had persuaded to resign from the US Supreme Court to assume the post of US permanent representative at the UN, called the Soviet proposal a prescription for renewed hostilities. He submitted instead a revised draft of an earlier US proposal that would take into account Israel's concerns for peace and security. The US draft resolution would have

---

panafricanperspective.com/Gamal-Abdel-Nasser.html.
3. "Record of Conversation between Polish Politburo Member Zenon Kliszko and Soviet Leader Leonid Brezhnev, Moscow, June 24, 1967," *Woodrow Wilson International Center for Scholars*.
4. See United Nations, *Yearbook, 1967*.

UNSC call for prompt discussions among the parties concerned with the goal of 1. establishing viable arrangements for the withdrawal and disengagement of armed personnel; 2. renouncing force regardless of its nature; 3. maintaining vital international rights; and 4. establishing a stable and durable peace in the Middle East.

The following day, June 14, the fifteen members of UNSC rejected the Soviet draft resolution in separate votes on each of its operative paragraphs. The first paragraph, on condemning Israel as the aggressor, received four affirmative votes and eleven abstentions, and the second, for the immediate and unconditional withdrawal of Israel's armed forces behind the 1949 Armistice Agreement lines, received six affirmative votes and nine abstentions.[5]

Following its defeat in UNSC, the Soviet Union asked, with urgency, the UN secretary-general to convene an emergency special session of UNGA. The fifth emergency special session of UNGA, attended by many heads of state and foreign ministers, opened on June 17, 1967. On June 19, the chairman of the Council of Ministers of the Soviet Union presented a draft resolution to UNGA that expanded the one-sided Soviet demands to UNSC and again completely ignored Israel's concerns for peace and security. According to this draft,

[UNGA would...]

1. vigorously condemn Israel's aggression;

2. demand that Israel immediately and unconditionally withdraw all its forces behind the armistice demarcation lines [of 1949];

3. demand that Israel should provide full and prompt compensation for all Egyptian, Syrian, and Jordanian losses; and

---

5. On the same day, UNSC unanimously adopted Resolution 237 (1967) to safeguard the human rights of the civilian population and of prisoners of war.

4. appeal to UNSC to take immediate, effective measures to eliminate all the consequences of Israel's aggression.[6]

Speaking the next day, June 20, Ambassador Goldberg restated the position of the US that the ultimate aim of UNGA…

> …must be nothing less than a stable and a durable peace in the Middle East. The USSR…had introduced a draft resolution essentially the same as that which the overwhelming majority of UNSC had refused to accept, and its one-sided condemnation of Israel as an aggressor would be neither equitable nor constructive. Its call for withdrawal of the Israel forces…would return the situation to that of 5 June, with opposing forces standing in direct confrontation and with no international machinery present to keep them apart… Rather than approve such a prescription for renewed hostilities, the US sought steps towards real peace based on five essential principles which the president of the US had enunciated the day before, on 19 June.

In an address at the State Department's Foreign Policy Conference for Educators, President Lyndon B. Johnson had postulated the following five essential principles for peace:

> The first and the greatest principle is that every nation in the area has a fundamental right to live and to have this right respected by its neighbors…

> Second, this last month, I think, shows us another basic requirement for settlement. It is a human requirement: justice for the refugees…

> A third lesson from this last month is that maritime rights must be respected… If a single act of folly was more responsible for this explosion [of war] than any other, I think it was the

---

6. For the texts of the draft resolutions submitted to UNGA and the votes cast, see United Nations, *Yearbook, 1967*.

arbitrary and dangerous announced decision that the Straits of Tiran would be closed...

Fourth, this last conflict has demonstrated the danger of the Middle Eastern arms race of the last twelve years. Here the responsibility must rest not only on those in the area but upon the larger states outside the area...

Fifth, the crisis underlines the importance of respect for political independence and territorial integrity of all the states of the area... This principle can be effective in the Middle East only on the basis of peace between the parties. The nations of the region have had only fragile and violated truce lines for twenty years. What they now need are recognized boundaries and other arrangements that will give them security against terror, destruction, and war.[7]

In accordance with these five principles, Ambassador Goldberg submitted a draft resolution whereby UNGA would endorse the ceasefire and decide that its objective must be a stable and durable peace in the Middle East, with the objective to be achieved through negotiated arrangements with appropriate third-party assistance. These arrangements should be based on:

> mutual recognition of political independence and territorial integrity, encompassing recognized boundaries that would provide security against terror, destruction, and war;
>
> freedom of innocent maritime passage;
>
> a just and equitable solution of the refugee problem;
>
> registration and limitation of arms shipments into the area; and

---

7. See Lyndon B. Johnson, "Address at the State Department's Foreign Policy Conference for Educators," *The American Presidency Project*, accessed on July 11, 2023, https://www.presidency.ucsb.edu/documents/address-the-state-departments-foreign-policy-conference-for-educators.

recognition of the right of all sovereign nations to exist in peace and security.[8]

Abba Eban, Israel's foreign minister, rejected, with indignation, Arab and Soviet charges against Israel, and he accused the Arab countries of unprovoked aggression. In May, he noted, Egypt had made a reckless decision to upset the security agreement that had been reached in 1957, and between May 14 and June 4, President Nasser and high officials of his government had made more than fifty declarations calling for Israel's annihilation.[9] How would any other member state have reacted, he asked, if a group of neighboring states had encircled it with hostile armies, had blockaded its coasts, and had announced their intention of waging a war of annihilation? With regard to Jordan, he emphasized that even after Jordan had opened fire on Jerusalem, Israel had offered King Hussein an opportunity to disengage by informing him that Israel would not attack any state that refrained from attacking it.

Eban categorically rejected the Soviet demand for Israel's complete and unconditional withdrawal behind the 1949 Armistice Agreement lines, emphasizing, as had US Ambassador Goldberg, that such withdrawal would restore the same situation from which the war had arisen. It would restore "the same frontiers, the same insecurity, the same blockade of waterways, the same belligerent doctrine, the same divided city…the same arms race, and, above all, the same absence of peace treaties requiring a mutual recognition of sovereignty."[10] All proposals or resolutions calling for a non-negotiated withdrawal, without a prior mutual commitment to peace, he declared, were prescriptions for a renewal of the conflict.

On July 4, 1967, UNGA rejected the Soviet draft resolution in separate votes on each of its four operative paragraphs and on its

---

8. United Nations, *Yearbook, 1967*.
9. For a selection of Yasser Arafat's own statements and those of his associates in the PLO calling for the destruction of Israel, see Appendix 3.
10. United Nations, *Yearbook, 1967*.

preamble, with each one of its parts failing to obtain not only the required two-thirds majority vote for passage but even a simple majority. The paragraph calling for condemnation of Israel as the aggressor was rejected by a vote of fifty-seven opposed to thirty-six in favor, with twenty-three abstentions, while the second paragraph on withdrawal behind the 1949 Armistice Agreement lines was turned down by a margin of forty-eight opposed to forty-five in favor, with twenty-two abstentions. The last two operative paragraphs and the preamble were all rejected by majorities of about three to two, similar to the vote on the first operative paragraph.[11]

Thus, UNGA had before it two additional draft resolutions in which the Soviet Union's call for Israel's withdrawal to the 1949 Armistice Agreement lines was retained, but its call for condemnation of Israel and its demand for reparations were dropped. These two drafts added calls instead for further UNSC action to deal in some fashion with the other outstanding Arab–Israeli issues. A seventeen-nation Afro-Asian draft resolution added a request for UNSC to "consider all aspects of the situation in the Middle East and seek peaceful ways and means for the solution of all problems—legal, political, and humanitarian—through appropriate channels." It failed to obtain the two-thirds majority required for UNGA adoption, receiving fifty-three votes in favor to forty-six against, with twenty abstentions.[12]

The second draft resolution, submitted by the twenty-member Latin American group, coupled an urgent request to Israel "to withdraw all its forces from all the territories it occupied as a result of the recent conflict," with an urgent request to "all the parties to end the

---

11. United Nations, *Yearbook, 1967*. Albania submitted an even more one-sided draft resolution calling for the condemnation of the US and the UK for assisting and directly participating in Israel's aggression and asking UNSC to confirm that Egypt alone had the right to decide whether to permit Israeli shipping in the Suez Canal and through the Tiran Straits. However, UNGA rejected this draft resolution by a vote of seventy-one against, with twenty-two in favor and twenty-seven abstentions.
12. United Nations, *Yearbook, 1967*, reproduced online on UNISPAL.

state of belligerency and endeavor to settle all issues peacefully." In addition, it asked UNSC...

> ...working directly with the parties, to:
>
> 1. implement the provision requesting Israel to withdraw all its forces from all the territories it occupied as a result of the recent conflict;
>
> 2. guarantee freedom of transit on the international waterways in the region; and
>
> 3. achieve an appropriate and full solution of the problem of the refugees and guarantee the territorial inviolability and political independence of the states of the region.

This draft resolution likewise failed to obtain the two-thirds majority required for adoption, receiving fifty-seven votes in favor to forty-three against, with twenty abstentions.[13] The US decided not to call for a vote on its own draft resolution.

After a week-long recess from July 5, UNGA resumed its emergency special session, which continued until July 21, 1967, when, before adjourning, it voted in Resolution 2256 (ES-V) to refer the Middle East issue to UNSC for urgent action.

Principles for Peace: United Nations Security Council Resolution 242 (1967)

Following the adjournment of UNGA's emergency special session, UNSC resumed its consideration of the situation in the Middle East. Before UNSC were complaints from Israel and Syria, from Israel and Jordan, and from Israel and Egypt regarding violations of the ceasefire at the borders between them, including incursions by Syrian-trained and Syrian-directed Palestinian guerrilla forces from Jordan into Israel. The most serious violation occurred on October 21, 1967, when

---

13. United Nations, *Yearbook, 1967*, reproduced online on UNISPAL.

Egypt sank the Israeli destroyer, Eilat, which was engaged in routine patrol in international waters off the Suez Canal. On October 24, Israel and Egypt both called for an urgent meeting of UNSC to deal with complaints regarding an exchange of fire between the Israeli and Egyptian forces on the banks of the Suez Canal. During the exchange, Israel shelled the Egyptian Suez Port and its industrial installations, including its petroleum refineries and fertilizer plants.

Thus, UNSC met on October 24 and 25, 1967 to consider the complaints. The Soviet Union submitted a draft resolution whereby UNSC would strongly condemn Israel for its act of aggression in the city of Suez and demand that Israel compensate Egypt for the damage. Recognizing that it did not have the information necessary to apportion blame, UNSC unanimously adopted instead, as Resolution 240 (1967), a neutral draft resolution, whereby UNSC 1. condemned the ceasefire violations; 2. regretted the resulting casualties and property damage; 3. reaffirmed the necessity of strict observance to the ceasefire resolutions; and 4. demanded that the member states concerned immediately cease all prohibited military activities in the area and cooperate fully and promptly with UNTSO.[14]

On November 7, 1967, Egypt again called for an urgent session of UNSC to consider the dangerous situation in the Middle East. Two draft resolutions setting forth the proposed principles for achieving peace in the Middle East were before UNSC, one submitted by the Afro-Asian members of UNSC—India, Nigeria, and Mali—and the other by the US. According to the three-nation draft resolution, UNSC would affirm the following principles for peace and the consequent calls for action in the Middle East:

> The occupation or acquisition of territory by military conquest is inadmissible; Israel's armed forces should therefore withdraw from all the territories occupied as a result of the recent conflict.

---

14. For the full text, see United Nations Security Council, *Resolutions*, accessed on August 9, 2023, https://www.un.org/securitycouncil/content/resolutions-0

Every state has the right to live in peace and complete security, free from threats or acts of war; all states in the area should therefore terminate the state or claim of belligerency and settle their international disputes by peaceful means.

Every state has the right to be secure within its borders, and consequently, all member states of the area must respect the sovereignty, territorial integrity, and political independence of one another.[15]

According to the US draft resolution, UNSC would…

> affirm that the fulfillment of [UN] Charter principles required the achievement of a state of just and lasting peace in the Middle East embracing withdrawal of armed forces from occupied territories, termination of claims or states of belligerence, and mutual recognition of and respect for the right of every state in the area to sovereign existence, territorial integrity, political independence, secure and recognized boundaries, and freedom from the threat or use of force;
>
> affirm further the necessity (a) for guaranteeing freedom of navigation through international waterways in the area, (b) for achieving a just settlement of the refugee problem, (c) for guaranteeing the territorial inviolability and political independence of every state in the area, through measures including the establishment of demilitarized zones, and (d) for achieving a limitation of the wasteful and destructive arms race in the area;
>
> request the secretary-general to designate a special representative to proceed to the Middle East to establish and maintain contacts with the states concerned with a view to assisting them in working out solutions in accordance with the purposes of this resolution; and

---

15. United Nations, *Yearbook, 1967.*

request the secretary-general to report to UNSC on the efforts of the special representative as soon as possible.[16]

On November 15, Ambassador Goldberg, in his explanation of the US draft resolution, stated that in formulating its proposal, the US delegation had urgently consulted with the members of UNSC and with the parties on both sides. Unanimous agreement existed that UNSC should act under Chapter 6 of the UN Charter dealing with the pacific settlement of disputes. Stemming in part from this agreement, the US had been guided by the following axioms of negotiation.

> First, only the parties themselves, through mutual accommodation, compromise, and peaceful means of their own choice, can make peace and impose peace. Peace, whether imposed by one side on the other or on both sides by any outside authority, including this council, cannot endure.
>
> Second, members of this council, both individually and collectively...can and must assist the process of accommodation between the parties.
>
> Third, to serve this purpose, the council must find a formula which will not prejudice the known positions of the parties on either side and which will not preclude the acceptance by either side of the assistance, encouragement, help, and guidance the UN can properly offer.
>
> Fourth, to arrive at such a formulation, it is essential that consultations be held with the parties on both sides as well as with the members of UNSC.

The US had held such consultations with both sides and was continuing to hold them. In the view of the US delegation, its draft proposal was the only draft resolution before UNSC that met these criteria and was "right in terms of the balance it strikes between conflicting

---

16. United Nations, *Yearbook, 1967*.

views and emotions and in terms of the cooperation it will elicit from all involved in the peace-making process it would put in train."[17]

In accordance with the third axiom that the UNSC resolution must not prejudice the known positions of either side, the US draft resolution omitted the three-power draft's first principle regarding the acquisition of territory by conquest as well as the consequent call for withdrawal from all the territories that had been occupied in the recent conflict. Such withdrawal would be prejudicial to Israel's known position, repeatedly stated in UNSC and UNGA, that withdrawal must be to secure and recognized boundaries. Israel's withdrawal could also not be a precondition for solving the many other problems relating to peace and security, a demand, made repeatedly by the Arab states and the Soviet Union, that UNSC had repeatedly rejected. Instead, withdrawal was tied to other principles included in the resolution for the achievement of peace, most notably to the principle of agreement on secure and recognized boundaries. The US draft resolution therefore deliberately omitted any call for withdrawal of armed forces to the positions held on June 4 or to the 1949 Armistice Agreement lines as well as any qualifying adjectives, such as "all" or "the" before "occupied territories." Instead, it called for the withdrawal of armed forces — only "from occupied territories." The extent of the required withdrawal was left unspecified, since withdrawal had to be to recognized and secure boundaries, which could be determined only by negotiated agreement between the two sides.

In his clarification of the meaning of the US proposal concerning withdrawal, Ambassador Goldberg emphasized:

> Historically, there have never been secure or recognized boundaries in the area. Neither the armistice lines of 1949 nor the ceasefire lines of 1967 have answered that description, although

---

17. United Nations Security Council, Official Records — 22nd Year, 1377th Meeting, Document S/PV1377 (November 15, 1967), paras. 54–58, accessed on August 10, 2023, https://digitallibrary.un.org/record/587206?ln=en.

the general armistice agreements explicitly recognize the necessity to proceed to permanent peace, which necessarily entails the recognition of boundaries between the parties. Now such boundaries have yet to be agreed upon. An agreement on that point is an absolute essential to a just and lasting peace just as withdrawal is... Secure boundaries must be mutually worked out and recognized by the parties themselves as part of the peace-making process.[18]

The principles concerning freedom of navigation and a just settlement of the refugee problem in the US draft resolution, Ambassador Goldberg noted, were as vital for peace as those relating to withdrawal. Declaring that the principal factor in precipitating the recent conflict was Egypt's decision not to permit ships of all states to pass through the Tiran Straits with equal freedom, he emphasized that freedom of navigation in the Tiran Straits, as well as in the Suez Canal, for all states, was essential for the achievement of peace. A just settlement of the refugee problem was also required, both on humanitarian grounds and for the achievement of peace in the region; and, he added, the nations of the area, with the help of the world community, must act with new determination and new energy to provide a just solution.

The key provision of the US draft resolution, Goldberg emphasized, was not the statement of principles, however, but the role of the special representative to be appointed by the secretary-general. He added in his concluding remarks:

> The peacemaking process is not quick or easy, nor is it a kind of magic which enables each side to realize its maximum demands... And the terms cannot be spelled out in advance; they must be spelled out on the ground. The crucial role which the special representative can play is to foster on both sides the

---

18. United Nations Security Council, Official Records—22nd Year, 1377th Meeting, Document S/PV1377 (November 15, 1967), para. 65, accessed on August 10, 2023, https://digitallibrary.un.org/record/587206?ln=en.

frame of mind essential to peacemaking—the pragmatic will to peace—which can face and overcome the undeniable difficulties in defining mutually acceptable terms.[19]

The Soviet deputy foreign minister, Vasily Kuznetsov, objected to the US draft resolution, because it did not acknowledge the inadmissibility of occupation of territory by conquest and did not call for complete withdrawal of forces from all territories occupied in the Six-Day War. He declared:

> The US draft leaves open the possibility that Israel's forces may not be withdrawn from all the Arab territories they have seized and that part of these territories may be kept by Israel. If this is not so, we hope that the US representative will give us a clear and unambiguous explanation to the effect that the US supports the withdrawal of Israel's forces from all the occupied territories to the positions occupied prior to 5 June 1967. It is obvious that the provision for the withdrawal of troops must be so clearly formulated as to leave no loopholes whereby anyone can interpret it in his own way. This is of course our basic position, and we require a clear answer with respect to it.[20]

Israel's foreign minister, Abba Eban, on the other hand, firmly rejected the three-power draft resolution, because it called for withdrawal without a peace treaty. Israel's policy, Eban again emphasized, was to respect the June 1967 ceasefire until Israel and the Arab states, through direct negotiations between them, signed peace treaties that would end the state of war, determine the agreed national frontiers of the States, and ensure mutually guaranteed security. He added:

---

19. United Nations Security Council, Official Records—22nd Year, 1377th Meeting, Document S/PV1377, paras. 67–75.
20. United Nations Security Council, Official Records—22nd Year, 1377th Meeting, Document S/PV1377, para. 117.

We cannot return to the shattered armistice regime. We should not seek to return to any system of relations other than a permanent, contractually binding peace; and we agree with those who have said, in [UNGA] and elsewhere, that fragile armistices and armistice lines must be superseded by agreed and secure national boundaries.[21]

The following day, Thursday, November 16, 1967, Lord Caradon, the representative of the UK, presented a third draft resolution to UNSC in the hope that it would receive general assent as a draft that was balanced and just. Lord Caradon declared:

We wanted to work with others…to devise a resolution which would take full account of the essential interests of both sides as they have stated them. We went to both sides… In the long discussions with representatives of Arab countries, they have made it clear that they seek no more than justice. The central issue of the recovery and restoration of their territories is naturally uppermost in their minds… The Israelis, on the other hand, tell us that withdrawal must never be to insecurity and hostility. The action to be taken must be within the framework of a permanent peace, and withdrawal must be to secure boundaries. There must be an end of the use of threat and fear of violence and hostility. I have said before that these aims do not conflict; they are equal. They are both essential. There must be adequate provision in any resolution to meet them both, since to attempt to pursue one without the other would be foolish and futile. So we have…endeavored, with the help of my brother members of [UNSC], to set out in a draft resolution what I believe will be recognized as a sincere and fair and honest attempt both to meet the just claims of both sides and also to discharge the high responsibility of this council.[22]

---

21. United Nations Security Council, Official Records—22nd Year, 1377th Meeting, Document S/PV1377, para. 105.
22. United Nations Security Council, Official Records—22nd Year, 1377th Meeting, Document S/PV1377, paras. 9–13.

The UK draft resolution retained the key points of the US draft regarding withdrawal of armed forces. Like the US draft, it called for withdrawal not to the position of June 4 or to the 1949 Armistice Agreement boundaries, as demanded by the Arab states and the Soviet Union, and not from "all" or "the" occupied territories. Rather, withdrawal was demanded only "from territories" occupied in the recent conflict, the extent of withdrawal tied to the need for secure and recognized boundaries. Withdrawal was also not to be a precondition for resolving the other Arab–Israeli issues regarding peace and security. Instead, as in the US draft, withdrawal was to take place in the context of the termination of belligerency and respect for the sovereignty, territorial integrity, and political independence of every state in the area.

The UK draft added in a preambular paragraph, however, the phrase, "emphasizing the inadmissibility of the acquisition of territory by war" together with "the need to work for a just and lasting peace in which every state in the area can live in security." The inclusion of this phrase meant that states could not claim the right of acquisition of territory by virtue of conquest, since as the Bulgarian representative noted, such a right would be an incentive for aggression.[23] Israel did not object to this phrase, because it did not claim the right of acquisition by virtue of conquest. It claimed the right to recognized and secure boundaries within a framework of a negotiated peace that would put an end to the Arab threats to annihilate it—threats to which it had been subjected throughout the two decades of its existence. The inclusion of this preambular paragraph, therefore, did not change the meaning of the operative paragraph regarding withdrawal, which, as Lord Caradon had repeatedly explained, made provision for Israel's just claim that withdrawal must be to secure and recognized boundaries.

In addition to the paragraph on withdrawal, the UK draft resolution, like the US draft, contained principles relating to freedom of

---

23. United Nations Security Council, Official Records—22nd Year, 1377th Meeting, Document S/PV1377, para. 137.

navigation, a just settlement of the refugee problem, and a guarantee of territorial inviolability and political independence. It omitted, however, any reference to the limitation of the arms race that the US had proposed. Again, as in the US draft, two additional paragraphs related to the work of the secretary-general's special representative. The UK draft was adopted unanimously as UNSC Resolution 242 and has served as the continuing basis for Arab–Israeli peace negotiations.[24]

When UNSC met the next day, it agreed to a Bulgarian proposal to adjourn the meeting to Monday, November 20 to give the delegates time for further consultations and for obtaining instructions from their governments. At the session on November 20, Soviet Deputy Foreign Minister Kuznetsov again insisted that "the crux of the problem in the Middle East is the withdrawal of Israel troops from all the Arab territories they have occupied." There could be no peace in the Middle East, he maintained, unless Israel would withdraw from all of the Arab territories it had occupied in the recent conflict. Accordingly, he submitted yet another Soviet draft resolution, whereby UNSC would urge, inter alia, that:

> The parties to the conflict should immediately withdraw their forces to the positions they held before 5 June 1967 in accordance with the principle that the seizure of territories as a result of war is inadmissible.[25]

Lord Caradon expressed surprise that the Soviet draft resolution did not provide for the appointment of a special representative to work with the parties to promote agreement between Israel and the Arab states. He emphasized that the achievement of peace in the Middle East involved two stages, with the adoption of a UNSC resolution on the principles for peace being only the first stage. The overriding test of success would come in the second stage, in the work that the

---

24. For the text of UNSC Resolution 242, see Appendix 4.
25. United Nations Security Council, Official Records—22nd Year, 1377th Meeting, Document S/PV1377, paras. 6–7.

special representative of the secretary-general was to undertake with the parties in the Middle East. It would be a mistake, he said, for UNSC to attempt in advance to specify exactly and, in detail, how the principles for peace were to be applied. He reported:

> I have been strongly pressed by both sides to make changes, particularly in the provisions regarding withdrawal. But I came to the conclusion that to make variations under pressure from one side or the other at this stage would destroy the equal balance which we had endeavored to achieve and would also destroy the confidence which we hoped to build on our effort to be just and impartial. I understand the intense feelings which are aroused not only by issues but also by words. Yet again, I say that I am convinced that it would be wrong, under pressure from either side, to detract from or add to the balanced formulation which we have endeavored to make both fair and clear.

Emphasizing once again that his text was prepared with the greatest care to take into account the Arab concern for withdrawal and the Israeli insistence that "withdrawal must be to secure boundaries," Lord Caradon expressed his conviction that his draft resolution offered "the best and indeed the only basis on which the practical cooperation of both sides can be won."[26]

Ambassador Goldberg announced that the US would vote for the UK draft resolution, because it was consistent with the policy enunciated by President Johnson on June 19 and reaffirmed by Goldberg in several interventions before UNSC. He noted:

> The draft resolution is non-prejudicial to and sufficiently mindful of the legitimate and vital interests of all parties to the recent conflict, so that they should be able to receive and cooperate

---

26. United Nations Security Council, Official Records—22nd Year, 1377th Meeting, Document S/PV1377, paras. 26–41.

with the UN special representative as he starts out on his difficult and historic peacemaking mission.[27]

In light of the new Soviet draft resolution, UNSC agreed to a Bulgarian proposal to adjourn until Wednesday, November 22 for further consultations. At the opening of the UNSC session on November 22, 1967, the Syrian delegate categorically rejected the UK draft resolution, objecting to its failure to condemn Israel for its aggression and to "its mere, vague call on Israel to withdraw its armed forces." The UK text, he complained, did not call for withdrawal to the pre-June 5 armistice lines and was…

> …almost nullified by the absence of any time limit or any *modus operandi* for ensuring this withdrawal… Moreover, this mention of withdrawal is made subject to a score of concessions to be imposed on the Arab countries, thus coupling it with conditions amounting to the liquidation of the whole Palestine question.[28]

The Indian representative, choosing to ignore Lord Caradon's repeated explanation that the UK proposal provided for Israel's just claim that withdrawal must be to secure and recognized boundaries, declared that he and the co-sponsors of the three-nation draft resolution interpreted the UK resolution as committing UNSC to the withdrawal of Israel's armed forces to the 1949 Armistices Agreement lines. On that basis, he announced, the three nations would not press for a vote on their own draft resolution.[29]

Lord Caradon welcomed the Indian decision not to press the three-nation resolution to a vote, but he repeated that the draft resolution was a balanced whole and that to add to it or to detract from it

---

27. United Nations Security Council, Official Records—22nd Year, 1377th Meeting, Document S/PV1377, para. 43.
28. United Nations Security Council, Official Records—22nd Year, 1377th Meeting, Document S/PV1377, paras. 11–12.
29. United Nations Security Council, Official Records—22nd Year, 1377th Meeting, Document S/PV1377, paras. 50–54.

would destroy the balance. Stating that every delegation was indeed entitled to state the separate and distinct policy of the government it represented, he added, "However, I am sure that it will be recognized by us all that it is only the resolution that will bind us, and we regard its wording as clear."[30] Ambassador Goldberg likewise declared,

> Various members of the Council have views of their own for supporting the UK text. The voting of course takes place not on the individual or discrete views and policies of various members but on the draft resolution. We will vote for that draft resolution. We do so in the context of, and because we believe it to be consistent with, US policy as expressed by President Johnson on 19 June and as subsequently reaffirmed in statements made by me.[31]

Following Ambassador Goldberg's brief statement, the UNSC president, calling attention to the decision by the representatives of India and the US and to a similar private indication by the Soviet representative not to press for a vote on their own drafts, put the UK draft to a vote. By a show of hands, UNSC unanimously adopted the UK draft as UNSC Resolution 242 (1967).[32] The representative of the Soviet Union then announced that he would not call for a vote on his draft resolution.

In accordance with Resolution 242, UN Secretary-General U Thant appointed Gunnar Jarring, the Swedish ambassador to the Soviet Union, as his special representative to assist Israel and the Arab states in their "efforts to achieve a peaceful and accepted settlement in accordance with the provisions and principles in this resolution." Jarring's shuttle diplomacy between the parties continued intermittently until 1973 but ended in failure.

---

30. United Nations Security Council, Official Records—22nd Year, 1377th Meeting, Document S/PV1377, paras. 55–62.
31. United Nations Security Council, Official Records—22nd Year, 1377th Meeting, Document S/PV1377, para. 63–64.
32. For the full text of UNSC Resolution 242, see Appendix 4.

Arab–Israeli Differences on Peace Principles Remain Unchanged

Speaking after the vote, the two sides made it abundantly clear that they remained as far apart as they had been beforehand. Abba Eban declared that after five months of international discussion, Israel's aims and policies remained "unchanged, unprejudiced, and intact." Israel, he emphasized, would respect and maintain the ceasefire agreements until Israel and the Arab states signed peace treaties, ending the state of war:

> Movement from the ceasefire lines can be envisaged only in the framework of a lasting peace establishing recognized and secure boundaries... [UNSC], like [UNGA], has consistently refused to endorse proposals which would have sought a return to the ambiguity, vulnerability, and insecurity in which we have lived for nineteen years. It has now adopted a resolution of which the central and primary affirmation is the need for "the establishment of a just and lasting peace" based on secure and recognized boundaries. There is a clear understanding that it is only within the establishment of permanent peace with secure and recognized boundaries that other principles can be given effect.[33]

Commenting on the statement of the Indian representative before the vote, Abba Eban added:

> The establishment of a peace settlement, including secure and recognized boundaries, is quite different from what he had been proposing, namely, withdrawal, without final peace, to demarcation lines. The representative of India has now sought to interpret the resolution in the image of his own wishes. For us, the resolution says what it says. It does not say that which it has specifically, and consciously, avoided saying... The crucial

---

33. United Nations Security Council, Official Records—22nd Year, 1377th Meeting, Document S/PV1377, paras. 85–88.

specifications to which he referred were discussed at length in consultations and deliberately and not accidentally excluded in order to be non-prejudicial to the negotiating position of all parties.[34]

Soviet Deputy Foreign Minister Kuznetsov, on the other hand, announced that although he would have preferred for UNSC to adopt his draft proposal on withdrawal, he had voted for the UK resolution as interpreted by the representative of India. Thus, although UNSC had repeatedly refused to adopt the many Soviet calls for withdrawal to the 1949 Armistice Agreement lines, he interpreted UNSC Resolution 242 as if the Soviet proposal had just been adopted. He maintained that in the resolution adopted by UNSC,

> Withdrawal of [Israeli] armed forces from territories occupied in the recent conflict becomes the first necessary principle for the establishment of a just and lasting peace in the Near East. We understand the decision taken to mean the withdrawal of Israel forces from all, and we repeat, all territories belonging to Arab states and seized by Israel following its attack on those states on 5 June 1967.[35]

The representatives of Syria, Egypt, and Jordan reaffirmed that the first and essential step toward peace lay in the immediate and complete withdrawal of Israeli armed forces from all the territories they had occupied in the recent conflict. There was no suggestion in their statements of any willingness to negotiate and sign a peace treaty with

---

34. United Nations Security Council, Official Records—22nd Year, 1377th Meeting, Document S/PV1377, paras. 93–94.
35. United Nations Security Council, Official Records—22nd Year, 1377th Meeting, Document S/PV1377, para. 119. In his book, *Palestine Peace, Not Apartheid*, former President Jimmy Carter echoes the Soviet and Arab position that UNSC Resolution 242 required Israel to withdraw to the 1949 Armistice Agreement lines and maintains that this has always been the position of the US as well.

Israel. On the contrary, the Arab refusal to negotiate had already been firmly asserted in a declaration on September 1, 1967 at a summit of the Arab heads of state in Sudan's capital, Khartoum, which became known as the Declaration of Three Noes. It stated, inter alia:

> The Arab heads of state have agreed to unite their political efforts at the international and diplomatic level to eliminate the effects of the aggression and to ensure the withdrawal of the aggressive Israeli forces from the Arab lands which have been occupied since the aggression of June 5. This will be done within the framework of the main principles by which the Arab states abide, namely, no peace with Israel, no recognition of Israel, no negotiations with it, and insistence on the rights of the Palestinian people in their own country.[36]

The goal of the Khartoum Conference was abundantly clear from its "insistence on the rights of the Palestinian people in their own country." The PLO Charter, established in 1964 by a decision of the summit of Arab kings and heads of state under Nasser's leadership, when the State of Israel existed only within the 1949 Armistice Agreement borders, had spelled out the meaning of this phrase. The PLO Charter, as previously noted, had declared the partitioning of Palestine in 1947 and the establishment of Israel illegal and null and void (article 17). It had denied the claim of any Jewish historic ties to Palestine and had pronounced null and void the Balfour Declaration and the Mandate for Palestine (article 18). The PLO Charter did not call for the establishment of a Palestinian state in the West Bank and Gaza, then held by Jordan and Egypt, respectively. On the contrary, it explicitly declared (article 24) that the PLO "does not exercise any territorial sovereignty over the West Bank in the Hashemite Kingdom of Jordan, in the Gaza Strip or in the Himmah Area [Israeli territory

---

36. "The Khartoum Resolutions; September 1, 1967," *The Avalon Project*, Yale Law School, accessed on August 7, 2023, https://avalon.law.yale.edu/20th_century/khartoum.asp#:~:text=The%20Arab%20Heads%20of%20State,the%20aggression%20of%20June%205.

then held by Syria]."[37] The Khartoum Resolutions' "insistence on the rights of the Palestinian people in their own country" was therefore only a euphemism for the continued Arab insistence on the liquidation of the State of Israel.

---

37. Palestine Liberation Organization, "Palestine National Charter of 1964."

– 22 –

Conclusion

THE ARAB–ISRAELI CONFLICT WILL NOT end unless and until the Arabs accept the Jewish State of Israel's right to exist within its ancient national and religious homeland. The *raison d'être* of Hamas and Hezbollah—financed and equipped by their patron country, Iran—is the obliteration of the State of Israel. But even the PLO and the Palestinian National Authority, which since 1988 have publicly declared their acceptance of Israel—after four decades of having promoted terrorism to annihilate Israel—insist they do not and will not recognize Israel as a Jewish state.

Difficult as it may be to believe in light of the top priority the world today assigns to the establishment of a state of Palestine, the Arab states launched their war against Israel without any thought of setting up such an independent state. They each had their own claim to all or part of Palestine, and their only concern was to abort the Jewish State before its birth and to liquidate it and its people after its birth. In a BBC radio interview just before launching the war of 1948, Azzam Pasha, secretary of the Arab League, gloated in anticipation, "This will be a war of extermination and a momentous massacre which will be spoken of like the Mongolian massacre and the Crusades."[1]

The Arabs lost their war of extermination of the Jews. Israel defeated all the invading armies of Egypt, Lebanon, Syria, Transjordan, and Iraq in a war that was very costly for both sides. It is this defeat that the Palestinians commemorate annually as their Nakba, their catastrophe, and it is this defeat for which they hold Israel, rather than

---

1. Cited in Collins and Lapierre, *O Jerusalem!*, 688, 456–457 and fn.

themselves and the Arab states, responsible. Had the Palestinians and the Arab states established a state of Palestine alongside Israel in accordance with the UNGA 1947 resolution for partition, however, there would have been no war, no Arab nor Jewish casualties, and no Arab or Jewish refugees. Instead of commemorating the Nakba, the Palestinian Arabs, like the Jews, would then have been able in the year 2011 to celebrate the sixty-third anniversary of their national sovereignty in their own independent state.[2] Commemoration of the Nakba as a tragedy for which the Arabs hold Israel, rather than themselves, responsible only indicates the Arab continuation of an existential war against Israel, which no territorial concessions can end.

But even the Arab defeat in the 1948 War of Independence did not end the Arab opportunity to set up a state of Palestine in accordance with the UNGA 1947 resolution for partition. For nearly twenty years from the end of the Mandate for Palestine on May 15, 1948 until their defeat in the Six-Day War in June 1967, the Arabs remained completely free to set up a state of Palestine. Under the 1949 Arab–Israeli Armistice Agreements, Egypt retained control of Gaza, and Jordan ruled the West Bank including East Jerusalem, which they had each seized in the war. For that entire period, the failure to realize the resolution's promise of a state of Palestine rests only with the Arabs themselves. But neither the Palestinians, nor the Arab states, nor the UN, nor the world at large gave any thought during those two decades to setting up an independent state of Palestine in Gaza and the West Bank. And it did not ever occur to anyone to charge Egypt and Jordan as illegal occupiers of Palestinian land, because the concept of a distinct Palestinian people with its own ethnic identity, entitled to its own independent state, which looms so large in world public opinion today, was still unknown then, as it had been unknown throughout the history of Arab and Moslem rule of the Middle East. It was unknown because no Palestinian language,

---

2. As noted in the preface, the manuscript of this book was completed in 2012.

literature, or religion exists, distinct from that of the Arab people as a whole. No state of Palestine was ever in existence. And Jerusalem was never an Arab capital. Even the name "Palestine" is not native to the Palestinian Arabs; rather, it is only a Roman name for the Land of Israel given by the Emperor Hadrian to the Land of Israel in his bitter anger over the heavy casualties the Jews had inflicted in their war of liberation under Bar Kochba (132–135 CE). Remarkably, neither Palestine nor Jerusalem even appears by name in the Koran.[3]

Even the Palestinian Arab leadership itself repeatedly demonstrated its own lack of any sense of possessing a distinct Palestinian identity. In 1920, when the Syrian Arabs crowned Feisal—leader of the Arab revolt in World War II—as their king, Palestine's Arab elders sought to have Palestine included as part of the kingdom of Syria. In 1948, Count Folke Bernadotte, appointed as the UN mediator in the Arab war against Israel, recommended that the area allotted for an Arab state in the UNGA 1947 resolution for partition be given not to the Palestinian Arabs but to Transjordan. As justification, Bernadotte cited this UN staff information:

> The Palestine Arabs have at present no will of their own. Neither have they ever developed any specific Palestinian nationalism. The demand for a separate Arab state in Palestine is consequently relatively weak. It would seem as though in existing circumstances, most of the Palestinian Arabs would be quite content to be incorporated in Transjordan.[4]

This assessment was confirmed in a 1950 referendum when, after Transjordan had seized the area still known at that time as Judea and

---

3. The only reference to Jerusalem in the Koran is an implicit reference, relating to the *Masjid Al Aksa* to which Mohammed was taken on his night journey (Sura 17:1), which, according to Moslem oral tradition, refers to the mosque on what the Moslems have named the *Haram al-Sharif*, the Moslem Noble Sanctuary, which is the Jews' Holy Temple Mount in Jerusalem.
4. Bernadotte, *To Jerusalem*, 113.

Samaria, the Palestinian Arabs overwhelmingly approved its annexation of the area as a newly renamed West Bank of a newly formed Hashemite Kingdom of Jordan.

✡ ✡ ✡

It was Yasser Arafat who first promoted the concept of a distinct Palestinian people possessing its own national identity, with entitlement to national sovereignty, when, around the year 1960, he founded the Fatah, whose constitution proclaims, "The Palestinian people have an independent identity and have complete sovereignty on all their lands (article 2)." Rejecting millennia of Jewish history rooted in the Land of Israel/Palestine and insisting instead that "the Israeli existence in Palestine is a Zionist invasion with a colonial expansive base (article 8)," the Fatah constitution calls for "armed struggle" that "will not cease unless the Zionist state is demolished and Palestine is completely liberated" (article 19). Even Arafat and his Fatah, however, never called upon Jordan and Egypt to establish a state of Palestine in the West Bank and Gaza, and they never called those countries occupiers of Palestinian land.

It is only against Israel, which regained Gaza and the West Bank from Egypt and Jordan in the 1967 Six-Day War, that the claim for the establishment of a state of Palestine has been directed, and it is only Israel that has been charged with occupying Palestinian land. No explanation has ever been provided, however, why land that was not considered occupied Palestinian land when it was ruled by Egypt and Jordan immediately became occupied Palestinian land as soon as Israel regained the land from the Arab states. The question is particularly profound since Israel, unlike Jordan and the West Bank, had received the legal right to close settlement on the land for development of the Jewish national homeland under the League of Nations 1922 Mandate.

Although the Arab states all shared Arafat's determination to demolish Israel and "liberate" Palestine, the Arab League firmly refused to accept the Palestinian claim to national statehood in the territory the Arab states ruled. True, the 1964 founding PLO Charter repeatedly refers to the Palestinian people and assigns it the vanguard role for the liberation of Palestine. And like the Fatah constitution, the PLO Charter rejects the legality of Israel's existence, insisting, "The partitioning of Palestine...and the establishment of Israel are illegal and null and void" (article 17). Likewise, "The Balfour Declaration, the Palestine Mandate System, and all that has been based on them are considered null and void" (article 18). Missing, however, is the Fatah claim to national sovereignty over all the Palestinian lands. Instead, the PLO Charter explicitly excludes the PLO from the exercise of "any territorial sovereignty over the West Bank in the Hashemite Kingdom of Jordan, on the Gaza Strip, or in the [Syrian-held] Himmah Area" (article 24).[5] Not surprisingly, Arafat refused to bring his Fatah into the PLO under this PLO Charter.

And the Arab states did not yield their own claims to Palestine even after Israel regained Gaza from Egypt, and the West Bank, including East Jerusalem, from Jordan in the 1967 Six-Day War. It is true that they included an expression of "insistence on the rights of the Palestinian people in their own country" in declaring their continued refusal to accept the existence of the State of Israel, whose extinction they had again threatened on the eve of the 1967 Six-Day War. Their Declaration of the Three Noes (Khartoum, Sudan, September 1, 1967) states, inter alia:

> The Arab heads of state have agreed to unite their political efforts at the international and diplomatic level to eliminate the effects of the aggression and to ensure the withdrawal of the aggressive Israeli forces from the Arab lands which have been occupied since the aggression of June 5. This will be done within the framework of the main principles by which the Arab states abide, namely, no peace with Israel, no recognition of

---

5. See Palestine Liberation Organization, "Palestine National Charter of 1964."

Israel, no negotiations with it, and insistence on the rights of the Palestinian people in their own country.[6]

This "insistence on the rights of the Palestinian people in their own country" did not include, however, a right to establish an independent state of Palestine in the West Bank and Gaza. Indeed, in the lengthy UN debates in both UNSC and UNGA on the Arab–Israeli conflict, the Arab states recognized no Palestinian people and no Palestinian claim to independent statehood—UNSC Resolution 242 on the principles for Arab–Israeli peace, adopted unanimously on November 22, 1967 (not quite three months after the Khartoum Declaration of Three Noes) does not even mention the Palestinians by name, let alone consider them a distinct national people entitled to its own national independence and sovereignty. It refers to the Palestinians only implicitly, as refugees, in a clause "affirming the necessity for achieving a just solution of the refugee problem." Resolution 242, inter alia…

> …affirms that the fulfillment of [UN] Charter principles requires the establishment of a just and lasting peace in the Middle East which should include the application of both the following principles:
>
> withdrawal of [Israeli] armed forces from territories occupied in the recent conflict;
>
> termination of all claims or states of belligerency and respect for and acknowledgment of the sovereignty, territorial integrity, and political independence of every state in the area and their right to live in peace within secure and recognized boundaries free from threats or acts of force.

The resolution deliberately kept the extent of withdrawal unspecified, leaving it to be decided only in the peace negotiations. The Soviet

---

6. For the full text, see "The Khartoum Resolutions; September 1, 1967," *The Avalon Project*, Yale Law School.

Union and the bloc of so-called NAM nations each submitted several substitute resolutions and amendments in both UNSC and UNGA to specify that Israel's withdrawal must be to the 1949 Armistice Agreement lines that had prevailed until June 4, 1967, but each UN body voted to reject all those proposals to specify or even to suggest such total withdrawal. Israel, along with the US, the UK (the resolution's sponsor), and several supporting countries, maintained in the UNSC session and long thereafter that the 1949 Armistice Agreement borders were indefensible and that the resolution called for secure borders to be reached by agreement in the peace negotiations. The Arabs and their supporters in the developing world and elsewhere have insisted, despite the history of the debates in UNSC and UNGA and the carefully chosen language of the relevant operative paragraph—that Resolution 242 nevertheless requires withdrawal to the 1949 Armistice Agreement borders.

Had Israel agreed at the time to the Arab interpretation, its withdrawal would have returned Gaza to Egypt and the West Bank to Jordan, not to the Palestinian people, who were not even mentioned in the resolution. The Palestinian prospects for the establishment of an independent state of Palestine might then have been no better than they had been until 1967, when the territory had been under Arab rule. And given the failure of the truly ancient Kurdish people in Turkey and Iraq to attract world support for their claims to statehood, there is little reason to assume that the world would then have showered the Palestinians with such lavish support for an independent state of Palestine as it has so zealously proffered under Israel's rule.

✡ ✡ ✡

The Arab states first accepted Arafat's claim to national sovereignty and the establishment of an independent state of Palestine only in 1974, when they were stunned by Egyptian President Anwar Sadat's decision to abandon the Arab goal of annihilating Israel and to begin instead military negotiations with Israel for saving his surrounded army. The military agreements led to Sadat's extraordinary trip to

Israel in November 1977 to address the Israeli Knesset concerning his desire to end the war and to open peace negotiations with Israel, negotiations which culminated in 1979 in a signed peace agreement between the two countries. Following Sadat's far-reaching shift in Egyptian policy, the PLO's Palestinian National Council announced a new policy (in Cairo on June 9, 1974), of the so-called "phased liberation of Palestine," according to which the PLO would establish an "independent combatant national authority for the people over every part of Palestinian territory that is liberated." In a significant blow to Hussein, who did not surrender Jordan's claim to the West Bank until fourteen years later, the Arab League reacted to the new turn of events by designating the PLO as "the sole legitimate representative of the Palestinian people" and approving its phased liberation policy for Palestine (in Morocco on October 28, 1974).

Ignoring the PLO's dedication to the annihilation of a UN member state, UNGA invited Arafat to address its 1974 session at which he defended his "armed struggle" against Israel with the argument that terrorism must be defined in terms of motivation. The PLO's "armed struggle" cannot be considered terrorism, he insisted, because its purpose is the liberation of Palestine, a right consecrated by the UN. Only Israel's resistance must be considered terrorism, because it is directed against Palestinian liberation. In lieu of his "freedom fighter's gun," Arafat offered the UN his "olive branch," calling for Israel to be replaced by a "democratic" binational state to which the millions of Arab refugees together with all their descendants would have a right of return, rendering Israel's Jews a minority in a newly formed Arab state.

On November 22, 1974, the UN, in its response to Arafat's address, adopted Resolution 3236 (XXIX), recognizing the PLO as the representative of the Palestinian people and reaffirming the Palestinian people's rights, inter alia, to national independence and sovereignty. The resolution also recognized "the right of the Palestinian people to regain its rights by all means consistent with the purposes and principles of the [UN Charter]" but took no position on Arafat's contention that terrorism must be defined in terms of the motivation of the perpetrators.[7] Omitted from this resolution is any mention of Israel or of UNSC Resolution 242, and its affirmation that a just and lasting peace requires the "acknowledgement of the sovereignty, territorial integrity, and political independence of every state in the area and their right to live in peace within secure and recognized boundaries free from threats or acts of force." Ignored likewise is UNSC Resolution 338 (1973) for a ceasefire in the Yom Kippur War, which called upon the parties concerned to implement Resolution 242.

In accordance with its recognition of the PLO as the representative of the Palestinian people, UNGA also adopted Resolution 3237 (XXIX), which granted the PLO permanent observer status in UNGA and all its subsidiary bodies.

Israel, seeing that Arafat's "olive branch" and his "freedom fighter's gun" were each aimed at putting an end to the Jewish State, banned Israeli dealings with the PLO. In 1985, following the shocking murder of a wheelchair-confined, American-Jewish passenger on a highjacked cruise ship, the US Congress likewise declared the PLO a terrorist organization. It prohibited all US dealings with the PLO "unless and until the PLO recognizes Israel's right to exist, accepts UNSC Resolutions 242 and 338, and renounces the use of terrorism."

✡ ✡ ✡

After 1982, when the PLO was driven out by Israel from Lebanon to Tunisia, where its political power began to erode, Arafat apparently came to recognize that his terrorist strategy for demolishing Israel served only to diminish rather than to enhance the prospects for the establishment of a Palestinian state. In 1988, in the midst of an ongoing Palestinian intifada that had erupted in the West Bank at the end of 1987—and following Hussein's official relinquishment of all Jordan's

---

7. Only in 2001, after the terrorist attack on the World Trade Center, did UNSC take a position on this issue, forcefully condemning all acts of terrorism regardless of motivation.

claims to the West Bank earlier in the year—Arafat transformed the Arab–Israel conflict with a surprise pronouncement of a new policy that replaced the strategy of "armed struggle" to demolish Israel with a call for an international conference to negotiate Palestinian–Israeli peace. The new policy was officially presented by the PLO's Palestinian National Council (in Algiers, November 15, 1988) in a newly issued Declaration of Independence of a New State of Palestine in the Land of Palestine with its capital at Jerusalem.[8]

The PLO Declaration of Independence cast aside the Fatah's language of armed struggle that "will not cease unless the Zionist state is demolished" and the past repeated rejections of UNSC Resolution 242 and of the UNGA 1947 resolution for partition. Instead, a political communiqué accompanying the PLO Declaration of Independence called for an international peace conference "on the basis of [UNSC] Resolutions 242 (1967) and 338 (1973)" with provision for "arrangements for security and peace among all the concerned states in the region." The communiqué emphasized, in this context, the PLO's "rejection of terrorism in all its forms." Most significantly, the declaration shrugged aside the PLO Charter's articles that rejected the UNGA 1947 resolution for partition as null and void and those that insisted on the illegality of the establishment of the State of Israel. Instead, it equated the Palestinian people's right to a state with Israel's right as a Jewish state, firmly basing the right of the Palestinian people to independence on "the adoption of [UNGA] Resolution 181(II) of 1947," which—the Declaration of Independence specifically noted—"partitioned Palestine into an Arab and a Jewish state."

Invited once again to address UNGA, Arafat confirmed the

---

8. United Nations General Assembly, Letter Dated 18 November 1988 from the Permanent Representative of Jordan to the United Nations, Addressed to the Secretary-General, Document A/43/827 (November 18, 1988), accessed on August 10, 2023, https://digitallibrary.un.org/record/50478?ln=en.

adoption of the new PLO policy in a speech on December 13, 1988.[9] He repeated the communiqué's call for an international peace conference based on Resolutions 242 and 338 as well as the PLO's "rejection of terrorism in all its forms." And, as in the text of the PLO Declaration of Independence, Arafat equated the right of the Palestinian people to a Palestinian state with the right of the Jewish people to a Jewish state. Calling the UNGA 1947 resolution for the partition of Palestine Israel's "birth certificate," Arafat based the Palestinian right to national sovereignty on that same resolution, again emphasizing that the resolution provided "for the establishment of two states: one Arab Palestinian and the other Jewish."

Two days later, on December 15, 1988, Arafat scored a resounding success in the UNGA, which, by a vote of 138 to 2 (the US and Israel), adopted Resolution 43/176 calling for an international UN peace conference on the Middle East, with the participation of all relevant parties, including the PLO, and based on UNSC Resolutions 242 and 338. Among its principles for peace, the resolution provided for "guaranteeing arrangements for security of all states in the region, including those named in Resolution 181(II) of 29 November 1947, within secure and internationally recognized boundaries."[10]

In addition, UNGA adopted, by a vote of 104 to 2, Resolution 43/177 to acknowledge the PLO's proclamation of the State of Palestine and to replace the designation PLO with the designation "Palestine" in the UN system. Resolution 43/177 reaffirmed Israel's right

---

9. United Nations General Assembly. Provisional Verbatim Record of the 78th Meeting, Held at the Palais des Nations, Geneva, on Tuesday, 13 December 1988: General Assembly, 43rd session, Document A/43/PV.78.
10. In the three years that followed—1989, 1990, and 1991—UNGA adopted resolutions containing the same language as in Resolution 43/176, calling for an international peace conference, with the participation of the PLO and guaranteeing security for the states named in Resolution 181(II) of November 29, 1947, with every Arab state again voting in favor. See UNGA Resolution 44/42, adopted by a vote of 153 to 3 on December 6, 1989; Resolution 45/68, by a vote of 144 to 2 on December 6, 1990; and Resolution 46/75, by a vote of 104 to 2 on December 11, 1991.

to exist as a Jewish state by beginning with the paragraph, "Recalling its Resolution 181(II) of 29 November 1947, in which, inter alia, it called for the establishment of an Arab State and a Jewish State in Palestine."

Every Arab state voted in favor of both resolutions, thereby unequivocally equating—as had both the PLO's Palestinian National Council in its Declaration of Independence and Arafat in his address to UNGA—the right of the Palestinian people to a Palestinian state as well as the right of the Jewish people to a Jewish state.

✡ ✡ ✡

The PLO's new policy announcement accepting Israel as a Jewish state opened the door to quick US recognition of the PLO as the representative of the Palestinian people. On December 14, 1988, the day after Arafat addressed UNGA, he held a press conference to spell out more explicitly his decision to meet the US requirements for opening a dialog with the US authorities. President Reagan responded immediately with a statement declaring that since the PLO had "accepted [UNSC] Resolutions 242 and 338, recognized Israel's right to exist, and renounced terrorism," he had authorized the State Department to enter a substantive dialogue with PLO representatives. Following this decision, George H. W. Bush launched the Arab–Israel peace process in 1991 at an international peace conference in Madrid that was co-chaired by the US and the Soviet Union, with the participation of Syria, Lebanon, Jordan, and Palestinian representatives.

Although the Madrid Conference itself achieved relatively little, the agreement of Arab states and Palestinian representatives to participate in a peace conference with Israel promoted the cause of peace in paving the way for many hold-out states, notably Russia and the Vatican, to establish diplomatic relations with Israel. The Madrid Conference served, in addition, as a launching pad for secret bilateral negotiations in Oslo, Norway between Israel and the PLO, which culminated in 1993 in the Oslo Accords, or the Declaration of Principles on Interim Self-Government Arrangements. The Oslo Accords, signed in President Clinton's White House, provided for the establishment of a PA to administer all territories that Israel had turned over to the Palestinians for self-government—initially, Gaza and Jericho but subsequently expanded to cover all the Arab populated cities as well as hundreds of peaceful West Bank villages. Intended to serve as the framework for future negotiations to resolve all outstanding "final status issues," the Oslo Accords aroused so much hope for the final resolution of the long-lasting Arab–Israel conflict that the Nobel Peace Prize in 1994 was awarded to Yasser Arafat, Yitzhak Rabin, and Shimon Peres. The Oslo Accords in turn paved the way for King Hussein's decision to enter bilateral peace negotiations with Israel, culminating, on October 26, 1994, in the signing of a peace treaty between Israel and Jordan.

Grave doubts about the value of the Oslo Accords soon began to grow in Israel and the US, however, as Arab terror against Israel, intensified rather than diminished, bringing into question the meaning of the PLO's repeated "renunciation of terrorism in all its forms." Unfortunately, President Reagan had failed to apply to the PLO his established policy toward the Soviet Union of "trust but verify," failing to verify whose terrorism Arafat and the PLO were so emphatically renouncing, particularly given Arafat's earlier insistence that terrorism must be defined in terms of motivation. According to Arafat's definition, presented before UNGA in 1974, the PLO's "armed struggle" for the "liberation of Palestine" could not be considered terrorism, and only Israel's resistance to the liberation of Palestine must be considered terrorism.

Indeed, the Palestinian National Council's dedication of the Algiers meeting to the "glorious intifada," which had erupted in 1987, and the call for its intensification, had shown that despite Arafat and the PLO's repeated "rejection of terrorism in all its forms," Israel could expect the continuation and even intensification of PLO terrorism. On July 25, 2000, confidence in Arafat's sincerity in accepting Israel's existence came crashing down when Arafat walked out on Prime Minister Ehud Barak's peace proposal at Camp David, followed only two months later by the eruption of the second intifada with its very heavy casualties.

✩ ✩ ✩

In 2002 and again in 2007, King Abdullah of Saudi Arabia submitted a peace proposal at an Arab League summit, which the Arab League unanimously approved and the PA has enthusiastically adopted.

The proposal requested Israel to agree to:

withdraw to the June 4, 1967 borders;

arrive at a just and agreed solution of the refugee problem in accordance with UNGA Resolution 194(III); and

accept an independent sovereign Palestinian state on the West Bank and Gaza territory occupied since June 1967, with East Jerusalem as its capital.

In exchange, the Arab states offered to:

consider the Arab–Israel conflict ended and to enter a peace agreement with Israel, with provision of security for all the states in the region; and

establish normal relations with Israel in the context of this comprehensive peace.

The Arab states' offer to establish normal relations with Israel in the context of a comprehensive peace agreement that would consider the Arab–Israel conflict ended and provide security for all states in the region represented a major step forward. Unfortunately, a steep divide, which remains far from easy to bridge, still exists on each of the final status issues of security, refugees, borders, settlements, and Jerusalem. This divide has become even more difficult to bridge since 2009, because negotiations have been repeatedly stalled by public declarations setting forth pre-conditions for negotiations, which have served only to harden positions.

Yet another serious difficulty was introduced by the PA's decision in 2011 to seek UN endorsement for a unilateral proclamation of a Palestinian state. Abbas and the world along with him appear to have completely erased from the pages of history the PLO's first unilateral proclamation of a state of Palestine in 1988. As discussed earlier, that proclamation was overwhelmingly supported in resolutions of UNGA, and it opened the door to the Arab–Israel peace process, but it yielded no state of Palestine, because Arafat walked out on serious peace negotiations with Israel in 2000. A request by Abbas in 2011 for UN endorsement of a second unilateral proclamation of a state of Palestine will undoubtedly also be approved by UNGA, but it is also bound to fail to yield a state of Palestine. Only a peace agreement reached through the resumption of serious peace negotiations in accordance with UNSC Resolutions 242 and 338 can yield a state of Palestine with provision of security for all states in the region.

This second Arab attempt to achieve a state of Palestine through UNGA is bound to be even less successful than the first attempt, because Abbas and the PA have since cast aside the transformative PLO decision of 1988 to equate the Palestinian right to national sovereignty with their recognition of the right of Israel to exist as a Jewish state. Arab acceptance of Israel as a Jewish state was embodied in the PLO's 1988 Declaration of Independence. It was reaffirmed in Arafat's address to UNGA, and it was incorporated in UNGA resolutions that were unanimously approved by all the Arab states. Unfortunately, Abbas and the PA, shrugging aside this unanimously adopted and repeatedly reaffirmed Arab decision in 1988, now insist they do not and will not accept Israel as a Jewish state.

The two-state solution they now propose is not two states for two peoples—an Arab state for the Palestinian people and a Jewish state for the Jewish people. Their two-state solution essentially calls for redividing Palestine only into two Palestinian states. One is a state of Palestine to be formally established in Gaza and the West Bank, with East Jerusalem as its capital, which the Arabs demand—and the progressive Western world evidently accepts with equanimity—must be ethnically cleansed of its entire Jewish population. The other is a Palestinian-controlled state that would replace the Jewish state of Israel, rendering its Jewish population a minority through a "right of return" of Arab refugees and their descendants, now numbering around five million people. This "peace plan" would wipe Israel off the map through diplomacy instead of "armed struggle." No Israeli government can be expected to accept such a two-state policy that appears to be a throwback to the 1974 PLO strategy for liquidating Israel through the "phased liberation of Palestine."

The gravest difficulty in putting an end to the Arab–Israeli conflict has been introduced by the recent merger of the PA with Islamist Hamas, whose founding charter calls explicitly for Israel's obliteration. Hamas even looks forward to an Islamic Judgment Day that promises wiping not just Israel but also the Jews off the map entirely, declaring (in article 7):

> The Day of Judgment will not come about until Moslems fight the Jews, killing the Jews, when the Jew will hide behind stones and trees. The stones and trees will say, "O Moslems, O Abdullah, there is a Jew behind me, come and kill him."[11]

The meaning of a comprehensive Arab–Israeli peace agreement, with provision of security for all states of the region, to be reached with such a schizophrenic PA of Fatah and Hamas, defies comprehension.

---

11. "Hamas Covenant," *The Avalon Project*, Yale Law School, article 7. Hamas even uses its TV programs to teach Palestinian children how Allah transformed the Jews into apes ("Hamas TV Cartoon Depicts Koran-Based Story of Jews Being Transformed into Apes," *MEMRI Special Dispatch*, No. 3128, September 7, 2010, accessed on August 10, 2023, https://www.memri.org/reports/hamas-tv-cartoon-depicts-koran-based-story-jews-being-transformed-apes).

Appendix 1

Excerpts from United Nations General Assembly Resolution 181(II) Concerning the Future Government of Palestine, November 29, 1947[1]

Plan of Partition with Economic Union

Part I. Future Constitution and Government of Palestine

A. Termination of Mandate, Partition, and Independence

1. The Mandate for Palestine shall terminate as soon as possible, but in any case not later than 1 August 1948.

2. The armed forces of the Mandatory Power shall be progressively withdrawn from Palestine, the withdrawal to be completed as soon as possible, but in any case not later than 1 August 1948…

3. Independent Arab and Jewish states and the Special International Regime for the City of Jerusalem, set forth in Part III of this plan, shall come into existence in Palestine two months after the evacuation of the armed forces of the Mandatory Power has been completed, but in any case not later than 1 October 1948. The boundaries of the Arab State, the Jewish State, and the City of Jerusalem shall be as described in Parts II and III below.

---

1. "Section 9: The Question of Palestine" in United Nations, *Yearbook, 1947–1948*.

[The thirty-three UN member states in favor:] Australia, Belgium, Bolivia, Brazil, Byelorussian S.S.R., Canada, Costa Rica, Czechoslovakia, Denmark, Dominican Republic, Ecuador, France, Guatemala, Haiti, Iceland, Liberia, Luxemburg, Netherlands, New Zealand, Nicaragua, Norway, Panama, Paraguay, Peru, Philippines, Poland, Sweden, Ukrainian SSR, Union of South Africa, USA, USSR, Uruguay, and Venezuela.

[The thirteen UN member states against:] Afghanistan, Cuba, Egypt, Greece, India, Iran, Iraq, Lebanon, Pakistan, Saudi Arabia, Syria, Turkey, and Yemen.

[The ten UN member states that abstained:] Argentina, Chile, China, Colombia, El Salvador, Ethiopia, Honduras, Mexico, United Kingdom, and Yugoslavia.

Appendix 2

United Nations Security Council Resolution 61, November 4, 1948[1]

The [United Nations] Security Council, having decided on 15 July 1948 that subject to further decision by the [UNSC] or [UNGA], the truce shall remain in force in accordance with Resolution 54 (1948) of that date and with Resolution 50 (1948) of 29 May 1948 until a peaceful adjustment of the future situation of Palestine is reached,

having decided on 19 August that no party is permitted to violate the truce on the ground that it is undertaking reprisals or retaliations against the other party and that no party is entitled to gain military or political advantage through violation of the truce,

having decided on 29 May that if the truce was subsequently repudiated or violated by either party or by both, the situation in Palestine could be reconsidered with a view to action under Chapter 7 of the Charter of the [UN],

takes note of the request communicated to the government of Egypt and the provisional government of Israel by the acting mediator on 26 October following upon the decisions adopted by [UNSC] on 19 October 1948 [and]

calls upon the interested governments, without prejudice to their rights, claims, or positions with regard to a peaceful adjustment of the

---

1. United Nations Security Council, Resolution 61—The Palestine Question, Document S/RES/61(1948) (November 4, 1948), accessed on August 10, 2023, https://documents-dds-ny.un.org/doc/RESOLUTION/GEN/NR0/047/86/PDF/NR004786.pdf?OpenElement.

future situation of Palestine or to the position which the members of the [UN] may wish to take in [UNGA] on such peaceful adjustment:

to withdraw those of their forces which have advanced beyond the positions held on 14 October, the acting mediator being authorized to establish provisional lines beyond which no movement of troops shall take place;

to establish, through negotiations conducted directly between the parties, or failing that, through the intermediaries in the service of the [UN], permanent truce lines and such neutral or demilitarized zones as may appear advantageous in order to ensure henceforth the full observance of the truce in that area. Failing an agreement, the permanent lines and neutral zones shall be established by decision of the acting mediator;

appoints a committee of [UNSC] consisting of the five permanent members together with Belgium and Colombia to give such advice as the acting mediator may require with regard to his responsibilities under this resolution, and in the event that either party or both should fail to comply with sub-paragraphs (1) and (2) of the preceding paragraph of this resolution within whatever time limits the acting mediator may think it desirable to fix, to study as a matter of urgency and to report to [UNSC] on further measures it would be appropriate to take under Chapter 7 of the Charter.

Appendix 3

A Selection of Calls from the Palestine Liberation Organization for the Annihilation of Israel

In his *Palestine Peace, Not Apartheid*, former US President Jimmy Carter quotes without comment Yasser Arafat's denial of any calls from the PLO for Israel's annihilation. In addition to the PLO Charter's call for Israel's annihilation, discussed in the main body of this book, the statements by Yasser Arafat and his PLO associates, presented below, are all uncompromising calls for the total destruction or liquidation of all of Israel. These statements are a small sample of numerous calls by various Arab government officials, Arab leaders, and Arab media outlets for Israel's annihilation.

"We shall never stop until we can go back home and Israel is destroyed... The goal of our struggle is the end of Israel, and there can be no compromises or mediations... The goal of this violence is the elimination of Zionism from Palestine in all its political, economic, and military aspects... We don't want peace—we want victory. Peace for us means Israel's destruction and nothing else."

Yasser Arafat, quoted in *Washington Post* (US)
March 29, 1970

✡ ✡ ✡

"I want to tell Carter and Begin that when the Arabs set off their volcano, there will be only Arabs in this part of the world... Our people will continue to fuel the torch of the revolution with rivers of blood until the whole of the occupied homeland is liberated…not just a part of it."

> Yasser Arafat, quoted in *Associated Press* (US)
> March 12, 1979

✡ ✡ ✡

"Peace for us means the destruction of Israel. We are preparing for an all-out war, a war which will last for generations… We shall not rest until the day when we return to our home, and until we destroy Israel."

> Yasser Arafat
> quoted in *El Mundo* (Venezuela), February 11, 1980
> and in *The Times* (UK), August 5, 1980

✡ ✡ ✡

"Fatah is a nationalist revolutionary movement bent on the complete liberation of Palestine [and] the liquidation of the Zionist entity, economically, militarily, politically, culturally, and intellectually."

> "The Fatah Congress Resolution," *Associated Press* (US)
> June 5, 1980

✡ ✡ ✡

"Without any doubt, the PLO is entirely in agreement with the [Fatah] resolution… We wish at any price to liquidate the State of Israel."

> Ibrahim Souss (PLO representative)
> quoted in *Europe No. 1 Radio* (France), June 16, 1980
> and in *The Times* (UK), August 5, 1980

✡ ✡ ✡

"The establishment of a Palestinian state over part of the Palestinian soil does not amount to a renunciation of the strategic aim. It is a pity that Israel realizes that…and knows that the establishment of such a state constitutes the reassertion of Palestinian identity and the beginning of the end for Israel."

> Shafiq al-Hut (director of the PLO's Beirut office)
> *Al-Anba*, Kuwait, March 20, 1983
> quoted in Barry Rubin, *Revolution Until Victory? The Politics and History of the PLO* (Harvard University Press, 1994), 70

✡ ✡ ✡

"The Palestinian people will achieve an independent Palestinian state, which will be the start of the liberation of the entire homeland. This is the beginning of the liberation and not its end or a halt along the borders of that state. The Palestinian state which shall arise shall be the beginning of the end of Israel."

> Salah Khalaf [Abu Iyad]
> *Al-Qabas*, Kuwait, November 10, 1984
> quoted in Harris O. Schoenberg, *A Mandate for Terror: The United Nations and the PLO* (New York, Shapolsky Books, 1989), 398–399

✡ ✡ ✡

"The so-called "State of Israel" was one of the consequences of World War II and should disappear, like the Berlin Wall has along with the other consequences of that war."

> Yasser Arafat and Colonel Muammar Gaddafi "Joint Statement"
> *BBC Summary of World Broadcasts*, January 8, 1990

✡ ✡ ✡

"The PLO will now concentrate on splitting Israel psychologically into two camps... We plan to eliminate the State of Israel and establish a Palestinian state. We will make life unbearable for Jews by psychological warfare and population explosion. Jews will not want to live among Arabs. I have no use for Jews. They are and remain Jews. We now need all the help we can get from you in our battle for a united Palestine under Arab rule."

Yasser Arafat
"Speech to Arab Diplomats in Stockholm"
Jerusalem Post, February 23, 1996

✡ ✡ ✡

"We are ambushing the Israelis and cheating them... If we agree to declare our state over what is now twenty-two percent of Palestine, meaning the West Bank and Gaza, our ultimate goal is the liberation of all historic Palestine from the River to the Sea... We distinguish the strategic, long-term goals from the political phased goals, which we are compelled to temporarily accept due to international pressure."

Faisal Husseini (PLO strategist)
quoted in *Al Arabi* (Egypt), June 24, 2001
and in *Jerusalem Report*, July 30, 2001

Appendix 4

United Nations Security Council Resolution 242, November 22, 1967[1]

The [United Nations] Security Council, expressing its continuing concern with the grave situation in the Middle East,

emphasizing the inadmissibility of the acquisition of territory by war and the need to work for a just and lasting peace in which every state in the area can live in security,

emphasizing further that all [UN] member states, in their acceptance of the Charter of the [UN] have undertaken a commitment to act in accordance with article 2 of the charter,[2]

affirms that the fulfillment of [UN] Charter principles requires the establishment of a just and lasting peace in the Middle East which should include the application of both the following principles:

---

1. United Nations Security Council, Resolution 242—The Situation in the Middle East, Document S/RES/242(1967).
2. Article 2 of the UN Charter sets out the principles that the Members and the UN shall pursue in fulfillment of the purposes of the United Nations set out in Article 1. These principles include, inter alia:
3. All Members shall settle their international disputes by peaceful means in such a manner that international peace and security, and justice, are not endangered;
4. All Members shall refrain in their international relations from the threat or use of force against the territorial integrity or political independence of any state, or in any other manner inconsistent with the Purposes of the United Nations.

affirms further the necessity

for guaranteeing freedom of navigation through international waterways in the area;

for achieving a just settlement of the refugee problem;

for guaranteeing the territorial inviolability and political independence of every state in the area, through measures including the establishment of demilitarized zones;

requests the secretary-general to designate a special representative to proceed to the Middle East to establish and maintain contacts with the states concerned in order to promote agreement and assist efforts to achieve a peaceful and accepted settlement in accordance with the provisions and principles in this resolution; [and]

requests the secretary-general to report to [UNSC] on the progress of the efforts of the special representative as soon as possible.

Bibliography

Abbas, Mahmoud. "The Long Overdue Palestinian State." *The New York Times*, May 17, 2011.

Aboul-Enein, Youssef. "The Heikal Papers: A Discourse on Politics and the 1967 Arab–Israeli War with Egyptian President Gamal Abdel Nasser." *Strategic Insights* 4, no. 4 (April 2005).

Acheson, Dean. *Present at the Creation: My Years in the State Department*. New York: W. W. Norton & Company, 1987.

African Union. "Charter of the Organization of African Unity, September 13, 1963." Accessed July 11, 2023. https://au.int/sites/default/files/treaties/7759-file-oau_charter_1963.pdf.

Aldington, Richard. *Lawrence of Arabia: A Biographical Enquiry*. London: Collins, 1969.

Arafat, Yasser. *Associated Press* (US), March 12, 1979.

Arafat, Yasser. *El Mundo* (Venezuela), February 11, 1980.

Arafat, Yasser. "Speech to Arab Diplomats in Stockholm." *Jerusalem Post*, February 23, 1996.

Arafat, Yasser. *The Times* (UK), August 5, 1980.

Arafat, Yasser. *Washington Post* (US), March 29, 1970.

Arafat, Yasser, and Colonel Muammar Gaddafi. "Joint Statement," *BBC Summary of World Broadcasts*, January 8, 1990.

Asquith, Herbert Henry. *Memories and Reflections*. Boston: Little, Brown, and Company, 1928.

Associated Press (US). "The Fatah Congress Resolution." June 5, 1980.

Bard, Mitchell G. "US–Israel Strategic Cooperation: The 1968 Sale of Phantom Jets to Israel." *Jewish Virtual Library*. Accessed

July 11, 2023. http://www.jewishvirtuallibrary.org/jsource/US-Israel/phantom.html.

Begin, Menachem. *The Revolt: Story of the Irgun*. Nash Publishing, 1977.

Ben-Gurion, David. *Israel: A Personal History*. New York: Funk & Wagnalls, Inc/Sabra Books, 1971.

Bentwich, Norman and Helen. *Mandate Memories 1918–1948*. New York: Schocken Books, 1965.

Bernadotte, Folke. *To Jerusalem*. Westport, CT: Hyperion Press, 1976.

Bethell, Nicholas. *The Palestine Triangle: The Struggle for the Holy Land*. New York: G. P. Putnam's Sons, 1979.

Biltmore Conference. *Declaration Adopted by the Extraordinary Zionist Conference at the Biltmore Hotel of New York City*. May 11, 1942.

Bowle, John, *Viscount Samuel*. London: Victor Gollancz, 1957.

Carroll, Michael K. "From Peace (Keeping) to War: The United Nations and the Withdrawal of UNEF." *Middle East Review of International Affairs* 9, no. 2 (June 2005).

Carter, Jimmy. *Palestine Peace, Not Apartheid*. London: Simon & Schuster, 2008.

Churchill, Winston. *Great Contemporaries*. London and Glasgow: Collins, 1937.

Churchill, Winston. *Palestine: Correspondence with the Palestine Arab Delegation and the Zionist Organisation*, White Paper, CMD 1700, London: His Majesty's Stationery Office, 1922.

Churchill, Winston. *The Second World War, vol. 2*, London: Cassell & Co., 1950–1955.

Clifford, Clark. *Counsel to the President: A Memoir*. New York: Anchor Books, 1992.

Clifford, Clark. "Recognizing Israel." *American Heritage* 28, no. 3 (April 1977): 7.

Clifford, Clark M., Rostow, Eugene V., and Barbara W. Tuchman, eds. *The Palestine Question in American History*. New York: Arno Press, 1978.

Clubb, Andrew. "T. E. Lawrence and the Arab Cause at the Paris Peace Conference." Accessed May 22, 2023. https://www.cliohistory.org/thomas-lawrence/paris.

Cohen, Michael J. "A New Look at Truman and 'Exodus 1947.'" *The Israel Journal of Foreign Affairs* 3, no. 1 (2009): 93–100.

Cohen, Michael. *Palestine: Retreat from the Mandate, the Making of British Policy 1936–45*. New York: Holmes & Meier, 1978.

Collins, Larry, and Dominique Lapierre. *O Jerusalem!* New York: Simon & Schuster, 2007.

Connell, John. *Wavell, Scholar and Soldier to June 1941*. London: Collins, 1964.

Crossman, Richard. *A Nation Reborn*. New York: Atheneum Publishers, 1960.

Crossman, Richard. *Palestine Mission*. New York: Arno Press, 1977.

Cruise O'Brien, Conor. *The Siege: The Saga of Israel and Zionism*. New York: Simon and Schuster, 1986.

Crum, Bartley. *Behind the Silken Curtain: A Personal Account of Anglo-American Diplomacy in Palestine and the Middle East*. Port Washington, NY: Kennikat Press.

Daniels, Jonathan. *The Man of Independence*. London: Victor Gollancz Ltd, 1951.

De Azcárate, Pablo. *Mission in Palestine 1948–1952*. Washington, DC: Middle East Institute, 1966.

Duff, Douglas. *Galilee Galloper*. London: J. Murray, 1935.

Duff, Douglas. *May the Winds Blow! An Autobiography*. London: Hollis and Carter, 1948.

Duff, Douglas. *Sword for Hire: The Saga of a Modern Free-Companion*. London: J. Murray, 1934.

Dugdale, Blanche E. C. *Arthur James Balfour, vol. 1, 1848–1906*. London: Hutchinson, 1936.

Erlanger, Steven. "The Saturday Profile: A Grande Dame of a Bygone Jerusalem." *The New York Times*, October 29, 2005.

Encyclopaedia Judaica, vol. 14. Jerusalem: Keter Publishing House, 1971.

Even-Shoshan, Abraham. *A New Concordance of the Torah, Prophets, and Writings*. Jerusalem, Kiryat Sefer/Baker Book House, 1989.

Forrestal, James V. *Forrestal Diaries*. New York: Viking Press, 1966.

Friedman, Isaiah. *Palestine—A Twice-Promised Land? The British, the Arabs, and Zionism, vol. 1, 1915–1920*. New Brunswick, NJ: Transaction Publishers, 2000.

Ganin, Zvi. *Truman, American Jewry, and Israel, 1945–1948*. New York: Holmes & Meier, 1979.

García-Granados, Jorge. *The Birth of Israel: The Drama as I Saw It*. New York: A. A. Knopf, 1949.

Garnett, David. *The Letters of T. E. Lawrence*. London: Spring Books, 1964.

Gilbert, Martin. *Exile and Return: The Struggle for a Jewish Homeland*. Philadelphia, PA: Lippincott, 1978.

Gilbert, Martin, ed. *Lloyd George: Great Lives Observed*. Englewood Cliffs, NJ: Prentice Hall, 1968.

Ginor, Isabella. "The Cold War's Longest Cover-Up: How and Why the USSR Instigated the 1967 War." *Middle East Review of International Affairs* 7, no. 3 (September 2003).

Glubb, Sir John Bagot. *A Soldier with the Arabs*. New York: Harper, 1957.

Grose, Peter. *Israel in the Mind of America*. New York: Schocken Books, 1984.

Hacohen, David. *Time to Tell: An Israeli Life 1898–1984*. New York: Cornwall Books, 1985.

Hamas, "Hamas Covenant 1988," *The Avalon Project, Yale Law School*. Accessed August 7, 2023. https://avalon.law.yale.edu/20th_century/hamas.asp.

Hanna, Paul. *British Policy in Palestine*. Washington DC: American Council of Public Affairs, 1942.

Hansard, House of Commons, Debates, vol. 248, cc751–7W, February 13, 1931.

Hansard, House of Commons, Debates, vol. 313, cc1331, June 19, 1936.
Hansard, House of Commons, Debates, vol. 326, cc2245–2361, July 21, 1937.
Hansard, House of Commons, Debates, vol. 326, cc2260–2261, July 21, 1937.
Hansard, House of Commons, Debates, vol. 326, cc2270, July 21, 1937.
Hansard, House of Commons, Debates, vol. 341, cc1992, November 24, 1938.
Hansard, House of Commons, Debates, vol. 341, cc1993–1994, November 24, 1938.
Hansard, House of Commons, Debates, vol. 347, cc2044 and cc2047, May 22, 1939.
Hansard, House of Commons, Debates, vol. 347, cc2045, May 22, 1939.
Hansard, House of Commons, Debates, vol. 347, cc2140, May 23, 1939.
Hansard, House of Commons, Debates, vol. 347, cc2142 and cc2144, May 23, 1939.
Hansard, House of Commons, Debates, vol. 347, cc2178, May 23, 1939.
Hansard, House of Commons, Debates, vol. 387, cc139, February 24, 1943.
Hansard, House of Commons, Debates, vol. 404, cc2242–2243, November 17, 1944.
Hansard, House of Commons, Debates, vol. 415, cc1927–1935, November 13, 1945
Hansard, House of Commons, Debates, vol. 426, cc970–971, July 31, 1946.
Hansard, House of Commons, Debates, vol. 426, cc1248, August 1, 1946.
Hansard, House of Commons, Debates, vol. 426, cc1253–1254, August 1, 1946.

Hansard, House of Commons, Debates, vol. 426, cc1257, August 1, 1946.

Hansard, House of Commons, Debates, vol. 433, cc1908, February 25, 1947.

Hansard, House of Commons, Debates, vol. 433, cc2007, February 25, 1947.

Hertz, Eli E. "Mandate for Palestine: The Legal Aspects of Jewish Rights." *Israel Forever Foundation*. Accessed August 8, 2023. https://israelforever.org/interact/blog/mandate_palestine_legal_aspects_of_jewish_rights.

Hope Simpson, Sir John. *Palestine: Report on Immigration, Land Settlement and Development*. London: His Majesty's Stationery Office, 1930.

Horowitz, David. *State in the Making*. New York: Alfred A. Knopf, 1953.

Hurewitz, J. C., ed. *The Middle East and North Africa in World Politics: A Documentary Record*. New Haven: Yale University Press, 1979.

Husseini, Faisal. *Al Arabi* (Egypt), June 24, 2001.

Husseini, Faisal. *Jerusalem Report*, July 30, 2001.

Ingrams, Doreen, ed. *Palestine Papers 1917–1922: Seeds of Conflict*. London: Eland, 2009.

Israeli Ministry of Foreign Affairs. "Arab Summit Decides to Divert Headwaters, Statement of the Council of the Kings and Heads of State of the Arab League Member Countries on its First Session, Cairo, 13–17 January 1964." Accessed July 10, 2023. https://www.gov.il/en/Departments/General/11-arab-summit-decides-to-divert-headwaters-13-january-1964.

Israeli Ministry of Foreign Affairs. "Highlights of Main Events, 1947–1974." Accessed July 10, 2023. https://www.gov.il/en/Departments/General/highlights-of-main-events-1947-1974.

Israeli Ministry of Foreign Affairs. "Letter from the Arab Higher Committee for Palestine concerning the Eric Johnston Scheme, 18 August 1955." Accessed July 10, 2023. https://www.gov.il/en/Departments/General/9-letter-from-the-arab-higher-committee-for-pal-

estine-concerning-thejohnston-scheme-18-august-1955.
Israeli Ministry of Foreign Affairs. "Memorandum by Secretary General Hammarskjold, August 1957." Accessed July 10, 2023. https://www.gov.il/en/Departments/General/35-memorandum-by-sec-gen-hammarskjold-1-august-1957.
Israeli Ministry of Foreign Affairs. "Message from Prime Minister Eshkol to King Hussein, 5 June 1967." Accessed July 11, 2023. https://www.gov.il/en/Departments/General/16-message-from-pm-eshkol-to-king-hussein-5-june-1967.
Israeli Ministry of Foreign Affairs. "Statement to the General Assembly by Foreign Minister Eban, 19 June 1967." Accessed July 11, 2023. https://www.gov.il/en/Departments/General/25-statement-to-the-general-assembly-by-fm-eban-19-june-1967.
Israeli Ministry of Foreign Affairs. "Statement to the Knesset by Foreign Minister Sharett, 15 June 1949." Accessed July 10, 2023. https://www.gov.il/en/Departments/General/2-statement-to-the-knesset-by-fm-sharett-15-june-1949.
Israeli Ministry of Foreign Affairs. "Statement to the Knesset by Prime Minister Eshkol, 12 June 1967." Accessed July 11, 2023. https://www.gov.il/en/Departments/General/23-statement-to-the-knesset-by-pm-eshkol-12-june-1967.
Israeli Ministry of Foreign Affairs. "Statement to the Knesset by Prime Minister Eshkol, October 17, 1966." Accessed July 11, 2023. https://www.gov.il/en/Departments/General/5-statement-to-the-knesset-by-pm-eshkol-23-may-1967.
Israeli Ministry of Foreign Affairs. "The Johnston Mission Fails: Summaries by Ambassador Johnston and General Burns." Accessed July 10, 2023. https://www.gov.il/en/Departments/General/10-the-johnston-mission-fails-summaries-by-amb-johnston-and-gen-burns-19-october-1958.
Israeli Ministry of Foreign Affairs, The Foreign Ministry of the Russian Federation, The Israel State Archives, The Russian Federal Archives, The Cummings Center for Russian Studies at Tel Aviv University, the Oriental Institute, the Russian Academy

of Sciences, eds., *Documents on Soviet–Israeli Relations 1941–1953*. Accessed July 10, 2023. http://www.tau.ac.il/~russia/series/book10.html.

Jabotinsky, Vladimir. *The Story of the Jewish Legion*. New York: B. Ackerman, 1945.

Jenkins, Joy. *Asquith: Portrait of a Man and an Era*, New York: Chillmark Press, 1964.

Jessup, Philip C. *The Birth of Nations*. New York: Colombia University Press, 1974.

Jewish Agency for Israel. *Jewish Zionist Education, vol. 7: World War II*.

Jewish Virtual Library. "Roots of the US–Israel Relationship." Accessed April 16, 2023. https://www.jewishvirtuallibrary.org/roots-of-the-u-s-israel-relationship.

Jewish Virtual Library. "Texts Concerning Zionism: Excerpts from Herzl's 'The Jewish State.'" Accessed April 16, 2023. https://www.jewishvirtuallibrary.org/excerpts-from-quot-the-jewish-state-quot.

Jewish Virtual Library. "The War of Independence: Letter from Dr. Bunche to the President of the Security Council, July 21, 1949." Accessed July 10, 2023. http://www.jewishvirtuallibrary.org/jsource/History/bunchlet.html.

Jewish Virtual Library. "Zionist Congress: First Zionist Congress & Basel Program." Accessed April 16, 2023. https://www.jewishvirtuallibrary.org/first-zionist-congress-and-basel-program-1897.

Johnson, Lyndon B. "Address at the State Department's Foreign Policy Conference for Educators." *The American Presidency Project*. Accessed on July 11, 2023. https://www.presidency.ucsb.edu/documents/address-the-state-departments-foreign-policy-conference-for-educators.

Jones, Martin. *Failure in Palestine*. London: Mansell, 1986.

Jordan History. "The Disaster of 1967." Accessed July 10, 2023. http://www.kinghussein.gov.jo/his_periods3.html.

Joseph, Dov. *The Faithful City: The Siege of Jerusalem, 1948*. London: Hogarth Press, 1962.

Katz, Samuel. *Battleground: Fact and Fantasy in Palestine*. New York: Taylor Productions, 2002.
Katz, Samuel. *Days of Fire*. Garden City, NY: Doubleday, 1968.
Kedourie, Elie. *England and the Middle East*. London: Mansell Publishing, 1987.
Kedourie, Elie. *The Chatham House Version*. Hanover, NH: Published for Brandeis University Press by University Press of New England, 1984.
Kirk, George. *The Middle East 1945–1950*. London: Oxford University Press, 1954.
Knightley, Phillip, and Colin Simpson. *The Secret Lives of Lawrence of Arabia*. London: Panther Books, 1971.
Koestler, Arthur. *Promise and Fulfillment: Palestine 1917–1949*. New York: Macmillan, 1949.
Koss, Stephen. *Asquith*. New York: Colombia University Press, 1976.
Kurzman, Dan. *Genesis 1948: The First Arab–Israeli War*. New York: Da Capo Press, 1992.
Laqueur, Walter. *A History of Zionism*. London: Tauris Parke, 2003.
Laqueur, Walter, ed. *The Israel–Arab Reader*. New York: Penguin Books, 2016.
Lawrence, A. W. ed. *T. E. Lawrence by His Friends*. New York: Doubleday, Doran and Co., Inc., 1937.
League of Nations Permanent Mandates Commission. *Minutes of the Seventeenth (Extraordinary) Session, Fifth Meeting, June 5, 1930*. Geneva, Switzerland.
Levine, Hillel. "Sugihara's List." *The New York Times*, September 20, 1994.
Lie, Trygve. *In the Cause of Peace: Seven Years with the United Nations*. New York: Macmillan, 1954.
Lorch, Netanel. *Israel's War of Independence 1947–1949*. Hartford, CT: Hartmore House, 1968.
MacDonald, Malcolm. *Palestine: Statement of Policy*, White Paper, CMD 6019. London: His Majesty's Stationery Office, 1939.

Mack, John E. *A Prince of Our Disorder: The Life of T. E. Lawrence.* Cambridge, MA: Harvard University Press, 1998.

Matthews, John P. C. "John Foster Dulles and the Suez Crisis of 1956." *American Diplomacy* (2006). *Gale Academic OneFile.* Accessed July 10, 2023. https://link.gale.com/apps/doc/A152745459/AONE?u=anon~fd8d4d89&sid=bookmark-AONE&xid=deee403c.

McDonald, James. *My Mission in Israel.* New York: Simon and Schuster, 1951.

Meinertzhagen, Colonel Richard. *Middle East Diary 1917–1956.* New York: Yoseloff, 1960.

Middle East Media Research Institute (MEMRI). "Hamas TV Cartoon Depicts Koran-Based Story of Jews Being Transformed into Apes." *MEMRI* Special Dispatch, No. 3128, September 7, 2010. Accessed August 10, 2023. https://www.memri.org/reports/hamas-tv-cartoon-depicts-koran-based-story-jews-being-transformed-apes.

Middle East Media Research Institute (MEMRI). "PA Chairman Mahmoud Abbas: I Will Never Recognize a Jewish State." *MEMRI*, Special Dispatch, No. 4235, November 1, 2011. Accessed August 10, 2023. https://www.memri.org/reports/pa-chairman-mahmoud-abbas-i-will-never-recognize-jewish-state-capturing-israeli-soldier.

Middlebury Institute of International Studies at Monterey. "6th Summit Conference of Heads of State or Government of the Non-Aligned Movement." Accessed August 7, 2023. http://cns.miis.edu/nam/documents/Official_Document/6th_Summit_FD_Havana_Declaration_1979_Whole.pdf.

Miller, Merle. *Plain Speaking: An Oral Biography of Harry S. Truman.* New York: Tess Press, 2004.

Mossek, Moshe, *Palestine Immigration Policy.* Totowa, NJ: London, 1978.

Murakami, Masahiro. *Managing Water for Peace in the Middle East: Alternative Strategies.* Tokyo: United Nations University Press,

1995. Accessed July 10, 2023. http://www.unu.edu/wwf/UNUwater-publications.html.

Nasser, Gamal Abdel. "A Political Testimony, July 23, 1970." *Pan-African Perspective*. Accessed August 10, 2023. https://www.panafricanperspective.com/Gamal-Abdel-Nasser.html.

Neumann, Emanuel. *In the Arena: An Autobiographical Memoir*. New York: Herzl Press, 1976.

Oren, Michael. "The Unwanted War That Made the Middle East" (California: June 24, 2002), Commonwealth Club of California Records, *Hoover Institution Library & Archives*, ID 2003c87_a_0001136, Record 2003C87.2862. Accessed July 11, 2023, https://digitalcollections.hoover.org/objects/3173/1967-the-unwanted-war-that-made-the-middle-east?ctx=473ba4dd-e459-41e1-96b2-79b35acf8b68&idx=3.

Palestine Liberation Organization. "Palestine National Charter of 1964." *Israeli Ministry of Foreign Affairs*. Accessed August 9, 2023. https://www.gov.il/en/Departments/General/11-national-covenant-of-the-palestine-liberation-organization-28-may-1964.

Palestinian National Council. "Palestinian Declaration of Independence," *MidEast Web*. Accessed August 7, 2023. http://www.mideastweb.org/plc1988.htm.

Parkes, James. *A History of Palestine from 135 AD to Modern Times*. New York: Oxford University Press, 1949.

Parkes, James. *Whose Land? A History of the Peoples of Palestine*. New York: Taplinger, 1971.

Pearlman, Moshe. *Ben Gurion Looks Back*. New York: Schocken Books, 1970.

Peel, Lord Robert. *Palestine Royal Commission Report*. CMD 5479. London: His Majesty's Stationery Office, 1937.

Prime Minister's Office (Israel). "PM Olmert's Remarks Following his Meeting with Russian President Putin, October 18, 2006." Accessed August 7, 2023. http://www.pmo.gov.il/PMOEng/Communication/EventsDiary/eventputin181006.htm.

Rabinowicz, Oskar K. *Winston Churchill on Jewish Problems: A Half-Century Survey.* London: Lincolns-Prager, 1956.
Rhodes James, Robert. *Winston S. Churchill: His Complete Speeches, 1897–1963, vol. 7—1943–1949.* New York: Chelsea House Publishers, 1974.
Rose, Kenneth. *Superior Person: Portrait of Curzon and His Circle in Late Victorian England.* London: Weidenfeld & Nicolson, 1969.
Royal Institute of International Affairs. *Survey of International Affairs, 1930.* London: Oxford University Press, 1931.
Rubin, Barry. *Revolution Until Victory? The Politics and History of the PLO.* Cambridge, MA: Harvard University Press, 1994.
Sachar, Howard M. *A History of Israel: From the Rise of Zionism to Our Time.* New York: Random House, 2013.
Safran, Nadav. *From War to War: The Arab–Israeli Confrontation 1948–1967.* New York: Pegasus, 1969.
Samuel, Edwin. *A Lifetime in Jerusalem: The Memoirs of the Second Viscount Samuel.* London: Vallentine Mitchell, 1970.
Samuel, Herbert Louis. *Memoirs.* London: Cresset Press, 1945.
Samuel, Maurice. *What Happened in Palestine: The Events of August 1929, Their Background and Their Significance.* Boston, MA: Stratford Company, 1929.
San Diego State University. "Constantinople Convention, 1888." *Department of Political Science.* Accessed August 7, 2023. https://loveman.sdsu.edu/docs/1888ConstantinopleConventionon.pdf.
Schoenberg, Harris O. *A Mandate for Terror: The United Nations and the PLO.* New York: Shapolsky Books, 1989.
Seliktar, Ofira. "Turning Water into Fire: The Jordan River as the Hidden Factor in the Six-Day War." *The Middle East Review of International Affairs* 9, no. 4 (June 2005).
Shaw, Walter. *The Report of the Commission on the Palestine Disturbances of August 1929,* CMD 3530. London: His Majesty's Stationery Office, 1930.

Sherwood, Robert E. *Roosevelt and Hopkins: An Intimate History*. New York: Enigma Books, 2001.
Slater, Leonard. *The Pledge*. New York: Pocket Books, 1971.
Souss, Ibrahim. *Europe No. 1 Radio* (France), June 16, 1980.
Souss, Ibrahim. *The Times* (UK), August 5, 1980.
Soustelle, Jacques. *The Long March of Israel*. New York: American Heritage Press, 1969.
Stein, Leonard. *The Balfour Declaration*. Jerusalem and London: Magnes Press and Hebrew University, 1983.
Storrs, Ronald. *The Memoirs of Sir Ronald Storrs*. New York: AMS Press, 1973.
Sykes, Christopher. *Crossroads to Israel*. Bloomington, IN: Indiana University Press, 1973.
The American Presidency Project. "Special Message to the Congress on the Middle East Situation, January 5, 1957." Accessed July 10, 2023. https://www.presidency.ucsb.edu/documents/special-message-the-congress-the-situation-the-middle-east.
The Avalon Project (Yale Law School). "The Khartoum Resolutions; September 1, 1967." Accessed August 7, 2023. https://avalon.law.yale.edu/20th_century/khartoum.asp#:~:text=The%20Arab%20Heads%20of%20State,the%20aggression%20of%20June%205.
The Group of 77 at the United Nations. "The Group of Seventy-Seven at the United Nations." Accessed July 11, 2023. http://www.g77.org.
Truman, Harry S. *Memoirs, vol. 1: Year of Decisions*. New York: Doubleday, 1955.
Truman, Harry S. *Memoirs, vol 2: Years of Trial and Hope*. New York: New American Library, 1965.
Truman, Margaret. *Harry S. Truman*. New York: William Morrow & Co, Inc., 1973.
United Nations Conciliation Commission for Palestine. Final Report of the United Nations Economic Survey Mission for the Middle East. Document A/AC.25/6 (December 28, 1949).

Accessed August 9, 2023. https://digitallibrary.un.org/record/1640579?ln=en.
United Nations Conciliation Commission for Palestine. Progress Report of the United Nations Conciliation Commission for Palestine to the Sixth Session of the United Nations General Assembly. Document A/1985 (January 23–November 19, 1951). Accessed August 9, 2023. https://www.un.org/unispal/document/auto-insert-186738.
United Nations General Assembly. Official Records of the 1st Special Session of the General Assembly: Volume 1, Plenary Meetings of the General Assembly, Verbatim Record, Document A/PV.68-79 (April 28–May 15, 1947). Accessed August 8, 2023. https://digitallibrary.un.org/record/3827201?ln=en.
United Nations General Assembly. 1st Special Session: 77th Plenary Meeting, Held on Wednesday, May 14, 1947. Document A/PV.77 (May 14, 1947). Accessed August 8, 2023. https://digitallibrary.un.org/record/3829520?ln=en.
United Nations General Assembly. 1st Special Session: 79th Plenary Meeting, Held on Thursday, May 15, 1947. Document A/PV.79 (May 15, 1947). Accessed August 8, 2023. https://www.un.org/unispal/document/auto-insert-178314.
United Nations General Assembly. 5th Emergency Special Session: 1545th Plenary Meeting. Document A/PV.1545 (July 3, 1967). Accessed August 10, 2023. https://digitallibrary.un.org/record/718801.
United Nations General Assembly. 124th Plenary Meeting, Held in the General Assembly Hall at Flushing Meadow, New York on Wednesday, November 26, 1947. Document A/PV.124 (November 26, 1947). Accessed August 8, 2023. https://digitallibrary.un.org/record/734598?ln=en.
United Nations General Assembly. 125th Plenary Meeting, Held in the General Assembly Hall at Flushing Meadow, New York on Wednesday, November 26, 1947. Document A/PV.125

(November 26, 1947). Accessed August 8, 2023. https://digitallibrary.un.org/record/734600?ln=en.

United Nations General Assembly. Ad-Hoc Committee/General Debate. Document GA/PAL/2 (September 26, 1947). Accessed August 8, 2023. https://www.un.org/unispal/wp-content/uploads/1947/09/ecb5eae2e1d29ed08525686d00529256_gapal02.pdf.

United Nations General Assembly. Ad-Hoc Committee/General Debate. Document GA/PAL/3 (September 29, 1947). Accessed August 8, 2023. https://www.un.org/unispal/wp-content/uploads/1947/09/a8c17fca1b8cf5338525691b0063f769_gapal03.pdf.

United Nations General Assembly. Ad-Hoc Committee/General Debate. Document GA/PAL/4 (October 2, 1947). Accessed August 8, 2023. https://www.un.org/unispal/wp-content/uploads/1947/10/a62f2fe8807066038525691b00658f74_gapal04.pdf.

United Nations General Assembly. Ad-Hoc Committee/General Debate. Document GA/PAL/5 (October 3, 1947). Accessed August 8, 2023. https://www.un.org/unispal/wp-content/uploads/1947/10/4d434db66697dc3f85256929006d26c5_gapal05.pdf.

United Nations General Assembly. Ad-Hoc Committee/General Debate. Document GA/PAL/12 (October 11, 1947). Accessed August 8, 2023. https://www.un.org/unispal/wp-content/uploads/1947/10/7b33678fe44b8dac85256929006e1e9e_gapal12.pdf.

United Nations General Assembly. Ad-Hoc Committee/General Debate. Document A/AC.14/SR.12 (October 13, 1947). Accessed August 8, 2023. https://www.un.org/unispal/document/auto-insert-205565.

United Nations General Assembly. Ad-Hoc Committee/General Debate. Document GA/PAL/73 (November 19, 1947). Accessed

August 8, 2023. https://www.un.org/unispal/document/auto-insert-214178.
United Nations General Assembly. Ad-Hoc Committee/General Debate. Document GA/PAL/74 (November 19, 1947). Accessed August 8, 2023. https://www.un.org/unispal/document/auto-insert-214134.
United Nations General Assembly. Ad-Hoc Committee/General Debate. Document GA/PAL/76 (November 20, 1947). Accessed August 8, 2023. https://www.un.org/unispal/document/auto-insert-214132.
United Nations General Assembly. Ad-Hoc Committee/General Debate. Document GA/PAL/80 (November 22, 1947). Accessed August 8, 2023. https://www.un.org/unispal/document/auto-insert-214186.
United Nations General Assembly. Ad-Hoc Committee/General Debate. Document GA/PAL/81 (November 22, 1947). Accessed August 8, 2023. https://www.un.org/unispal/document/auto-insert-214177.
United Nations General Assembly. Declaration of State of Palestine—Palestine National Council, Annex III, Document A/43/827, S/20278 (November 15, 1988). Accessed August 7, 2023. https://www.un.org/unispal/document/auto-insert-178680.
United Nations General Assembly. Letter Dated 18 November 1988 from the Permanent Representative of Jordan to the United Nations, Addressed to the Secretary General. Document A/43/827 (November 18, 1988). Accessed August 10, 2023. https://digitallibrary.un.org/record/50478?ln=en.
United Nations General Assembly. Provisional Verbatim Record of the 78th Meeting, Held at the Palais des Nations, Geneva, on Tuesday, 13 December 1988: General Assembly, 43rd session, Document A/43/PV.78 (January 3, 1989). Accessed August 7, 2023. https://digitallibrary.un.org/record/55459?ln=en.
United Nations Palestine Commission. First Special Report to the Security Council: The Problem of Security in Palestine.

Document A/C.21/9 (February 16, 1948). Accessed August 9, 2023. https://unispal.un.org/pdfs/AAC21R9.pdf.
United Nations General Assembly. Resolution 181(II) — Future Government of Palestine. Documents A/PV.128 and A/RES/181(II)[A] (November 29, 1947). Accessed August 9, 2023. https://digitallibrary.un.org/record/671195?ln=en and https://digitallibrary.un.org/record/667160?ln=en.
United Nations General Assembly. Resolution 194(III) — Palestine: Progress Report of the United Nations Mediator. Document A/RES/194(III) (December 11, 1948). Accessed August 9, 2023. https://digitallibrary.un.org/record/210025?ln=en.
United Nations General Assembly. Resolution 1237(E-S III) — Questions Considered by the Security Council at Its 838th Meeting. Document A/Res/1237(E-S III) (August 21, 1958). Accessed August 9, 2023. https://digitallibrary.un.org/record/207462?ln=en.
United Nations General Assembly. Resolutions Adopted by the General Assembly during Its 1st Emergency Special Session. Document A/3354 (November 1–10, 1956). Accessed August 9, 2023. https://digitallibrary.un.org/record/228961?ln=en.
United Nations General Assembly and United Nations Palestine Commission. Memorandum from the Jewish Agency: Acts of Aggression by Arab States. Document A/AC.21/JA/12 (February 2, 1948). Accessed August 9, 2023. https://www.un.org/unispal/document/auto-insert-211102.
United Nations Security Council. Attack on As Samu — SecCo Action/the Palestine Question (Last Consideration of Item) — SecCo Verbatim Record. Document S/PV.1328 (OR) (November 11, 1966). Accessed August 9, 2023. https://www.un.org/unispal/document/auto-insert-180759.
United Nations Security Council. Egyptian-Israeli General Armistice Agreement. Document S/1264/Rev. 1, Dee. 13 (February 24, 1949). The Avalon Project. Accessed July 10, 2023. https://avalon.law.yale.edu/20th_century/arm01.asp.

United Nations Security Council. Letter Dated 6 October 1964 Addressed to the President of the Security Council by the Representatives of Algeria, Iraq, Jordan, Kuwait, Lebanon, Libya, Morocco, Saudi Arabia, Sudan, Syrian Arab Republic, Tunisia, United Arab Republic, and the Arab Republic of Yemen. Document S/6003 (October 8, 1964). Accessed August 9, 2023.

United Nations Security Council. Official Records—22nd Year, 1377th Meeting. Document S/PV1377 (November 15, 1967). Accessed August 10, 2023. https://digitallibrary.un.org/record/587206?ln=en.United Nations, *Yearbook of the United Nations, 1947–1948*. New York: United Nations Department of Public Information, 1948.

United Nations Security Council. Report of the Secretary General on Measures Taken by Israel to Change the Status of the City of Jerusalem. Document S/8052 (July 10, 1967). Accessed August 10, 2023. https://digitallibrary.un.org/record/520093?ln=en.

United Nations Security Council. Resolution 50 (1948). Document S/801 (May 29, 1948). Accessed August 20, 2023. https://documents-dds-ny.un.org/doc/RESOLUTION/GEN/NR0/047/75/PDF/NR004775.pdf?OpenElement.

United Nations Security Council. Resolution 59 (1948). Document S/1045 (October 19, 1948). Accessed August 20, 2023. https://documents-dds-ny.un.org/doc/RESOLUTION/GEN/NR0/047/84/PDF/NR004784.pdf?OpenElement.

United Nations Security Council. Resolution 61—The Palestine Question. Document S/RES/61(1948) (November 4, 1948). Accessed August 10, 2023. https://documents-dds-ny.un.org/doc/RESOLUTION/GEN/NR0/047/86/PDF/NR004786.pdf?OpenElement.

United Nations Security Council. Resolution 62. Document S/1080(1948) (November 16, 1948). Accessed August 19, 2023. https://documents-dds-ny.un.org/doc/RESOLUTION/GEN/NR0/047/87/PDF/NR004787.pdf?OpenElement.

United Nations Security Council. Resolution 95—The Palestine Question. Document S/RES/95(1951) (September 1, 1951). Accessed August 9, 2023. https://documents-dds-ny.un.org/doc/RESOLUTION/GEN/NR0/072/14/PDF/NR007214.pdf?OpenElement.pdf.

United Nations Security Council. Resolution 228—On Israeli Military Actions against Jordan. Document S/RES/228(1966) (November 25, 1966). Accessed August 9, 2023. https://digitallibrary.un.org/record/90503?ln=en.

United Nations Security Council. Resolution 242, The Situation in the Middle East, Document S/RES/242(1967) (November 9, 1967). Accessed August 7, 2023. https://documents-dds-ny.un.org/doc/RESOLUTION/GEN/NR0/240/94/PDF/NR024094.pdf?OpenElement.

United Nations Security Council. Revised Draft Resolution [on Complaint by Lebanon in Respect of a Situation Arising from Interference of the United Arab Republic (Egypt) in the Internal Affairs of Lebanon, Document S/4050/Rev.1 (July 18, 1958). Accessed August 9, 2023. https://digitallibrary.un.org/record/536919?ln=en.

United Nations Security Council. Revised Draft Resolution [on Complaint by Lebanon in Respect of a Situation Arising from Interference of the United Arab Republic (Egypt) in the Internal Affairs of Lebanon, Document S/4055/Rev.1 (July 22, 1958). Accessed August 9, 2023. https://digitallibrary.un.org/record/536964?ln=en.

United Nations Security Council. Water Works in Demilitarized Zone—Vetoed Draft Resolution. Document S/3151/Rev.2 (January 22, 1954). Accessed August 9, 2023. https://digitallibrary.un.org/record/539477?ln=en.

United Nations Special Committee on Palestine. Report of the United Nations Special Committee on Palestine, vol. 2: Report to the General Assembly, Document A/364 (September 3, 1947). Accessed August 8, 2023. https://digitallibrary.un.org/

record/563036?ln=en.

United States Government. *Foreign Relations of the United States: Diplomatic Papers*, 1936, vol. 2. Washington DC: United States Government Publishing Office.

United States Government. *Foreign Relations of the United States: Diplomatic Papers*, 1939, vol. 1. Washington DC: United States Government Publishing Office.

United States Government. *Foreign Relations of the United States: Diplomatic Papers*, 1939, vol. 4. Washington DC: United States Government Publishing Office.

United States Government. *Foreign Relations of the United States: Diplomatic Papers*, 1942, vol. 4. Washington DC: United States Government Publishing Office.

United States Government. *Foreign Relations of the United States: Diplomatic Papers*, 1943, vol. 4. Washington DC: United States Government Publishing Office.

United States Government. *Foreign Relations of the United States: Diplomatic Papers*, 1944, vol. 5. Washington DC: United States Government Publishing Office.

United States Government. *Foreign Relations of the United States: Diplomatic Papers*, 1945, vol. 8. Washington DC: United States Government Publishing Office.

United States Government. *Foreign Relations of the United States: Diplomatic Papers*, 1946, vol. 7. Washington DC: United States Government Publishing Office.

United States Government. *Foreign Relations of the United States: Diplomatic Papers*, 1947, vol. 5. Washington DC: United States Government Publishing Office.

United States Government. *Foreign Relations of the United States: Diplomatic Papers*, 1948, vol. 5. Washington DC: United States Government Publishing Office.

United States Government. *Foreign Relations of the United States: Diplomatic Papers*, 1949, vol. 6. Washington DC: United States Government Publishing Office.

United States Government. *Foreign Relations of the United States: Diplomatic Papers,* 1964–1968, vol. 18. Washington DC: United States Government Publishing Office.

United States Government. *Foreign Relations of the United States: Diplomatic Papers,* 1964–1968, vol. 34. Washington DC: United States Government Publishing Office.

United States National Archives. "Letter to General Eisenhower Concerning Conditions Facing Displaced Persons in Germany." In *Public Papers of the Presidents,* September 29, 1945, no. 152.

United States National Archives. "Statement by the President on the Problems of Jewish Refugees in Europe." *Public Papers of the Presidents,* November 13, 1945, no. 187.

Urofsky, Melvin. *We Are One!: American Jewry and Israel.* Garden City, NY: Anchor Press, 1978.

Van Paassen, Pierre. *The Forgotten Ally.* Washington, D.C.: Top Executive Media, 2005.

Wasserstein, Bernard, ed. *The British in Palestine: The Mandatory Government and Arab-Jewish Conflict.* Oxford: Blackwell Publishing, 1991.

Webb, Sidney (Lord Passfield). *Palestine: Statement of Policy by His Majesty's Government in the United Kingdom.* CMD 3692. London: His Majesty's Stationery Office, 1930.

Weisgal, Meyer. *The Letters and Papers of Chaim Weizmann, Series A,* vol. 7. London: Oxford University Press, 1975.

Weisgal, Meyer. *The Letters and Papers of Chaim Weizmann, Series A,* vol. 10. London: Oxford University Press, 1977.

Weisgal, Meyer. *The Letters and Papers of Chaim Weizmann, Series B,* vol. 2. New Brunswick, NJ: Transaction Books, 1983.

Weisgal, Meyer, Carmichael, Joel, and David Ben-Gurion, eds. *Chaim Weizmann: A Biography by Several Hands.* New York: Atheneum, 1963.

Weiss, Martin A. "Arab League Boycott of Israel." *Congressional Research Service.* Accessed July 10, 2023. https://crsreports.congress.gov/product/details?prodcode=RL33961.

Weizmann, Chaim, *Trial and Error: The Autobiography of Chaim Weizmann*. New York: Schocken, 1949.

Weizmann, Vera and David Tutaev. *The Impossible Takes Longer: The Memoirs of Vera Weizmann, Wife of Israel's First President*. New York: Harper & Row, 1967.

Welles, Sumner. *We Need Not Fail*. Boston, MA: Houghton Mifflin Co., 1948.

Wilson, Evan. *Decision on Palestine: How the US Came to Recognize Israel*. Stanford, CA: Hoover Institution Press, Stanford University.

Wilson, Harold. arold. *The Chariot of Israel: Britain, America, and the State of Israel*. London: Weidenfeld and Nicolson/Michael Joseph, 1981.

Wolf, Aaron T. "Hydropolitics along the Jordan River: Scarce Water and Its Impact on the Arab–Israeli Conflict." *United Nations University*. Accessed July 10, 2023. https://collections.unu.edu/view/UNU:8714.

Woodhead, John. *Palestine Partition Commission Report*, CMD 5854. London: His Majesty's Stationery Office, 1938.

Woodrow Wilson International Center for Scholars (Virtual Archive). "On Soviet Policy following the Israeli Aggression in the Middle East—Report by Comrade L. I. Brezhnev to the Plenum of the Central Committee of the Soviet Communist Party, Held on 20 June 1967." Accessed August 7, 2023. https://digitalarchive.wilsoncenter.org/document/soviet-policy-following-israeli-aggression-middle-east.

Woodrow Wilson International Center for Scholars (Virtual Archive). "Record of Conversation between Polish Politburo Member Zenon Kliszko and Soviet Leader Leonid Brezhnev, Moscow, June 24, 1967." Accessed July 11, 2023. https://digitalarchive.wilsoncenter.org/document/record-conversation-between-polish-politburo-member-zenon-kliszko-and-soviet-leader-leonid.

Wyman, David S. *The Abandonment of the Jews*. New York: Garland Publishing, 1989–1991.

Index

1888 Constantinople Convention, 562
1949 Armistice Agreements, 557–60, 561–62, 574–575, 594, 599, 617–23, 645–46

A
Abbas, Mahmoud
    attempts to admit Palestine as a UN member state, xii, 654
    op-ed article, ix, x, 381
    refusal to accept Israel as a Jewish state, x–xi, 654
Abdullah, King (brother of Feisal), 96, 97, 164, 173n53, 205, 388–89, 433, 464, 481–82, 486, 519, 527, 539–40, 653
"absorptive capacity" concept regarding immigration, 84, 106–07, 135, 152, 159–61, 162–64, 290
acceptance of the State of Israel. See recognition of a Jewish state
Acheson, Dean, 296–97
Agnon, S. Y., 72n16
agriculture
    concerns about immigration policies' effects on, 131–32, 135–36
    development of the Negev, 355–56
    Hope Simpson Report conclusions about, 134–35
    regional water development project for Israel, Jordan, Lebanon, and Syria, 566–67, 581–85
    work in Syria's demilitarized zone, 562–63, 569
Aldington, Richard, 40–41
Algeria, 570, 571, 607
Alkabetz, Shlomo Halevi, xvii
Allenby, Edmund, 59
Al Qibla (newspaper), 25–26
Amer, Field Marshal, 608
Amery, Leopold, 183–84, 206, 208n37

Anglo-American Commission of Inquiry, 257–63, 264–80
Anglo-Egyptian Treaty of 1936, 544, 548, 572n20
Anglo-French Joint Declaration, 50–54
Anglo-Transjordanian Treaty, 389, 549–50
anti-Semitism, 8–11, 48–49, 62–63n2, 76, 328, 568n13
Arab Revolt
    link to psychological absorptive capacity, 162–64
    against the Ottoman Empire, 38–39, 40–44, 46–47, 54
    in Palestine (1936-39), 144–55, 188–89
the Arab world
    appeasement of, 73, 136–37, 150, 182–84, 255–56
    appointment of a new mufti (1921), 79–83
    Arab-African solidarity, 588–89
    Arab Headwater Diversion Plan, 584–85
    Arab-Jewish relations, xi, 94, 128–29, 222–23, 238, 301, 325, 337–39, 504–05, 511, 610
    Arab League, 211, 375, 387, 464, 561, 566–67, 582–86, 643–44, 653
    Arab Legion, 388–91, 433, 459, 460, 465
    Arab Liberation Army, 377–78, 526
    Arab refugees in Israel, 495–01, 507–09, 564–67, 655
    Arab-Soviet alliances, 349
    attacks against Jewish settlers, 377, 379
    attitudes regarding continuing the war against Israel, 526–27
    benefits of Jewish immigration, 160–61, 166–67
    continued refusal to accept the UN resolution, 381–82, 408
    effects of the Balfour Declaration on, 156–57, 171–72
    exclusion of Palestine in Britain's promise of Arab independence, 50–54, 156–57
    fedayeen terrorist attacks, 563
    fellaheen ("landless tenants"), 159, 163–64
    freedom to establish a state of Palestine, 641
    guerilla war response to the UNGA partition resolution, 373–82
    immigration, 166–67
    invasion of Israel immediately following independence, 459–65
    Jericho conference (1948), 539–40
    Jerusalem Arab elders, 52–53
    Joint Arab Defense Pact, 587
    massacres of Jews in Palestine (1929), 73, 113, 117–34, 214
    meaningful work programs, lack of, 567

Nashashibi and Husseini families, 67–68, 77–83, 147–48
Palestine as another Arab state, 168, 173–74, 183, 337–38, 376
Palestinian identity, lack of a distinct, 641–42
pan-Arab nationalism, 47–48, 577, 615
Paris Peace Conference negotiations, 24–32
refusal to accept Arab refugees from Israel, 499, 564–57
rejection of Herbert Samuel's representative government policy, 89–91
"right of return," 499–501, 507–09, 538n8, 564–67, 655
San Remo Agreement, 31–32
Supreme Moslem Council, 82
unification of Arab Palestine with Transjordan, 539–40
United Arab Command, 584
welfare structure, 499, 567

Arafat, Yasser
concept of a Palestinian identity, 643
Declaration of Independence of a State of Palestine, xi–xii, xiv, 648–51
Fatah, 587, 593–94, 643, 644
invitation to address the UNGA, 647–48
as the leader of the PLO, 587

Aranha, Oswald, 363–64
armistice negotiations, 534–36, 546, 548–54, 557–60, 561–62
Armour, Norman, 353
arms
British sale of arms to Iraq, 387
Czech smuggling of military equipment and arms to Israel, 393–94n42
disarmament of the United Resistance, 264, 271–72, 277–78, 280, 284–85
embargo on shipments of arms to Palestine, 393, 408, 466, 545, 591
Israel's request for arms from the US, 569–70
Jewish disappointment in US assistance with, 427
Soviet-Arab deals, 591–93, 616
Soviet-Egyptian deal, 569–70
weapons and ammunition, removal of, 122
weapons smuggling by both sides, 487, 529

army, Jewish, 188–92
Arslan, Amir, 374
Ashbee, Charles R., 50
Asquith, Herbert Henry
feelings about the Jews, 11

opposition to Palestine, 8–10
political downfall, 12–15
relationship with Venetia Stanley, 12–15
visit to Palestine, 11
WWI ammunition crisis, 6
Asquith: Portrait of a Man and an Era (Jenkins), 11–15, 12n17
assassination of Mediator Bernadotte, 516–18
Aswan Dam financing, 570–72
the Atlantic Charter, 225–26
Attlee, Clement, 169–70, 193, 207, 246–47, 251, 252–57, 277–78, 281–83, 284–85, 295, 297, 299n42, 326
Austin, Warren, 328, 331, 332–33, 400–02, 403–06, 409–10, 412, 450–51, 468
Azcárate, Pablo de, 383–84n20

B
Badeau, John S., 582–83
Baghdad Pact, 571
Balfour, Arthur James, 3–5, 7n6, 32, 110, 111
Balfour, Sir John, 465–66
Balfour Declaration
 Arab response to the, 24, 25–32, 171–72, 314
 ban on distribution of the, 50
 changes to the, 16–17, 32–37, 329n29
 dual obligation of the, 85–86
 effect on WWI alliances, 6–8, 156–57, 171–72
 Herbert Samuel's interpretation, 85–86, 87–91, 104–06
 opposition to the, 47–48, 70–71n15
 and the promise of a Jewish homeland, 435
 text of the, 18, 100
 US support for the, 17–18, 22
Bandung Conference, 571
Barak, Ehud, 612n59
Barker, Sir Evelyn, 287
Bar Kochba, Shimon, xv–xvi
Baruch, Bernard, 366
Basel Program, 2–3
Beeley, Harold, 266–67, 311, 348, 460, 480, 482
Begin, Menahem, 139–40n44, 198, 203–04, 249–50, 285, 286, 315, 317, 612
Belgium, 364

Belt, Ambassador (Cuba), 452
Ben-Gurion, David, 1, 66n9, 71–72n15, 112, 141–42n2, 187, 199, 202, 215–16, 248–49, 263, 314, 372–73, 412, 431n30, 455, 473–74, 482–83, 484, 487, 489–90, 523–25
Bentwich, Norman, 80
Ben Zvi, Yitzhak, 121
Berendsen, Sir Carl, 423–24
Berle, Adolf A., 365–66
Bernadotte, Count Folke, 470–71, 472–85, 486, 487, 492–97, 501–11, 516–18, 642
Bevin, Ernest, 141–42n2, 258–60, 269–70, 277–79, 304, 305–06, 307–08, 318, 319, 325–26, 348, 388–89, 422, 459, 460–61, 463–64, 465–66, 475, 521–22, 525, 528–29, 542–43, 551–56
Biltmore Program, 199–202
Bols, Louis, 44, 55, 58, 60
Bolshevik Revolution, 49
Bowman, Humphrey, 75
boycott of Israel, 518–19n27, 561
Brezhnev, Leonid, 600, 602n46, 605, 615–16n1
Britain as an Arab ally in the fight against a Jewish state
    alliance with Transjordan against the other Arab states, 540
    Anglo-Transjordanian Treaty, 389
    assumption that the Arab states would quickly defeat Israel, 459–61
    British interference in armistice negotiations, 553–54
    naval blockade preventing immigration, 385–86
    offer of assistance to Egypt, 387–88
    public demand for Arab and Jewish cooperation, 382
    refusal to withdraw Mandate forces in a timely manner, 383, 392–93
    unequal treatment of Arabs and Jews, 386–87, 391–93, 471
    US requirements for getting Britain to comply with the resolution, 40
British government
    Anglo-American Commission of Inquiry, 257–63, 264–80
    conflicts with the United States, 465–68, 543–44
    disagreement over the Labour government's Palestine policy, 541–42
    House of Commons' vote on the Palestine Mandate, 110
    House of Lords' vote on the Palestine Mandate, 110
    Labour Party, 245–51, 254–55, 261, 541
    parliamentary debate about the partitioning of Palestine, 168–72
    reactions to the UNSCOP committee report, 324–26

rejection of the Anglo-American committee report, 277–80
rejection of the partitioning of Palestine, 172–78
reversal of policy regarding the recognition of Israel, 554–55
British Mandate for Palestine, ix–x, xv, 19–24, 32–37, 61, 97–98, 104–11, 137, 158–61, 329n29, 350, 442, 446–48
Brook, Sir Norman, 288, 292–93
Bunche, Ralph, 315, 383–84n20, 470, 480n39, 510, 516, 527, 534–36, 557, 559
"Burma Road," 486, 491
Bush, George H. W., 651
Byrnes, James, 242–43, 292

C
Cadogan, Alexander, 309, 357, 384, 421–22, 463
Cafferata, Mr. (British police), 124–27
Campbell, Sir Ronald, 387–88
Caradon, Lord, 630, 631–33, 634–35
Carter, Jimmy, 582n3, 583–4n6
certificates issue, one hundred thousand, 196, 253, 255–57, 258, 259, 261, 268, 274–76, 278, 281–83, 289–90, 292, 295, 307–08
Chamberlain, Neville, 180, 182, 185, 189
Chamoun, Camille, 577, 580
Chancellor, John, 113, 127–28
The Chariot of Israel: Britain, America, and the State of Israel (Wilson), 14
Chaytor, E. W. C., 46
Chehab, Fuad, 580
Chile, 362, 370
Chovevei Zion ("Lovers of Zion") movement, 1–3
Christianity
    Gospels records regarding the Holy Temple, xiii
Churchill, Winston
    acceptance of Herbert Samuel's policies, 99–100
    Arab Revolt, interest in the, 42–43n10
    comments about the Arab population, 167
    partitioning of the Palestine Mandate, 92, 97–98, 164, 208
    as prime minister, 189, 192–93
    reactions to Bevin's anti-Israel behavior, 556–57
    response to the White Paper of 1939, 184–85, 189, 192–98, 204–08
    support for a Jewish army, 190

support for a Jewish state, 92–93, 99, 110, 169, 197, 216n48, 457, 541–42, 556–57
White Paper (1922), 25, 104–08, 183
withdrawal of support for Zionism, 213–16, 294–95
Clarke, Ashley, 471
Clayton, Sir Gilbert, 48n19, 73–74, 91n51
Clemenceau, Georges Benjamin, 22, 28–29, 45
Clifford, Clark, 369, 407–09, 418n8, 431–32, 434–43, 450, 454, 520
Cohen, Benjamin, 441, 529
Cold War alliances, 344–45, 348, 568–69, 571, 576, 596
Colombia, 451
Comay, Michael, 495–96
communism, fear that a Jewish state would lead to, 219, 408, 542–43
Conciliation Commission for Palestine, 509–10, 522, 552
conflict of interest, 478–79
Congreve, Walter, 100–01
Costa Rica, 361–62
Cox, Sir Percy, 96–97
Creech Jones, Arthur, 301, 306, 336–37, 350, 427–28
Crossman, Richard, 48n20, 238–39n48, 260, 265, 269–70, 275, 279–80, 288–89
Cruise O'Brien, Conor, 35–37, 56, 68, 320
Crum, Bartley, 227, 265–66, 269, 272, 279
Cunningham, Sir Alan, 272, 303
Curzon, Lord George, 19–20, 32–36
Cyprus refugees, 386, 426n23, 475, 555
Czechoslovakia, 488n53

D
D'Arcy, John, 271–72
Davar (newspaper), 248
Declaration of Independence (Israel), 448–50
Declaration of Independence of a State of Palestine, xi–xii, xiv, 648–51
Declaration of Three Noes, 638–39, 644–45
Deedes, Wyndham, 80
Der Judenstaat ("The Jewish State") (Herzl), 2
Dewey, Thomas E., 525
Dill, John, 149–50, 152–53
disarmament of the Jews in Palestine, 264, 271–72, 277–78, 280

displaced persons camps, 106, 251, 253, 262–63, 267–68, 274–75, 293–94, 298–99, 300, 318–20, 346–47
Disraeli, Benjamin, 9n11, 11n14
Douglas, Ambassador, 422, 475, 510–14, 528, 532–33
dual obligation to the Arabs and the Jews, 85–86, 258, 314
Duff, Douglas, 75–76, 114, 117–18, 120–21, 122, 125n23, 128, 144–45
Dugdale, Blanche, 4, 15n21
Dulles, John Foster, 529, 569–71

E
Eban, Abba, 416n5, 484, 492, 551, 610, 613, 621, 629–30, 636–37
economic development and employment, 135–36, 138–39, 499
Economic Survey Mission for the Middle East, 565–66
Eden, Anthony, 168, 173–74, 195–96, 208, 210–11, 225, 541, 570–71
Egypt, 387–88, 401, 410, 460, 519, 523–25, 539, 543–44, 546–48, 557–58, 561–62, 568, 569–70, 592, 596–97, 623–24, 646–47
Einstein, Albert, 268–69
Eisenhower, Dwight, 574–75
Eisenhower Doctrine, 578
The Encyclopaedia Judaica, 65–66
Epstein, Eliahu, 440–41
Eshkol, Levi, 598–99, 606, 610, 611
Ethiopia, 145–46, 361, 364
Exodus 1947 (refugee boat), 318–20

F
Faisal, Amir, 518
Faisal II, King, 577
famine and water shortages in Jerusalem during the truce period, 484–87
Farouk, King, 547–48
Fatah, 587, 593–94, 643, 644
Fawzi, Mohammed, 601
Feisal (son of Hussein), 24–30, 38–47, 53, 96–97, 157–58, 373, 642
financial issues
    financing of the Arab Revolt, 148
    with the proposed partitioning of Palestine, 177–78
Fishman, Judah Leib, 202
Forrestal, James V., 394n43
Fourteen Points statement of principles, 19, 21, 22

France
    French Mandate in Syria, 38–39, 43–46
    negotiations with Britain regarding the Middle East, 20–24
    Suez Canal crisis, 574, 576
    UN vote for partition, 364
Frankfurter, Felix, 29–30
Franks, Sir Oliver, 544–45, 548–49, 551, 554–55

G
Galilee, 515
Galilee, Western, 507, 515n19
García-Granados, Jorge, 319, 320, 382–83, 392–93, 423, 446, 456–57
Gass, Oscar, 293n27
Gaulle, Charles de, 605–06
geographic boundaries negotiations, 23–24, 164–65, 170, 176, 209–10, 290–91, 321–22, 343, 352n30, 354–56, 371, 507, 511–12, 537, 549, 627–28
Germany
    financing of the Arab Revolt, 148
    immigration to Palestine during and after the Holocaust, 86, 106, 143–44, 180, 188, 214, 227, 229–30, 293–94, 318–20
    Nazi occupation of Austria and Czechoslovakia, 182
    support of Arab goals in Palestine, 148
Ginsburg, David, 441
Glubb Pasha, 388, 389–91, 391–92n38, 464–65, 489n54, 540
Goldberg, Arthur, 617–18, 619, 620–21, 626, 627–29, 633–35
Goldmann, Nahum, 296
Golomb, Eliyahu, 204
government of Palestine
    attitudes regarding Arab-Jewish relations, 128–29, 136–40
    establishment of a legislative council, 146–47
    establishment of an Arab-controlled government, 519
    Herbert Samuel's representative government plan, 86–91
    proposed Constitution for Palestine, 106
gradualism approach to the establishment of a Jewish state, 62–63
Grady, Henry F., 288–93
grand mufti. See al--Husseini, Haj Amin (grand mufti)
Grauel, John, 319
Greece, 360–61, 362, 364, 370

Grey, Sir Edward, 62
Grigg, Sir Edward, 216–17
Gromyko, Andrei, 310–11, 332, 446
Grose, Peter, 17–18
Group of 77 (G-77), 590
Guatemala, 361, 451

H
Hadrian, xv–xvi
Haganah (Jewish self-defense force), 139–40n44, 155, 202–04, 263–64, 271–72, 283–84, 285–88, 315, 379–80, 386
Haifa, 497–98, 507
Haiti, 360–61, 365–66
Halifax, Lord, 179
Hall, George, 251
Hamas
   Charter of 1988, xivn10
   mission and ideals, 382, 640, 655
Hammarskjöld, Dag, 575–76, 601
Harrison, Earl G., 252–54
Harry S. Truman (Truman), 414, 415–16
Hashemite Kingdom of Jordan. See Jordan (formerly Transjordan)
Hebrew as the language of the Jewish people, xv
Hebron massacre (1929), 123, 124–27
Heikal, Mohamed, 600
Henderson, Arthur, 141–42n2
Henderson, Loy, 254n15, 311n3, 329–32, 341–44, 349, 352–53, 358–60, 394, 396, 482
Herzl, Theodor, 2–3
Hezbollah, 640
Hilldring, John, 330–32, 354
Himmler, Heinrich, 470n21
History of Zionism (Laqueur), 243–44
Hitler, Adolf, xivn10, 145–46, 182, 215
the Holocaust, xiv–xv, 86, 106, 143–44, 180, 188, 193–98, 214, 227, 229–30, 238, 252, 260, 262–63, 293–94, 435
Holy Temple (Jerusalem), xii–xiv, xv, xvi–xviin11
Hoo, Victor, 315
Hope Simpson, Sir John, 134–36

Hope Simpson Report, 134–36, 159
Hopkins, Harry, 239, 240
Horowitz, David, 367n56, 368
Hos, David, 141–42n2
Hoskins, Harold, 222, 224–25, 229–30
Hull, Cordell, 219–21, 228–29, 232
Hurley, Patrick J., 205, 223
Hussein, King, 577, 595, 604–05, 606, 621, 647, 652
Husseini, Jamal, 313n6, 337–38
al-Husseini, Abd al-Qadir, ix, 379–80
al-Husseini, Haj Amin (grand mufti), xivn10, 55–57, 59, 77–83, 115–17, 144, 145–48, 153–54, 337n4, 379, 388, 497–98, 566–67
Hussein (Sharif of Mecca), 24–26, 53, 96
Hutcheson, Judge, 274, 275, 296

I
Ibn Saud, King, 24n13, 188, 205, 227, 237–40, 300–01, 345–46
immigration
    1920s ordinances, 65–66
    "absorptive capacity" concept, 84, 106–07, 135, 152, 159–61, 162–64, 290
    accusations of foreign infiltration, 437n35
    Arab immigration to Palestine, 166–67
    benefits of Jewish immigration for the Arab community, 160–61, 166–67
    under Bernadotte's proposal, 480–81
    British naval blockade preventing, 385–86
    during the ceasefire (1948), 474–78
    Cyprus refugees, 386, 426n23, 475, 555
    displaced persons camps, 251, 253, 262–63, 267–68, 274–75, 298–99, 300, 318–20, 346–47
    illegal, 182, 385, 428–29
    Labour Party's call for increased Jewish immigration to Palestine, 246–47, 254–55, 261
    MacDonald letter interpretation, 141–44
    of military age personnel, 472, 474–77, 502–03
    one hundred thousand certificates issue, 196, 253, 255–57, 258, 259, 261, 268, 274–76, 278, 281–83, 289–90, 292, 295, 307–08
    opposition to Jewish immigration to Palestine, 75–76, 98, 105–07, 131–32, 135–36, 138–39, 166, 179–80, 209, 210, 328–29
    policies by Herbert Samuel, 83–86, 105–07

refugee boats, 193–96, 283, 318–20
by those fleeing during the Holocaust, 86, 106, 143–44, 180, 188, 193–98, 214, 227, 229–30, 238, 252–57, 293–94
under the truce proposal, 426
under a trusteeship plan, 305
White Paper of 1939 policies, 181–82, 188, 251
India, 256n18, 624–25, 634, 636–37
internationalization, 492
Iran, 640
Iraq, 352n30, 460, 577, 605
Irgun Tzvai Leumi (National Military Organization), 139–40n44, 155, 187, 202–03, 249–50, 263–64, 283–84, 288, 315–16, 316–18, 324, 516
Israel Defense Forces (IDF), 487–88
Israel (formerly Palestine)
   Arab boycott of, 518–19n27, 561
   Arab invasion immediately following independence, 459–65, 472–73
   attacks to drive Egypt out of the Negev and defend Israel, 543, 546–48
   battles during the truce period, 487–91
   Declaration of Independence, 448–50
   defeat of all invading armies, 640–41
   demand for sovereignty, 482–83
   false charges against, 597–98, 603
   food and water supplies, 484–87
   G-77 attacks against, 590
   international recognition, 450–53, 451–53, 456–58, 555–56, 615, 638–39
   key assumptions for a UN ceasefire, 474
   naming of, 441
   official establishment of, 440–48
   perceived scrutiny from the UN observers, 502
   Six-Day War victory, 609–10
   Suez Canal crisis, 573–77
Italy, 148

J
Jabotinsky, Vladimir, 46, 49, 56–57, 78n25, 108, 139–40n44, 318
Jaffa
   massacre (1921), 73
   reallocation of, 356

Jamali, Dr. (Iraq), 344–45, 357, 374
Japan, 196
Jarring, Gunnar, 635
Jenkins, Roy, 11–15
Jerusalem
    Arab East Jerusalem, xviii
    biblical holiness of, xviin11, 469
    demilitarization of, 492–94
    famine and water shortages, 484–87
    Herbert Samuel's personal feelings about, 63–64
    internationalization of, 492
    invasion (1948), 464–65
    proposal of governance by Transjordan, 481–84
    reunification of, 611–13
    Truce Commission's control of, 492
    UN objection to the reunification of, 612–13
    UN trusteeship over, 371, 423n15, 443–44, 447
Jessup, Philip, 445, 450–51, 452, 537
Jesus Christ, xiii
the Jewish Agency, 187, 203–04, 245–46, 263, 271, 272, 284–86, 295–96, 298, 299, 338, 377, 412, 433–34, 440–41, 445
Jewish army, 188–92, 222
The Jewish Frontier (journal), 248
Jewish history, challenges to
    Arab claims during the UN ad-hoc committee meeting, 345
    Arab rejection of Jewish history, 373, 586, 638
    Christian proof of Jewish history, xiii
    denial of the existence of the Holy Temple, xii–xiv
    Montagu thesis regarding Judaism as just a religion, 15–17
    Peel Commission's review of, 156
    PLO redefinition of the Jewish people, xix–xxi
Jewish holy books and writings
    the bible as the original Mandate, 314–315n7
    importance of Jerusalem in, xix–xx
    Jerusalem Talmud, xvii
    Masorah, xviin12
    Mishnah (Jewish Oral Torah), xvi–xvii
Jewish Legion, 46
the Jewish National Council, 448, 449

Jewish religious practices
    accessibility to the holiest Jewish sites, 337, 465n13, 611, 613–14
    Sabbath observance, 285
    separation of men and women during prayer services, 113–14, 133
    Tishah B'Av commemoration, 119
Jewish Revolt (1945), 263–64
Jewish-Roman wars, xv–xvi
Johnson. Herschel, 347, 354–55, 355–56, 358
Johnson, Lyndon B., 591, 606
Johnston, Eric, 566, 581
Joint Arab Defense Pact, 587
Jones, Morgan, 170–71
Jordan (formerly Transjordan)
    establishment as an independent state, 97, 539–40
    Jordanian rule of Jerusalem, xviii, 613–14
    UAR interference complaint, 577–78
Jordan-Yarmouk River water development plan, 566–67, 581–85
Joseph, Dov, 372, 380n15, 386, 485–86
Judea and Samaria (later the West Bank), 459, 539–40, 558, 587, 642–43

K
Karo, Yosef, xvii
Kastel, 379–80
Kaukji (leader of Arab Liberation Army), 526
Kedourie, Elie, 83
Keeley, James, 498
Keith-Roach, Edward, 113–14
Kennan, George, 394, 463, 466–67
Kennan-Henderson policy recommendations, 394–97
Kennedy, John F., 591
Kfar Etzion, 390–91
Khartoum Resolutions, 638–39, 644–45
al-Khouri, Faris, 479
Khrushchev, Nikita, 576
Kirkbride, Sir Alexander, 389–90, 460, 465
Koestler, Arthur, 350–51n29
the Koran, xiii, 642
Kosygin, Alexei, 596–97
Kuznetsov, Vasily, 629, 632, 637

L

Labour Party (Britain), 245–51, 254–55, 261, 541
land purchase restrictions for Jews, 84–85n38, 87–89, 98, 131–32, 138–39, 188
land transfers and population exchanges, 165–66, 168, 182, 246–47, 274
Laqueur, Walter, 243–44
Latrun, 465, 486
Lawrence, T. E. ("Lawrence of Arabia")
    and Chaim Weizmann, 39n1, 47
    as a champion of the Arab cause, 40–41, 43–47, 94–97
    as a mentor and advisor to Feisal, 38–40
    Paris Peace Conference role, 27
    political career and reputation, 38–39, 46–47
League of Nations
    British Mandate for Palestine, ix–x, xv, 19–24, 32–37, 61, 97–98, 104–11, 137, 158–61, 329n29, 350, 442, 446–48
    Mandates Commission, 132–34, 186
    Palestine Commission, 163–64
Lebanon
    armistice agreement with Israel, 558
    invasion of Israel immediately following independence, 376, 459
    UAR interference complaint, 577–80
Lehi (militant organization), 187, 203, 213–14, 324, 516
Levant federation proposal, 224–25
Liberia, 361, 364, 365
Lie, Trygve, x, 398, 401–02, 406, 411–12, 448, 461–64, 470, 475
Litani River, 23–24
Lloyd, Lord, 190, 193–94
Lloyd George, David, 8, 10–11n13, 14, 19–20, 60, 62, 103–04, 157
London Conference of 1939, 178–80
London Conference of 1946, 297–303
Lovett, Robert, 350n28, 351–52, 354, 359, 403–04, 417–18, 428, 432–34, 436–43, 467–68, 476, 520, 547–48, 550–55
Lowenthal, Max, 431–32
Luke, Sir Harry, 72–73, 116, 118–19, 126–27
Luria, Yitzchak, xvii
Lydda, 488–89, 495n65, 507

M

Macdonald, James, 491, 519–20, 528, 541, 545, 550
Macdonald, John, 485, 494, 547
MacDonald, Malcolm, 160–61, 177–78, 179, 188
MacDonald, Ramsay, 141–43
MacMichael, Sir Harold, 154, 209
Macmillan, Sir Gordon, 459
the Madrid Conference, 651
Magnes, Judah, 273
mandate. See British Mandate for Palestine
Mapai (Jewish Workers' Party in Palestine), 248
Marcus, David ("Micky"), 486
Marshall, George, 306, 331, 332–33, 335, 342–44, 354, 385–86, 393, 400, 404–07, 409–10, 417–19, 429, 432, 435–40, 510–15, 517, 520–22
martial law, threat of, 150, 151–53
Marxist-Leninist doctrine, 348
Masorah, xviin12
massacres in Palestine. See also pogroms
    Jaffa (1921), 73
    Kfar Etzion (1948), 390–91
    Shaw Commission Report on the 1929 massacres, 119–21, 124–26, 130–34
    widespread (1929), 73, 113, 117–29, 214
May the Winds Blow: An Autobiography (Duff), 120–21, 122n16
McClintock, Robert, 351–53, 424–25, 514–16, 532
McDonald, James G., 268, 278–79
McMahon, Sir Henry, 24–25
McMahon-Hussein Agreement, 24–27, 53
McNeil, Hector, 530
Meinertzhagen, Richard, 41, 44–45, 54, 58–60, 62–63n2, 69, 81–82, 95–96, 101–02, 103, 111, 128–29, 198, 215, 261–62, 284n9, 317–18n11, 457–58
Memoirs, vol. 1: Year of Decisions (Truman), 327–28
Memoirs, vol. 2: Years of Trial and Hope (Truman), 308, 346, 416n5
Memoirs (Samuel), 9–10n12, 70
Memories and Reflections (Asquith), 10–11n13, 11
Mesopotamia, 50–51
migration to the Holy Land, 19th century, xvii–xviii
military. See also Haganah (Jewish self-defense force); Irgun Tzvai Leumi

(National Military Organization); Israel Defense Forces (IDF); Jewish army; Lehi (militant organization)
  demilitarization of Jerusalem, 492–94
  international contributions of armed forces, 359, 408–09, 445
  and security recommendations, 408–09
  United Arab Command, 584
Mishnah (Jewish Oral Torah), xvi–xvii
Montagu, Edwin, 13–15, 15–17, 19, 91n51
Morrison, Herbert, 148–49n12, 185–86, 207, 293–94
Morrison-Grady Plan, 293–98, 302
Moslem religion
  and the Hebrew Bible, xiii
  Mosque of the Dome of the Rock forged photos, 117n9
  Nebi Musa holiday, 54–55
  Supreme Moslem Council, 82
  US desire for good relations with the Moslem world, 344
  zikr ritual, 115–16
Motza massacre (1929), 123
Mount Scopus agreement, 494–94
Moyne, Lord, 194–95, 209–10, 213–14
Murray, Wallace, 212–13, 218–21, 222, 226, 229–30, 236, 240
Mussolini, Benito, 145–46

N
Nakba ("Catastrophe"), 381, 641
Nasser, Gamal Abdel, 568, 569–74, 575–77, 582–88, 601–02, 608, 615–17, 621
National Water Carrier (NWC) diversion plan, 566–67, 581–85
the Negev, 354–56, 459, 482, 511–13, 517, 519–28, 530–37, 552, 558
the Netherlands, 364
Neumann, Emmanuel, 268
The New York Times (newspaper), ix, 240, 381
New Zealand, 595–96
Niles, David, 244, 330–31, 431–32
Noel-Baker, Philip, 148, 185
Nokrashi Pasha, 387–88
Non-Aligned Movement (NAM), 588, 617
Nuri Said, 151

O

Occupied Enemy Territories Administration (OETA), 38, 47, 52, 60, 61
oil concerns, 205, 236, 240, 408, 607
Operation Nachshon, 379–80
Oren, Michael, 611
Organization of African Unity (OAU), 588–89
Ormsby-Gore, William, 153, 168–69, 175n55
the Oslo Accords, 651–52
Ottoman Empire
    division of the, 20–22, 51
    laws against Jewish religious rights, 71–72

P

Paassen, Pierre van, 30–31, 41–42, 82–83n34, 126–27, 191
Palestine Conciliation Commission, 509–10, 522, 552
Palestine (later Israel)
    1929 massacres of Jews, 73, 113, 117–34, 214
    as another Arab state, 168, 173–74, 183, 204–05, 218–19, 337–38
    Cairo War Office, 103–04
    capture of adjacent areas by various Arab countries, 376–77
    continuous Jewish ties to, xv–xviii, xix–xxi
    disarmament of the Jews in, 264, 271–72, 277–78, 280
    geographic boundaries negotiations, 23–24, 164–65, 170, 176, 209–10, 290–91, 321–22, 343, 352n30, 354–56, 371, 507, 511–12, 537, 549, 627–28
    history of the name "Palestine," 642
    Jewish army, 188–92
    as the Jewish national home, 105, 157, 158, 180, 183, 198–202, 204–05, 237, 300, 329n29, 372–73, 412–13
    Jewish territorial gains, 380
    Jewish violence in, 263–64, 275, 283–88
    land purchase restrictions for Jews, 84–85n38, 87–89, 98, 131–32, 138–39, 162n38, 188
    military and security recommendations, 408–09
    one hundred thousand certificates issue, 253, 255–57, 258, 259, 261, 268, 274–76, 278, 281–83, 292, 295, 307–08
    Ottoman laws against Jewish religious rights in, 71–72
    population exchanges and land transfers, 165–66, 168, 182, 246–47, 274
    provincial autonomy, 290–91

representative government plan, 86–91
Roman conquests of, xv–xvi
trusteeship plan, 230–31, 305, 328, 394–95, 420–24
as two independent states with an economic union between them, 356–57
as a unitary bi-national state, 273, 353n31
Palestine Peace, Not Apartheid (Carter), 582n3, 583–4n6
Palestinian Authority (PA)
"right of return," 382, 499–501, 538n8
Palestinian Liberation Organization (PLO)
charters, xii–xiii, xix, 586–87, 638–39, 644
Declaration of Independence of a State of Palestine, xi–xii, xiv, 648–51
establishment of the, 585–86
intifada, 652–53
lack of plans for an independent sovereign Palestinian state, 586–87, 638–39, 644
"phased liberation" policy, xi, 647
Paraguay, 361, 370
Paris Peace Conference (1919-20), 19–20, 22, 24–32, 45–46, 97
Parker, William L., 225–26
Parkes, James, xviii, 16
partitioning of Palestine. See also United Nations General Assembly (UNGA); United Nations Special Committee on Palestine (UNSCOP)
Arab reaction to the, 345–46, 347, 363, 373–82, 641
British government's rejection of the, 172–78
British parliamentary debate regarding, 168–72
by Churchill, 92, 97–98, 164, 208
financial considerations, 177–78
Jewish stance on, 295, 299, 371–73, 410
London Conference (1946) discussions, 303–05
Peel Commission proposal, 164–66
revisions to previously adopted policies, 209–10
Soviet Union support for the, 348–50
UNSCOP recommendations, 320–22
Woodhead Commission, 174–78
Pasha, Ahmed, 471
Pasha, Azzam, 375, 464n12, 472–73, 496–97, 509, 640
Passfield, Lord and Lady (Sydney and Beatrice Webb), 128–30
Passfield White Paper (1930), 136–43

Patria (refugee boat), 193–95
peace
    Arab-Israeli differences on peace principles, 636–39
    Arab League summit peace proposal (2002/2007), 653
    Declaration of Three Noes, 638–39, 644–45
    LBJ's five essential principles for, 619–20
    the Madrid Conference, 651
    the Oslo Accords, 651–52
    requirements for a lasting peace in the Middle East, 625–26
    UNSC's responses to threats to peace, 461–64, 468–69
    US position about the ultimate aim of the UNGA, 619
Pearson, Lester, 576
Peel Commission
    objectivity of the, 155–56
    paradoxical conclusions of the, 161–62
    partitioning proposal, 164–66
    purpose of the, 150–51, 152–53
    Weizmann-Feisal Agreement, 27–31, 44–45n14, 157–58
"phased liberation" policy, xi
the Philippines, 360–61, 364–65, 370
Plumer, Herbert, 112–13
Podgorny, Nikolai, 600
pogroms. See also massacres in Palestine
    Jerusalem Jewish Quarter (1921), 101
    Passover (1920), 54–58, 77–78
Poland, 238, 452
population exchanges and land transfers, 165–66, 168, 182, 246–47, 274
Prebisch, Raul, 590
presidential campaigns of 1944, 234–37
Proskauer, Joseph, 366–67

Q
al-Qawuqji, Fawzi, 377, 378n9

R
Ramla, 488–89, 495n65, 507
Reagan, Ronald, 651, 652
recognition of a Jewish state
    Arab reactions to, 441–42, 561, 644–45, 650–52

Clifford-Lovett negotiations, 438–43
   by other countries, 450–53, 456–58, 555–56, 615, 638–39
   strategic advantages of recognition, 435, 455
   Truman's plan for, 431–43
   by the US, 434, 450–56
   by the Vatican, 504
Rees, M. van, 132, 133–34
refugees
   Arab, 495–501, 507–09, 538–39, 564–67, 655
   at the center of today's Arab-Israeli conflict, 495, 499, 655
   in Cyprus, 386, 426n23, 475, 555
   expulsion of Jews by all Middle East and North African Arab countries, 499
   Jewish refugees from Jerusalem and other Arab-occupied areas, 508, 538–39
   refugee boats, 193–95, 283, 318–20
   treatment of, 499, 538–39
   World War II, 193–98, 227, 229–30, 238, 252–57, 262–63, 268, 283, 293–94, 318–20, 346–47, 437n35
Rendel, George, 168, 172–73, 175
resources
   famine and water shortages in Jerusalem during the truce period, 484–87
   opening the road to the Negev to deliver supplies, 523–25, 551–52
Revisionists (Union of Revisionist Zionists), 108–09, 155, 318
Richmond, Ernest, 73–74, 79, 80–81
"right of return," 382, 499–501, 507–09, 538n8, 564–67, 655
Roman conquests of Palestine, xv–xvi
Romania, 195
Romulo, Carlos, 364–65
Roosevelt, Eleanor, 332, 393, 411, 529
Roosevelt, Franklin
   correspondence with Arab countries, 227–28, 231, 243
   illness and death, 238, 242–43
   meeting and correspondence with King Ibn Saud, 237–40, 237–42
   opinion on immigration, 167, 219–20, 252
   as a politician supporting both sides, 238–44, 346
   pro-Arab attitude, 238–40, 241–42
   pro-Zionist attitude, 205, 218, 223, 232–33, 235–37, 242
   trusteeship plan for Palestine, 230–31
   and the White Paper of 1939, 220–21, 233

Rosenman, Samuel, 416, 430–31
Rosenwald, Lessing, 268
Ross, John, 425–26
Rusk, Dean, 351, 395–97, 418n8, 427, 450, 453n55
Russia/Soviet Union. See Soviet Union/Russia

S
Sadat, Anwar, 600, 646–47
Safed (Tzfat)
    as the center of mysticism and Kabbalah, xvii
    massacre (1929), 123–24
Samuel, Edwin, 70n14, 118–19
Samuel, Herbert
    appointment of anti-Zionists to key posts, 68–76
    correspondence with Feisal, 29–30
    desire to appease both the Arabs and the Jews, 66–68, 80–83, 85–86
    gradualist approach to the establishment of a Jewish state, 62–63, 67
    as head of the civilian administration of Palestine, 60–66
    immigration policies, 83–86, 105–07
    interpretation of the Balfour Declaration, 85–86, 87–91, 104–06
    memorandum from, 8–10
    personal feelings about Jerusalem, 63–64
    plan to establish a representative government in Palestine, 86–91
Samuel, Maurice, 115, 116–17, 124, 125–26
sanctions against Israel, 528–29
San Remo Peace Conference, 31–32, 45
Saudi Arabia, 151, 373, 376, 410
Saunders, Mr. (Chief of police), 121
Sayre, Ambassador, 450–51, 451–52
security and order
    Arab invasion immediately following independence, 459–65, 472–73
    Baghdad Pact, 571
    concerns regarding the unrestricted admission of Arab refugees, 496
    demilitarization of Jerusalem, 492–94
    international contributions of armed forces, 359, 408–09, 445
    rights of the Jewish community and the non-Jewish community, 137
    UNSC's responses to threats to peace, 461–64, 468–69
    US military and security recommendations, 408–09
Selassie, Haile, 145–46

Seven Pillars of Wisdom (Lawrence), 42–43
Sharett, Moshe, 565
Shaw, John, 271
Shaw Commission Report on the 1929 massacres, 119–21, 124–26, 130–34
Shertok, Moshe, 355–56, 402–03, 424–28, 431n30, 433–34, 476–78, 483–84, 493, 496, 501–02, 504, 509, 524, 531
Siam (Thailand), 370
Silver, Abba Hillel, 201–02, 232–33, 249, 302, 323–24n22, 338–39, 368–69, 402, 425–26
Sinclair, Sir Archibald, 171–72, 193
Singleton, Sir John, 275
Six-Day War
  accusations of US and UK participation in the, 607
  ceasefire, 608–09
  closure of the Tiran Straits, 602, 605, 628
  fighting, 606–08
  Israel's victory, 609–10
  Soviet Union's demand for a return to 1949 Armistice Agreement lines, 617–23, 645–46
  Soviet Union's role in instigating the, 600–01
  three-power draft resolution for withdrawal following the, 624–25, 627, 629–30
  UNSC meetings prior to the, 602–04
  weapons amassed by the Arab states, 605
Smuts, Jan, 318
Sneh, Moshe, 204, 263–64, 287–88
A Soldier with the Arabs (Glubb), 390n34
Southern Syria, 209–10
Soviet Union/Russia
  accusations of infiltration among Jewish refugees, 437n35
  anti-Israel campaign, 591–99
  anti-Semitism in, 49, 568n13
  Arab-Soviet alliances, 349, 591–99, 615–17
  demand for Israel's return to 1949 Armistice Agreement lines, 617–23, 645–46
  ending of diplomatic relations with Israel, 609
  expansionism, fears of, 266
  hostility towards Israel, 568–69
  as a key power in the Middle East, 571–72, 576–77

    military equipment and political support to Arab states, 591–93
    official position regarding Palestine, 310–11
    recognition of Israel, 451
    Soviet-Egyptian arms deal, 569–70
    support for partition, 348–50, 406
    support of the UAR, 578
    UN voting rights, 339n8
Spain's support of the British Mandate, 110–11
Stabler, Wells, 481n41
Stalin, Joseph, 349–50
Stanley, Venetia, 12–15
State Department, US. See under United States
Stettinius, Edward R., 236, 237, 326–27, 365
Stimson, Harry, 228–29, 232
Storrs, Sir Ronald, 52–53, 57, 68–72, 78–79, 81–82, 223–24
Struma (refugee boat), 194–95
Suez Canal, 561–62, 572–75, 576–77, 623–24
Sugihara, Chiune, 196
Sword for Hire (Duff), 114–15n4
Sykes-Picot Agreement, 20–22, 51
Syria
    acceptance of the Six-Day War ceasefire agreement, 608–09
    as an area of exclusion, 25
    Anglo-French Joint Declaration, 50–54
    anti-French Arab campaign for, 38–40, 43–46
    Arab Liberation Army, 377–78
    armistice agreement with Israel, 558, 594, 599
    attacks against Israel, 593–94
    Baath regime, 593, 596, 597–98
    conflict of interest issue at the UNSC, 478–79
    defense pact with Egypt, 596–97
    demilitarized zone interference, 562–63, 569
    desire for independence, 28–29
    effect of civil war on Syrian refugees, 497
    Franco-Syrian Treaty of Alliance, 146
    governance of Palestine, 52–53
    invasion of Israel immediately following independence, 459
    military intrigues, 38–47
    objection to the UNGA partition resolution, 374, 376, 410

plan to make Feisal king of Greater Syria, 44–45, 96
recognition of Israel, 452
surrender of Damascus, 43–44
United Arab Republic (UAR), 577–80

T
Talib, Saiyid, 96
Taufiq Pasha, 388–89
Tedder, Lord, 469
Temple Mount, xvi–xviin11, 611. See also Western Wall of the Temple Mount
terrorism
    intimidation from, 154
    PLO's defense of, 652
Thailand (Siam), 370
Thant, U, 599, 601–04
Tiran Straits, 602, 605, 628
Transjordan (later Jordan), 23–24, 97–98, 158, 167, 207, 270, 290, 376, 388–90, 459, 460, 480–83, 506–07, 512, 519, 539–40, 546, 555, 558, 642
truce periods
    battles during the, 487–91
    ceasefire order, 524–25
    duration, 490
    famine and water shortages in Jerusalem during the, 484–87
    immigration under the truce proposal, 426
    opening the road to the Negev to deliver supplies, 523–25, 551–52
    UNSC Truce Commission and truce proposals, 424–29, 484–87, 492
Truman, Harry S.
    Anglo-American committee activities, 267, 276–77, 281–83, 289–90, 296–97
    campaign pledge regarding Israel's boundaries, 513, 520, 525–26, 532–33
    and Clement Attlee, 252–57, 281–83, 295, 297
    conversations with Weizmann, 355, 368, 415–17, 430–31, 531–32, 545–46
    correspondence with Arab leaders, 243n58, 300–01, 379
    criticism of, 252, 347n20, 407, 415–16
    immigration stance, 252–57, 258–60, 289, 298–301, 307–08, 327–28
    London Conference of 1946, 298–301

714 INDEPENDENCE

    mobilization of support for the UN resolution, 367–69
    Negev negotiations, 355–56, 520–21
    recognition of a Jewish state, 431–43, 450–56, 455–56, 525–26
    reliance on George Marshall, 435–36, 438–39
    role of career officials in government, 454n56
    shock of Warren Austin's abandonment of partition speech, 414–19
    support for partition, 346–47, 359, 399–400, 407, 415–16
    UNSCOP decisions, 326–28
Truman, Margaret, 414, 415–16
"Truman's Trusteeship Proposal," 411–13, 417–19
trusteeship plan, 230–31, 305, 328, 394–95, 420–24
two-state solution
    Arab version, 382, 654–55
    requirements for, xxi
    resettlement of Arab refugees, 501
    unfulfillment of, ix, 654–55

U

Uganda settlement offer, 3–5
Union of Revisionist Zionists, 108–09
United Arab Command, 584
United Arab Republic (UAR), 577–80
United Kingdom. See Britain/British entries
United Nations Economic and Social Council, 481
United Nations Emergency Force (UNEF), 575–76, 601
United Nations General Assembly (UNGA). See also partitioning of
    Palestine; United Nations Special Committee on Palestine (UNSCOP)
    ad-hoc committee, 335–39, 345, 357–60
    Arab guerilla war response to the UNGA partition resolution, 373–82
    attempts to convince other countries to vote for partition, 363–70
    First Committee, 420, 422–24, 443–47, 537
    headquarters and meeting places, 447n46
    historic resolution, passage of the, 370–73
    mediator, appointment of a, 444–45, 469–71
    member states, 339–40
    Palestine commission, 383, 392–93, 397–98, 403, 419–20
    plenary session, 360–70
    request for a unilateral proclamation of a Palestinian state, 654
    requests for a special session, 397, 399, 401, 404–06, 409–10, 419

INDEX 715

Resolution 43/177 (1988), xi–xii, 650–51
Resolution 53 (1948), 487
Resolution 54 (1948), 487–88
Resolution 62 (1948), 535–36
Resolution 181 (1947), ix–xii, 370–71, 373–75, 382, 419–20, 425, 448, 477–78, 479–80, 498, 552, 560
Resolution 194 (1948), 499–501, 538, 543, 552, 564–65
Resolution 273 (1949), 560
Resolution 997 (1956), 574–75
Resolution 998 (1956), 575
Resolution 1000 (1956), 575
Resolution 1001 (1956), 575
Resolution 1237 (1958), 579–80
Resolution 2253 (1967), 612–13
Resolution 2254 (1967), 613
Resolution 3237 (1974), 648
roles of the US and the UK, 510–16
Rules of Procedure, 446
special session, 309–12, 419–24, 453
Sub-Committee 9, 424, 444–46
Sub-Committee 10, 443–44, 446–47
sub-committees under the ad-hoc committee, 353–57
UK-China draft resolution for establishing a conciliation commission, 536–39
unanimous recommendations, 321
US attempts to overturn the partition resolution, 393–403
US delegation's support of partition, 331–33
virtual trusteeship, 509–10
vote for partition, ix–x
voting rules, 339
United Nations Information System on Palestine (UNISPAL), ix
United Nations Relief and Works Agency (UNRWA), 382, 499, 538n8, 565, 567
United Nations Security Council (UNSC)
    armistice negotiations, 534–36, 546, 548–54, 557–60, 561–62
    axioms of negotiation, 626–27
    Bernadotte's proposals for governing Israel, 479–84, 506–10
    enforcement measures, 398–99, 401, 420–21, 523
    Israel's application for UN membership, 540, 542, 560

lack of condemnation for Arab attacks on Israel, 592–93, 592–96
powers of the, 397, 398, 401
request for a cease and desist from hostile military action, 468–69
Resolution 50 (1948), 472, 474–79, 549–50
Resolution 61 (1948), 530–31, 534, 536
Resolution 66 (1948), 552
Resolution 73 (1949), 560
Resolution 95 (1951), 562, 573, 604n48
Resolution 118 (1956), 573
Resolution 228 (1966), 595–96
Resolution 233 (1967), 607
Resolution 234 (1967), 608
Resolution 235 (1967), 608–09
Resolution 240 (1967), 624
Resolution 242 (1967), 635, 645–46, 648, 649–50
Resolution 338 (1973), 648
Soviet Union's demand for Israel's return to 1949 Armistice Agreement lines, 617–23, 645–46
Syria's conflict of interest, 478–79
threats to peace, 461–64, 468–69
Truce Commission and proposal, 424–29, 484–87, 492
"Truman's Trusteeship Proposal," 411–13, 417–19
UK-China draft resolution about restoring the status quo ante in the Negev, 527–31, 539
US State Department position paper, 398–412
United Nations Special Committee on Palestine (UNSCOP). See also partitioning of Palestine; United Nations General Assembly (UNGA)
Arab opposition to the, 312, 313
Arab states' reactions to the committee's report, 322–24
British reactions to the committee's report, 324–26
committee members, 312
Exodus 1947 (refugee boat) incident, 318–20
Irgun death sentence response, 316–18
Jewish reactions to the committee's report, 323–24, 338–39
meetings and visits, 312–14
report recommendations, 320–22
responsibilities, 311–12
US response, 326–33, 335, 341–44, 347
United Resistance, 263–64, 271, 277–78, 283–88

United States
　allegations of double-dealing against the Jews, 85–86, 258, 269
　Anglo-American Commission of Inquiry, 257–63, 264–80
　calls for Arab restraint following the UNGA resolution, 377–79
　conflicts with Britain, 465–68, 543–44
　Congressional resolutions regarding Palestine as a Jewish state, 231–32
　false charges against, 598
　fear of hostilities between Arabs and Jews in Palestine, 224–25
　importance of maintaining good relations with the Moslem world, 344
　involvement in UNSCOP decisions, 326–33
　Jewish community's responses to Israel issues, 520
　mobilization of support for the UN resolution, 367–69
　recognition of a Jewish state, 431–43, 450–56
　recognition of Transjordan, 555
　State Department concerns about Palestine, 228, 257, 306, 328–33, 351–53, 393–403, 398–412, 418n8
　support for the British Mandate, 109, 212
　switch position possibilities, 342–43
　and Zionism, 216n48, 217
Uruguay, 451
Ussishkin, Menachem, 57–58

V
the Vatican, 504

W
Wadsworth, George, 330, 352n30
War of Liberation. See Jewish-Roman wars
water resources
　Arab Headwater Diversion Plan, 584–85
　regional water development project for Israel, Jordan, Lebanon, and Syria, 566–67, 581–85
　shortages in Jerusalem during the truce period, 484–87
Waters-Taylor, Bertie Harry, 55–57, 59–60, 68n10, 81–82
Wauchope, Sir Arthur, 143–44, 146–47, 150–51, 152
Wavell, Sir Archibald, 256n18
weapons. See arms
Webb, Sydney and Beatrice (Lord and Lady Passfield), 128–30
Weisgal, Meyer, 431n30

Weizmann, Chaim
    agricultural concerns about the Negev, 355
    and Balfour, 4–5, 16–18
    chemistry background, 4, 5–6
    concerns about anti-Semitism and anti-Zionism, 102–03, 136–37, 261
    concerns about Herbert Samuel's representative government policy, 88–90
    concerns about pogroms, 57
    conversations with Truman, 355, 368, 415–17, 430–31, 531–32, 545–46
    desire for a Jewish state, 175–76, 187, 198–99, 413
    immigration stance, 84n37, 89, 107, 163
    opposition to the 1930 Passfield White Paper, 139–40
    Paris Peace Conference, 31–32
    and the Peel Commission, 155–56, 169
    request for the establishment of a Jewish army, 189–90
    support for partition, 323n21, 368, 415
    and T. E. Lawrence, 39, 47
    work to allow Jewish land purchases, 98–99n11
    World Zionist Congress, 3, 302
Weizmann-Feisal Agreement, 27–31, 44–45n14, 157–58
welfare structure, 499, 567
Welles, Sumner, 223, 369
the West Bank (formerly Judea and Samaria), 459, 539–40, 558, 587
Western Wall of the Temple Mount, 113–14, 115, 119, 133, 611, 613–14. See also Temple Mount
White Paper of 1922 (Churchill), 104–08, 183
White Paper of 1930 (Passfield), 136–43
White Paper of 1939
    Churchill's response to the, 184–85, 189, 192–98, 204–08
    criticism of the, 183–86, 207–08, 274
    immigration policies, 181–82, 188, 251
    League of Nations Mandates Commission response, 186
    Roosevelt's response to the, 220–21
Williams, Thomas, 167
Wilson, Evan, 233–34, 235, 267
Wilson, Harold, 14, 193n10, 247–48, 251, 419, 606
Wilson, Woodrow, 17–18, 19, 22, 157, 407
Wingate, Orde, 155, 188–89
Wise, Stephen, 232–33, 240, 268, 520

Woodhead Commission, 174–78
World War I, 5–6, 6–8, 156–57, 171–72
World War II
    accusations of foreign infiltration, 437n35
    the Atlantic Charter, 225–26
    British anxiety about war with Germany and Italy, 182–83
    displaced persons camps, 106, 251, 253, 262–63, 267–68, 274–75, 293–94, 298–99, 300, 318–20, 346–47
    end of, 217, 262
    Jewish contributions to the British military, 190–92
    refugees, 193–98, 227, 229–30, 238, 252–57, 262–63, 268, 283, 293–94, 318–20, 346–47, 437n35
    tabling of decisions about Palestine until after, 207, 224–25
World Zionist Congress, 302

Y
Yemen, 592
Yom Kippur (1928), 113–15
Young, Hubert, 100
Yugoslavia, 340n9, 451n50

Z
Zangwill, Israel, 107–08n25
Zionism
    Biltmore Program, 199–202
    British opposition to, 101–02, 136–37, 265–67
    Chovevei Zion ("Lovers of Zion") movement, 1–3
    Curzon's changing attitude regarding, 32–37
    demand for Palestine to be an independent Jewish state, 198–202
    effect of the intrigues on, 58–60
    Hussein's response to, 26
    international responses to, 236, 262, 311, 348
    Jewish opposition to, 90n47, 268, 366–67
    Labour Party's pro-Zionism campaign, 245–51, 254–55, 261
    origins of, xix–xx
    PLO's attacks on, 586
    US government opposition to, 244
Zionist Executive, 92, 104, 108, 186
Zionist Organization, 23, 28–29, 108, 130–31n31

About the Author

JACOB LOUIS MOSAK received his PhD in 1941 from the University of Chicago, where he taught in its economics department and was associated with the Cowles Commission for Research in Econometrics in 1944. He was the author of several books on world economics and was best known for his book *General-Equilibrium Theory in International Trade* (1944).

During World War II, Mosak served as the regional head of the Office of Price Administration and as the director of economic stabilization in the Office of War Mobilization and Reconversion. In 1947, he joined the United Nations, rising to the rank of assistant secretary-general as the United Nations' chief economist. He guided the work of a staff of economists from all parts of the world and was in charge of many expert committees. He dealt with major international economic issues before the United Nations General Assembly and the Economic and Social Council. During World War II, he held high-level posts in several wartime economic agencies of the United States government in Washington, DC. He was also an adjunct professor at Columbia University.

After his retirement, Dr. Mosak devoted decades to researching the history of the Arab–Israeli conflict. He passed away in 2013, six weeks short of his hundredth birthday.